1940

1940

FDR, Willkie, Lindbergh, Hitler— the Election amid the Storm

SUSAN DUNN

Yale UNIVERSITY PRESS

New Haven & London

Yale University Press books may be purchased in quantity for educational, business, or promotional
use. For information, please e-mail sales.press@yale.edu (U.S. office) or sales@yaleup.co.uk
(U.K. office).

Designed by James J. Johnson
Set in Ehrhardt Roman type by Westchester Publishing Services
Printed in the United States of America by

Library of Congress Cataloging-in-Publication Data
Dunn, Susan, 1945–
1940 : FDR, Willkie, Lindbergh, Hitler—the election amid the storm / Susan Dunn.
pages cm
Includes bibliographical references and index.
ISBN 978-0-300-19086-1 (hardback : alk. paper)   1. Presidents—United States—
Election—1940.   2. Roosevelt, Franklin D. (Franklin Delano), 1882–1945.   3. Willkie, Wendell L.
(Wendell Lewis), 1892–1944.   4. Lindbergh, Charles A. (Charles Augustus), 1902–1974.   5. United
States—Politics and government—1933–1945.   6. Isolationism—United States—History—20th
century. I. Title.
E811.D86 2013
973.917—dc23

2012047739

A catalogue record for this book is available from the British Library.

This paper meets the requirements of ANSI/NISO Z39.48-1992 (Permanence of Paper).

10 9 8 7 6 5 4 3

To the memory of my parents

Ruth Lesser Dunn,
who fled Germany in 1938 and came to the United States

and

U.S. Army Captain Carl Dunn,
who served in Panama during World War II

Contents

Illustrations follow page 88

Chapter 1

Mystery in the White House

O N THE MILD NOVEMBER MORNING OF ELECTION DAY, November 5, 1940, Franklin Roosevelt, his wife, Eleanor, and his mother, Sara, cast their votes in Hyde Park's little town hall.[1] "Your name, please," said the young chairwoman of the election board. "Franklin D. Roosevelt," came the hearty reply.[2] She nodded but did not ask his occupation, as she had four years ago when Mr. Roosevelt replied, "Farmer." This time the question was unnecessary, she said, "because everybody knows who he is."[3]

Outside, a jovial Roosevelt posed patiently for photographers. "Will you wave to the trees, Mr. President?" asked one of them. "Go climb a tree!" Roosevelt said with a laugh before obediently waving at the trees for the cameras.[4] Dutchess County, with its majestic elms and maples, its farms and tranquil estates along the Hudson River, was Franklin Roosevelt's boyhood home, the place to which he always returned—yet he could be sure that this year, as in 1932 and 1936, he would fail to carry the county.

That morning, Roosevelt's Republican opponent, Wendell L. Willkie, and his wife, Edith, accompanied by their 20-year-old son, Philip, a student at Princeton, voted at Public School 6 on Madison Avenue and Eighty-Fifth Street in New York City, a few blocks from their apartment on Fifth Avenue. During the campaign, the thoughtful, pro-business Willkie had attacked Roosevelt's economic policies, arguing that they stifled growth. But Willkie was also an internationalist who repeatedly stressed to voters that "our way of life is in competition with Hitler's way of life." He adamantly ruled out any compromise with fascist aggression or with "religious and racial persecution or the destruction of human lives and liberty." As the Willkies entered the

1

school, people on the sidewalk cheered, "We want Willkie!" Surrounded by flashing news cameras, the boyishly handsome candidate smiled broadly and waved to the crowd. Before returning home, he drove through Central Park and then along Riverside Drive. Afterward he rested and then left for his headquarters at the Commodore Hotel.[5]

Ten miles away, in Englewood, New Jersey, Charles Lindbergh and his wife, Anne, lunched at the home of Anne's mother, Elizabeth Morrow, before going to the polls. Lindbergh hoped that Willkie would win the presidency. "I do not believe he is a great leader," he confided to his diary that day, "and I doubt that he has much understanding of the problems in Europe, but regardless of these failings, I think he would be far preferable to Roosevelt."[6] The fearless young aviator with a disarming smile, whose unprecedented thirty-three-hour, trans-Atlantic flight in the single-engine, single-seat *Spirit of St. Louis* in May 1927 had thrilled the world, was now the principal spokesman for American isolationism. Intoxicated with admiration for Nazi Germany's advances in aviation, he had hammered Roosevelt for failing to appease Hitler, sourly blaming him for having "alienated the most powerful military nations of both Europe and Asia."[7] Lindbergh's wife pitched in, too. Anne Morrow Lindbergh's eloquent, best-selling book *The Wave of the Future*, published just that October, predicted a new dynamic and dazzling age of fascism in the United States.

No candidate ever felt secure until the votes were counted, commented Roosevelt's attorney general Robert Jackson. FDR, too, Jackson said, "never overlooked or discounted the possibilities of defeat."[8] In 1932, Roosevelt had easily triumphed over incumbent Herbert Hoover, carrying forty-two states to Hoover's six. Four years later, at Hyde Park on election night, as the astonishing results trickled in, FDR leaned back in his chair, blew a ring of cigarette smoke at the ceiling, and exclaimed, "Wow!"[9] He had beaten the moderate Republican Alf Landon of Kansas by a vote of 27,752,309 to 16,682,524 and by 523 electoral votes to 8. Only the states of Maine and Vermont had gone for Landon. "ROOSEVELT ELECTED BY LANDSLIDE," announced newspapers all over the country on November 4, 1936.[10] It was a "Democratic tidal wave," marveled the *Washington Post*.[11] The confetti and ticker tape that rained down on the crowd in New York's Times Square on election eve "reached blizzard proportions," according to the *New York Times*.[12]

But this time was different. Now the president had good reason to be nervous. He had a strong and intelligent opponent in Wendell Willkie, who for months had been pounding away at the "third-term candidate." In addition,

Lindbergh and the powerful isolationist movement had mounted a virulent offensive against Roosevelt, and the GOP had made a striking comeback in the 1938 midterm elections. Though Democrats kept their majorities in both chambers of Congress, Republicans picked up eight Senate seats, nearly doubled their strength in the House, and even gained a dozen new governorships.[13] Two days after that election, syndicated columnist Walter Lippmann wrote that it was "not too rash" to predict a total Republican victory in 1940.[14]

In November 1940, voters all over the country were once again judging their president. They could think back to the abyss of the Great Depression and the avalanche of legislation during FDR's first and second hundred days, new programs that gave Americans new economic security, protection for their homes and farms, labor rights, a minimum wage, and even electricity. But in the last six months, a shift had taken place as the international crisis eclipsed the New Deal. This year, the election was taking place against a background of world catastrophe as Japanese warplanes attacked China and as European democracies from Norway to France yielded to the shocking speed of Hitler's army of fire and steel, his relentlessly advancing troops, tanks, and screaming dive-bombers.[15] While politicians on all sides of the political spectrum spoke about the importance of preparedness and a strong defense, American boys registered not for Civilian Conservation Corps camps or for Works Progress Administration jobs but instead for the country's first peacetime draft, and tens of thousands of workers flocked to new jobs in defense plants that were turning out planes, ships, and weapons.

The weekend before Election Day, the Gallup poll reported that Roosevelt still held the lead but that there appeared to be a strong trend toward Willkie. George Gallup, the head of the American Institute of Public Opinion, a Republican and a Willkie supporter, judged that it would be the closest election in a quarter century.[16] The competing Dunn survey of indicators of public opinion was less circumspect, confidently predicting that Willkie would win with 364 electoral votes.[17] "This fellow Willkie is about to beat the Boss," said a worried Harry Hopkins, FDR's close advisor.[18]

And all around the country, Willkie received enthusiastic endorsements from the largely Republican national press. A rare editorial voice in Roosevelt's corner was the *Chicago Defender*, the nation's largest African American newspaper. "No administration in our history," the *Defender* reminded its readers, "has done more than the New Deal to achieve economic and social democracy. . . . It would be suicidal for the masses to place their faith in Wendell Willkie who promises everything from a bag of peanuts to a shooting star."[19] But almost every major newspaper in America favored Willkie. "His election as President would be most likely to preserve the traditional restraints and balances of the American system of government," wrote the *New York Times* as it condemned Roosevelt's "impatience" with the two other branches of government.[20] "The indispensable man in this time of national crisis is Wendell Willkie," editorialized the *Los Angeles Times*.[21] Papers like the *Hartford Courant* and the *Washington Post* concurred. If Willkie is elected, the *Post* wrote, "we are willing to predict that he will make a truly great President of the United States."[22] William Allen White, the famous editor of the *Emporia* (Kansas) *Gazette* and Theodore Roosevelt's old friend, also came out for Willkie. Whereas FDR had always lived on inherited wealth, White wrote, Willkie had risen from modest origins in Indiana to the pinnacle of success as the head of the Commonwealth and Southern Corporation, the nation's largest electric utility holding company. The GOP candidate "has what it takes," White concluded. "And best of all he is fighting for the old hard way of American life. We are for Willkie."[23]

Also rooting for Willkie were the Nazis. "Despite Willkie's almost outdoing the President in his promises to work for Britain's victory," wrote CBS's sharp foreign correspondent William Shirer from Berlin, "the Nazis ardently wished the Republican candidate to win." Shirer surmised that the Germans believed that even if Willkie turned out to be their enemy, they would at least have several months of indecision before he could hit his stride, a period of delay from which they could profit.[24]

It was a bleak autumn. Across the Atlantic, the hooked-cross Nazi flag fluttered atop the Eiffel Tower in Paris,[25] and German soldiers goose-stepped in frightening precision up the Champs-Elysées with a brass band every day at noon. Meanwhile, Luftwaffe planes barreled out of the sky over Britain, carpeting London, Liverpool, and Midland industrial centers with thousands of tons of high-explosive bombs and tens of thousands of incendiary devices.[26] In late October, Pierre Laval, the blatantly anti-British vice premier of unoccupied Vichy France, approvingly declared that democracy was dead all over the world. His evidence: the almost unopposed Nazi victories in Europe. The future of France, Laval asserted confidently, lay in collaboration with Germany.[27]

The humanism of Western civilization and the essence of Christian morality, the peerless legacy of the Enlightenment and Thomas Jefferson's immortal affirmation of the inalienable human rights of life, liberty, and the pursuit of happiness all stood on the brink of annihilation. On November 5, 1940, a front-page story in the *New York Times* reported that British planes were bombing Italy's Adriatic ports to help Greece fend off an Italian assault.

On that day, while much of the world reeled from violence and chaos, an orderly, free election was calmly taking place in the United States at its regular, constitutionally appointed time. Millions of American men and women woke up in their peaceful towns and cities. They had breakfast, walked or drove to the polls, cast their votes, and then, as usual on a late-autumn Tuesday, went to work. In those democratic rituals and ordinary routines of everyday life lay certitude, safety, and happiness.

"Hold on to your hats, boys, I'm going to run for a third term!" cried a sprightly, tap-dancing Franklin Roosevelt in the fall of 1937. Cheers from the balcony and a chorus of boos from the expensive orchestra seats loudly commingled in the Music Box Theatre in New York. Every evening, Broadway star George M. Cohan transformed himself into a nimble FDR in the sparkling Kaufman, Rodgers, and Hart musical spoof *I'd Rather Be Right*. The president had not seen the show, but he enjoyed what he had heard about it. "Grace—take a law," Roosevelt would often say to his secretary Grace Tully when he wanted to dictate something, happily borrowing a line from the show.[28]

While Cohan's president buoyantly sang out his political intentions, the real Franklin Roosevelt played a cautious and even mystifying game. Indeed, for three more years, the president, with his usual finesse, would tap-dance around the possibility of running for an unprecedented third term.

In another more political theater known as the White House, Roosevelt performed at his twice-weekly press conferences. On Tuesday afternoons and Friday mornings, reporters filed into his office, eager to pepper him with questions. Sitting behind his desk, a cigarette in a holder jutting rakishly from his mouth, the president smiled in welcome. He excelled at cultivating friendly relations with journalists—if not with their typically Republican publishers. Usually in a genial mood and often quite candid—"I cannot tell a lie—like George Washington," he occasionally said—Roosevelt was ready for a laugh, even if only at his own jokes.[29]

Would the president care to comment on suggestions that he run for a third term? a reporter asked in June 1937, just eight months after Roosevelt's reelection victory. Mr. Roosevelt listened to the question and replied that the weather was very hot. The *New York Times*'s reporter Robert Post tried again. "Mr. President, would you tell us now if you would accept a third term?" "Put on a dunce cap and go stand in the corner," the president said to Post with a laugh.[30]

But over the next two years, speculation naturally mounted as reporters persisted in trying to glean some insight about his intentions. By June 1939, the president showed his impatience. When another intrepid reporter asked once more if he would be a candidate in 1940, for a few seconds, the president did not answer. Then, dropping his customary amiable façade, he admonished him to go stand in a corner—this time without a laugh.[31] But reporters still drooled for news, and the president finally realized that showing irritation at third-term questions got him nowhere. Humor and deft evasion were not only more effective but also, as the *New York Times* wrote as 1939 drew to a close, "infinitely more puzzling."[32]

For Europe, the year of 1939 was cataclysmic, climaxing in the German-Soviet nonaggression pact, the Nazi invasion of Poland, and British and French declarations of war against Germany. But in the United States, for Americans seeking relief from crises abroad, 1939 was the year of the Riddle.

In offices and living rooms, on railroad trains and buses, in city luncheonettes, small-town corner drugstores, and farm kitchens—all over the nation, wherever politics was discussed—people debated the president's intentions. "All-Absorbing Political Riddle," proclaimed one headline in the *New York Times*. A Washington columnist noted with satisfaction that the third-term mystery "is good for several million words of conversation daily."[33]

By not talking about his intentions, Walter Lippmann observed, FDR had indeed bestowed upon the nation a timely and welcome "diversion from the grim realities of the world." And the president's game was becoming "subtler and subtler," Lippmann wrote. With little more to go by than a few skillfully planted clues, some true and some false, Americans, like Agatha Christie's popular fictional detective, the elegant Hercule Poirot, had to resort to "imagination, intuition, and brain-power" to figure out how FDR's mind worked and solve the third-term puzzle.[34]

In December 1939 in the ballroom of the Willard Hotel in Washington, the riddle in the White House provided fodder for a musical skit at the all-male winter dinner of the Gridiron Club, the prestigious organization of American journalists. While the president and a crowd of tuxedoed foreign ambassadors, Supreme Court justices, cabinet members, and other Washington insiders watched, a group of reporters, dressed as Democratic Bedouins, gathered around an eight-foot-tall papier-mâché Sphinx that wore an engaging Roosevelt smile and sported a long cigarette holder at a jaunty angle. The Bedouins crooned:

> One alone can make it known
> You, alone, what is your decision?
> Will you run? Or are you done?
> Will you be, eternally, the one

To hold our party's nomination?
We come to you, the way we always do.
It rests with you alone.[35]

The flesh-and-blood president, marvelously beguiled, asked that the Sphinx be donated to the presidential library and museum he was planning in Hyde Park.[36]

Skits were also performed that night at the competing Gridiron Widows dinner, hosted by Eleanor Roosevelt in the White House. A Gridiron wife, playing the role of Mrs. Roosevelt, suggested staging a roundup to look over possible 1940 first ladies and see how they "will carry on the splendid work begun by Franklin and myself. That is," she added significantly, "if there is to be a change in first ladies."[37]

The White House mystery became the standard fare for political entertainment. At the March 1940 Women's National Press Club dinner, comedienne Gracie Allen observed that the solution to FDR's problem would be for future presidents to "run for the third term first." Gracie also announced that she was running for president on the Surprise Party ticket; she had no running-mate, however, because, as she explained, she would tolerate no vice in her administration. Another skit at that dinner featured Franklin and Eleanor in retirement, relaxing in rocking chairs in Hyde Park. "Maybe, Franklin, we should have stayed on after all, and attended to things for a third term," mused Eleanor. "Well," the former president replied, "they've got to learn to take care of themselves sometime."[38]

At a traditional Democratic event for politicians and their guests, the Jackson Day dinner in 1940, only seven months before the party's nominating convention, the president acknowledged that he had provided the country with a spellbinding pastime. "You know, there are a lot of riddles in the National Capital," he told the guests at the Mayflower Hotel in Washington. "I, myself, am supposed to be a self-made riddle."[39] Not entertained by the president's wit—or by his refusal to solve the riddle—were two expected presidential aspirants seated at the head table, Vice President Jack Garner, puffing on his cigar, and Postmaster General and national Democratic Party chair Jim Farley. Though Roosevelt was joking publicly about the speculation, he refused to end it. As the *Los Angeles Times* wrote that same month, "he doesn't say yes, and he doesn't say no; he just keeps on smiling and looking pleased."[40]

The stellar performance of the Sphinx-in-Chief, his artistry in withholding information, confounded, exasperated, and amused the press. "When what a man does *not* say plus the manner of his saying it becomes what reporters call the natural 'lead of the story,'" commented the *Wall Street Journal*, "it's a tough assignment and no fooling." Across the country, columnists veered from judging that the president was "overplaying this riddle game which he finds such fun" to surmising that Roosevelt was a riddle to himself. "His intention when he goes to bed at night," speculated columnist Mark Sullivan, "may not remain his intention when he arises in the morning."[41]

Intensely private, Roosevelt had no bent for self-explanation or public confession.

"You won't talk frankly even with people who are loyal to you and of whose loyalty you are fully convinced," Harold Ickes once complained to him. "You keep your cards close up against your belly."[42] Even Robert Sherwood, Roosevelt's brilliant speechwriter, had given up on trying to fathom the bewildering complexity of his boss's psyche. "One may speculate endlessly and fruitlessly," he remarked, "as to what went on in that mysterious mind."[43] Indeed, with a keen taste for suspense, in the mid-1930s, FDR had suggested to a friend the outline for a mystery novel—a millionaire disappears and starts a new life— and was pleased to see the novel completed by others and published in 1936.[44]

Especially on the third-term question, Roosevelt was cryptic, calm, and cool. "It is a game with me," he mischievously told Henry Morgenthau, his secretary of the treasury, in early 1940. "They ask me a lot of questions, and I really enjoy trying to avoid them."[45] "The political pot boils," he wrote to a relative in March 1940, "but I lose no sleep over that."[46]

A *New York Times* headline in early February 1940 announced that the "Roosevelt Enigma Overshadows All Else."[47]

"I want to get up to Hyde Park," Franklin Roosevelt had told Bob Jackson in the late fall of 1937, dismissing early rumors that he might run again for the presidency in 1940. The 55-year-old president, some of his friends said, had no desire to tempt fate, for he knew the tremendous strain of the presidency. Indeed, while there was only one living former president, Herbert Hoover, six widows of presidents were still living. Still, Roosevelt seemed to carry the burden of high office with greater ease than most of his predecessors.[48] FDR described to Jackson the post-presidential life he envisaged for himself, that of an elder statesman, like Thomas Jefferson, enjoying life on his Hudson River Valley estate, surrounded by friends, family, and his library.

The president delighted in chatting with family, friends, and advisors about the old days in Hyde Park and making varied plans for his retirement.[49] They all believed that his intention was to retire. One evening in early 1940, Secretary of Labor Frances Perkins brought Daniel Tobin, the president of the Teamsters Union and a political ally, to meet with Roosevelt in the White House. "Mr.

President, you just have to run for the third term," Tobin said. "Don't talk to me about your fishing trips next winter—you are going to be right here in the White House." "No, Dan, I just can't do it," objected the president. "I have been here a long time. . . . You don't know what it's like. And besides, I have to take care of myself. . . . I have to have a rest. I want to go home to Hyde Park. I want to take care of my trees. I have a big planting there, Dan. I want to make the farm pay. I want to finish my little house on the hill. I want to write history. No, I just can't do it, Dan." Unsatisfied, Tobin persisted: the president owed it to the nation to serve for another term. Roosevelt smiled, Perkins recalled. "You know," he said, "the people don't like the third term either."[50]

Nor, in their private conversations, did Roosevelt hint to Perkins herself that he might run again. She later wrote that when she discussed with him the possibility of their introducing legislation after the 1940 election, he laughed and said, "Well, how do you know there's going to be any next year for us? Papa won't be around." When she tried in other ways to fathom his intentions, "he would just laugh and I could get nothing positive out of him," she said.[51] The facts seemed to corroborate the president's words. As his second term drew to a close, he signed a three-year contract with *Collier's* magazine to write articles for an annual salary of $75,000.[52]

Sam Rosenman, a New York judge who was also one of the president's closest political advisors, believed that a wearied FDR was truly looking forward to retirement in Hyde Park; Rosenman himself planned to buy property nearby so that he could help the president write his memoirs.[53] Rosenman knew that the past few years had been bumpy, with more political setbacks than triumphs. The political atmosphere in Washington had quickly turned toxic in the wake of FDR's 1936 landslide, when he shocked even members of his own party with a scheme to "pack" the conservative Supreme Court with pro–New Deal justices. The proposal had been rejected in the Senate by a vote of 70 to 20—and 53 of those negative votes had come from Democrats. In a parliamentary system, Roosevelt would have been forced to resign after what amounted to a vote of "no confidence." On top of that, the New Deal itself had stalled, harmed by the recession of 1937–1938. And then there was lingering resentment among some Democrats over the president's attempt to "purge" conservatives from the party by supporting liberal challengers in the 1938 primaries. And now Europe was engulfed in war. Why would Roosevelt not seek respite from the crushing demands of the White House?

To others, too, FDR confessed a desire to quit the increasingly unmanageable world of Washington. On August 4, 1939, a month before Germany invaded Poland, Montana's senator Burton Wheeler chatted with the president in the White House and told him that he thought it would be a mistake to seek a third term. "He immediately interrupted me, by saying casually, 'Of course, it would be a mistake,'" Wheeler wrote in his autobiography.[54] Conversing with his ambassador to Great Britain, Joseph P. Kennedy, the president pleaded exhaustion. "Joe, I can't take it. What I need is one year's rest," he said when the two men met in the White House in late 1939. But he added the all-important caveat: "I just won't go on unless we are in war."[55] And the president had a not dissimilar conversation with Senator George Norris of Nebraska. "I am tied down to this chair day after day, week after week, and month after month," he complained to Norris late in his second term. "And I can't stand it any longer. I can't go on with it." His attitude left Norris stunned. "This is war," he told FDR, "and in war the life of one person means nothing."[56]

But political realism was playing a role in Roosevelt's reluctance to run again. "I would have much more trouble with Congress in my third term," he said to Norris in February 1940, "and much more bitterness to contend with as a result of my running for a third term than I have ever had before."[57] And in chance remarks he made to friends, FDR revealed another side of his thinking: he suggested that after four years of retirement and a blundering, reactionary government in Washington, he might be called back to run for a third term in 1944.[58]

The women in Roosevelt's family all thought he would and should retire, especially after a fainting spell he suffered in February 1940 was diagnosed as a very slight heart attack.[59] His formidable mother, Sara, thought that the setbacks and frustrations of his second term in office had aged him prematurely.[60] Of course this patrician grande dame had never wished for her son to enter vulgar politics in the first place. The president's 34-year-old daughter, Anna, told reporters that she too did not favor a third term for her father because he needed a rest. But, she added, "it always has been a woman's prerogative to change her mind."[61] As for his wife, Eleanor, who had become the White House champion of young people, African Americans, sharecroppers, and the poor during FDR's first two terms in the White House, she admitted that she had never asked her husband what he himself really wanted to do. "In his mind, I think, there was a great seesaw," she later wrote. "Sometimes one is at a loss oneself to know just how one feels." Still, she guessed that he preferred to return to Hyde Park, play the role of elder statesman, and tend to his papers and new presidential library.[62]

The president also worked overtime to convince Jim Farley, who had expertly managed his first two presidential campaigns, that he had no interest in a third term. But Farley remained skeptical after a meeting with Roosevelt in Hyde Park in July 1939.

On Sunday, July 23, Farley arrived at Springwood, the Roosevelt family's Hyde Park estate, for an overnight stay. Looking for the president, Farley came across him whirling down a winding dirt lane in his blue Ford, accompanied by his private secretary and confidante Missy LeHand, who had worked for him since the early 1920s. Farley climbed into the backseat. For years the two men had worked closely together, but recently their relationship had grown distant and strained—in part because of Farley's own presidential ambitions. "Jim hasn't altogether given up hope that he may be the nominee next year," commented Harold Ickes, "nor has he gotten over the idea that he might be nominated for Vice President."[63] But Roosevelt felt strongly that his postmaster general needed to establish his own credentials first by running for governor of New York. "He could then go before the people as an administrator," FDR told Robert Jackson in late 1937, "but . . . he's not going to do it and I wouldn't go to him about it at this time."[64]

After their drive, the threesome enjoyed iced tea and cake on the porch of Springwood. In the evening, Eleanor and a few friends and relatives joined them for dinner. Later, the president and Farley retired to a small study. As they sipped vodka, the conversation meandered—conditions in the South, the appointment of a new secretary of the navy, America's role in the world crisis. Finally Roosevelt got around to the burning questions on Farley's mind: the third term and the president's evaluation of the Democratic field for 1940.

Just a few weeks earlier, on July 6, Farley had spoken with Vice President Garner. The two men spilled out their hearts to each other. "With tears in his eyes," Farley wrote in the notes he took of their meeting, Garner insisted that "he did not want to be president, but he felt he was the only one at the moment who could head up opposition to the third term."[65] For his part, Farley told Garner that he opposed a third term but "did not want a living soul to know it." The vice president promised secrecy. Farley felt that, after six years of loyal service to the president and the party, it was his turn, though he had not yet decided if he would announce his candidacy. Convinced of Garner's friendship for him, Farley believed that if the Texan got the nomination, he would choose Farley as his running-mate.[66]

Now, in Hyde Park, Farley and Roosevelt discussed the list of Democratic hopefuls and possibles while Farley struggled to fathom the president's true thoughts. FDR judged that Garner, as an anti–New Deal conservative from Texas, was "just impossible." He and Farley both turned thumbs down on Montana's isolationist senator Burton Wheeler as well as on agriculture secretary Henry Wallace, who had never been elected to public office. "I don't think he has *It*," remarked FDR. Nor did he think sufficiently well of the former Indiana governor Paul McNutt, even though McNutt had managed to balance his state budget and expand welfare and relief programs.[67] The possibility of a bid by Farley himself went curiously unmentioned, as did one by the experienced Cordell Hull, even though Roosevelt had expressed to Hull his hope that the secretary of state would be his successor.[68]

Finally the conversation turned to the one essential question: the third term. "Jim, I am going to tell you something I have never told another living soul," said the president, lowering his voice to a confidential whisper. "Of course, I will not run for a third term." The news came as a burst of sunlight and hope for Farley.[69]

After that revelation, Roosevelt swore Farley to secrecy. He did not want his decision to become known prematurely. The important thing, he stressed, was that the Democratic nominee, whoever he might be, remain sympathetic to his administration and, if elected, continue its progressive policies. Afterward, Farley told reporters only that he and the president had had an "interesting" chat. Any other statement, he added, must come from Mr. Roosevelt himself.[70]

It had been a strange visit for Farley. FDR had claimed to have no interest in a third term but had disparaged every potential candidate for the nomination, creating the impression that he could identify no viable candidate other than himself. If he had analyzed the situation more deeply, Farley might have guessed that Roosevelt's casual criticism of all other potential candidates revealed more truth about the president's own ambition and intentions than his dreamy plans for retirement and the presidential library being built on the Hudson. One suspicious and perceptive reporter, covering the story in the summer of 1939, wrote that the library project might be a "false scent." "We urge you to look back at this column six months hence; the joke may be on us."[71]

Roosevelt was directing and starring in an intricate Machiavellian political drama, in which he was shrewdly maneuvering for control and playing for time. By not throwing his hat in the ring, he could play the role of president, not candidate; and by refusing to state publicly that he would not run again, he managed not only to remain a potential candidate but also to avoid the weakened and politically impaired status of a lame duck. Not even those in Roosevelt's inner circle could tell if he had planned all of this complex maneuvering or if he was truly ambivalent and hesitant about running again. He seemed simultaneously to be running and refusing to run. "It was certain that by hiding his plans," wrote historian James MacGregor Burns, "Roosevelt was adding to the confusion, and that he was expecting to benefit from it."[72] Indeed, by prolonging the mystery of his intentions, by giving mixed signals at every opportunity, Roosevelt increased his chances of controlling the convention.

A calculating politician with an instinct for perfect timing, FDR had learned never to make critical political decisions far in advance. Although he may have been "genuinely unsure of his own desires," commented Burns, his political genius was "to keep open alternative lines of action, to shift from one line to another as conditions demanded, to protect his route to the rear in case he wanted to make a sudden retreat, and, fox-like, to cross and snarl his trail in order to hide his real intentions."[73]

And more than any other situation, the subject of a third term required precisely such an elusive, labyrinthine, and carefully orchestrated performance by a supremely adept master politician and Sphinx—and in this case, one with a pyramid-sized ego and inventive talent for camouflage. This was, after all, the inscrutable man who had once told his treasury secretary Henry Morgenthau, "Never let your left hand know what your right hand is doing."[74]

And so, by neither making his intentions clear nor anointing a potential successor, Roosevelt profited from the confusion, uncertainty, mystery, and suspense he created[75]—and there was no way of smoking him out.

Chapter 2

George Washington and
Franklin Roosevelt: Duty or Ambition?

NO CONSIDERATION UNDER HEAVEN THAT I CAN FORESEE," the president wrote after seven increasingly contentious years in office, "shall again draw me from the walks of private life."[1] The year was 1796, and the president was George Washington.

Not only was Washington adamantly opposed to serving for a third term, he hadn't even wanted to serve for a second one. His most ardent wish, he told James Madison in May 1792, was to "spend the remainder of my days (which I cannot expect will be many) in ease and tranquillity." Only when beseeched by Madison, Hamilton, and Jefferson did the General consent to allow his name to be placed in nomination for a second four-year term.[2]

Washington decided to serve for two terms—and two terms only—for private reasons, not to create a precedent or a tradition. On the contrary, in 1788 he had written to his young friend Lafayette, "I can see no propriety in precluding ourselves from the services of any man who in some *great emergency* shall be deemed universally most capable of serving the public." The dangers of one-man rule—of a president who would seek to "perpetuate himself in office"—could be realized, he wrote, only in "the last stage of corrupted morals and political depravity." And at that grim point, term limits would be of no consequence.[3] As for his own decision to step down from office, he emphasized only his fatigue in his 1796 Farewell Address: "Every day the increasing weight of years admonishes me more and more that the shade of retirement is as necessary to me as it will be welcome." After a lifetime of public service, he was simply bone tired. He would die at the age of sixty-seven, one year and nine months after leaving office.

During the debates at the Constitutional Convention in Philadelphia in the sultry summer months of 1787, the blueprint for the presidential office had taken shape slowly. Some delegates wanted a vigorous executive; others warned against the "foetus of monarchy." Two thorny issues preoccupying the delegates were the length of the president's term and his eligibility for reelection. Three Virginians—James Madison, George Mason, and Edmund Randolph—suggested a seven-year term without reeligibility, while others proposed single terms of eleven, fifteen, and even twenty years.[4]

But Alexander Hamilton was not afraid of presidential power. This brilliant, forward-looking Founder desired a robust and energetic leader unconstrained by a limited term in office. Perceiving no danger in a republican version of an "elective Monarch," Hamilton proposed an executive elected for life, empowered to govern during good behavior. He considered a president elected for a limited term and ineligible for reelection a "Monster" who would inevitably be lured into abusing his power "by this constitutional disqualification." The "English model," Hamilton concluded, "was the only good one on this subject."[5]

Hamilton's colleague Gouverneur Morris, who represented Pennsylvania, also spoke up at the Constitutional Convention in favor of a strong president, noting that the new American union would be so extensive in size that it required an executive "with sufficient vigor to pervade every part of it."[6] But Morris added another key dimension to the discussion: ego. He understood that some ambitious men possessed a passionate drive for fame and glory, and he wanted to harness that drive to public service. Therefore, though he preferred that presidential terms be of "short duration"—perhaps just two years—an excellent president should have the chance to be rewarded for his public service with the possibility of reelection an indefinite number of times. Glory would be attached to such repeated public affirmations, and, Morris pointed out, the "love of fame is the great spring to noble and illustrious actions." Niccolò Machiavelli would have agreed with Morris. "A well-regulated republic," he wrote in the early sixteenth century, "should open the way to public honors to those who seek reputation by means that are conducive to the public good."[7] It would thus be a win-win situation: the people would gain an effective and talented leader, while the leader would gain the public esteem and fame he craved.

Ultimately, the convention leaned toward Morris's argument. The president "shall hold his Office during the Term of four Years," read the

Constitution. No mention whatsoever was made of term limits. In *The Federalist*, the series of newspaper essays written before the state-ratifying conventions by Hamilton, James Madison, and John Jay in defense of the Constitution, Hamilton forcefully made the case for unlimited presidential tenure. Term limits for the chief executive, he held in *Federalist* No. 72, would discourage the president from undertaking new projects, diminish inducements to good behavior, deny the community the advantage of his experience, and jeopardize political stability. There would surely be certain situations when the president's continuance in office would be "of the greatest moment to the public interest or safety." Most important in a republic founded on popular sovereignty, the decision on a president's tenure in office should be made by voters. Reeligibility in office, he wrote, was "necessary to *enable the people*, when they see a reason to approve his conduct, to continue him in his station." It was a point that Morris and others had made in Philadelphia. If the president was to be "the Guardian of the people," Morris had said, "let him be appointed by the people."[8] And the people at large "would choose wisely," added Massachusetts delegate Rufus King.[9]

Hamilton saw a sufficient guarantee of responsible leadership in the unrestricted right of the people to choose their own leaders combined with the possibility of the president's impeachment for misconduct, which he described as being "sentenced to a perpetual *ostracism* from the esteem and confidence, and honors and emoluments of his country." As the modern equivalent of "ostracism"—the banishment of leaders for ten years by popular vote in ancient Athenian democracy—impeachment was still a way to remind leaders of the power of the *demos*, the people.[10]

It was ironic that Hamilton, who was no acolyte of democracy, trusted the people's judgment in regard to the duration of presidential terms, but Thomas Jefferson, probably the most democratically minded of the Founders, rejected the idea of leaving such a key decision to the people. Upon receiving a report in February 1788 about the convention's deliberations, Jefferson wrote from Paris, where he was serving as minister to France, that he "strongly disliked" the absence of term limits. It would be "productive of cruel distress to our country," he predicted, and could permit the president to become effectively "an officer for life."[11] Living up to that belief, President Jefferson simply quit after two terms. "Genl. Washington set the example of voluntary retirement after 8. years. I shall follow it," he wrote in 1805, adding that the "indulgence and attachments will keep a man in the chair after he becomes a dotard." In the spring of 1807, Jefferson also admitted that he was "panting for retirement."[12]

But in the Constitution, the Hamiltonian vision had won out: there was no stipulation about limits on presidential terms.

A hundred and thirty years later, where did Roosevelt himself stand on the issue of term limits? It was hardly clear. He seemed to be of two minds, oscillating between Jefferson and Hamilton.

FDR had always expressed a strong preference for Jefferson's generally democratic ideas over Hamilton's typically more elitist ones. Indeed, FDR broke ground for the Jefferson Memorial in Washington, placed the Virginian's face on the first-class three-cent postage stamp, and hailed him as the savior of the ideals of the Revolution. But it was Hamilton who, like FDR, had favored an expansive national government led by an activist executive and who had ridiculed the folly of laissez-faire economics. Hamilton had even been the good friend of Roosevelt's paternal great-grandfather, who named one of his sons Hamilton and the other one Alexander Hamilton.[13]

On many occasions, Roosevelt adopted a Jeffersonian approach to the question of term limits. At a Democratic Victory dinner in March 1937, Roosevelt, in an affable mood, amused the audience by telling of a conversation he had had a few days earlier with a congressional friend. "John," the president said, "I am by no means satisfied with having twice been elected president of the United States by very large majorities. I have an even greater ambition." At that point, his friend sat up on the edge of his chair, looking stricken as horrid thoughts raced through his mind. "So, in order to relieve his anxiety," Roosevelt continued, "I went on to say: 'My great ambition on January 20, 1941, is to turn over this desk and chair in the White House to my successor . . . with the assurance that I am at the same time turning over to him a nation intact, a nation at peace, a nation prosperous.'"[14]

In the spring of 1939, Roosevelt again expressed his approval of presidential term limits, praising the president of the Philippines, Manuel Quezon, who opted to follow the Washingtonian tradition of serving no more than two terms in office. "To my mind," wrote Roosevelt, "he is right in setting a precedent in regard to a second term because, after all, he is the George Washington of the republican form of government experiment in the Far East."[15]

But that restrained attitude toward power and public service, in fact, clashed with Roosevelt's inner Hamilton, his deeper and perhaps more unconscious drives for power, recognition, and an esteemed place in history. One reporter recalled a story about a dinner conversation in the mid-1930s in which the president, thinking creatively along Hamiltonian lines, said that if Booth had missed his aim, it would have been President Lincoln's "duty" to run in 1868 for a third term in order to complete the wise reconstruction of the South.[16] Duty, perhaps. But, as Morris had stressed at the Constitutional Convention and as Hamilton had noted in *Federalist* No. 72, the desire for reward and the love of fame are "the strongest incentives of human conduct." And ego and ambition were clearly large components of Roosevelt's psyche.

"There's one issue in this campaign," FDR had told a friend in 1936, when he sought reelection, "and people must be either *for me* or *against me.*"[17] A few days before the election that year, in a fiery speech in Madison Square Garden, he personalized the campaign and placed himself at the center of the great ideological struggle of the decade when he declared that the economic royalists "are unanimous in their hate for *me* and I welcome their hatred!" And, bristling at the conservative Democrats who opposed much of the New Deal and then sought to run for reelection on his coattails, he lashed out at them for making a "clear misuse of *my own name.*"[18]

And FDR could learn from his distant cousin Theodore Roosevelt the political and psychological costs of prematurely giving up power. As William McKinley's vice president, TR took office after the president was assassinated and served out the last three years of McKinley's second term in office. Then, after winning the presidency on his own in November 1904, a youthful, 46-year-old TR had impetuously announced that he would not run again for the White House in 1908. The two-term tradition, he said at the time, was a "wise custom."[19] But by the spring of 1908, he seemed tortured by his impulsive promise. "Having given my word to the people at large as to what I would do," he wrote to a friend, "I never felt the slightest hesitancy . . . as to the proper course to follow. *But* the developments of the last year or two have been so out of the common that at times I have felt a little uncomfortable as to whether my announced decision had been wise. *But* I think it was wise."[20]

In 1910, finding himself jobless, restless, powerless, and disapproving of the policies of his handpicked successor, William Howard Taft, TR decided to reenter the political arena. "I am ready and eager to do my part," he said, "in helping solve problems which must be solved." Though TR expressed some pro forma hesitation about running once more for the presidency, he said that he would accept the GOP nomination to run in 1912 if it were offered to him "simply and solely because the bulk of the people wanted a given job done, and for their own sakes, and not for mine, wanted me to do that job."[21] His mask of selflessness scarcely disguised the gigantic ego and ambition that drove him into the 1912 race that ended with the victory of Woodrow Wilson.

In 1957, Brain Truster Rex Tugwell would look back at Franklin Roosevelt's career and observe that at the core of FDR's being was a "ferocious drive."[22] But unlike his cousin Theodore, who knew only how to shoot from the hip, Franklin Roosevelt instinctively acted and reacted with infinitely more self-mastery, subtlety, and finesse.[23]

If Alexander Hamilton had returned to Planet Earth in 1940 and discovered Europe falling into a vicious fascist abyss and Great Britain, whose government and economy he so admired, facing mortal danger, he would surely have voiced dismay at the sacralization in the United States of the two-term tradition. Indeed, among all his objections to term limits, the one that overshadowed all the others was the possibility that the nation might be involved in a war. "It is *evident*," he had crisply written in *Federalist* No. 72, "that a change of the chief magistrate, at the *breaking out of a war*, or at any similar crisis, for another, even of equal merit, would at all times be detrimental to the community, inasmuch as it would substitute inexperience to experience, and would tend to unhinge and set afloat the already settled train of the administration."[24]

And Hamilton would also have objected to some Americans' reverence for George Washington's Farewell Address—most of which he himself had ghostwritten—and his recommendation that the young republic "steer clear of permanent alliances." At "Keep-America-Out-of-War" rallies in 1940, Hamilton would have heard speakers declaring that "we have by no means escaped the foreign entanglements and favoritisms that Washington warned us against."[25] But Hamilton knew better—not only that it was Jefferson, not Washington, who used the phrase "entangling alliances" in his Inaugural Address, but also that Washington's point was more nuanced and realistic. In his Farewell Address, Washington advised that "we may safely trust to temporary alliances for *extraordinary emergencies*." In addition, in his own draft for that address, Washington had underscored that if the young American republic adopted neutral conduct and remained at peace for the next twenty years, it would expand its economy, develop its might, and be able "*to bid defiance, in a just cause, to any earthly power whatsoever.*"[26]

There would have been no hesitation, no question in Hamilton's mind about coming to the aid of Great Britain. "We think in English," he had said in 1789, encapsulating the profound intellectual and cultural ties binding the United States and Great Britain.[27] "Who of us lives if England dies?" the eminent British political scientist and Labor Party member Harold Laski asked a century and a half later.[28]

In the spring of 1940, Laski published his book *The American Presidency*, just in time to influence the thinking of Franklin Roosevelt and other politicians before the Democratic Party's nominating convention that July. "The war has made the folly of slavish devotion to any mechanical tradition grimly obvious," he wrote, urging Americans to free themselves from "servitude to the past." Laski's Hamiltonian premise was that robust leadership in the United States could come only from the chief executive—there was no other source of direction for the nation as a whole. Only a powerful and effective president could determine the nation's foreign policy and deal with Nazi Germany's lethal challenges to democratic nations; and only he had the "immense power to shape public opinion."[29]

Not only Americans but the rest of the civilized world, Laski contended, desperately needed strong presidential leadership from the United States— the leadership of a Franklin Roosevelt. Laski dedicated a copy of his book to FDR, "with deep respect and affection." On the basis of that dedication, newspaper columnists Joseph Alsop and Robert Kintner surmised that "Professor Laski on the presidency is also the President on the presidency"[30] and that Roosevelt indeed intended to run for a third term.

But was Roosevelt, the consummate politician, improviser, and master of timing, the courageous and unwavering internationalist savior for whom Laski and the rest of the civilized world cried out?

Chapter 3

Walking on Eggs

W E SHUN POLITICAL COMMITMENTS WHICH MIGHT ENTANGLE us in foreign wars," President Roosevelt told his audience in Chautauqua, New York, in August 1936, as if harkening back to Washington's 1796 Farewell Address. That same week, the State Department made it clear that, despite the fact that Italian troops as well as Nazi bombers, tanks, and advisors were supporting the military uprising against the republican government of Spain, the United States would remain completely neutral in the Spanish civil war.[1]

Was Roosevelt really willing to wear the isolationist label? No—and yes. "We are not isolationists," he hedged in Chautauqua, "except in so far as we seek to isolate ourselves completely from war." As assistant secretary of the navy, he had observed war for himself on French and Belgian battlefields. In Chautauqua he remembered that summer of 1918. "I have seen blood running from the wounded," he said. "I have seen men coughing out their gassed lungs. I have seen the dead in the mud." No act of his administration, he promised, as if holding up a pacifist banner, would produce or promote war. Still, though he had just strengthened the isolationist cause, he injected a note of realism by reminding Americans that uncertainty always reigned. "So long as war exists on earth," he said, "there will be some danger that even the Nation which most ardently desires peace may be drawn into war."[2] Already in 1935, he had recognized that the world had entered nightmare years; people were "very ready to run after strange gods," he wrote to Secretary of State Cordell Hull, but added weakly that "common sense" made him loath to change America's foreign policy of neutrality.[3] In the fall of 1935, he refused to sign on to the League of Nation's sanctions against Italy, just when Italian dictator Benito Mussolini was preparing to attack Ethiopia.[4]

In January 1936, in his State of the Union message, Roosevelt had acknowledged that the prospects for peace had grown more remote. "To say the least," he admitted, "there are grounds for pessimism." There were "marked trends" in Europe and Asia toward aggression, an increase in armaments and shortened tempers—all the elements that could lead to the tragedy of general war. But to halt that aggression, Roosevelt offered lame and insufficient remedies: a limitation on world armaments; the exertion of America's "moral influence" against repression and autocracy; and an embargo on American arms to all belligerents.[5] Congress responded a month later by passing the Second Neutrality Act, which renewed the rigid provisions of its 1935 predecessor, prohibiting arms shipments, loans, or credit to belligerents while making no distinction between aggressor nations and their victims. Though the bill stripped the president of the power to act against aggressors and extend military aid to democracies struggling for survival, Roosevelt nevertheless signed onto it, issuing a statement approving the policy of neutrality.[6]

"We've got to get into this war," the 34-year-old FDR had repeatedly argued in 1916 when he served as assistant secretary of the navy, as if echoing his cousin Theodore's bellicose stand.[7] But two decades later, the grim realities of the mechanized mass slaughter of modern warfare erased any romantic enthusiasm that Americans may have once harbored for war. And cementing their aversion for armed conflict was a highly effective and revealing 1934 Senate investigation, approved by the president and led by Republican Gerald Nye of North Dakota, into corruption, bribes, and excessive profits in the arms industry. In the mid-1930s, Roosevelt had decided that American policy would be one of defense, not offense.

In 1936, with reelection and his political future at stake, opportunism and expediency were the name of the game. On the subject of domestic policy, Roosevelt could hardly have been more confrontational, uncompromising, and implacable in his calls for the overthrow of the "economic royalists" whose hatred he famously and defiantly welcomed. But on the subject of foreign policy, his campaign strategy during that electoral season was one of passive avoidance of world problems. Fearful that an emphasis on foreign affairs might alienate supporters of the New Deal who were also isolationists, Roosevelt largely ignored foreign policy in his presidential campaign. In his annual message in January 1936, he had warned that certain leaders in Europe "have not pointed the way either to peace or to good will," and he suggested that Americans "take cognizance of growing ill-will." But a year later, in January 1937, his Inaugural Address on a cold and wet day contained not a single sentence on international affairs. Instead he focused on the "one third of a nation ill-housed, ill-clad, ill-nourished," his words echoing his first inaugural speech in March 1933, when he underscored that his top priority was "putting our own national house in order." Then he had made no mention of the new German chancellor, Adolf Hitler, who had been appointed thirty-three days earlier, on January 30, 1933.[8]

In October 1937, the president moved a little closer to adopting a more robust foreign policy—but then stepped back. As Italy and Germany increased their aid to Spanish fascists and monarchists and as Japanese bombers and tanks reduced cities in northern China to ruins, slaughtering thousands of retreating Chinese troops, machine-gunning rescue workers, and strafing U.S. gunboats, Roosevelt gave a tough-minded talk—known as his "quarantine" speech—in Chicago, the city at the heart of the isolationist movement.

Without mentioning any countries by name, he denounced the "reign of terror and international lawlessness" that threatened the very foundations of civilization. One reporter noted that the president's face was "set hard," that he spoke very slowly, his every sentence showing "worry and a determination to take action against international anarchy." Peace-loving nations, the president told Americans, could no longer ignore the violations of treaties or seek "escape through isolation or neutrality." His implicit suggestion was that the United States would reverse its hands-off policy, emerge from the cocoon of isolation, and play a more active role in world affairs. He declared that, just as in the case of a viral epidemic, it had become necessary to "quarantine" the violators of peace in order to protect the health of the community. A noble plan—but also enigmatic. Just how did the president intend to "quarantine" the aggressors?[9]

The following day, at a press conference, Roosevelt told reporters that the lead in their articles should be that the nation was "actively" engaged in the search for peace. "I can't tell you what the methods will be," he said vaguely. "We are looking for some way to peace."[10] Reporters pressed him for more specifics. What about economic sanctions? "Sanctions" was a "terrible word to use," the president replied. They were "out of the window." Did the quarantine belong solely to the "moral sphere"? someone asked. "No, it can be a very practical sphere," he answered. When one reporter suggested that the speech had presented "an attitude without a program," FDR did not disagree. "We are looking for a program." Another reporter asked whether there wasn't a conflict between what the president had outlined and the Neutrality Act. "They seem to be on opposite poles to me," said the reporter, Ernest Lindley.

"Put your thinking-cap on, Ernest," the president replied. But he never answered Lindley's question—or offered the nation the program he said he was searching for. That left a range of possibilities for people to speculate about, from a multilateral agreement breaking off diplomatic relations with the belligerents to naval blockades of Germany and Japan.[11]

Despite the ambiguity of the president's talk, some of the nation's more internationally minded politicians and newspapers reacted positively to it. Colonel Frank Knox, the Republican nominee for vice president in 1936 who would join Roosevelt's cabinet in 1940, praised the speech as "magnificent." Senator Elbert Thomas, a Democrat from Utah, pronounced it "extremely timely." The quarantine talk was "statesmanlike in theme and compelling in argument," wrote the *Atlanta Constitution*, concluding that "the call today is no longer merely to make the world safe for democracy, but to make the world itself safe from the conflagration of hate and destruction. . . . The militaristic, war-diseased nations must be *quarantined.*" Other newspapers editorialized that FDR was "right, wholly right" and expressed approval that the president "at last has spoken in this vein, offering at least a hint that he will adopt a stronger foreign policy." The *New York Times* praised Roosevelt for expressing "the increasing indignation in this country" over predatory governments that flouted international law.[12]

But those newspapers represented a small minority of voices, for there was no "increasing indignation" at gangster nations. As indeterminate and hazy as Roosevelt's speech was, the nation's response was "quick and violent—and nearly unanimous," Sam Rosenman, the president's advisor and speechwriter, later wrote.[13] A Gallup poll taken after Roosevelt's speech showed that 69 percent of Americans—and 75 percent in the isolationist Midwest—wanted Congress to pass stricter neutrality laws.[14] Asked if America should take part in another war like World War I, 95 percent of respondents answered "No!" and demanded that the government do "everything possible to keep us out of foreign wars."[15]

In Congress, the president's quarantine talk sparked fury and even calls for impeachment. Republican isolationists like Massachusetts representative George Tinkham and New York's Hamilton Fish, the ranking member of the House Foreign Relations Committee, threatened to impeach the president for having "torn to shreds" America's neutrality laws. Newspapers across the country echoed the *Hartford Courant*'s accusation that FDR had "arbitrarily divided" the world's nations into two groups, one of peace-loving nations, the other of international gangsters. "In brief," the *Courant* concluded, "the United States would be perpetually busy fighting other people's battles all over the world." Even if the foundations of civilization were seriously threatened, wrote the isolationist *Boston Herald*, "this time, Mr. President, Americans will not be stampeded into going 3,000 miles across water to save them."[16]

"It's a terrible thing," FDR said to Rosenman, "to look over your shoulder when you are trying to lead—and to find no one there."[17] Ten days after his quarantine speech, the president wrote to Endicott Peabody, his old headmaster at Groton, and complained that he was "fighting against a public psychology of . . . 'Peace at any price.'" Two days later, in a letter to another friend, he was slightly more optimistic. "As time goes on," he wrote, "we can slowly but surely make people realize that war will be a greater danger to us if we close all the doors and windows than if we go out in the street and use our influence to curb the riot."[18]

And yet, just one week after his quarantine talk, FDR broke the spirit of any promise to isolate aggressor nations when he hosted Vittorio Mussolini, the dictator's son, at a White House tea, deaf to the shouts of protest coming from members of the Italian Anti-Fascist Committee parading on the sidewalk outside the Italian Embassy.[19] "We are sure, Mr. President," the head of the committee had written optimistically to Roosevelt after hearing his talk, "that you will continue to maintain the courageous stand you have taken in your Chicago speech by refusing to meet this person who typifies the lawlessness of the aggressor nations whom you wish to put in quarantine."[20]

The quarantine speech turned out to be a trial balloon, swiftly punctured by political realities and FDR's failure to prepare a plan of action.[21] The president reaped the worst of both worlds, leaving internationalists frustrated and isolationists enraged. The safest course, carped Prime Minister Chamberlain, was for Britain to count on America for nothing "except words."[22]

During those critical years between 1936 and 1940, FDR in fact neither satisfied the internationalists' desire that America play a more vital role in world affairs nor disabused isolationists of the comforting illusion that the nation's neutrality laws and arms embargoes—which one historian termed "the American Maginot line"[23]—would keep them out of war. With an eye cocked on isolationists in the halls of Congress as well as on the newspaper world and opinion polls, he had saddled himself with a makeshift foreign policy. Roosevelt seemed to "float almost helplessly on the flood tide of isolationism," wrote historian James MacGregor Burns, "rather than to seek to change both the popular attitudes and the apathy that buttressed the isolationists' strength."[24]

In 1938, the president was still searching for a foreign policy to ward off American involvement in war. In his State of the Union message to Congress on January 3, he called for the nation to be "adequately strong in self-defense" and requested increased appropriations for a major rearmament program to deter aggressors. But cautiously taking his cue from public opinion polls, he once again stressed his goal of keeping the nation at peace and out of war.

Just a week later, isolationists demonstrated their clout when a proposal for a new constitutional amendment curtailing the president's power in foreign affairs almost passed in Congress. Representative Louis Ludlow, a Democrat from Indiana, wanted to require that a national referendum be held before any declaration of war could be issued. "Such an amendment would cripple any President in the conduct of our foreign relations," Roosevelt sternly warned.[25] By a close margin of 209 to 188, the House refused to take the resolution out of committee for consideration on the floor. But more than a hundred Democrats had joined a majority of Republicans in trying to wrest the bill out of committee.

"I am in the midst of a long process of education," FDR wrote to a friend in February, "and the process seems to be working slowly but surely."[26] He had made similar claims before, but there was still little evidence that he was actively working to educate the public about the possibility of war or that his lessons were paying off. So strong was isolationist sentiment in the nation that when German tanks rolled into Austria on March 12, 1938, the president of the United States—trying to rally his New Deal supporters as he struggled with an economy in recession and prepared for midterm elections—said and did nothing.[27]

Roosevelt's ambassador to France, William Bullitt, was less circumspect. In September, the crisis over Germany's determination to annex the Sudetenland, a region in Czechoslovakia with a majority German population allegedly oppressed by the Czechs, was escalating. Speaking in Bordeaux on September 3, 1938, Bullitt used the occasion to announce that France and the United States were "united in war as in peace." American newspapers had a field day, reporting that Roosevelt was bent on carrying the nation into war. Two days later at a press conference in Hyde Park, a reporter asked Roosevelt if the United States had allied itself "morally" with France and Great Britain in a stop-Hitler move. The president answered vaguely and then blamed journalists for misinterpreting Bullitt's remarks.[28]

A few days later, on September 12, Roosevelt listened on the radio as Hitler spoke to a frenzied crowd of thirty thousand people in Nuremberg. Announcing that he had placed on his own head Germany's "thousand-year-old crown," the Führer proclaimed German invincibility and poured scorn on the democracies of Europe. With fist-clenching and manic gesticulations, he threatened Czechoslovakia with war while also proclaiming Germany's peaceful intentions, all to zealous, frenzied shouts from the audience of *"Sieg Heil!"*[29] "I have never heard Adolf so full of hate," wrote CBS radio's Berlin-based correspondent William Shirer, "his audience quite so on the borders of bedlam. What poison in his voice!"[30]

After Hitler's speech, Roosevelt sent his emissary, Harry Hopkins, to the West Coast to inspect the aircraft industry with the aim of expanding it for war production. "The president was sure then," Hopkins later wrote, "that we were going to get into war."[31] But even if Hopkins's perception was correct, the president still said nothing to the public about the likelihood of war.[32] On the contrary, on September 27, as the Sudeten crisis was nearing a climax, he issued a public message to all nations appealing for peace. With Hitler poised to invade Czechoslovakia, the president stressed his hope that international disputes could be resolved by "pacific means," by the "resort to reason rather than by the resort to force," while undermining any leverage he might have had with a careful avowal that the United States had "no political involvements" and "no obligations" in Europe. To Hitler's intransigent response that same day, blaming the Czechs, Roosevelt simply repeated his hope that peaceful solutions would be found.[33] While FDR spurned urgent pleas for help from the president of Czechoslovakia, he agreed to make one foreign commitment—to the safe, friendly neighbor of Canada. Should that dominion ever be invaded by air, land, or sea, the United States would be there to help.[34]

Then came Munich, the sad symbol of appeasement. On September 29, 1938, Hitler struck a deal in that German city with the British prime minister Neville Chamberlain and the French prime minister Edouard Daladier. Unwilling to risk a war, the two heads of government chose conciliation. They allowed Germany's Führer to send in his troops to occupy the Sudetenland, thereby putting the rest of Czechoslovakia at his mercy. The concessions he had made to Germany spelled "peace with honor" and "peace for our time," a smiling Chamberlain told a London crowd as he stood on the balcony at 10 Downing Street. "Good old Chamberlain!" shouted people in the crowd.[35]

Five months earlier, Winston Churchill—a lone, indignant, responsible voice pleading for the British to face up to the Nazi peril—had bitterly predicted that such a pact would "lead us straight to war." The Nazi regime, he said, "elated by this triumph, with every restraint removed, would proceed unchecked upon its path of ambition and aggression. . . . After an interval, long or short, we should be drawn into a war."[36] Roosevelt, too, feared that Chamberlain was taking a very long chance in making a deal with a criminal nation; continued appeasement, he thought, would probably fail. But with his own options limited and despite his harsh view of Chamberlain, he sent a congratulatory wire to the British prime minister. "Good man," he wrote.[37] While England continued to sleep, the men of Munich ruled the roost.

In mid-October, Roosevelt met with Ambassador Bullitt in the White House and admitted to being very troubled by his reports about the European situation. At a press conference the morning after that meeting, when a reporter commented upon his "snappy" new suit, FDR replied that he certainly did not feel snappy, having "sat up last night hearing the European side of things from Ambassador Bullitt."[38] He made news at that press conference with an announcement that his administration would undertake a deep study of the nation's defense requirements. Reporters interpreted his remarks as signaling a possible turning point. The electrifying headline in the *New York Times* the next day read: "ROOSEVELT MOVES TO RUSH EXPANSION OF ARMY AND NAVY."

On one issue the Roosevelt administration did not waver or waffle: the relaxation of immigration quotas for refugees. During the first years of Nazi persecution of Jews and others, the White House remained mostly passive as immigration policy was set by State Department officials who were largely indifferent to the plight of Hitler's victims.[39]

On Liberty Island in October 1936, the president commemorated the fiftieth anniversary of France's gift of the Statue of Liberty, the glorious symbol of light and hope for immigrants making their way to America's shores. After noting that for over three centuries "a steady stream of men, women and children followed the beacon of liberty," Roosevelt closed the door. "Within this present generation," he said, "that stream from abroad has largely stopped. We have within our shores today the materials out of which we shall continue to build an even better home for liberty." No more room in the inn.[40]

The immigration acts of 1921 and 1924 had imposed tight restrictions on the flow of immigrants to the United States. In 1930, during the economic crisis, President Hoover curtailed immigration even more, reducing the annual quota from Germany, for example, from about 60,000 to only 26,000. Under Roosevelt, even that shrunken allotment went unfilled. Between 1933 and 1937, only 30,000 refugees entered the United States from Germany, whereas the quota would have permitted nearly 130,000.[41] Politics played a key role as the president yielded to the widespread fear, fanned by his labor union allies, that increased immigration would aggravate unemployment and add more public charges to the relief rolls. FDR's political antennae were also sensitive to anti-Semitism, not only the hatred whipped up by demagogues like the Catholic radio priest Father Charles Coughlin, but anti-Semitism in its quieter, more pervasive forms. Indeed, Gunnar Myrdal, the Swedish expert on American race relations, hypothesized that anti-Semitism in the United States in the 1930s was probably "somewhat stronger than in Germany before the Nazi era."[42]

By the time of Munich, Hitler's war against German Jews was clear. At the Nazi party conference in Nuremberg that September, Hitler had explained why he and his followers fought "with such fanaticism" against Jews in Germany. "National Socialism desires to establish a true community of the people," the Führer shouted, "because we . . . can never suffer an alien race."[43] Two months later, on November 9, 1938, came Kristallnacht, "the night of shattered glass," when across Germany the Hitler Youth, the Gestapo, and the SS murdered Jews, attacked their shops, smashed their windows, ransacked their homes, set synagogues ablaze, and shipped tens of thousands of them off to concentration camps. Nor was this to be the end of it. "How the Jews are treated in Germany," threatened Joseph Goebbels, the Nazi propaganda minister and architect of Kristallnacht, "will depend on their own good behavior and above all on the good behavior of Jews abroad." Speaking to a crowd of seventy thousand four days after Kristallnacht, he added that ownership of all Jewish enterprises would be transferred to Aryans and Jewish influence eliminated from the German economy.[44]

At a press conference a week after Kristallnacht, President Roosevelt expressed "shock" over the German persecution of Jews. But would he consider offering sanctuary to Jewish refugees? one reporter asked. He had given the subject a great deal of study, he replied, but declined to be more specific. What about raising immigration quotas? another reporter asked. No, Roosevelt said, he did not contemplate that.[45] The president did order that the visas of some fifteen thousand Germans and Austrians be extended indefinitely and that consular officials suspend, at least temporarily, enforcement of the "likely to become a public charge" clause they had used in order to deny visas to Jews impoverished by Nazi confiscations.

Yet only in the middle of 1939, after Germany announced that it would expel one hundred Jews a day from the Reich, was the German quota finally filled.[46] At the same time, though, the administration denied permission to nine hundred desperate German-Jewish refugees aboard the German liner *St. Louis* to disembark in the United States after they were refused sanctuary in Cuba. When the *St. Louis* idled near the east coast of lower Florida, a Coast Guard patrol boat, as the *New York Times* reported in a front-page story, stood by to prevent possible attempts by passengers to jump off and swim ashore.[47]

Ultimately, the ship returned to Europe, its passengers allowed to stay in Britain and in the soon-to-be Nazi-occupied Belgium, Holland, and France.

Fierce opposition to immigration came from senators like Georgia's Richard Russell and North Carolina's Robert Reynolds, who denounced "alien coddling" and proposed legislation to seal American borders against immigration for at least five years.[48] At the same time, New York senator Robert Wagner and Massachusetts representative Edith Rogers introduced a bill that would admit twenty thousand refugee children. "It is all right for you to support . . . the bill," wrote FDR to Eleanor, "but it is best for me to say nothing."[49] His silence effectively doomed that effort. Russell-Reynolds did not pass either, but after the German conquest of Poland, Americans' fear that spies, saboteurs, and fifth columnists might slip into the country had the effect of reducing immigration to a trickle.

Roosevelt's efforts to internationalize the refugee problems were hardly more effective in saving lives. His endorsement of Jewish immigration to Palestine was met by a cold British refusal. The British claimed that there was neither vacant land in Palestine suitable for crops nor room for immigrants who had not inhabited the region for many centuries. FDR's plea to Mussolini to open Ethiopia to Jewish refugees was similarly brushed aside.[50]

FDR's boldest initiative came in July 1938 when, at his call, representatives of thirty-one countries—but not Germany—convened in Evian, France, to discuss the crisis of Jewish refugees.[51] Yet the president sent as his representative no high official or diplomat, but only a businessman-friend, Myron Taylor, who was authorized to promise nothing more than that Jewish refugees would be eligible for the existing German and Austrian quota of thirty thousand immigrants a year. With Americans setting so mean an example, most countries echoed the French delegate's complaint that France had reached "the extreme point of saturation" and could do nothing more for refugees.[52]

The Evian conference gave birth to the Intergovernmental Committee on Political Refugees (ICPR), which became the new object of hope and disappointment for the persecuted of Europe. Impotent and meagerly funded, this international organization was now responsible for finding safe havens for the increasing numbers of Hitler's victims. And where would those safe havens be? At an ICPR meeting in Washington in October 1939, FDR proposed that the delegates try to resettle several million people in "comparatively vacant spaces on the earth's surface"—places like Madagascar, Angola, Alaska, and South America. It was his "hope," he said, that the work would be carried on with "redoubled vigor."[53]

But on this subject, the world's statesmen, including Roosevelt, demonstrated no vigor. FDR was first and foremost a politician accountable to American voters, and as such he was obliged to make difficult trade-offs and painful compromises. Among those compromises was his failure to respond with greater urgency to the nascent Holocaust. Although no other national leader did more than he did to help rescue Jews, he did not do enough.[54]

Why didn't the president speak openly with the American people about the gravity of the situation in Europe? demanded his pugnacious interior secretary, Harold Ickes. But Roosevelt merely responded that people would not believe him.[55] And when he did attempt to warn Americans about an uncertain future, he softened his message with captivating charm and wit. America's actions in the next few years would have an immeasurable bearing on "the history of the human race for centuries to come," he told an audience in North Carolina in December 1938, underscoring that democracies around the world "look to us for leadership." But, with a broad smile, he also reassured his listeners in Chapel Hill that he was "an exceedingly mild-mannered person—a practitioner of peace, both domestic and foreign" and that there was absolutely no truth to the rumor that he "breakfasted every morning on a dish of 'grilled millionaire.'"[56]

In early 1939, Roosevelt began to push for massive expansion of aircraft production, military aid—including planes—for the European democracies, and the lifting of the arms embargo. In his State of the Union address in January 1939, in addition to requesting almost a billion and a half dollars for defense out of a total budget of nine billion, he called for reform of the arms embargo. The current complete arms embargo, he said, operated unevenly and unfairly and was actually helping the aggressors by denying aid to the victims. But then, once again, he waffled and backtracked.

On January 31, the day after Hitler publicly predicted the "annihilation of the Jewish race in Europe," Roosevelt invited members of the Senate Military Affairs Committee to meet with him privately in an effort to persuade isolationists on the committee that fundamental changes in American foreign policy were necessary. Making the argument that the strengthening European democracies would help insulate America from another horrific war, he repeated his administration's desire to lift the arms embargo. According to a transcript of the meeting, he also uttered words to the effect that "the frontiers of the United States are on the Rhine." One of the senators, Josh Lee of Oklahoma, clapped his hands, but the others sat in stony silence.[57] When those candid remarks were leaked to the press, the president retreated and forcefully denied having made any such comments. Reporters must have listened to some "boob," he said, asserting that his administration remained opposed to entangling alliances and in favor of world trade for everybody.[58] One senior official in the British Foreign Office remarked in March 1939 that predicting the course of American foreign policy was "as simple as trying to weigh a wild cat on the kitchen scales."[59]

In April 1939, FDR wrote a conciliatory message to Hitler and Mussolini, suggesting a ten-year guarantee of peace for Europe in return for American cooperation in talks on trade and armaments. The president fully realized that his message was hardly likely to spur an agreement, but it was a safe bet that Hitler's rejection of it would smoke out his ruthlessness and mendacity and reveal his brazen belligerence. Visiting Mussolini in Rome, Hermann Goering, the supreme commander of the German air force, saw the letter and advised the Duce not to bother to answer it. The American president, he said, obviously "was suffering from an incipient mental disease."[60] The official German press sneered that the proposal had a "Jewish taint."[61] And Hitler's response? In a two-and-a-half-hour speech to the Reichstag on April 28, he gave his answer. William Shirer said that, with this performance, the Führer reached a new level in "sheer eloquence, craftiness, irony, sarcasm and hypocrisy."[62]

After proclaiming his admiration and friendship for England, Hitler denounced its "new policy of encirclement of Germany" and revoked the naval agreement of 1935 with Great Britain that barred the sinking of passenger ships. Then, tearing up another treaty, he revoked the German nonaggression pact with Poland. "Herr Roosevelt!" Hitler exclaimed, "I fully understand that the vastness of your nation and the immense wealth of your country allow you to feel responsible for the history of the whole world and for the history of all nations. I, sir, am placed in a much more modest and small sphere." In fact, all he had ever done, said the Führer modestly, was assert "my abhorrence of war." The master of demagoguery assured the American president that, contrary to rumors that he intended to attack "Finland, Latvia, Estonia, Norway, Sweden, Denmark, the Netherlands, Belgium, Great Britain, Ireland, France, Portugal, Spain, Switzerland, Liechtenstein, Luxemburg, Poland, Hungary, Turkey, Iraq, the Arabias, Syria, Palestine, Egypt and Iran," none of those countries felt in the least threatened by Germany.[63] As the Führer mockingly pronounced the names of all of those nations which, of course, Germany would never dream of attacking, his audience in the Reichstag rocked with laughter, captivated by their leader's wit.

Hitler showed his true hand and his appetite for lawless aggression, wrote one perceptive *Washington Post* columnist who, reading between the lines, called his speech the *Mein Kampf* of 1939. While some French politicians who were committed to appeasement read a pacific intention into the speech, on Capitol Hill, adjectives such as "defiant" and "sinister" were heard among congressmen. Even Senator William Borah, an isolationist from Idaho who sat on the Senate's Foreign Relations Committee, expressed disappointment. The Führer's speech, he said, had put an end to discussions of peace. But other isolationists saw reasons for hope. Montana's Burton Wheeler dismissed the talk as something only for "home consumption"; Senator Gerald Nye of Iowa thought it opened the door for economic negotiations with Germany; and Congressman Hamilton Fish asserted that there would be no war "unless the hate and warcrazy administration in Washington goads the British and French into it."[64]

In late August, when the president received the devastating news that Germany had signed a nonaggression pact with the Soviet Union and that Hitler's invasion of Poland was imminent, there was little he could do other than send a last plea to Hitler for a nonmilitary resolution. A week later, the Führer replied.

In the middle of the night on September 1, 1939, FDR was awakened by an emergency phone call from Bullitt in Paris. He learned that more than one million Nazi troops had stormed into Poland and that German planes were bombing Warsaw. "It's come at last," the president sighed. "God help us."[65]

Hours later, General George C. Marshall was sworn in as army chief of staff with the rank of four-star general. The challenges he faced were staggering. "You certainly left me on a hot spot," Marshall wrote to his predecessor, the retiring general Malin Craig. Indeed, Marshall faced an unprecedented situation. During World War I, he had served in France as a director of training and planning and afterward as aide-de-camp to General and Army Chief of Staff John Pershing. But twenty years after World War I, military mobilization could encompass the entire planet as well as all of the resources of the United States. As military historian Mark A. Stoler wrote, Marshall would have to "move beyond many of the concepts and boundaries he had lived with throughout his life." Within days, the general asked for authorization for a rapid expansion of the regular army. Ranked only eighteenth in the world—just ahead of Bulgaria's—the army consisted of nine understrength divisions, one hundred and seventy-five thousand men all told. But Marshall found Roosevelt too cautious. The president permitted only a small increment—the addition of one hundred thousand men by voluntary enlistments to the armed forces and National Guard—and pared the army's requests for money for training and equipment.[66]

Two days later, when the British and the French declared war on Germany, FDR sought once again to reassure Americans that the nation would not send its soldiers abroad to fight. "Let no man or woman thoughtlessly or falsely talk of America sending its armies to European fields," he said in a fireside chat on Sunday, September 3. And yet, there was another side to the president's message that evening, one that was more revealing of his true thinking than his routine statement of neutrality. "Passionately though we may desire detachment," he said, "we are forced to realize that every word that comes through the air, every ship that sails the sea, every battle that is fought does *affect the American future*." And finally, he told Americans that, despite the nation's neutrality, they did not have to remain neutral in thought. "Even a neutral," he said in conclusion, "cannot be asked to close his mind or his conscience." But thoughts and words were not actions; on the contrary, they were an easy, passive way out of a commitment to military action abroad that neither the president nor his fellow citizens were yet willing to make.[67]

After delivering his talk, the president learned from his aides that three hours earlier, the Germans had torpedoed the British passenger liner *Athenia*. But unlike Americans' outraged and bellicose reaction to the sinking of the *Lusitania* in 1915, the attack on the *Athenia* sparked little protest—even though 28 of the 246 Americans on board lost their lives.[68]

In the fall of 1939, there seemed to be something almost schizophrenic in Roosevelt's war policy. The president requested more money for the army, asked the Federal Bureau of Investigation to arrest spies and investigate subversive activities, lashed out at isolationists as a fifth column, called for a special session of Congress to repeal the arms embargo, and closed U.S. waters to belligerents.[69] But he also told reporters a week after Germany's invasion of Poland that there was "no thought in any shape, manner or form of putting the Nation . . . on a war basis."[70] In a message to Congress on September 21, Roosevelt once again assured Americans that he would be guided by "one single hard-headed thought—keeping America out of this war."[71] And so, at the same time that he was taking a variety of measures to build up American military strength, the president hedged his words in public and above all waited for events to force his hand.

"Have you noticed," he wrote Frank Knox on October 4, 1939, "that I have been trying to kill all war talk?" The following day he confided in Lord Tweedsmuir, the governor general of Canada, that he was "*almost literally walking on eggs.* I am at the moment saying nothing, seeing nothing and hearing nothing."[72]

That same week the Senate continued its debate on a new neutrality bill, one that would modify the arms embargo and allow the sale and shipments of arms to the Allies—France and Britain. The debate had been dragging on for months. But finally, after numerous postponements, filibusters, compromises, emasculating amendments, votes, and conferences,[73] the bill passed.

On November 4, almost a year after he had proposed changes to the arms embargo in his annual message, the president signed the Neutrality Act of 1939. The new legislation at last repealed the arms embargo, making it possible for the United States to provide military aid—in non-American ships and on a "cash and carry" basis—to the democracies fighting for survival. It was a belated step, but also a courageous one, for that month a *Fortune* magazine poll reported that only 20 percent of Americans favored aiding the European democracies and 54 percent favored trade with both sides—Nazis and Allies alike.[74] Still, Senator William Borah of Idaho, who opposed these changes to the neutrality law, scoffed that "cash and carry" meant that America would help the Allies defend civilization "provided you pay cash."[75]

In mid-December 1939, Roosevelt invited William Allen White to spend a night at the White House. He wanted White to sit with him "on the sofa after supper and talk over small matters like the world problems." Though still a staunch Republican, White had become FDR's informal and occasional advisor.[76] In his letter, Roosevelt once again confided to White the intractable dilemma he faced. American public opinion, he wrote, "is patting itself on the back every morning and naively thanking God for the Atlantic and Pacific Oceans," as if those expanses of water made the United States invulnerable to attack. And while the world situation was getting progressively worse, Americans continued to underestimate "the serious implications to our own future."[77] But he proposed no course of action, no antidote to American somnolence.

At the Gridiron Club winter dinner in December, Raymond Clapper, the club's president, opened the evening's entertainment with pointed remarks about the antiwar mood in Washington. "While democracies in Europe fight to save themselves," he said, "Democrats in America decide to save themselves by not fighting. In 1916 the Democratic slogan was 'He kept us out of war.' In 1939, the Republican slogan is 'We kept HIM out of war.'"[78]

Roosevelt's annual message to Congress in January 1940 contained more of the same confusing signals. There was a "vast difference," he said, "between keeping out of war and pretending that this war is none of our business."

The world would be a "shabby and dangerous place," he remarked, if it were subjected to the rule of a few dictators. But then he changed tack and insisted that the isolationists had no monopoly on calling themselves the "peace bloc." All "right thinking" Americans, he asserted, could accept that label.

FDR was still "puzzling a good deal over ways to wake the country up to its world position," commented Rex Tugwell in February 1940.[79] Well, if he was puzzled, so was everyone else. What in fact was the difference between "keeping out of war" and rejecting the idea that "war is none of our business"? What did it mean to object to criminal dictatorships while seeking shelter in the "peace bloc"? Years earlier, FDR had spoken cogently about the importance of political leadership in a tumultuous world. The "blame for the danger to world peace," he said in a speech in late 1933, "lies not in the world population but in the *political leaders* of the population."[80] But political leaders, as he knew well, have constituencies to court, refractory members of their own party to conciliate, and opposition parties to handle. Roosevelt "could utter brave words," remarked one White House insider, "but, when deals were called for, he was hogtied by the prevailing isolationist sentiment."[81] Though FDR was supremely skilled in communicating and connecting with Americans, he had no unambiguous, resounding message about America's role and responsibility in the international crisis.

While the president was ruminating Hamlet-style over how and in what direction to lead, Hitler and his Nazi army acted.

On April 9, 1940, German troops advanced across the undefended border of Denmark. Offering no resistance, within a few hours Denmark fell to the Nazi grip. At the same time, there was another surprise attack in Norway: Nazi destroyers emerged from low-lying clouds, torpedoing gunboats in the port of Narvik. All along the coast, German vessels disgorged thousands of infantrymen who invaded Norway's port cities. In two days, Germany had taken over the country's main ports. Prime Minister Chamberlain sent British warships to help the Norwegians. "I pray God the Germans will not attack in the West," FDR wrote to his ambassador to Belgium, John Cudahy, a week after the German lightning strikes, "but judging by the Scandinavian action, they are complete experts at hiding their moves."[82]

On May 7, Dutch citizens were surprised by an announcement that all military leaves were immediately canceled, all reserves were called up for active duty, and all telephone lines reserved for military use. Across the border in Belgium, however, no precautions were taken; people went about their business with little sense of threat. But that day, Roosevelt's minister in The

Hague reported to Washington that Germany had issued ultimatums to the Dutch and Belgian governments; an assault on the two countries was expected within twenty-four or forty-eight hours. "I am much depressed and much occupied with world affairs," FDR again wrote to Cudahy on May 8. "The news today is very bad, and, of course, my hope, being of the Netherlands on my Father's side and of Belgium on my Mother's side, is that both nations will resist the rumored ultimatum to the bitter end."[83]

On May 10, with blinding speed, German warplanes, parachutists, infantry divisions, and tanks burst across the frontiers of Holland, Belgium, and Luxembourg. Nazi troops would "decide the destiny of the German people for a thousand years," exulted the demonic Adolf Hitler.[84] Neville Chamberlain resigned that day, and Winston Churchill was called to Buckingham Palace to accept the post of the King's First Minister. Five days later, German tanks and armored cars smashed through French defenses, rolling across the hills and fields of northern France. In the area of Sedan, near the borders of Belgium and Luxembourg, the French Ninth Army collapsed. As the shocking events in Europe unfolded, President Roosevelt spoke at a meeting of the Pan-American Scientific Congress in Washington. "I am a pacifist," he told the three thousand scientists in an address that was broadcast internationally. "You, my fellow citizens of twenty-one American Republics, are pacifists too. But I believe that by overwhelming majorities in all the Americas you and I, in the long run if it be necessary, will *act* together to protect and defend by every means at our command our science, our culture, our American freedom and our civilization."[85]

On May 15, five days after he was chosen prime minister, Churchill urgently wired the American president. "The scene has swiftly darkened," he wrote, imploring Roosevelt to send Great Britain thirty or forty reconditioned World War I destroyers and several hundred aircraft. "We expect to be attacked here ourselves," the 66-year-old prime minister gravely wrote, signing his telegram "Former Naval Person," a reminder that both he and Roosevelt had occupied similar positions during the First World War.[86] Churchill knew that if France, too, fell to the Nazis, Britain would be left standing alone against Hitler. But during that critical month of May, Roosevelt did not act and even turned away Churchill's urgent plea for destroyers. At a cabinet meeting a few days later, Harold Ickes heard the president say that he believed the odds were in favor of Germany. "And it certainly looks that way," Ickes sighed.[87]

The events of the tumultuous spring of 1940 forced FDR to "hit on all cylinders about seventeen hours a day," as he wrote to his daughter, Anna.[88] Meeting with dozens of people, dictating letters, reviewing reports and cables, scanning maps, making decisions, he had no time to leave his desk for lunch or watch evening movies upstairs in the White House. Though total war looked more and more likely, the president still had not decided upon a course of action.[89]

At the White House on May 13, General George Marshall, Treasury Secretary Henry Morgenthau, and a few others convened with the president to discuss more aggressive preparedness measures. It was evident, Marshall later recalled, that the president "was not desirous of seeing us." When Morgenthau broached the subject of appropriations for expanding and training the army and building bombers, the president was short with him. "Well, you filed your protest," Roosevelt snapped. "Well, Mr. President," said Morgenthau, "will you hear General Marshall?" In reply, Roosevelt insisted that he already knew "exactly" what Marshall would say. "There is no necessity for my hearing him at all."[90]

But Marshall persisted. "Mr. President, may I have three minutes?" The general usually was a team player. "I never haggled with the President," he later said. "I swallowed the little things so that I could go to bat on the big ones." Now, the issue was big, and world events forced him to think, plan, and lead on a global level. Talking for far more than three minutes, Marshall outlined the disastrous state of American military forces and equipment. Not only was war matériel in desperately short supply, but no more than fifteen thousand troops could go into combat at any one time—at a moment when the Germans had two million men equipped and trained for combat. Roosevelt listened quietly to the torrent of words. "If you don't do something," Marshall concluded, "and do it right away, I don't know what is going to happen to this country." He had broken through the logjam. "He stood right up to the president," an impressed Morgenthau wrote in his diary.[91] After the meeting, the secretary of the treasury congratulated the general. "You did a swell job, and I think you are going to get about 75% of what you want."[92]

Following those intense discussions,[93] the president addressed a joint session of Congress on May 16, 1940. As he tightly gripped the rostrum, reporters could see the whiteness of his knuckles. Soberly, forcefully, he asked members of the Senate and House of Representatives to "examine, without self-deception, the dangers which confront us," and he also asked Americans to "recast their thinking about national protection." Assailing the isolationist reverie of untroubled detachment from the wars in Europe, he pointed out that the world had entered a new age of air power and surprise bombing raids. Impregnable fortifications no longer existed. Not even the vast reaches of the

Atlantic and Pacific oceans could protect the American continent. No longer could the United States be considered invulnerable. From the fjords of Greenland, a Danish colony at risk of Nazi invasion, it was only hours by air to Newfoundland, Nova Scotia, and New England. And from the islands of the South Pacific, it was only several hours to the west coast of South America.[94]

With an emphatic tone of urgency, the president called on Congress to appropriate immediately more than a billion dollars for the army, navy, and air force and for the production of ships, tanks, and fifty thousand planes a year. The nation's defenses had to be invulnerable, its security absolute. It was a formidable task, especially because, since the end of the First World War, the armed forces had languished, undermanned, underfunded, and under-equipped. "Defense cannot be static," Roosevelt said. "Defense must grow and change from day to day." He prayed for peace, he told Congress, "but I am determined to face the fact *realistically* that this nation requires also a *toughness* of moral and physical fiber. Those qualities, I am convinced, the American people hold to a high degree."[95]

Realism and toughness: two qualities that Roosevelt prized. But since 1936, when events in Europe began to spiral out of control, neither his actions nor his words had been sufficiently realistic or tough. Especially in the election year of 1940, the president remained unwilling to move too far beyond public opinion. "Governments, such as ours, cannot swing so far or so quickly," the president wrote to Helen Reid, the publisher of the interventionist *New York Herald Tribune*. "They can only move with the thought and the will of the great majority of our people."[96]

But had the people moved ahead of him? According to a Gallup poll taken in June 1940, five out of eight Americans now believed that the United States would eventually be drawn into war, and, after the collapse of so many European democracies, a vast majority of Americans was now anti-Nazi and deeply sympathetic to Britain and France—so much so that the British ambassador Lord Lothian prematurely informed London that in the United States "isolationism is dead." Although 92 percent still opposed American entry into the European war and only 7 percent wanted the country to declare war on Germany, 65 percent believed that Germany would eventually start a war against the United States.[97]

Roosevelt found the greatest public support on the question of aid to the Allies: almost three quarters of Americans believed that the United States was "not doing enough" to aid the Allies, while only 6 percent thought America should give less help and 20 percent thought that "what we are doing is about right."[98] The pollsters, however, knew that Americans' opinions about the wars raging in Europe fluctuated, as did their sympathies for the victims of fascist aggression. Roosevelt's popularity, too, ebbed and flowed, rising with the wrath of Americans after each new act of German belligerence—and then waning as each emergency faded from the headlines.[99]

Roosevelt's task was enormously difficult. In addition to trying to remain sensitive to American public opinion, he was receiving contradictory advice from his closest advisors. While Harold Ickes faulted him for a *"lack of aggressive leadership,"*[100] General Marshall faulted his enthusiasm for aiding Great Britain. Though not opposed to the principle of such military aid, Marshall wanted first to make sure that Britain would survive, that American war matériel supplied to Britain would not fall into Nazi hands, and that assistance to Britain would not hinder America's buildup of its own forces.[101] If the United States was found to have given away the matériel needed for its own mobilization, remarked one of Marshall's planners in mid-June, "everyone who was a party to the deal might hope to be found hanging from a lamp post."[102]

Caution over military aid to the Allies, oscillating public opinion, a refractory Congress unwilling to give up the dream of neutrality, and a potent isolationist movement—everything conspired to complicate Roosevelt's ability to lead.

It was in the spring of 1940 that Franklin Roosevelt decided to run for a third term. He had been toying with the idea for months if not years, and, if he harbored any lingering doubts, Hitler and Mussolini helped him make up his mind. In May 1940, a headline in the *Washington Post* insightfully asked, "Will the European War Shatter an American Tradition and Elect a Third Term President?"[103] After Germany invaded Denmark and Norway, Sam Rosenman later commented, the president "became determined to stay in the White House until the Nazis were defeated." Frances Perkins also saw the events in Europe as the turning point for Roosevelt. "It seemed to me just inevitable that he would be the Democratic Presidential candidate," she said.[104]

Attorney General Robert Jackson, too, felt that war—and war alone—compelled the president to run for a third term. Jackson believed that, as far as domestic policy was concerned, the president had given virtually all that he had to give to the country during his first four years—he had pulled out everything that was in his bag of tricks. "Really, there was not much in the second four—a little, but not much," Jackson said. "There would have been no justification for a third term, except for the foreign situation. . . . It was foreign affairs only that warranted it." Jackson was even convinced that a third term for the president was "far to be preferred to a first term, an experimental term, a trial term, a novitiate, for a man without experience."[105]

The other men and women in the president's inner circle believed that it was probably too late for Americans to search for a new leader who would keep them out of war. What the nation needed was a proven leader, a leader who had the skills, experience, self-confidence, and courage to wage war and who was deeply committed to the idea of man's responsibility for the welfare and safety of his fellow man.

On July 5, 1940, Roosevelt held a press conference in the newly finished Franklin D. Roosevelt Library in Hyde Park. As he sat behind a mahogany desk in the room that was to be his private study one day, reporters peppered him with questions about his long-range vision for the nation. He thought for a moment and then sketched out his ideas. "You might say there are certain freedoms. The first I would call 'freedom of information,' which is terribly important." The second was freedom of religion, the third was freedom of expression "as long as you don't advocate the overthrow of government." The fourth, "freedom from fear, so that people won't be afraid of being bombed from the air, or attacked, one way or the other, by some other nation." The reporters scribbled his words down on their notepads. "Does that cover it pretty well?" Roosevelt asked. After a pause, one of the reporters spoke up. "Well, I had a fifth in mind which you might describe as 'freedom from want.'" "Yes," said the president, "that is true. I had that in mind but forgot it. . . . That is the fifth, very definitely." With the help of that friendly reporter from the *Philadelphia Inquirer*, he had hammered out what would become the key themes of his Four Freedoms address in the winter of 1941. Hitler's version of freedom, FDR noted at his press conference, was nothing more than freedom for the Nazis to "dominate and enslave the human race." While the Nazis stood for human slavery, the United States and its allies, he said, stood for human freedom and security.[106]

Little did Roosevelt know that his characterization of the Nazi ideology was an understatement. In May 1940, the German minister of agriculture, Richard-Walther Darré, had given a speech to high Nazi officials in Berlin, in which he outlined the vision and goals of the Reich. "A new aristocracy of German masters (*Herrenvolk*) will be created," Darré said. "This aristocracy will have slaves assigned to it, these slaves to be their property and to consist of landless, non-German nationals. . . . We actually have in mind a modern form of medieval slavery which we must and will introduce because we urgently need it in order to fulfill our great tasks. These slaves will by no means be denied the blessings of illiteracy; higher education will, in future, be reserved only for the German population of Europe."[107]

During his first presidential campaign in 1932, FDR had remarked, "It's a terrible job. But somebody has to do it."[108] Seven and a half years later, in the spring of 1940, the job had become infinitely more terrible. But despite his vague and contradictory stances, his tergiversations and equivocations, Roosevelt's mind and heart were firmly anchored in the internationalist camp. And he was sufficiently confident about his own talent for leadership to want to remain in the White House.

And yet, isolationists wielded formidable power in Washington as well as across the country. "We have many of our compatriots and even more friends among the citizens of the United States who are favorably disposed toward us," Darré had boasted to his listeners in Berlin.[109] Indeed, as Roosevelt campaigned a third unprecedented time for the presidency, he would confront the prodigious challenge of trying to defend human freedom while walking on eggs.

Chapter 4

Lindbergh and the Shrimps

D EAR FRISKY," President Roosevelt wrote in May 1940 to Roger Merriman, his history professor at Harvard and the master of Eliot House. "I like your word 'shrimps.' There are too many of them in all the Colleges and Universities—male and female. I think the best thing for the moment is to call them shrimps publicly and privately. Most of them will eventually get in line if things should become worse."[1]

To designate young isolationists, who deluded themselves into believing that America could remain aloof, secure, and distant from the wars raging in Europe, Roosevelt liked the amusing term "shrimps"—crustaceans possessing a nerve cord but no brain. In that critical month of May 1940, he finally realized that it was probably a question of when, not if, the United States would be drawn into war. Talk about neutrality or noninvolvement was no longer seasonable as the unimaginable dangers he had barely glimpsed in 1936 erupted into what he termed a "hurricane of events."[2]

On the evening of Sunday, May 26, 1940, days after the Germans began their thrust west, as city after city fell to the Nazi assault, a somber Roosevelt delivered a fireside chat about the dire events in Europe.

Earlier that evening, the president had distractedly prepared drinks for a small group of friends in his study. There was none of the usual banter. Dispatches were pouring into the White House. "All bad, all bad," Roosevelt grimly muttered, handing them to Eleanor to read.[3] But in his talk, as he tried to prepare Americans for what might lie ahead, he set a reflective, religious tone.

"On this Sabbath evening," he said in his reassuring voice, "in our homes in the midst of our American families, let us calmly consider what we have done and what we must do." But before talking about his decision to vastly increase the nation's military preparedness, he hurled an opening salvo at the isolationists.

They came in different sizes and shapes, he explained. One group of them constituted a Trojan horse of pro-German spies, saboteurs, and traitors. While not naming names, he singled out those who sought to arouse people's "hatred" and "prejudices" by resorting to "false slogans and emotional appeals." With fifth columnists who sought to "divide and weaken us in the face of danger," Roosevelt declared, "we must and will deal vigorously." Another group of isolationists, he explained, opposed his administration's policies simply for the sake of opposition—even when the security of the nation stood at risk.[4]

The president recognized that some isolationists were earnest in their beliefs and acted in good faith. Some were simply afraid to face a dark and foreboding reality. Others were gullible, eager to accept what they were told by some of their fellow Americans, that what was happening in Europe was "none of our business." These "cheerful idiots," as he would later call them in public,[5] naively bought into the fantasy that the United States could always pursue its peaceful and unique course in the world. They "honestly and sincerely" believed that the many hundreds of miles of salt water would protect the nation from the nightmare of brutality and violence gripping much of the rest of the world.

Though it might have been a comforting dream for FDR's "shrimps," the president argued that the isolationist fantasy of the nation as a safe oasis in a world dominated by fascist terror evoked for himself and for the overwhelming majority of Americans not a dream but a "nightmare of a people without freedom—the nightmare of a people lodged in prison, handcuffed, hungry, and fed through the bars from day to day by the contemptuous, unpitying masters of other continents."[6]

Two weeks after that fireside chat, on June 10, 1940, Roosevelt gave another key address about American foreign policy. This time it was in the Memorial Gymnasium of the University of Virginia in Charlottesville, to an audience that included his son Franklin, Jr., who was graduating from the Virginia Law School. That same day, the president received word that Italy would declare war on France and was sending four hundred thousand troops to invade the French Mediterranean coast. In his talk, FDR deplored the "gods of force and hate" and denounced the treacherous Mussolini. "On this tenth day of June, 1940," he declared, "the hand that held the dagger has plunged it into the back of its neighbor."[7]

But more than a denunciation of Mussolini's treachery and double-dealing, the speech finally gave a statement of American policy. It was time to "proclaim certain truths," the president said. Military and naval victories for the "gods of force and hate" would endanger all democracies in the western world. In this time of crisis, America could no longer pretend to be "a lone island in a world of force." Indeed, the nation could no longer cling to the fiction of neutrality. "Our sympathies lie with those nations that are giving their life blood in combat against these forces." Then he outlined his policy. America was simultaneously pursuing two courses of action. First, it was extending to the democratic Allies all the material resources of the nation; and second, it was speeding up war production at home so that America would have the equipment and manpower "equal to the task of any emergency and every defense." There would be no slowdowns and no detours. Everything called for speed, "full speed ahead!" Concluding his remarks, he summoned, as he had in 1933 when he first took the oath of office, Americans' "effort, courage, sacrifice and devotion."[8]

It was a "fighting speech," wrote *Time* magazine, "more powerful and more determined" than any the president had yet delivered about the war in Europe.[9] But the reality was actually more complicated.

On the one hand, the president had taken sides in the European conflict. No more illusions of "neutrality." And he had delivered a straightforward statement of the course of action he would pursue. On the other hand, he was not free to make policy unilaterally; he still had to contend with isolationists in Congress. On June 10, the day of his Charlottesville talk, with Germans about to cross the Marne southeast of Paris, it was clear that the French capital would soon fall. France's desperate prime minister, Paul Reynaud, asked Roosevelt to declare publicly that the United States would support the Allies "by all means short of an expeditionary force." But Roosevelt declined. He sent only a message of support labeled "secret" to Reynaud; and in a letter to Winston Churchill, he explained that "in no sense" was he prepared to commit the American government to "military participation in support of the Allied governments." Only Congress, he added, had the authority to make such a commitment.[10]

"We all listened to you last night," Churchill wired the president the day after the Charlottesville address, pleading, as he had done earlier in May, for more arms and equipment from America and paring down his request for destroyers from "forty or fifty" to "thirty or forty." "Nothing is so important," he wrote. In answer to Churchill's urgent appeal, the president arranged to send what he cleverly called "surplus" military equipment to Great

Britain. Twelve ships sailed for Britain, loaded with seventy thousand tons of bomber planes, rifles, tanks, machine guns, and ammunition—but no destroyers were included in the deal. Sending destroyers would be an act of war, claimed Senator David Walsh of Massachusetts, the isolationist chairman of the Senate Naval Affairs Committee. Walsh also discovered the president's plan to send twenty torpedo boats to Britain. Flying into a rage, he threatened legislation to prohibit such arms sales. Roosevelt backed down—temporarily—and called off the torpedo boat deal.[11]

Even as Nazi troops, tanks, and planes chalked up more conquests in Europe, the contest between the shrimps and the White House was not over. On the contrary, the shrimps still occupied a position of formidable strength.[12]

The glamorous public face and articulate voice of the isolationist movement belonged to the charismatic and courageous Charles Lindbergh. His solo flight across the Atlantic in May 1927 had catapulted the lanky, boyish, 25-year-old pilot onto the world stage. "Well, I made it," he said with a modest smile upon landing at Le Bourget airfield in Paris, as thousands of delirious French men and women broke through military and police lines and rushed toward his small plane. When he returned to New York two weeks later, flotillas of boats in the harbor, a squadron of twenty-one planes in the sky, and four million people roaring "Lindy! Lindy!" turned out to honor him in a joy-mad city, draped in flags and drenched in confetti and ticker tape. "No conqueror in the history of the world," wrote one newspaper, "ever received a welcome such as was accorded Colonel Charles A. Lindbergh yesterday."[13]

On May 19, 1940, a week before the president gave his fireside chat denouncing isolationists and outlining plans to build up American defenses, Lindbergh had made the isolationist case in his own radio address. The United States was not in danger from a foreign invasion unless "American people bring it on" by meddling in the affairs of foreign countries. The only danger to America, the flier insisted, was an "internal" one.

Though the president had explained that the Atlantic and Pacific oceans could no longer provide safe boundaries and could not protect the American continent from attack, Lindbergh insisted that the two vast oceans did indeed guarantee the nation's safety. "There will be *no invasion* by foreign aircraft," he stated categorically in his reedy voice, "and no foreign navy will dare to approach within bombing range of our coasts." America's sole task, he underscored, lay in "building and guarding our own destiny." If the nation stuck to a unilateral course, avoided entanglements abroad, refrained from intervening in European affairs, and built up its own defenses, it would be impregnable to foreign incursions. In any case, he stressed, it was pointless for the United States to risk submerging its future in the wars of Europe, for the die had already been cast. "There is no longer time for us to enter this war successfully," he assured his radio audience.

Deriding all the "hysterical chatter of calamity and invasion," Lindbergh charged that President Roosevelt's angry words against Germany would lead to "neither friendship nor peace."[14]

Friendship with Nazi Germany? Surely Lindbergh realized that friendship between nations signifies their mutual approval, trust, and assistance. But so starry-eyed was he about German dynamism, technology, and military might and so detached was he from the reality and consequences of German aggression and oppression that even on that day of May 19, when the headline in the *Washington Post* read, "NAZIS SMASH THROUGH BELGIUM, INTO FRANCE" and when tens of thousands of desperate Belgian refugees poured across the border into France, Lindbergh said he believed it would make no difference to the United States if Germany won the war and came to dominate all of Europe. *"Regardless of which side wins this war,"* he stated in his May 19 speech without a whiff of hesitation or misgiving, "there is no reason . . . to prevent a continuation of peaceful relationships between America and the countries of Europe." The danger, in his opinion, was not that Germany might prevail but rather that Roosevelt's antifascist statements would make the United States "hated by victor and vanquished alike."[15] The United States could and should maintain peaceful diplomatic and economic relations with whichever side won the war. Fascism, democracy—six of one, half a dozen of the other. His defeatist speech could not have been "better put if it had been written by Goebbels himself," Franklin Roosevelt remarked two days later.[16]

As the mighty German army broke through French defenses and thundered toward Paris, the dominance of Germany in Europe seemed obvious, inevitable, and justified to Lindbergh. Why, then, he wondered, did Roosevelt persist in his efforts to involve the nation in war? "The *only reason* that we are in danger of becoming involved in this war," he concluded in his May 19 speech, "is because there are *powerful elements* in America who desire us to take part. They represent a *small minority* of the American people, but they control much of the machinery of influence and propaganda." It was a veiled allusion to Jewish newspaper publishers and owners of major Hollywood movie studios. He counseled Americans to *"strike down* these elements of personal *profit* and *foreign* interest."[17] While his recommendation seemed to border on violence, he was also reviving the centuries-old anti-Semitic myth of Jews as stateless foreigners, members of an international conspiratorial clique with no roots in the "soil" and interested only in "transportable" paper wealth.[18]

"The Lindberghs and their friends laugh at the idea of Germany ever being able to attack the United States," wrote radio correspondent William Shirer, stationed in Berlin. "The Germans welcome their laughter and hope more Americans will laugh."[19] Also heartened by Lindbergh's words was the German military attaché in Washington, General Friedrich von Boetticher. "The circle about Lindbergh," von Boetticher wrote in a dispatch to Berlin, "now tries at least to impede the fatal control of American policy by the Jews."[20] The day after Lindbergh's speech, the defiant Hollywood studio heads, Jack and Harry Warner, wrote to Roosevelt to assure him that they would "do all in our power within the motion picture industry . . . to show the American people the worthiness of the cause for which the free peoples of Europe are making such tremendous sacrifices."[21]

Who could have foreseen in 1927 that Lindbergh, whose flight inspired a sense of transatlantic community and raised idealistic hopes for international cooperation, would come to embody the fiercest, most virulent brand of isolationism? Two years after his feat, Lindbergh gained entrée to the Eastern social and financial elite when he married Anne Morrow, the daughter of Dwight Morrow. A former J. P. Morgan partner and the ambassador to Mexico, Dwight Morrow would be elected as a Republican to the United States Senate in 1930, just before his death in 1931. Charles and Anne seemed to lead charmed lives—until their 20-month-old son was snatched from his crib in their rural New Jersey home in March 1932. Muddy footprints trailed across the floor in the second-floor nursery to an open window, beneath which a ladder had stood. "The baby's been kidnapped!" cried the nurse as she ran downstairs. The governor of New York, Franklin Roosevelt, immediately placed all the resources of the state police at the disposal of the New Jersey authorities. Two months later, the small body was found in a shallow grave. A German-born carpenter who had served time in prison for burglary, Bruno Hauptmann, was charged with the crime; Lindbergh identified his voice as the one he heard shouting in the darkness of a Bronx cemetery when he handed over $50,000 in ransom.[22]

Carrying a pistol visible in a shoulder holster, Lindbergh attended the trial in January 1935, sitting just a few seats away from the accused. After Hauptmann's conviction and move for an appeal, Eleanor Roosevelt oddly and gratuitously weighed in, second-guessing the jury and announcing that she was a "little perturbed" that an innocent man might have been found guilty.

But the conviction stood, and Hauptmann would be executed in the electric chair in April 1936.[23]

In December 1935, in the wake of the trial, Charles and Anne, harassed and sometimes terrified by intrusive reporters as well as by would-be blackmailers, fled to Europe with their 3-year-old son, Jon. "America Shocked by Exile Forced on the Lindberghs" read the three-column headline on the front page of the *New York Times*.[24]

Would the crowd-shy Lindbergh and his wife find a calm haven in Europe? The Old World also has its gangsters, commented a French newspaper columnist, adding that Europe "suffers from an additional disquieting force, for there everyone is saying, 'There is going to be war soon.'" The Nazi press, however, took a different stance. "As Germans," wrote the *Deutsche Allgemeine Zeitung* with an absence of irony, "we cannot understand that a civilized nation is not able to guarantee the safety of the bodies and lives of its citizens."[25]

For several years the Lindberghs enjoyed life in Europe, first in England, in a house in the hills near Kent, and later on a small, rocky island off the coast of Brittany. In the summer of 1936, the couple visited Germany, where they were wined and dined by Hermann Goering, second only to Hitler in the Nazi hierarchy, and other members of the party elite.[26] Goering personally led Lindbergh on an inspection tour of aircraft factories, an elite Luftwaffe squadron, and research facilities. The American examined new engines for dive bombers and combat planes and even took a bomber up in the air. It was a "privilege" to visit modern Germany, the awestruck Lindbergh said afterward, showering praise on "the genius this country has shown in developing airships."[27] Photographers snapped pictures of Charles and his wife, relaxed and smiling in Goering's home.[28] Lindbergh's reports on German aviation overflowed with superlatives about "the astounding growth of German air power," "this miraculous outburst of national energy in the air field," and the "scientific skill of the *race*."[29] The aviator, however, showed no interest in speaking with foreign correspondents in Germany, "who have a perverse liking for enlightening visitors on the Third Reich," William Shirer dryly noted.[30]

In Berlin, Lindbergh's wife, Anne, was blinded by the glittering façade of a Potemkin village. She was enchanted by "the sense of festivity, flags hung out, the Nazi flag, red with a swastika on it, *everywhere*, and the Olympic flag, five rings on white." The Reich's dynamism was so impressive. "There is no question of the power, unity and purposefulness of Germany," she wrote effusively to her mother, adding that Americans surely needed to overcome their knee-jerk, "puritanical" view that dictatorships were "of necessity wrong, evil, unstable." The enthusiasm and pride of the people were "thrilling." Hitler himself, she added on a dreamy, romantic note, "is a very great man, like an inspired religious leader—and as such rather fanatical—but not scheming, not selfish, not greedy for power, but a mystic, a visionary who really wants the best for his country and *on the whole* has rather a broad view."[31]

On August 1, 1936, Charles and Anne attended the opening ceremonies of the Olympic Games in Berlin, sitting a few feet away from Adolf Hitler. As the band played "Deutschland über alles," blond-haired little girls offered bouquets of roses to the Führer, the delighted host of the international games. Theodore Lewald, the head of the German Organizing Committee, declared the games open, hailing the "real and spiritual bond of fire between our German fatherland and the sacred places of Greece founded nearly 4,000 years ago by Nordic immigrants." Leaving the following day for Copenhagen, Lindbergh told reporters at the airport that he was "intensely pleased" by what he had observed. His presence in the Olympic Stadium and his warm words about Germany helpfully added to the luster and pride of the Nazis.[32] Also present at the Olympic games, William Shirer overheard people in Nazi circles crow that they had succeeded in "making the Lindberghs 'understand' Nazi Germany."[33]

In truth, Lindbergh had glimpsed a certain unsettling fanaticism in Germany, but, as he reasoned to a friend, given the chaotic situation in Germany after World War I, Hitler's achievements "could hardly have been accomplished without some fanaticism." Not only did he judge that the Führer was "undoubtedly a great man," but that Germany, too, "has more than her share of the elements which make strength and greatness among nations."[34] Despite some reservations about the Nazi regime, Lindbergh believed that the Reich was a "stabilizing factor" in Europe in the 1930s. Another visit to Germany in 1937 confirmed his earlier impressions. German aviation was "without parallel in history"; Hitler's policies "seem laid out with great intelligence and foresight"; and any fanaticism he had glimpsed was offset by a German "sense of *decency* and value which in many ways is *far ahead of our own.*"[35]

In the late spring of 1938, Lindbergh and his wife moved to the tiny Breton island of Illiec, where Charles could carry on lengthy conversations with his neighbor and mentor, Dr. Alexis Carrel, an award-winning French scientist and eugenicist who instructed the flier in his scientific racism. In his 1935 book *Man, the Unknown*, Carrel had laid out his theories, his criticism of parliamentary democracy and racial equality. Asserting that the West was a "crumbling civilization," he called for the "gigantic strength of science" to help eliminate "defective" individuals and breeds and prevent "the degeneration of the [white] race." In the introduction to the German edition of his book, he praised Germany's "energetic measures against the propagation of retarded individuals, mental patients, and criminals."[36]

In the fall of 1938, Charles and Anne returned to Germany. In October, at a stag dinner in Berlin hosted by the American ambassador and attended by the Italian and Belgian ambassadors as well as by German aircraft designers and engineers, Goering surprised the aviator by bestowing on him, "in the name of the Führer," Germany's second-highest decoration, a medal—the Service Cross of the Order of the German Eagle—embellished with a golden cross and four small swastikas. Lindbergh wore it proudly that evening. Afterward, when he returned from the embassy, he showed the medal to Anne, who correctly predicted that it would become an "albatross."[37]

The Lindberghs wanted to spend the winter in Berlin, and Anne even found a suitable house in the Berlin suburb of Wannsee. They returned to Illiec to pack up for the move, but changed their plans when they learned of Kristallnacht. "My admiration for the Germans is constantly being dashed against some rock such as this," Lindbergh lamented in his diary, expressing dismay at the persecution of Jews at the hands of Nazi thugs. Concerned that their taking up residence in Berlin might cause "embarrassment" to the German and American governments, he and Anne rented an apartment in Paris instead. And yet, Lindbergh's deep admiration for Germany was not seriously dampened.[38] On the contrary, crossing the border from Belgium into Germany in December 1938, Lindbergh was captivated by the fine-looking young German immigration officer whose "air of discipline and precision," he wrote, was "in sharp contrast to the easygoing pleasantness of Belgium and France."[39] Germany still offered the striking image of the virility and modern technology he prized. The spirit of the German people, he told John Slessor, a deputy director in Britain's Air Ministry, was "magnificent"; he especially admired their refusal to admit that anything was impossible or that any obstacle was too great to overcome. Americans, he sighed, had lost that strength and optimism.[40] Strength was the key to the future. It appeared eminently rational and fair to Charles Lindbergh that Germany should dominate Europe because, as he wrote, "no system . . . can succeed in which the voice of weakness is equal to the voice of strength."[41]

In April 1939, Lindbergh returned to the United States, his wife and two young sons following two weeks later. A few years earlier he had discussed with his British friends the possibility of relinquishing his American citizenship,[42] but now he decided that if there was going to be a war, he would remain loyal to America. Even so, on the same day that he and Anne discussed moving back to America, he confessed in his diary that, of all the countries he had lived in, he had "found the most personal freedom in Germany." Moreover, he still harbored "misgivings" about the United States; critical of the "short-sightedness and vacillation" of democratic statesmen, he was convinced that, in order to survive in the new totalitarian world, American democracy would have to make "great changes in its present practices."[43]

Back on American soil in April, Lindbergh immediately launched into a tireless round of meetings with scientists, generals, and government officials,[44] spreading the word about the remarkable advances in aviation he had seen in Germany and pushing for more research and development of American air and military power.[45] Though he believed in American isolation, he also believed in American preparedness.

On April 20, 1939, Lindbergh had a busy day in Washington: first a meeting with Secretary of War Harry Woodring and then one with President Roosevelt at the White House. After waiting for forty-five minutes, the aviator entered the president's office. "He is an accomplished, suave, interesting conversationalist," Lindbergh wrote later that day in his diary. "I liked him and feel that I could get along with him well." But he suspected that they would never agree on "many fundamentals" and moreover sensed that there was "something about him I did not trust, something a little too suave, too pleasant, too easy. . . . Still, he is our President," Lindbergh concluded. He would try to work with him, he noted, cautiously adding that "I have a feeling that it may not be for long."[46]

Emerging after half an hour from a side exit of the executive mansion, Lindbergh found himself besieged by photographers and reporters. The boisterous scene was "disgraceful," the camera-shy aviator bitterly judged. "There would be more dignity and self-respect among African Savages." After their meeting, neither Lindbergh nor the White House would shed any light on what had been discussed. Rumors would later surface that, at that April meeting or several months later, the president had offered the aviator a cabinet appointment, but such rumors were never substantiated.[47]

From the White House that April day, Lindbergh went to a session of the National Advisory Committee for Aeronautics (NACA) and spoke about the importance of establishing a program to develop technologically advanced aircraft. While he backed the NACA's recommendation that the government allocate $10 million for a West Coast research center, not even that represented sufficient progress in Lindbergh's mind. It would still leave the United States "far behind a country like Germany in research facilities," he wrote in his diary. "We could not expect to keep up with the production of European airplanes as long as we were on a peacetime basis."[48]

Lindbergh was unrelenting in his message about military preparedness.[49] One scientist who listened carefully to him was Vannevar Bush, the chairman of the NACA and head of the Carnegie Institution, a research organization in Washington. After several more meetings that spring, the two men agreed that a plan was needed to revive the NACA. Bush "soaked up" Lindbergh's opinions, wrote Bush's biographer G. Pascal Zachary. Indeed, so impressed was Bush that he offered Lindbergh the chairmanship or vice chairmanship of the NACA—an offer the aviator declined. Early in 1940 Bush received another report from Lindbergh that repeated his alarm about a serious lack of engine research facilities in the United States and called for "immediate steps to remedy this deficiency."[50]

Deeply concerned after reading Lindbergh's recommendations, Bush drafted a proposal for the creation of a National Defense Research Council (NDRC), an organization that would supervise and fund the work of American engineers and scientists. On June 12, 1940, Bush met for the first time with President Roosevelt in the Oval Office. He handed him his memo—four short paragraphs on a single sheet of paper. It was enough, one of Bush's colleagues later wrote, to convince the president of the need to harness technology for possible war. Taking out his pen, he wrote on the memo the magical words, "OK—FDR."[51]

During the war, two thirds of the nation's physicists would be working under Vannevar Bush. One of the secret projects he supervised until 1943, when it was turned over to the army, was known as Section S1. The S1 physicists sought to unlock energy from the fission of atoms of a rare isotope of uranium. And among the starting places for that work as well as for Bush's creation of the NDRC were his informative and disturbing conversations with Charles Lindbergh.[52]

In June 1940, as France fell to Nazi troops and planes, Lindbergh turned to memories of his father for reassurance and wisdom. "Spent the evening reading Father's *Why Is Your Country at War?*" he wrote in his diary.[53] That 1917 book justified the son's alarm at the prospect of America's entry into another European war. Charles Lindbergh, Sr., a progressive Minnesota Republican who died in 1924, had served in the House of Representatives from 1907 to 1917. His young son, Charles, ran errands and addressed letters for him and occasionally was seen in the House gallery, watching his father on the floor below. Although Lindbergh, Sr., had been a follower of Theodore Roosevelt, on the question of American participation in the First World War, he and the bellicose TR parted company.[54]

Why Is Your Country at War? was a long-winded, turgid antiwar tract, arguing that the United States had been drawn into the war by the machinations of "cowardly politicians," wealthy bankers, and the Federal Reserve Bank. The senior Lindbergh did not oppose the violence of war per se. Rather, this midwestern agrarian railed against the injustice of a war organized and promoted as a for-profit enterprise by the "wealth grabbers" of Wall Street, people like the Morgans and the Rockefellers. Ironically, the men of the "power elite" whom he most despised might have included his son's future father-in-law, Dwight Morrow, a Morgan partner—though Lindbergh, Jr., later told an interviewer that he believed that his father and Dwight Morrow would probably have liked each other. At bottom, the elder Lindbergh's screed was a rambling, populist, socialist primer that offered radical remedies for the twin evils of war and capitalism.[55]

When his book appeared in print, Lindbergh, Sr., had to defend himself—not against the charge that he was anticapitalist, which would have been true, but rather against the charge that he was pro-German. He was hung in effigy and taunted as a "friend of the Kaiser."[56] Though there was nothing pro-German in the book, the accusations contributed to his defeat when he ran for governor of Minnesota in 1918. "If you are really for America first," he wrote in his own defense, "then you are classed as pro-German by the big press[es] which are supported by the speculators."[57]

Like his father, Charles Lindbergh, Jr., would also face allegations that he was pro-German. But in his case the indictment rang true.[58]

In the aviator's mind, Germany had it made. In England there was "organization without spirit," he would tell a radio audience in August 1940. "In France there was spirit without organization; in Germany there were both."[59] Indeed, the more Lindbergh had lived among the English people, the less confidence he had in them. They struck him, he wrote, as unable to connect to a "modern world working on a modern tempo." And sadly, he judged that it was too late for them to catch up, "to bring back lost opportunity."[60] Britain's only hope, as he once mentioned to his wife, was to learn from the Germans and to adopt their methods in order to survive. Nor did he have confidence or respect for democracy in the United States. On the American continent, he felt surrounded by mediocrity. Writing in his diary in the summer of 1940, he bemoaned the decline of American society—"the superficiality, the cheapness, the lack of understanding of, or interest in, fundamental problems." And making the problems worse were the Jews. "There are too many places like New York already," he wrote, alluding to that city's Jewish population. "A few Jews add strength and character to a country, but too many create chaos. And we are getting too many."[61]

Was Lindbergh a Nazi? He was "transparently honest and sincere," remarked Sir John Slessor, the Royal Air Force marshal who met several times with Lindbergh. It was Lindbergh's very "decency and naiveté," Slessor later said, that convinced him that the aviator was simply "a striking example of the effect of German propaganda." One of Lindbergh's acquaintances, the journalist and poet Selden Rodman, also tried to explain the aviator's affinity for Nazi Germany. "Perhaps it is the conservatism of his friends and the aristocratic racial doctrines of Carrel that have made him sympathetic to Nazism," Rodman wrote. "Perhaps it is the symbolism of his lonely flight and the terrible denouement of mass-worship and the kidnapping that have driven him to the unpopular cause because it is unpopular; that always makes the Byronic hero spurn fame and fortune for guilt and solitary persecution."[62]

For his part, Lindbergh knew that many of his views were unpopular in certain circles, but, as he told a nationwide radio audience in 1940, "I would far rather have your respect for the sincerity of what I say than attempt to win your applause by confining my discussion to popular concepts."[63] Mistaking sincerity for intelligence and insight, he considered himself a realist who grasped that German technological advances had profoundly and irrevocably altered the balance of power in Europe. The only issue, he once explained to Ambassador Joseph Kennedy, was "whether this change will be peaceably accepted, or whether it must be tested by war."[64] Priding himself on his clear-eyed understanding of military strength, he darkly predicted in June 1940, before the Battle of Britain had even begun, that the end for England "will come fast."[65]

The playwright Robert Sherwood, whom FDR would draft in the summer of 1940 to join his speechwriting team, may have come closest to the truth about Lindbergh. The aviator, he dryly commented, had "an exceptional understanding of the power of machines as opposed to the principles which animate free men."[66] As Sherwood suggested, Lindbergh may simply have been naive about politics, ignorant about history, uneducated in foreign policy and national security, and deluded by his infatuation with German technology and vigor. Perhaps he did not fully appreciate, Sherwood said, the extent to which the German people "are now doped up with the cocaine of world revolution and the dream of world domination."[67]

Despite his exuberant enthusiasm for Germany, his disenchantment with democracy, the zealous applause he received from fascists in the United States and in Germany, his admiration for the racial ideas of Alexis Carrel, his increasingly extremist and anti-Semitic speeches, and the fact that his simplistic views mirrored Nazi propaganda in the United States, Lindbergh seemed to want what he believed was best for America.[68] And yet Franklin Roosevelt may have been instinctively correct in his own less nuanced view.

"I am absolutely convinced that Lindbergh is a Nazi," FDR said melodramatically to his secretary of the treasury and old Dutchess County neighbor and friend, Henry Morgenthau, in May 1940, two days after Lindbergh's May 19 speech. "If I should die tomorrow, I want you to know this." The president lamented that the 38-year-old flier "has completely abandoned his belief in our form of government and has accepted Nazi methods because apparently they are efficient."[69]

Others in the White House shared that assessment. Lindbergh, Harold Ickes sneered, pretentiously posed as a "heavy thinker" but never uttered "a word for democracy itself." The aviator was the "Number 1 Nazi fellow traveler," Ickes said.[70] The delighted German embassy wholeheartedly agreed. "What Lindbergh proclaims with great courage," wrote the German military attaché to his home office in Berlin, "is certainly the highest and most effective form of propaganda."[71] In other words, why would Germany need a fifth column in the United States when it had in its camp the nation's hero, Charles Lindbergh?

Chapter 5

Isolationists: The War Within

I N THE LATE 1930S, while Hitler was issuing an ultimatum to Czechoslovakia and exhorting his military chiefs to "act brutally! Be hard and remorseless! Be steeled against all signs of compassion!," a ferocious debate raged in the United States about American foreign policy.[1] It was a bitter, divisive clash between isolationists and internationalists—more virulent than the debates over communism in the late 1940s, McCarthyism in the early 1950s, or Vietnam in the 1960s. Families and friends, churches, universities, and political parties found themselves torn apart.[2] Even an isolationist like Herbert Hoover pleaded for both sides to use "cool judgment" and put an end to the "ferocity" of the public debate.[3]

Charles Lindbergh was the heroic, celebrated spokesman for the isolationists, but in fact isolationists and anti-interventionists came in all stripes and colors—ideological, economic, ethnic, geographical. Making up this eclectic coalition were farmers, union leaders, wealthy industrialists, college students, newspaper publishers, wealthy patricians, and newly arrived immigrants. There were Democrats, Republicans, socialists, communists, anticommunists, radicals, pacifists, and simple FDR-haters. While the least isolationist region was the South, with its strong military tradition and cultural and blood ties to Great Britain, the most isolationist region of the country was the inland, insulated Midwest and the Plains states.[4] But nonregional factors also played a role: isolationists included Americans of Scandinavian and German origin who championed strict neutrality, Italian-Americans who admired Mussolini, and Irish-Americans who cheered for anyone fighting against England.

Among those who wanted the United States to remain uninvolved in European wars were the former president of the United States Herbert Hoover and a future president, Gerald Ford; the advertising executive Chester Bowles, who would serve in the administrations of Roosevelt, Truman, and Kennedy;[5] and labor leader John L. Lewis, the president of the United Mine Workers and the Congress of Industrial Organizations.

In the halls of Congress, senators and congressmen of all political persuasions jumped on the isolationist bandwagon. There were populist Farm-Laborites like Henrik Shipstead and Ernest Lundeen of Minnesota; independents like George Norris of Nebraska; and left-wing American Laborites like New York's Vito Marcantonio. And there were Democrats like Senators Rush Holt of West Virginia and David Walsh of Massachusetts, who believed that it was "not our concern" what kind of governments other nations have and insisted on a foreign policy of "mind your own business."[6] Democrat Burton Wheeler of Montana, a senator since 1923, supported FDR on most New Deal legislation but deserted the Roosevelt administration on war-related issues. "I do not want to see the American people dragged into a war for . . . driving fascism from the world," Wheeler said in 1937, promising his constituents to vote for "every single piece of legislation that will stop war and keep us out of war."[7]

But it was especially Republicans who possessed, as Robert Sherwood put it, the "isolationist fetish."[8] Among the isolationists were conservative Republicans like Herbert Hoover, Senators Robert Taft of Ohio and Arthur Vandenberg of Michigan, and Congressman Hamilton Fish, who represented FDR's own New York district. Heaping scorn on the interventionists who wanted to "police the world with American blood and treasure," Fish defined the struggle as "Americanism against Internationalism."[9] Progressive Republicans, too, wanted no part of the European conflict: men like Hiram Johnson of California, Lynn Frazier of North Dakota, Robert La Follette of Wisconsin, William Borah of Idaho, and Gerald Nye of North Dakota, the most isolationist state in the nation.[10] They all spoke out for noninvolvement and, as Nye said, for a *reasonable* approach to Germany by our government."[11] In April 1940, Nye told a college audience that nothing in the European war was "worthy of the sacrifice of one American mule, much less one American son." Norwegian-Americans in his home state protested the idea that one mule was worth more than their recently invaded mother country of Norway. But Nye refused to retreat from his position, and years later he would blame the Norwegian-American vote in North Dakota for his defeat in 1944.[12] For his part, Senator Johnson, who had been Theodore Roosevelt's progressive running-mate in 1912 and had crossed party lines in 1932 to support FDR, stated in October 1939 that it was "idiotic" to believe that Hitler could conquer Europe.[13]

Few Republicans in Congress expressed interest in resisting fascism or even in building up America's defense capability. In 1939, 122 Republicans in the House of Representatives voted against an increase in the Army Air Corps, while only 5 Republicans voted in favor. By a similar margin, House Republicans also voted against a repeal of the arms embargo.[14]

But Washington did not have a monopoly on isolationism. Many distinguished intellectuals were isolationists—such as the president of the University of Chicago and educational reformer, Robert Maynard Hutchins, and the respected historian Charles Beard. A former president of the American Political Science Association and the author of *An Economic Interpretation of the Constitution of the United States*, Beard had been a New Deal stalwart and a critic of laissez-faire capitalism and rugged individualism.[15] But in 1936 he published *The Devil Theory of War: An Inquiry into the Nature of History and the Possibility of Keeping Out of War* and became a vocal opponent of FDR's attempts at internationalism. In an appearance before the House Naval Affairs Committee in February 1938, Beard ridiculed Roosevelt's foreign policy as a "new racket," scoffed at the idea that "the Fascist goblins of Europe" could threaten North or South America, and admonished the president to halt his "gratuitous advice and insults to foreign governments."[16] The United States, he insisted in his 1939 book *America in Midpassage*, should "not attempt to carry the Atlas load of the White Man's Burden . . . to settle the difficult problems of European nations." Instead the nation should simply concentrate on making America's own civilization "more beautiful."[17] The following year, in *A Foreign Policy for America*, Beard again insisted that the United States concentrate solely on solving "the grave social and economic crises at home." In the margin of his copy of Beard's book, a scornful FDR scribbled, "40 years hard and continuous study has brought forth an inbred mouse."[18]

An intellectual whose isolationism was saturated with fascism was Lawrence Dennis. Harold Ickes called him the "Brains of American fascism."[19] In 1936 the Harvard-educated Dennis published the futuristically entitled *The Coming of American Fascism* and, in 1940, *The Dynamics of War and Revolution*. Dennis effused about Nazi dynamism and fawned over Hitler's "genius." Convinced that Germany's triumph over the Allies was "imminent," Dennis hammered Roosevelt—"a semi-paralyzed country squire"—for alienating the inevitable fascist victors. Democracy and capitalism were played out and moribund, Dennis argued, calling for a new "discipline and direction" for American society, for "more collectivism and less individualism."[20] Meeting with one of the editors of *Fortune* magazine in early 1941, Dennis explained that he did not fear a Hitler-dominated Europe because he believed, as he said, "that the United States would have to develop a Hitler of its own, and a Nazified America would be strong enough to balance off a Nazified Europe."[21]

Joining these authors in whipping up isolationist sentiment were publishers like William Randolph Hearst with his nationwide chain of newspapers, Joseph Patterson of the *New York Daily News*; Colonel Robert R. McCormick, owner of the *Chicago Daily Tribune*; and Oswald Garrison Villard, the former publisher and editor of the *Nation* magazine and grandson of the great abolitionist William Lloyd Garrison.

Isolationists also included major industrialists, like automobile manufacturer Henry Ford. In 1916, Theodore Roosevelt had scolded Ford for his pacifism during the First World War, pacifism that, in the 1930s, morphed into pro-German isolationism.[22] Not only did Ford pledge in a company newsletter to cooperate in helping the Führer achieve his goals of "honor, liberty and happiness for Greater Germany," but he refused to permit his American plants to fill orders involving engines and weapons for the British.[23] In gratitude for the military vehicles manufactured at the Ford-Werke plant in Cologne, Hitler rewarded Henry Ford with the Grand Cross of the German Eagle. In 1945, a U.S. Army report would accuse the German branch of Ford of serving as "an arsenal of Nazism, at least for military vehicles."[24]

Other powerful business leaders were less ideologically driven than Ford and merely put trade and profits and the continuation of the status quo ahead of everything else. James Mooney, the vice president for overseas operations of the General Motors Corporation, advocated doing business with the totalitarian nations if they provided nonaggression guarantees to the United States. A recipient of a medal for "distinguished service to the Reich," Mooney participated in the conversion of the General Motors plant in Russelsheim from automobile manufacturing to engine production for German bombers. "If the Bokseviki are to be kept out of the Baltic and the Balkans," Mooney warned upon returning to the United States from Europe in December 1939, "only Germany can do the job."[25] The president of General Motors, Graeme Howard, also supported business with Germany; in his 1940 book, *America and a New World Order*, he argued that appeasement was a rational option and a far better one than "blind intervention."[26] Torkild Rieber, chairman of the board of Texaco, shipped oil and other petroleum products to Germany, helping the Nazis stockpile fuel. When his close ties with the commercial attaché at the

German embassy were made public in the spring of 1940, Rieber was forced to resign.[27]

Isolationists had multiple and complex grounds for their opposition to American intervention in the war. Some were pacifists—men like socialist Norman Thomas, and the founders of the "Keep America Out of War Congress" Robert La Follette and Oswald Garrison Villard.[28] Others, like Robert M. Hutchins and Herbert Hoover, a Quaker, were haunted by memories of the First World War and the wanton and meaningless destruction of young lives, so powerfully commemorated by writers of the 1920s like Erich Maria Remarque and John Dos Passos.[29]

American communists surged into the isolationist ranks. Between 1935 and 1939, they had toed the Soviet Union's antifascist line and even supported the New Deal as a rampart against the fascist tide. But when Stalin signed the Nazi-Soviet Non-Aggression Pact in August 1939, they made a 180-degree shift, denouncing Roosevelt as a warmonger who obeyed the dictates of America's economic royalists. In September 1940, they formed the American Peace Mobilization (APM). Although it never built up much of an organization, the APM kept a perpetual picket line and peace vigil in front of the White House—that is, until June 22, 1941. On that day, Hitler invaded the Soviet Union, and American communists made another abrupt about-face, fleeing from the stain of isolationism and demanding full American aid for the Soviet Union and Great Britain.[30]

There were also anticommunist isolationists. Viewing communism as a grave threat to American capitalism and democracy, they hailed Nazi Germany as a bulwark against the spread of Bolshevism. Though the Nazi-Soviet Pact demolished their pro-German stance, they continued to cling to anticommunism. After the German attack on the Soviet Union, they were horrified by the idea that the United States might find itself allied with Russian communists. One vocal isolationist organization argued that the Roosevelt administration could hardly ask Americans to take up arms "behind the red flag of Stalin" and reminded American Catholics of Pope Pius XI's 1937 encyclical affirming that communism was "intrinsically wrong" and that no Christian "may collaborate with it in any undertaking whatsoever." Agreeing with those sentiments, Senator Bennett Champ Clark of Missouri asked if American boys would be sent to their deaths "singing 'Onward Christian Soldiers' under the bloody emblem of the Hammer and Sickle."[31] And Charles Lindbergh declared at a rally in 1941 that he would "a hundred times rather see my country ally herself with . . . Germany with all her faults" than with the godless Soviet Union.[32]

Few isolationists, however, were willing to sign on to Charles Lindbergh's racial theories and follow him down the path to the master race. "Our bond with Europe is a bond of *race* and not of political ideology," Lindbergh emphasized to a radio audience in October 1939. "Racial strength is vital, politics, a luxury." He fervently believed that a purely Aryan Germany would provide an invincible safeguard for the white race, galvanizing the collective strength and will of Europe to protect white Europeans against Russians and other Slav and "Asiatic intruders"—non-Aryan lesser breeds like Mongol Khans, Turks, Persians, Czechs—and, of course, Jews. He was convinced that a war against Germany would have the disastrous effect of diluting America's "most priceless possession, our inheritance of European blood." The only war worth fighting, in his mind, was one to preserve the European race, and in *that* war he wanted America to fight "side by side" with the Nazis. His words, in fact, echoed Hitler's *Mein Kampf*: "The State [is] only a means to an end and as its end it considers the preservation of the racial existence of men."[33]

More appealing to isolationists than Lindbergh's racialism was the age-old prejudice of anti-Semitism. Scattered throughout the isolationist ranks were dyed-in-the-wool Jew-haters like Joe McWilliams, the head of the American Destiny Party;[34] the pro-Hitler William Dudley Pelley, founder of the "Silver Shirt Legion," whose members, called "Silver Shirts," wore Nazi-like silver uniforms;[35] the expatriate poet Ezra Pound, who had embraced Italian fascism and wrote articles with titles like "The Jew, Disease Incarnate"; and Father Charles Coughlin, the Detroit radio priest who reprinted the notorious anti-Semitic tract "The Protocols of the Elders of Zion" in his periodical *Social Justice* in order to promote his belief that a Jewish conspiracy was pushing the country into war.[36] Henry Ford's isolationism was also steeped in anti-Semitism. In 1920, he had paid for the publication and distribution of a four-volume anthology of hate called *The International Jew: The World's Problem*; it included articles entitled "The Historic Basis of Jewish Imperialism," "How Jews in the U.S. Conceal Their Strength," "How Jews Gained American Liquor Control," and "The Jewish Associates of Benedict Arnold."[37]

Many isolationists shared a sense of defeatism. Why make sacrifices and spend the national treasure to defend worn-out European nations destined to succumb to the overwhelming might of Nazi Germany? A June 1940 editorial in the *Wall Street Journal* entitled "A Plea for Realism" maintained that "our job today is not to stop Hitler" but rather to become accustomed to his rule. "Hitler has already determined the broad lines of our national life for at least another generation," the *Journal* peremptorily decided. "European totalitarianism has made obsolete our American way of life, temporarily at least; permanently, unless we modernize our thinking and our national planning."

As nation after nation folded before the Nazi onslaught, Charles Lindbergh added his own brand of military defeatism to the mix, preaching that it was "improbable" that the Allied armies could recover their strength in time to defeat the Axis powers. Any such effort would mean ten to thirty years of warfare at the cost of millions of lives, and the final result would be the downfall of all European civilization and "the establishment of conditions in our own country far worse even than those in Germany today."[38]

The isolationists' defeatism was linked to their recurring theme of the fundamental fragility of democracy; it seemed axiomatic to them that democratic government and participation in another world war were mutually exclusive. As early as 1936 President Roosevelt had called on Americans to have confidence and "faith in the soundness of democracy in the midst of dictatorships," but many isolationists were convinced that personal liberty and economic freedom in the United States would not survive if the nation went to war with Germany.[39] America would find itself transformed "into practically a Fascist state," wrote Herbert Hoover, certain that the inevitable wartime restrictions on individual rights would be permanent.[40] Ohio's senator Robert Taft similarly warned in May 1940 that if the United States entered the war under New Deal leadership, it would mean dictatorship at home with complete socialization of property and the permanent end of private enterprise and local self-government.[41] Leading isolationists fervently insisted that "capitalism cannot survive American participation in this war."[42] The day after Paris fell to German troops, Charles Lindbergh also voiced certainty that "if we decide to fight, we *must* turn to a dictatorial government, for there is no military efficiency to be lost."[43] Perhaps Hoover, Taft, and Lindbergh had forgotten that when both Germany and the United States were devastated in 1932 by the Great Depression, it was Germany and not America that met the crisis by turning to dictatorship.

Summing up the defeatist position in the summer of 1940, Robert Sherwood took sharp aim at the "grotesque fallacy that a totalitarian system is efficient and therefore must conquer a democratic system which is necessarily inefficient, incompetent, obsolete." It was a cliché repeated by "stupid people everywhere," Sherwood acidly concluded. And in the spring of 1941, Roosevelt would also voice scorn for the defeatist mentality, remarking that "there are some timid ones among us who say that we must preserve peace at any price— lest we lose our liberties forever. To them I say this: . . . Our freedom has shown its ability to survive war, but our freedom would never survive surrender."[44]

Still other isolationists focused their efforts on the sins of British and French colonialism. In the fall of 1939, Ambassador Kennedy informed President Roosevelt that Britain was fighting not for principle but merely for self-interest, "for her possessions and a place in the sun just as she has in the past."[45] The University of Chicago's Robert Hutchins maintained that there were more victims of French and English colonialism in Indochina, Africa, and India before 1939 than there were victims of Nazi aggression after 1939. His fellow pacifist, Norman Thomas, declared Western imperialism a "curse to mankind." Indeed, despite the Anglo-American bond of a common language and a shared democratic tradition, there were many people in the United States who, though they may have felt culturally allied with Britain, were highly critical of British imperialism. Senator Wheeler charged that Britain was "the greatest aggressor in the pages of history,"[46] while Senator Lundeen pointed out that in the previous 150 years, the British had engaged in fifty-four wars and the French in fifty-three.[47] The predatory British, commented Senator Borah, were focused solely on the "realization of their imperialistic scheme."[48]

Another creative group of isolationists formed the "Make Europe Pay War Debts" Committee. Their idea was to block efforts to send more aid to the Allies by stoking Americans' anger at the European nations that had failed to repay American loans from the First World War.[49] The German chargé d'affaires in Washington, Hans Thomsen, gave financial assistance to that organization and boasted to his handlers in Berlin that he and his intermediary agent "entertained the closest relations" with the committee.[50]

Some isolationists blamed the British and the French, some blamed the Jews, some blamed Roosevelt, and some blamed Woodrow Wilson for promising that World War I would be the "war to end all wars." Some embraced fascism, others pacifism, and still others business as usual with the dictators. But what they all had in common was an inability or unwillingness to grasp that this world crisis was fundamentally and profoundly different from that of 1914 when a web of political alliances—and not totalitarian dictators—plunged the world into war. Refusing to confront the complex world in which America was inextricably entangled, they were convinced that a self-sufficient United States could chart its own independent course. Protected by two vast oceans and therefore immune from foreign attack, the United States, they reassuringly told one another, could remain safely unaffected by the turbulent events in Europe and Asia—unaffected, that is, *if* it resisted meddling in the affairs of other nations. Calling themselves the "peace bloc"[51] and serving what they saw—narrowly and myopically—as America's self-interest in a world aflame, their mission was to convince Americans that any aid to the Allies was synonymous with a commitment to a war that would necessarily lead to the destruction of self-government in the United States.

Much of the energy for the isolationist movement was supplied by college students, the very people who would be called to serve their country in time of war. Yale students were particularly active and effective. One student at Yale Law School, R. Douglas Stuart, Jr., the son of a vice president of Quaker Oats, began organizing his fellow Yalies in the spring of 1940. He and two other students, Gerald Ford, the future American president, and Potter Stewart, the future Supreme Court justice, drafted a petition stating, "We demand that Congress refrain from war, even if England is on the verge of defeat." Their solution to the international crisis lay in a negotiated peace with Hitler. Other Yale students—including Sargent Shriver and Kingman Brewster, the chairman of the *Yale Daily News*, future president of Yale and ambassador to the Court of St. James—joined their isolationist crusade.[52]

After dropping out of Yale, Stuart devoted himself full-time to the isolationist cause. Working to enlarge the isolationist circle, he and Brewster met with politicians in Washington as well as at both the Republican and Democratic Conventions in June and July 1940. Many of the people they spoke with suggested that they contact retired general Robert Wood, the board chairman of Sears, Roebuck who had served during World War I. Wood agreed to act as their group's temporary chair.[53] The students also sparked the interest of wealthy corporation heads from Stuart's hometown of Chicago, prominent attorneys, former government officials, and writers. Their growing organization soon included powerful men like Colonel Robert McCormick of the *Chicago Tribune*; Hugh Johnson, a retired brigadier general whom FDR had fired in 1934 as head of the National Recovery Administration; William Regnery, a Chicago textile manufacturer; Minnesota meatpacker Jay Hormel; Sterling Morton, the president of Morton Salt Company; United States Representative Bruce Barton of New York; Philip La Follette, the former Progressive governor of Wisconsin; John T. Flynn, a columnist for *The New Republic*; retired diplomat William Castle; and Lessing Rosenwald, the former chairman of Sears.[54]

The isolationist movement that began at Yale evolved into the America First Committee (AFC), the spearhead of isolationism in the nation. Although nominally a nonpartisan and politically neutral organization, in fact it was composed largely of Republicans and longtime anti–New Dealers. America First was not a pacifist organization; on the contrary, it stood for preparedness and a strong national defense—a professional, mechanized army, a modern air force, and a two-ocean navy. The group even threw the charge of defeatism back at the interventionists, claiming that it was they who lacked faith in America's ability to defend itself and stay out of the war. On September 5, 1940, Hugh Johnson officially launched the America First Committee with a nationwide radio broadcast. The first directors' meeting was convened on September 21, and the committee's first newspaper advertisements appeared in early October. There would soon be several hundred chapters and almost a million members, two thirds of whom resided in the Midwest.[55] Charles Lindbergh would officially join America First in April 1941, serving as the committee's principal spokesman and chief drawing card at its rallies.[56]

Seeking to brand itself as a mainstream organization, America First struggled with the problem of the anti-Semitism of some of its leaders and many of its members. At first, the AFC included some token Jews: Rosenwald; Florence Kahn, a former Republican congresswoman from California; and Sidney Hertzberg, the first publicity director of the AFC's New York chapter. But a few months after the group's founding, Rosenwald caused a stir by resigning from the national committee, unwilling to serve alongside a notorious anti-Semite like Henry Ford. In a move to avoid more negative publicity, the AFC removed from its executive committee not only Ford but also Avery Brundage, the former chairman of the U.S. Olympic Committee who had ejected two Jewish runners from the American track team in Berlin in 1936.[57] Still, the problem of anti-Semitism remained; some chapter leaders spewed anti-Semitic accusations, while others invited anti-Semitic speakers to address their members. The chairman of an Indiana chapter wrote that "Jews or their appointees are now in possession of our Government," and a Kansas chapter leader pronounced FDR and Eleanor "Jewish" and Churchill a "half-Jew." The Salt Lake City chapter hosted the rabidly anti-Semitic former congressman Jacob Thorkelson of Montana. Making matters worse, America First explicitly "welcomed" the support of Father Coughlin's followers. Though most of its members were probably patriotic, well-meaning, and honest in their efforts, the AFC would never be able to purge itself of the taint of anti-Semitism.[58]

In the spring of 1940, students across the nation participated in peace rallies: students on the right cheered at America First rallies; left-leaning students flocked to rallies sponsored by the leftist Keep America Out of the War Congress.[59] At the University of Chicago, they carried banners reading "The Yanks Are Not Coming!" At the University of Michigan, the Fire Department hauled down a swastika-emblazoned flag that students had hoisted to the top of the campus flagpole; in New York City, at Columbia, Barnard, and the College of the City of New York, ten thousand students participated in demonstrations. Eighty-eight percent of Columbia students, according to one survey, opposed the entrance of the United States in the European war.[60] Maury Maverick, the ultraliberal mayor of San Antonio, reported that students at the University of Texas, including his own son, could not accept that there was even a remote possibility of their having to fight.[61]

President Roosevelt had come face to face with the anger of isolationist American youth at a February 1940 meeting of the left-wing American Youth Congress. Standing in a chilly rain on the south lawn of the White House, the student activists booed the president when, referring to the recent Soviet invasion of neighboring Finland, he called on them to oppose all dictatorships, communist as well as fascist.[62] At that meeting, when Theodore Roosevelt's grandson Archibald Roosevelt, a slight young man in horn-rimmed glasses, tried to read a resolution aloud to the audience denouncing the invasion of Finland, he was declared out of order and wrestled to the ground.[63] In June, the president met again with a delegation of the American Youth Congress. As he explained to the two hundred young Americans why the Nazi conquest of western Europe threatened the nation's security, members in the audience complained that the president was abandoning the economic mission of the New Deal. When one member of the audience loudly grumbled that "we have had demonstrated here tonight that democracy does not exist in the United States," the president decided to limit himself to saying tersely, "That is some statement."[64]

Still, the tide of American opinion was changing. As country after country fell to the Nazi storm that spring, more and more Americans sympathized with the plight of the Allies. A majority had come to favor military aid for Britain and France, and by the end of September, a majority—and 70 percent of southerners—believed that it was critically important to aid Great Britain against Hitler's Nazi army *"even at the risk of war."*[65]

Williamstown, Massachusetts. Friday, June 14, 1940: Three hundred alumni, undergraduates, and faculty members of Williams College packed into Jesup Hall on the bucolic campus in the Berkshires. Without a single dissenting voice, they approved resolutions calling for universal compulsory military training and service and the immediate creation of military training camps. Chairing the meeting, William H. Curtiss of the class of 1906, a lieutenant-colonel who received the Croix de Guerre for his service in France in World War I, asserted his faith that Williams men in 1940 would not hesitate to serve their country.

Two days later, the president of the college, James Phinney Baxter, who would play a key role in the Office of Strategic Services during World War II, gave the Sunday Baccalaureate address to an overflow audience of graduating seniors and their families. Already in 1937 Baxter had condemned the Neutrality Act, and now he lamented the nation's failure to take a stand in support of the moral values of democracy. Williams College had been virtually alone among American colleges and universities when it terminated exchanges with German universities in 1936. Since German students wishing to study abroad had to prove their enthusiasm for the Nazi regime in order to qualify for a certificate of "political responsibility" from the Ministry of Education, Williams concluded that those students would not come to the small men's college in Williamstown "with an open mind." Two years later, a group of Williams students, including the editor of the college newspaper, the future political scientist James MacGregor Burns, and Woodrow Sayre, the grandson of Woodrow Wilson, demonstrated the school's commitment to open minds by contacting the librarian of the Vienna National Library and offering to purchase all the books that the library had deemed "non-Aryan" and was about to destroy.[66]

In Cambridge, Massachusetts, the same weekend, Secretary of State Cordell Hull addressed Harvard alumni and students at graduation ceremonies. "Our American history has not been achieved in isolation from the rest of mankind!" he exclaimed to the cheers of the audience.[67] A Harvard professor of government, William Yandell Elliott, also spoke, asserting that the United States was already at war with Nazi Germany and called for the United States to enter the conflict as a full military belligerent. Referring to those who advocated all aid for the Allies "short of war," he declared that, "for myself, today more than ever, I ask, why 'short of war?'"[68]

At Yale on Monday, June 17, seniors attending a graduation event heard alumnus Henry Stimson, a Republican who had served as secretary of war under William Howard Taft, call for repeal of American neutrality acts, for the acceleration of military help to the Allies, and for immediate, compulsory universal military service. The rally ended with students voting for a resolution advocating a draft. Two days later, the British ambassador, Philip Kerr, the Marquess of Lothian, addressed university alumni after receiving an honorary degree at graduation. Warning his listeners against the "illusion" that American security would not be affected by the fall of Britain, Lord Lothian pleaded for "arms, airplanes and machines. We want from you everything you can send us, as quickly as you can send it. They may make all the difference."[69]

On June 16, another rally took place in Boston, sponsored by the "Committee to Defend America by Aiding the Allies." "The blood-drenched Hitler is at our gates!" Colonel Henry Breckinridge warned a crowd of twenty thousand. Breckinridge had been personal counsel to Charles Lindbergh, but now he went on the attack against his former friend. "Can a man who is both intelligent and honest . . . try to lull the American people into a false sense of security?" he asked. "If he is intelligent and not a knave he knows that there are not 3,000 miles of open water between America and Europe for aviation but small hops by Greenland and Iceland." If America did not generously come to the aid of the Allies, he warned, it would find itself the only free nation "in a world of conquering tyrants."[70]

The "Committee to Defend America by Aiding the Allies" had been founded by William Allen White that past January.[71] More than a hundred local chapters and "youth divisions" around the country were quickly formed. Referred to by some of its members as the "Let's Get in the War Now Society,"[72] the "Committee to Defend America" pushed for the United States to throw its economic and moral weight—all aid "short-of-war," they called it—behind the Allies. Their "STOP HITLER NOW!" ads were published in dozens of newspapers and won praise from President Roosevelt.[73]

Among the other founding members of White's bipartisan committee were the governors of New York, Maine, and Rhode Island; New York's mayor, Fiorello La Guardia; the presidents of Harvard, Columbia, and Yale; a hundred of the nation's most famous historians and scholars; and Broadway and Hollywood stars and writers. Religious leaders like theologian Reinhold Niebuhr came on board. Indeed, Niebuhr condemned the pacifist clergymen who had created the "Churchmen's Campaign for Peace through Mediation." Their movement "has no trace of religious idealism," he wrote, furious that these Christian pacifists urged Americans, in the name of the Sermon on the Mount, to feel "love" for Hitler.[74]

Perhaps the most surprising member of White's committee was Charles Lindbergh's mother-in-law, Elizabeth Morrow. Unlike Charles and Anne, she was an internationalist who spoke out often and passionately for immediate military aid to the Allies. "The French and the British are fighting tonight for all the things we honor in life," Elizabeth Morrow declared in a June radio broadcast. Explicitly rejecting her son-in-law's refusal to take sides in the conflict, she called for Americans to give the Allies not just "admiration and advice" but "everything we have"—food, money, airplanes, ships, and anything else that could help them in their death-struggle against Germany. She was acting and speaking only for herself and for "members of my family," she said—pointedly excluding her son-in-law and daughter from that intimate group.[75] They got the hint.

"Mother is being used for the superb publicity effect of her connection with Charles," Anne Morrow Lindbergh bitterly noted in her diary. Indeed,

White would later tell an audience in New York's Town Hall that "the really smart trick we pulled . . . was that we put Lindbergh's mother-in-law on the air—and was that a face card? It was!" Anne was all the more bitter because she understood that her isolationism had in fact isolated her. "I am hurt," she wrote in her diary in October 1940, "by the growing rift I see between myself and those people I thought I belonged to. The artists, the writers, the intellectuals. . . . I feel exiled from them. I have become exiled for good." Anguished, in her diary she poured out her doubts about her and Charles's adamant isolationism. "I wonder where Daddy would stand? Probably behind the committee," she wrote. "We are alone and probably always will be from now on."[76]

Chapter 6

Dark Horse

G ANGBUSTER THOMAS E. DEWEY, the Republican district attorney of Manhattan, will be the next president of the United States. So predicted fifty Washington newspaper correspondents polled by *Newsweek* in April of 1939, fourteen months before the Republican National Convention.[1] The 38-year-old Dewey might have been a bit young as well as inexperienced in national and international affairs, but he had proven himself a tough, aggressive prosecutor, successfully locking up some of the most notorious gangsters of the Depression era, like Lucky Luciano, "Legs" Diamond, and "Dutch" Schultz, and deftly prosecuting and jailing the notorious American Nazi leader Fritz Kuhn.[2] He inspired a popular radio program called *Gangbusters* as well as the 1937 movie *Marked Woman* starring Humphrey Bogart and Bette Davis. Now the hard-hitting DA itched to take on FDR in the ring.

According to the reporters' predictions in the *Newsweek* poll, a Republican ticket with Dewey in the top spot and Ohio's 50-year-old senator Robert Taft as his running-mate would trounce the probable Democratic ticket of John Garner and Jim Farley. The Republicans were going to carry the country in 1940, prophesied columnist Raymond Clapper at the April 1939 Gridiron Club dinner in Washington, "if Tom Dewey has to put every Democrat in jail!"[3]

But not everyone thought that Dewey was a shoo-in. "I'd watch Willkie," wrote *New York Times* columnist Arthur Krock in February 1939. "If he is a Republican—is he?—you can't wholly count out Willkie." Still, Krock admitted that Willkie was the "darkest horse in the stable."[4] More surprised than anyone else by Krock's column was Wendell Willkie himself. He couldn't imagine himself running for office and "making the equivocating statements which a candidate for office usually must make," he told White House insider Ben Cohen later that year. Cohen relayed their conversation to Roosevelt, reporting that Willkie thought he was "too outspoken" to succeed in government.[5]

Others seriously doubted that a former Democrat could win the GOP nomination. The head of the vast Commonwealth and Southern Utilities Corporation that controlled the power supply of millions of Americans, Willkie had been a Democrat, albeit an ambivalent one, and would register as a Republican only in the fall of 1939.[6] A few years earlier, in 1935, he had accepted a refund for the $150 he gave to FDR's 1932 campaign. "I am still a Democrat," he said, "but not a Socialist. Therefore, I feel I am entitled to a refund."[7] In 1936, he wrote that he continued to consider himself "an ardent Democrat" but acknowledged that Roosevelt "still causes me great worries and concern."[8] When a reporter in 1940 asked him why he finally left his party, he shot back, "I did not leave my party. My party left me. I am a Jeffersonian Democrat and I have never deviated from the principles of Thomas Jefferson."[9]

By early 1940, Dewey was still leading the Republican pack. Republicans believed that with him they finally had a fighting chance to recapture the White House. He cut an attractive, dapper figure with his wavy black hair, pointed nose above a jet-black mustache, and quick-darting eyes. And he was an effective speaker. Once interested in a career as an opera star, he knew how to use his melodic voice. When he accepted a GOP draft to run against New York's Democratic governor Herbert Lehman in 1938, Dewey sought to present himself as an energetic achiever and an aggressive fighter, eager to replace the "tired and unwilling leadership" of the New York Democratic establishment.[10] When anti-Semitism targeting Lehman crept into the campaign, Dewey took the high road. "I condemn and despise any support based upon racial or religious prejudice," he said. In the past, the governorship of New York had been a stepping-stone to the White House, but Dewey lost the race against Lehman. Still, his fans barely noticed. "You're a sure bet for 1940!" a voice cried out to him from the crowd of his supporters on that disappointing election night.[11]

Two years later, campaigning for the GOP presidential nomination, the New York DA in shining armor excited Republican crowds. At his rallies across the Midwest, audience members almost bowled him over as they strained to shake his hand. A January 1940 poll showed 60 percent of likely Republican voters favoring Dewey, while 16 percent were for Michigan's senator Arthur Vandenberg, 11 percent for Taft, with Massachusetts senator Henry Cabot Lodge, Herbert Hoover, 1936 presidential nominee Alf Landon, and Charles Lindbergh all trailing far behind in the single digits.[12] By early May, Dewey soared to 67 percent in the polls. It was "obvious," wrote the *New York Times*, that

Dewey was the leading contender.[13] The Republican convention appeared locked up. "Don't you realize that Franklin Roosevelt is the easiest man in the world for me to beat?" the self-confident Dewey boasted to a reporter.[14]

But in that May 8 poll, appearing for the first time and garnering 3 percent, was the dark horse identified by Arthur Krock—Wendell Willkie. A few weeks earlier, appearing on a popular radio show called *Information Please*, in which a guest matched his or her erudition and wit against four permanent panel members, Willkie had captivated the audience with his knowledge, humor, and charm.[15] "I never had a better time in my life," Willkie said after the show.[16] An enthusiastic *Life* magazine profile of him commented that "by performances like this, Wendell Willkie has won for himself an astonishing popularity outside the regular Republican fold" and quoted columnist Raymond Clapper's opinion that Willkie "is doing more than anyone else to bring businessmen back into political responsibility."[17] In late May, he climbed up to 10 percent, with Dewey slipping to 56 percent.[18]

By June 12, less than two weeks before the start of the Republican Convention in Philadelphia, Dewey had fallen to 52 percent and Willkie had jumped to 17 percent, putting Willkie in second place.[19] Three days before the convention opened, Dewey dropped another five points, while Willkie gained twelve.

Whether the candidate would be Dewey, Taft, or Willkie, many journalists were convinced that the signs of the times—the slow economic recovery, lingering unemployment, dissension among the Democrats, and the widespread desire for a return to "normalcy"—all pointed to a Republican victory in 1940. The only unknown factor, they conceded, was the possibility of war.

"As a nation, we must face a bitter truth," Dewey declared as he campaigned for the nomination. "This has become a gangster world. I know something about gangsters."[20] Indeed, he had rounded up mobsters in the poultry business, trucking, loan sharking, and prostitution, but until the convention, the Manhattan DA had expressed no interest in going beyond the borough of Manhattan to take on the Nazi mob in Europe. In a skit performed at the Gridiron Club dinner in April 1940, a reporter asked the young man playing the part of Dewey what he would do about Hitler and Mussolini. "Indict them!" replied the DA.[21]

But the real-life Dewey took a mostly isolationist stand for much of his campaign, repeating at his rallies that the United States must "keep its hands wholly out of the European war."[22] He was heeding the advice of his chief foreign policy advisor, a New York lawyer named John Foster Dulles, who viewed Hitler as nothing more than a "passing phenomenon."[23] Following suit, Dewey dismissed the chatter of imminent war. "There is no fever so contagious as war fever," he said in a speech in Dallas in late May. "It might even sweep this country off its feet." Still, he hedged his bets, remarking that Americans should not be blind to the possibility that they might have to defend themselves. But with what? Though Republicans had consistently voted against increasing defense appropriations, Dewey hypocritically blamed Roosevelt for "our hopelessly inadequate defenses."[24] And only toward the end of his campaign, late in June, did Dewey soften his stand on help to the Allies, conceding that the United States, while "steadfastly refusing" to send American forces to Europe, could give "all proper aid"—that is, surplus weapons not needed for America's own defense—to the victims of aggression.[25]

Rather than take on Hitler, Dewey relished attacking Franklin Roosevelt. When one Democrat at a small Midwestern rally demanded, "What have you got against President Roosevelt?" Dewey shot back, "Nine million people out of jobs!" Among the president's misdeeds, Dewey included Roosevelt's "vested interest" in continued unemployment, his hostility to the spirit of enterprise and harassment of business, his "crew of fuzzy-minded theorists," and his failure to build up the army, navy, and air force and ensure that the country was "impregnable to attack." Dewey promised to give hope and courage to a nation "in despair as a result of incompetent government." "Roosevelt must go!" he shouted out at his rallies.[26]

In November 1938, when Dewey went down to defeat in the gubernatorial race in New York, Robert Taft of Ohio won a seat in the United States Senate. The serious, stiff, and pedantic freshman senator—a "stuffed shirt," according to White House Brain Truster Rex Tugwell—was the son of the former president and Chief Justice William Howard Taft.[27] Three decades earlier, a Taft had moved into the White House as a Roosevelt moved out; it could happen again. A graduate of Yale and Harvard Law School—first in his class at both schools—Bob Taft had worked in Washington and Paris as a legal advisor to Herbert Hoover in the American Relief Administration during and after the First World War. Before joining the Senate, he had served for a dozen years in the Ohio state legislature. The most conservative of the GOP contenders, the pro-business and isolationist Taft hammered away in his campaign speeches at Roosevelt, pounding the New Deal for its deficit spending and its "sympathy for communist ideals."[28] In fact, Taft stressed that the real danger to democracy lay in the White House, not in Hitler's Nazified Germany. In a speech that would prove damaging to his campaign, he told an audience in St. Louis on May 20 that there was "a good deal more danger of the infiltration of totalitarian ideas from the New Deal circle in Washington than there will ever be from any activities of the communists or the Nazi bunds."[29] In response, FDR told syndicated columnist Walter Winchell at a White House tête-à-tête that Taft was "a horse's aft." Winchell wanted to quote the president, but his editors at the *New York Mirror* vetoed that idea. "I got it from FDR!" Winchell protested. "How can it be in bad taste?"[30]

In 1939, Taft had taken some enlightened stands in foreign affairs. He had been one of only eight Republican senators to support Roosevelt in repealing the arms embargo, and he supported military aid to the Allies on a "cash and carry" basis, that is, if the Allies paid for and transported the war matériel themselves. But in 1940, candidate Taft headed straight for the isolationist camp. Opposing any other forms of assistance to the Allies, he reasoned that it would be immoral to spend American dollars to help them, because then "it would be cowardice not to support them also with men." And although he touted military preparedness, on June 19, the eve of the GOP Convention, he was one of only five senators to vote against a bill to defray the cost of accelerated defense spending through an increase in the income tax and a tax on excess corporate profits.[31] In seven months, he went from belonging to the GOP internationalist minority favoring aid to the Allies to voting with the GOP isolationist minority opposing more spending on defense. "I am absolutely opposed to the William Allen White Committee," he wrote to a friend, "and thoroughly in sympathy with the America First Committee."[32]

Taft was Lindbergh minus the anti-Semitism and the Order of the German Eagle. He baldly accused FDR of trying to divert attention away from his domestic failures by "ballyhooing the foreign situation" and "stirring up prejudice" against Germany. Like Lindbergh, who ridiculed the Democrats' "hysterical chatter" about war, Taft railed against Roosevelt for provoking "needless excitement" about war. On May 18, just when Nazi troops were knifing through Europe and sympathy for the Allies was increasing even in the isolationist Midwest, Taft spoke in Topeka, Kansas, scoffing at the "screaming headlines" and the glut of newspaper articles devoted to Europe. It was no time for Americans to be "wholly absorbed in foreign battles," he said. Americans should let Europe deal with its own problems and instead focus on problems at home. All the Roosevelt administration's talk about war was nothing but a cynical scam, a "cover" to keep the New Deal "sneaking on."[33]

Just as Lindbergh's father had influenced his son's thinking, so had Taft's father influenced his son's outlook with his memorable statement in 1917 that the United States was "not a knight-errant country" telling other nations that we didn't like their forms of government.[34] And like Lindbergh, Taft accepted the prospect of American accommodation to Hitler. A German victory, Taft asserted, would neither weaken American defenses nor destroy trade. "I don't understand why if peace is once restored we could not trade as well with Germany as with England," he said, although his preference was for minimal foreign trade with any nation. The senator did not welcome a German victory—which would mean, he acknowledged, the triumph of "ruthless force over every principle of justice"—but he judged that a Nazi-dominated Europe was far preferable to American participation in the war. A few weeks before the convention, as France was falling to the onslaught of Hitler's planes and tanks, Taft privately admitted having doubts about his hard-line view, but in public he neither softened his tone nor changed his position.[35]

Shortly after the 1938 midterm election, Michigan's Arthur Vandenberg, eager for alternatives to GOP losers like Hoover and Landon, had welcomed the "new ideas, new blood" of men like Dewey and Taft.[36] But in 1940, Vandenberg wanted the presidential nomination for himself. A respected, hard-working veteran politician and reliable anti–New Dealer who had written two superficial books about his hero Alexander Hamilton, the 56-year-old Vandenberg had bolstered conservative ranks in the Senate since 1927. Unlike Dewey, he declined to mount a vigorous campaign and refused to compete in the mostly unimportant state primaries, which were popularity contests more than anything else. "Imagine killing yourself to carry Vermont!" he scoffed.[37] In domestic politics, he professed to seek a middle path and called on the GOP to be neither "reactionary at the right nor radical at the left." Though he hammered the New Deal's fiscal policies, he never sought to abandon its progressive achievements. In a magazine article he authored in early 1940 entitled "The New Deal Must Be Salvaged," he endorsed New Deal reforms but argued that they would be better administered by Republicans.[38]

On the question of the war in Europe, Vandenberg took a steady isolationist line. In 1939, he voted against repeal of the arms embargo. "Protected by a great ocean on either side, the United States need fear no other nation," he said, "if we mind our own business." In May 1940, he conceded that America would be safer if the Allies won the fight against "the anti-Christ" Hitler, but he still insisted that the United States "cling relentlessly" to a policy of noninvolvement and neutrality. Still, he sought to cleanse himself of the isolationist brand; resorting to word games, he labeled his position "insulationism." Whereas isolation was impossible in the modern world, he argued that complete "insulation"—through impregnable national defense against the Nazi scourge—would give the United States the protection it needed. But on the eve of the GOP Convention, as the crisis in Europe took an even more vicious turn, some Republican pundits believed, according to the *New York Times*, that Vandenberg's "rigid stand for complete 'insulation'" could only hurt his candidacy. Even in the traditionally isolationist Midwest, the *Times* reported, there was a "grim, unemotional feeling" that the United States should do more to help the Allies.[39]

Also a candidate for the nomination was the 66-year-old Herbert Hoover, the only living ex-president. A decade earlier, he had been the morose leader of a dazed and somnolent administration, "frozen," as Roosevelt memorably said in 1936, "in the ice of its own indifference." In 1930, tens of millions of Americans were without any income whatsoever; cities like Toledo and Akron staggered under unemployment of up to 80 percent.[40] But Hoover had insisted on reining in government spending; his remedy for the Depression was to rely on local governments and community chests to help the unemployed and the homeless. The primary duty of government, he announced again and again, was to hold down government expenditures. Blind to the old men begging or selling apples for five cents on the streets, indifferent to the young men standing slumped, hollow-eyed, in breadlines that stretched block after block, covering themselves at night with newspapers they called "Hoover blankets," the president was stunningly unwilling to reach out to desperate Americans. Years later in his memoirs, he maintained that there had been a shrewd plot by "some Oregon or Washington apple growers' association" to raise their prices by organizing the unemployed to sell apples on street corners. "Many persons left their jobs for the more profitable one of selling apples," Hoover wrote.[41]

And yet, during and after the First World War, Hoover brought his Quaker values to his work as an efficient and compassionate administrator of food relief for millions of starving people in Europe. In 1939 he organized relief for Finland after the Soviet invasion, and in May 1940 he agreed to head a relief commission for Belgium. Intimately acquainted with the ravages of war, Hoover buttressed his isolationist warnings with his own emotional memories of "the filth, the stench, the death, of the trenches . . . the dumb grief of mothers, wives, and children." At the Somme in France, he had witnessed unending rows of trenches packed with a million and a half men, advancing "like ants" under the thunder from ten thousand guns. Before the battle was over, more than a quarter million of them would be dead, their lives thrown away.[42]

Hoover wanted no part of war ever again. He even opposed building up American defenses, making the bizarre case in 1939 that rearmament would arouse fear of America and "make us suspect of the whole world." The United

States, he allowed, could sell "defensive" weapons to the belligerents in Europe—though it was militarily impossible to distinguish between offensive and defensive weapons. But if America entered the war, he warned in a speech in October 1939, "we shall have sacrificed liberty for generations." As for the Nazis' barbaric cruelty, he observed with inane irrelevance that "chivalry is certainly dying in our world."[43]

By the spring of 1940, however, Hoover's thinking had evolved on the question of preparedness, if not on the question of help for the Allies. Although he was convinced that neither the United States nor the Western Hemisphere was in any danger of invasion by Hitler, in May, he nevertheless endorsed the president's proposals for national defense spending. "The president is right," he stated. "There can be no partisanship upon the principle of national defense. . . . We must be thoughtfully and scientifically armed."[44] And a May 26 Gallup poll that asked Republicans, "Which candidate would handle this country's foreign affairs the best?" showed the former president leading the pack with 22 percent.[45]

Hoover confided to his closest associates that he wanted to make a comeback,[46] but how could Republican leaders be enthusiastic about a man who had resoundingly lost the 1932 election with 59 electoral votes to FDR's 472?

As German planes and tanks plunged the peaceful democracies of Europe into bloodshed and despair, Republicans found themselves in an increasingly vulnerable position. With their isolationism hung like an albatross around their necks, their leading candidates for the presidential nomination all had shortcomings—Dewey, young and politically inexperienced; Taft, distant and doctrinaire; Vandenberg, abstruse with his overly subtle distinction between isolationism and insulationism; Hoover, out of touch. And that left . . .

Wendell Willkie. He was the only Republican candidate, wrote Walter Lippmann, who did not misjudge the international situation.[47] Speaking forthrightly about the need for American involvement in the international crisis, Willkie stressed that America had a vital interest "in the continuation in this world of the English, French and Norwegian way of life." Indeed, he later revealed that he made up his mind to run for the Republican presidential nomination when he realized that the other Republican hopefuls would not budge from their isolationist lines. "It was only after failing to convince those gentlemen that I decided," he wrote.[48]

Isolationists and Old Guard conservatives indeed wielded power in the GOP. They were "still living among cobwebs and mothballs," the governor of New Jersey, Harold Hoffman, complained after the 1936 election, in which

Alf Landon had garnered a pitiful 8 electoral votes to Roosevelt's 523. "This feeble leadership tramps bravely backward," Hoffman said, "passing the milestones of our history in reverse, its eye set firmly on its goal—the rediscovery of the kerosene lamp!"[49] The GOP desperately needed new blood and fresh ideas.

Although several staunch conservatives, like Robert Taft and Connecticut's John Danaher, were elected to the Senate in 1938, moderates had also been making inroads. In 1936, joining veteran Senate moderates and internationalists like Warren Austin of Vermont, William Barbour of New Jersey, and Frederick Hale of Maine, newcomers came in: New Hampshire's Styles Bridges and Massachusetts's Henry Cabot Lodge, followed by South Dakota's Chan Gurney in '38. Also in 1936 and 1938, running successfully for governor of their states were liberal Republicans like Harold Stassen of Minnesota, William Vanderbilt of Rhode Island, Leverett Saltonstall of Massachusetts, and George Aiken of Vermont. It was time for the GOP to "purge" itself of reactionary elements, Aiken declared, lamenting that "we have become a party of old men." For his part, Saltonstall, sounding just like a New Dealer, said that it was the duty of government to do everything within its power to solve the problems of poverty, unemployment, capital, and labor.[50] So in 1940, the time seemed right for Wendell Willkie, too, to challenge the conservative leadership of the party and steer it toward the center.

Willkie grew up in Elwood, Indiana; his father was a public-spirited lawyer, engaged in the local school system as well as in wiping out the town's red-light district; his mother was the first woman admitted to the Indiana bar. At Indiana University before the First World War, Willkie's fellow students had known him as a campus activist and hell-raiser. Sporting his usual red turtleneck sweater, he led the campus Democratic club, where he spouted socialist ideas.[51] So fascinated was he by socialism that he successfully petitioned the Economics Department to include a course on that subject. Elitist fraternities aroused his ire—he joined one only in his senior year, to please his girlfriend.[52]

After graduation, he spent a year teaching history and coaching basketball at a high school in Kansas. "[You] actually taught us history and made us like it!" one of his students later wrote to him. She remembered that one day a month he declared a holiday from history, and, sitting on his desk and swinging his long legs, read O. Henry stories to his students.[53] The versatile young teacher also organized the debating club. One of the questions his team debated was, "Should American presidents be elected for a six-year term without the possibility of reelection?" He spent one summer working in Puerto Rico, where the poverty and conditions on sugar plantations, he later said, deeply influenced his thinking.[54] In 1915, he headed to law school at Indiana

University, where he won prizes as well as the role of "Class Orator" at graduation.[55] After briefly practicing law in Elwood, Willkie enlisted in the army on the day the United States declared war on Germany. After a long training program, he was sent off to France, where, fortunately for him, he arrived too late to fight in any battles. Still, he was able to use his legal knowledge to defend fellow soldiers who went AWOL.[56]

The war over, the young man began an impressive, successful career in business, taking a job in 1919 with the Firestone Tire and Rubber Company in Ohio. After that, he went to work for an Akron law firm.[57] In 1929, the head of the giant public utilities holding company Commonwealth and Southern hired him as its general counsel in New York. By 1933, Willkie was the company's president.

An active Democrat who backed liberal and internationalist causes, Willkie had a particular interest in civil rights and fought against the Ku Klux Klan in the 1920s. In 1928 he served as a delegate to the Democratic Convention, where he voted for Al Smith and battled—unsuccessfully—for platform planks condemning the Klan and endorsing the League of Nations.

During FDR's first term, nearly all the New Deal policies on labor and welfare, conservation, and social security appealed to him. But by the late 1930s, concerned about the concentration of power in the White House and the expansion of the national government, Willkie had come to distrust Roosevelt. In 1936, he split his vote, supporting Lehman over Dewey in New York's gubernatorial contest and casting his vote in the presidential race for Landon. He especially objected to the Public Utility Holding Company Act of 1935. Aimed at curbing the influence of huge utility holding companies that dominated the market for electrical power in the United States, the act permitted holding companies to control only "a single integrated system" of power in a limited geographical area. Recognizing that what would remain of Commonwealth and Southern after its breakup under the act would not be able to compete with the publicly owned Tennessee Valley Authority's ability to provide low-cost electricity, Willkie decided to sell out to the government. After several years of litigation, he won a stunning settlement of $78,000,000 for all of Commonwealth and Southern's electrical power assets in Tennessee. Hamming it up in front of newsreel cameras as TVA director David Lilienthal, a fellow Hoosier, handed him the check in August 1939, Willkie thanked him in his best home-boy style. "This is sure a lot of money for a couple of Indiana farmers to be kicking around," he said.[58]

Willkie was proving himself a natural, engaging performer. In January 1938, an appearance on a radio show called *America's Town Meeting of the Air* had raised his profile in the public eye. He and Assistant Attorney General Robert Jackson—both Democrats—debated the subject, "How can government and business work together?" Willkie called for a truce between the antagonists. "I hope that at last we can have done with the epithets, the calling of names, the catchwords," he said, "such as economic royalists, Bourbons, moneyed aristocrats."[59] Jackson, on the other hand, blamed big business for the Depression and spoke about the government's responsibility to provide Americans with jobs and security. They both made compelling arguments, but it was Willkie with his low-key defense of private enterprise who charmed the audience. If Willkie was an amateur, remarked one journalist, so was Babe Ruth. Columnist Joseph Alsop wrote that Willkie reminded him of "the best kind of English Conservative"—one who is for "liberal measures, conservatively administered."[60]

Editorial writers, economists, and some influential, moderate Republicans began to think of the wayward Democrat and impressive businessman as a possible presidential contender. So far, only two men had won the presidency without having previously run for or held public political office—Zachary Taylor and Ulysses Grant, both hero-generals. Maybe the utilities magnate could be the third, just the ticket to the White House the GOP had been looking for. Willkie had a proven "leadership capacity," wrote syndicated columnist David Lawrence in May 1939, observing that Willkie could satisfy Republicans' longing for improved government relations with business. That month, the *New York Times* editorialized that an article Willkie had recently published in the *Atlantic Monthly* contained precisely the right free enterprise formula for putting "idle men and idle money" back to work. In July 1939, his picture appeared on the cover of *Time* magazine. He was still too much of a liberal to suit old-line Republicans, *Time* wrote, admitting that the talk about his being presidential material was "mildly fantastic." Still, according to *Time*, he was "obviously going places."[61]

In the summer of 1939, Willkie participated in a "Round Table" seminar in the Berkshires in western Massachusetts, sponsored by *Fortune* magazine, which later printed reports of the discussions. Willkie's comments greatly impressed one of the participants, *Fortune*'s managing editor, Russell Davenport.[62]

In August, Davenport invited him to spend the weekend with friends—including Davenport's boss Henry Luce, the publisher of *Time*, *Life*, and *Fortune*—at his country home in Connecticut. Willkie "radiated a stunning combination of intellect and homely warmth," commented Davenport's wife, Marcia. While the other guests enjoyed golf, tennis, and bridge, Willkie spent the entire time sprawled in a wicker armchair, one leg thrown over the arm, drinking whiskey, chain-smoking, and talking about politics, war, and the economy. He criticized the "monopolistic governmental theories of the New Deal" and was "equally outspoken in opposition to what was then the classic isolationist position of the Republican Party," Marcia Davenport later recalled. And as he poured out his ideas, Russell Davenport took notes. There was a "chemical reaction" between Davenport and Willkie, Henry Luce later wrote. But Luce, too, believed that they had found a man who ought to be president of the United States.[63]

Politically intuitive, Willkie was following George Washington's carefully honed script. He presented himself not just as a successful businessman but as a former soldier in France,[64] a man who had no taste for power but was willing to accept the people's call to serve. "I am utterly devoid, I believe, of political ambition," Willkie wrote in a note of thanks to columnist David Lawrence, who had promoted him as a potential presidential candidate, "but no man could be honest and at the same time indifferent to the suggestion . . . that he was qualified to lead the country."[65] In a series of magazine articles Willkie wrote that year, he outlined his pro-business plan for economic recovery. The Roosevelt administration, he argued, had taken over many of the functions of private enterprise, restricted free competition, and discouraged the use of private capital for development and job creation. Among his practical suggestions for the future, he proposed that innovative, risk-taking entrepreneurs not be taxed, that capital gains taxes be eliminated, and that *safe* investments—like Treasury securities—be taxed instead.

Willkie stressed a pragmatic, nonpartisan approach to problem-solving and thought his program could command the support of Republicans and Democrats, conservatives as well as New Dealers. "This is a campaign of revitalization which looks forward rather than back; which is not political in its nature," he wrote in June 1939.[66]

Willkie was beginning to sound like a candidate. When reporters questioned him about a run for the White House, he left the possibility open. "Of course, it isn't going to happen," he modestly told an audience in January 1940 at Wooster College in Ohio, "but if the nomination were given to me without any strings I would have to accept it. No man in middle life and in good health could do otherwise."[67] Even Harold Ickes was impressed. "Willkie is undoubtedly a man of affairs and ability," Ickes wrote after attending a packed meeting of the Economic Club in February 1940 at which Willkie presided. "He makes a distinctly favorable impression and he is no man's fool. He handles himself well on his feet and has the self-confidence that a successful man ought to have."[68]

In February, Russell Davenport exhorted his candidate to begin "hitting the country with a bang." But by April 1940, he was forced to realize that Willkie had not yet become a "political reality." "But why in the hell don't we make him one?" he wrote to newspaperman Raymond Clapper. It was up to GOP progressives to rally to Willkie and turn him into a popular political figure. That spring, Davenport resigned from his job at *Fortune*, opened Willkie headquarters in Manhattan, and served as top advisor and campaign manager, though his wife, Marcia, remarked that the title of campaign manager was laughable since Willkie was the "most unmanageable of men."[69] Davenport's wise strategy was to skip the primaries in the spring of 1940; only about a quarter of the states even held Republican primaries, and the votes in those contests were merely "advisory" and not binding on delegates at the national convention.[70] Moreover, among the GOP candidates, only Dewey devoted energy and resources to competing in the primaries. Instead Davenport wanted to focus on Willkie's image as a political outsider and on name-recognition by rounding up high-power advertising executives like New York's Bruce Barton, who had been elected to Congress in 1938, to market the Willkie name.[71]

The biggest gun to join the Willkie team was Henry Luce, who, like Willkie, was deeply committed to the interventionist cause. In 1938, Luce visited Germany; but unlike the Lindberghs, who marveled at its prosperity, dynamism, and festive atmosphere, Luce remarked on the shabbiness, the terrible food, even the shortage of toilet paper. The conditions in Germany, he wrote, were "the worst I have encountered in years." Even more distressing was the "intensity" of German anti-Semitism. In November 1939, his wife Clare Boothe Luce's anti-Nazi comedy, *Margin for Error*, opened on Broadway. One character, an official in a German consulate in the United States, exuberantly announces that "our primary objective is to spread Germanic Kultur— That's why from now on I carry a gun!" In May 1940, Luce and his wife were in Brussels just when German troops began storming across the Belgian border. Though he was a Republican who deeply distrusted FDR, Luce said he was almost tempted to support the president. "The remarks of Roosevelt . . . sound wonderful here," he wrote, noting that he intended to join the ranks of the third termers unless the GOP came up with a good candidate. The only sign of hope, he added, was "Davenport's man," Wendell Willkie.[72]

In the spring of 1940, Luce mobilized his powerful publishing empire for Willkie. *Fortune* devoted its April 1940 issue to articles about Willkie and to one written by him—with help from Davenport—entitled "We, the People." Willkie's essay "made a terrific splash," commented one Republican insider.

Reprinted in *Reader's Digest*, it conveyed his progressive and internationalist credo. Though agreeing with the New Deal ethos that the government needed to be responsible for the security and well-being of its citizens, Willkie took aim at Roosevelt's management of the New Deal, charging that many of the programs impeded economic recovery with an antibusiness philosophy.[73] Two weeks after his article appeared, hundreds of speaking invitations poured in.[74] In May, *Life* gave him an eleven-page spread. "A vote for Willkie," *Life* wrote, "is a vote for the best man to lead the country in a crisis." In June, a week before the Republican Convention, *Time* put Willkie on its cover for the second time. While Dewey was "fumbling" and Taft was running toward "the wrong goal posts, Willkie seized the ball," *Time* wrote. His candidacy, the article concluded, was "decidedly within the realm of possibility today."[75]

In addition to Luce, Willkie also won over media giants like Roy Howard, publisher of the Scripps-Howard newspaper chain; John and Gardner Cowles, the brothers who owned Minneapolis newspapers along with the *Des Moines Register* and *Look* magazine; and Ogden and Helen Reid, the publishers of the interventionist *New York Herald Tribune*, the voice of the Republican establishment in the Northeast. And he also won the backing of corporate executives like Thomas Lamont, the director of J. P. Morgan, and Walter Mack, Jr., the president of Pepsi Cola.[76]

While Willkie had the support of titans in the publishing, broadcasting, and financial worlds, other less powerful people were also climbing on board. Unbeknownst to Willkie and Davenport, a zealous Willkie movement had begun in April 1940, initiated single-handedly by Oren Root, Jr., a young, 29-year-old Wall Street lawyer, Princeton graduate, and grandnephew of Theodore Roosevelt's secretary of state, Elihu Root.[77] Root realized that the lead Dewey held in convention delegates chosen in state primaries would amount to little at the national convention, and he was convinced that the thoughtful Willkie offered better answers to the problems besieging the nation and the world. And so he decided to conduct a test and see whether support for Willkie was deep and widespread—or merely a *Time* invention.[78]

Root mailed out eight hundred fliers containing excerpts from Willkie's "We, the People" article to Princeton and Yale alumni who were no more than fifteen years out of college—men who were young enough to still be idealistic and old enough to be seriously interested in the future of their country. A few days later, he sent out twenty thousand more. He asked for no money, only signatures. To Willkie himself, Root penned a charming letter, praising his "colossal qualifications" for the presidency and noting, too, that the name of Root "catches the political eye." "Beyond that," he wrote, "I am only one of the millions of citizens who most ardently desire your nomination and election as President."[79]

Willkie as well as his supporters Davenport and Lamont had serious misgivings about Root's activities and even asked him to cease and desist his unauthorized publicity. Willkie still maintained the posture of a noncandidate—reluctant but, like FDR, willing to serve if the people called upon him to do so. He would officially announce that he was a candidate only in mid-June, twelve days before the GOP Convention was set to begin. In the meantime, he and his advisors felt that his public stance of ambivalence was at odds with Root's all-out spirited efforts. And so Root and Davenport met for lunch. Won over by the enthusiastic young lawyer, Davenport—who was hardly more experienced in politics than Root or Willkie—convinced Willkie to issue a statement saying that he neither approved nor disapproved of Root's efforts. Green light for Root. He took a friendly leave of absence from his job, with the blessing of his law firm. "Well, Oren, my boy," one partner said to him, "how is the great politician feeling today? You are doing a wonderful job. Keep it up."[80]

By the end of April, two hundred thousand people had signed up as Willkie supporters. Now Root put a small ad in the *New York Herald Tribune*, this time asking for more than signatures. "Wendell Willkie for President!" the ad read. "Help Oren Root, Jr., organize the people's demand for Willkie. Send Root a contribution to 15 Broad Street, New York." Checks poured into Root's new office, a windowless room in midtown Manhattan. "My telephone has not stopped ringing," he boasted to a reporter. Willkie-for-President clubs sprang up around the country, often led by a town's affluent and progressive businessmen and lawyers. Willkie's fraternity brothers from Indiana also pitched in, spreading the message.[81] The movement led by Ivy Leaguers was spreading to the grass roots. Across the country there were five hundred Willkie Clubs and several million signatures on petitions calling for Willkie's nomination.[82]

In May 1940, Willkie made his political debut with a speech in St. Paul that was also broadcast on the radio—air time that was paid for by Gardner Cowles. While pounding the Roosevelt administration for the growing deficit and for abandoning the "principle of free enterprise," he did not disagree with the president on foreign affairs. "On behalf of our own peace and our own spiritual values," he said, "we should give to the democracies such assistance as we can, short of war." The enthusiastic reception his speech received in St. Paul, he later said, helped him make up his mind to run.[83]

Over the next six weeks, though still not a declared candidate for the GOP nomination, Willkie held rallies in the Midwest and West and gave radio talks and interviews. He was articulate, charming, and witty—but only beginning to master public speaking and the art of connecting with his audience. For half an hour, he would read dryly and mechanically from his prepared text and then, when the broadcast ended and the tepid applause was over, he would cheerfully toss aside the dull text, remove his glasses, and, to the delight of his audiences, turn political evangelist. "Now I'm off the air," he would announce with obvious relief. "And I don't have to use so much of that damn fine language!" Audiences roared in approval. "We've got to get rid of that bunch!" he would shout to more cheers. The "Willkie boom" was spreading through the country and even making inroads in the midwestern "isolation belt," reported the *New York Times* in May, in an article headlined "WILLKIE SHEDDING 'DARK HORSE' ROLE." Finding his own voice, Willkie was coming on strong. "I'm the cockiest fellow you ever saw," Willkie gleefully declared to a crowd in Kansas in June. "If you want to vote for me, fine. If you don't, go jump in the lake and I'm still for you!"[84]

In 1940, Willkie projected the image of a likeable, expansive, relaxed, and thoroughly approachable and countrified Indiana businessman and lawyer—even though he lived on Fifth Avenue in Manhattan. Energetic, 6'1", burly, boyish, with tousled brown hair, rumpled suit, and a warm chuckle, the 48-year-old Willkie was often described as "shaggy" and a "bear of a man." The *New Yorker*'s Janet Flanner commented that he possessed something that GOP candidates had lacked since Theodore Roosevelt: masculine charm.[85] Intelligent and well-read, Willkie was comfortable socializing with fellow members of New York's prestigious Century Club. He was candid and forthright in his opinions—taking on the Ku Klux Klan in Ohio and even lashing out at Thomas Dewey for denying equal protection to some of the targets of his prosecutions—including hated defendants like Fritz Kuhn, the head of the pro-Nazi German-American Bund.[86] He penned book reviews for the *Harvard Law Review* as well as numerous articles for the *Atlantic Monthly*, the *Saturday Evening Post*, and other magazines. He said that what interested him most were justice and the survival of democracy. "Whenever I go into a town or city anywhere in America," he once remarked, "one of the first things I ask is, 'What are the bookselling facilities here?' and then, 'What sort of courts do you have?' If people read books, I've found, and are interested in justice, they're also interested in democracy."[87]

To the outside world, he appeared to be a family man, married to Edith Wilk Willkie, a librarian from Indiana whom he had wed before leaving for France in the war. Their son Philip was a student at Princeton. In truth Wendell and

Edith led separate lives—she mostly in Indiana and he in New York, in a book-filled apartment at the elite address of 1010 Fifth Avenue, directly across the street from the Metropolitan Museum of Art. "She's plain vanilla," commented Indiana congressman Charles Halleck approvingly. The anti–Eleanor Roosevelt, Edith dressed well and avoided discussions of public affairs. "I don't know why you would want to interview me," she said to a reporter for the *Christian Science Monitor* in June 1940. "You know, I'm no career woman." When that reporter did interview her a short time later for an article that appeared on June 12, the day Willkie finally declared himself a candidate, she toed the campaign line. "As a matter of fact, my husband has never mentioned the Presidency at home," she said. "I myself hardly think of Wendell as a candidate for that high office, and I don't even know that he thinks of himself as a candidate, but he is interested in the Republican Party adopting some of his principles."[88]

Reporters in those days did not seek to dredge up the contradictions in Willkie's All-American image, and many still portrayed him not as a powerful New York businessman but as a homespun Hoosier. After all, Indiana didn't have a Fifth Avenue overlooking Central Park or, as Rex Tugwell observed, a Dutchess County.[89] Nor did reporters expose what they knew about Willkie's personal life, that his romantic relationship with his wife had collapsed and that he had an attractive, accomplished mistress. Since 1937, he had shared his life with Irita Bradford Van Doren, the book editor for the *New York Herald Tribune* who was the ex-wife of the biographer and literary critic Carl Van Doren. Their liaison was common knowledge among "everybody," Frances Perkins later remarked, noting that Irita "was really a woman of great brains and intelligence" who helped Willkie write his best speeches. A charming and gracious Alabama native who had grown up in Florida—"she was not pretty, but she was beautiful," commented foreign correspondent William Shirer—Irita introduced Wendell to New York's literary and academic world as well as to her bosses, *Tribune* owners Ogden and Helen Reid, who became two of his boosters. "Everybody knows about us," Willkie once said, "all the newspapermen in New York."[90] Indeed, so open was his relationship with his mistress that he once held a press conference in her apartment—and reporters didn't even bother to mention it.[91]

"You whom I admire inordinately and love excessively," Willkie wrote to Irita. But of course it was understood that he could not risk a possible future in politics with a divorce from Edith and a remarriage to Irita. In November 1945 the intertwining of their love story and Willkie's presidential campaign would become the basis for a Broadway play, *State of the Union*, and three years later for a Hollywood movie of the same title starring Spencer Tracy and Katharine Hepburn.[92]

On the eve of the Republican Convention, Willkie was out of step with GOP leaders on the international crisis. He said he thought that FDR has done "a pretty good job" on military preparedness and help for the Allies and scoffed at the naiveté of Republican partisans who thought it wise to be 100 percent opposed to the president's foreign policy. Conducting a kind of cost-benefit analysis, he reached the commonsensical conclusion that if the United States helped France and Britain "lick Hitler now," America would be saved from spending billions of dollars on armaments. In May 1940, he suggested that Secretary of State Hull ask the Allies what help, short of an expeditionary force, they needed. Britain and France, he underscored, were America's first line of defense against Hitler.

And Willkie saw Hitler clearly for what he was, a tyrant with an unquenchable thirst for conquest and destruction. Hitler had spent the last seven years, Willkie said, "organizing a great nation with one unified aim, to fight, to conquer, and to kill." Unlike Taft, Hoover, and Lindbergh, Willkie could not envisage any kind of political or economic relationship with Nazi Germany. Hitler's "ideals of war and bloodshed don't fit with our ideas of peace and commerce," he declared. "The fruits of his labor are hate and death. The fruits of ours are happiness and life. He shall not enter here!"[93] On May 11, the day after Germany invaded Norway and Denmark, Willkie insisted that there was one thing all Americans could agree on: "The British and French way of life shall continue in this world!"

Where Willkie departed from the Roosevelt administration was in his attitude toward business and free enterprise. The New Deal, he charged, had set up too many roadblocks for business and investment. And yet, even on the question of private enterprise, Willkie was no dyed-in-the-wool, laissez-faire conservative. He commended Theodore Roosevelt and Woodrow Wilson's attempts to rein in the excesses of the financial elites, and he recognized that, during the 1920s, Wall Street financiers and businessmen had been drunk with money and power. The New Deal deserved praise for correcting the "startling abuses" in industry and financial institutions.[94] But while he had no interest in rolling back reforms and regulations, he contended that too many agencies and commissions created by the New Deal—like the Securities and Exchange Commission and the National Labor Relations Board—had too much control over business and labor. Instead of eliminating monopolistic control, the Roosevelt administration had merely moved the ownership of

Charles and Anne Lindbergh in Berlin with Aviation Minister Hermann Goering, July 1936. (Bayerische Staatsbibliothek München/Fotoarchiv Hoffmann)

German-American Bund Rally, Madison Square Garden, February 1939. (U.S. Department of Defense)

Assistant Secretary of the Navy Franklin D. Roosevelt in London, July 1918. (Franklin D. Roosevelt Presidential Library and Museum)

"The Oldest Mistake in the World,"
September 21, 1940. (Princeton
University Library)

1940 Republican Party Campaign
Broadside.

(The New Press)

Willard Combes, July 1940.

Former president Herbert Hoover (right) and Wendell Willkie meet in Colorado Springs, August 1940. (© 1940 The Associated Press)

Willkie campaigns in his hometown of Elwood, Indiana, August 17, 1940. (© 1940 The Associated Press)

Willkie officially accepts the GOP nomination in Elwood, Indiana, August 17, 1940. (Library of Congress)

London during the Blitz, Autumn 1940. (Franklin D. Roosevelt Presidential
Library and Museum)

FDR signs America's first peacetime draft law, September 16, 1940. From left:
Secretary of War Henry Stimson; Andrew May, chair of the House Military Affairs
Committee; General George Marshall; and Morris Sheppard, chair of the Senate
Military Affairs Committee. (© 1940 The Associated Press)

FDR waving to the crowd in the Brooklyn Academy of Music, November 1, 1940.
From left: Governor Herbert Lehman; Franklin D. Roosevelt, Jr.; Mrs. William
Good; President Roosevelt; and, at extreme right, James Farley. (© 1940
The Associated Press)

David Low, November 4,
1940. (British Cartoon
Archive and *London Evening
Standard* © Associated
Newspapers Ltd. / Solo
Syndication)

FDR's third presidential inauguration, January 20, 1941. (Franklin D. Roosevelt Presidential Library and Museum)

monopoly to government. "Today it is not Big Business that we have," he said. "It is Big Government. The abuses that corrupted the 1920s have been transferred from Wall Street to Washington."[95] He explained that his goal was to find a balance between "the rights of the individual and the needs of society," and he defined that balance as the essence of liberalism. "The true liberal," he instructed his listeners, "is as much opposed to excessive concentration of power in the hands of government as . . . in the hands of business."[96]

Weaving together foreign and domestic policy—his internationalist and pro-business positions—Willkie portrayed Roosevelt as having harmed the national defense as well as the domestic economy by divisively pitting government and labor against business. In mid-May 1940, Willkie proposed bringing together labor and the "industrial brains" of the country and assigning defense-related work to every factory in the nation so that the army, navy, and air force could be immediately and adequately equipped.[97] But despite Willkie's criticism of the administration's attitude toward business, his proposed remedies did not satisfy the GOP's Old Guard. For those conservative Republicans, Willkie was an interloper and a renegade. But he made it clear that the antipathy was mutual, insisting that he was completely opposed to "returning to the . . . days of Harding and Coolidge."[98]

While the Old Guard viewed Willkie with suspicion, many progressive Republicans rushed to join his team. William Allen White discerned in him a "strong, manly, intrepid citizen" who also had a talent for impertinence. His independence of mind and even his tendency to blurt out what he was thinking captivated White. He was delighted to discover a Republican candidate who, as he wrote, was "not afraid to spit in the eye" of organized pressure groups—whether labor unions or the archconservative pro-business Liberty League.[99] There was "something fundamentally democratic about Wendell Willkie that is no political veneer," cheered the *Christian Science Monitor* in early June. "He makes the plutocrats shiver, the *Monitor* added, "when he talks about . . . the right of labor to assemble and talk. And he turns the New Dealers pop-eyed by his utilities record."[100]

Willkie's independence was his big draw: he could appeal to interventionists on foreign policy, to labor on union rights, and, from his perch as utility head, to pro-business conservatives on economic issues. Asked by a reporter what he thought his chances were of becoming president, he replied, "I feel very good and I am having a lot of fun."[101]

Wendell Willkie's positions on the world crisis mirrored those of Roosevelt—so much so that on May 16, 1940, the day the Gallup poll pronounced Willkie a "dark horse,"[102] syndicated foreign affairs columnist Dorothy Thompson, writing from Paris, urged the GOP to let FDR run unopposed with Willkie as his running-mate. Thompson knew Willkie well; she and Irita Van Doren were colleagues at the *Herald Tribune*, and she and her ex-husband, the novelist Sinclair Lewis, were old friends of the Davenports.[103] Thompson considered the utilities magnate an "enlightened Republican." "I write this article as a battle rages in Belgium, on the border between Belgium and France and all along the French-German front," she wrote, warning her readers that the outcome of the war was by no means certain. Echoing Alexander Hamilton, she underscored that, at such a time of crisis, it was "not wise to make any change in the presidency." Roosevelt's handling of foreign affairs was "masterly," she wrote, and as vice president, Willkie would back him up. Both men inspired confidence and both were on the side of the masses.[104]

"Do try to get this silly business of Wendell Willkie out of her head," FDR wrote to a friend after reading Thompson's column.[105] Willkie shared Roosevelt's amusement at the idea of a joint ticket. "I am sure I would be the last person President Roosevelt would want to have on the same ticket with him," he said.[106] But Thompson accurately fathomed the two men's alignment on foreign policy.

Willkie's foreign policy advisor, Raymond Buell, one of *Fortune*'s editors, was a passionate interventionist. He believed, as he told Henry Luce, that Americans "must come to realize that the defense of Britain is as important to us as the defense of Pearl Harbor."[107] He argued against the obsolete "fatuity" of isolationism in his book *Isolated America*, which was the subject of a glowing front-page review from historian Allan Nevins in the *New York Times Book Review* in May 1940.[108] Buell proposed a bipartisan agreement on the European crisis—one that included planes and destroyers for the British, repeal of the Neutrality Act, and support for compulsory military service—provided that Roosevelt renounced a third term. It was a plan that went nowhere.[109] And yet, the question remained: would the delegates at the GOP Convention choose a Republican version of Franklin Roosevelt? Would they nominate Wendell Willkie, a man whom some—like Dorothy Thompson—viewed more as FDR's political partner than as his political adversary?

Willkie's support for the Allies appeared to be unwavering. At an elegant dinner party in New York in early June 1940, attended by newspaper magnates, financiers, and the British ambassador, Lord Lothian, as well as Robert Taft and Dorothy Thompson, Willkie declared that he would vote for Roosevelt before voting for a Republican who opposed helping Britain and France. His remark pleased most of his fellow guests—especially Lord Lothian, who later commented that Willkie "went all out for war." But the hot-tempered Taft exploded, his wife later wrote, "with a loud pop." A most inelegant screaming match ensued.[110]

Three weeks before the start of the GOP Convention in Philadelphia, all bets were off. Turner Catledge, a political reporter for the *New York Times*, wrote that "all calculations in the Republican race must be made virtually on a day-to-day basis," so volatile was the world and national situation.[111]

"Who? Who? Who?" hooted a chorus of reporters dressed as owls at a Gridiron Club dinner that spring, attended by President Roosevelt, cabinet members, diplomats, and all the Democratic and Republican candidates.

"Whom will they nominate?" the owls asked to the laughter of the crowd.

> Whom will they elevate?
> Roosevelt, Garner, Farley, McNutt?
> Vandenberg, Taft, Dewey, Tut Tut!
> Who in this room tonight,
> Who has the answer right?
> Who? Who? Who?[112]

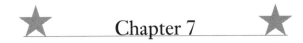

Chapter 7

Home Run for the White House

T HE WHOLE IDEA WAS "COCKEYED," Roosevelt said at his press conference on May 24, 1940, when a reporter asked him if he was thinking
about building a coalition cabinet with Republicans. Such conjectures
were a "newspaper dream," the president scoffed—almost resentfully, one
journalist wrote. Reporters were simply barking up the wrong tree. Still, they
had thought they were onto something, because Frank Knox, the Republican
vice presidential candidate in 1936, had recently been seen entering the White
House. But now the question was "all settled," wrote columnist Mark Sullivan, and the "coalition cabinet idea is out."[1]

Less than a month later, on June 20, the president announced the appointments of two prominent Republicans to his cabinet. Henry Stimson would
become the new secretary of war and Knox secretary of the navy. Home run
for the White House.

In 1940, a year of crisis in Europe and Asia, it made sense for the president to reach out to Republicans to try to forge a common foreign policy, especially at a time when isolationists, Nazi sympathizers, and fifth columnists,
as he had remarked in his fireside chat on May 26, wanted nothing more than
to spread discord and induce political paralysis.[2] But 1940 was also an election
year, and how better for the president to broaden his support and take some
wind out of Republican sails than by recruiting respected members of the
GOP—and on the very eve of the party's convention? A canny political strategy of divide and conquer.

For several months, Roosevelt had been assiduously courting the 66-year-old
Knox, a "Rough Rider" who had fought beside Theodore Roosevelt in the Battle

of San Juan Hill and then served as a colonel in the army in France during World War I. Knox later bought two newspapers, the *Chicago Daily News* and the Manchester (N.H.) *Union-Leader*. When he ran for vice president in 1936, he denounced the Roosevelt administration as "blundering, visionary and fanatic" and lashed out at the New Deal's "crackpot ideas," which, he said, contained "something of Karl Marx" but "equally as much of Groucho Marx."[3]

Roosevelt might well have harbored a grievance against Knox—after all, the president had a taste for crushing his enemies. "I'm a mean cuss at heart," Roosevelt once said to Frances Perkins, who had witnessed his vindictive streak. But Perkins was also acquainted with the Franklin Roosevelt who adapted to new circumstances and whose personal rule was "Be flexible in all dealings with human beings."[4] In the case of Frank Knox, FDR held no grudge. Indeed, his invitation to this biting critic was a supremely self-confident move. And he had good reason to reach out to him. Knox was an outspoken and perspicacious internationalist, as early as 1937 writing antifascist editorials for his *Chicago Daily News*, the rival paper to that city's isolationist *Daily Tribune*. After Roosevelt's "quarantine" speech in October 1937, Knox penned an editorial not only praising the president's talk but calling for immediate repeal of the Neutrality Act, which, he wrote, tied the president's hands "in advance in his momentous task of guiding the nation at a time of international turmoil."[5] In September 1939, on the day after German forces invaded Poland, Knox editorialized that Americans should put politics aside and rally behind their president; a few days later, calling for national unity, he suggested that FDR create a bipartisan cabinet.[6]

May 1940 found Knox writing to William Allen White that "there is no longer any such thing as isolation."[7] In a page-one editorial he wrote for the *Daily News*, Knox warned of an attack on the United States by Germany and Japan and called for Americans to speed up arms production, equip both naval and army air fleets, and repeal the arms embargo. He passionately advocated for extending every form of help, short of war, to the Allies, who, he said, "are now fighting the bestial monster that is making a shambles of Europe." And he proposed training ten thousand college students to be military pilots, while he himself helped organize nine privately financed volunteer training camps. Military aid for Britain was crucial not only to American security but also to America's soul. The roots of American national life, Knox stressed, "lie embedded in British soil. From a cultural standpoint it would be a calamity for us if British life were uprooted and replaced by a Nazi growth."[8]

Roosevelt had begun his active courtship of Knox in December 1939, tendering an offer of the position of secretary of the navy.[9] Earlier that year, after a long illness, Secretary of the Navy Claude Swanson had died, and the position was still open. As a former assistant secretary of the navy, FDR felt that he understood the navy so well that he would in fact run it himself no matter who was in charge. Still, the department needed a head. "You of all the Republican leaders," Roosevelt wrote to Knox, "have shown a truer understanding of the effect which the international situation will of necessity exert on our domestic future." Hopeful that Knox would join his team, the president diplomatically suggested that they put the campaign attacks behind them. "I, too, was inexperienced in national campaigns in 1920," FDR wrote, "and later regretted many of the things I said at that time." But with the European war still in an early stage, Knox was not ready to accept the president's invitation, though he promised to serve in any capacity "if an emergency arose." Roosevelt wrote back that, if a real crisis developed, "I would still want you as part of such an Administration. Also, I hope much that you will run down to see me from time to time to talk over events as they occur. In this job I need every angle from every part of the country."[10]

Instead of Knox, the president promoted Charles Edison, the assistant secretary of the navy and the son of Thomas Edison, to the post. But Edison quickly proved a timid, listless administrator, who, as Knox had warned Roosevelt at their December meeting, failed to comprehend the seriousness of the rapidly deteriorating world situation.[11] In short, Edison was hardly better than the isolationist, obstructionist secretary of war, Harry Woodring.[12] Both men had to go.

In late May 1940, as Nazi troops pushed deeper into France, Roosevelt and Knox met again. This time Knox accepted FDR's offer—still unofficial—for the job of secretary of the navy or possibly, if Knox preferred, secretary of war. Knox told the president that he was at his service and afterward mentioned to a friend that it would have been "damnably near treason" to do otherwise.[13]

With one Republican in his fold, Roosevelt had his eye on another for a wartime cabinet position: Henry Stimson.

In early June, Grenville Clark, a wealthy New York lawyer who had helped organize military training camps before the First World War, enlisted FDR's old advisor, Supreme Court justice Felix Frankfurter, to lobby the president for Stimson's appointment as secretary of war. Unlike the Rough Rider, newspaperman, and politician Frank Knox, Stimson was a well-connected, decorous, independently wealthy patrician, a graduate of Yale and Harvard Law. A staunch, lifelong Republican, the 73-year-old Stimson had served as a U.S. attorney under Theodore Roosevelt and, under Taft, as secretary of war, acquiring the nickname "Light Horse Harry" in part because he rode horseback every day and in part because he worked quickly. During World War I, he had fought in France and attained the rank of colonel. In 1927, Coolidge appointed Stimson governor-general of the Philippines; and in 1929, Stimson joined the Hoover administration as secretary of state.[14] Stimson was hardly youthful, but Frankfurter assured Roosevelt that as secretary of war, he would have energetic help in an assistant like 49-year-old Judge Robert Patterson, who had also served in World War I, earning a Distinguished Service Medal for heroism.[15]

Roosevelt and Stimson had clashed a decade earlier. In 1930, when FDR ran for a second term as governor of New York against Charles Tuttle, Republicans had mobilized Secretary of State Stimson to proclaim in a radio address from Washington that, as the nation was sinking into the Depression, FDR had "shown his unfitness to deal with the great crisis now confronting New York State." FDR had replied that the Washington establishment should "rest assured that we of the Empire State can and will take care of ourselves and our problems."[16]

But Stimson would soon earn Roosevelt's admiration for advocating international resistance to the Japanese invasion of Manchuria in 1931 and, in 1935, for supporting American membership in the World Court. And the appreciation was mutual. In January 1933 Stimson went to Hyde Park to confer with President-elect Roosevelt about foreign affairs. "I was really touched, overwhelmed by the kindness which he showed me," Stimson later said about that first meeting.[17] In 1939, Stimson's star rose further when he made several important and well-received speeches in favor of repeal of the arms embargo. In March 1939, the *New York Times* printed his powerful 3,500-word letter calling for a robust, interventionist foreign policy. "Shall we bury our heads in the sands of isolationism," he asked, "and timidly await the time when our security shall be lessened and perhaps destroyed by the growing success of lawlessness around us?" American isolationists failed to see that the Axis nations' "extreme brutality" and contempt for freedom of speech, thought, and all the "moral and humane ties which bind human society together" constituted "a complete reversal of the whole trend of European civilization" and the most serious attack ever waged on the principles of democracy. Although Stimson distanced himself from what he termed Roosevelt's "novel and haphazard experiments" with the nation's economy, he nevertheless concluded that the president, in carrying out a foreign policy "adequate to meet the emergency of the present world," should have the support "of all parties and citizens."[18]

Frankfurter's suggestion that Stimson be named war secretary "struck fire" with Roosevelt, the justice noted.[19] It would put the right man in the right place and cement the bipartisan makeup of FDR's team.

Enter Stimson and Knox. Exit Woodring and Edison.

Send the "small-bore" Woodring to Paris as ambassador, Harold Ickes had advised in February 1940. According to the acid-tongued Ickes, Woodring was "a misfit and incompetent."[20] In fact, the conflict between the isolationist Woodring and the interventionist assistant secretary of war Louis Johnson had virtually paralyzed the War Department at a critical time.[21] Making matters worse, Woodring was interested in the "social side of his position," Jim Farley said. "Instead of working hard all day," Farley complained, "he has handled his Department in a perfunctory way and lets others handle the show."[22] Ickes and Farley were not alone in their contempt for Woodring; others, including one of Woodring's fellow isolationists, disapproved of the war secretary's obvious dislike for the commander in chief, a dislike that verged on disloyalty. "Woodring is just about as fond of Roosevelt as I am," wrote William Castle, Hoover's undersecretary of state. "Really he should not criticize unless he is willing to get out."[23]

In March 1940, after Roosevelt's trusted envoy, Undersecretary of State Sumner Welles, returned from Berlin, Rome, Paris, and London with discouraging reports about everything in Europe except the temper and determination of the British,[24] the president decided to ask his secretary of war about the possibility of an attack on the United States. Methodically he questioned Woodring. Was the army prepared for a possible bombardment of Washington? What would the secretary of war do if the bridges over the Potomac were destroyed? How could troops, equipment, and supplies on a large scale be moved from the coast to the interior of Virginia? What if the railroad bridge in Washington was blown up? Could the two existing highway bridges carry heavy freight cars and small artillery? Woodring's vague responses left the president deeply unsatisfied. By mid-May, FDR's mind was made up. He would get rid of Woodring.[25]

In early June, as a hundred divisions of German troops bore into the heart of France from four different directions in the north, and as Britain withdrew three hundred thousand of its troops and fifty-three thousand French troops from the northern French port of Dunkirk, the White House saw to it that British ships in American ports were loaded with arms and munitions, overriding the War Department and bypassing the uncooperative Woodring, who complained about "frittering away" war matériel overseas.

Then, on Monday, June 17, the same day that the defeated French government requested armistice terms from Nazi Germany, the secretary of war challenged the president's authority and refused to approve the transfer of a dozen bombers to Britain, insisting that such a sale violated the Neutrality Act and stripped the nation of needed defenses.[26]

Two days later, Woodring was out. On June 19, he received a polite but cool letter from FDR. "Because of a succession of recent events both here and abroad, and not within our personal choice and control," the president wrote in his letter of dismissal, "I find it necessary now to make certain readjustments." Lowering the boom, he asked point blank for Woodring's resignation, though he offered a consolation prize—the governorship of Puerto Rico—in the hope that Woodring might refrain from joining the isolationist chorus. But Woodring declined the governorship, pointedly commenting that he hoped FDR would continue his "pronounced non-intervention policy." Not wishing to escalate the tensions between them, Roosevelt sent a diplomatic response. "Don't worry about maintaining the non-intervention policy," he reassured Woodring. "We are certainly going to do just that." Looking back on Woodring in 1946, Treasury Secretary Morgenthau pronounced the secretary of war a "fourth-rate" former governor of Kansas "who not only couldn't see that our frontier was the Rhine but couldn't see across the Hudson River."[27]

Woodring "literally had to be dynamited out of his post," wrote Harold Ickes, while Secretary of the Navy Edison had been more gently removed, in March accepting FDR's suggestion that he run as the Democratic candidate for governor of New Jersey, a post he would win in November. Now Roosevelt was free to assemble a new team.[28]

His first move was to call Frank Knox on the morning of June 19, the day of his letter of dismissal to Woodring. After exchanging some pleasantries, the president officially extended an offer to serve as the next secretary of the navy. Knox readily accepted, but, hoping to play an active role at the upcoming GOP Convention and work for an interventionist party platform as well as an interventionist candidate, he asked if the president could postpone the announcement of his appointment until after the convention. Roosevelt pointed out that if the convention nominated an isolationist, Knox would look like a disgruntled politician, abandoning his party for FDR's cabinet after losing the fight. The new secretary of the navy accepted the president's reasoning. Then FDR phoned Stimson to offer him the War Department. Stimson knew that his name had been mentioned for the job but was astonished that Roosevelt had listened to the suggestion and acted on it. "He told me that Knox had already agreed to accept the position of Secretary of War," Stimson wrote in his diary a week later. "The President said he was very anxious to have me accept because everybody was running around at loose ends in Washington and he thought I would be a stabilizing factor." Stimson asked for a little time to consult his wife and four hours later called the president to say that he considered his invitation "a call to duty."[29] Accepting the new position, Stimson emphasized to the president his strong commitment to compulsory universal military training. The stars were aligned, for, just the previous day, Roosevelt had read the press accounts of Stimson's outspokenly internationalist speech at Yale, in which he had called for a draft, and told Stimson that, as Stimson wrote in his diary, "he was in sympathy with me."[30]

On June 20, the same day that Edward Burke of Nebraska introduced a bill in the Senate for compulsory military service, the president made the new appointments public. They reflected, he said, "the overwhelming sentiment of the nation for *national solidarity* at a time of world crisis and in behalf of national defense and nothing else."[31] By adding the words "nothing else," Roosevelt sought to quash speculation that he had made a calculated political move. The appointments would indeed nicely bolster his position for a possible run in 1940 and, conveniently, they would also spark dissension in the Republican ranks. But more important, the president had assembled a strong, internationalist bipartisan team, committed to the buildup of the nation's military defenses in response to the escalating crisis in Europe.

For his part, Army Chief of Staff George Marshall was relieved to see Woodring go and, though anxious at first at the prospect of working with Stimson, came to have great respect for the new secretary of war. Six days after the appointment was announced, Marshall visited Stimson and his wife at their summer home on Long Island. "They are both delightful people. . . . We talked until almost midnight," Marshall wrote to his wife afterward. Over the next several years, Marshall's refrain would be, "Thank heaven we have a Stimson with us." During the war, the door between their offices would always be open.[32] Also happy about the appointments of Stimson and Knox was the British ambassador, Philip Kerr, the Marquess of Lothian. A few years earlier, Lord Lothian had been a member of the pro-German "Cliveden Set" in England, but by 1939 he had come to loathe and fear Hitler and fascism. "The president has now strengthened his national position," Lothian reported to London in June, "by securing two outstanding Republican personalities to fill two key defense positions . . . [that] notoriously needed strengthening."[33] Ironically, the four boldest interventionists in the president's cabinet now were present and former Republicans—Stimson, Knox, Harold Ickes, and Henry Wallace.

"CAPITAL SURPRISED," shouted the headline in the *New York Times* on June 21, the day after Roosevelt announced the two appointments. "Master Stroke by Roosevelt Stuns G.O.P.," read the headline in the *Atlanta Constitution*; its reporter called FDR's appointments a "demolition bomb tossed into the Republican camp." Indeed, on the eve of the Republican National Convention in Philadelphia, Roosevelt's naming of two distinguished Republicans to his cabinet caught the GOP by surprise. In their bewilderment and helpless outrage, some Republicans impulsively read Stimson and Knox out of their party, sputtering that they were "fifth column" saboteurs who had committed "an act of party treachery." John Hamilton, the party chairman, growled that Stimson and Knox were no longer "qualified" to speak as Republicans, while the *Chicago Daily Tribune* charged that the appointments of the two interventionists were a White House ploy to try to saddle the GOP "with the responsibility for wasting the billions appropriated for national defense."[34]

On the Senate floor, the startling news of the two appointments broadsided isolationists. After a moment of stunned silence, Bennett Champ Clark, a Democrat from Missouri, leaped up and cried, "Who?" Isolationists in both parties called for Senate hearings on the appointments. In addition to demanding a Senate investigation into Woodring's sudden and unexplained resignation, Senator Nye insisted that President Roosevelt resign and turn the presidency over to Vice President Garner. Only Garner, Nye said, could restore confidence in the government.[35]

Most moderate Republicans, however, kept their cool. Joseph Martin, the House minority leader, judged that Republicans should treat the appointments as a "compliment" to the GOP. After all, he pointed out, Roosevelt was apparently forced to turn to the Republicans to fill key defense posts because he couldn't find such qualified men in his own party.[36] Vermont's Warren Austin, the ranking Republican on the Senate Military Affairs Committee, called on members of his party to stop acting like fools and give Stimson a fair hearing.[37] Massachusetts governor Leverett Saltonstall remarked that with the appointments of Stimson and Knox "the strength of the Cabinet has been enormously increased."[38] William Allen White acknowledged that the president's naming of Stimson and Knox was an "obviously planted time bomb" designed to throw confusion into the Republican leadership. But, speaking out for the moderate and interventionist wing of the party, he warned that

Republicans should not let FDR goad them into the isolationist corner. If the GOP adopted a "peace at any price platform," White said, they would surely hand the election over to the Democrats.[39]

Just four days before the Republican Convention was set to open, Roosevelt had made a brilliant move, in both policy and politics. He not only strengthened his cabinet with two dedicated and talented internationalists and expertly played the patriotism card by including members of the opposition in his administration, he also widened the breach within the GOP between isolationists and internationalists. And what better way to set the stage for an election than by dividing and weakening the rival party? Now he could sit back and watch them spar and grumble. Indeed, while he reached out to the GOP in order to form an inclusive government in a time of national crisis, Republicans like Alf Landon, Thomas Dewey, and Herbert Hoover showed themselves unwilling to give even the appearance of transcending partisan party politics. Landon, to whom FDR had briefly considered offering a cabinet seat, declared that he preferred "the vitality of the two-party system," and Dewey blasted what he called the president's "continuous reliance on political strategy instead of statesmanship." Though Hoover refrained from criticizing his former secretary of state Henry Stimson, the ex-president maintained that a coalition cabinet would mean the "suspension of all democratic processes" and spell a direct road to dictatorship.[40]

It would have been so much smarter, commented Harold Ickes, if Republicans had accepted Martin's suggestion that they take the Stimson and Knox appointments in stride and congratulate the president on his perspicacity in turning to the GOP to fill pivotal positions. "Instead of that," Ickes wrote, "they played right into the President's hands."[41]

 Chapter 8

The Republicans in Philadelphia

TWO LIFE-SIZED PAPIER-MÂCHÉ ELEPHANTS, adorned with big red and yellow circus blankets sporting the name of Robert Taft, waggled their trunks and nodded to passersby on the sidewalk outside the Taft headquarters in Philadelphia. Near the Dewey headquarters, a "highway Pullman"—an unusually large campaign bus complete with seven beds and a kitchenette—attracted the curiosity of crowds. At the Arthur Vandenberg headquarters, as aides prepared for a reception, one of them informed reporters that they would see "no stunts." The senator, said the aide with a hint of resignation in his voice, "won't stand for any circus stuff." Still, Vandenberg fans carried signs reading, "Welcome Van, you're the man!"[1]

It was late in June, and the Republican Convention was about to begin.

What is a national political convention? Every four years, for five raucous and hectic days, delegates and politicos expectantly come together to formulate a party platform and nominate a president and a vice president. Bands play, quartets sing, organizations throw lavish cocktail parties and receptions, delegates parade through the aisles, supporters cheer at the names of their candidates and jubilantly shout out their slogans. Politicians give speeches, some interesting, some interminable. Rumors circulate, offers are proffered, deals are brokered, bargains are sealed, names are placed into nomination, state delegations dramatically cast their votes. Chaotic, emotional, theatrical—and quintessentially a part of the American political scene. But this convention was unusual. It was unbossed and even unled. "From the moment they came to town," wrote *Time*, "Republicans of all stripes agreed wholeheartedly that this was 'the damnedest convention that ever was.'"[2]

Hundreds of reporters from all parts of the country worked the convention hall, hunting out stories.[3] There were columnists and cartoonists from Damon Runyon and William Allen White to Walter Lippmann, Dorothy Thompson, and Herbert Block. One newspaper story described the candidates' headquarters—Dewey's 78 rooms at the Walton Hotel, Taft's 102 rooms at the Benjamin Franklin Hotel, and Vandenberg's 48 at the Adelphia. Willkie's boast that he had reserved only a two-room suite at the Benjamin Franklin was somewhat exaggerated, though it was true that some of his top strategists had no hotel space.[4]

"I have no campaign manager, no campaign fund, no campaign headquarters. All the headquarters I have are under my hat!" Willkie merrily told reporters as he chatted casually with them on the sidewalk. "If I accidentally am nominated and elected President of the United States," he added, "I shall go in completely free of any obligations."[5] Indeed, publisher John Cowles, who spoke with Willkie several times during the convention, later said that, although several important Republicans approached Willkie with proposals to swing votes his way in return for certain favors and agreements, the independent Willkie turned them all down, making no commitments to anyone.[6]

But others in Philadelphia worried about the candidate's political inexperience and the amateur quality of his entourage. When two *New York Times* reporters asked Willkie who his floor manager was at the convention, he purported to be mystified and beseeched them for suggestions—though at the 1932 Democratic Convention, he himself had served as a lieutenant on the convention floor for presidential hopeful Newton Baker, Woodrow Wilson's secretary of war. But that show of innocence was precisely Willkie's appeal. Unrehearsed, spontaneous, candid, uncalculating, he appeared to be conducting an impromptu candidacy—and winging it successfully.[7] Indeed, columnists Alsop and Kintner reported that nine tenths of the chatter at the convention centered on Willkie—his personality, his background, his ideas.[8]

The convention got under way on the evening of Monday, June 24, in the huge Philadelphia Convention Hall, gaily decorated with red, white and blue bunting, banners, and statues of eagles. In sweltering 90-degree heat, made even worse by the blazing lights, Harold Stassen, the blond-haired, 33-year-old, politically moderate governor of Minnesota, gave the keynote address. After welcoming the delegates, he launched into an hour-long speech that revealed the difficulty Republicans had in formulating policy on the war. Stassen offered no criticism of the Stimson and Knox appointments, pointing out, on the contrary, that those two Republican internationalists would greatly improve Roosevelt's cabinet. "It is only regrettable," he said, "that we cannot change the entire Cabinet and the man who heads it with equal abruptness!" But, to the applause of the crowd, he also expressed the "earnest hope" of keeping the nation out of the conflict and declared that the United States was "too woefully weak" to provide the Allies with military matériel. He called for national preparedness but excluded compulsory military training, which he branded a "method of Hitler and Mussolini and Stalin."[9]

Across the ocean on that same evening, fighting came to an end in France. Two days earlier, on June 22, in a railway carriage in Compiègne—the same place and same car in which a humiliated Germany had signed the 1918 armistice—a beaten France signed an armistice with its German conqueror. Not a single public figure in France raised his voice to condemn the surrender, Charles de Gaulle would later complain.[10] Now, on June 24, the German government announced a second armistice between Italy and France. Loudspeakers in Berlin blared forth news of the victory: The "war in the West is over!"[11] Throughout Germany, people celebrated; Hitler's newspaper, the *Völkische Beobachter*, exulted that Paris, a "city of frivolity and corruption, of democracy and capitalism, where Jews had entry to the court, and niggers to the salons," would never rise again.[12] And in Paris itself, an excited Hitler paraded through the streets of his new conquest. After touring the Opera, the Champs-Elysées, the Arc de Triomphe, and Napoleon's tomb, he decided against demolishing the city. "In the past I often considered whether we would not have to destroy Paris," he said to his architect, Albert Speer. "But when we are finished in Berlin, Paris will only be a shadow. So why should we destroy it?"[13]

The terms of the armistice spelled a crushing, humiliating defeat for France. The northern part of the country became a province of Germany under military occupation. France was required to pay for that occupation as well as "reparations for injustices done to the German empire." Unoccupied southern France would be governed by a puppet regime, under the 84-year-old Marshal Philippe Pétain. "Certainly our parliamentary democracy is dead," Pétain would soon tell the French people, as he committed France to collaboration with Nazi Germany and the "new order."[14]

For days, tens of thousands of desperate French men, women, and children had been hurriedly packing a few of their belongings and fleeing Paris. "Anything that had four wheels and an engine was pressed into service," wrote reporter Virginia Cowles. "We saw terrible sights. All along the way cars that had run out of petrol or broken down were pushed into the fields. Old people, too tired or ill to walk any farther, were lying on the ground under the merciless glare of the sun."[15] William Shirer arrived in Paris on June

17 and described the scene. Streets were "utterly deserted," he wrote, "the stores closed, the shutters down tight over all the windows. It was the emptiness that got you."[16]

Winston Churchill had sent an emissary to France on a last-ditch mission to warn the government, in Churchill's words, "how dearly France would have to pay for capitulation to Hitler," and he assailed the decision of the French military to accept such devastating terms. One of both Churchill and Roosevelt's immediate concerns was the disposition of the powerful French Fleet and how to keep its vessels, anchored in ports in North Africa and the Far East, out of German hands. For his part, Hitler announced that the conflict with Britain remained to be "resolved."[17] With Germany commanding the entire coast of Europe from Norway to the border of fascist-friendly Spain, Britain now stood alone.

Newsmen in Philadelphia reported that word of those heart-stopping events barely penetrated the convention hall, which was, one journalist noted, "like a fiercely lighted, sealed theatrical museum." Comfortable and well-dressed, happily engaged in political ritual, the sixteen thousand people inside the arena appeared unconcerned with the calamity in France. "There is neither discussion nor purpose nor any consciousness of the terrible reality just ahead," wrote a gloomy William Allen White in a dispatch from Philadelphia that was published on Tuesday, June 25. He described the delegates as "entirely innocent, so puerile in their political attitude, walking in the grooves laid down by dead politicians, the moldy traditions of other days."[18]

But *New York Times* reporter Anne O'Hare McCormick found the convention thrilling. The real news story in Philadelphia, she wrote, was the "unique exhibit of free assembly, free speech and a free press for an opposition party," something that, after the fall of France, she wrote, could take place nowhere on the continent of Europe. In America, "nobody throttles the convention orators. Nobody curbs the criticism of the Administration. Nobody censors the reports."[19] As for White's allegation that the delegates suffered from catastrophic political blindness and naiveté, a cartoonist named H. E. Homan offered a different perspective. Captioned "The Uninvited Guest," his drawing showed the ominous figure of Hitler standing in the middle of the convention hall.[20] But it remained to be seen how the delegates would react to that lurking demonic presence. Would they forthrightly confront the Nazi leader—or cower in his shadow?

On Tuesday evening, June 25, while the world listened tensely to radio broadcasts about the fall of France, the convention's chairman, Joe Martin, the

House minority leader from Massachusetts, introduced the convention's evening speaker, Herbert Hoover.

The former president still held out hopes for the party's nomination. A week earlier, he had received an unexpected boost from John L. Lewis, the president of the United Mine Workers and the Congress of Industrial Organizations. Speaking in Philadelphia to a meeting of the National Association for the Advancement of Colored People, Lewis insisted that Hoover had been unfairly blamed for the Great Depression and that the economic recovery that was supposedly well under way in 1932 was sabotaged by none other than FDR and his New Deal. Roosevelt alone, Lewis bizarrely maintained, was responsible for the economic turmoil of the 1930s, for the domestic hardships that posed a far greater danger to American democracy "than all the dictators of foreign lands."[21]

Now at the convention, people cheered, whistled, and clambered onto chairs to better see Herbert Hoover as he marched down the long aisle to the speaker's platform. Closest to the stage in the best seats were the contingents from Maine and Vermont—the only states that had stuck with the Republican nominee Alf Landon in 1936. Taking his stand before the microphone, Hoover waved shyly at the audience. Then, in a monotone voice, he proceeded to read his prepared speech, forcing members of the audience to shout, "Louder! Louder!" as they struggled to hear the words lost in his bulldog chops.[22] His message was predictably replete with denunciations of the incompetence of the "totalitarian liberals" in the Roosevelt administration. On the one hand he expressed resentment at FDR's "sapping our stamina and making us soft," and, on the other, criticized him for having been too hard on Hitler and Mussolini. Leaders, he advised, should "keep cool" and avoid "provocative speech" that could incite war.

Hoover conceded that there could be no such thing as American isolation from the wars enveloping much of the world, but he warned against overreaction to the German military machine. "Every whale that spouts is not a submarine," he quipped. He gave a firm yes to national preparedness but an equally firm no to universal military training. Yes, Hoover acknowledged, "we will have to deal with totalitarianism in all of Europe," but Americans would be served by their "morals" in dealing with it.[23] Trapped among his contradictions and vacillations, he seemed uncomprehending of the meaning and consequences of fascist world dominance.

Hoover's only answer to German aggression was for the nation to retreat meekly into a modestly armed bunker. But the *Hartford Courant*, whose editor was Hoover's friend, congratulated him on his "fighting message" that courageously taught Americans how to "establish stamina, character and ideals."

The *Washington Post* hailed his "lucid thinking" and called his talk "a peroration of high literary merit, of great spiritual beauty."[24]

On June 25, the day of Hoover's convention speech, a full-page advertisement appeared in dozens of American newspapers. It read: "To the Delegates to the Republican National Convention and to American Mothers, Wage Earners, Farmers and Veterans: STOP THE MARCH TO WAR!! STOP THE INTERVENTIONISTS AND WARMONGERS! STOP THE DEMOCRATIC PARTY!" Sponsored by the "National Committee to Keep America out of Foreign Wars," the ad was signed by Hamilton Fish, the ranking Republican on the House Foreign Affairs Committee, along with fifty current and former members of Congress.[25] At the time, Americans did not suspect that the German chargé d'affaires in Washington had secretly paid half the cost of the ad.[26]

In the late afternoon on Wednesday, June 26, the chair of the Resolutions Committee presented the party platform to the delegates. Inevitable were the numerous planks excoriating Roosevelt's New Deal as a disaster for America and promising that Republicans would put idle men and idle capital back to work, create new wealth and profits, limit the rights of workers in order to provide more "fairness to employers," and shift responsibility for social security to the states.

The plank on national defense and foreign policy represented a compromise hammered out at stormy meetings chaired by the subcommittee's moderate-leaning chair, Alf Landon. The isolationist bloc on the committee, led by Hamilton Fish and Massachusetts senator Henry Cabot Lodge, Jr., pushed for a rigidly noninterventionist plank. With a secret subsidy of $3,000 from Hans Thomsen of the German embassy, Fish had partially paid the expenses for several dozen isolationist members of Congress, all elected for the first time in the 1938 Republican resurgence, to travel to Philadelphia and testify before the platform committee.[27] Headed by the reactionary Karl Mundt of South Dakota, they demanded a resolution unequivocally opposing any American involvement in the war in Europe.[28]

The opening sentence of the final version of the plank set the tone: The party was "firmly opposed to involving this Nation in foreign war." Then followed a long recital of the enormous economic cost to the United States of World War I, leaving the impression that money was one of the main reasons behind Republican isolationism.[29] The plank sensibly called for the building up of national defenses, but it placed "upon the New Deal full responsibility for our unpreparedness." The authors of the platform, so many "somersaulting weasels," wrote one reporter, neglected to point out that a majority of Republicans in Congress had consistently voted against military appropriations, including new planes for the army and more battleships for the navy.[30]

Regarding the issue of help for Hitler's opponents, the committee members expressed sympathy for the nations "whose ideals most closely resemble our own." But they rejected use of the word "allies"—just as the Democrats would do in their own platform—as if that word implied too much attachment and responsibility to the European nations struggling for survival. As for aid to those European democracies, the plank pronounced the GOP in favor of "the extension to all peoples fighting for liberty . . . of such aid as shall not be in violation of international law." Where the Republican platform differed most sharply from the Democratic one was in its fear of any escalation of tension with Hitler. Thus the plank attacked "the explosive utterances by the president directed at other governments which serve to imperil our peace."[31]

The foreign policy plank suited "both the triumph of democracy and the collapse of democracy," commented H. L. Mencken, fully grasping the acrobatic feat of the somersaulting weasels. It seemed to approve "both sending arms to England and sending only flowers."[32] Others voiced similar astonishment at the know-nothing platform. "Did you ever see a dream walking?" asked columnist Raymond Clapper. "Well, I did. It's the Republican National Convention. . . . They mumble a platform that has less relation to the reality around us than Grimm's *Fairy Tales*."[33] Though Hamilton Fish declared himself pleased that the GOP was determined to keep the country out of war, progressives like William Allen White saw Republican isolationism as a political dead end. "Why the Republican Party wants to monkey-doodle around after the Fascist vote in this country," White wrote, "is beyond my understanding." If the GOP "bleats like sheep for peace at any price, my beloved party will not even carry Maine and Vermont."[34] And most disappointed of all was Alf Landon himself, who, as the subcommittee's chair, had been forced to make compromises he found barely tolerable. The GOP plank on foreign policy was "lousy, weasel-worded, and two-faced," he wrote a month later to publisher Roy Howard.[35]

Some moderates and progressives like White wanted to debate the plank on the convention floor but were dissuaded from doing so by Willkie's supporters who were fearful of antagonizing the isolationists.[36] That restraint, however, did not stop the members of Fish's group from trying to sabotage a Willkie candidacy. They called for the convention to nominate a *real* Republican who had "a past record consistently supporting Republican policies and principles" and who would not lead the nation into a foreign war.[37]

Who would be the Republican choice? Would the GOP go with front-runner Thomas Dewey, who had won most of the primaries that spring and could boast a well-organized, professional campaign team? He had come out for "all proper" aid to the Allies—by which he meant outdated "surplus" war matériel—but he sternly warned against any other involvement in the war.

Or would delegates gravitate toward Robert Taft, who was against compulsory military training, condemned the appointments of Stimson and Knox, and attacked the Democrats as the "war party"? Unfortunately, even the Ohioan's own publicity director admitted privately that his emotionally distant candidate spoke "as if he were submitting a brief in a probate case rather than addressing an audience." Taft had made efforts to humanize himself with voters, but they all fell flat. He was the "No. 1 Republican Bumbler," wrote *Time* two weeks before the convention, recognizing his perfect record of "putting his foot in his mouth." In late May, on the same day that Republican leaders like Alf Landon advised him to go slow on isolationism, pointing out that even in the Midwest, sentiment was increasing for more substantial aid to the Allies, Taft plowed ahead with his strongest pitch yet for complete American neutrality and isolation.[38]

For his part, FDR guessed that Taft would get the Republican nomination, but neither Taft nor Dewey suited Walter Lippmann.[39] Their speeches, he commented during the convention, "make Mr. Neville Chamberlain seem like a far-sighted and strong statesman." Both men gave the impression, he wrote, of "being always surprised, always unprepared, always confused by the course of events. Even at the eleventh hour there is no slightest evidence that Messrs. Taft and Dewey have any idea, any policy, any program designed to prepare their country for what lies ahead." He called Taft's complacency "terrifying" and sneered that Dewey changed "his view from hour to hour." They had, in effect, assured "Hitler that he could safely disregard America and go to war." Apathetic leaders like them had doomed democracy in Europe and would doom it in America, too. In short, Lippmann maintained, the GOP was walking in its sleep and offering no positive leadership.[40]

Dewey was still only the young district attorney of New York; Taft had been a senator for a mere eighteen months; Hoover had already been crushed under a Roosevelt landslide; and Vandenberg had no national following. Where could the GOP find some fire and spark?[41]

Willkie was a colorful maverick in a sea of gray. "I have no managers, no ghost writers, no workers—except voluntary ones!" he had exclaimed to reporters as the convention got under way. Unlike Dewey, Willkie had no convention delegates in his pocket. And so he made himself available to anyone and everyone in Philadelphia who wanted to meet him and speak with him. For eighteen hours a day, he addressed group after group. Vigorous and frank—as well as, according to *Time*, "shaggy, haggard, hoarse, sweating, strange"—he responded to all their questions. "Nothing is off the record," he said, "so shoot, ask anything you want . . . any damn thing in the world!" Willkie's powerful supporters in the publishing world pitched in. *Time*'s June 24 issue contained a three-page article on his "spectacular campaign," and the *Saturday Evening Post*, *Look*, and *U.S. News* also devoted feature articles to him.[42]

It had been a shrewd decision on the part of Willkie's team of advisors to run an unprecedented media campaign and skip the nonbinding popularity contests of primary elections. For example, in the New Jersey primary, Dewey had rolled up 340,000 votes, while Willkie received 25,000 as a write-in candidate. But though the entire New Jersey delegation was nominally pledged to Dewey, a third of the delegates indicated that they would vote for Willkie. In addition, many state delegations were committed to their favorite sons—at least on the first and second ballots.[43] Indiana's delegates, on the other hand, declined to commit themselves to Willkie—and some were openly hostile to him.[44] As a result of primaries and favorite son loyalties, only 276 out of the 1,000 convention delegates arrived in Philadelphia pledged to candidates: about 150 bound to Dewey and the other 126 split among the rest.

And making the primaries all the more moot were the alarming reports coming out of Europe on the eve of the convention. There might as well have been no primaries at all, columnist Mark Sullivan thought, convinced that, because of the European crisis, the convention delegates would be "practically all uncommitted and open-minded."[45]

On the subject of that crisis, Willkie was the only candidate who took—well, at least most of the time—an assertive position against fascist aggression. When asked if he favored military aid to Britain, he replied, "I favor all possible aid to the Allies without going to war." Still, reporters spotted some discrepancy. A week before the convention, Willkie had declared in a speech at the Hotel St. George in Brooklyn that the United States must stay out of war at all costs. Which is it? asked a reporter. Willkie said he stood by the Brooklyn speech. After all, he knew that, in order to be nominated and then run successfully against Roosevelt, he would need the support of traditional Republicans, including isolationists.[46] But in truth Willkie was as committed to resisting fascism and helping the Allies as was Frank Knox, Roosevelt's new secretary of the navy. Knox had written to Willkie that past March to say that he "would crawl on my hands and knees from here to Washington if, by that act, I could bring about your nomination."[47]

It would also take skillful maneuvering for Willkie to overcome his Democratic past, for many panicked Republicans thought it would be political suicide to nominate a man who had only recently joined the GOP. "Well, Wendell," said an Indiana delegate, "you know that back home in Indiana it's all right if the town whore joins the church but they don't let her lead the choir the first night." Indeed, forty congressmen and several senators sent an anti-Willkie letter to all the convention delegates, insisting that the party's candidate "must be a Republican in heart as in speech" and could not be "tainted with New Dealism" or interventionism.[48]

But the Willkie tide seemed palpable. "I will vote for Willkie on the first ballot," declared Governor Stassen, bestowing upon the internationalist Willkie the backing of his isolationist state. "We must have a president who can mobilize and unify our country to make it strong. Willkie is the best fitted man for the job." In addition to Stassen, who agreed to serve as Willkie's floor manager, the youthful governors of Connecticut, Rhode Island, Massachusetts, Colorado, and Oregon came on board for Willkie.[49] His star was quickly rising as more and more people voiced doubts about the other candidates.

Dewey and Taft looked for ways to halt the momentum toward Willkie. In a move to pool their resources and their strength, they each proposed the vice presidency to the other, an offer both men stubbornly refused. Dewey also offered the vice presidency to Vandenberg and promised that the Michigan senator could "write his own ticket." Vandenberg politely declined—"My place on the Senate Floor is more important than on the Senate rostrum," he said—and instead, he offered the vice presidency on a Vandenberg ticket to Dewey.[50] For his part, Taft requested Hoover's support and reportedly offered him the position of secretary of state, but, still a hopeful himself, Hoover, too, demurred. In the end, by refusing to unite and cooperate with one another against the unexpected ascension of Wendell Willkie, conservative, anti-interventionist Republicans would relinquish their clout.[51] "Anything may happen," said the cool Vandenberg.[52]

On Wednesday evening, four candidates were placed into nomination. On Thursday, voting would take place. Dewey was the first to be nominated. A New York politico and government attorney praised his strength and courage, his record of bringing "safety and confidence" to the citizens of New York, and his determination to "keep us out of war." Unfortunately, many of Dewey's supporters had not yet arrived in the convention hall, and the floor demonstration for him was brief and muted. The second candidate placed in nomination was Frank Gannett, an isolationist newspaper publisher from Rochester, New York.[53] The demonstration for Gannett began at 8:57 p.m.

and ended at 9:00. Then Robert Taft was nominated by Grove Patterson, the editor of the *Toledo Blade*, who said that he was speaking for Ohio, "the mother of presidents." Extolling the senator's background and experience, Patterson assured the audience that the Ohio senator would swiftly undo the "quack remedies" and "Russianized economic system" of the Roosevelt administration. Taft supporters joyously paraded around the convention floor.

Finally Charles Halleck, a 39-year-old congressman from Indiana, placed in nomination his fraternity brother, Wendell Willkie.[54] Willkie's advisors had asked Joe Martin to give the nominating speech for Willkie, but Martin had already accepted the convention chairmanship, and besides, he said, "I don't think your man Willkie has a chance."[55] The Indiana delegation itself was split, and some conservative Hoosiers had even made threats against Halleck.

After slugging down a few stiff drinks, Halleck headed to the speaker's podium. When he began his talk, a blast of boos almost blew him off the platform. "I just couldn't believe it," he later said. "But I kept going." As the crescendo of hostility rose from the floor, especially from the Ohio delegation supporting Taft, Joe Martin stepped forward to the rostrum, placed his arm on Halleck's shoulder, and quieted the crowd. Halleck soldiered on. With interruptions, his talk, which he had timed at eighteen minutes, took forty-five minutes to deliver.[56]

Halleck answered complaints that Willkie was a businessman with no political experience and that, until recently, he had been a Democrat. "I'd rather have a public utility man as president," he shouted, "than a president with no public utility!" And was the Republican Party a closed corporation? he demanded. Did a man have to be born into the GOP? A loud chorus of "No!'s" echoed throughout the convention hall, mostly from the galleries that had been carefully packed with Willkie supporters.[57] The speech itself was scarcely controversial—it did not even mention foreign policy—but Halleck's seal of approval helped Willkie with Republican isolationists and conservatives, especially from the Midwest. While Willkie's fans in the galleries chanted "We want Willkie! We want Willkie!," delegates on the floor paraded through the aisles. Watching quietly from the gallery was Irita Van Doren, worried, according to a friend, that she had now lost Wendell forever.[58]

On Thursday morning, a few more candidates were nominated: Vandenberg, Oregon's senator Charles McNary, Senator Styles Bridges of New Hampshire, and two others. No one, however, came forward to nominate Herbert Hoover.

That day, George Gallup also issued a statement saying that, although his national poll measuring the popularity of Republican candidates was not complete, he could say that a swing toward Willkie in public opinion had recently trended "sharply upward."[59] And, for the first time in its history, the influential Republican newspaper, the *New York Herald Tribune*, published a front-page editorial. It was an endorsement of Willkie—a coup orchestrated by *Tribune* writers Dorothy Thompson and Irita Van Doren and publisher Helen Reid. "Extraordinary times call for extraordinary abilities," the editors wrote, urging convention delegates to vote for Willkie, the man "uniquely suited" to respond to the urgent crises sweeping the globe. "Such timing of man and the hour does not come often in history," they concluded.[60]

· Columnists in the nation's leading newspapers were also pushing for a Willkie nomination that week. Arthur Krock wrote that while Republicans pussyfooted around every important issue and put out a "timorous platform," Willkie was the only candidate who dodged no questions and dared to say what he thought. "He is at once a novelty, a sparkling political prism and a thrilling entertainment," Krock excitedly wrote. Walter Lippmann effused that Willkie possessed "the insight, the character and the magnetism of which leadership is composed." Republicans were lucky, he added, to have a candidate who could compete on equal terms with a leader like Roosevelt.[61] With eminent columnists, advertising executives, and publishers on the Willkie team, commented the *Christian Science Monitor*, it was safe to say that "no presidential campaign in American history ever had such resources in the way of prima donna publicists."[62]

Balloting began on Thursday, June 27, another sweltering day in Philadelphia. An eager crowd of seventeen thousand delegates, alternates, and spectators jammed into the convention hall. Mrs. Willkie sat in the upper balcony, while her husband remained in his hotel room. Chain-smoking, drinking whiskey, munching on a steak dinner, and conferring with his aides, he listened to the radio coverage along with millions of others. He appeared, a *New York Times* reporter wrote, in "high good humor."[63]

On the first ballot, Dewey led with 360 votes to 189 for Taft and 105 for Willkie. Vandenberg had 76 and, though Hoover had not been nominated, a small handful of votes went to him anyway, though none from his home state of California. The winner would need the backing of 500 delegates plus one. Dewey's plan was to throw all his might into the first ballot in order to demonstrate early on his overwhelming strength, whereas the Willkie camp had the opposite approach. Charles Halleck, one of Willkie's strategists, had arranged for some delegates to hold their votes for Willkie in reserve, which would limit his first ballot support, but, in the crucial battle of perception and momentum, show him making a significant advance in each round of voting. "If we ever lost strength," Halleck said, "we were dead."[64]

The second ballot exposed the failure of Dewey's blitzkrieg strategy as he lost momentum, slipping to 338 while Taft jumped to 203 and Willkie shot up to 171. Trailing behind was Vandenberg with 73 votes. The convention floor was a scene of agitated confusion, of intrigue and bargaining, hopeful cheers and moans of disappointment. During the voting, Martin repeatedly begged delegates to keep their seats as they scurried around the hall, trying to pick up the latest information on what was going on.[65]

Between the second and third votes, there were frenzied attempts at negotiations. Harold Stassen cornered Alf Landon, a Dewey supporter, in an elevator for fourteen minutes, the *Washington Post* reported. Afterward, Stassen issued a statement to the press: "No announcement now. Mr. Landon and I had a very fine and thorough review of the situation."[66] Taft, meanwhile, hoped to persuade Hoover to hand over his few delegates, but the former president clung to the idea that the convention might deadlock and that he would emerge the nominee. Still, the Ohio senator confidently predicted victory on the fourth or fifth ballot. "The results of the first and second ballots are very encouraging," he told reporters.[67] At one point, Vandenberg turned toward Courtney Letts de Espil, the American wife of the Argentinean ambassador. "Courtney," he said, with a small smile, "tell me what Willkie has that I haven't got." "Well, Arthur," she replied half-mockingly, "he has a mop of unruly curly black hair that to most women is almost irresistible." "I hadn't thought of that," Vandenberg said, passing his hand across his balding head.[68]

On the third ballot, Dewey sank further, down to 315. And, just as Halleck had planned, Willkie's gains in the New York, New Jersey, and Massachusetts delegations now lifted him to 259.[69] One New Jersey delegate who was committed to Dewey heard his own family shouting down to him from the galleries to switch to Willkie.[70] With each convert, a deafening roar filled the hall. "We want Willkie! We want Willkie!" The psychological momentum was now undoubtedly with the dark horse. He "caught fire," Joe Martin later commented.[71] Taft was not losing support, but neither was he gaining much, locked in third place with 212. Vandenberg ran a consistent fourth with 72. At that point, Dewey pleaded for an adjournment to the next day, but the Willkie forces were determined to forge on—and they had Joe Martin, the convention chair, in their corner. Taft, too, was willing to continue, hoping that Vandenberg would throw his support to him. And Taft reportedly sent his brother-in-law to Dewey headquarters to see once again about a Taft-Dewey alliance against Willkie.[72] "Dewey is definitely out," Willkie exclaimed. There was little doubt that he had captured the energy in the hall. "It's a race between the senator and myself," he said.[73]

At 10:00 p.m. on Thursday, the convention voted for a fourth time. The chaos was now so great that delegates could not even hear Martin bang his gavel for order. The clamor only mounted as Willkie raced ahead, now grabbing the lead with 306 votes, as more state delegations swung to him. Taft advanced to second place with 254, while Dewey's downfall accelerated, plunging him to the third spot with 250. Vandenberg and Hoover were also sinking, though more gently, from their modest heights. Was the momentum now with Taft? For an instant, Willkie thought so. "It has been a grand fight," he glumly said.[74] At the same time, however, his ally, Joe Martin, conferred with Landon. "I told Landon that Willkie appeared to be well on the way to victory," Martin said, "and that Landon ought to do what was best for his state."[75]

Then, for a fifth time, state delegations announced their votes. A delegate from the state of Washington declared that Washington was casting its 16 votes "for a *real Republican*, Senator Robert Taft." Scolding him, Joe Martin declared that "*all* the candidates before this body are Republicans!"[76] Taft increased his strength with more votes from Arkansas and Iowa. In fact, Taft had been holding onto strong leads in the midwestern, western, and southern states while Willkie's strength was coming from the East. As Landon rose to announce the decision of the Kansas delegation, a hush fell over the hall. "Kansas gives all of its 18 votes to Wendell L. Willkie," stated Landon unemotionally, in his midwestern twang, to shouts of joy and wild applause. By then, facing reality, Dewey had released all his delegates and joined Vandenberg in the double digits with 57 votes. Now Willkie sprinted from 306 to 429 as Taft also rose, to 377. "My word, Wendell, you're going to get this thing," Edith Willkie said to her husband when she returned to their hotel.[77]

Now Taft's leading supporter, Ohio's governor John Bricker, wanted an adjournment until the morning, hoping to give Taft a chance to buttonhole the delegates who had remained loyal to Dewey, Vandenberg, and Hoover. But the Willkie forces, tasting victory, were determined to press on. The decision of Joe Martin not to adjourn would again prove crucial.[78]

At 12:30 a.m., delegates voted a sixth time—and now the lead swung back and forth several times between Willkie and Taft. Taft made gains in Colorado and California, but Willkie picked up votes in Florida and Illinois. People in the galleries shouted, "We want Willkie! We want Willkie!" "Well, if you'll be quiet long enough," Joe Martin announced, "maybe you'll get him!" Then Vandenberg's campaign manager declared that the senator had released his home state's delegates and that Michigan now gave one vote to Hoover, two to

Taft, and thirty-five to Willkie. Delirium in the galleries. Willkie was only a handful of votes away from victory. Meanwhile Charles McNary, the favorite son of Oregon, released his state's delegation, which promptly cast its votes for Willkie. Taft's only hope was Pennsylvania, but that state passed. When Virginia cast its sixteen votes for Willkie, he went over the top. He had won. "Charlie, I predicted to you that I'd be nominated on the sixth ballot," Senator Vandenberg said to Halleck. "I had the right ballot but the wrong man."[79]

The drama had reached its conclusion. Governor Bricker moved to make the vote for Willkie unanimous. Joe Martin polled the delegates a last time, as state chairmen jumped up to change their votes. As was traditional at party conventions, the final ballot was unanimous: 988 for Willkie—and zero for everyone else.[80] It was 2:00 a.m., and the startling, exhausting session was over.

It was "one of the greatest upsets in the history of the convention system in America," wrote a *New York Times* reporter.[81] "As usual, the people were far ahead of their leaders," editorialized the *New York Herald Tribune*.[82] "The people have saved the Republican politicians from themselves," rejoiced journalist Raymond Clapper. "Mr. Willkie's nomination is a triumph for public opinion."[83] The selection of Willkie, agreed the *Los Angeles Times*, "was not made in the convention hall but in the living rooms, crossroads grocery stores, street corners and other informal meeting places of tens of thousands of Republican communities throughout America." Henry Luce's *Time* magazine unabashedly cheered that "the people had won."[84]

New myths of the "people's" takeover of the Republican Party and Willkie as the "people's" candidate were born, even though much of Willkie's strength and popularity had been engineered by powerful media barons like Luce and Howard and advertising giants like Bruce Barton, the New York congressman who had been an executive with one of the nation's great advertising firms. The GOP, the party of business and Wall Street, had hardly fallen into the hands of the "people." The electoral successes over the past four years of moderate senators and governors confirmed only their influence in the party, not their ascendancy. As for the Republican Old Guard, the enthusiasm for Willkie—they called it "fanaticism"—left them baffled and dazed. Many of them feared that a President Willkie would be too independent and not the amenable and controllable time-server they preferred.[85]

Even with a fractured GOP, at a time of unprecedented world crisis, Willkie's candidacy was of historic importance. With the anti-interventionists like Hoover, Taft, Vandenberg, and Dewey unable to coordinate their efforts and agree on a joint slate, the party had chosen a man who was moderate on domestic policy and an interventionist on foreign policy.[86] Willkie might have disapproved of aspects of Roosevelt's management of the New Deal, but he embraced most of its core values and achievements. And his and Roosevelt's fundamental agreement on foreign policy signaled to Americans the critical importance of a bipartisan approach to the European crisis. The isolationist Republican platform still reflected the thinking of the party's conservatives, but it now meant little to the party's nominee and new titular head.[87]

On the other side of the Atlantic, the British called the nomination a "miracle," viewing it as a sign of the end of American isolationism. The British ambassador, Lord Lothian, assured London that if Willkie won in November, Britain would have a friend in the White House. Editorial writers in England rejoiced that "whether Mr. Roosevelt decides to stand for a third term or not, a President will be elected on whom we can rely for substantial aid." The London *Daily Express* happily remarked that "aid for us ceases to be an issue in American politics. Both sides are for it."[88]

Willkie's candidacy, however, did not spell good news for the Germans. After the convention, Hans Thomsen grumbled to the German Foreign Ministry that Willkie was "not an isolationist," that his nomination was "unfortunate for us," and that not even Willkie's "pure German descent" had diverted him from the cause of the Allies. The only difference between Roosevelt and Willkie, Thomsen underlined, was "one of methods and not of beliefs."[89]

The Nazi press in Germany, on the other hand, committed to blocking a Roosevelt victory, cheered Willkie's nomination, claiming that he would lead no crusades against the "new Europe." German papers gloated that his "attitude toward world events is the same as Lindbergh's."[90] They did not know their man.

At dawn on Friday, June 28, Willkie met with his advisors to discuss a running-mate. The vice presidential candidate would be chosen that afternoon, at the convention's final session.

Willkie had hinted to Connecticut's governor Raymond Baldwin that he wanted Baldwin on the ticket with him. An early presidential hopeful himself, the moderate governor had given a speech at the convention seconding Willkie's nomination, imploring those he called "Republicans by heredity" to welcome to the party ranks those of other political faiths who now recognized that "only through the Republican Party can the destiny of America be richly fulfilled."[91] But Willkie's advisors as well as GOP leaders wanted him to choose Oregon's senator Charles McNary. A progressive westerner and a champion of farmers, McNary had supported much of the New Deal, including the Wagner Act and the Social Security Act, and he was especially enthusiastic about New Deal public power projects. But he was also a strong isolationist who had voted against crucial measures to increase American preparedness and provide help to the Allies. Republicans believed that he would give geographical and ideological balance to the ticket. In addition, McNary knew about the legislative process from the inside. Vandenberg enthusiastically pronounced McNary "the best legislator who ever sat in the Senate of the United States."[92]

While Baldwin politely stepped aside, both Willkie and McNary had to swallow hard. As soon as he arrived in Philadelphia, the Oregon senator, who wanted the presidential nomination for himself, had begun criticizing Willkie, labeling him a tool of Wall Street and a former Democrat and insisting that the party's candidate had to be someone who stands for "traditional Republican ideas"—a Taft or a Vandenberg if not himself.[93] Describing the convention as a "mess" and grumbling that Willkie was "not supposed to be nominated," McNary had returned to Washington on Thursday, where he sourly announced that he would not accept second place. On Friday, when Joe Martin phoned to offer him the vice presidential slot, the Oregon senator flatly turned it down. "Hell no, I wouldn't run with Willkie," he bristled. But in the end McNary came around and accepted the summons—for the "sake of the party," he said.[94]

And Willkie, too, had come around. "You'd make a perfect team," Joe Martin told him. The Willkie-McNary ticket made sense, said Charlie Halleck, because McNary was public power and West Coast and Wendell was private power and East Coast—via Indiana.[95] And perhaps most important, McNary's presence on the ticket was a signal to isolationists that they were welcome in Wendell's world.

When the convention was called to order on Friday afternoon for the vice presidential balloting, the delegates' seats and the visitors' galleries were half-empty—it looked like Madison Square Garden in the early morning hours of a six-day bicycle race, wrote one reporter.[96] There wasn't much more drama than that—no sooner did the roll call of the states begin than the only other candidate for the nomination, Representative Dewey Short of Missouri, an extreme isolationist, took himself out of the running, and the vote for McNary was declared unanimous. "I'll be a good soldier," McNary announced from Washington.[97]

Minutes later, Willkie and his wife arrived. Breaking with tradition, he had decided to address the convention in person, as Franklin Roosevelt had in

1932 in Chicago. "Republicans wanted to see if Mr. Willkie would dare to do it," wrote one reporter. "He did."[98] With the convention hall now packed with Willkie fans, Mr. and Mrs. Willkie, accompanied by deafening cheers, applause and music, walked down the aisle to the speakers platform. Brightly colored balloons and a blizzard of confetti rained down from the ceiling. After a three-minute ovation, Willkie gave a brief, informal message of thanks to the convention. It was not an occasion to speak about "policies or principles," he said, but rather simply to express his appreciation and his sense of dedication to the cause. He alluded to the wars in Europe by noting that he stood for building up American defenses and preserving "the democratic way of life." American democracy was "the last firm untouched foothold of freedom in all the world." He promised an aggressive campaign that would "bring unity to America . . . the unity of labor and capital, and agriculture and manufactures, and farmer and worker and all classes."

In conclusion, he asked for his party's support. "And so, you Republicans, I call upon you to join me, help me. The cause is great. We must win." His choice of words— "you Republicans" instead of "we"—was unfortunate and telling.[99] Was he not entirely one of them? Years later, his son Philip remarked that, like an outsider, his father always talked about "the Republicans"—never "us" or "we."[100] The band played and then Willkie stepped forward to say, "Now I am going to sleep for a week."[101]

Quickly, all the losers came on board—or at least gave the appearance of doing so. "Am I glad I ran? Tremendously!" Dewey effused, adding that he was ready to give "every possible support to my party"—and presumably also to the unmentioned Willkie. Taft announced that he would "work just as hard for Mr. Willkie as I would for myself." And Vandenberg declared that "Willkie has captured the imagination of the American people. . . . I am going to put my shoulder to his wheel." In private, however, they were more candid. Taft groused about the overwhelming press attention given to Willkie. The party's nominee "took the wrong side" on almost every issue, he said, and, moreover, Willkie didn't know "anything about the Republican Party." For his part, Dewey blamed "Wall Street" for Willkie's success, and Vandenberg confided to Charles Lindbergh that, if Willkie were elected, Republicans will "certainly have a problem child on their hands."[102]

An idealistic young man—played by Jimmy Stewart—from a western state, with no political experience or money but with deep grass-roots support, unexpectedly found himself appointed to a Senate seat in the popular 1939 film

Mr. Smith Goes to Washington. Now another idealist, with the same tousled hair and rumpled suit, was headed toward the center of power. It was too early to call Willkie "a wonder-worker," wrote columnists Joseph Alsop and Robert Kintner, "but he has about him the atmosphere of success which, in itself, is almost half the battle."[103]

In the White House, people breathed sighs of relief. "Well, now I think we can sleep quietly and peacefully," Frances Perkins remarked.[104] Willkie's nomination was a "Godsend to the country," said FDR, overheard by his speechwriter Robert Sherwood.[105] With the GOP nominee largely in agreement with the White House on international policy, Roosevelt and his inner circle were cheered that the nation would not be fractured along interventionist-isolationist lines. The fact that Republicans had chosen Willkie to represent them, commented Sherwood, meant that there would be a "continuity of American foreign policy regardless of the outcome of the election." And perhaps there would be essential continuity in domestic policy, too, for Willkie seemed to take for granted, as he would state during his fall campaign, that "the legitimate, proper object of government is to do for the people what they need to have done but cannot do for themselves"—words that could have easily been spoken by Franklin Roosevelt and that could hardly have been more antithetical to the credo of limited government and rugged individualism long embraced by the Republican Old Guard.[106]

But had the GOP's choice of a man who basically shared FDR's convictions on the war squelched FDR's most compelling reason—or pretext—for seeking another four years in the White House? So in tune were Willkie and FDR on foreign policy that the *New York Times* peremptorily editorialized that Roosevelt's "clear duty" was now to announce that he would refuse his party's nomination. It would be counterproductive, the *Times* argued, for the president to provoke an unnecessary debate over the third term. Walter Lippmann concurred. Delivered from his fear that the Republican Party would turn its back on Great Britain, Lippmann contended that it would now be "unpatriotic" for FDR and the Democrats to disrupt the country by a "useless and destructive conflict" over a third term. Would Willkie's ardent admirers now come forth with the inspired suggestion that it would be highly "unpatriotic" for the Democrats to offer a ticket of *any* kind in opposition to Mr. Willkie? wondered bemused columnist Ernest Lindley.[107]

But Willkie's supporter Raymond Clapper reached the opposite conclusion, arguing in his column that the GOP's choice of "the strongest possible candidate" meant that Roosevelt, by far the most popular Democrat, would have no choice but to run.[108] As for Willkie himself, he seemed to want nothing more than to climb into the ring with Roosevelt. "Bring on the Champ!" he exuberantly cried. "Come on and let's swap blows!"[109] At a press conference the day after the GOP Convention, glowing with self-confidence, he told reporters that he would be happy to meet with Mr. Roosevelt. "One should be courteous to one's predecessor," he said with a smile.[110]

Chapter 9

Roosevelt's Game

OLONEL WASHINGTON APPEARS AT CONGRESS *IN HIS UNIFORM*, and by his great experience and abilities in military matters, is of much service to us," wrote John Adams in 1775 to his wife, Abigail, from Philadelphia, where the Continental Congress was meeting.[1] Why did George Washington bring to Philadelphia the old blue military uniform he had worn during the French and Indian Wars in the 1750s and donned only once since then, when he posed for a portrait? It was a brilliantly calculated theatrical gesture designed to remind delegates to the Congress of his military background—and it worked like a charm. They unanimously elected him commander in chief of the new Continental Army. Never actively seeking the command, he had simply presented himself in the costume of a former military officer who, though highly reluctant to take on once again the responsibilities of power, was willing to do so at the fervent behest of others. "I feel a great distress from a consciousness that my abilities and military experience may not be equal to the extensive and important trust," he said upon accepting his commission on June 16, 1775. "However, as the Congress desire it, I will enter upon the momentous duty."[2]

"It was utterly out of my power to refuse this appointment," he disingenuously wrote a few days later to his wife, Martha, adding that "a kind of destiny" had imposed this high position and burden on him. Not self-interest but destiny, not ambition but duty, not desire but self-sacrifice.[3] For the next twenty years, Americans would again and again entrust him with power, because he always appeared loath to accept it. Throughout his political career, Washington carefully masked his driving ambition and need for respect and glory by staging himself as a self-sacrificing, public-minded citizen-soldier who, though yearning, like the victorious Roman general Cincinnatus, to return to his plow and his private, peaceful rural life, was willing to take on the reins of power and patriotically answer his country's call—that is, provided that call was unanimous. He would decline to engage in contests for office but would accede to a compelling draft.

Fast-forward a hundred and fifty years.

"Like most men of my age, I had made plans for myself, plans for a private life. . . . Today all private plans, all private lives, have been in a sense repealed. . . . All those who can be of service to the Republic have no choice but to offer themselves for service."[4] Words that might have been spoken by Washington but that would be uttered by Franklin Roosevelt in the summer of 1940. Like Washington and Cincinnatus, FDR supposedly longed to retire to his country estate situated on a lovely river, but, since it had become a question of the very survival of the Republic in a time of unprecedented international crisis, he was willing to sacrifice himself for his country.

And yet, unlike George Washington, Roosevelt never expressed a lack of self-confidence. Whereas Washington dwelt in his first inaugural address on the "magnitude and difficulty" of the task facing him as well as on his own "deficiencies," Roosevelt had struck an uncompromising note of self-assurance in his own first inaugural address in 1933. The original draft of his speech had contained a Washingtonian line expressing humility—"The people . . . have made me the instrument, the temporary humble instrument, of their wishes." But FDR crossed out the word "humble" and instead would self-confidently declare, "I assume *unhesitatingly* the leadership of this great army of our people!"[5] In 1940, he aspired to remain at the center of power.

The year 1928 was the exception. That year he had not wished to run for governor of New York. Polio had struck him in the summer of 1921, and seven years later, he wanted more time to spend in Warm Springs, Georgia, not only to recover his strength but also to build up the Warm Springs Institute for Rehabilitation that he had founded there. And already an astute politician with keen political instincts, he feared that the Democratic candidate for president that year, New York governor Al Smith, would go down to defeat and take other Democrats along with him. But Smith and other New York politicos, desperate to keep the governor's mansion in Albany in Democratic hands, pushed Roosevelt's reservations and qualms aside. "Well, if I've got to run for governor, there's no use in all of us getting sick about it!" Roosevelt said in October 1928, after the Democratic State Convention in New York nominated him by acclamation.[6]

Against his own inclinations and the advice of his close advisors, FDR accepted the party's call.

Although Roosevelt had been truly reluctant to run in 1928, that script would nevertheless serve as the template for the very different circumstances of 1940. Right up to the July convention, FDR would appear uncertain and hesitant about running again. And then he would finally yield to the party's draft and to the nation's overwhelming and irresistible summons to duty. Of course, FDR did not really leave the decision passively to others. With infinite skill and subtle vulpine dissimulation, he would manipulate the process, ingeniously orchestrating the calls from politicians and party rank and file for a third term.

Roosevelt had "harpooned and torpedoed" all other potential candidates for the Democratic presidential nomination, charged Colorado's Democratic senator Edwin Johnson in March 1940. The party was "foundering in confusion," Johnson fumed. "A year ago, the Democrats had a dozen attractive prospective candidates. Had political developments been permitted to take their course, many of these able men would have grown in public esteem with the months."[7]

But Johnson was wrong. The president had not torpedoed other candidates. In fact, he had done the opposite, encouraging all possible aspirants to run. That tack was far more creative and effective than sabotaging fellow Democrats. In 1938, he had spurred Harry Hopkins, the head of the Works Progress Administration and soon-to-be secretary of commerce, to think about throwing his hat in the ring. To aid his friend, FDR was photographed at baseball games and on fishing cruises with Hopkins at his elbow. "This was not by accident," commented Robert Sherwood.[8] Early in his second term, Roosevelt had also urged his assistant attorney general Robert Jackson to run for governor of New York, a perfect jumping board for a White House run in 1940. "I think he was entirely sincere," Jackson later wrote.[9] FDR indicated to his 68-year-old secretary of state Cordell Hull, who was highly experienced in foreign affairs, that he would be a fine successor; he suggested to his agriculture secretary Henry Wallace as well as to Paul McNutt, the former Indiana governor and head of the Federal Security Agency, that they contemplate a run; he did nothing to dampen the presidential hopes of Burton Wheeler after a Wheeler-for-President organization was launched in Montana;[10] he let Senate majority leader Alben Barkley of Kentucky know early in 1940 that "some of the folks here at the White House" were rooting for him as the next Democratic nominee; and he told Governor Herbert Lehman of New York that he deserved the vote of his state delegation at the Democratic Convention.[11] Even the visiting Joseph P.

Kennedy, Roosevelt's hyper-ambitious ambassador to Great Britain who salivated at the idea of occupying the White House, found himself flattered as a possible presidential candidate by FDR, who urged him to run in the Massachusetts primary.[12] In other words, instead of discouraging Democrats from vying for the party's nomination, Roosevelt cheerfully welcomed them all to the arena. Playing on their ambition and their vanity, flattering and manipulating them, he pulled the strings—and finally let them twist and dangle in the wind.

By deftly enlarging the field, Roosevelt left almost a dozen rivals to divide the anti–third term opposition, weaken one another or get discouraged—like Paul McNutt—and drop out.[13] And as long as there was no clear front-runner among them to offer an appealing alternative to the New Deal or to unite the many factions in the Democratic Party, the talk about a third term for Roosevelt would continue. And that third-term buzz—along with the impossibility of FDR's transferring his huge popularity and charismatic personality to someone else—effectively put a ceiling on the prospects of any rising stars.[14] "I had more or less taken for granted that Roosevelt would run for a third term," remarked Frances Perkins, "after I began to observe that there were no important people's heads showing above the general melee of people who would be likely candidates for President."[15]

Complicating matters even more, FDR insisted that any Democratic presidential nominee would have to pass his own litmus test in order to earn his blessing. His distant cousin Theodore Roosevelt had taught him that key lesson. TR had, after all, handpicked William Howard Taft to succeed him in 1909, convinced that Taft would continue the progressive policies of his Square Deal. But Taft's indifference to TR's legacy came as a crushing disappointment, spurring TR to challenge Taft in 1912. Franklin did not want to take that same chance. He declared that if the Democratic Party chose a candidate in 1940 who was lukewarm about the New Deal, he would simply turn his back on the party. "If we nominate conservative candidates or lip-service candidates on a straddle-bug platform," FDR told a convention of Young Democrats in August 1939, "I personally, for my own self-respect . . . will find it impossible to have any active part in such an unfortunate suicide of the old Democratic Party."[16]

But no politician measured up to his stringent criteria. Only candidates who were "progressive liberals at heart" would do, he remarked in a letter to Illinois's governor Henry Horner in March 1940. That criterion, he added, "eliminates a good many people whose names you and I could readily agree on." The second criterion was to pick a liberal ticket that could win. But here, too, he spotted problems. "Some liberal combinations would obviously be weak, others would be strong—at least as strong as it is possible to find," he wrote to Horner. At any rate, he judged, it was too early to make a selection. And it was also possible, he observed, that the few remaining viable candidates "may stub their toes in the next four months." And so that left . . . perhaps just himself? But then he quickly reminded his friend that it was "sheer defeatism" to suggest that no other Democrat could be elected.[17]

When FDR's secretary Missy LeHand asked him if he was at all worried about finding a successor, he confidently replied that "God would provide." Well, God had better get busy pretty soon, Missy said. Eleanor also discussed this with her husband. Shouldn't he make a "definite effort" to prepare someone to take over in 1941? she asked. People had to prepare themselves, he answered brusquely.[18]

Name the Nominee was a game Roosevelt often enjoyed playing. "What about our Democratic candidate? Who will he be?" the president asked Harold Ickes one day in early June 1940. "I think that he was teasing me," Ickes wrote in his diary, adding that the president was in "high good humor."[19]

That spring, dozens of rumors and counter-rumors bounced around the Washington stratosphere. Except to strenuously deny having said that Jim Farley could not be elected president because he was Catholic, FDR declined to respond to any of the stories—or to hush them all by clarifying his position on a third term. "If I once start, you know, interpreting or answering questions about things written in columns," he said at a press conference in March 1940, "there is no end. I could not do it."[20]

So the rumors did not stop. According to one story, Roosevelt intended to run and had asked two of his most loyal supporters to draft a third-term agenda for him. Another story had FDR planning to run again—with Cordell Hull as his running-mate—but stipulating that, if elected, he would serve only as long as the emergency existed. Other reports conjectured that the president kept alive talk of a third term to dodge the status of lame duck.[21]

For her part, Eleanor Roosevelt believed that her husband not only enjoyed the rumor mill but played an active role in stirring it up. He would sometimes reveal confidential information to precisely those people who he knew would leak it, she later wrote. "There were times when I felt that Franklin was indiscreet. However I came to realize that he had his own reasons for doing it." She herself was not privy to confidential information about the third term; when questioned by reporters in April 1940, she tersely replied, "I'm in a vacuum about it."[22]

One person did grasp the president's intentions: Jim Farley. At their meeting in Hyde Park in the summer of 1939, Roosevelt had assured Farley that he would not run for a third term. A year later, in the summer of 1940, Farley returned to Hyde Park for another luncheon and tête-à-tête with the president. It was one week before the Democratic Convention, and Farley was still very much thinking of himself as "presidential timber," in Frances Perkins's words.[23] After the two men had a pleasant conversation over lunch with Harry Hopkins, Steve Early, Missy LeHand, and Eleanor, photographers arrived to take their pictures. Roosevelt and Farley smiled warmly and joked, like the old friends they were, for the cameras. But as soon as the photographers left, the temperature dropped.

"I want to come up here," Roosevelt told Farley, gesturing toward the library and the new house, called Top Cottage, that he had constructed as his own private retirement retreat. "Jim, I don't want to run and I'm going to tell the convention so," FDR said. But Farley wanted more—he wanted a commitment. "If you make it *specific*, the convention will not nominate you," he pressed, adding that if the Democrats had no other candidate than FDR, they deserved to lose. The smiles and the pretense of warmth vanished.

"What would you do if you were in my place?" the president finally asked. Farley replied that, first of all, he never would have waited as long as Roosevelt had waited to make his position known. And second, he would have followed the example of General William Tecumseh Sherman in 1884 and stated unequivocally that he would refuse to run if nominated and refuse to serve if elected. But Roosevelt would not go for the bait. "Jim, if nominated and elected I could not in these times refuse to take the inaugural oath," he said, "even if I knew I would be dead within thirty days." Then, Farley later wrote, Roosevelt "talked on aimlessly about the third term."[24]

Farley could barely contain his rage. He felt double-crossed. He was "the maddest white man I've ever seen," remarked Roosevelt's press secretary Steve Early, who drove Farley around the Hudson Valley countryside to cool him off. Meeting with reporters afterward, Farley tersely stated that his meeting with Mr. Roosevelt had been "entirely satisfactory" and that he would not reveal what was said. "It is up to the President to discuss his own plans. He was extremely frank with me and I was frank with him, but I will not divulge what he told me." Nor would he comment on reports that he would quit politics to head the New York Yankees.[25]

In the fall of 1939, though hoping for the 1940 nomination for himself, Farley had conceded that if the "very existence" of the United States was imperiled, he would support a third term for Roosevelt. But by April 1940, he curtly dismissed the idea that the international situation cried out for Roosevelt at the helm. It was silly to believe, he wrote, "that one man can keep us out of war better than the other fellow." In June 1940, he had complained to Raymond Clapper that the president was behaving selfishly. After making sacrifices for Roosevelt and serving him loyally for years, Farley believed that the president was "unfair not only to me but to Hull, Garner and the other fellows who have been mentioned as candidates."[26] His July 1940 meeting with Roosevelt in Hyde Park confirmed his judgment and eliminated any lingering doubt in his mind about FDR's intentions. Now Farley knew the score.

"The Boys Are Hopeful," read the caption of a cartoon that appeared in the *New York Times* in May 1940. It showed New Deal politicians, dressed as firemen, anxiously waiting in the fire station for the signal to descend the sliding pole and jump onto the FDR truck. Most Democratic politicians wanted nothing more than for the hugely popular Franklin Roosevelt to stay in office for a third term—and continue to bestow upon them all the perks that came with majority party status.[27]

Roosevelt's inner circle, too, welcomed the prospect of another four years in the White House.[28] As Farley pointed out a year before the 1940 convention, "after Roosevelt leaves Washington they will be out of the picture and they know it."[29]

In a *Look* magazine article in 1939, Interior Secretary Harold Ickes put the issue on a somewhat loftier plane, arguing that to deny the people the opportunity to decide for themselves whether they want the president for a third term "is to deny democracy itself."[30] Commerce Secretary Harry Hopkins, too, publicly called for a third term for the president. "First, last and all the time," Hopkins declared in his native Iowa, "my choice for President is Franklin D. Roosevelt!"[31] And at Jackson Day dinners in January 1940, Roosevelt boosters, including Robert Jackson and Henry Wallace, called on the president to run again. A third term was "imperative," Wallace declared.[32]

The third-term push gained a momentum of its own. Speeches were given, articles and books written, resolutions announced, clubs formed. "We must draft him!" declared Judge John Gutknecht of Chicago, the founder of a club called "The Third Termers of Chicago." The Young Democrats, meeting in Pittsburgh, endorsed a third term. "It is not for Roosevelt to tell us that he wants a third term," one enthusiastic delegate shouted, "but it is rather for us to tell Roosevelt that we want a third term!"[33]

In the halls of Congress, too, Democrats banged the third-term drum. No one knew more about foreign affairs than Roosevelt, said Senator Elmer Thomas of Oklahoma, arguing that 1940 was an "abnormal year" and that "whether it be the first, second, third or fourth term is not as important as competent leadership."

Senator Kenneth McKellar of Tennessee informed a reporter that Roosevelt was "inordinately popular" in his state. "He can have the delegates," McKellar said, "and can carry the State in November." On the Senate floor, McKellar and Arizona's senator Henry Ashurst read aloud George Washington's letter to Lafayette, in which the nation's father had outlined the reasons why the framers opposed presidential term limits.[34]

The anti-third-term tradition was going the way of the dodo bird, wrote Yale Law School professor Fred Rodell. In his book *Democracy and the Third Term*, published early in 1940, Rodell argued that if a president intended to turn himself into a dictator and destroy American democracy, he didn't need a third term to do so. On the contrary, he could accomplish that in eight days, eight weeks—or in two terms as easily as in three. Brain Truster Rex Tugwell agreed, labeling the two-term tradition "a bogey" promoted and sanctified by people who sought to advance their own selfish purposes. It was in the interest of the anti–New Dealers, Tugwell argued in an article he wrote for the *New Republic*, to have weak government in Washington and an amateur in the White House.[35]

Of course, not all Democrats were pleased by the idea of a third term for Roosevelt, and some scrambled for a way to block it or at least to show their displeasure. Vice President Garner, who at seventy-one had one last chance for the presidency, saw Roosevelt's possible run for a third term as more evidence of his arrogance and ruthlessness. "Jim," Garner said to Farley, "the two of us can pull together to stop Roosevelt." A contingent of anti–New Deal Democratic senators wanted to pull the plug on FDR, including Carter Glass and Harry Byrd of Virginia, Pat McCarran of Nevada, Nebraska's Edward Burke, Ellison "Cotton Ed" Smith of South Carolina, Sheridan Downey of California, and Millard Tydings of Maryland. For his part, Rush Holt of West Virginia proposed an anti-third-term resolution, but dropped it after losing his primary in May.[36]

But not surprisingly, it was Republicans who most passionately defended what conservative columnist Frank Kent called "the oldest and most deeply cherished of American political traditions."[37] This cherished tradition, however, was largely a fiction. Before Franklin Roosevelt, the thirty-second president, only ten other presidents had been elected to two terms: Washington, Jefferson, Madison, Monroe, Jackson, Lincoln, Grant, Cleveland, McKinley, and Wilson. Seven first-term incumbents who ran for a second term in office lost their elections: John Adams, John Quincy Adams, Van Buren, Cleveland, Benjamin Harrison, Taft, and Hoover. For much of the nation's history, most presidents served just one term. The two-term tradition was more myth than tradition.[38]

Still, the objections to a third term were too powerful for Roosevelt to over-come, contended Alf Landon, predicting that the president would go down to a "crushing defeat."[39] A former Harvard president, A. Lawrence Lowell, also weighed in, warning that "a third term for Roosevelt is a long step toward Nazi-fying American institutions." Lewis Douglas, Roosevelt's former budget direc-tor who headed the "Democrats for Willkie" club, insisted that a third term was "contrary to all American principles and is a real threat to democracy,"[40] and the *Washington Post* editorialized that a third term was an "affront" to American traditions that would "compromise democracy in behalf of dictator-ship."[41] For their part, conservative newspaper columnists ridiculed the "Roose-velt or doom" scenario. "Beware the Third Termites," one of them wrote.[42]

Grasping for historical examples to make their case, the third-term foes reminded Americans that Andrew Jackson, in his State of the Union message in December 1829, had urged Congress to limit presidents to one term in office in order to secure the government's "efficiency" and "integrity." And between Jackson and Lincoln, no president would serve more than a single term in office.

In 1895, Democrats opposed the idea of a third term for their own unpop-ular Democratic president, Grover Cleveland. They included in their 1896 platform—on the one hundredth anniversary of George Washington's deci-sion to decline a third term—an anti-third-term plank. It was the "unwritten law of this Republic," they maintained, that no president should serve a third term in office.[43]

Three decades later, when President Calvin Coolidge—who had risen from the vice presidency to serve out the final year and a half of Warren Harding's term and then won the presidency himself in 1924—was being urged by Old Guard Republicans to run for another term in 1928, Coolidge declined. "If I take another term," he said, "I will be in the White House till 1933. . . . Ten years in Washington is longer than any other man has had it . . . too long!"[44] But Coolidge's decision to step down did not stop Wisconsin's progressive Republican Robert La Follette from proposing a Senate resolution stating that presidents should be limited to two terms in office. The resolution's wording—that any departure from the "time honored" two-term tradition "would be unwise, unpatriotic and fraught with peril to our free institutions"—mirrored that of two previous House resolutions, one passed overwhelmingly in 1875, opposing a third term for President Grant after he made noises about possibly running again, and another in 1907, pushed briefly by southern Democrats fearful that Theodore Roosevelt might be tempted to try for another term in office, despite his public declaration in 1904 that he would not run again.[45] In February 1928, progressive Republicans like George Norris of Nebraska and

William Borah of Idaho joined Democrats to pass La Follette's resolution by a vote of 56 to 26.

That seemingly decisive vote not only carried no constitutional weight but also masked a deeper reality of uncertainty and opportunism. William Borah, who said on February 7, 1928, that it was "perfectly safe" to leave the question of a third term to the judgment of the people because there could be "exigencies which might justify a third term," voted three days later for the third-term ban.[46] Also voting for the resolution banning a third term were liberal Democratic senators like Alben Barkley of Kentucky and Robert Wagner of New York, who would make an about-face a dozen years later when they supported a third term for Franklin Roosevelt. And one *Republican* who voted *against* the 1928 anti-third-term resolution was none other than Wendell Willkie's running-mate, Charles McNary, who in 1940 would reverse himself to denounce the "zealous third term partisans."[47]

And where did average Americans stand on the issue? A poll released on July 24, in the middle of the 1940 Democratic Convention, found that 59 percent of all Americans opposed a ban on a third term; 86 percent of Democrats were against such a ban; and 92 percent of Democrats still believed in Roosevelt's leadership and wanted him to remain their president after 1940.[48]

Even Hollywood directors dueled over the third term. In their movie *Remember the Night*, which opened in January 1940 and starred Barbara Stanwyck and Fred MacMurray, director Mitchell Leisen and screenwriter Preston Sturges took a swipe at FDR. In one scene, a gift box is wrapped in an old newspaper that, when spread out, displays a front-page photo of Theodore Roosevelt and the bold, banner headline "Roosevelt Refuses Third Term."[49] But director Alexander Hall was friendlier toward the president. In his movie *He Stayed for Breakfast*, which made its debut in August 1940, the hero, a former French communist played by Melvyn Douglas, tells a pal that he is going to leave Paris and move to the United States. "I'm going to vote for Roosevelt," Douglas boasts. But it takes five years to become a citizen over there, his friend explains. "He'll still be running," Douglas cheerfully replies.[50]

Chapter 10

The Democrats in Chicago

D
ID THE WHITE HOUSE TEAM REALLY HAVE NO PLAN for the convention in Chicago? Harold Ickes asked the president in early July. Was
there no strategy, no floor leader, no one chosen to make the nominating speech? The president tersely replied that he had nothing to suggest, leaving Ickes dumbfounded.[1]

On July 9, a week before the Democratic Convention, Roosevelt parried
questions at a press conference. One reporter remarked that FDR's military
aide and poker companion, General Edwin ("Pa") Watson, had bet a few hundred dollars with a friend that Mr. Roosevelt would be renominated and reelected. Would the president care to comment? Well, no matter who won the
bet, the money would fall into good hands, the president pleasantly replied,
still a master at dodging questions. Another reporter reminded the president
of his promise to disclose his political plans at a time and place of his own
choosing. Would that time come before the convention? Well, that question
was just too "iffey" to be answered, FDR said. Couldn't the president give a
hint about a third term, asked a reporter who hoped to announce the story that
evening on his radio broadcast. Not a bad idea, said the president. At what time
would the broadcast occur? he asked. "Why—why, at 11:15 tonight," the excited reporter replied. Mr. Roosevelt's mobile face registered profound disappointment. Oh, what a shame that it would be on so late, he said. He would be
in bed by that time. The headline of the story the next day read: "Third Term
Still Secret; 'Sphinx' to Be in Bed.'"[2]

On Friday, July 12, with the convention scheduled to begin that Monday, the president, bored with the "will he or won't he" clamor, slipped out of

Washington for a weekend cruise on the Potomac with Sam Rosenman, Missy LeHand, and a few other friends. While Roosevelt sailed on the gentle river, delegates were trickling into the Chicago hotels.

Secluded on his boat, Roosevelt appeared neither interested nor involved in the convention. He had given no clear directions to anyone. He seemed happy to leave convention delegates with the impression that he wanted them to make their own decision. But from backstage—unobtrusively and indirectly—he was pulling the strings.[3]

One string was his strategy. By keeping his intentions a secret, he had neutralized the other presidential hopefuls, almost frozen them in place. None could campaign energetically for the nomination without seeming to go against the president. Setting up the Garner-for-President headquarters in Chicago, Garner's campaign manager told reporters that "we've always gone on the assumption that the president would not run again." But, he diplomatically added, "of course, Mr. Roosevelt can have the nomination again if he wants it." Burton Wheeler followed that script. "Frankly," he said, "if President Roosevelt is out, I am a candidate. But if he wants it he can get the nomination and there is no use kidding yourself." As for Jim Farley, the most he would say before the convention about his own presidential aspirations was "everything will be all right. Time will take care of anything."[4] In this limbo, Garner, Wheeler, Farley, and others remained possible candidates, and the convention appeared open to a variety of outcomes. But in fact FDR had positioned himself to take the nomination without dogged opposition. He scarcely needed to raise a finger.

Another of the strings was the selection of Chicago itself. FDR had pressed for the convention to be held in the Windy City, not because of the massive Chicago Stadium, which one reporter said was as "ugly as the underside of a railroad bridge," but because he could rely on Mayor Edward Kelly. The mayor had been one of the original sponsors of the "Draft Roosevelt" movement, and the president expected him to pack the galleries with supporters. But Kelly did even more than that.[5]

"The salvation of the nation rests in one man!" Kelly declared in his welcoming speech at noon on Monday, July 15, the convention's opening day. He noted that the president was tired of the burdens of his office, and he admitted that Roosevelt had rebuffed all his suggestions that he run again. But the world was now facing multiple catastrophes that transcended the president's personal desires. "We must overrule his comfort and convenience," Kelly roared, "and draft Roosevelt!"

More than a greeting and greater than an endorsement, it was an urgent demand, a panicked plea in a time of world crisis. It was even a disclosure of God's will. "God has sent a guardian of our liberties," Kelly intoned, "the kind of a man that mankind needs, our beloved president, Franklin D. Roosevelt." Sent by God! What more could anyone ask? But Kelly went even further. "We are praying for a man who will give, if need be, of his life's blood, a man who may be crucified but never corrupted, a man who will recognize this as the call of civilization itself!" Roosevelt the savior, the son of God![6]

Kelly had explicitly promised not to nominate FDR in his welcoming speech, but he did precisely that. Roosevelt had not wanted the convention to seem over before it began. Nor did he want people to think that he was actively seeking the nomination. Perhaps it was fortunate, as far as the president was concerned, that the stadium was two-thirds empty and that people cheered only halfheartedly when they heard Kelly pronounce the president's name.[7]

One of the strings that Roosevelt tried to pull, however, got tangled. On that first morning of the convention, he placed a call to Jim Farley, still the chair of the Democratic National Committee. Very tentatively he mentioned to Farley that there were a lot of stories in the paper "about there being no need for a ballot." His implicit—and understood—suggestion was that he might simply be nominated by acclamation. "That's perfectly silly," Farley shot back, insisting that any effort to prevent a ballot would "wreck the Democratic Party in November." Two days earlier, Farley had spoken in Chicago with former attorney general Homer Cummings, who had agreed to serve as the president's ears at the convention. Cummings recalled that he urged Farley to "handle things in a big way and in a generous way so that there would develop no quarrel between him and the president"—advice that Farley had difficulty in swallowing. Although FDR was the first choice of nine out of ten Democrats, according to the June 29 Gallup poll, Farley had improbably convinced himself that he would be a stronger candidate against Willkie than the president.[8]

The tone at Monday's evening session was decidedly blander. In the sprawling, smoke-filled stadium, a crowd of more than twenty thousand delegates and spectators listened to Jim Farley hail the accomplishments of the party and the "Administration." The "Administration," he said, had saved the country from economic collapse and had started it anew on the road to prosperity. And he promised that "the next Administration" would keep the nation at peace. Generalities and platitudes abounded. The November election, he declared, would present Americans with a stark choice between the GOP and the Democratic Party, between a party unable to cope with the problems of the twentieth century and the party that had made the United States "the last stronghold of genuine democracy in a world of violence and ruthless force." Who would be foolishly willing to turn the government over to "inexperienced hands?" he demanded.

Speaking for more than twenty minutes, never once did Farley utter the magical name of Franklin Roosevelt. The only people he referred to were Thomas Jefferson and Andrew Jackson. Still in the game, he was not about to ignite cheers or demonstrations for his nemesis. But the odds were heavily against him.

After Farley's welcoming talk, Speaker of the House William Bankhead of Alabama gave the keynote address that evening, a speech that the White House had vetted and trimmed to prevent any premature Roosevelt eruptions. In addition to his role as Speaker, Bankhead was known as the father of the glamorous, scandalous, deep-voiced actress Tallulah Bankhead. "Daddy warned me about men and alcohol," she once said. "But he never warned me about women and cocaine."[9]

Following instructions, Speaker Bankhead outlined the accomplishments of the Democrats. Thirteen times he mentioned "this Democratic Administration," but only twice did he refer to "the President," and neither time by name.[10] It was an uninspiring talk, pro–New Deal and resolutely antiwar, designed to placate isolationists and cause no waves.

Indeed, there were no winds to allow waves to swell. Despite all of the Sphinx's painstakingly elusive responses, most of the delegates already knew the dénouement. They felt no suspense; they expected no surprise revelation. "This convention is like a mystery story in which everybody knows the answer to the mystery," remarked Maury Maverick, the ultraliberal mayor of San Antonio. In Chicago for the convention, Harold Ickes agreed. The gathering, he noted, was "dead and cold. Everything was dull and bogged down."[11]

Just a few weeks earlier, eager GOP delegates had swarmed into the convention hall in Philadelphia. Everyone was abuzz, talking about the candidates, attending parties, luncheons, even fashion shows. Every hotel had something going on. Wide-open, unscripted, and undirected, the GOP Convention had possessed all the elements of an exciting whodunit: suspense, surprises, twists, and an unexpected, breathtaking conclusion as the dark horse candidate sprinted across the finish line. But at the Chicago convention, there was nothing, one disappointed person said, to pump up your blood pressure.[12]

Even the city seemed subdued. Hotel lobbies and the surrounding streets were quiet—there was none of the usual boisterous, cheerful mayhem of a convention town. Hotel managers groaned about the lack of cocktail parties and other entertainment for the delegates. In the convention hall, too, there was little color or spark—just a sea of plain black-and-white signs. A huge portrait of FDR covered one end of the hall, and a smaller picture of Vice President Garner adorned the other.[13]

It had been very different in 1932, in the depths of the Great Depression. Then, morose Republican delegates had listlessly renominated their hapless president, Herbert Hoover, while energized Democrats, eager to take on Hoover and his failed administration, fought for their candidates—New York's governor Franklin Roosevelt, the former New York governor Al Smith, House Speaker Jack Garner, and Virginia's former governor Harry Byrd.

But in Chicago, people asked, "If not Roosevelt, who?" Though Walter Lippmann opposed a third term, he acknowledged that Roosevelt "is the first choice, with no second choice, for millions of voters." No other Democrat, he wrote, "has any real popular following." Indeed, no one else stood out, though several—Jack Garner, Burton Wheeler, Jim Farley, Paul McNutt, and Cordell Hull—hoped, against all odds, for the nomination. And hope was about all they had, since they could not openly campaign or build a popular following so long as Roosevelt had not declared his intentions. Alas, the convention was, as one reporter wrote, "as dead as last month's newspaper." Another journalist, desperate for a story, shared with his readers his hunch that Roosevelt would make "a dramatic exit."[14] But there would, in fact, be no such chaotic turn of events.

Many of the delegates sported campaign buttons that read "Just Roosevelt." But since it was "Just Roosevelt," some of them wondered just what they were doing in Chicago. So predetermined was the outcome, wrote the *New York Times*, that most delegates wanted to get the thing over with and go home before the weekend.[15] And that sense of a fait accompli was exactly what Roosevelt had wanted to avoid.

The drab and dull Tuesday afternoon session simply marked time. After Speaker Bankhead called the convention to order at noon, the band played "Dixie" to the applause of southern delegates, and a dozen girls in colorful costumes, members of the Young Democrats of America, paraded across the platform.[16] "Did you delegates get an eyeful of those beautiful young girls? Now what chance has Mr. Willkie got?" Bankhead asked the crowd.

There was a feeling of real unhappiness and apathy at the convention. "I was being accosted by leaders of delegations and members of Congress," Harold Ickes wrote in his diary, "all wanting to know what the word was, but I had none to give them. I did not even pretend that I knew." On Tuesday afternoon, Ickes fired off a telegram to the president. "THIS CONVENTION IS BLEEDING TO DEATH," he informed Roosevelt, urging him to come to Chicago and provide the "inspiration of leadership" to the "nine hundred leaderless delegates milling about like worried sheep." Working himself into a nervous frenzy, Ickes ended his 600-word telegram with two autocratic imperatives: "You should insist that the convention take a platform of your own dictation. . . . You should insist upon a candidate for Vice President who sees eye to eye with you."[17]

The president had not confided to Ickes—or to anyone else—what role, if any, he would play in the convention. He had not told even his closest advisor, Harry Hopkins, the congenial, 50-year-old widower who had recently moved into the White House with his daughter.[18] Everyone who walked through his door wanted something, FDR once said, except for Harry Hopkins, who wanted only to serve.[19]

Roosevelt had sent Hopkins to Chicago in late June to discuss the convention with Mayor Kelly. Now Hopkins was back in town for the big event. Though Kelly had conferred upon him the august title of "Deputy Sergeant at Arms," Hopkins's job was to act as confidential liaison with the White House. In the bathroom of his hotel suite—the only room in which privacy could be assured—Hopkins had a direct telephone line to the president. And yet, even he remained in the dark about Roosevelt's intentions. And no more in the loop than Hopkins was South Carolina's senator James Byrnes, Roosevelt's floor manager at the convention.[20]

The one person in charge was the president himself—and he declined to go to Chicago. "Absolutely no" was his answer in private. "Too many promises will be extracted from me if I go." But his public response was more diplomatically crafted. The key element of his strategy was to play the Washingtonian role of a statesman far too preoccupied with world crises to involve himself in the crude and vulgar fray of party politics. At his press conference on that same Tuesday, he explained that he had no time to focus on the events taking place in Chicago. None of the convention news, he solemnly said, was equal in importance to the information on national defense that he had just been discussing with reporters. "Wouldn't you put the safety of the country ahead of anybody's convention?" he asked.[21]

On Tuesday evening, the mood was expectant. Something had to happen, people felt. Some story had to break.

At 9:00 p.m. the meeting came to order. First a rabbi prayed for unity, a band played, delegates and spectators sang, and politicians paid tributes to one another. An hour later, Presiding Officer Alben Barkley of Kentucky, the Senate majority leader, came forward in his white summer suit to give the main address of the evening, carried on radio stations across the country. Without any preamble, he launched into his seventeen-page speech. Aiming for some humor, he said that the Republicans nominated Wendell Willkie because they were afraid to nominate anyone who had been a Republican for more than two years. People laughed, and newspaper reporters noted an "electric tension in the air like a gathering thunderstorm." Jokingly, Barkley referred to Hoover, to the accompaniment of the jeers and boos of the crowd. The speech was like that, platitudes mingling with mild crowd-pleasers, as Barkley went on to declare that for the past seven years the government had been working to strengthen American democracy. And then, departing from his prepared text, he spoke three magic words—Franklin Delano Roosevelt.[22]

Pandemonium ensued, giving pro-Roosevelt delegates a chance to work off steam. The stadium pipe organ crashed out "Anchors Aweigh" and Roosevelt's 1932 theme song, "Happy Days Are Here Again"; confetti rained down from the galleries; delegates cheered, yelled, rang cowbells, blew police whistles and automobile horns, waved their state banners, and stomped around the stadium for twenty-five minutes. Florida's senator Claude Pepper led a chorus of delegates in shouting "We want Roosevelt!" and singing "God Bless America" to the accompaniment of a forty-piece band. Grinning, Barkley rapped his gavel for order now and then in perfunctory fashion, spreading his arms in a helpless gesture, pointing forlornly to the pages of his speech. But the noise did not stop. "Will the delegates kindly return to their seats?" he shouted. The delegates roared back, "NO!" as they continued to cheer for Roosevelt.[23]

When the hall calmed down, Barkley resumed his talk. "My friends," he slowly began with a smile—and then skipped through the rest of his speech, tossing aside whole pages and abbreviating the talk more and more—with no noticeable gaps—as he went along. Finally, at ten past 11:00, with the crowd again growing restive, he came to the climax. "I have an additional message from the president of the United States," he said. Suddenly silence descended on the convention hall.

Paraphrasing the gist of the message that the White House had telephoned to him that afternoon, Barkley told the delegates that he and other close friends of the president "have long known that he has no wish to be a candidate again. The president has never had, and has not today, any desire or purpose to continue in the office of the President, to be a candidate for that office, or to be nominated by the convention for that office. He wishes in all earnestness and sincerity to make it clear that all of the delegates to this convention are free to vote for any candidate."[24]

With that, Barkley left the podium. The president had said nothing about declining the nomination or refusing to run if drafted by the convention. Like George Washington, Roosevelt understood that power may come to those who appear not to seek it. His perfectly timed announcement had all the "earnestness and sincerity" of a brilliantly calculated performance.

A steady buzz filled the stadium, and then an unknown voice bellowed into the amplifying system: "ROOSEVELT! . . . ROOSEVELT! . . . ROOSEVELT!" again and again and again, almost hypnotically. Quizzically delegates looked at one another. No one was quite sure who had the microphone or where the voice was coming from. Only later did it become known that Mayor Kelly had planted his superintendent of sewers in a basement room with a microphone, and it was he who chanted Roosevelt's name. After a few minutes of confusion, the state delegations joined in, shouting, "Massachusetts wants Roosevelt!" "Illinois wants Roosevelt!" "America wants Roosevelt! Humanity wants Roosevelt!" People laughed when someone shouted, "Willkie wants Roosevelt!" and again when another person yelled, "The whole United States wants Roosevelt!" Delegates whistled and cheered, over and over as the organ once again launched into "Happy Days Are Here Again." Barkley spurred the demonstration to even greater heights by holding a picture of Roosevelt over his head. At midnight, one group shouted, "Suspend the rules! Vote now!"

On the convention floor, chewing gum violently, blinking back tears, Jim Farley presented, one reporter wrote, "the most pathetic picture in the Stadium." From the galleries above, spectators quietly observed the frenetic spectacle below. And eight hundred miles away in the White House, listening intently to the radio in his second-floor study, its walls adorned with pictures of ships and of the Hudson Valley, was Franklin Roosevelt.[25]

One reporter at the convention grasped the situation perfectly. "Mr. Roosevelt, in announcing that he had never been a candidate for a third term, had made himself more of a candidate than ever." And that was the general consensus. "Great statement," said Paul Lewis, a member of the Pennsylvania delegation, in telegraphic style. "Don't care whether he wants it or not; going to give it to him." Claude Pepper held that Roosevelt was "the people's candidate and they will have no other." "The American people know this man, they trust him and they want him," Harry Hopkins said, predicting that FDR would be nominated the next evening by acclamation. And Harry Truman of Missouri simply yelled that "the country wants Roosevelt!" Joyous telegrams addressed to Bankhead poured into Chicago. "We rose with Roosevelt," one read; "why wilt with Willkie?"[26]

Only a few skeptics and nonbelievers voiced dissent. Worth Clark of Idaho, a Wheeler supporter, told reporters that he thought Roosevelt's statement was not "definite" and that it left the delegates just as uncertain as before. Anti–New Dealer Millard Tydings of Maryland, the favorite-son candidate of his delegation and of no one else, engaged in wishful thinking, declaring that he believed Roosevelt was "sincere" in wanting to leave the White House.[27] And Jim Farley tersely said that he had no comment.

After almost an hour of cheering and parading around the stadium for Roosevelt, Barkley called the meeting back to order. James Byrnes announced that on Wednesday the convention would ratify the party platform and then, mincing no words, he boldly told the delegates that "tomorrow night, you can finish the job of drafting Franklin D. Roosevelt!"[28]

On the evening of Wednesday, July 17, delegates, alternates, and spectators jammed into every available inch of space in the Chicago Stadium. People were sitting in the aisles, standing along the walls, while outside a crowd of ten thousand, some with tickets, struggled to get in. In the White House, Roosevelt listened to the proceedings on the radio, surrounded by his usual group of intimates—Sam Rosenman, "Pa" Watson, Steve Early, Missy Le-Hand, his secretary Grace Tully, and several others.

At 8:20 Barkley pounded his gavel and called the session to order. A minister gave the invocation; an Irish tenor sang the national anthem, and a chorus offered songs for every region of the nation—"In Old New York," "Sewanee River," "On the Banks of the Wabash," and "Home on the Range." Then New York's senator Robert Wagner, the chairman of the Resolutions Committee, came forward to read aloud the party platform, which was adopted at 9:30—but not before a roar of groans and jeers drowned out Minnesota representative Elmer Ryan's proposal for an anti-third-term plank.[29]

The key plank, entitled "We Must Strengthen Democracy against Aggression," was not significantly different from that of the Republicans. The Republicans were "firmly opposed to involving this Nation in foreign war," and the Democrats, too, promised to keep the country out of war "except in case of attack," a phrase insisted upon by the White House. The GOP platform favored aid to "all peoples fighting for liberty," and the Democratic platform similarly promised help for the "peace-loving and liberty-loving peoples" under siege. Both parties pledged material aid to the European democracies that was "consistent with law" and America's own self-defense; and neither the Democrats nor the Republicans were willing to use the word "allies" to describe those liberty-loving nations. If the Republican plank on foreign policy was, in the words of Alf Landon, "weasel-worded and two-faced," the Democratic plank was no less so.[30]

While Senators Wheeler, Walsh, and McCarran as well as former war secretary Woodring wanted the platform to state unequivocally that the party stood for "nonintervention in the political and military affairs of the Old World," German agents were working behind the scenes for a similar pledge.[31] It was later revealed that the German chargé d'affaires, Hans Thomsen, who had subsidized the attendance of isolationist congressmen at the GOP Convention in Philadelphia, did the same at the Chicago convention. In his memo of July 19, 1940, to the German Foreign Ministry, Thomsen credited embassy staff with sending "several reliable isolationist Congressmen" to Chicago "in order to exert influence on the delegates with the purpose of including . . . in the Democratic platform . . . a pledge of nonparticipation in a European war." Thomsen hastened to reassure his superiors in Berlin that no one was aware of his behind-the-scenes machinations.[32] For his part, Burton Wheeler pronounced himself pleased with the isolationist plank. Assuring his supporters that he had obtained everything he wanted, he withdrew his name from the presidential race.[33]

Despite all the foreign policy debates, compromises, and clandestine Nazi maneuvers that took place in the resolutions committees of both party conventions, by the time the fall campaigns were under way, world events as well as the two presidential candidates themselves would render both parties' platforms equally irrelevant.

Finally the real spectacle was about to begin on Wednesday evening. First came nominating speeches and the roll-call of the states.

"Alabama!" was called. Senator Lister Hill came forward to place Franklin Roosevelt's name in nomination. "This is no time for untried hands to pilot the ship," he said in a lackluster speech. "I am proud to offer . . ."—his microphone failed. A few seconds later, he continued: "I place in nomination for President of the United States, Franklin Delano Roosevelt!" The demonstration for the president swept over the convention like a forest fire, one reporter wrote.[34] In an instant, the aisles were once again full of marching, cheering delegates—even though, as Harold Ickes observed, the crowd had pretty well shouted itself out the night before. Signs popped up throughout the hall, reading, "We Want Roosevelt!" "Give Us Roosevelt!" "Roosevelt and Humanity!"

"Arizona!" Arizona seconded the nomination.

"Arkansas!" Arkansas yielded to Virginia. The Old Dominion's 82-year-old senator Carter Glass rose to nominate James Farley. "I come from a sickbed," Glass defiantly told the crowd in a hoarse voice, "to present to this convention the name of a great Democrat, James A. Farley of New York!" Denouncing the betrayal of the two-term tradition, the conservative Glass, who had declined to vote for the Social Security Act in 1935, likened Farley to Thomas Jefferson, Virginia's own champion of limited and frugal government who had cemented that two-term custom. Then Glass confided to the crowd that he had received two anonymous protests that Farley was a Catholic. "That made me more determined than ever to put this great man in nomination!" he shouted, reminding his listeners that one of Jefferson's three greatest achievements was the Virginia Statute of Religious Freedom. A five-minute demonstration for Farley ensued, disrupted by a chorus of boos from the public galleries.[35] Now Farley, who had served brilliantly as the shrewd and tireless campaign manager for Franklin Roosevelt in 1932 and 1936, stood adamantly opposed to his old friend—the break between them was sealed. And now there was no chance that Roosevelt could simply be chosen unanimously.

"California!" The head of the California delegation praised Roosevelt.

"Connecticut!" Senator Francis Maloney seconded the nomination of Roosevelt. "It's no time to take off our national armor!" he cried.

Eventually the Maryland delegation was called, and a long-winded delegate nominated Millard Tydings.

Massachusetts seconded Farley.

Then Texas came forth with Jack Garner's name. Though the Texas delegation was committed to their favorite son Garner on the first ballot, it was bitterly split. Feelings ran so high that a young John Connally, the future governor of Texas, jumped over a row of chairs to prevent a fistfight between his boss, Congressman Lyndon Johnson, a Roosevelt man, and another delegation member who supported Garner.[36]

At 12:15 a.m., two and a half hours after the nominating process began, the delegates prepared to cast their votes.

Each time a delegation announced its vote for Roosevelt, joyous howls filled the air. The Maryland delegation split its vote between Tydings and Roosevelt, and Massachusetts and New York both split their votes between Farley and Roosevelt. On the first ballot, Roosevelt—the candidate who still hadn't said yes to his nomination—had 946½ votes, Farley 72½, Garner 61, Tydings 9½, and Hull, who had not been officially nominated, 5. One hundred and forty-eight votes had been cast against Roosevelt. Earlier that evening, Harry

Hopkins had let it be known that Roosevelt would refuse the party's nomination if more than 150 delegates voted against him. The convention had come perilously close to that limit.[37]

The Texas delegation then jubilantly announced that it was switching the forty-six votes of the Lone Star State from favorite son Garner to Roosevelt. Other states followed suit. Then Farley, the good soldier who had recently told reporters that "anybody that knows anything about me knows that Jim Farley is a Democrat," took the floor. Dramatically surrendering to Roosevelt, he moved that the rules be suspended and that Roosevelt be nominated by acclamation.[38] Over the next hours and days, delegates and reporters would fuss over whether Roosevelt had been named by "acclamation" or "unanimously" or simply on the "first ballot." But the result was the same.

At 2:00 in the morning, the session was over. For the first time in American history, a president had been nominated to serve a third term. In the presence of the deathbed of the two-term tradition, no one at the convention other than Elmer Ryan and Carter Glass had publicly voiced objections.[39]

"Boy, I'm tired," sighed Hopkins as he sat with friends in a Chicago nightspot. "Wonder what they'd do if I took off my shoes?" he said with a grin. A cartoonist for the Cleveland Press imagined the scene at the White House. Under the title "Imagine His Surprise" an aide tells FDR, "Chief—you're nominated!" and the president, springing out of his chair, replies in utter amazement, "Who? Me?"[40]

But all the frantic cheering notwithstanding, the mood among the delegates in Chicago was sour and frustrated. Many felt that they had been used—cast in the role of puppets, some grumbled—and that the convention had been all sewed up before it began.

The events the following day would only deepen that mood.[41]

The nomination belonged to Roosevelt. Easily done. But he wanted more.

On Thursday, July 18, the convention's final day, delegates would choose the vice presidential nominee, a selection process for the second fiddle that had rarely caused a rumpus in the past. There was a large stable of vice presidential possibilities—McNutt, Byrnes, Bankhead, Hull, Texas representative Sam Rayburn, and another Texan, Jesse Jones, the Federal Loan administrator whom FDR's son Elliott intended to nominate. Vice President Garner told a reporter that he would "consider it a real honor" to be nominated a third time. Though Burton Wheeler disdained the vice presidential nomination, he improbably convinced himself that he was the White House's first choice; Robert Hutchins, the isolationist president of the University of Chicago, thought he, too, had a chance; and the overly self-confident Harold Ickes informed the president that he would not refuse the position.[42]

The three names on Roosevelt's short-list, according to Sam Rosenman, were Hull, Henry Wallace, and Byrnes. The president was ready to back Hull, Rosenman noted, if the secretary of state wanted the job, but Rosenman had become convinced that he wasn't interested. On Wednesday evening, Roosevelt placed a phone call to Hull, asking him to be his running-mate. "No, by God!" and "By God, no!" he replied, just as Roosevelt had anticipated. Now the president had the green light to wring out of the convention Wallace, the 52-year-old Iowan who had been FDR's secretary of agriculture since 1933.[43]

Confiding in Frances Perkins, Roosevelt had outlined his reasons. If something happened to the president, Wallace would be a good substitute for him. No isolationist, the Iowan understood the crisis rapidly engulfing the world, and he had a wide following among farmers in the Midwest, where isolationist sentiment was at its strongest. "He is good to work with," Roosevelt told Perkins when she phoned him from Chicago during the convention, "and he knows a lot, you can trust his information. He digs to the bottom of things and gets the facts. He is honest as the day is long. He thinks right. He has the general ideas we have. He is the kind of man who can do something in politics. He can help the people with their political thinking. Yes, I think it had better be Wallace." Perkins agreed with her boss.[44]

Neither of them needed to reassure the other that Wallace had been a brilliant, innovative, and energetic secretary of agriculture who brought the New Deal to the heartland. When he took over the department, it had forty thousand employees; by 1940, it had more than three times that number. Under Wallace, the department had become a behemoth that oversaw the nation's food supply and touched almost every aspect of the lives of tens of millions of rural Americans, from education and electrification to crop management and soil conservation, from the nation's first food stamp and school lunch programs to credit, refinancing, and antipoverty projects.[45]

The first to hear the news about Roosevelt's choice was Mayor Kelly. He phoned the president to congratulate him right after the roll-call vote. When FDR told him that he wanted Wallace, Kelly voiced some doubts. Listening to one side of the conversation, Sam Rosenman heard the president adamantly inform Kelly that his running-mate would be Wallace—or no one. The mayor quickly stepped into line and spread the word. When Harry Hopkins heard the news, he phoned Rosenman at the White House to double-check on the story. It was true. There would be "a hell of a lot of opposition," Hopkins warned, remarking that there were at least ten candidates who had more support than Wallace. "Well, damn it to hell," Roosevelt barked at Hopkins, overheard by Grace Tully, "they will go for Wallace or I won't run and you can jolly well tell them so." In the dark hours of Thursday morning, Rosenman phoned Wallace. He was the man, Rosenman told him, voicing the hope that Wallace would "play ball with the boss."[46]

Many Democrats, however, were not ready to play ball. Some criticized Wallace for being a dreamer and a visionary; others lambasted him as a poor campaigner; still others noted that he had been a Republican until 1932. But to a great extent, the opposition to Wallace was not directed at him personally, but rather at the heavy-handed manner in which the White House sought to impose him on the convention. James Byrnes placed a call to the president to protest the choice. But he, too, learned that the president's mind was made up. Agreeing to try to put Wallace over, Byrnes underlined that he was not sure it could be done.[47] The reward for his efforts would soon be a seat on the Supreme Court.

As for Jim Farley, he considered Wallace a "wild-eyed fellow" and a mystic. "Jim, Henry's not a mystic, he's a philosopher, a liberal philosopher, and I'm sure that he'll be all right," Rosenman heard the president tell Farley on the phone. But Farley refused to go along. He would vote instead for Jesse Jones or Bankhead. "I feel the Democrats want a Democrat," Farley snapped, referring to Wallace's Republican past, "and I do not consider Wallace one." Their conversation ended abruptly. Even Harold Ickes chimed in with a cautionary telegram from Chicago, describing the opposition to Wallace and suggesting that he himself would be a better choice. "I would be honored to be considered as your running mate," Ickes wrote. With a laugh, the president handed the telegram to Rosenman. "Dear old Harold," he said. "He'd get fewer votes even than Wallace in that convention." So bitterly disappointed was Ickes that he groused in his diary, "So far as the Vice Presidential candidates are concerned, I prefer McNary to Wallace."[48]

The bitterness in Chicago was palpable. Whether it was because delegates were weary at the end of the week, or because they resented what some commentators called "presidential bossism" and wanted the freedom at least to choose the vice president, or because Hopkins, Byrnes, and other Roosevelt allies were working the floor all day, threatening them that the president might well refuse the nomination if he did not get his man, many were in a rebellious mood. "Ugly rough words were exchanged, fiery challenges were shouted, tempers flared," wrote one reporter. Wallace proved to be a hard sell. On the convention floor, Governor Ed Rivers of Georgia turned to his neighbor, Governor Leon Phillips of Oklahoma, to ask what he thought of Wallace. "Why, Henry's my second choice," said Phillips. "That so?" said Rivers. "Who's your first choice?" Without the hint of a smile, Phillips replied, "Anyone—red, white, black or yellow—that can get the nomination."[49]

Before the convention spiraled out of control, Frances Perkins phoned the president from Chicago to issue one more warning that a fight over Wallace was coming. Unwilling to go to Chicago himself, FDR offered the excellent suggestion that Eleanor fly to Chicago instead. Perkins phoned Eleanor. "Things look black here," she said. "I think you should come."[50] Reluctantly Eleanor agreed to bring a message of harmony to the convention.

The Thursday afternoon session passed uneventfully with the hall only half full. The session had been called to listen to the president's reply to his nomination, but no reply was forthcoming. After some entertainment and speechifying, the delegates were sent back to their hotel rooms until 7:00 p.m.[51] When the evening session got under way, before the balloting for vice president began, Alben Barkley introduced Eleanor Roosevelt.

Standing on the speaker's platform, she faced the stadium full of edgy delegates. When the cheers subsided, the crowd fell silent. "Any man who has an office of great responsibility today faces a heavier responsibility perhaps than any man has ever faced before in this country," Mrs. Roosevelt told the delegates. The party's nomination for the presidency—especially in the crisis year 1940—was a "very serious and a very solemn thing." Because a third term for her husband would be highly stressful, she said, he was "entitled" to have Wallace's assistance. She also noted that her husband would not be able to do the usual campaigning because he had to be constantly on the job. Her high-minded message was that all Americans similarly had to sacrifice their personal preferences, rise above partisan considerations, and give their full efforts to their country. Her words, aimed at healing the breaches within the party, induced only a brief calm—though Jim Farley later commented that she saved the day for the president.[52]

Moments after she sat down, the roll-call started. The Alabama delegation came first, nominating its own "most brilliant and beloved son," Speaker William Bankhead. The band played "Dixie" while supporters cheered for twenty minutes. Then Arizona yielded to Maryland, which nominated Jesse Jones, sparking yells of approval from the Texans on the floor. Roosevelt's son Elliott, a Texas delegate, seconded Jones's nomination.[53] So resentful were many delegates of the White House's heavy-handed tactics that they were happy to root for any candidate who was not forced upon them, but Jones declined the nomination.

Then Arkansas yielded to Iowa, whose chairman, Frank O'Connor, exclaimed that "Iowa, the greatest agricultural state in the union gives to this convention and the Democratic Party its great and illustrious son, Henry A. Wallace!," a man of "ripe experience for these ominous times." A roar of cheers greeted the nomination as Iowans waved their stalks of corn. But an equally thunderous storm of boos broke out on the floor and in the galleries. Grabbing the microphone, one mutinous delegate hollered that "just because the Republicans have nominated an apostate Democrat, let us not for God's sake nominate an apostate Republican!" Others cried, "We want a Democrat!" Even the band, which accompanied all the other demonstrations, fell strangely silent.[54]

Minutes later, Oklahoma announced, to euphoric stomping and clapping, that it wanted to draft Paul McNutt. But McNutt, the handsome, white-haired favorite of the convention, was a Roosevelt loyalist. Stepping up to the podium to withdraw his name, he was drowned out by chants of "We want McNutt!" "Please, please let me speak," he asked and tried to begin. "In the first place, I want to express"—but shouts and hurrahs cut him off. "Will the convention grant me the privilege of speaking?" he pleaded. "NO!" the delegates roared back. He waited them out, and when the crowd finally calmed down, he went on. "It is necessary that we be and remain a united party. . . . America needs strong, logical, liberal and able leaders in the kind of world we live in today. We cannot take chances now. We must have leaders who have demonstrated what they can and will do. . . . Franklin D. Roosevelt is such a leader, he is my leader, and I am here to support his choice for Vice President."[55] Though he did not mention Wallace by name, his words prompted a deafening cataract of boos, louder than anything before.

Others also withdrew from the race, to more catcalls and boos. Sam Rayburn declined the nomination and instead yielded to Roosevelt's request that he make a seconding speech for Wallace, though in that speech he made it clear that he did so only from loyalty to FDR, "following the wish of our great leader, the greatest president since Thomas Jefferson!" Still, people jeered.[56]

On the platform sat a stoical Henry Wallace. His suffering was intense, observed Frances Perkins. "There was no outlet for it. There was nothing to do. He had to just sit there and take it." His distraught wife turned to Eleanor Roosevelt and plaintively asked, "Why are they so opposed to Henry?" In fact, the rowdy crowd had merely transferred its foul mood and frustration from the White House to Wallace. The delegates could not afford to show their spite to Roosevelt, as Perkins later explained, but they could punish Wallace with their display of cruelty.[57]

Finally it would be a contest between Wallace and the 66-year-old Bankhead, who though in poor health refused to withdraw.

In the White House Oval Room, a dour Roosevelt, his face grim and set, played solitaire as he listened on the radio to the extraordinary events in Chicago. He paid little attention to the people listening along with him that night—Steve Early, Sam Rosenman, Missy LeHand, Pa Watson and his wife, and several others.[58]

Steeling himself for the worst—a Bankhead nomination that would signal the convention's rejection of his authority—Roosevelt set his playing cards aside and asked for paper and pencil. Rosenman later commented that he had never seen Roosevelt looking so determined. He scribbled a harsh message for the convention, telling delegates that he would not participate in a party divided between liberalism and reaction and that he would free the party to make that choice by declining the nomination. The bottom line was that, since the convention refused his leadership, he would not agree to be its candidate. "Sam, take this inside and go to work on it; smooth it out and get it ready for delivery," the president said, handing Rosenman the sheet of paper. Then he went back to his game of solitaire.[59]

Outside the president's study, Rosenman sat down and read Roosevelt's cold, adamant words as Missy and Pa Watson leaned over his shoulder to see what FDR had written. "Sam, give that damned piece of paper to me—let's tear it up," Pa Watson impulsively suggested, close to tears. "The only thing that's important to this country is that fellow in there. There isn't anyone in the United States who can lead this nation for the next four years as well as he can." Only Missy was glad, hopeful that her boss would be spared another four-year sentence in Washington. But fortunately the president's message would never be delivered.[60]

In Chicago, after three hours of nominating and seconding speeches and tornadoes of booing, the balloting finally began. At first, Bankhead held the lead. "For God's sake, do you want a president or a vice president?" Byrnes pleaded, trying to beat back support for Bankhead. A misinformed Elliott Roosevelt spread the story that his father was open to Wallace, McNutt, or Bankhead—a rumor quickly quashed.[61]

The mood in the Oval Room was tense. The president and his friends listened to the delegates call out their votes. Roosevelt put aside his cards and tallied the numbers himself.[62]

Finally it was the turn of New York. Earlier in the roll-call, its delegation had passed. Now Bronx political boss and soon to become Farley's successor as chair of the national party, Ed Flynn, announced to the convention that New York—and Roosevelt—wanted Wallace. The Illinois delegation made a similar announcement, greeted with cheers and boos.

When the balloting was over at eight minutes after midnight, Wallace had 627 votes to Bankhead's 327. Jesse Jones, Farley, Barkley, and a few others had a scattering of votes. Then Bankhead's brother, Alabama senator John Bankhead, moved that the rules be suspended and that Wallace be nominated unanimously.[63] Barkley declared that the motion carried while a chorus of voices shouted, "NO!"

A few well-wishers rushed over to Wallace to offer their congratulations. Then the vice presidential nominee started toward the microphone to deliver his prepared message of acceptance—remarks he had already distributed to the press. But James Byrnes abruptly stopped him midway. "Don't do it, Henry," he ordered, reminding Wallace that the radio audience would hear the explosive resentment in the hall. "You'll ruin the party if you do."[64]

And so it was a done deal. Through the most extraordinary machinations and ploys, begun months earlier and culminating at the convention with threats and ultimatums, the president had gotten all he wanted—his own nomination and that of his handpicked vice president. Franklin Roosevelt was in "absolute command" of the Democratic Party, wrote *Time*.[65]

In the White House, Roosevelt prepared to give the one acceptance speech of the evening. "He looked weary and bedraggled," remarked Sam Rosenman. He was wheeled into his bedroom, where he freshened up, coming out a few minutes later his usual jaunty self. He and his friends went downstairs to the radio broadcasting room. They were all happy and smiling—except for Missy LeHand, who was in tears.[66]

Unlike in 1932 when he had flown to Chicago to accept the party's nomination, this time FDR renounced any spectacle or grandstanding. He made his speech to the convention—and to the nation—by radio. As his assured and resonant voice filled the stadium, delegates and spectators fell silent.

Sitting at a desk before the microphones in the dungeon-like room at 1:20 a.m. Eastern Standard Time, Roosevelt accepted the nomination quietly. Only "the nocturnal life" of the nation caught his words, wrote *Time*—the taxi drivers, the sleepless passengers in deluxe trains, the patrons in bars and restaurants. Workers and farmers were long since asleep.[67]

What mattered to him most, the president said, was not the nomination of his party but rather, in this time of world crisis, the call from the American electorate. Since he had unofficially "drafted into the service of the nation" so many men and women, taking them away from their private affairs and asking them to make sacrifices for their country, he could not decline a summons to duty when it came from them. Underscoring that a military draft would soon be "necessary and fair," he told Americans that his "conscience" would not let him turn his back upon a call to service.

He thanked the delegates for their selection of Henry Wallace—Wallace's "first-hand knowledge of the problems of Government in every sphere," he said, qualified him for the position—and he thanked Jim Farley for his party leadership. And then he turned to the burning issue of the fascist regimes that sought "not to set men free but to reduce them to slavery." FDR left no doubt that he intended to pursue anti-Hitler, pro-British policies. "I do not regret my consistent endeavor to awaken this country to the menace for us and for all we hold dear." Nor did he have patience for the fashionable notion that democracy could not compete with the energy and decisiveness of fascism. Americans, he declared "will never willingly descend to any form of this so-called security of efficiency which calls for the abandonment of other securities more vital to the dignity of man." And as if responding to Lindbergh's defeatist charge that Roosevelt's biting denunciations of the Nazi onslaught would lead to "neither friendship nor peace" with Germany, the president strongly affirmed that he would "not now soften the condemnation expressed by Secretary Hull and myself . . . for the acts of aggression that have wiped out ancient liberty-loving, peace-pursuing countries which had scrupulously maintained neutrality." In Berlin, the German ambassador to the United States, Hans Heinrich Dieckhoff, reacted predictably to Roosevelt's message, angrily branding the speech an "outrageous provocation" that proved the president's "fanatical hatred" of Germany and Italy.[68]

At 1:05 a.m. Central Time, the convention adjourned.

The unimaginable had happened. The Democrats had broken with the 150-year-old two-term tradition and renominated a president who, with guile and steel, had bent his party to his will. The GOP had nominated a party newcomer who had never held office and never participated in party affairs. One candidate had been born to wealth and privilege but embraced the interests of the poor; the other was a self-made utilities magnate with ties to Wall Street. What they both had in common was a commitment to social justice and equality and a lucid understanding of the grave crisis abroad. They both knew that 1940 was not a year to fight the election of 1936 all over again and debate the New Deal. On the contrary, the one central issue of the campaign had been decided in Germany.

Isolationists were not pleased with the choice they were left with. The Socialist candidate for president, Norman Thomas, groused that Willkie and Roosevelt agreed on so many key matters that any debate between them "would involve little more than personalities and oratorical generalizations." Though Burton Wheeler had assured his colleagues that he would "support the nominees of the party, irrespective of who are nominated," he decided to throw his support to Thomas for president.[69] And while other frustrated isolationists slammed the "Willkievelt" twins, a rumor circulated that a third-party movement would emerge, with Wheeler as the presidential nominee and Lindbergh as a possible vice presidential candidate.[70] For his part, Lindbergh said he considered Wheeler the "most able" of the anti-interventionist senators, but he expressed no interest in a joint ticket. "Don't worry about my running for Congress or any other office," the aviator reassured a friend. "It is just one of those rumors that start, God knows where."[71]

The Democrats and the Republicans had in fact made wise choices in their presidential nominees. Though neither Roosevelt nor Willkie was about to abandon political ploys, campaign rhetoric, or the day-to-day opportunism of electoral politics, they both understood that it was also time for courageous leadership. Both men, Robert Sherwood judged, were well qualified to speak for the true interests of their nation and to lead it into the next decade. With either candidate, America's future would be in safe hands. The more dangerous contest, Sherwood believed, was not between Roosevelt and Willkie but between them and the extreme isolationists.[72]

In his acceptance speech to the convention, Roosevelt, ever the political animal, had warned that if power passed to "untried" hands, an inexperienced president might seek compromise with fascist powers. But that was merely campaign talk. "He's grass-roots stuff," the president remarked to columnist Walter Winchell about Willkie. "The people like him very much. His sincerity comes through with terrific impact. . . . We're going to have a heck of a fight on our hands with him."[73]

Chapter 11
Willkie Runs Alone

TRETCHED OUT IN A LOUNGE CHAIR AT THE MAJESTIC BROADMOOR Hotel in Colorado Springs, Wendell Willkie listened to the Democratic Convention on the radio. Eager to challenge the reigning champ, he was disappointed when it appeared that the president might withdraw from the race. But the raucous floor demonstrations for Roosevelt on Tuesday evening lifted Willkie's spirits. "Boys," he said, "I think my worries are over." On Wednesday evening, while delegates in Chicago were casting their votes for the party's presidential candidate, Wendell Willkie and his wife, Edith, were in Central City, Colorado, attending a music festival in the deserted gold mining town. When the performance of *The Bartered Bride* was over, Willkie turned on the radio to see if his prediction that Roosevelt would be nominated on the first ballot had come true. He pronounced himself "gratified" when it was clear that Roosevelt had indeed won the nomination. "The battle's on!" Willkie roared, promising a "great campaign." He added that voters would have the opportunity "to pass on the sanctity of our two term tradition," but he did not go as far as Senator Vandenberg and other Republicans who likened the nomination of Roosevelt to "political dictatorship" and "totalitarianism."[1]

When the Republican Convention ended in June, Willkie and his wife, who agreed to play the customary role—right out of central casting—of the devoted political spouse, left immediately on a brief cruise with Russell Davenport and Roy Howard, who was mobilizing his Scripps-Howard newspaper chain for Willkie. Raymond Buell, the interventionist who was Willkie's new foreign policy advisor, later remarked that he was "taken aback" by his candidate's apparent friendship with Howard. According to Buell, who was a strong internationalist, Howard had clearly revealed his isolationist and "fascist" pro-clivities, and his newspapers, as the British Foreign Ministry itself grumbled, were one of the principal vehicles for American appeasers.[2] Moreover, How-ard had recently declined a personal request from President Roosevelt that he undertake a confidential mission to South America and speak to newspaper editors and publishers there about fifth-column activities.[3] After the cruise, Willkie spent a few days in New York and Washington before retreating in early July for a five-week working vacation at the picturesque Broadmoor, a sprawl-ing 3,000-acre resort on a large man-made lake under the shadow of Chey-enne Mountain. Seeking rest, recuperation, and recreation, he hiked in the Pike's Peak landscape, swam every morning, and spent afternoons reading.

He worked, too, logging hundreds of phone calls, holding daily press brief-ings, and meeting with dozens of visitors, some of whom were helpful, others who were, according to his aide Sam Pryor, "screwballs." He showed up at cam-paign rallies in Salt Lake City, Cheyenne, and Des Moines, attended a rodeo, watched a parade, gave impromptu speeches, and went to an Iowa conference on farming. And he worked on polishing the official acceptance speech he was scheduled to give in August in his hometown of Elwood, Indiana.[4] Visiting Willkie at the Broadmoor, William Allen White offered to help put the finish-ing touches on the speech. "I want to let an artist at phraseology take a look at it," the candidate said.[5]

Buoyed by support from newspapers in Tennessee and Texas, Willkie an-nounced that he would campaign actively in the South, optimistic that he could capture those two states as well as North Carolina, as Herbert Hoover had done in 1928. He also welcomed support from the presidents of Yale and Harvard as well as from disgruntled onetime Roosevelt supporters and Demo-crats like Nebraska's senator Edward Burke and former budget director Lewis Douglas. Especially pleasing to him was an endorsement from T. Jefferson Coolidge, the former undersecretary of the treasury who had resigned in pro-test from FDR's administration. "I give you my whole-hearted support. An end must be made of centralized power, personal rule and uncontrollable spending," telegraphed the great-great-great-grandson of Thomas Jefferson, FDR's hero.[6]

Though Willkie referred to his weeks at the Broadmoor as "a most *strenu-ous* vacation," most of his advisors grumbled that he was doing too little to prepare for the fall campaign, set to begin two weeks after Labor Day. During this critical period of international crisis and electoral politics, Willkie re-mained strangely remote amid the Rocky Mountains. Indeed, while President Roosevelt acted the part of national and world leader, making crucial decisions every day and forgoing a partisan role, the GOP nominee permitted the exuberant fire of his insurgency in Philadelphia to die a cold death. He was letting things slide, Charles Halleck said. "He was just giving interviews to every crackpot magazine reporter that came along."[7] A *New York Times* reporter shared that impression, remarking that Willkie read too many books and talked to too many people.

A newspaper editor whom Willkie had invited to Colorado, Paul Smith of the *San Francisco Chronicle*, discovered that the GOP candidate had brought only one secretary with him to the Broadmoor. For years, Willkie had headed one of the largest holding companies in the nation, but he seemed not to have the faintest idea of what a presidential campaign entailed. Entering the Willkies' suite, Smith found that lone secretary sitting motionless, staring, "as if hypnotized," at a high mound of mailbags, while Wendell and his wife scurried from room to room, answering the constantly ringing phones. Although Willkie insisted that everything was shaping up "splendidly," Smith, who would later join the campaign, decided to take him in hand and organize a staff and a switchboard.[8] Another editor had also implored the candidate to professionalize his campaign. But Willkie waved off such advice, stubbornly replying that the "amateurs won the nomination and they can win the election." To drive that point home, at one talk in Iowa, the candidate proudly addressed the Willkie Club members as his "fellow amateurs." Later asked if the Willkie campaign was truly run by amateurs, Halleck gave a crisp "Yes."[9]

In Colorado Springs, Willkie held court, meeting with Alf Landon, Thomas Dewey, Herbert Hoover, and other Republican dignitaries. The former president, who had administered food relief to war-torn Europe during the First World War, arrived for his tête-à-tête at the Broadmoor armed with a proposal that the United States ship food to the European countries occupied by Nazi Germany. Not only the British but also many Americans—like William Allen White—rejected that plan outright, arguing that such aid would only help Germany's war efforts by relieving the Nazi regime of the task of feeding millions of people. "Are we to feed Dutch workmen, making airplanes for the German air fleet, or Belgian miners mining coal for the German munitions factories?" asked one of Hoover's angry critics.[10]

At one point during his afternoon with Hoover, Willkie learned that FDR's son Elliott, on his way to a fishing trip in Wyoming, was also staying at the Broadmoor. Picking up the phone, Willkie invited the young man to join him, General Hugh Johnson, and Hoover for cocktails. "I wouldn't go too strong on that," objected Hoover. But Willkie wanted an open forum. "In my campaign I intend to discuss problems on the issues, not on personalities," he replied. "I've never met him. Let's have him come up." While Hoover squirmed, frowned, and tapped his foot restlessly, Willkie graciously asked Elliott to "stay for a bite." FDR's son happily accepted the invitation from the man he had recently described to reporters as "the epitome of all that the New Deal has fought since it came into power." Willkie told the young Roosevelt that he had a great deal of respect for his father but felt that "it was time for the country to take a new direction." For his part, Elliott wished Willkie good luck. The two smiling men posed for photographers and newsreel cameramen. "We had a delightful time," Elliott later said.[11] Left out of the love fest, Hoover regretted having journeyed to the Broadmoor. Still, he dutifully played the part of loyal soldier and assured reporters that Willkie would be the next president of the United States. But Hoover would soon pay Willkie back. On a modest, three-speech swing through the West and Midwest in October—his only contribution to the campaign—Hoover poured his energy into bashing Roosevelt and the New Deal while mustering only halfhearted confidence in Willkie. "You are far more likely to get into war with Franklin Roosevelt," he told a crowd in Lincoln, Nebraska, "than with Wendell Willkie."[12]

Another visitor to Colorado Springs was Nelson Rockefeller, the 32-year-old president of New York's Rockefeller Center and grandson of the founder of Standard Oil. The young Rockefeller was a Willkie supporter, but he had just received an invitation from FDR to serve in the Office of Inter-American Affairs. Just as the president had appointed Republicans Stimson and Knox to key cabinet positions, he wanted the Republican Rockefeller to be part of the new agency set up not only to promote cooperation with Latin America but also to monitor—and eliminate—German influence there. Should he take the job? Rockefeller asked Willkie. Though the GOP candidate had recently told reporters that, if elected, he would not keep Stimson and Knox in his cabinet, now Willkie showed his true bipartisan and patriotic colors. "If I were president in a time of international crisis and if I asked someone to come to Washington to help me in foreign affairs, and if that man turned me down—well, I don't need to tell you what I would think of him!"[13] Rockefeller accepted the appointment and would win praise for his excellent work as coordinator of Inter-American Affairs.

Joe Martin, the new national chairman of the Republican Party, also made the trek to Colorado Springs. Right after the convention, Willkie had agreed to do a little housecleaning—and dump John Hamilton as the GOP national party chair and ask Martin to take over his duties. At the Republican Convention, Hamilton had made some decisions that were favorable to Willkie, and, as national party chairman since 1936, he had worked to revitalize the party at the grass roots and foster some degree of party unity. But his isolationist positions and vindictive diatribe against Stimson and Knox had angered GOP moderates like William Allen White and *Herald Tribune* publishers Ogden and Helen Reid. So conservative was John Hamilton that New York's rabidly anti–New Deal congressman Hamilton Fish, who had been a follower of Theodore Roosevelt's Progressives, had implored him to "liberalize your leadership and policies or the Republican party dies."[14] Even so, the dismissal of Hamilton greatly weakened Willkie's standing with party regulars.[15]

Meeting with Martin in New York shortly after the convention, Willkie offered him the position of national party chair. But Martin had no stomach for a job that would also entail many of the responsibilities of a campaign manager for Willkie. "I had no desire to jeopardize my standing with Republicans in the House," Martin wrote, "by running the campaign of a candidate toward whom many of them were all but openly hostile." But Willkie poured on the charm. "I have never known a man so hard to say *no* to," Martin wrote in his memoirs. "He had a great Midwestern simplicity and enthusiasm. As he talked on, I became conscious of the fact that I *liked* Willkie." "Are you going to be with me, Joe?" the nominee asked at the end of their long tête-à-tête. "Yes, Wendell," he replied, realizing he had no escape route left. "It looks as though I am." "I've got my man!" Willkie bragged afterward to the press.[16]

The reaction at *Time* over the new appointment was sheer ecstasy. Luce's flagship magazine had criticized Willkie's nonprofessional staff and lamented that "something was lacking in the Republican campaign." Now, *Time* cheered, Martin would expertly fill that vacuum. He was the "equivalent of Franklin Roosevelt's Man Farley." Still, the magazine diagnosed that Martin had his work cut out for him in trying to unify and reenergize the "creaking, long inactive" GOP.[17]

Martin agreed that his new job placed him, as he later wrote, "on top of a powder keg," for it was an almost impossible task to make peace among the party's quarreling factions. Conservatives in the Hoover mold resented the young newcomers and "hotheads" surrounding Willkie and were rankled to see the Republican nominee trying to "out-Roosevelt Roosevelt" on social reform.[18] Moderate Republicans like Alf Landon, meanwhile, believed that any taint of the Hoover Old Guard was "poison" and would cost the Republicans votes in November.[19] Would it be possible for moderates like Martin and Willkie to lead a united GOP?

In early August, Martin arrived at the Broadmoor with advice about healing the breach in the GOP—a breach that Democrats thirsted to exploit. With divisive issues like compulsory military service coming before Congress,

Martin advised Willkie to tread softly and refrain from taking a position on every bill. "Wait and see how the questions come up in the campaign. There will then be some issues on which you will want to comment, but let's avoid these unnecessary conflicts as much as possible."[20] Willkie's running-mate, Charles McNary, offered similar counsel. "In politics," McNary said, "you'll never get in trouble by not saying too much."[21]

But that practical and prudent advice did not suit Willkie's frank and forthright style. One observant reporter noted that he was "handicapped by a natural candor which makes him speak his mind honestly in spite of his immediate self-interest. . . . He does not wear the politician's habitual mask of restraint."[22] For his part, Willkie proudly accepted that description. "One receives a great deal of advice," he said later during the campaign. "Most of it is free and it is worth just that." His friends liked to repeat that "Wendell L. Willkie's closest advisor is Wendell L. Willkie."[23]

What the GOP nominee most wanted was to conduct an unconventional campaign, one that rejected all the worn stereotypes, stale arguments, and the corruption of political machines. "I know the American people are tired of the old political game," he told a *New York Times* reporter. "I know they are tired of it because I am tired of it."[24]

On Saturdays, Elwood, Indiana, a town of eleven thousand people, always came to life as farmers and townspeople poured into the downtown. And so Willkie chose a Saturday afternoon, August 17, to deliver his official acceptance speech. Located in north central Indiana, Elwood was no longer the bustling little city it had been at the turn of the century: the huge glass plant had closed, and the tin plate factory was shuttered.[25] But Elwood could still boast several foundries, furniture factories, banks, a hotel, movie theaters, and a newspaper. When the town's leaders learned that Willkie would make his acceptance speech there, they called for a "rejuvenation" campaign that included removing tumble-down buildings, cleaning the streets, and sprucing up gardens and lawns. They rented hundreds of acres of farmland to park the thousands of vehicles they expected to arrive.

On August 17, right on cue, a horde of visitors, estimated at between 150,000 and 250,000, cascaded into the town. Drivers of 60,000 cars found parking space on city streets and in cornfields, while 800 policemen, borrowed from nearby cities, tried to keep traffic moving. Vendors peddled Willkie souvenirs—flags, stamps, cards, drinking glasses, hats, and neckties. Hoosiers paraded through the main streets as dozens of bands played "Back Home

Again in Indiana." People cheered and waved flags, despite temperatures that soared above 100 degrees. "I personally saw a thermometer on somebody's porch that read 112," said Marcia Davenport.[26]

Sporting a flat-topped straw hat, the candidate arrived with his wife and her mother from nearby Rushville, where they had just spent the night. And then, the awful discovery: Willkie had left the text of his speech behind. A special police motorcade sped back to retrieve it. Saved! Then Joe Martin asked to have a look at the speech. "This is it," Willkie said, handing him the typewritten pages. "Well, this isn't the way we do it in Washington," was all Martin said, appalled that the text had not been typed in large, legible letters and triple spaced so that Willkie would not have to keep his eyes glued to the page.[27] And from there, many people felt, it was all downhill.

In the large park that had been transformed into an open-air amphitheater, Willkie stepped onto the podium. For ten minutes, the crowd gaily cheered. Then, tossing away his chewing gum, he launched into his speech, heard by Americans nationwide on the radio. Already wilting from the withering heat, exhausted after just a few hours of sleep, he read from his text in a droning voice, rarely changing tone or adding emphasis.

The speech itself was intelligent, forthright, and, in some respects, courageous. He did make some stylistic errors: he oddly spoke of himself in the third person—"This young man was born and raised in Elwood. He attended the Elwood public schools. . . ." And occasionally he sank to the level of empty generalizations: "We must fight to preserve America as a country in which every girl and boy has every opportunity for any achievement." But most of what he said was clear and thoughtful.

Describing himself as a long-standing liberal, he declared that he had fought for many of the reforms of progressives like La Follette, Theodore Roosevelt, and Woodrow Wilson "before another Roosevelt adopted—and distorted—liberalism." On domestic policy, he took a few powerful swings at FDR—criticizing him for hostility to business and for setting class against class. But he also acknowledged the accomplishments of the New Deal—from collective bargaining and fair labor standards to social security and federal regulation of securities markets. The purpose of those policies was "a *better distribution of the wealth* and the earning power of the country," he told his listeners. Though applause had followed every paragraph of Willkie's speech, this time the response was tepid.[28] As sweat dripped from his forehead in the oppressive heat, he recouped, arguing that the New Deal had become exhausted. Instead of aiming for economic growth and increased production, "it seeks safety." A continuation of such policies, he darkly warned, would lead to "economic disintegration and dictatorship."

As for foreign relations, Willkie opposed the direct involvement of the United States in the European war and, taking a page from the isolationist handbook, criticized the president for his "inflammatory statements and manufactured panics," wondering aloud if he was "deliberately inciting us to war." But then he proceeded to proclaim his basic agreement with Roosevelt's policies. Putting himself at odds with many in his party, especially in the heavily isolationist Midwest, Willkie asserted that he, too, stood for military preparedness, assistance for the Allies, and even compulsory universal military service.[29]

Hoping to tame the isolationists within his own party by criticizing and rejecting their vision of the United States as an impregnable fortress, detached from the rest of the world, Willkie concluded that a British defeat would be a "calamity" for the United States that "any lover of democracy must view with consternation." He would try as president to maintain peace, he said, but "in the defense of America and of our liberties *I should not hesitate to stand for war.*" It was a brave statement that reflected his genuine beliefs—and also a radical departure from the imprudent, offhand remark he had made immediately after accepting his party's nomination in Philadelphia. At an informal press conference, he had told reporters that there was "no basis to the claim that I am an interventionist." But in Elwood, Willkie truthfully pointed out that "no man can guarantee peace. Peace is not something that a nation can achieve by itself. It also depends on what some other country does."[30]

If there were any isolationists or anti-Semites in the crowd in Elwood, they could not have been happy. Not only did Willkie recommend all aid to Great Britain short of war, he went on to denounce the Nazis' oppression of Jews, "a race that has done so much to improve the culture of those countries." The misery and suffering caused by the Nazis' "medieval persecution," Willkie said, "make us resolve to preserve our country as a land free of hate and bitterness, of racial and class distinctions. I pledge you that kind of an America."

The little town of Elwood, he noted, seemed far removed from the shattered cities, the gutted buildings, and the stricken men, women, and children of Europe, but the war raging across the Atlantic would surely and inevitably affect Americans' daily lives. Indeed, Americans "instinctively" knew, he said, that they were not isolated from those suffering people. If elected, Willkie added, he would ask Americans to serve their country selflessly. "We cannot rebuild our American democracy without hardship, without sacrifice, and without suffering." As for his own service, he repeated the recent words of Winston

Churchill, when he took over as prime minister from Neville Chamberlain—"I have nothing to offer you but blood and tears, toil and sweat."

Wrapping up his speech, Willkie challenged President Roosevelt to debate the issues of the campaign—the nation's inadequate defenses, the languishing economy, and the dictatorial third term. That demand brought the audience to its feet, and for the first time that afternoon, people loudly cheered.

Later that day, streams of visitors and cars poured out of Elwood. Vendors hawked their remaining souvenirs at sharp discounts. Willkie flags priced originally at a quarter went for 10 cents.[31]

The day after Willkie's talk, heavy rain poured down over Indiana, the first powerful rainstorm in weeks. "Modesty forbids me from taking credit," Willkie told reporters with a smile. He could, however, take credit for the thousands of telegrams of congratulations that flooded his headquarters. Republican senators predictably pronounced the speech "one of the greatest in our generation." The more objective Gallup poll recorded an impressive rise in Willkie's approval rating. In Ohio, a state that had voted for the winning candidate in every presidential election since 1900 and was considered a reliable barometer of national sentiment, Willkie polled 53 percent to 47 percent for Roosevelt. A Republican victory in November was "in the stars," William Allen White predicted.[32]

Willkie was pleased to inform reporters that reactions to his talk seemed generally very favorable. "There undoubtedly is some adverse editorial comment," he added, "but honestly I haven't heard of any."[33]

Well, adverse comment there was. The first wave came from Willkie's own supporters. Joe Martin fretted that "his performance was flat," and Charles Halleck groused that the speech "wasn't worth a damn and it was too hot." Then journalists piled on. "The crowd had waited too long. It was too hot. And Willkie had much to learn as a speaker," reported *Time*. Though *New York Times* columnist Arthur Krock was a fervent Willkie supporter, his criticism was even harsher. He carped that Willkie had written a dry essay to be silently read, not a lively, inspiring speech to be delivered and heard. Krock then launched into an elocution lesson, taking Willkie to task for his pronunciation. He had said "Amarrica" for America and "forn" for foreign. How could the Hoosier compete with Roosevelt's "golden voice" and "Groton-Harvard" accent? Krock wondered. Next to the grave events of the day, the columnist admitted, his criticism might be considered petty, but he contended that Willkie's listless delivery prevented his audience from grasping his message.[34]

President Roosevelt himself had no comment. "He even went to the extremity of failing to listen to Willkie's speech," wrote the *Hartford Courant*, adding that, according to Washington insiders, "Mr. Roosevelt was afraid of Willkie." While it was unlikely that FDR feared his opponent, Washington Democrats delighted in hammering the talk. Indiana's Democratic senator Sherman Minton snapped that "it was the worst major political speech I ever listened to," and, in backhanded praise, New York's Sol Bloom, the chair of the House Foreign Affairs Committee, hailed it as "a great Democratic speech" in which Willkie had endorsed virtually all of President Roosevelt's domestic and foreign policies.[35]

Nothing, however, compared to the roasting Willkie received from Harold Ickes. Almost immediately, the acid-tongued Ickes obliged the president by taking to the radio to blast the Republican candidate as the "rich man's Roosevelt, the simple, barefoot Wall Street lawyer." Ickes acknowledged that Willkie supported the basic achievements of the New Deal as well as the essence of FDR's foreign policy. To turn that against the Republican nominee, Ickes pointed out that Willkie was, in fact, at odds with own party. Then, targeting Willkie's criticism of Roosevelt, Ickes said that it was "unpatriotic demagoguery" to make accusations against the man who had become, in his words, "the world's *symbol* of fearless support of democratic principles, the emblem of the world's faith in freedom." Willkie had no "warrant," Ickes insisted, to disparage the president.

Furthermore, Ickes decreed, there would be no debates. The president "cannot adjourn the Battle of Britain in order to ride the circuit with Mr. Willkie," he said. But if Willkie was so eager for a debate, Ickes wittily added, he could challenge his running-mate instead. After all, the GOP candidate was obviously at "greater variance" with the isolationist McNary than with the president.[36] Seconding that idea, a Democratic senator from Illinois quipped that, since Willkie had promised to bring unity to America, "he might begin by obtaining a degree of unity with his distinguished running mate." Willkie responded only to say that Ickes's speech was "unworthy of answering."[37]

Unlike the hyperpartisan interior secretary, the new secretary of war, Henry Stimson, found much to praise in his fellow Republican's speech. It was "fine, brave and sensible," Stimson wrote, and had "gone far to hamstring the efforts of the little group of isolationists to play politics." Roosevelt's attorney general Robert Jackson was also kind. He was also probably correct in remarking that "no man could live up to the expectations that were aroused in the hearts of the people opposed to Roosevelt" after Willkie's remarkable nomination in Philadelphia. "They expected a messiah. Then Willkie got up at Elwood in August 1940 and made . . . a very ordinary campaign speech." But, ever the loyal Democrat, Jackson added that as Willkie's speech went "flatter and flatter," his own spirits flew higher and higher, and those of his Republican friends sank lower and lower. "The actor," Jackson concluded, "could not live up to the billing."[38]

Ten days after Willkie's address in Elwood, his running-mate, Senator Charles McNary, delivered his own acceptance speech at the Fair Grounds in Salem, Oregon. It was a bland and uninspiring performance, larded with such platitudes as "What we need in times like these is more democracy, not less" and "the Republican Party this year lifts the standard of hope." He spoke about the problems of farmers, endorsed federal development of hydroelectric power, and, mentioning the foreign crisis and the importance of preparedness, criticized the Roosevelt administration "for neglecting our defenses, both spiritual and material." The most notable feature of the address was that McNary pronounced the name of his running-mate only once—in the first sentence of his long talk when he affirmed his "loyalty to the candidate for president, the able, magnetic and forceful Wendell L. Willkie." After that, the magnetic and forceful Wendell Willkie simply disappeared. And just as worrisome to Republicans was McNary's announcement that he would make only four or five speeches that fall. The senator said that he would let Willkie "carry the ball."[39]

Two days later, on August 29, Henry Wallace gave his own acceptance speech to a crowd of seven thousand Democrats in the Des Moines Coliseum and, by radio, to Americans across the nation. Wallace spoke almost entirely about the world crisis, pronouncing the Nazi Führer's name so often— twenty-one times—that the *Chicago Daily Tribune* asked, "Who's he running against, Hitler?" But Wallace dwelt even more on Roosevelt—naming him twenty-two times—as the unique symbol of democracy around the world and especially in the stricken nations. His replacement, Wallace said, "even if it were by the most patriotic leadership that could be found, would cause Hitler to rejoice. I do not believe the American people will turn their backs on the man that Hitler wants to see defeated."[40]

"The last vestige of democracy is gone!" cried one listener—not because Wallace was suggesting that it would be unpatriotic for any candidate to dare to oppose his running-mate but rather because some radio stations carrying Wallace's speech cut off a football game between the College All-Stars and the Green Bay Packers. "The Democrats lost the football vote," grumbled another fan. "The guy's talking about Hitler. What do I care about Hitler? I want the football game!"[41]

Buffeted by the stinging criticism of his Elwood speech, Willkie vowed that he would avoid scripted radio addresses and instead exploit his ability to speak off-the-cuff in an informal, "down to earth" manner with ordinary folks. He decided that, when his campaign began in mid–September, he would board a special train and stump the country, stopping mostly in small towns and villages, carrying his gospel to "the common people" at the grass roots. Only one or two major speeches, he told reporters, would be read from a text and "two, perhaps only one" would be delivered over national radio hookups. Asked if he intended to chat over the radio without a prepared address, he replied, "Why, of course."[42] Or so he thought. Though he would make off-the-cuff remarks in some small towns, he would, in fact, make dozens of speeches at large rallies in major cities; his words would be carried live on nationwide radio, the texts released and printed in the nation's newspapers.

But four weeks lay between the August 17 acceptance address and Willkie's opening rally on September 16 in Kansas. He decided to spend that late-summer month with his wife, Edith, in Rushville, her hometown. By making that town—and a three-story brick house on loan to them—his temporary home and base of operations, he hoped to downplay the image of himself as a Wall Street insider and come across as—well, not exactly as a farmer. "There is one error I want to correct," he candidly told reporters, "this talk of being a Rush County farmer. I am purely a conversational farmer." Though he owned five farms there, he set the record straight. "I have never done a stroke of work on a Rush County farm in my life, and I hope I never have to."[43] During those weeks in Rushville, he told the newspapermen, he would make a few side trips but would give no important campaign talks—unless, he added, the president changed his mind and accepted his challenge to a series of debates.[44]

Life was slow and quiet in Rushville, and Willkie accomplished little there. "He rocked and talked on the front porch of the house on Harrison Street," wrote *Time*, "visited his temporary office over the Rexall Drug Store on Main Street, and, as casually as the postman, popped into the Lollis Hotel, where newsmen gathered."[45] The candidate's operations in Rushville were all improvised; he held press conferences in his mother-in-law's living room and scrambled to find enough chairs for all the reporters. Nor did he provide them with interesting news, forcing them to scrounge for stories. One day, the dispatch from Rushville in the *New York Times* was about a huge watermelon that someone had mysteriously placed on Willkie's front porch. Another day, he led a group of reporters on a tour of his farms and effused about the good life on the soil. "Why should any one with a few thousand dollars laid away invest in stocks and bonds while there is fine land to buy?" he asked, revealing his insensitivity to the plight of most Americans who, still reeling from the Depression, hardly had "a few thousand dollars" stashed away to buy land or stocks. The transition from Fifth Avenue to the Midwest did not come easily to Willkie. Posing for photographers, he shunned overalls for a dark business suit. To please his advisors, he dutifully attended church—but admitted to newsmen that he usually slept late on Sunday mornings. He is "the frankest talker in American politics," wrote reporter Damon Runyon.[46]

But frankness and indiscipline went hand in hand. By counting on his talent for speaking extemporaneously, the candidate did little to prepare himself for the rigors of the fall campaign. "The result was," Charles Halleck later said, "when we started out hardly any speeches were ready, hardly any."[47] Even though Willkie insisted that the election would be won by nine-tenths publicity and only one-tenth organization, many members of his team were appalled by the disorganization that had persisted from Colorado Springs to Rushville.

The Willkie campaign faced two other critically important challenges: the candidate needed to come up with a coherent, consistent, and rousing campaign message and he had to rally GOP leaders and their organizations behind him.

But what message, what strategy, would help him connect not only with the Republican base, including its Old Guard and isolationists, but also with moderate independents, anti-third-term Democrats, and first-time voters? His speech in Elwood illustrated the problem: he had agreed with so much of the president's internationalist and progressive agenda that, on the one hand, he alienated members of his own party, and, on the other, he seemed to be telling potential Democratic and independent converts that they could trust him to do the same as Roosevelt, only better.[48]

Willkie also needed to overcome his own disdain for party politics and his implicit decision to adopt a style of personal leadership rather than party leadership. Whether he was bragging about his own "amateur" status or describing his campaign as a "people's movement" or addressing delegates in Philadelphia as "you Republicans," he seemed content to run alone rather than with a well-organized party team behind him.[49]

This "merely personal campaign" was not sufficient, Walter Lippmann judged; the candidate needed the loyal and wholehearted support of the GOP organization to get results and win the election. "Crusades cannot be led by any one reclining in an easy chair on the veranda of a summer hotel," Lippmann scolded, "and popular movements cannot be put in cold storage for two months and then be set moving again." The conservative *Chicago Daily Tribune* also grumbled that the candidate was neglecting if not spurning his party. By swinging on his front porch in Rushville without actively seeking out the views, counsel, and support of GOP leaders, editorialized the *Tribune*, Willkie "may dynamite whatever unity is left in the Republican Party."[50]

Many Republican conservatives were indeed unenthusiastic about Willkie, and he displayed little interest in winning them over. He treated the Republican Party, in the words of historian James MacGregor Burns, "as an allied but somewhat alien power."[51] At the Broadmoor, for example, he had met with Thomas Dewey. His old rival pledged to campaign for him and even offered the assistance of several of his aides, including his pollster and his economic advisor. But when Dewey peppered him with advice about campaigning, Willkie dispensed with charm and snapped, "Tom, since when did the party make you the nominee?"[52] In early July, Willkie high-mindedly announced that he would reward no one with government jobs in exchange for support or campaign contributions. Though he was discarding the patronage system that was the glue of party politics, he said that he relished the prospect of entering the White House "completely unfettered." But in early September, he would backtrack, assuring GOP leaders who came to meet with him in Rushville that a Willkie administration would not deprive them of the power of patronage.[53]

If conservative Republicans were ambivalent about Willkie because they saw him as a progressive and an interventionist, moderates were ambivalent about him because they wanted to see more of that progressivism and interventionism. Willkie should stop this "cracker-barrel dawdling," grumbled Henry Luce. "Running for president may be fun for Mr. Willkie, but it's a goddamn serious thing for 130 million Americans and maybe for the world." On economic issues, Luce wanted more nerve from Willkie. The candidate had not "disavowed the stupid, idle-rich, backward-looking economic royalists—all the people whom I really hate worse than Roosevelt," Luce told Russell Davenport in the summer of 1940. And Luce wanted more guts from Willkie on foreign policy, too. "America will never be ready for any war," the publisher warned, "until she makes up her mind that *there is going to be a war.*" Whereas he criticized Roosevelt for willful blindness to the horrifying reality in Europe, he did not see Willkie either as a "real fighter—a Republican fighter." Neither candidate, he judged, was honest and frank with the

American people. "Ten billions for defense," Luce wrote, "and not one word for courage?"[54]

While Ickes pummeled Willkie and Republicans carped about their candidate and while both Roosevelt's and Willkie's campaigns languished in the summer heat, Alfred Hitchcock stepped forward with a powerful reminder of just what was at stake in this election. "Ever been in Europe?" a newspaper publisher asked his flippant, lackadaisical reporter, Johnny Jones, played by Joel McCrea, in the beginning of Hitchcock's gripping new movie, *Foreign Correspondent*.[55]

"No."

"What's your opinion of the present European crisis, Mr. Jones?"

"What crisis?"

"I'm referring to the impending war, Mr. Jones."

"Oh that! Well, to tell you the truth, I haven't given it much thought."

"You don't keep up with our foreign news, do you? How would you like to cover the biggest story in the world today?"

"Give me an expense account and I'll cover anything."

"You'll get an expense account. What Europe needs is a fresh, unused mind. You think you can dig up some news in Europe?"

"I'll be happy to try, Sir."

After suspenseful encounters with fifth columnists in Dutch windmills and with assassins on the steps of the Peace Palace in Amsterdam, Joel McCrea winds up in London as German bombers are wreaking night-long destruction on the city. Curiously, *Foreign Correspondent* opened on August 16, but the bombing of London did not begin until August 22. That June, after production ended in Hollywood, Hitchcock had returned to his native England, where he found people in fact anxiously expecting Nazi bombing to begin shortly. Quickly he decided to add a final scene to the movie and asked the Academy Award–winning screenwriter Ben Hecht to draft it. In that last scene, Johnny Jones, no longer an insouciant, detached reporter, seriously addresses Americans on a radio hookup from London, a city under terrifying siege.[56]

"Hello America," he grimly says to his radio audience back home, reminiscent of radio journalist Edward R. Murrow's dramatic transatlantic broadcasts that had debuted in June.[57] "I've been watching a part of the world being blown to pieces. A part of the world as nice as Vermont, Ohio, Virginia and California and Illinois. I've seen things that make the history of savages read like Pollyanna legends. All that noise you hear isn't static. It's death coming to London. Yes, they're coming here now. You can hear the bombs falling on the streets and the homes. This is a big story. You're part of it. It's too late to do anything here except stand in the dark and let them come. It's as if the lights were out everywhere except in America. Keep those lights burning. Cover them with steel, ring them with guns, build a canopy of battleships and bombing planes around them. Hello America. Hang on to your lights. They're the only lights left in the world."

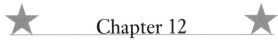

Chapter 12

An Army of Citizen Soldiers

Topping Roosevelt's list of national priorities in the spring of 1940 was military preparedness, beginning with an increase in the production of weapons, planes, ships, and other war matériel. But what about a ready army and ready soldiers? In early 1940, the regular army and the National Guard numbered at best five hundred thousand troops, compared to several million in Germany.[1]

"Dear Grennie, I see no reason why [you] should not advocate military training," FDR wrote on May 18 to his 57-year-old Harvard friend Grenville Clark. But Roosevelt was in fact ambivalent about Clark's proposal for compulsory military service. The president told him that he favored "universal service of some kind so that every able-bodied man and woman would fit into his or her place." With America not yet involved in the war in Europe, he could not envisage a compulsory program devoted exclusively to military training. And it was also a question, as he wrote to Clark, of "what one can get from the Congress." But Clark persisted. When he sought a meeting with the president a few weeks later to discuss military service again, a cautious Roosevelt firmly declined. "The answer is NO," FDR told his aide Pa Watson. "The time is not ripe yet—put it off until a little later."[2]

On the subject of compulsory military service, the president wavered, shifted, and hedged—especially in public. In his address to Congress on May 16, 1940, Roosevelt described the ominous developments in Europe and called for vast new appropriations for defense—but made no mention of increasing military manpower. On the contrary, he simply expressed his "confidence in our officers and men."[3] In a fireside chat ten days later, he voiced satisfaction that the number of enlisted men in the army had doubled since 1933. And at a press conference on May 28, he assured reporters that "we are *not* talking at the present time about a draft system, either to draft men or women or money or all three."[4] In a message to Congress later that week, he inched slightly forward, suggesting a system of "national service" that was not confined to the military. But he offered few details beyond the statement that the nation's defense required the immediate training of young people "for employment in industry and in service in the Army and Navy."[5] He made no mention of compulsory military service.

Eleanor Roosevelt, however, did just that. In her "My Day" newspaper column of July 11, she heaped scorn upon the 240 "educators" who had signed a petition published in newspapers the previous day opposing military conscription. They were talking about "the world of a year ago, not the world as it is today," she wrote. "Above all, we should accept the fact that democracy requires service from each and every one of us, not just from those who happen to want to volunteer."[6]

For his part, the president was less forthright. Only after his army chief of staff, General Marshall, testified in Congress on June 4 about the "tragic shortage" of manpower in the army and after newspapers criticized the White House for its "total silence" on that essential question did Roosevelt give the nod to a draft. At his press conference on June 7, he responded favorably to a *New York Times* editorial outlining a system of compulsory military service. Though he declined to commit himself to the plan, he stated that he "liked it."[7]

Oops. Had he spoken too freely? Ten days later on June 18, he backtracked. He had not meant to "imply that there should be compulsory military training for every boy in this country," he told the reporters that morning. "Perhaps I should not have spoken so fast," he hedged. He had used the word "military" in a broad sense, he explained, claiming that he meant to refer to *all* facets of defense.[8]

Conceding that the country was heading to "some form of universal government service," he called for an approach that would not only train men for the army and navy but also create one cadre of uniformed communications and aviation technicians and another of non-uniformed technicians engaged in war production.[9] What about the girls? one reporter asked. Yes, women should be included, Roosevelt agreed. A year of public service would have a salutary effect on the nation's morale, he said, adding with a smile that the reporters might also toughen themselves up in a Civilian Conservation Corps camp. Was he changing his policy from neutrality to belligerency? a reporter asked. He was too busy to open his thesaurus, the president laughingly replied.

The very next day, another shift. This time, Steve Early, the president's press secretary, announced that the administration's plan to train two million young people was for vocational "peacetime training in which military preparedness would have *no part.*"[10]

In that election year, FDR was acutely sensitive to public opinion. "Governments, such as ours," he wrote in May, "can only move in keeping with the thought and will of the great majority of our people." But was he lagging behind majority opinion? In June, while he was still toying with a concept of "national service" that deemphasized military training, pollster George Gallup reported a "spectacular rise" in the number of Americans favoring compulsory military service for young men, with 64 percent of Americans nationwide supporting a draft. But that spring, the president remained "apathetic" on the subject of a draft, historians J. Garry Clifford and Samuel Spencer noted in their book, *The First Peacetime Draft.* In the months leading up to the Democratic National Convention, Roosevelt's strategy was to let others take the lead on selective service.[11]

First to lead was Grenville Clark. A lieutenant colonel in World War I, a Republican, and a Wall Street lawyer, Clark had been a casual friend of FDR's for decades. They had both grown up in the same elite New York circles, attended Harvard, and served together as young law clerks in 1907. Thirty years later, they were photographed in their top hats, sitting near each other, under a steady drizzle, at ceremonies in Cambridge commemorating Harvard's three hundredth anniversary.[12]

On May 8, 1940, Clark met with Colonel Henry Stimson, Frank Knox, Judge Robert Patterson, and a few other middle-aged friends at the Harvard Club. They were all members of the "Plattsburg Movement," a group of upper-class, well-educated pace-setters who had initiated a voluntary program in 1915 that trained one hundred thousand men for military service. Ultimately the Plattsburg Movement provided 80 percent of all the officers who commanded American combat troops in World War I. Now, with the group reconstituting itself as the nation faced the possibility of another war, the main topic on their agenda was national compulsory military training and service. Meeting for a second time on May 19—the same evening that Charles Lindbergh gave his tough-talking radio speech, ridiculing the "hysterical chatter of calamity and invasion"—Clark and his friends agreed on a strategy for selling their proposal to Congress. And thanks to the help of one of their members, Julius Ochs Adler, the vice president and general manager of the *New York Times*, their initiative received front-page coverage.[13]

Clark also discussed his plan with George Marshall. Though the army chief of staff declined to lend his official support to Clark's movement, he privately directed members of his staff to help Clark draft his proposal.[14] And within a few weeks, Marshall came fully on board. "Now, you veterans know," the general underscored at a June 19 meeting of the Veterans of Foreign Wars, "that an army—a large army—can not be recruited, equipped and trained overnight. It is a long and tedious process. We must get down to hard pan and carry out our preparations without vacillations or confusion."[15]

While many members of Congress, though sympathetic, would not commit themselves to Clark's proposal, he did find two who were willing to affix their names to the Selective Service Training bill. On June 20, the same day that the president announced the appointments of Stimson and Knox to his cabinet and two days before the surrender of France, Nebraska's Edward Burke introduced Clark's bill on the Senate floor, and the following day, James Wadsworth of New York introduced the same bill in the House. Clark and the Plattsburg group "scored by getting their proposal before Congress at a crucial moment," wrote historians Clifford and Spencer.[16]

Ironically, neither Burke, a Democrat, nor Wadsworth, a Republican, was an FDR ally. On the New Deal, Burke had a mixed record; he had supported the Social Security Act but opposed the Wagner Act, and recently he had voted against the president on court-packing and on a bill for reorganizing the executive branch of government. In April 1940, he lost his primary election and would soon bolt the Democratic Party and support Willkie. But the Nebraska senator had long been a stout interventionist who injected a dose of morality into foreign policy, and on the draft he was a democrat with a small "d." "One of the main objects of the bill," Burke said, "is our desire to have this country show the world that its citizens feel they have a duty to their country. No voluntary enlistment program can do the same thing." In the fall of 1939, as the Senate debated the arms embargo, he had pleaded for its repeal. "There is a time for compromise, for yielding, for appeasement," he stated. "That hour is past. We need a rebaptism in the faith and the courage of our fathers."[17]

Wadsworth, a New York Republican who, since 1915, had served in the Senate and then in the House of Representatives, was a staunch conservative, one of only thirty-three House members to oppose the Social Security Act in 1935 and one of eighty-nine to vote against the Fair Labor Standards Act. But he was also a resolute supporter of a ready army and had helped draft and promote passage of the National Defense Act of 1920, establishing a peacetime army consisting of a regular professional army, a national guard, and civilian reserves. In May 1940 he warned against repeating an old pattern of delay. "Our trouble has always been that we have waited and waited and postponed and postponed," he said, "until all of a sudden we woke up and found ourselves unprepared."

FDR would not have chosen these two New Deal foes to lead the charge for military preparedness, but the British, for their part, were ecstatic. "The change in American thinking since May 10th has been overwhelming," Lord Lothian, the British ambassador to Washington, wrote home on July 1.[18]

But would the Burke-Wadsworth bill pass in Congress? It was a long shot in this election year, said James Byrnes, unless "his Excellency"—as he called FDR—gave it his full support. Without that, Byrnes felt, military conscription did not stand "a Chinaman's chance."[19] And the president was not yet prepared to commit himself, placing him at odds with Henry Stimson, his brand-new secretary of war. At his press conference on July 9, Roosevelt would say only that he was mulling over the bill as well as a proposal of his own that included compulsory nonmilitary as well as military service for young men and women.

In early July, one of the first people to testify in favor of Burke-Wadsworth before the Senate Military Affairs Committee was Grenville Clark. He pointed out that a voluntary system was not only inadequate but also undemocratic and unfair and that only compulsory service would preserve the nation's economic life, institutions, "and even our physical integrity." Sharply parting ways with the president, Clark emphasized that the bill under consideration contemplated no training for anything but military purposes—"*nothing whatever.*"[20]

Then it was Army Chief of Staff George Marshall's turn. "Let General Marshall, and only General Marshall, do all the testifying," Morgenthau had written to Roosevelt in a succinct message earlier that spring. The general would be a strong and articulate advocate for military preparedness, Morgenthau wrote; he was an orderly, careful thinker—and on party politics not only was he neutral, he had never even voted. "My father was a Democrat, my mother a Republican, and I am an Episcopalian," Marshall once said. Marshall spoke before the Senate and House Military Affairs Committees at fifteen separate hearings on the Selective Service Training bill. At one session, on July 12, he stated categorically that "we must have more men as quickly as possible." The need for compulsory service was "hardly debatable." At another hearing, he was asked if Burke-Wadsworth would mean a "peacetime" draft. "If you will pardon me," Marshall said, "I think it is a time of peril."[21]

A seasoned expert in dealing with Congress, Marshall appeared in a civilian business suit at the hearings, perceptively opting for a nonmilitarist and nonconfrontational image. He also knew how to steer clear of the clash between isolationists and interventionists: he always argued that military preparation was key for defending the American continent and deterring aggressors. "Whereas presidential proposals were attacked as partisan and manipulative," wrote military historian and Marshall biographer Mark Stoler, "almost anything suggested or supported by the chief of staff came to be seen as in the national interest. . . . He deliberately avoided discussion of all political issues that could be considered partisan and consistently phrased his arguments in terms of managerial objectivity and nonpartisan national security."[22]

Secretary of War Stimson also testified before the House Military Affairs Committee, framing his support for the draft as an obviously necessary response to an extraordinarily dangerous world situation. "I have seen the forces of lawlessness gather force like a prairie fire growing nearer and nearer to our country," he said. When one committee member suggested that many people feared that a draft would hasten the nation into war, Stimson replied, "I think just the opposite. I think it will make others hesitate to attack us." Upon hearing a first-term Republican representative from Illinois muse aloud that "somehow it has not been fixed in my mind that this selective service is necessary," Stimson expressed his astonishment. "I am surprised," he said, "that any one who has read . . . of the lawlessness of the world by which we are surrounded, even if only in press accounts, does not realize we live in a world more dangerous to us than ever before."[23]

And Roosevelt? Where did he stand? A master of political timing, he would not make his position clear until after the Democratic Convention. His first hurdle at the convention was to block an anticonscription plank in the party platform. The second hurdle was to secure the nomination. Only then, after he himself had been "drafted" by his party into running for a third term, would it be politic for him to speak about sacrifice, service, and a military draft. "Today," FDR said in his acceptance speech to the convention on July 18, "all private plans, all private lives, have been in a sense repealed by an overriding public danger." Referring to military service, he remarked that "most right-thinking persons are agreed that some form of selection by draft is as necessary and fair today as it was in 1917 and 1918."[24] Now he and millions of young men were in the same position, he said. They were all obliged to do their duty and serve their country.

On Thursday, August 1, the thermometer in Washington, D.C., climbed to 100 degrees. These were the dog days of summer. But a thousand people showed up at the Raleigh Hotel for an antidraft rally, sponsored by the Youth Committee Against War, to listen to socialist Norman Thomas and Senators Burton Wheeler, Rush Holt, and Gerald Nye denounce compulsory military service. "We can and are winning this fight on conscription," Holt declared. "Show me a dictatorship," he shouted, "and I'll show you conscription!" After he charged that Secretary of War Stimson had been "war-mongering" for twenty years, a World War I marine sergeant rushed the speakers' platform and scuffled with Holt and Nye. "Throw him out!" people yelled. After order was restored, Senator Nye echoed Holt, insisting that conscription was "a move to shanghai American youth into totalitarianism and militarism." The need for a draft was a "fiction," offered Norman Thomas, who supported a purely volunteer system. It was a strange idea for a socialist who believed in equal rights, commented columnist Ernest Lindley, to hire somebody else to do the job.[25]

Over the summer, isolationist organizations of every stripe—from the Young Communist League to the German-American Bund—mobilized their members in opposition to Burke-Wadsworth, their extremist arguments drowning out more moderate voices of opposition, like those of the Quakers.[26] Labor leader John L. Lewis weighed in, equating the draft with dictatorship and fascism. Not to be left out, Father Coughlin labeled Burke-Wadsworth a "communist plot" inspired by "a Hitlerized president and his American Gestapo." Playing a lesser role in the debate, Charles Lindbergh had sternly warned that past June that, since America was "not a military nation," it could overcome that heavy disadvantage only by "the building of a tremendous armed force and the establishment of a dictatorial government." Though he kept "mum" on the subject of conscription, wrote *Life* magazine in early August, "his championing of Nazi appeasement is the best possible anti-conscription propaganda."[27]

All summer, denunciations of a peacetime draft poured into Congress. "Keep letters and wires coming," wrote Senators Burton Wheeler and Hiram Johnson to an isolationist activist. "They are having tremendous effect . . . running 100–1 or 70–1 against the bill." Even Democratic congressman Adolph Sabath of Illinois, the chairman of the House Rules Committee, felt the sting of the antidraft movement and urged Roosevelt on August 2—the day the president came out in support of a compulsory universal military service draft at a press conference—"to state that the Burke Wadsworth bill is not your bill."[28]

But all those anticonscription letters in fact stood in sharp contrast to the true feelings of the majority of Americans. A July 28 Gallup poll showed that 67 percent of Americans were in favor of compulsory military training, up from 50 percent in May and 64 percent in June; by August 11, 71 percent of Americans supported conscription. Even Republicans in that August poll favored the draft by 60 percent—and so did 71 percent of union members, despite the vociferous opposition of Lewis and AFL president William Green.[29]

There was a feeling that the president was "not very hot" about the conscription bill, one reporter remarked to the president at a White House press conference on August 2. Well, it depended on which paper people read, FDR replied. After alluding to the contradictory editorials in the newspapers that morning—some demanding action ("quick-quick-quick") and others recommending delay ("My Lord! why rush this thing?"), he zeroed in on the bottom line. "You cannot get a sufficiently trained force," he stated, "by just passing an Act of Congress when war breaks out, and you cannot get it by the mere volunteer system. . . . I not only hope, but I definitely believe, that the Congress is going to do something about it, because it is very important for our national defense."

"There is a very quotable sentence right there, if you will permit it," said one hopeful reporter.

"What is it?" asked the president.

"That you are distinctly in favor of a selective training bill . . ."

"And consider it essential to adequate national defense," added the president, finishing the reporter's sentence. "Quote that."

"Ought women to be trained in service for their country?" another reporter asked.

"Not in legislation at the present time." Roosevelt did not specifically mention Burke-Wadsworth, but his meaning was perfectly clear. The bill had his blessing, even though, as he told Eleanor three days later, he feared that his support for a draft could lead to "political disaster" in the fall.[30]

The president turned up the heat on Congress, too. He had recently received a letter from Vic Donahey, a first-term Democratic senator from Ohio, informing him that the draft would be a "political disaster" in Ohio and that the senator felt compelled to vote against it. On August 3, Roosevelt replied to Donahey—and sent copies of his letter to Alben Barkley and Jimmy Byrnes. "I would be derelict in my duty if I did not tell the American people of the real danger which confronts them at the present time," FDR wrote. He implored Donahey to think only of the safety of the nation and banish "political considerations" from his mind.[31] Donahey would vote against the draft and would also decline to run for reelection. His Senate seat would be taken over by Harold Burton, a Republican supporter of the draft whom Truman would appoint to the Supreme Court in 1945.

Mostly it was Grenville Clark and his colleagues who were drumming up support for Burke-Wadsworth from behind the scenes, tirelessly working the House and Senate. They "practically wore out shoe leather tracking down and buttonholing Senators and Representatives," commented Lieutenant Colonel Lewis Hershey, the executive secretary of the joint army and navy selective service committee.[32]

On August 5, when senators would have preferred to be on vacation rather than stuck in the sweltering Capitol, they began debate on Burke-Wadsworth. Well, not exactly debate.

"Liar," "rat," "slacker," were among the slurs hurled across the chamber floor. Rush Holt, on his way out after losing in the Democratic primary in West Virginia, got into a shouting match with Sherman Minton of Indiana, a staunch New Deal loyalist who would later serve on the Supreme Court. Holt began his long diatribe by denouncing conscription as a doctrine that came from foreign shores and that was "incubated in the banks and law firms of Wall Street." He then went on to attack Clark, Stimson, and the *New York Times*. Finally Senator Minton spoke up. "I am sick and tired and impatient of being lectured by a member of a slacker family," Minton said. He reminded senators that, while he himself was serving in France in 1917 and 1918, Holt's father "was preaching that people should not raise any food to send to me and my comrades who were fighting for this country in France. The father of the senator from West Virginia sent his eldest son Matthew, who was eligible for service, to hide away in South America to avoid the draft." Now Holt turned his rage against Minton. There was no "dirty, filthy, low job" that the Roosevelt administration could not get "the senator from Indiana to do," Holt wildly charged. Majority leader Barkley intervened, chastising Holt for violating Senate rules by impugning Minton's motives.[33]

Aside from the personal aspersions, anticonscription senators from both parties repeated three main arguments: the United States faced no threat from abroad; compulsory military service would destroy American democracy; and a voluntary system was sufficient.

With his straggly hair and wearing the steel-rimmed glasses that gave him a menacing air, Burton Wheeler hammered the draft, predicting that it would "slit the throat of the last democracy still living!" Compulsory military service, he warned, would result in "a country where robbery and murder will run riot." A peacetime draft in 1940 would be "a stepping-stone toward the destruction of everything we have been fighting to preserve," agreed Nevada's Pat McCarran. Robert Taft prophesied that conscription "would lead directly to totalitarianism." He and Vandenberg blamed the president for not giving a "ringing call for volunteers." Senator Bennett Champ Clark considered the whole proposal a sham response to a manufactured emergency, designed to "take advantage of the hysteria which is now sweeping over the country." And looking into his crystal ball, Senator Ernest Lundeen announced that "if Japan ever fights America, it will not be in the Hawaiian region . . . the Japanese are too clever to come over and tackle us here."[34]

On the other side, Tom Connally of Texas dismissed the idea of a volunteer force, pointing out that Ohio, Montana, and Michigan, the home states of Taft, Wheeler, and Vandenberg, had the poorest enlistment records in the country.[35] Also pitching in to support compulsory service, Roosevelt's longstanding foe Millard Tydings of Maryland, a conservative anti–New Deal Democrat, said, to the applause of the spectators in the Senate galleries, "I would rather have it and not need it than need it and not have it." Seconding that message, Tennessee's Arthur Stewart warned his fellow senators against acting like "Chamberlains of America."[36]

In mid-August, some commentators estimated that forty-one Senate Democrats and eight Republicans supported the draft and sixteen remained uncommitted. Scrambling for a way to block passage of the bill, opponents tried to divide southern and northern Democrats by introducing an amendment to end racial discrimination in the military; when that failed, they focused on watering down Burke-Wadsworth with a host of other amendments, from a ban on beginning the draft until Congress issued a declaration of war to an amendment, proposed by Connecticut's senator Francis Maloney, that would postpone the draft until the end of the year, to see if enough volunteers signed up. If they did not, then on January 1, the president would be authorized to institute the draft. The Maloney amendment became the rallying point for opponents of the draft. Unless the Roosevelt administration revved up its engines, wrote a *New York Times* reporter, the Maloney amendment was "in the bag."[37]

As bombs rained down on English cities that August, interventionists fought any postponement of the draft. "All this talk of wait, wait, wait, wait, and wait," bristled Henry Stimson, "and we're confronted with an enemy who does not wait."[38]

In August, the president had to deal with another urgent issue: military aid for Great Britain. Since June, Churchill had been pleading for American warships; it was "a matter of life or death," he wrote to Roosevelt. In July he repeated that the key to British survival in the next few months was the transfer of fifty or sixty old destroyers to Britain. "In the long history of the world this is the thing to do *now*," Churchill implored. The president wanted to help, but for weeks he hesitated. He knew that the isolationists in the Senate and House were waiting to axe any such aid to Britain. In late June, Congress had forbidden the sale of military supplies unless army and navy chiefs deemed them unessential to the national defense, and naval officers had indeed testified about the destroyers' potential value to the U.S. Navy. Roosevelt moreover had recently told Jim Farley that he put Britain's chances of holding out at about one in three, and he as well as navy commanders feared that, if Britain fell, the American warships would be lost to Germany.[39]

For several weeks, a novel plan for a way to provide Britain with those ships had been percolating in interventionist circles. In July, when Henry Luce dined at the White House, he suggested to Roosevelt that the United States might consider supplying destroyers to Great Britain in exchange for military bases in Newfoundland, Bermuda, Jamaica, St. Lucia, Trinidad, Antigua, and British Guiana. In its next issue, *Time* ran an unusually long article that pointed out the vital importance of Caribbean bases, especially for defending the strategically crucial Panama Canal.[40]

In early August, Secretary Knox, with Roosevelt's approval, presented the idea of an exchange of destroyers for bases to the British ambassador, Lord Lothian. "We realize your situation and we want to help," Knox told Lothian. He explained to the ambassador that in order to get a bill through Congress, there had to be some element of reciprocity. "England has naval bases along the Atlantic Coast that are very essential to our own defense," Knox said. "I know how reluctant England would be to surrender sovereignty over these lands. . . . But would England consider transferring to the United States . . . such land for naval and air bases as we might need for our own fleet?" Lothian could not commit his government to such an exchange and sent a cable to Churchill that night.[41]

But before signing any deal with Britain, Roosevelt needed support in Congress. "Honestly, Dave, these islands are of the utmost importance to our national defense," Roosevelt wrote to David Walsh, chairman of the Senate Naval Affairs Committee. "I am absolutely certain that this particular deal will not get us into war and, incidentally, that we are not going into war anyway unless Germany wishes to attack us." Though Walsh refrained from publicly attacking FDR's plan, he remained skittish. "I always favored the obtaining of naval and air defense bases in the Western Hemisphere," he told reporters, but underscored his fear that the transfer of ships to Britain could have "serious consequences."[42]

The president also wanted bipartisan cover for the deal, and he asked William Allen White to see if he could get Wendell Willkie's approval. But Willkie demurred. His "general views" on foreign policy were already known, he told White, and he declined to make any commitments about "specific executive or legislative proposals." White wrote to FDR that there weren't "two bits of difference" between the two candidates and regretted that the GOP candidate was unwilling to make a public statement.[43] Even Thomas Dewey had tried serving as an intermediary. Visiting Willkie at the Broadmoor, Dewey offered to come out in support of the deal if that would make it easier for him to endorse it, too. But Willkie, apparently under pressure from isolationists like Hoover, tartly replied that he did not need Dewey's help.[44]

As the Battle of Britain grew ever more critical and intense, the commander in chief acted—courageously, unilaterally, and peremptorily. On August 13, Roosevelt and his cabinet decided to bypass Congress and simply furnish Great Britain immediately with at least fifty destroyers and other war matériel. In exchange, Churchill had agreed to grant the United States a ninety-nine-year lease "free from all rent" for British naval and air bases in Newfoundland, Bermuda, and the Caribbean.[45] At his press conference on August 16, Roosevelt announced that negotiations were under way to finalize the exchange.

The following day, August 17, Willkie accepted his party's nomination in his speech in Elwood. Although the previous week he had stated that it was not "appropriate" for him to enter into "advance commitments" like the destroyers-for-bases exchange, in Elwood he quoted FDR's pledge in Charlottesville to "extend to the opponents of force the material resources of this nation" and remarked that he was in agreement with the president's proposals "as I understand them." But if he was vague and inconsistent about the destroyers deal, at least there was no doubt in his mind which way to go on the subject of compulsory military service. Undeterred by Joe Martin's warning that conscription was "Roosevelt's responsibility not yours" and that he should "go slow on this thing," Willkie listened instead to Grenville Clark, who urged him to make a clear statement in favor of a draft "with no weasel words."[46]

"We must not shirk the necessity of preparing our sons to take care of themselves in case the defense of America leads to war," Willkie declared in Elwood. "I cannot ask the American people to put their faith in me without recording my conviction that some form of selective service is the only democratic way to secure the trained and competent manpower we need for national defense." A principled Willkie stated that compulsory conscription, unlike a volunteer system, was "the most democratic way of creating an army" and would oblige "the sons of the rich as well as the sons of the poor and all others" to serve. His endorsement of the draft, pronounced a relieved Henry Stimson, was "a godsend."[47] Though Robert Taft declared himself "satisfied" because, as he explained, Willkie had not used the word "compulsory," another isolationist, California's Hiram Johnson, correctly grasped that Willkie's speech "broke the back of the opposition to the conscription law. He slapped every one of us . . . who were thinking American and acting American." Willkie's support for selective service not only rallied many people to Burke-Wadsworth but, equally important, removed compulsory service as a divisive campaign issue.[48]

On Saturday, August 17, the day of Willkie's acceptance speech in Indiana, Franklin Roosevelt traveled to a remote spot in New York, near the Canadian border, to meet with the Canadian prime minister William Mackenzie King. After the two leaders discussed a plan of cooperative action for hemispheric defense, the president told reporters that the United States would never passively stand by and see Canada threatened. Almost with "tears in his eyes," Stimson wrote later in his diary, the Canadian leader thanked Roosevelt for his "most tremendous encouragement to the morale of Great Britain and Canada."[49] In private, Roosevelt and Mackenzie King also discussed the critical importance of selective service, and when the text of Willkie's Elwood speech and his words of support for selective service came through on the president's wire, they were elated. FDR in fact had been hoping that Willkie would voice support for compulsory military service and had tried unsuccessfully to arrange a meeting with him two days before his nomination in Philadelphia and later that month.

Broaching the subject of American politics, the prime minister asked the president what he thought his chances were in the upcoming election. FDR replied that he thought his chances were "very good" unless peace were made in Europe, which would leave him out on a limb; if the nation entered a period of "reconstruction," he said, Americans might seek a businessman in the White House. Still, the president joked that he and the prime minister had stolen "half the show" that day from Willkie.[50] In reality, they stole less than half, because, on the front page of the next day's *New York Times*, the headline "U.S.-Canada Ties Welded by President and Premier" was sandwiched in between two larger and more eye-catching headlines: "WILLKIE

FOR DRAFT TRAINING" and "R.A.F. BOMBS BIG NAZI PLANTS; RAIDS ON ENGLAND RENEWED."

In late August, with the debates on selective service in Congress approaching their end and with the possibility that the Maloney amendment would pass, Julius Ochs Adler, the general manager of the *New York Times*, suggested to Roosevelt that it was time for him, too, to take a strong stand. "Have someone ask me at my next conference," the president replied, welcoming a planted question.[51]

On Friday, August 23, the president met with reporters. "Just plain ain't no news," he said as the press conference began. Right on cue, *Times* reporter Charles Hurd posed the first question.

"Mr. President, would you care to comment on the wisdom of this Senate proposition to postpone conscription to January first and give the volunteer system a further trial?"

The reply was quick and strong. "Personally, I am absolutely opposed to the postponement because it means in these days—and we all know what the world situation is—nearly a year of delay." Time was of the essence, he underscored. "If we put off increasing the Army to its definite needs, until sometime next spring, it is going to put off the whole defense program, as a whole about a year." The "gist" of the matter, he said, was that he wanted the Burke-Wadsworth legislation passed right away. It had been introduced in June, he reminded reporters, and "they are still talking. . . . That is why I am asking for action now." Indeed, members of Congress talked and talked—and on the day after the president's press conference, they defeated majority leader Barkley's motion to cut off Senate debate.[52] At such a politically sensitive moment— the beginning of the election season—Roosevelt's firm statement demonstrated the courage to lead.

On August 26, Roosevelt corresponded with an Illinois newspaper editor who was worried that selective service might harm the president's chances for reelection. FDR shared that doubt, he wrote, but added that "there are some occasions in the national history where leaders have to move for the preservation of American liberties and not just drift with what may or may not be a political doubt of the moment." That same day, at a press conference, Wendell Willkie emphasized to reporters that his comments at Elwood were a definite endorsement of *immediate* conscription and pointed out that some opponents of the draft had attempted to distort his position. "Any interpretation of my stand on the conscription bill that holds I am for its passage at some time other than *now* is erroneous."[53]

But could Willkie speak for GOP senators? In fact, many of them were backing and empowering the Democratic insurgents—Wheeler, Clark, Holt, Walsh, McCarran, Gillette, and others—in their ferocious opposition to the draft. More than half the Republicans in the Senate and two thirds in the House would ultimately vote against conscription. Though Willkie's running-mate, Senator Charles McNary, was in favor of the draft, he remained silent on the issue and chose not to participate in the Senate debate. People wondered if Willkie could lead the country when he seemed unable to lead his own party. If elected, commented Walter Lippmann in his column on August 27, Willkie would be a "president without a party."[54]

As the summer weeks drew to an end, the debate limped on. More amendments were proposed—among them an important one. Senators Richard Russell of Georgia and John Overton of Louisiana proposed giving the president the authority to seize any industrial plant whose owner refused to accept government defense contracts. Russell argued that no industry should shirk cooperation and participation in the nation's defense program while the government was drafting young men to serve for a dollar a day. The president agreed. "The principle of eminent domain or eminent use," Roosevelt said in a speech to the Teamsters Union in early September, "is as old as democratic government itself." It would be a rare occurrence for a plant owner to refuse to aid in the munitions and other defense requirements of the nation, he said, but if such a case did arise, "the Government cannot stand by, helpless in its efforts to arm and defend itself. No business is above government."[55]

But now Willkie curiously took the opposite stance. He decided to impugn the Russell-Overton amendment for "sovietizing" American industry and handing over to the national government "absolute and arbitrary control over virtually our entire economic system." It was just a "catch phrase," he said, to compare conscription of wealth and industry with the conscription of men. Willkie's opposition to Russell-Overton was a timely gift to Democrats; now they had the green light to hammer him for being partial to big business—willing to conscript boys but not the men of wealth and power who controlled American industry. Willkie's stand on the Russell-Overton amendment also posed a problem for him with Senate Republicans who were evenly split on it. Interestingly, conservatives like Vandenberg who objected to the conscription of men were in favor of the conscription of industry. "Property cannot claim a sanctity which is refused to human life," the Michigan senator said. Exacerbating the rift in the GOP by challenging Willkie's personalistic leadership, the conservative *Chicago Daily Tribune* accused the Republican nominee of attempting to run the party "like a corporation head handing down orders to subordinates. On questions of policy he asks neither advice nor counsel."[56]

Hardly a week after Willkie slammed Russell-Overton, he had to backtrack. The reason? Several newspapers pointed out that the Republican platform of 1932 had explicitly and presciently approved an act just like Russell-Overton. "We believe that in time of war," that platform read, "every material resource in the nation should bear its proportionate share of the burdens occasioned by the public need and that it is a duty of government to perfect plans in time of peace whereby this objective may be attained in war." Willkie was reduced to saying that his earlier position had been misunderstood, painfully explaining that he favored emergency conscription of industry but not through "the capricious determination of one man."[57]

On August 28, the same day that it was proposed, the Russell-Overton amendment quickly passed in the Senate by a vote of 69 to 16—with 9 Republicans voting for it and 8 against. The Maloney amendment went down, 50 senators voting against and 35 in favor. But most important, the Senate passed Burke-Wadsworth as amended by a vote of 58 to 31—with Republicans again evenly split.[58] That day, a front-page headline in the *New York Times* announced "2 LONDON ATTACKS; Nazis Strike at 20 Cities." "Every time Hitler bombed London we got another couple of votes," said Lieutenant Colonel Lewis Hershey, delighted at the outcome.[59] It remained to be seen how the House would vote the following week.

On September 3, during a tour of defense plants, President Roosevelt held a press conference aboard his private train. Squeezing into the tiny vestibule of his car, reporters listened to him announce that the exchange of destroyers for bases was official and finalized. Now the two English-speaking democracies were bound tightly together.[60]

Churchill had wanted to announce the leasing of bases to America as a spontaneous gesture of friendship, but a pragmatic Roosevelt publicly framed the deal as a shrewd Yankee bargain. The United States acquired eight valuable British bases in the Western Hemisphere—some as outright "gifts," others with ninety-nine-year leases. In exchange Britain received fifty World War I vintage destroyers. Roosevelt had also insisted on a public commitment from Churchill that, if Britain were forced to surrender to the Nazis, the British fleet would be sent abroad "for the defence of other parts of the Empire."[61]

But what about Congress? a reporter asked. Did the exchange require Senate ratification? "It is all over; it is all done," Roosevelt snapped. There was nothing more to discuss. Indeed, he had bypassed Congress—but he had the approval of Justice Felix Frankfurter and Attorney General Robert Jackson, who wrote a memo citing the Supreme Court's 1936 decision in *United States v. Curtiss-Wright*, which recognized the exclusive power of the president in international affairs.[62]

Roosevelt also informed reporters that he had the 137-year-old precedent on his side of Thomas Jefferson's Louisiana Purchase, also a critical response to the exigencies of the situation. As he closed the deal with France, Jefferson had said that the government refused to be bound by the "metaphysical subtleties" of the Constitution.[63] James Monroe and Robert Livingston, Jefferson's emissaries, had gone to Paris to negotiate with Napoleon's foreign minister Talleyrand, Roosevelt explained, and brought back a signed contract for the Louisiana territories. "It was a fait accompli," FDR told the reporters, conveniently neglecting to mention that the Senate in fact ratified the Louisiana Purchase treaty in 1803 by a vote of 24 to 7.[64] But for his part, Walter Lippmann believed firmly in the necessity of FDR's bold stand. "In our fear of strong government," he astutely wrote in his column, "we must not forget that wherever democracy has been overthrown from within or conquered from without, the disaster has been preceded by a period of indecision, weakness, confusion." Indeed, FDR would later comment that had he followed the advice of the constitutional legalists, "the subject would still be in the tender care of the Committees of the Congress!"[65]

Roosevelt's brave stand hit the front pages of the nation's newspapers like a bombshell. The eight-column headline in the *New York Times* read: "ROOSEVELT TRADES DESTROYERS FOR SEA BASES; TELLS CONGRESS HE ACTED ON OWN AUTHORITY; BRITAIN PLEDGES NEVER TO YIELD OR SINK FLEET." A *Times* reporter based in London wrote that "it would be impossible to overstate the jubilation in official and unofficial circles." In America, too, internationalists like Henry Luce applauded Roosevelt. Not only did the bases complete a defensive ring around the Caribbean and provide outposts against attack from the Atlantic, but, as *Time* pointed out, the bases had a "preventive" value, too, for now the nation's enemies would be denied their use.[66] "Mr. Roosevelt is a handy man in a trade," editorialized the *Atlanta Constitution*. The deal marked the "ebb of the totalitarian tide," wrote the *Christian Science Monitor*. Even Colonel Robert McCormick, the publisher of the isolationist *Chicago Daily Tribune*, recognized a good deal when he saw one. "Now, thank God," he said in a radio address on September 8, the Caribbean was "an American lake." [67]

Even so, Roosevelt knew that the exchange could be risky in an election year—and according to Bernard Baruch, who met with FDR in Tennessee over the Labor Day weekend, the president was even concerned that he might be impeached. But the survival of Britain was far more important. "Grace, Congress is going to raise hell about this," FDR said to his secretary Grace Tully, "but even another day's delay may mean the end of civilization."[68] For his part, Churchill also understood the deep meaning of the exchange and its implications for the Anglo-American collaboration. The two English-speaking democracies would now be "somewhat mixed up together" for their mutual advantage, Churchill declared in the House of Commons on August 20. It would be an unstoppable process, he said. "Like the Mississippi, it just keeps rolling along. Let it roll! Let it roll on full flood, inexorable, irresistible, to broader lands and better days!"[69]

A Gallup poll on September 6 showed that most Americans—58 percent of Republicans and 63 percent of Democrats—favored the deal.[70] But that did not dampen the isolationist chorus. Connecticut's senator John Danaher charged that the president had unilaterally committed the nation to the war. In the House, George Tinkham of Massachusetts called FDR a "lawless dictator," and Hamilton Fish—whom Frank Knox labeled the "prize jackass of the whole bunch down there"—declared that now Hitler would be perfectly justified in declaring war on the United States.[71] And from Wendell Willkie came the judgment that the destroyers-for-bases deal, neither debated in public nor approved by Congress, was "the most arbitrary and dictatorial action ever taken by any President in the history of the United States."[72] Several years later, Willkie admitted that he regretted those words more than anything else he had said in the campaign.[73]

While Willkie flailed about, chameleon-like, still unsure how to position himself, the president had risked a bold measure in an election year and acted responsibly and courageously. On September 9, glistening with fresh coats of paint, the ships were transferred to British command.[74]

On September 3, the day FDR announced the destroyers deal and a week after the Selective Service Training Act was passed in the Senate, debate on Burke-Wadsworth began in the House of Representatives. On the first day, dozens of young left-wing antidraft protesters, wearing "Stop Conscription" buttons, poured into the House galleries, zealously applauding the opponents of the bill. "American conscription is American fascism," hollered one protester before guards ejected him from the chamber.[75]

"We cannot afford to indulge in a 'wait and see' policy," said Representative Wadsworth, reminding House members that "others have indulged in that and they have perished." And that was about as rational as the debate got. "We have created an hysteria of imminent invasion," declared New York representative Vito Marcantonio, a member of the left-wing American Labor Party. "What are we arming for?" One of the few women in Congress, Frances Bolton, a Republican from Ohio, exclaimed that God alone knew what Mr. Roosevelt "will do with our boys." When an Ohio Democrat, Martin Sweeney, accused Roosevelt of following Woodrow Wilson in taking the nation needlessly into war, another Democrat, Beverly Vincent of Kentucky, a World War I veteran, muttered that Sweeney was a "traitor." Sweeney swung at Vincent and Vincent landed a hard right to Sweeney's jaw before House members separated the two pugilists.[76]

Contributing his wisdom to the debate, Hamilton Fish offered the thought that conscription would mean importing "the very essence of Nazism and Hitlerism into the United States." It was ironic, as Clifford and Spencer observed, that Fish, a product of the Plattsburg Movement and the recipient of the Croix de Guerre in the First World War, now found himself bitterly opposed to his old colleague Grenville Clark. Recognizing that Burke-Wadsworth would pass, Fish decided to propose an amendment similar to Maloney's; it would postpone draft registration for sixty days to see if four hundred thousand men would volunteer for military service. If they did, the draft would not go into effect. "Tempus fugit," commented Roosevelt at his press conference. "I hope," said Willkie, resisting GOP pressure, "the Fish amendment is eliminated," prompting the congressman's retort that Willkie had "fallen for the propaganda of the interventionists and the eastern press and columnists."[77]

The Fish amendment passed in the House by a vote of 185 to 155, but a version of the Russell-Overton amendment also passed, one proposed by Representative Joseph Smith of Connecticut that replaced the seizure of industrial plants with "mandatory rental" and added a provision for the criminal prosecution of noncooperative plant owners. The final vote in the House on Burke-Wadsworth was 263 in favor and 149 against, with 211 Democrats and 52 Republicans voting for the bill and 33 Democrats and 112 Republicans voting no.

Then came the last stage: the reconciliation of the two different versions of the bill by a Senate-House conference committee. On Monday, September 9, Roosevelt phoned every conferee, informing them that "the bombing of London was much worse than the newspapers say" and urging them to move conscription out of conference and get it passed. The reports from London in the newspapers, in fact, were bad enough. The "Blitz," the mightiest air assault ever and the first intended to terrorize a civilian population, had begun the previous day. For eight hours, wave after wave of German bombers, fifteen hundred in all, rained relentless death and destruction on London, on its crowded buses, theaters, factories, gasworks, power stations, railroad yards, docks, warehouses, and shipyards. In the sky above the London office of the *New York Times*, the bombers looked like "swarming bees," a reporter wrote. The office shook as if from an earthquake, and the staff was ordered to take shelter.[78]

Alarmed by the reports, members of the Senate-House committee voted to eliminate the Fish amendment; they set the age range for eligibility at 21 to 35; and they substituted for Russell-Overton the House's Smith plan for mandatory forced rental of defense industries and for criminal prosecution of uncooperative plant owners.

On Saturday, September 14, the new bill was quickly passed in the Senate—in just thirty minutes—and the House, in an hour. A majority of Republicans in both chambers, however, voted against conscription. And whereas 88 House Republicans voted against the draft bill and 46 voted in favor in 1940, when that bill came up for renewal in August 1941, 133 Republicans would vote against it and only 21 in favor, ensuring that the bill would be reauthorized by a razor-edged margin of only one vote.[79]

Most Americans, however, approved of selective service and rewarded Roosevelt with a boost in his poll numbers. On September 16, he signed the Selective Service Training Act. Standing behind him were Stimson; Andrew May of Kentucky, chair of the House Military Affairs Committee; Morris Sheppard of Texas, chair of the Senate Military Affairs Committee; and General George Marshall—in the civilian attire he wore in public before Pearl Harbor. Movie cameras whirred and flash bulbs popped. "America stands at the cross-roads of its destiny," Roosevelt said. "A few weeks have seen great nations fall. We cannot remain indifferent to the philosophy of force now rampant in the world. . . . We must and will marshal our great potential strength to fend off war from our shores. Our decision has been made."[80]

Notably absent from the ceremony was the person who had contributed the most to the success of the legislation, the private citizen who had inspired and crafted the bill and skillfully organized and pushed for its passage. "I want to tell you what a fine job—in fact unique job—you have done in getting it drafted and passed," Stimson wrote to Grenville Clark the day after the signing. "If it had not been for you no such bill would have been enacted at this time. Of this I am certain." James Wadsworth also wrote to Clark, thanking him for letting him introduce the bill "and, what is more important, you gave me a chance to serve in a great cause." On vacation in New Hampshire, Clark replied that the draft was "the sine qua non to any real effort to stand up to Hitler et al. Much more needs to be done to that end but without this I don't think we'd have got to first base." Not only was the Burke-Wadsworth bill the first peacetime draft in American history, but, equally unusual, it was drafted by a group of private citizens and, in the words of *Fortune* magazine, led by the "Statesman Incognito," Grenville Clark.[81]

After the ceremony, Roosevelt left by train for Alabama to speak at the funeral of Speaker Bankhead, who had died suddenly, shortly after the final vote in the House. On the train, the president and Sam Rosenman discussed selective service. "From a political point of view," said Rosenman, "there couldn't have been a worse time for them to have passed this bill. The actual drawing of numbers will probably take place right smack in the middle of the campaign, and of course you are going to be blamed for it in a great many homes." "I guess you're right," replied Roosevelt. "But if we really do a great job of telling American fathers and mothers how necessary this is . . . maybe it won't be so bad."[82]

That evening George Marshall addressed the nation on the radio. "I fear that we expect too much of machines," he said. "Success in combat depends primarily upon the development of the trained combat team. . . . It demands a standard of discipline which will prevail over fatigue, hunger, confusion, or disaster. Given the opportunity to prepare himself, the American makes the finest soldier in the world, and for the first time in our history we are beginning in time of peace to prepare against the possibility of war. We are starting to train an army of citizen soldiers. . . . If we are strong enough, peace, democracy, and our American way of life should be the reward."[83]

That past summer, before the Democratic Convention, an anti-Roosevelt button had warned "Draft Roosevelt and He'll Draft You."[84] But most Americans were not so easily scared—either by the prospect of a third term for Roosevelt or by a military draft. The draft will remove the "morass of disgrace" that separated drafted men and volunteers, said Sergeant Alvin York, the head of the Fentress County draft board. York, a Tennessee backwoodsman and conscientious objector who was drafted in the First World War and became a national hero by single-handedly disabling 32 German machine guns and capturing 132 German officers and soldiers, said he faced a dilemma:

selective service gave his county a six-month quota of two men "and we have 40 boys wanting to go for a year of training."[85]

Forty-five million young men would register for the draft, and ten million would be drafted. In the 1941 movie *You're In the Army Now*, comedians Jimmy Durante and Phil Silvers joined the exuberant chorus singing "I'm Glad My Number Was Called!"

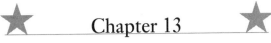

Chapter 13

Campaigning 101

"THE NEXT FEW MONTHS WILL BE DIFFERENT from the usual national campaigns of recent years," Roosevelt informed the convention delegates in Chicago when he accepted their nomination in July. He would continue to travel to inspect national defense projects. But, given the fast-moving events all over the world, he would have to abandon all journeys from the Alleghenies to the Pacific Coast because, in times of emergency, he said, he would need to be back at his desk in a few hours. Of course, he would still hold regular press conferences and speak with Americans on the radio. But there would be no real campaigning by the old campaigner. "I shall not have the time or the inclination to engage in purely political debate," he stated, though he made it clear that he would respond to any "deliberate or unwitting falsifications of fact, which are sometimes made by political candidates."

Thus the president made the eminently rational and shrewd decision to stage himself as a nonpolitical commander in chief, dedicated to the defense of the nation, too occupied and preoccupied with matters of major importance to go out and plead for votes. He would concentrate solely on foreign policy and military preparedness, and although he intended to suspend fireside chats, he did not preclude talking "educationally" with the appeasers and semi-appeasers. When a reporter at one of his press conferences in August asked him a question about one of Willkie's positions, he answered, to laughter, "I don't know nothing about politics."[1]

Of course, Roosevelt, a master politician and maestro of timing, knew well that his "nonpolitical" appearances at defense plants and naval stations would only enhance his image as a purposeful leader, focused on strengthening the nation's military capability so that the United States might perhaps be able to stay out of war. As for the partisan resonances of his public appearances, he joked when he spoke to a convention of Teamsters in early September that he was in a sort of quandary because he did not know whether he was delivering a political speech or not. So, he added, he would throw himself on the indulgence of the radio companies "for in one case we will pay and in the other case we will not pay."[2]

September and early October saw him making trips to dedicate new dams, defense factories, and naval ordnance plants. On Labor Day, he dedicated the Chickamauga Dam in Chattanooga, praising the Tennessee Valley for assuming "its share of responsibility for national defense." At the Great Smoky Mountains National Park, he spoke about two different kinds of conservation: the first was relatively simple—the preservation of pines, dogwoods, trout, and thrushes. The second involved the more serious task of preserving democratic institutions. And the key was preparedness and defense. To meet the greatest attack ever launched against the freedom of the individual, he said, "we must prepare beforehand, for preparing later may and probably would be too late."[3]

At Fort Meade and at Aberdeen Proving Ground in Maryland, he conferred with army officers about their work, viewed mobile artillery, and, against a background of guns, planes, tanks, and ships, was photographed watching army maneuvers and gazing at aircraft carriers under construction. The men and women who worked in the plants he visited, he wrote to his son-in-law, "get a real enthusiasm and speed up production during the days following my visit." And as for the western and midwestern states that the president was unable to see firsthand, he reassured their governors that they too would get their share of new defense industries.[4]

Indeed, the nation was humming with new jobs, new defense plants, textile mills producing material for military uniforms, and army camps. The economy was springing back to life—the first time since 1929.

"I really meant it when I told the Convention I could not do campaigning myself," Roosevelt told Connecticut's senator Francis Maloney in August.[5] He was more than happy to let others—especially Broadway and Hollywood actors, writers, and musicians—campaign for him. In September Eleanor hosted a celebrity picnic at her Hyde Park cottage, Val-Kill. Over barbecued hamburgers, the president and the first lady chatted and joked with Katharine Hepburn, Lorenz Hart and Richard Rodgers, Edna Ferber, Thornton Wilder,

John Gunther, William Saroyan, Moss Hart, and Douglas Fairbanks, Jr. Along with stars like Henry Fonda, Groucho Marx, and Humphrey Bogart, they spoke and sang on radio shows for FDR during the campaign season. Roosevelt's son Franklin, Jr., also played his part. "My old man is going to keep us out of war!" he exclaimed to the delight of crowds. Willkie was a "very fine man," he told one audience, adding that "I think my old man is a little more capable." The crowds loved hearing him refer to the president as "my old man." When he once left out that laugh line, FDR sent him a telegram. "You did a grand job only I wanted to hear you say 'my Old Man!' "[6]

Also doing a grand job was Roosevelt's running-mate, Henry Wallace. "You have made a glorious start!" Roosevelt wired him after his running-mate's acceptance speech in late August. Harold Ickes had predicted that the shy Wallace would bomb, but he was pleasantly surprised when the vice presidential candidate proved to be an aggressive, effective, and sometimes acerbic campaigner. "Henry is doing extremely well on the stump," Ickes wrote in his diary. "He is a new man." In New Mexico, Wallace was able to switch into Spanish to converse with Mexican-Americans; he penned an article on "Judaism and Americanism" for a Jewish magazine; and he sought the support of independents by reminding audiences of his Republican background and his father's service in the cabinets of Presidents Harding and Coolidge.[7]

But what really saved Wallace from bombing was not his talent but rather Wendell Willkie himself. Republicans—through the intermediary of the publisher of the *Pittsburgh Post-Gazette*—had acquired acutely embarrassing letters that Wallace had written in 1933 and 1934 to a mystic philosopher named Nicholas Roerich, his "guru." Describing himself as a "searcher for methods of bringing the inner light to outward manifestation and raising outward manifestation to the inner light," Wallace had reached out to Roerich to be his spiritual guide. Perhaps even more damaging for the campaign, the letters, according to Robert Jackson, also contained "intimations about the mental health condition of the President."[8]

Shortly after the Democratic Convention in Chicago, Harry Hopkins somehow obtained photostatic copies of the letters and immediately realized that they were radioactive. "Sam, is there any way to get Wallace off the ticket now, or is it too late?" Hopkins frantically asked Sam Rosenman.[9] A White House meeting was quickly convened. As Roosevelt, Robert Jackson, Steve Early, Pa Watson, and a few others listened, Hopkins reported on the contents of the letters. But the president made light of the situation, skeptical that letters not involving a woman could prove so fatally embarrassing. "How ridiculous!" he said. Wasn't it possible to invent a sexual liaison for Henry? he laughingly proposed to Jackson. "Bob, you've got the FBI. . . . Can't you turn this into a romance?"[10]

Ultimately it was Willkie who rescued Wallace. The self-protective candidate understood that any smear of Wallace would only trigger revelations about his own private life. Though his wife, Edith, accompanied him on his campaign tour through the states, he communicated by telephone at least once a day with Irita Van Doren. In the elite circles of Washington and New York, their relationship was no secret. "Awful nice gal," FDR said. At one point he considered leaking the story. "We can spread it as a word-of-mouth thing," Roosevelt suggested, "or by some people *way, way down the line*." In fact, the details of Willkie's affair were already spreading around the country, he added. But in the end, the president decided to do nothing. "No, no, I don't think so," he said to Frances Perkins. "Those things always boomerang." Still, if the campaign got dirty, the White House was prepared to leak the story.[11]

But Willkie decided not to play rough. Trying to ensure his own privacy as well as Wallace's, he gave the order to keep the guru letters under seal. According to another version of the episode, however, it was Joe Martin who saved Wallace's skin. Martin later wrote that the decision to kill the guru story was his and that he wanted at all costs to avoid the appearance that the GOP was resorting to "a last minute smear." One of the rare hints of the guru letters appeared in a *Time* magazine profile of Wallace in late September. Conceding that Wallace was a significant "agricultural theoretician" and a voracious reader, *Time* slyly portrayed him as a "savant, dreamer and mystic" whose hobbies were astrology and numerology. The article concluded with a not-so-subtle reminder of the "weight that would fall upon his shoulders if anything should happen to the President."[12]

While Roosevelt avoided the usual round of campaign speeches and partisan political activities, he assumed that the election would not be an extremely bitter, polarizing, and divisive one, as would have been the case if an Old Guard conservative like Hoover or a younger isolationist like Taft or Vandenberg were the nominee. On the other hand, he knew that running against the internationalist and moderately liberal Willkie could make for a tougher election fight precisely because his likeable, articulate, and witty opponent would probably cut into the independent vote.[13] But in the early fall of 1940, it was unlikely that FDR could have imagined that, within six weeks, both he and Willkie would both be pandering to the isolationist crowd.

One of Roosevelt's tactics to limit Willkie's appeal was never to pronounce his name. Instead he referred to him as the "gentleman from Indiana" or as the GOP candidate or simply as his opponent. "There are a great many people who never heard of him," Roosevelt said. "Why should I advertise him?" FDR's own well-known—if not magical—name, he realized, was a great political asset. When voters go to the polls on Election Day, the president explained to Frances Perkins, many of them look over the list of candidates and "vote for people whose names they know." He was not about to give free publicity to his opponent.[14]

The problems facing Willkie, however, were more challenging than that of his opponent's refusal to mention him by name or to engage him in debate. While Roosevelt skillfully presented himself as a diligent, active, vigorous soldier-statesman with no time to indulge in self-serving campaign politics, the GOP candidate, the political outsider, was left on the sidelines to react to the president's deeds. When Willkie labeled the appointments of Stimson and Knox "a political trick" or denounced the president's handling of the bases-for-destroyers deal as an executive agreement that bypassed Congress or when he criticized his visits to defense plants as taxpayer-funded "make-believe military inspection trips," he found himself forced to box against a phantom opponent and carry on a one-sided partisan debate. As elusive as he was, the president controlled events and called the tune. Even in Willkie's speeches, Roosevelt occupied center stage—the scene-stealing charismatic villain in the starring role.[15]

After a long dormancy between his acceptance speech in Elwood in mid-August and the end of his sojourn in Rushville in September, Willkie's campaign awakened when his train finally rolled out of Indiana on September 12. The plan was for a whirlwind journey through thirty-one states—the most extensive campaign tour ever made by a presidential candidate, remarked the *New York Times*.[16] Carrying Willkie, his wife, and his brother Edward along with two bodyguards, thirty staff members, forty-six reporters, mimeograph machines and cases of beer, the twelve-car train headed to Chicago. After the kickoff rally on September 16 in Coffeyville, Kansas, the candidate and his entourage would travel through the Southwest, up the Pacific Coast, east to New England and the Mid-Atlantic states, and back to the Midwest and end with a final rally on November 2 in Madison Square Garden. Along the way, he intended to address crowds from the rear platform of his train.

Willkie's itinerary reflected the harsh challenges he faced in the electoral college. Roosevelt's tremendous popularity in many states was unassailable, with polls giving him between 75 and 85 percent in the entire southern region of the country and 59 percent on the Pacific Coast. In the Mountain states, he dipped to 53 percent. To win, Willkie needed to target regions where FDR's support fell under 50 percent: states in the nation's broad heartland as well as in New England and the Middle Atlantic. According to George Gallup, eight states were in the bag for Willkie: Colorado, Indiana, Iowa, Kansas, Maine, Nebraska, South Dakota, and Vermont. He needed to hold onto slim leads in Idaho, Illinois, Michigan, Missouri, New Hampshire, New York, North Dakota, Ohio, Pennsylvania, and Wisconsin, but he also had to tip into his column Massachusetts, Connecticut, and perhaps Minnesota, too. And yet, the candidate and his advisors did not employ a strategy that focused on the key battleground states.[17]

His campaign trip would be no less daunting a challenge physically, too—especially for his vocal cords. Unused to speaking into a microphone, he shouted out his speeches—and shouted himself hoarse. At one talk, his voice gone, he mutely held out his arms to the crowd with a rueful smile. His advisors called on a Hollywood doctor to help him. As his raspy voice degenerated into squawks, squacks, and croaks before giving out altogether, he finally and reluctantly canceled several speeches on doctor's orders. "He needs a policeman, not a doctor," commented his physician.[18] "Mr. Willkie is losing his voice," President Roosevelt said one morning, with a twinkle in his eye, to his doctor, Ross McIntire. "I think it would be a grand gesture on your part if you would get in touch with his doctors and offer them your own favorite prescription for treating such trouble. We've got to keep him talking." But perhaps Willkie's gravelly utterances were not altogether a liability. "His husky voice, his earnest appearance and his vehement gestures," remarked one reporter, "have carried conviction."[19]

At his first stop in Chicago in mid-September, Willkie sped around the city for nine hours, speaking in stockyards, factories, and nickel-hamburger luncheonettes, hitting hard to break Roosevelt's hold on the labor vote. Hammering the president and the New Deal for the continuing unemployment (although employment was increasing by seven percent in 1940), he promised jobs and a strong America with factories producing at full speed. But it would be an uphill struggle to convince voters that he was a friend to labor. The following day, Ed Flynn, the Democratic Party chairman, armed with documents and company vouchers, charged that subsidiary companies of Willkie's Commonwealth and Southern Utilities Corporation had hired labor spies from the Pinkerton National Detective Agency to engage in "ruthless anti-labor activities." Willkie immediately shot back that his company had merely hired Pinkerton "inspectors" to ride in the street cars it operated to check on fares and methods of operation. The heads of the subsidiaries and even a union official also denied Flynn's charges, but the accusations hurt the campaign.[20]

In the stench of Chicago stockyards, the GOP candidate spoke earnestly to people in bloodied aprons, occasionally using profanity to impress the mostly silent workers. Only in the financial district was the reception tumultuous, as Willkie was showered with a ticker tape blizzard. In a ballpark on the South Side, he hoarsely implored a crowd of eight thousand African Americans to leave the New Deal and come back to the party of Lincoln, promising to end racial discrimination and appoint qualified "colored citizens" to federal civil service jobs. The reception, reported the *Washington Post*, was respectful, if not enthusiastic, as people cried out, "We want jobs!"[21]

On September 16, in Coffeyville, Kansas, where the young Willkie had taught history and coached the high school basketball team in 1913 and 1914, the campaign finally got into full gear. Willkie had sent two journalists ahead of him to collect some local stories for him about poverty and unemployment in Coffeyville, but what they found instead was healthy prosperity—a profitable municipal electric plant, public swimming pools, and low taxes. On the afternoon of Willkie's speech, men, women, and children lined the streets festooned with banners and flags, cheering his motorcade. A large, enthusiastic crowd—estimates of its size ranged wildly from fifteen thousand to sixty-seven thousand—applauded the candidate in Willkie Park, freshly named for the town's former teacher, while thousands of others heard the speech on loudspeakers set up throughout the city. It was the most exciting day in Coffeyville since October 5, 1892, people said, when the Dalton gang raided a Coffeyville bank and eight people were killed.[22]

In his speech, Willkie claimed that American democracy was in danger "from without and from within" and pleaded with voters to save American government and the American way of life—"the most precious thing in the world"—from another four years of Roosevelt. The president had strained democratic institutions to the breaking point, he charged, predicting that by the end of a Roosevelt third term, Americans would be living under a totalitarian government. After his speech, Willkie was driven to the Coffeyville high school. On a classroom door a sign read: "This is the Room Where Wendell Willkie Taught." "Oh no, this isn't it," he said. He found his old room and wrote on the blackboard, "No Third Term—Wendell Willkie."[23]

The following day he traveled to the Texas Panhandle, hoping to make inroads on the Democrats' hold over the South. In Amarillo he told a small crowd of Texans that they had to decide between two great traditions, the

80-year-old tradition of the South voting Democratic and the 160-year-old tradition that no president served for more than two terms.[24] Then it was on to the coast.

"California Willkie Tide Rises," announced the *Los Angeles Times* during his swing through the state three days later. Seventy thousand people chanting, "We want Willkie!" filled the Los Angeles Coliseum on September 19. In San Diego, Santa Ana, Inglewood, and Long Beach, people shouted their approval. Only in Fresno, in the San Joaquin Valley, made famous in John Steinbeck's *The Grapes of Wrath* as the destination of "Okies" fleeing the Dust Bowl, did reporters spy desperately poor people near Willkie's rally— "itinerant workers in ragged overalls, lying in a state of such indifference or exhaustion that they gave no sign they knew the crowd was there."[25] In San Francisco's Civic Auditorium, where Hoover's offer to introduce Willkie to the crowd was turned down, the crowd of fifteen thousand stood and cheered their candidate. Willkie gave an important speech on foreign policy, proclaiming that Britain was "our only remaining friend" and that the United States had to aid her "to the limits of prudence and effectiveness." He also called for economic assistance for besieged China. "Thanks for coming out," he told people afterward on the streets of the city. "This is a tribute to my cause, the preservation of America!" In Berkeley, he was greeted by students cheering, "We want Roosevelt!" Heading back east a few days later, Willkie received a rousing reception in Omaha, where he spoke about the difficulties faced by farmers. Taking a swipe at those who "preach disunity and class discord," he pleaded for unity and sacrifice on the part of all.[26]

On his swing back through the Midwest, in small, rural towns and in the downtown urban business districts, he received warm receptions and ticker tape parades. But in the factory sections of cities and towns like Detroit, Pontiac, Flint, and Toledo, where Willkie hoped to pry away some union votes from FDR, loyalty to the president and the New Deal proved especially intense. Willkie was forced to cancel several meetings at automobile plants. People in the streets booed, held up "Roosevelt Forever" signs, and pelted the candidate's motorcade with tomatoes, overripe cantaloupes, and rotten eggs.[27] When one splattered Mrs. Willkie's dress, she remarked to reporters, to the consternation of her husband, that the eggs had been thrown "by some poor boy whose family probably is on relief." The missiles tracked the nominee beyond the Midwest. "Willkie Hit by Potato When He Enters Boston," a newspaper headline reported during one of his campaign stops in New England.[28]

Willkie's plan was to reach every part of the country and speak, in his homey, down-to-earth style, to every voter he could reach. Well, at least every voter minus 51 percent of them. "If I am elected," he told an audience of labor men in Pittsburgh on October 3, "I will appoint a secretary of labor, an outstanding and an actual representative of labor." A great applause line—until he added the wildly impolitic remark, "The job of Secretary of Labor is a man's job!" A gratuitous slap at Frances Perkins, the only woman until then ever to have held a cabinet post, but also a thoughtless put-down of all working women. Five hundred telegrams protesting Willkie's blunder poured into Perkins's office, half of them, she wrote, from Republican women. For his part, Roosevelt could only laugh with satisfaction. "That was a boner Willkie pulled," he said to Perkins.[29]

Willkie had secured the help of media magnates like Luce and Howard, and he was well served by the force and charm of his personality, candor, intelligence, and wit. But he also needed a strong, winning campaign message. His trump card, Roosevelt's unprecedented bid for a third term, was gaining no traction. Willkie himself acknowledged that many people were reluctant to embrace a new leader at a critical moment in history. "People say we ought not to change horses in the middle of the stream," he had remarked in Detroit in his hoarse, earnest voice. "Well, for one thing, what are we doing in the middle of the stream? How did we get there? The man who got us in is not the right one to get us out!" Speaking in upstate New York, he dismissed the notion that a man who had served eight years in the presidency was more experienced and better fit to lead than a newcomer. By that logic, Willkie said, "you will come to the conclusion that Louis XIV, the worst despot in history, was the best ruler because he served the longest."[30]

But handicapping Willkie's condemnation of a third term were his own words. The founding fathers "knew, as we know," he had written in the June 4, 1940, issue of *Look* magazine, that the number of years the president served "was of no importance. Had they made the president's term two, six or 12 years, it would have made little difference." Democracy stands or falls, he explained, on the "attitude" of the individuals who hold office "for *whatever number* of years." Just as he had suggested in that article, Democrats and many independents simply ignored the third-term question as the worldwide crisis worsened: Luftwaffe aircraft dumping their bombs on London every day and every night; the Japanese joining the Axis alliance and moving into Indochina; Italy preparing to storm Greece.

Willkie would continue throughout his campaign to refer to Roosevelt as the "third term candidate," mocking him as the "indispensable man," but that theme became a rapidly wasting asset. An advisor suggested to Harry Hopkins that the president "quote key paragraphs" from the *Look* article, and the Democratic National Committee also took action, distributing to party leaders a "Third Term Catechism," packed with useful, short quotations from the Founders with which to quickly counter any objections to a third term.[31]

Apart from Willkie's mockery of the third-term candidate, which usually took up a large portion of his speeches, what would be his core campaign messages on domestic and foreign affairs? At his rallies, people heard pleas for unity at home, praise for the principles of democracy and for private enterprise, and calls for racial and religious tolerance. He continued to voice strong support for the New Deal—"no one in the nation leans toward social security more than I do," he told a crowd in the Bronx.[32] He painted compassionate descriptions of "undernourished children living in houses without enough sanitary facilities," of anxious mothers and overworked fathers, over whose heads "constantly hangs the fear of loss of work, the fear of injury and loss of earning power, the fear that old age will find them without security and without hope." He made heartfelt pleas for expanding and reinforcing the social gains of the New Deal. But he also lambasted the New Deal's "aimless management" that, he said, had doubled the national debt. The "boys of the New Deal," he told a small crowd in Belen, New Mexico, had been on the "most drunken orgy of spending in history." His speeches contained substantive ideas for creating jobs, revitalizing industry, and speedily building up America's defenses. Too substantive, perhaps. In a mid-October swing through upstate New York, he analyzed, in mind-numbing detail, the weakness of American military defenses by tracing it to the shortcomings of the government's negotiations with private arms manufacturers, who, he claimed, needed more government help to amortize their corporate debt and increase their depreciation allowances.[33]

He discussed the rights of labor in speeches in Seattle and Pittsburgh. Declaring that he was "100 per cent determined" to protect labor's safeguards, he outlined a program ranging from the extension of social security benefits and protection against unemployment to cooling-off periods before strikes or lockouts and simpler regulations of big business. In midwestern centers like Omaha and Minneapolis, he focused on the interdependence of agriculture and industry. The problems of the farmer, laborer, businessman, investor, and consumer were all one, he thoughtfully explained. "Those horses must pull together." Though he approved of much of the administration's farm program, he faulted the New Deal's "elaborate economic theories" for hurting the farmer and failing to get at the root of the problem. Pointing to the imbalance between farm population and farm share of the national income, he called for less bureaucracy, more local control, and a variety of new measures from farm-to-market roads to cooperative marketing and an end to crop control.[34]

Most of his ideas were sensible and intelligent. He sought to appeal to a wide range of moderates, independents, and Republicans with praise for New Deal reforms as well as tributes to free enterprise. But he sounded some odd and contradictory notes as he ventured down new paths of attack. Flinging red meat to hard-core Republican crowds, he blasted the president for "our very rapid drift toward totalitarianism." In several speeches, he introduced the theme of "state socialism" and, more ominously, "national socialism," with its Nazi resonances. The Roosevelt administration seemed to be imposing "national socialism" on Americans, he warned, emphasizing that such policies threatened to turn citizens into servants of the state. "I cannot say that my opponent is *consciously* aiming at State socialism," he allowed, but "*every major economic policy* of the New Deal is pushing in that direction."[35]

On foreign affairs his message was often just as confusing. At the same time that he pummeled the president for "deliberately inciting us to war" and creating "manufactured panics," he sought to portray himself as a strong defender of the nation, who, as he had stated in Elwood, would "*not hesitate to stand for war.*" Walter Lippmann, in private, had suggested to Willkie that he present himself as a "strong, competent man," and Willkie followed that advice, criticizing Roosevelt as a hapless appeaser. "Let's have a Winston Churchill government in the United States!" he cried. "Away with the Chamberlains, and let us preserve democracy in America!"[36] Instead of "standing up and fighting for democracy," he charged in Joliet, Illinois, on September 14, Roosevelt had "telephoned Hitler and Mussolini and urged them to sell Czechoslovakia down the river." It was an irresponsible, wholly invented allegation that troubled Willkie supporters like Lippmann. "He goes off half-cocked," Lippmann wrote to a friend, "and instead of presenting himself as a kind of solid and reliable force . . . he makes a very erratic impression." Willkie's wild charges, however, did not stop the *New York Times* from editorializing that "whatever overstatement there may be in some of these accusations, they contain too much truth . . . for the Administration to be able lightly to brush them aside."[37]

In truth, it was impossible to tell where Willkie finally stood. While he berated Roosevelt as a false friend to European democracies, he also pledged that, if elected, he would send no American boy to the shambles of a European war—and he added that he meant it![38] Hammering FDR in Joliet, Willkie said, "One day he is an interventionist, the next day he is an isolationist," words that neatly described the GOP candidate himself.[39] "He began by demanding that the President debate with him," declared Robert Jackson in a nationwide radio address on October 9, "but he has shown that there was no need for it. He debates with himself, taking both sides of every issue."[40] A few weeks later, in Madison Square Garden, Henry Wallace would sketch out, to the laughter of the crowd, the GOP nominee's contradictory and perpetually shifting stands. "Just what does he mean?" Wallace asked in mock bewilderment. "Or does he know what he means? Does *anyone* know what he means?"[41]

In late September, the Willkie team was worried; the campaign was in a slump. A recent Gallup poll gave Roosevelt 453 electoral votes to only 78 for Willkie. Campaign contributions that Willkie expected from businessmen were going to Roosevelt instead.[42] In public his advisors put on a good face, maintaining that the campaign was on track and would gain momentum in the final stretch. But in private there was panic. The campaign had lost steam during Willkie's lackadaisical sojourns in Colorado Springs and Rushville. In neither place, according to his advisor Raymond Buell, had Willkie and his team thought up "a program of attack against the New Deal, in the intellectual sense, or lay the basis for a party organization."[43] The Willkie boom must have been a "flash in the pan," wrote the *Atlanta Constitution* in a September 21 editorial entitled "Wilting Willkie." Still, it wasn't too late. Many voters remained undecided, columnist Ernest Lindley pointed out. With a few lucky breaks for Willkie, he wrote, the pendulum could still swing his way.[44]

Seven hundred daily newspapers had already come out for Willkie, compared to 216 for Roosevelt. But Roy Howard, the owner of the Scripps-Howard newspaper chain, nevertheless wrote letters to dozens of other publishers pleading for more pro-Willkie editorials and articles. "The yammering about his slump is phony," Howard wrote, praising Willkie for sticking to his principles and refusing to "stoop to demagogic appeals."[45] Within days, editors responded. Newspapers from the *Chattanooga Times* to the *Hartford Courant* acclaimed the GOP candidate's ideas and accomplishments. The *Washington*

Post, for example, hailed his uncontroversial comment that the United States was "not a static society" as a statement of "profound truth."[46]

Henry Luce's *Time* also did its best, lavishing praise on a speech Willkie gave in Detroit on September 30. "Gather your families together on our great national holidays," the candidate had solemnly said. "Read to your children the sacred words of the Declaration of Independence, or the Gettysburg Address. These are the living creeds of our American faith." If this was hokum, it was "magnificent hokum," cheered *Time*. "If these words were reasons to vote for Wendell Willkie, they were good reasons. For Mr. Willkie could win only if people had faith—not simply in him—but in his own faith in such words."[47]

And yet, this fresh avalanche of publicity orchestrated by the media magnates could not offset the persistent confusion and disorganization in Willkie's campaign. Supporters who raised funds were ignored; phone calls went unreturned; last-minute schedule changes were frequent. "Seldom has there been more chaos in a presidential campaign," wrote Raymond Clapper in his column in late September. "If the Willkie Administration in the White House functioned with no more unity, coordination, and effectiveness than the Willkie Administration in the campaign, then the Government would be almost paralyzed." One member of the candidate's entourage devoted fifteen minutes to convincing a dignified-looking stranger to vote for Willkie, only to hear him reply, "I agree with every word you say. I'm Mr. Willkie's masseur."[48] Others commented about large contributions made to Republican state organizations being grossly wasted. In Phoenix, Arizona, there were five headquarters for Willkie on the main street. When Willkie made a visit to his running-mate's home state of Oregon on September 22, McNary was nowhere to be seen. The two GOP nominees in fact never developed a cordial working relationship, though the two vice presidential candidates, McNary and Wallace, friends since the 1920s, spent hours chatting amicably together during the campaign.[49]

Adding to the disarray was Willkie's aborted attempt in late September to dump Joe Martin as party chair. According to rumors, Martin had been overheard to say that his candidate would probably lose in November. "He is double-crossing me," Willkie fumed to John Hamilton, the arch-conservative he had recently ousted as party chair. Would Hamilton take over the chairmanship once again? he asked. A dumbfounded Hamilton calmed Willkie down with a reminder that if the GOP took over the House, Martin would be the Speaker, and Willkie could not risk antagonizing him. The greatest mistake he made in the campaign, Willkie confided to Raymond Buell, was the Martin appointment.[50]

But a more serious problem surfaced when a Gallup poll published on October 6 showed that Willkie had slipped to 44 percent of the popular vote from 45 percent in September and 49 percent in August, when the pollster, calling the race a dead heat, gave Willkie 284 electoral votes to 247 for Roosevelt. Gallup now showed Roosevelt holding 499 electoral votes with Willkie shriveling down to 32. Was it possible for Willkie to regain momentum? His sagging poll numbers suggested to some GOP leaders and pundits that Republican voters—especially isolationist-leaning ones—were more excited when he flayed the president for being a warmonger than when he ridiculed him as an appeaser. According to *Time*, Willkie was not giving Republicans what they wanted to hear—"griddle-hot partisan talk."[51]

And so, with Republican leaders begging him to go on the warpath, Willkie cooked up more griddle-hot talk. Even as he continued to make clear his loathing for fascism and rejection of compromise with Nazi Germany, he escalated his attacks on Roosevelt. Backtracking from his descriptions of the president as an appeaser, Willkie berated him now for being a warmonger who imprudently insulted the Axis powers and was steering the nation toward an armed conflagration.

In December 1939, Willkie had told White House insider Ben Cohen that he could not "imagine himself making the equivocating statements which a candidate for office usually must make." And in early September, before kicking off his campaign, he had idealistically stated, "I will not compromise my principles or modify my basic philosophy to gain the office of president." But by the fall, he found himself making precisely those shady compromises. "You can't do anything until you're elected," his advisor Sam Pryor once pragmatically counseled. "And to get elected you have to make compromises. After you're elected, you can be as radical as you want." Isolationists in his audiences could cheer themselves hoarse, but Willkie's new tack cost him the support of backers like Lippmann and Dorothy Thompson and brought him into alliance, as his biographer Steve Neal commented, with people for whom he had contempt—rabid isolationists like Hamilton Fish and Charles Lindbergh.[52]

"Is there any one who thinks that the President is sincerely and honestly trying to keep us out of war?" Willkie demanded in a speech at Theodore Roosevelt High School in the Bronx on October 8. "No! No!" came shouts from the audience, while a few yelled back "Yes!" Now the Republican candidate charged Roosevelt with maneuvering the country toward war. The president must come clean, he demanded, and tell the nation whether there were "any international understandings to put America into this war that we, the citizens of the United States, do not know about." Repeating the isolationist article of faith that waging war and preserving democracy were mutually exclusive, he said that civil liberties and the American way of life could not be preserved if the nation went to war. Later that same day, in a radio broadcast, he again stated that, intentionally or not, "this administration is rapidly pushing us toward war, and also is pushing us toward a totalitarian state."[53]

As for whether or not the United States would ultimately enter the conflict, he told reporters in the Bronx that "if I am President, the people of the United States are going to decide that question." Was he suggesting a post-election national referendum on entering the war? In early 1938, an isolationist Democratic congressman from Indiana, Louis Ludlow, had proposed just such a scheme. He had unsuccessfully called for a constitutional amendment stipulating that, absent an actual invasion by a foreign force, the United States could not engage in warfare unless such action was approved in a nationwide vote.[54]

The candidate's lurch toward anti-interventionism seemed to be paying off. "In the last few days Mr. Willkie's vigorous and valiant drive has been taking hold," editorialized the *Christian Science Monitor* approvingly on October 14, while the *New York Times*, which had already endorsed Willkie in September, happily noted that the errors its candidate had made earlier in the campaign had been repaired. On that same day, the British ambassador to the United States made the same diagnosis. Willkie "seems to be recovering," Lord Lothian wrote to the Foreign Office in London. "He is indefatigable in presenting himself and his views to the electorate. Inner ring Democratic circles are becoming alarmed." And the latest Gallup poll showed Willkie picking up three more states: Illinois, Indiana, and Michigan.[55]

In Syracuse, New York, in mid-October, Willkie again accused the president of being both a dictator and a warmonger, of following "the pattern of dictatorship—the usurpation of power by manufactured emergencies." Three days later in St. Louis, Willkie was greeted with a hundred-car parade and miles of streets lined with cheering people throwing confetti. To the applause of twenty-seven thousand people in the St. Louis arena, he again pounded the Roosevelt administration, this time attributing the global conflagration to the president's failed economic policies. At bewildering length he quoted from Winston Churchill, who in 1937 and 1938 had expounded on the importance to world peace of an economically strong and prosperous United States.

Willkie went on to attribute the rise of fascism in Europe, the Nazi Blitzkrieg, and the fall of France to the unfulfilled promises of the New Deal. "Let us be very very clear about this," he declared in his speech, "the fact that the New Deal stopped the recovery that was coming about in 1937 helped wreck France and England and helped to promote Hitler." And, once again, he charged that Roosevelt intended to take the country into war. "We do not want to send our boys over there again. If you elect me, I will not send them over. By the same token I believe if you reelect the third-term candidate, *they will be sent.*" His words seemed a repudiation of the Wendell Willkie who, more bellicose than FDR, had told the crowd in Elwood that he would "not hesitate to stand for war."[56]

Willkie also appeared to backtrack on his passionate commitment to help Great Britain. Earlier that fall, in San Francisco, he soberly warned that "if Britain falls we are utterly and savagely alone"; in Cleveland, days after the announcement in Berlin of the "Tripartite Pact" among Germany, Italy, and Japan, he had pledged to aid the heroic British people "even if it meant the sacrifice of some speed in building up our own airfleet"; and in Boston on October 11, he repeated his resolve "to do everything in our power to strengthen those heroic British people." But on October 17 in St. Louis, looking for a way to please isolationists without entirely abandoning Britain, he blamed the Roosevelt administration for forcing the nation to "make the awful choice as to whether to supply Britain first or ourselves first. We cannot supply either one adequately, much less both." In other words, it was Roosevelt's fault that the United States could no longer safely afford to aid its ally. The day after his St. Louis speech, Gallup showed Willkie climbing back to 117 electoral votes but still trailing Roosevelt by 10 percent in the popular vote.[57]

In the Chicago Stadium on October 22, Willkie declared that if Roosevelt's "promise to keep our boys out of foreign wars is no better than his promise to balance the budget, they're already almost on the transports." That same day, in Milwaukee, he said that "the American people desire, desire with all of their hearts, peace, peace, peace!" And the path to peace, peace, peace in a world staggering from the fascist rampage was, in his mind, straightforward, simple, and Jeffersonianly poetic: the nation had only to become "strong in the arts of peace, the arts of industry and the pursuit of happiness."[58]

"I think we have them on the run," an optimistic Willkie had written to Senator Vandenberg on that day.[59] But while he was urging the nation to master the "arts of peace," the front-page headline in the *New York Times* that morning read "Nazi Fliers Foiled by London's Smoke." Rising from the countless smoldering bombed-out buildings in East London, thick smoke had forced German bombers to bypass the city and drop their missiles over Liverpool, Glasgow, and Bristol instead.[60] Even so, those grim reports of terror bombings did not give Willkie pause.

Despite his increasingly strident attacks on the president, Willkie could not compete on the stump with the master communicator. "You—people like you," he had declared to his audience in Springfield, Illinois, flailing about almost helplessly for the right words, "who can understand, who must understand—must join me, must join these other fine men in this crusade to stop this thing in America."[61] With tens of thousands of words in the English language, he needed a more compelling one than "thing" to describe the lethal threat to American self-government. But Willkie was not the gifted extemporaneous speaker he thought he was, nor was his team of amateur speechwriters up to the task. His verbal struggles were devoid of ringing phrases and emotional lift.[62]

For eight years, Americans had gathered around their radios in their living rooms and kitchens, listening attentively to Roosevelt's fireside chats. Those talks had inspired the affection, confidence, and trust of Americans reeling from the dislocations of the Great Depression. "Together we cannot fail," he had said in his very first fireside chat in 1933. With his warm, melodious voice, precise, unhurried pronunciation, studied inflections and emphases, and deliberately slow, rhythmic cadences, Franklin Roosevelt spoke to his listeners as if confiding in them, poring over their problems with them, carefully laying out his plans. Never talking down to them, he knew just how to reach their intelligence as well as their emotions.

But many of Willkie's talks, though they contained thoughtful proposals for economic, agricultural, and labor reform, drowned in lengthy quotations, abstruse jargon and minutiae, fabricated allegations, tangled syntax, and lackluster phrases. Roy Howard, Henry Luce, and others complained that Russell Davenport was writing all the candidate's speeches, with only occasional input from advisors like Raymond Buell, Henry Cabot Lodge, Raymond Moley, and sometimes from Luce himself.[63] Making matters worse, Davenport had "a platitudinous, moralistic approach," Buell remarked. He fumed that Willkie's speech in Yonkers, New York, on September 28 was "one of the worst yet in its vapid optimism and lack of content." In that speech, after humbly expressing gratitude to all the people who had come out to listen to him over the previous two weeks—"I was deeply touched"—Willkie rambled through scattered attacks on the New Deal and the president—"the man whose trademark is on this depression, the man whose foreign policies helped to disrupt the democratic world"—renunciations of the "petty spirit" of partisanship, and acknowledgments of the "stupendous task" ahead. Finally he made a vow: "I pledge a new world."

Though the Republican crowds who heard Willkie in person often found him appealing and gallant, over the radio "his speeches sounded harsh, hurried and diffuse," remarked one of Willkie's critics, describing his talks as "short-range blasts of birdshot rather than pinpointed high explosive shells."[64]

That critic's name was Robert Sherwood, and he had just come on board as Roosevelt's speechwriter.

Chapter 14

Enter Robert Sherwood

W HAT ARE YOU WARMONGERS UP TO NOW?" Harry Hopkins heat-
edly demanded when he once again encountered the glamorous bon
vivant and dramatist Robert Sherwood in the summer of 1940 at
the Long Island home of a mutual friend. The 44-year-old Sherwood had already
won Pulitzer Prizes for two of his plays—in 1936 for *Idiot's Delight* and in 1939 for
Abe Lincoln in Illinois. His latest play, *There Shall Be No Night*, about the Russian
invasion of Finland, had recently opened on Broadway. It was about men who
fight against barbarism, wrote *New York Times* critic Brooks Atkinson, "not for
glory, but humbly to preserve the tradition of freedom . . . to fulfill the destiny
of civilization."[1]

Hearing himself greeted as a warmonger, Sherwood assumed that Hopkins was joking, but he answered seriously that he was working on a campaign
to transfer fifty American destroyers to the Royal Navy. "Don't you realize,"
Hopkins shot back, "that a public demand like that would be a big embarrassment to the President—especially now, with an election coming up? Don't
you know that our country is neutral?" Sherwood felt himself getting angrier
and angrier that a man so close to Roosevelt could be such a blatant isolationist. "The whole country's isolationist," Hopkins snapped, "except for a few
pro-British fanatics like you." Sherwood later recalled that he answered Hopkins "with a tirade of much more vehemence and eloquence than I can usually
summon." When the playwright's harangue was over, Hopkins grinned. "All
right then," he said, "why don't you get out and say these things to the people?" It had all been an elaborate test. "Hopkins pulled that same goading
tactic on a great many people to find out just how sound their arguments were

and how sincere was their advocacy of them," Sherwood wrote. "But one could never be entirely sure if it was a trick, for sometimes this was his method of telling an overzealous proponent to pipe down."[2] In any case, Sherwood passed Hopkins's exam with flying colors. A+.

The result of this "interview" was an invitation for Sherwood to join the White House speechwriting team. For the next five years, while modestly considering himself "a transient with a temporary visa in the realm of politics," Sherwood would work closely with Roosevelt's other excellent speechwriters: Sam Rosenman, the president's old friend from his New York gubernatorial days; Hopkins himself, who stepped down as commerce secretary in August 1940; the poet Archibald MacLeish; and, on occasion, Carl Sandburg. And of course he also worked with the master editor himself, Franklin Roosevelt—the former president of the *Harvard Crimson*. Until Pearl Harbor, Sherwood would live in the White House alongside the president, Rosenman, and Hopkins.[3]

As a young man, Sherwood had been an internationalist. Fresh out of Harvard in 1917, he had joined the Plattsburg Movement, signing up for its Officers Training Camps. Rejected by the American army because, at 6' 7", he was deemed too tall, he enlisted in the Forty-Second Battalion of the Canadian Black Watch and was sent to France. After being gassed and wounded twice fighting in that devastating, futile war, he became a self-described pacifist and until 1938 was a passionate advocate for international disarmament. "I believed that war was a hideous injustice," he wrote, "and that no man had the right to call himself civilized as long as he admitted that another world war could conceivably be justifiable." When war erupted in Europe in 1939, Sherwood found himself, as he later wrote, "in a frenzy of uncertainty." He knew all the arguments for keeping the United States out of another war, but he also knew that Hitler posed a lethal threat to all the decent democracies of the world. A speech Charles Lindbergh gave in October 1939 removed any lingering confusion, for the aviator's words proved to him "that Hitlerism was already powerfully and persuasively represented in our own midst." It was after hearing that talk that Sherwood made up his mind to speak out in protest against the "hysterical escapism which . . . pointed our foreign policy toward suicidal isolationism."[4]

"What do you think the president ought to say?" Hopkins asked Sherwood when they met in New York in October 1940. He was hoping for some input from Sherwood for a Columbus Day speech in Dayton, Ohio, that Roosevelt was scheduled to give later that month. Soon Sam Rosenman joined the discussion. He had been writing speeches for FDR since their time in the governor's mansion in Albany and believed he had mastered the art of writing "the way [Roosevelt] spoke." After the three men tossed around some ideas, Rosenman suddenly slapped a pencil on the dining room table and said, "Well, gentlemen, there comes a time in the life of every speech when it's got to be written." Sherwood later commented that this was his "induction" into working with Hopkins and Rosenman.[5] They decided to use the occasion to assure the nations in North and South America that the United States was determined to defend the hemisphere even as it gave military aid to Great Britain.

Roosevelt's stop in Dayton was part of a swing through cities and towns in Pennsylvania and Ohio. It was billed as another military inspection tour— "I have come here to educate myself," the president told a crowd in Pittsburgh. He visited flood control engineering projects and new public housing for defense workers. He went to steel mills that produced armaments for battleships and saw, at close range, the reduction of ore and the pouring out of molten metal. One reporter noted that the trip, which brought out cheering throngs of supporters—especially in the poorer towns—had "all the fervor and trappings of an old-fashioned political campaign."[6]

In Dayton, one hundred and fifty thousand people lined the streets, joyously waving at the president as he drove by in his motorcade. But he chose to give his Columbus Day address away from the crowds and on a radio hookup from the dining car of his railroad train. Only a small staff was present as newsreel cameras recorded the speech under blazing lights.

He began by noting that the anniversary of the Italian explorer Christopher Columbus's discovery of the New World was an occasion to remember that the Italians who came "in welcome waves of immigration" to America's shores had made invaluable contributions; they helped "create the scientific, commercial, professional and artistic life of the New World." Four months after the president had slammed Italy for stabbing France in the back, his appreciative nod to the Italian-American community was an attempt to recoup his losses among those traditionally Democratic voters.

Then Roosevelt movingly described America as a community of immigrants who shared the same ideals and aspirations. "Men and women of courage, of enterprise, of vision," he said, formed "a new human reservoir." They came not for economic betterment alone "but for the personal freedoms and liberties which had been denied to them in the Old World. They came not to conquer one another but to live with one another. They proudly carried with them their inheritance of culture, but they cheerfully left behind them the burden of prejudice and hate." Contrasting the Nazis' ideology of racial superiority and conquest with the spirit of international cooperation that reigned in the Americas, Roosevelt said that no group in the New World had any desire to subjugate or dominate the others.

Rejecting the defeatist propaganda that "repeats and repeats that democracy is a decadent form of government," Roosevelt triumphantly announced that "we reject that thought. We say that *we are the future!*" With that affirmative statement came an unwavering promise of support for Great Britain, "almost *the last free people*" still fighting to hold the "dictator countries" at bay. "Our course is clear. Our decision is made," he said. "The men and women of Britain have shown how free people defend what they know to be right. Their heroic defense will be recorded for all time." "Viva la Democracia!" he concluded. "Long Live Democracy!"[7]

A tremendous amount of work went into the preparation of almost all of Roosevelt's speeches—discussions over breakfast in the president's bedroom, group brainstorming for days, all-night drafting sessions, more discussions over martinis in the Oval Study, fact-checking, multiple drafts, vetting by the departments of War and State, timing the talk down to the second, and typing it on special limp paper so that there would be no rustling noises when the president turned a page. And yet FDR was happiest, commented Robert Sherwood, when he could express himself in simple, homey, even trite phrases.[8] The sentences and vocabulary of his Dayton talk were indeed simple and straightforward; the discussion of America as a nation of immigrants was welcoming and inclusive; short, optimistic phrases like "We are the future" were memorable and reassuring; the black and white antitheses—liberty vs. hate, democracy vs. dictatorship—sparked a combative adrenalin rush; certain phrases were repeated and rhythmically orchestrated; the use of the word "our"—such as in "our course is clear" and "our decision is made"—created feelings of solidarity, purpose, and confidence. A+ for Sherwood, Rosenman, and Hopkins.

The three speechwriters listened to the Dayton address on the radio, Sherwood holding a carbon copy of the text to compare it with the words the president spoke. "I thoroughly enjoyed his expression of pleasure," Rosenman later said. "Since Sherwood was a playwright, he should have been used to hearing his lines spoken by others; but, as he said to me, 'When Roosevelt does it—it's different!'"[9] Even with his extensive Broadway experience, Sherwood still marveled at the "unfailing precision" with which FDR enunciated his points, "his grace in reconciling the sublime with the ridiculous." In Roosevelt, he found a born actor, one with a perfect sense of timing and an actor's range of emotion. "No mere politician, and certainly no mere ghost writer,"

Sherwood wrote, could put into speeches "the same degree of conviction and the same deep spiritual quality that he conveyed."[10]

Roosevelt was an eager and skilled participant in the speechwriting process, too. He paid special attention to punctuation, not because he wanted grammatical correctness but because it was an aid to him when he read the speech aloud. He liked dashes, not commas, because they were clearer visual aids. "Grace!" Sherwood would hear FDR say to his secretary Grace Tully. "How many times do I have to tell you not to waste the taxpayers' commas?"[11]

But were FDR's eloquent words in Dayton enough for a win in November? He had given a talk about unity, democracy, and heroic resistance to oppression, but hardly a rousing, partisan campaign speech. On October 10, one new opinion research organization, the Rogers Dunn Survey, concluded that Willkie would win in November with an astounding 334 electoral votes. In mid-October, the more established—since 1935—Gallup poll showed Willkie slightly edging up to 45 percent of the popular vote from 44 percent earlier in the month and judged that six midwestern states were shifting toward the Republican. The results indicated a comfortable lead for Roosevelt, but Gallup took pains to explain that a change of just a few percentage points could swing a large number of electoral votes to one candidate or the other. When the Gallup organization asked Americans how they would vote if there were no war in Europe, 53 percent of those surveyed replied that they would cast their ballots for Willkie.[12]

Those poll numbers and the opposition to Roosevelt in much of the nation's press worried many Democrats around the country—congressmen, governors, mayors—who were on the ballot in November and whose political fates were tied to Roosevelt's coattails. Especially worrying to them were the Republican scare tactics. Posters in Philadelphia read, "SAVE YOUR CHURCH, DICTATORS HATE RELIGION, VOTE THE STRAIGHT REPUBLICAN TICKET." German-speaking people in Iowa were told that if Roosevelt was reelected their sons would be sent to Germany to fight against their relatives. Policyholders received notices from their insurance companies informing them that Roosevelt's election would make their policies relatively worthless; isolationists mailed telegrams to doctors warning that a Roosevelt victory would spell socialized medicine; and an advertisement in the *Chicago Daily Tribune*, paid for by a Chicago bank, urged depositors to vote for Willkie if they wanted to protect their savings.[13]

Roosevelt's advisors and staff—along with hundreds of Democrats and independents across the nation—pleaded with him to "*do something!*" It was time for the president to "smash Willkie," they said.[14] Over dinner at the White House one evening, Roosevelt's son Franklin, Jr., also urged his father to be more active. "Are the party workers out ringing doorbells?" the president asked. When his son nodded his head, he said, "Good. Then they're not relying upon me." But others, including Harry Hopkins, were also concerned about Willkie's recent gains in the polls. They advised against making a "scorching attack" on Willkie, but wanted the president to make the most of his sharp wit, "the deft sarcastic touches" that he had used so skillfully in the past.[15]

Hopkins's prodding and especially Willkie's campaign itself finally changed Roosevelt's mind. He was deeply angered by Willkie's cries of dictator and warmonger. "I am fighting mad," FDR told Harold Ickes, as he embraced the idea that rousing campaign speeches instead of presidential aloofness were now required.[16] He and his advisors decided on a series of major political addresses in the two climactic weeks of the campaign: Philadelphia on October 23; Madison Square Garden on October 28; Boston on October 30; Brooklyn, New York, on November 1; Cleveland on November 2; and a concluding radio speech on November 4, election eve. What about a speech a little farther out west, more removed from the capital? a sympathetic Washington columnist asked the president. That idea, FDR wrote back, was, "as Al Smith would say, 'outta de winder.'"[17]

Snapping into action, Roosevelt gave his first true campaign speech of the 1940 season in Philadelphia—and used it to allay Americans' fears about war. Two weeks earlier Willkie had spoken in the city of brotherly love, but much larger and noisier crowds turned out for FDR. Now, the president responded to Willkie's wild accusations that he had made deals with foreign powers and that he would replace American democracy with a totalitarian government. In the convention hall, jammed with sixteen thousand people, he said he would set the record straight and "answer falsifications with facts." It was one thing for a candidate to urge the repeal of social security or the elimination of the truth-in-securities act. "But it is an entirely different thing," he explained, "for any party or any candidate to state, for example, that the president of the United States telephoned to Mussolini or Hitler to sell Czechoslovakia down the river; or to state that the unfortunate unemployed of the nation are going to be driven into concentration camps; or that the social security funds of the Government of the United States will not be in existence when the workers of today become old enough to apply for them; or that the election of the present Government means the end of American democracy within four years."

It was simple, he said, to repeat and repeat and repeat falsehoods "with the idea that by constant repetition and with no contradiction the misstatements will finally come to be believed." In fact, all the "fantastic misstatements" of his adversaries, he charged, launching into rough accusations himself, resembled "techniques of propaganda, created and developed in dictator countries." Taking a swipe at the Republican press that had been on the attack against him since 1933, he said that he did not believe that the repetition of deliberate misstatements would prevail "in a democracy like ours, where the radio and a *part* of the press—I repeat, where the radio and a *part* of the press—remain open to both sides."

The current campaign of fabrications, Roosevelt explained, was calculated to "create fear by instilling in the minds of our people doubt of each other, doubt of their Government, and doubt of the purposes of their democracy." But the vast majority of Americans would not be scared by "this blitzkrieg of verbal incendiary bombs," he said, neatly attributing to his opposition a softer version of the tactics of the Axis powers. And so he would continue to answer falsifications with facts. "I will not pretend that I find this an unpleasant duty. I am an old campaigner, and I love a good fight!"

Turning to the domestic front, he delivered several knockout punches to Willkie's courtship of the labor vote. All the "crocodile tears" that the Republicans were shedding for American workers were no more than a cynical charade, Roosevelt said. "Back in 1932, those leaders were willing to let the workers starve if they could not get a job. Back in 1932, they were not willing to guarantee collective bargaining. Back in 1932, they met the demands of unemployed veterans with troops and tanks. Back in 1932, they raised their hands in horror at the thought of fixing a minimum wage or maximum hours for labor. They never gave one thought to such things as pensions for old age or insurance for the unemployed." Then came the clincher: "In 1940, eight years later, what a different tune is played by them! . . . It is a tune with overtones which whisper: 'Votes, votes, votes!'" The crowd erupted in laughter, cheers, and applause.

Republicans suddenly wanted to claim ownership of those New Deal reforms, he continued. "They believe in them so much," he said with low chuckles, artfully mocking the newly minted progressives of the GOP, "that they will never be happy until they can clasp them to their own chests and put their own brand upon them. If they could only get control of them, they plead, they would take so much better care of them, honest-to-goodness they would!"[18]

It was Rosenman, Sherwood, and Hopkins at their best. The combination of Roosevelt's acting talent and their fiery, derisive words was unbeatable.[19]

Finally, after scornfully grinding Willkie and the Republicans into dust, Roosevelt returned to the central issue—and he was categorical and truthful: the nation was arming itself not for conquest or intervention in foreign disputes but for its own self-defense. "We will not participate in foreign wars and we will not send our army, naval or air forces to fight in foreign lands outside of the Americas except in case of attack. It is for peace that I have labored," he concluded. "And it is for peace that I shall labor all the days of my life."

Every day that fall, the president read intelligence reports from Tokyo, Moscow, Chungking, Athens, and London, outlining the grim and explosive world situation. At dawn on October 28, Italian troops launched their attack on Greece. On a day when Hitler was meeting with Mussolini in Florence, Italian warplanes pounded Greek defenses, bombing the port cities of Patras and Piraeus. Living up to his malignant credo of "duty and struggle and conquest," Mussolini began the assault half an hour before the expiration of an ultimatum demanding that Greece cede strategic air and naval bases to Italy so that "il Duce" could use them against the British fleet in the Mediterranean. Greece's long coastline and fine harbors represented an enormous prize for the Axis powers: a navy and an air force that possessed those bases would have control over the entrances to the Adriatic Sea and the Black Sea straits as well as over much of the eastern Mediterranean. The British, fearing that the Axis would next move toward the Suez Canal and the oil reserves of the Middle East, promised all possible assistance to Greece. "We are with you in this struggle— your cause is our cause," wrote King George VI to General John Metaxas, the Greek premier. "We will give you all the help in our power. We fight a common foe and we will share a united victory." Two days later, Hitler promised his partner Mussolini that "no one now will snatch victory from us."[20]

On the day that Italy attacked Greece, Roosevelt went on a fifty-eight-mile journey through New York's boroughs, stopping at groundbreaking ceremonies for two new tunnels connecting the outer boroughs to Manhattan, the Brooklyn Battery Tunnel and the Queens Midtown Tunnel. The crowning event of the day was a huge Democratic rally in Madison Square Garden at which FDR as well as Governor Herbert Lehman, Senator Robert Wagner, Jim Farley, and a few other notables would speak. The president finally arrived there at 10:00 p.m., exhausted from the talks and crowds of the day. But in front of the jubilant throng of twenty-two thousand, he came alive, energized by their ear-splitting cheers, applause, whistles, and shouts of "We want Roosevelt!"[21]

He began by discussing the crisis in Europe. "I am quite sure that all of you will feel the same sorrow in your hearts that I feel," he said, "sorrow for the Italian people and the Grecian people, that they should have been involved together in conflict."[22] This time there was no mention of Italy stabbing its neighbor in the back. On the contrary, seeking votes, votes, and more votes, he placed victim and aggressor on the same level—expressing empathy for both populations.

And then came the real meat of the speech: an attack *not* on Wendell Willkie but on the GOP and the lies it spread, its phony allegations that Roosevelt had neglected defense and that the nation was militarily unprepared. He was going to nail up those falsehoods to dry on the barn door "the way when I was a boy up in Dutchess County we used to nail up the skins of foxes and weasels."

"For almost seven years the Republican leaders in the Congress kept on saying that I was placing too *much* emphasis on national defense. And now today," the president sneered, his voice oozing the "deft sarcastic touches" that Hopkins had recently counseled, "these men of great vision have suddenly discovered that there is a war going on in Europe and another one in Asia! And so, now, always with their eyes on the good old ballot box, they are charging that we have placed too *little* emphasis on national defense." The president boasted that the army, air forces, and navy were at the highest level of efficiency and fighting strength that they had ever been in peacetime. Of course, he added, in light of the world crisis, work was going forward to make America's defenses even stronger.

Playing the role of prosecuting attorney, Roosevelt announced that he would proceed "now to *indict* these Republican leaders out of their own mouths." Quoting from the *Congressional Record*, he read aloud one congressman's words: "The facts are that we have the largest and most powerful Navy we ever had." "Now, who do you suppose made that statement a little over two years ago?" he asked with a grin. "It was not I. . . . It was the ranking Republican member of the House Committee on Foreign Affairs, Republican leader, Hamilton Fish."

Next he quoted from the even more damaging words of Herbert Hoover: "We shall be expending nine hundred million dollars more than any nation on earth. We are *leading* the arms race." Hoover's words were followed by Vandenberg's: "I rise in opposition to this super-super Navy bill. I do not believe it is justified by any conclusive demonstration of national necessity."

Roosevelt arrived at his closing argument: "Today they proclaim that this Administration has starved our armed forces, that our Navy is anemic, our Army puny, our air forces piteously weak. Yes, it is a remarkable somersault." His speechwriters added a little icing to the cake with words from a famous nineteenth-century song: "On the radio these Republicans orators swing through the air with the greatest of ease; but the American people are not voting this year for the best trapeze performer."

And who were the politics-playing leaders of this Republican circus who voted against increasing naval appropriations, against constructing more battleships and planes, against repeal of the arms embargo? They included the Republican candidate for vice president, Senator McNary, as well as Senators Vandenberg and Nye. Right on cue, the crowd roared and booed at the mention of their names. And who were some of the other culprits? "Now wait," the president said with glee, "a perfectly beautiful rhythm—Congressmen Martin, Barton, and Fish!" The audience howled with laughter, eager to hear the names again. The president did not disappoint. Great Britain, he said, would never have received an ounce of support from the United States if the decision had been left to—MARTIN, BARTON, AND FISH! The audience deliriously took up the refrain, blissfully chanting it aloud with the president.[23]

The unforgettable triplet of Martin, Barton, and Fish was Sherwood and Rosenman's masterstroke. In their first draft, they had listed them as Barton, Fish, and Martin. Then they changed the order and handed the new line to the president. He read it aloud. "His eyes twinkled and he grinned from ear to ear," Rosenman observed. Not only was the rhythm contagious, but, commented Sherwood, the crowds loved such "organized exercises of derision." And this particular exercise in derision worked marvelously, for without ever mentioning Wendell Willkie by name, FDR's speechwriters had memorably linked him to the obstructionists in the GOP. "When I heard the president hang the isolationist votes of Martin, Barton, and Fish on me and get away with it," a rueful Willkie later said, "I knew I was licked."[24]

Roosevelt did not stop there. After convicting Republicans of "timidity, weakness, and short-sightedness," he wanted to score one more point. Eight days before the election, he sought to prove that he was committed not just to peace but to neutrality as well. "By the Neutrality Act of 1935, and by other steps," he told his listeners in Madison Square Garden and his radio listeners across the nation, "we made it clear to every American, and to every foreign nation that we would avoid becoming entangled through some episode beyond our borders. Those were measures to keep us at peace. . . . Since 1935, there has been no entanglement and," he categorically and chimerically promised, "*there will be no entanglement.*"[25]

It was bewildering to hear the president embrace the Neutrality Act, for people who remembered recent history knew that, at the time, the White House had opposed its core provision—the arms embargo that did not distinguish between aggressor nations and their victims. But with the nation dominated by powerful isolationist sentiment, the Neutrality Act had passed both chambers of Congress by almost unanimous votes.

When Roosevelt signed the bill into law in 1935, he had issued a statement making his reservations clear. Though he recognized that the act met the needs of the present, he noted that history was filled with unforeseeable situations that called for "some flexibility of action." Indeed, the act's "inflexible provisions," he underscored, "might drag us into war instead of keeping us out."[26] When the neutrality legislation came up for renewal the following year, the world situation had worsened, but the president was focused on the upcoming election of 1936 and declined to counter the isolationist tide. Three years later, in 1939, he worked successfully behind the scenes for reform of the Neutrality Act and repeal of the arms embargo, freeing him to send the Allies much needed war matériel.

Finally, after taking credit in Madison Square Garden for the Neutrality Act that he had in fact opposed, the president asked Americans to cast their votes once again for him because, he said, he knew best how to ensure a peaceful future. "I am asking the American people to support a continuance of this type of affirmative, realistic fight for peace." Throwing Willkie's accusations back at him, he sternly warned that the election of his opponent would place the government "in the inexperienced hands of those who in these perilous days are willing recklessly to imply that our boys are already on their way to the transports."

This time, Robert Sherwood was less than pleased. He judged the Madison Square Garden speech "one of the most equivocal of Roosevelt's career." Years later, Sherwood would deeply regret yielding to the isolationists' "hysterical demands for sweeping reassurance." But in October 1940, he felt strongly that the risk of future embarrassment was negligible compared to the risk of losing the election.[27]

In October 1940, as Election Day approached, both Roosevelt and Willkie were fighting for their political lives. Like all politicians, their number one priority was winning the election. If the two internationalists needed to talk peace, peace, peace to win, then so be it. If they had to shade or disguise the truth, if Willkie had to hurl fabricated accusations at his opponent about phone calls to Hitler and Mussolini and inadequate and unsanitary housing for the hundreds of thousands of young men about to be drafted, if Roosevelt had to absurdly embrace the Neutrality Act, if Sherwood had to betray his own conscience, then so be it.[28] Their concessions to isolationists and their promises of peace were equally dismal and unrealistic. They were playing their assigned parts in the customary campaign script, wrangling for votes, vying for a knockout punch, hiding their true thoughts and positions—and concealing their fundamental agreement on many crucial issues.

At noon on October 29, the day after Roosevelt's Madison Square Garden speech, Brigadier General Lewis Hershey and Selective Service Director Clarence Dykstra walked onto the stage of Washington's Departmental Auditorium. Camera lights illuminated a ten-gallon glass fishbowl—the same one used in the draft lottery of 1917—filled with nine thousand blue capsules, each containing a different registration number. The hall was crowded with cabinet members, senators, congressmen, young men, anxious parents, and reporters. The buzz quieted when the president, on the arm of his appointments secretary Pa Watson, walked slowly onto the stage.

His words broadcast across the nation, Roosevelt gravely addressed the American people. "This is a solemn ceremony," he began. "It is accompanied by no fanfare—no blowing of bugles or beating of drums. There should be none." Explaining the reason for the selective service lottery, he said, "We are mustering all our resources, manhood and industry and wealth to make our nation strong in defense. For recent history proves all too clearly, I am sorry to say, that only the strong may continue to live in freedom and in peace."

Then he addressed the young men who would be called up for military training. "You will be members of an army," he said, "which first came together to achieve independence and to establish certain fundamental rights for all men. Ever since that first muster, our democratic army has existed for one purpose only: the defense of our freedom." After carefully outlining the mechanics of the draft, he read aloud from letters he received from three clergymen, representing Catholic, Protestant, and Jewish faiths, who expressed their "love and respect for democracy" and their belief that Americans wanted peace but not "a peace whose definition is slavery or death." The priest, minister, and rabbi assured the young men of "our active comradeship and prayer." In conclusion, the commander in chief told the young men that "you have the confidence, and the gratitude, and the love of your countrymen. We are all with you in the task which enlists the service of all Americans—the task of keeping the peace in this New World of ours."[29]

Stepping forward, Secretary of War Henry Stimson, his eyes blindfolded, put his left hand in the jar, took out the first capsule he touched, and handed it to the president. Across the country, the 1.4 million young men between the ages of 21 and 35 who had registered for the draft anxiously waited to hear the order in which they might be called for induction. President Roosevelt glanced at the newsreel cameramen, waited for their nod, and then slowly intoned, "Drawn by the secretary of war, the first serial number is one—fifty—eight." That registration serial number, held by about six thousand young men, became Draft Order No. 1. People heard a sharp, quickly repressed little scream from the rear of the auditorium. It was a woman who heard the president announce the number of her 21-year-old son. The same number also belonged to another member of the audience, a 34-year-old employee of the Civil Service Commission. "I didn't know whether to stand up and salute or just remain quiet," he said later to reporters.[30] Other officials, cabinet officers, and members of Congress proceeded to draw eighteen more serial numbers. Then, continuing into the night, a long procession of veterans drew the tiny capsules from the bowl. The lottery went on until 5:00 a.m. the next day. Hours later, the numbers of the eight hundred thousand men called to service would be repeated on the radio and reported in newspapers.

Many people had expected Roosevelt to delay the lottery until after the election. "It was a brave decision on the part of the President," Stimson wrote later that day. "It showed good statesmanship [and] the solemn nature of the occasion . . . served to change the event of the Draft into a great asset in his favor." Indeed, by putting his responsibilities as commander in chief ahead of his political campaign, Roosevelt made up for his dubious promises of peace. But the following day, the results of the latest Gallup poll showed FDR dropping slightly from 55 percent to 53 percent and Willkie climbing by the same amount, from 45 percent to 47. The numbers were trending toward Willkie, announced George Gallup, who pronounced the race neck-and-neck.[31]

Chapter 15

Franklin and Joe

O N SUNDAY, OCTOBER 27, 1940, the phone rang in Roosevelt's Oval
Room while he and Sam Rayburn, the new Speaker of the House,
and the young Lyndon Johnson were having lunch. "Ah, Joe, it is so
good to hear your voice," Roosevelt said to his ambassador to Great Britain.
"Come to the White House tonight for a little family dinner. I'm dying to talk
to you." With that, continuing to exude his usual warmth on the phone, he
turned to his Texas guests and drew his finger, like a razor, across his throat.[1]

The 52-year-old Joseph Patrick Kennedy had just arrived from London at
the airport in New York, preceded by rumors that he might publicly come out
against Roosevelt. Though Kennedy was not popular with Boston Brahmins
or Jews, he was loved in his hometown by Irish-Catholics who were no friends
of England, and his endorsement of Willkie might well cost the president the
seventeen electoral votes of the Bay State. Republicans like Henry Luce and
General Robert E. Wood, the acting chairman of America First, were said to
be steering him in that direction. To friends in London, the ambassador had
boasted that he could "put 25 million Catholic votes behind Wendell Willkie
to throw Roosevelt out."[2]

For almost two months, Kennedy had been yearning to return to the
United States. Ignoring taunts of cowardice from the British press, he had
moved his large family out of London during the Blitz and into a seventy-
room mansion he rented in Sunningdale, west of the capital. Though the
president no longer trusted his reports or his judgment and had sent World
War I hero Colonel William J. "Wild Bill" Donovan to Britain for a true picture

of the situation, he nevertheless enjoined Kennedy to remain at his post. Perhaps he believed—as Washington insiders and columnists Joseph Alsop and Robert Kintner suggested—that his ambassador would cause him less harm in London than at home. FDR was well aware that Kennedy "has less than no remaining fondness for his chief," Alsop and Kintner reported in early October, before the ambassador's return home. "The instant he gets through the customs," they wrote, he was sure to spew out his opinions to every available American listener in sight.[3]

Roosevelt and Kennedy were both Harvard graduates, and there the similarity ended. One was a product of the small, secure circle of the wealthy, well-bred, and well-read Hudson Valley gentry; the other, the son of an East Boston saloon keeper. Born into the vulnerable world of Irish immigrants, the striving Kennedy managed, by pluck, luck, and a measure of underhandedness, to become extremely wealthy, making millions in stock speculation, the movies, liquor importing, oil ventures, real estate, and corporate reorganization. In 1932, he had been a generous supporter of FDR, who in turn satisfied the Boston Irishman's eagerness for public office by naming him the first chairman of the Securities and Exchange Commission and then director of the Maritime Commission. Backing FDR again in the 1936 election, Kennedy published a campaign book, *I'm for Roosevelt*, in which he wrote that the gravest danger to democracy in America resided in the "unreasoning malicious ill-will displayed by the rich and powerful against their common leader." This time FDR rewarded Kennedy with the ambassadorship to the Court of St. James, a decision he would have much cause to regret. Appointed in 1938, Kennedy became a "trouble-maker," as Roosevelt would call him in October 1940, "entirely out of hand."[4]

In London, Kennedy had gravitated toward Britain's appeasers and apologists for the Nazis, becoming the "prize exhibit," in the words of historian Michael Beschloss, of the Cliveden set, Lord and Lady Astor's circle of Germanophile British aristocrats. Harold Nicolson, a member of Parliament, remarked that the ambassador was warmly greeted by the decadent upper class "who hope that he may bring with him a little raft of appeasement on which they can float for a year longer before they are finally submerged."[5] Kennedy was "Germany's best friend in London," effused the Reich's ambassador to Britain, Herbert von Dirksen, who did not seem to disagree with Kennedy's advice that Germany conduct its anti-Jewish measures less publicly and without so much "loud clamor." Kennedy himself, von Dirksen reported to Berlin, "understood our Jewish policy completely; he was from Boston and there, in one golf club and in other clubs, no Jews had been admitted for the past 50 years. . . . Such pronounced attitudes were quite common, but people avoided making so much outward fuss about it."[6]

Kennedy was impressed by letters from his friend Charles Lindbergh, in which the aviator described Germany's military strength as "greater than that of all other European countries combined," and he passed those letters on to Prime Minister Chamberlain. In Chamberlain, Kennedy found a "warm friend," as Beschloss observed. "He shared the prime minister's dread of war and communism." Kennedy became proudly convinced that the prime minister's agreement with Hitler at Munich was a direct result of his own intervention.[7] "Do you think the Lindbergh memorandum had anything to do with Chamberlain's decision at Munich?" reporter Walter Winchell asked Kennedy in 1939. "I think it was the decisive factor in his mind," Kennedy bragged with his usual self-assurance.[8] For his part, Lindbergh supported Kennedy's claim. The ambassador had "taken a large part in bringing about the conference," the flier wrote.[9] A few weeks before Munich, Kennedy had sent the State Department the draft of a speech he intended to deliver in Aberdeen, Scotland, in early September; his text included the line, "I can't for the life of me understand why anybody would want to go to war to save the Czechs." The White House immediately struck the astounding language from the speech. "If Kennedy wants to resign when he comes back, I will accept it on the spot," Roosevelt said to Henry Morgenthau.[10]

A few weeks after the Munich conference, in a speech he gave in October 1938 at a Trafalgar Day dinner in London sponsored by the British Navy League—a talk that the State Department apparently neglected to vet— Kennedy was more explicit about his belief that both Britain and the United States needed to make concessions to Germany. Although he allowed that there were some "divergences" between fascism and democracy, he discerned no moral issue in the conflict between fascism and democracy. "There is simply no sense, common or otherwise," he stated, to the dismay of many of the dinner guests, "in letting these differences grow into unrelenting antagonisms. After all, we have to live together in the same world." The headline in the *New York Times* the following day read, "KENNEDY FOR AMITY WITH FASCIST BLOC, Urges That Democracies and Dictatorships Forget Their Differences in Outlook." Someone should put a "muzzle" on him, wrote one irate columnist.[11]

In late August 1939, on the eve of Germany's invasion of Poland, Kennedy found common ground with Chamberlain's close advisor Horace Wilson; the two agreed that Poland needed to submit to Hitler's ultimatum and surrender the Polish port of Danzig to Germany. For a week the ambassador tried without success to convince Washington to pressure Poland to give in to the Führer's extortion. On September 2, 1939, the day after Hitler launched his attack on Poland, Roosevelt and his friends were playing poker in the White House. With a straight face, Harold Ickes said that he had just heard that Chamberlain was enlarging his cabinet "so he can give Joe Kennedy a place on it." Everyone laughed.[12]

But Kennedy only became more outspoken, more alarmist and defeatist, arguing that it was pointless for America to aid Britain because English democracy was sick and would not recover. "I personally am convinced," Kennedy wrote to Roosevelt on September 3, 1939, the day Britain declared war on Germany, "that, win, lose or draw, England will never be the England that she was and no one can help her to be." Britain, he wrote, had passed its peak. The "signs of decay, if not decadence, here, both in men and institutions," were all too apparent, and war would merely hasten the inevitable decay. America, he counseled, should not attempt to "re-create what has disappeared." A month later, in a gossipy letter to FDR's secretary Missy LeHand, Kennedy confessed that he could not understand what the British were fighting for, but, he added, "one isn't supposed to say this out loud."[13]

Kennedy has "always has been an appeaser and always will be an appeaser," Roosevelt sneered in October 1939, telling Henry Morgenthau that the ambassador was "just a pain in the neck to me."[14]

In late September 1940, as the lights went out again in the city and as terrorized Londoners scrambled into the Underground for shelter from another night of bombs and fire, hoping perhaps to catch a few hours of sleep, Kennedy fired off another memo to Washington. "I cannot impress upon you strongly enough," he cabled the State Department, "my complete lack of confidence in the entire conduct of this war. . . . Imagining for a minute that the English have anything to offer in the line of leadership . . . would be a complete misapprehension." It did not occur to him that the British Empire and its new prime minister, the indomitable Winston Churchill, were now America's only viable ally in a struggle against world catastrophe. Kennedy saw Britain only as a burdensome albatross, and as the Blitz intensified, he cautioned Roosevelt not to let himself be caught "holding the bag in a war in which the Allies expect to be beaten." Off the record, he told columnist Frank Kent that he knew with certainty that "Germany is going to win the war."[15]

Democracy was certainly not doomed in the western world, insisted the young author of a new book, *Why England Slept*. On the contrary, there was no doubt, he wrote, that "in the long run" it was the superior form of government "because it is based on a respect for man as a reasonable being." In the short run, however, democratic governments had to compete with systems built solely for war, and therefore the United States could not afford to be, as England had been, "asleep at the switch."[16] Confronted with totalitarian aggression, democratic nations, he stressed, had to guard against fear and inertia. The United States could not again withdraw from Europe, as it did after the First World War when, as the young author held, the United States "refused to do anything to preserve the democracy we had helped to save. We thought that it made no difference to us what happened in Europe. We are beginning to realize that it does."

In the summer of 1940, *Why England Slept* jumped to the top of the bestseller list—with the help of the author's father, who purchased copies in bulk. It was the senior thesis of a 23-year-old Harvard political science major named John F. Kennedy. Its publication—and its foreword, written by Henry Luce— were testimony to the influence of Joseph P. Kennedy. Though the ambassador had shepherded the book into print, his son rejected his father's defeatism. "Dad is a financial genius," Jack once said, "but in politics he is something else." He concluded his book with an urgent appeal to the United States to get "our armaments and the people behind these armaments . . . prepared . . . *even to the ultimate point of war.* There must be no doubt in anyone's mind, the decision must be automatic: if we debate, if we hesitate, if we question, it will be too late."[17]

While reviewers showered John F. Kennedy with praise—*Why England Slept* should be "required reading," wrote the *Wall Street Journal;* it was "a notable textbook for our times" judged the *New York Times*—Ambassador Kennedy had become virtually persona non grata in the White House. Key administration officials crossed the Atlantic to confer with counterparts in Churchill's government, consistently bypassing the ambassador. The "Jew influence in the papers in Washington," Kennedy fumed, had eroded his reputation. "I either want to run this job or get out," he wrote in August to Secretary of State Hull. But Hull would not even grant him home leave. The administration had placed him in a "very embarrassing situation," Kennedy told the president. "Frankly and honestly I do not enjoy being a dummy."[18]

More and more resentful, he decided that if the president did not soon grant his request for a leave, he would strike back. He penned a virulent article—"an indictment of President Roosevelt's administration for having talked a lot and done very little," he called it—and instructed a friend in New York to publish it if he had not returned to the United States by the first of November. In that case, his resignation—often threatened—was certain.[19]

It was finally time for the president to speak in private with his envoy and try to make peace. "I know what an increasingly severe strain you have been under during the past weeks," FDR cabled Kennedy on October 17, inviting him to return home "and get some relief." Roosevelt told his ambassador that he was anxious to talk with him about the "present situation." But, he added, he was "specifically" requesting that Kennedy make no statement to the press on his way over or upon his arrival in New York "until you and I have had a chance to agree upon what should be said."[20]

Upon landing at La Guardia Field on Sunday, October 27, Kennedy was handed a personal letter from the president. "Thank the Lord you are safely home," FDR wrote. "I do hope you & Rose can come down Sunday p.m.—we expect you both at the White House."[21] For one evening, Roosevelt the Seducer would mount a charm offensive, masterfully concealing his displeasure, acting as if there were no bad blood at all between him and the ambassador.

"I have nothing to say until I have seen the President," Kennedy obediently told reporters at the airport in New York, before his flight to Washington. "After I have seen the President I will make a statement."

"Do you intend to resign?" a reporter asked.

"No statement." Then, turning to his wife, he asked, "Where's Teddy? I don't see Teddy," referring to their 8-year-old son.[22]

It was a small dinner party at the White House. Joining the president and the ambassador and his wife were Missy LeHand and Senator James Byrnes and his wife. "Be sure to butter Joe up when you see him," the president had reminded his secretary Grace Tully earlier that day. Before dinner, Roosevelt and Kennedy shared their warm memories of the early days of the New Deal. Then, over the Roosevelts' usual Spartan Sunday supper of scrambled eggs, sausages, and toast, and rice pudding for dessert, Kennedy described conditions in London. Halfway through dinner, Jimmy Byrnes interjected that he thought it would be a great idea if Kennedy went on the radio that Tuesday and gave a speech for the president. FDR agreed that it would be "essential to the success of the campaign." But Kennedy said nothing. Then the president turned to Rose Kennedy, showering her with his charm, relating stories he knew about her father, John "Honey Fitz" Fitzgerald, the colorful former mayor of Boston.[23]

The ambassador had hoped for a private tête-à-tête with the president after dinner, but when Roosevelt made no move, Kennedy abruptly announced that he would just have to say what he had on his mind in front of everybody. "In the first place," he began, "I am damn sore at the way I have been treated."

A flood of resentments, grievances, and hurts streamed forth. White House envoys like Sumner Welles, who had conducted official business in London, had ignored him. No one had consulted or even informed him about the bases-for-destroyers deal. His influence with the Churchill government was nil.[24]

To Kennedy's surprise, Roosevelt offered neither defense nor rebuttal but nodded understandingly. In fact, the president said, Kennedy was being charitable. No one in the State Department should have dared to treat him with such disregard. After the election, there would be a "real housecleaning," he promised, assuring Kennedy that in the future he would receive the respect and gratitude he deserved. The next portion of the dialogue, as historian Michael Beschloss noted, "remained a mystery." Later Kennedy told Clare Boothe Luce, "I simply made a deal with Roosevelt. We agreed that if I endorsed him for President in 1940, then he would support my son Joe for governor of Massachusetts in 1942." Kennedy's son John, however, offered a different version of the conversation; he said that Roosevelt dangled in front of his father the prospect of being FDR's chosen heir for the presidency in 1944. And, as Beschloss discovered, a third, grimmer version of what was said that night came from James Roosevelt, who, Beschloss wrote, "believed his father warned Kennedy that abandoning him now would mark him as a Judas Iscariot for the rest of his life" and that Kennedy's desertion of Roosevelt would forever ruin his sons' careers.[25]

However it transpired, at the end of the evening, Roosevelt again asked Kennedy to give a radio talk endorsing his reelection, and now the ambassador agreed. "All right, I will," he said, but, his raw wounds only partially soothed, he added, "I will pay for it myself, show it to nobody in advance, and say what I wish." In minutes it was all arranged. Kennedy would speak on nationwide radio on Tuesday evening. Then he left for New York, while his wife, Rose, accepted FDR's invitation to spend the night at the White House.

When the news broke that Kennedy would speak on the radio, many assumed that the disgruntled ambassador would come out for Willkie. Others were more circumspect. The ambassador's intentions, wrote a *Washington Star* reporter, were "as much of a mystery as ever."[26]

On the evening of Tuesday, October 29, one week before Election Day, Joseph Kennedy delivered a nationwide address on the Columbia Broadcasting System. He had just returned from war-torn Europe, he began, and proceeded to give his views on the role of the United States in the world crisis "in the most critical election year of our existence." That reminder of the upcoming election hinted that this might be a political speech. The Nazi "philosophy of blitzkrieg" and "unbridled force and terrorism," he said, made diplomatic negotiations obsolete. The only path now open to the United States was rearmament. "It is today our guarantee of peace." The mention of the word "peace" oddly led him to praise an unlikely hero, his friend Neville Chamberlain. Criticism of Chamberlain, Kennedy argued, "in my judgment is not justified." The Munich Pact gave Britain a much-needed respite during which it could prepare for eventual war. "Can anyone imagine," he asked, "what would have happened to England if the blitzkrieg of the summer of 1940 had occurred in September of 1938?" In Kennedy's mind, the former prime minister was a leader with keen foresight, not a hapless appeaser caving in to a power-mad dictator. Continuing along that line, he gave the standard isolationist warning about the fatal consequences of war on American democracy. When war is declared, Kennedy said, "democracy—our freedoms—all become jeopardized." Britain itself, he strangely claimed, had already been obliged to "go totalitarian."[27]

Finally came the meat of the speech. "In this atmosphere charged with war and revolution . . . the people of America must make a solemn decision. Which of two men will lead the destinies of our people for the next four years?" He acknowledged that there had been disagreements between himself and the president and that they had sharply different views on some issues. "In normal times," Kennedy said, "I might be persuaded that the best interests of the country called for no third term." But the third term should now be the least of Americans' considerations. So gigantic were the problems facing the United States that the third-term issue simply appeared "insignificant by comparison."

The next president, Kennedy emphasized, would have to cope with staggering difficulties. "Already Hitler's conquered nations," he said, "make the advances of Napoleon appear puny." Therefore it was too late to train a green hand. Though the other candidate was "full of goodwill and general capacity," he was nevertheless "lacking in the vital government experience." Then he clinched the deal. "In the light of these considerations, I believe that Franklin D. Roosevelt should be reelected President of the United States."[28]

"WE HAVE ALL JUST LISTENED TO A GRAND SPEECH MANY THANKS," the president immediately wired Kennedy. "LOOKING FORWARD TO SEEING YOU ALL TOMORROW EVENING."[29]

"I've had a glorious day here in New England," the president told the crowd in the Boston Garden on October 30, adding—with perfect comedic timing—that there was only one thing he regretted. He had not been able to visit "my two favorite states of Maine and Vermont"—a witty reference to the only two states in the union that had voted against him in 1936. But in comparison with the ecstatic crowd in Madison Square Garden two days earlier, the laughter this time was muted. Still, the audience was pleased to hear his salute to "that Boston boy, beloved by all of Boston, *my* Ambassador to the Court of St. James, Joe Kennedy." His speechwriters had wanted him to say "*our* Ambassador," but Roosevelt insisted that "my" was not only correct but a way to underscore his close tie with Kennedy.[30]

Before arriving in Boston, Roosevelt had made campaign stops in New Haven, Meriden, Hartford, and Worcester, speaking off-the-cuff to crowds from the rear platform of his train. In New Haven, Roosevelt, who usually radiated optimism, slipped and said, "Win or lose, I hope to see you again!" Between stops, he and Sherwood, Hopkins, and Rosenman labored on the speech for that evening. Telegrams were streaming in from Democratic politicos, still running scared that Willkie's accusations of warmongering might be sticking. They urged the president to assure voters again that he would not take the country to war. "But how often do they expect me to say that?" an exasperated Roosevelt asked. "I've repeated it a hundred times." "I know it, Mr. President," Sherwood replied, "but they don't seem to have heard you the first time. Evidently you've got to say it again—and again—and again."[31]

After his joke about Maine and Vermont, the president launched without further preamble into another stern rebuttal of GOP accusations that his administration had been slow to increase military defenses. Republicans in Congress had again and again voted against all new appropriations. "What kind of political shenanigans are these?" Roosevelt asked. "Can we trust those people with national defense?"

In fact, hundreds of ships were being built, he said, some right in the Boston Navy Yard, "one of the best." Private shipbuilding yards and aircraft factories hummed with activity; indeed, an economic boom was accompanying the boom in defense industries. "You citizens of Seattle who are listening tonight," he said, "you have watched the Boeing plant out there grow. . . . You citizens of Southern California can see the great Douglas factories. . . . You citizens of Hartford who hear my words: look cross the Connecticut River at the whirring wheels and the beehive of activity which is the Pratt and Whitney plant I saw today." In Buffalo, St. Louis, Paterson, and other cities, new defense plants were producing engines for tens of thousands of new military planes. "The productive capacity of the United States . . . will make, and is making us, the strongest air power in the world. And that is not just a campaign promise!" he declared as the audience burst into cheers.[32]

Most crucially, the president had more than doubled the size of the army and the National Guard, and 800,000 young men would soon be trained for military service. Debunking GOP charges that soldiers would not be properly housed, he assured the audience that all those young men would be well trained, well housed, and well fed with "constant promotion of their health and their well-being." And just as critical for the survival of Western civilization, the president announced plans to supply Great Britain with 12,000 additional planes. Britain's orders for military planes now totaled more than 26,000, requiring the construction of new plants to meet the needs of both the United States and Britain.

And then, he told the audience that he had "one more assurance" to give to all mothers and fathers, one that was consistent with his policy of "all aid short of war." "I have said this before, but I shall say it *again and again and again*: Your boys are not going to be sent into any foreign wars." Before arriving in Boston, Rosenman had reminded the president that he could repeat the wording of his recent speech in Philadelphia: "We will not send our army, navy or air forces to fight in foreign lands . . . except in case of attack." But Roosevelt saw no need to include those last five words. "If somebody attacks us, then it isn't a foreign war, is it?" he snapped. When the overflowing crowd in the Boston Garden heard the unequivocal statement that American boys were not going to be sent into foreign wars, they burst into the only deep-throated cheers of the evening.[33]

They may have believed him—or they simply may have longed to believe him and hear what they passionately wanted to be true. But a mid-October Gallup poll showed that most Americans were not as committed to nonintervention as the audience reaction suggested. On the contrary, although a majority of Americans hoped that the nation would stay out of war, a majority also favored aiding Britain even at the risk of war. In fact, most Americans had not been bamboozled by the isolationists' reckless campaign against intervention. For his part, pollster George Gallup believed that the president could have done more to educate and lead public opinion. The best way for the president to influence opinion on a certain issue, Gallup said, was to "talk about it and favor it." But the isolationist drumbeat nevertheless had had an impact on Roosevelt, who had a conservative view of what was politically possible and chose to take a go-slow approach and reassure Americans of a calm future. "Whatever the peril," wrote Robert Sherwood, "he was not going to lead the country into war—he was going to wait to be pushed in."[34]

The president's rash, categorical promise that the United States would not participate in foreign wars was also an effective swipe at Willkie, for, that same evening, the GOP candidate was repeating to a crowd in Baltimore that "on the basis of [Roosevelt's] past performances with pledges to the people, if you re-elect him you may expect war in April 1941." But whereas Willkie was indulging in chimerical predictions of war—predictions that were, contrary to Willkie's intention, welcomed in Great Britain—Roosevelt was offering the opportunistic message of increased defense production, more military aid to Britain, and the promise of peace. As one reporter noted, the president was playing his audience "as a musician handles a fine violin."[35]

Roosevelt then switched subjects entirely. Moving from defense to agriculture, the principal province of his running-mate Henry Wallace, he spoke about his administration's many programs from soil conservation and farm mortgages to rural electrification. But Republicans, he noted, had voted against all the New Deal bills designed to aid farmers. "Listen to this," Roosevelt said. "Last summer, only a few weeks after the Republican National Platform had been adopted endorsing commodity loans for the farmers, the Republican members of the House marched right back into the Halls of Congress and voted against commodity loans for the farmers, 106 to 37!" And casting a nay vote, he noted, was none other than the party chairman, the "farmers' friend," Congressman Joe Martin of Massachusetts.

At the mention of his name, the crowd stirred, awaiting the rousing threesome of Martin, Barton, and Fish. Gradually FDR worked his way to it. "What I particularly want to say on the radio to the farmers of the Nation . . . is that Republican National Chairman Martin voted against every single one of the farm measures that were recommended by this Administration." Indulging in a prediction of his own, he offered that "perhaps Brother Martin will be rewarded for this loyal service to the principles of his party" by being appointed secretary of agriculture. "He is one of that great historic trio," Roosevelt exclaimed, "which has voted consistently against every measure for the relief of agriculture—MARTIN, BARTON AND FISH!" The hall erupted in joyous laughter and applause.

Roosevelt relished their reaction. "I have to let you in on a secret," he said, building up suspense. "It will come as a great surprise to you. And it's this: I'm enjoying this campaign! I'm really having a fine time!"

And then, more seriously, he countered the notion that democracy was, as Lindbergh and his wife claimed, outmoded and doomed. "We can assert the most glorious, the most encouraging fact in all the world today," the president declared, "the fact that democracy is *alive*—and going strong. We are telling the world that we are free—and we intend to remain free and at peace. We are free to live and love and laugh."

Three short verbs, all beginning with the letter "l"—borrowed perhaps from the line "live, love, laugh and be happy" in Al Jolson's 1926 hit song "When the Red Red Robin"—contributed to a powerful finale, stirring in its simplicity and brevity.[36] The speech had sparked a gamut of emotions in the audience: excitement, confidence, anger, joy, derision, laughter, pride, patriotism. His tone had moved from affable to belligerent to sarcastic to inspirational.

His final message was an emphatic, lyrical statement of the national ethos of inclusivity, solidarity, and strength. "In our own American community," Roosevelt said, "we have sought to submerge all the old hatreds, all the old fears, of the old world. We are Anglo-Saxon and Latin, we are Irish and Teuton and Jewish and Scandinavian and Slav—we are American. We belong to many races and colors and creeds—we are American. . . . We face the future with confidence and courage. We are American."

Chapter 16

The Fifth Column

L ET THERE BE NO MISTAKE ABOUT THIS," declared Governor Herbert
Lehman at the New York State Democratic Convention on September 30,
1940. "Nothing that could happen in the United States could give Hitler,
Mussolini, Stalin and the government of Japan more satisfaction than the defeat
of the man who typifies to the whole world the kind of free, humane government
which dictators despise—Franklin D. Roosevelt!" The following day the *New
York Times* shot back in an editorial, accusing Lehman of having made the "reckless" statement that a vote for Willkie was a vote for Hitler. But a front-page story
in the *Times* on October 4 in fact contradicted the editorial page. "The Axis is out
to defeat President Roosevelt," wrote Herbert Matthews, the paper's star foreign
correspondent stationed in Rome. Hitler and Mussolini hoped for a Willkie win
"because of the President's foreign policy and because of everything for which he
stands in the eyes of the Italians and Germans. . . . Therefore the normal strategy for the Axis is to do something before Nov. 5 that would somehow have a
great effect on the electoral campaign." Days after Matthews's story appeared,
he was suddenly expelled—temporarily, as it turned out—from Italy. The Italian government's communiqué charged that Matthews had "falsely stated that
Italy and the Axis would interfere in the United States Presidential elections."[1]

While Matthews's story in the *Times* might have been news to most American readers, for months the German embassy in Washington had been hard at
work trying to sabotage the reelection of Franklin Roosevelt.

"It is no exaggeration to say that for the president foreign policy considerations
outweigh all those of a domestic nature in the preparation for the election cam-

paign," wrote one analyst of the American political scene in early February 1940. Although Roosevelt had not said that he intended to run again for office, continued this commentator, there was no evidence that he intended to retire from political life. "In addition to his strongly developed pretensions to leadership and his vanity vis-à-vis world opinion, he believes that in these critical times he must make the 'sacrifice' of another 4-year term."[2]

The author was not Walter Lippmann, Arthur Krock, Joseph Alsop, or any other American columnist. These acute, clinically cool observations were passed on in code to the Foreign Ministry of the Third Reich by the German chargé d'affaires in Washington, the 49-year-old Hans Thomsen. While Roosevelt's masterful sphinx-like performance puzzled most American pundits, Thomsen saw right through it. "The timing and strategy of the nomination will doubtless be so cleverly synchronized," Thomsen continued in his February report to the German Foreign Ministry, "that not only will the wind be taken out of the sails of the Republicans but Roosevelt will also be able to take over the role of Cincinnatus, to whom his country appeals in its hour of need." As for the two-term tradition, Thomsen noted that although some Americans objected to a third term, the "masses" were sticking with Roosevelt.[3]

Thomsen was attuned not only to American public opinion but to the political, historical, and psychological dimensions of the upcoming contest— even to the historians' comparisons of the selfless George Washington and Cincinnatus, the Roman aristocrat who answered his country's call, led its army to victory, and then returned to his farm and plow. But Thomsen did more than comment astutely on the American political scene. As an inventive, hardworking, and circumspect subversive agent, he was determined to shape that scene to Germany's benefit.[4]

Thomsen's top priorities were to convince Americans that fascist aggression posed no danger to them, to discourage them from pouring billions of dollars into national defense and military aid for the Allies, and, finally, to engineer Roosevelt's defeat in 1940. Fortunately, he failed on all scores. And when his machinations and clandestine contacts with American politicians, antiwar activists, and writers were eventually exposed, they only served to discredit the isolationist movement and help the very man he had wanted to beat.

At his disposal Thomsen had money, a cohort of isolationist congressmen, senators, and authors, and a bag of dirty tricks. Still, it would be an uphill struggle. First of all, American public opinion was swinging sharply against the Third Reich. "The attack on peaceful Scandinavia showed that Germany does not recoil from anything," he lucidly reported in April 1940 to Berlin. German conquests that spring were robbing isolationists of all their best slogans and thinning their ranks. A few weeks later, Thomsen informed his handlers in Germany that the invasions of Holland and Belgium had so "narrowed down the moral and political ground on which we can operate here in America that only a tight-rope walker could keep his balance on it."[5]

Second, as a Nazi agent hoping to influence American public opinion, Thomsen had to proceed with extreme caution. He knew that the German embassy and German consulates had come under investigation by the FBI as well as under the suspicious watch of the Special Committee to Investigate Un-American Activities, chaired by Texas congressman Martin Dies. Thus the chargé d'affaires grasped that it was absolutely critical that his actions and support for American isolationists take place entirely behind the scenes. Any leaks, stolen documents, or suggestions that isolationists received encouragement or financial support from the German government, he wrote, would spell "political ruin" for his American friends and devastate German propaganda efforts. And so Thomsen, who periodically sent the Foreign Office meticulous accounts of all of his expenditures, requested special permission to destroy all financial records related to his press and propaganda activities.[6]

Thomsen also urged the Foreign Ministry to prevent the German press and radio from even mentioning isolationists like Lindbergh or Coughlin so as not to taint them with a pro-German label.[7] Offering similar advice, the German ambassador to the United States, Hans Heinrich Dieckhoff, who had been recalled in November 1938 after Kristallnacht, recommended from his office in Berlin that the German press lie low and "continue on the whole its reserved attitude . . . so that the president would not be able to use the argument that Germany was interfering in the election campaign."[8] Unfortunately for this strategy, the German press couldn't resist endorsing Willkie. In mid-October the *Frankfurter Zeitung*, an authoritative press organ of the Reich, carried a front-page editorial denouncing Roosevelt as a warmonger who "strengthened the English in their illusions" and endorsing Willkie, whose position on the war in Europe "bears more weight."[9]

But Nazi support revolted Willkie to the core. At the same time that the *Frankfurter Zeitung* gave him their vote of confidence, Willkie alerted Americans to the insidious presence of German agents in their midst who spread their nefarious propaganda and, he said, even sought to "entrap American businessmen by the lure of commercial profit." Hammering home his point, he quoted from Joseph Goebbels, Hitler's malignant minister of propaganda, who said that "nothing will be easier than to produce a bloody revolution in the United States. . . . We shall be able to play upon many strings there." In fact, Goebbels's propaganda machine in Berlin, as the *New York Herald Tribune*'s foreign correspondent Sidney Freifeld pointed out, did try to use the American press to plant stories as well as fictional "interviews" with key German officials, including Hitler and Goering, who expounded on their peaceful intentions. But for the most part, the American press was immune to Berlin's propaganda campaign.[10]

The German embassy was particularly embarrassed by what it called the "mistaken methods" and "clumsy actions" of the pro-Nazi German-American Bund and its leader, Fritz Kuhn. Members of the embassy and consulate staffs were prohibited from having any connection with the Bund.[11] Kuhn and his followers, sneered columnist Walter Winchell, constituted a veritable fifth column of "Ratzis."[12] The Bund's bizarre mass rally to celebrate George Washington's birthday in February 1939 in Madison Square Garden, though "unquestionably well-meaning," wrote the German general consul in New York to his home office, "has done no service to the German cause in the United States." Indeed, the rally presented a surreal picture: on the stage adorned with stars and stripes and the Bund's swastika-embellished shield, beneath a gigantic picture of George Washington, a Nazi-uniformed drum and bugle corps played. Storm troopers also in Nazi uniforms and wearing black iron crosses filled the aisles; a color guard carrying Bund and Nazi flags paraded down the center aisle as the twenty-two thousand mostly uniformed people in attendance stood erect and raised their arms in the Nazi salute. These "five-cent Hitlers" had all sworn an oath, reported the *New York Times*, to "exterminate with all their power the stinking poison of red Jewish infection in America."[13]

Taking the stage to address the crowd was the national Führer of the Bund movement, Fritz Kuhn, who claimed to have been one of Hitler's original followers in Munich in 1923. Dressed in full Nazi regalia, he launched into a denunciation of insidious Jewish control of both the American government and Wall Street. And railing against the Jewish-owned press and movie industry, he attacked the "campaign of hate" they waged against the Bund. In the arena festooned with banners reading "Wake up America—Smash Jewish Communism" and "Stop Jewish Domination of Christian America," Kuhn won appreciative laughter and applause when he called for Americans to throw out of office President "Frank D. Rosenfeld" and elect a white American instead. Speakers after him demanded the Nazification of America, calling for the swastika's adoption as the national symbol and suggesting that

American citizens hail one another with the Nazi salute. Bund members forcibly ejected the *Herald Tribune*'s anti-Nazi columnist Dorothy Thompson from the Garden, while fifty thousand anti-Nazi protesters filled the streets outside, trying to break up the rally.[14]

American officials did not regard the Bund as merely a noxious gang of starry-eyed pretend Nazis. In late 1939, New York district attorney Thomas Dewey successfully prosecuted Kuhn, who had become a naturalized American citizen in 1935, for embezzlement. Kuhn would be stripped of his citizenship in 1943, interned in Texas, and deported after the war. Roosevelt had ordered the FBI to investigate all Nazi activities within the United States. Working closely with FBI director J. Edgar Hoover, the president authorized mail inspection and wiretaps of all those suspected of subversive activity, including espionage, counterespionage, and sabotage.[15]

While the Bund rallies that aped Hitler's mass gatherings in Nuremberg embarrassed the German cause in America, Thomsen knew that far more damaging to Germany's goal of keeping America out of the war would be any acts of sabotage on American soil that could be tied to Berlin. Thomsen reminded the Foreign Ministry that sabotage and the sinking of American ships were among the factors contributing to America's entry in the First World War. "I therefore request," he wrote to Berlin in 1939, "that the possibility of German sabotage in the United States of America not be used either politically or for propaganda purposes *in any manner whatsoever.*" The aim, after all, was to shore up the isolationists' position and not undermine their argument that the United States was not directly threatened by the Axis powers.[16]

The most prudent strategy, the chargé d'affaires realized, was to tread gently and let American isolationists do most of his work for him. It would be highly effective, he told the Foreign Ministry in June 1940, "if American politicians themselves provide *enlightenment* regarding our political aims and the mistakes of Roosevelt's foreign policy."[17]

The inventive Thomsen channeled funds to a variety of isolationist organizations and clandestinely sponsored the "Committee to Keep America Out of Foreign Wars." A week before the GOP Convention, Thomsen had advised Berlin that "the rapidly thinning ranks of the isolationists among the Republicans . . . must be supported in their struggle in Philadelphia. To this end a well-camouflaged lightning propaganda campaign might well prove useful." It was he who suggested—and partly paid for—the "STOP THE MARCH TO WAR" ads that appeared in American newspapers and were signed by Hamilton Fish and others. Such ads, Thomsen informed Berlin, would be an effective "counterblast" to the "Stop Hitler Now" ads of the White Committee.[18]

The energetic Thomsen also helped finance the "Make Europe Pay War Debts Committee" and gave it $3,000 to publish a pamphlet attacking the liberal, antifascist New York newspaper, *PM*. And he maintained what he described as "good relations" with the America First Committee, supporting it, as he boasted to the Foreign Ministry, "in various ways."[19] Indeed, although America First made an effort to keep pro-fascists and pro-Nazis out of its chapters, some of them did in fact infiltrate the organization. Wayne Cole, the preeminent historian of the isolationist movement, wrote that there was at least some truth to the accusation that America First, despite the earnest efforts of its leaders, was a "Nazi transmission belt." For example, one of America First's most active speakers, Laura Ingalls, would be convicted in 1942 of failure to register as a German agent, and another speaker would be convicted for failure to register as a Japanese agent.[20]

One of Thomsen's propaganda tactics was to keep in close touch with several senators and congressmen and encourage them to publish and distribute their most persuasive isolationist speeches. The congressional franking privilege, he reassured his tightfisted handlers in Berlin, enabled him to keep the cost of this propaganda campaign "disproportionately low." One speech that had particularly impressed Thomsen was given by Senator Nye in April 1939 during debates on the lifting of the arms embargo. Nye had assembled all the isolationist arguments "in a particularly striking manner," Thomsen told the Foreign Ministry, happily reporting that the senator printed and distributed a hundred thousand copies under his own frank. Then, in the summer of 1940, Nye permitted the German embassy to circulate another hundred thousand copies of his passionate statement through the "Make Europe Pay War Debts Committee." That committee also paid for the mass distribution of an essay by historian Charles Beard called "Giddy Minds and Foreign Quarrels."[21]

Among Thomsen's chief operatives was an odd duck named George Sylvester Viereck. Born in Germany in 1884, Viereck came to America as an adolescent. A fervent Germanophile, Viereck admitted that he was "dazzled" by Adolf Hitler, whom he had met in 1923 and whom he continued to consider a "genius," even though Viereck did not share his hero's vicious anti-Semitism. On the contrary, in 1928 Viereck penned a strange semi-pornographic book called *My First Two Thousand Years: Confessions of a Wandering Jew*, in which, trying to come to terms with his own homosexuality, he identified with a gifted Jew, a contemporary of Christ, who searches for life's ideal in a synthesis of the male and female principles.[22]

Before he was convicted in 1941 for failing to register with the State Department as a Nazi agent, Viereck was on the German payroll as a pro-Nazi hack writer and propagandist. He maintained helpful contacts with congress-men like Hamilton Fish, who used his franking privilege to mail out hun-dreds of thousands of reprints of Nazi propaganda, and Senators Ernest Lundeen and Rush Holt. They would be known in the U.S. Attorney Gen-eral's office as "Viereck's Capitol Hill Squad"—Viereck wrote speeches for them and encouraged them to create the "Make Europe Pay War Debts Com-mittee." In addition, Viereck founded the Flanders Hall publishing house, an isolationist press that would turn out twenty books in less than two years.[23]

Thomsen repeatedly turned to Viereck for help, using him, for example, to persuade ultra-isolationist congressman Jacob Thorkelson of Montana to insert a wholly fabricated "interview" with Adolf Hitler into the *Congressional Record* and permit the embassy to mail out copies of it. The fictional interview had Hitler telling a reporter that American fears of him were "flattering but grotesque" and calling the idea of a German invasion of the United States "stupid and fantastic."[24] Thorkelson also inserted into the *Congressional Rec-ord* wildly anti-Semitic tracts, like one entitled "British-Israel Is True" that railed against the contamination of Great Britain by Jews.[25] Thomsen also requested permission from Berlin to spend $3,000 to circulate two hundred and fifty thousand copies of a September 1940 radio speech by Rush Holt in which the soon-to-be ex-senator fulminated against military conscription. The speech, wrote Thomsen, contained "splendid material."[26]

Another minor coup for Thomsen came in late March 1940 when the Ger-man government released diplomatic documents supposedly discovered in the Polish Foreign Office after the Nazis captured Warsaw in September 1939. The papers, whose authenticity was never established, purported to show that Am-bassador Kennedy as well as the American ambassador to France, William Bullitt, had promised American as well as British assistance to Poland and gave assurances that the United States would "finish" any war in Europe on the side of the Allies. In truth, even if Kennedy and Bullitt had made such promises, neither ambassador had the authority to commit the United States to military action or anything else. But a delighted Thomsen reported to his home office that the publication of the so-called White Paper came as a "bombshell," noting that an embarrassed Roosevelt had to deny that the doc-uments were authentic. Right on cue, to Thomsen's utter satisfaction, two isolationists in Congress, Hamilton Fish and North Carolina senator Robert Reynolds, demanded a congressional investigation. Whether or not the docu-ments were genuine, editorialized the isolationist *Chicago Daily Tribune*, the White House's "consistent" interventionist stand "is in itself damning."[27]

Thomsen also embarked upon a variety of literary projects. He played a key role in the publication of antiwar books, including *Country Squire in the White House*, a bestselling attack on FDR by America Firster and *New Republic* columnist John T. Flynn that was also serialized in the *Chicago Daily Tribune*; *The Dynamics of War and Revolution*, by Lawrence Dennis, the nation's foremost fascist theorist—the embassy distributed fifteen hundred free copies of the book to American colleges and universities; *America Wake Up*, a pro-Nazi primer by the pseudonymous An Beneken; and *War, War, War— Veritas Vincit*, by the anonymous "Cincinnatus," described by Thomsen as "a very sharp indictment of the American Jews and their strawman Roosevelt."[28]

Another of Thomsen's pet projects involved funneling $20,000 to an American literary agent, William C. Lengal, to promote the publication of articles and books by five isolationist writers during the fall presidential campaign. Thomsen's chosen authors were 69-year-old novelist Theodore Dreiser, who would argue in his antiwar book, *America Is Worth Saving*, that America must not "pull the British Lion's chestnuts from the fire"; George Creel, an investigative journalist who had served as the head of Woodrow Wilson's propaganda organization, the Committee on Public Information, and would write a series of articles for the *American Mercury* debunking the idea of fifth-column activity; Sylvia Field Porter, a widely respected financial writer for the liberal *New York Post*, who gave the "housewife's point of view"; a literary critic named Burton Rascoe, who slammed compulsory military conscription; and 60-year-old popular novelist Kathleen Norris, president of the National Legion of Mothers of America, who offered the contradictory advice that mothers equip themselves with guns to pick off enemy parachutists and that Americans not heed the people trying to frighten the nation into war. "None of the authors knows who is behind the publisher's offer," Thomsen boasted to his home office.[29]

The German Library of Information, housed in the same building with the German Consulate in New York, also provided a steady flow of Nazi propaganda. In addition to distributing books, pamphlets, records, and movies, all free of charge, and even subsidizing a bookstore in New York that sold pro-German books, the library gave out twenty-five thousand weekly program guides for German shortwave radio broadcasts originating in Europe and Shanghai. One of the most popular programs was the anti-British broadcast by Lord Haw Haw, a committed fascist who renounced his British nationality and became a German citizen. "He has a titanic hatred for Jews and an equally titanic one for capitalists," remarked Berlin correspondent William

Shirer. In addition, Thomsen called upon Viereck, the library's public relations advisor, to help edit its weekly magazine, *Facts in Review*, which had a circulation of two hundred thousand. An August 1940 issue contained the reassuring thoughts of Hermann Goering, whose Luftwaffe had recently begun the Battle of Britain. America simply could not be invaded by air or sea, Goering maintained. "No one would be so idiotic as to attempt an invasion."[30]

In the days leading up to the 1940 election, Thomsen tried for one final propaganda coup: he sought to plant in American newspapers a fabricated story claiming that Roosevelt had long been planning to intervene in the European war, even before Germany invaded Poland. Unable to gain any traction in the mainstream press, the chargé d'affaires found one newspaper willing to take the bait, the local weekly *New York Enquirer*, whose owner, an arch-isolationist named William Griffin, would be indicted in 1942 for sedition and conspiracy to "impair the morale and loyalty of American armed forces." In a typically inflated and self-congratulatory dispatch, Thomsen bragged to the Foreign Ministry that, for the occasion, the *Enquirer* had put out an enlarged edition of a quarter of a million copies. Still, Thomsen worried that his role might be discovered, thereby furnishing Roosevelt "the desired occasion for rupture of diplomatic relations" and termination of his own stay in Washington.[31] And who would want to leave Washington for Berlin?

Chapter 17

Final Days, Final Words

"WHAT CHANGE HAS COME OVER US?" demanded Charles Lindbergh in a nationwide radio address on October 14, at the height of the fall campaign season. "Where is the *blood* of such leaders as Washington, Jefferson and Lincoln, blood that stood firm on American soil?" Whereas Roosevelt underscored that, no matter the race, color, or creed, "we are American," Lindbergh made blood the test of patriotism, loyalty, and leadership.

As if he were himself campaigning for the presidency, he regaled his audiences with his own formula for great leadership. "We have not confidence in our leaders," he said. "We have not confidence in their *efficiency* or in their judgment," in their ability to turn "adversity and hardship into *virility* and *success.*" Blood, efficiency, virility, success: Lindbergh injected all the fascist code-words into his prescription for American leadership.

Lindbergh insisted that "the first step must be to assure ourselves of leadership which is entirely and *unequivocally American,*" as he told a radio audience three weeks before the November election. "There must not be even the remotest question of foreign influence involved." It was "amazing," he said in his talk, that he was forced to "plead for American independence in a nation with a heritage such as ours." Reminding his listeners that Americans had fought a revolutionary war against "foreign control," he voiced dismay that the nation's independence and destiny "were never more in jeopardy than they are today." In addition to stooping to the insinuation, long heard in conservative, anti-Semitic, and pro-fascist circles, that FDR had Jewish ancestors, that his real name was Rosenfeld, the aviator was also displaying his ignorance of the key roles that foreigners like Lafayette, General de Rochambeau, Admiral de Grasse and the French fleet—and even the Caribbean-born Alexander Hamilton himself—played in the American War of Independence.

His thinking and values influenced by German Nazis and French fascists like his friend, the eugenicist Alexis Carrel, Lindbergh warned that the policies of interventionists like Roosevelt would be "*fatal* to our nation." He urged Americans to vote for "men, regardless of their party, who will lead us to *strength* and peace." The United States desperately needed leaders "whose promises we can trust, who know where they are taking us, and who tell us where we are going!"[1]

Despite his dread of a Roosevelt victory—"no one I know trusts Roosevelt," he had written a few weeks earlier—Lindbergh had minimal interest in endorsing the president's rival and never even pronounced Willkie's name in public. He supported the GOP candidate *faute de mieux*—"I wish that someday I could vote for a President in whose leadership I had real confidence," he would write on Election Day.[2] But his wife, Anne Morrow Lindbergh, was far more enthusiastic: she saw in the GOP candidate a perspicacious, forthright leader who knew where he wanted to take the nation. "At least he knows we cannot turn backwards and has some conception of the *forces of the future*," Anne wrote.[3] Did she think that Willkie would subscribe to the vision of the future she had outlined in her latest book? Published in early October 1940, at the height of the election season, her elegant, lyrical essay *The Wave of the Future*, fewer than fifty pages long and costing one dollar, sold tens of thousands of copies and jumped to the top of the bestseller list. American readers eagerly drank of her exquisite prose—until they tasted its foul poison.

The conflict taking place in Europe between democratic and fascist nations, she argued in *The Wave of the Future*, was not between good and evil, but rather between the forces of the past and those of the future. Fascism was energetic and dynamic; democracy inefficient, exhausted. Disdainfully she pointed to the "decay, weakness, and blindness into which all the 'Democracies' have fallen since the last war." The quotation marks with which, over and over, she skeptically surrounded the word "democracy" relegated self-government, perhaps the greatest achievement of the Enlightenment, to the irrelevance of a quaint, worn-out past.

In Germany, however, a "new conception of humanity" was struggling to come to birth. "But because we are blind we cannot see it, and because we are slow to change, it must *force* its way through the heavy crust violently—in eruptions." There might be some maleficent elements in the birth of the new order, she conceded, "but the *greatness* remains," and "*no price* could be too high" to reach it. The leaders in Germany and Italy "have felt the wave of the future and they have leapt upon it," using modern social and economic forces. "The evils we deplore in these systems are not in themselves the future. They are *scum on the wave of the future*," she wrote dismissively, borrowing her metaphor from Lawrence Dennis, the theoretician of fascism who had similarly written that the misdeeds of the Nazis were merely the "foam" on that unstoppable fascist wave.[4] There were indeed far worse sins, Anne wrote, than armed aggression, invasion, persecution, and religious intolerance; more blameworthy in her opinion were transgressions "such as blindness, selfishness, irresponsibility, smugness, lethargy, and resistance to change."

Her message to American readers was twofold. First, they must not intervene in the battles waging in Europe. "I do feel that it is futile," she wrote, "to get into a hopeless 'crusade' to 'save' civilization."

Second, they must embrace the wave of the future. The United States, she believed, had to "work out in moderation what the rest of the world is fighting out in bloodshed, intolerance and hate." Fascism in the United States, she wrote in her little book, should be "peculiarly American, crisp, clear, tart, sunny, and crimson—like an American apple," as American as the "white steeples of New England or the skyscrapers of New York; as American as a boy's slang, as backyard life in small towns, as baseball and blue jeans." In other words, the American brand of Nazi totalitarianism would be as innocent and uncomplicated as Norman Rockwell's images of small-town life on the covers of the archconservative weekly magazine the *Saturday Evening Post*. Americans could simply skim off the scum of Nazism and let pure and sparkling waves of fascism wash up on their shores.[5]

She called *The Wave of the Future* "A Confession of Faith"—something that is "not seen, but felt; not proved, but believed; not a program, but a *dream*." Her heartfelt "faith" in the fascist tide was sad, if not grotesque. She was convinced that she was making, as she improbably told her mother, "the *moral* argument for isolationism—which I think no one has yet presented."[6] But the cloudy mysticism, emotional and metaphorical evasions, and political naiveté, along with her loyalty to her husband, not only blinded her to breathtaking, unfathomable evil and to the incontrovertible moral argument for opposing fascism but also prevented her from seeing that history and politics, tyrannies and self-governing democracies, are made not by magical waves or lunar-controlled tides but by free, rational human agents who make—and are accountable for—their own political, military, moral, and criminal decisions. As for the upcoming election, her candidate of choice, Wendell Willkie, would surely have been repelled by her vision of a future of vibrant fascism. "I see an America from which *democracy will arise to a new birth*," Willkie passionately declared in a speech in New Jersey in late October, "an America which will once more provide this war-torn world with a clear glimpse of the destiny of man."[7]

Lindbergh's *The Wave of the Future*, Harold Ickes acidly remarked, was "the bible of every American Nazi, Fascist, and appeaser."[8] Others were equally repelled by the idea that fascism represented a salutary revolutionary tide. In an article entitled "Or Is It 'The Wave of the Past'?," Columbia University history professor Allan Nevins insisted that it was abhorrent to think that the crimes of Hitler and Mussolini represented only the "froth and spray on a great wave of the future." Hardly an "anticipation of man's most modern needs," Nevins wrote, Lindbergh's futuristic vision was in reality "a step toward the old Stone Age" and a "resuscitation of medievalism." It negated "the great progressive forces of our time," he argued, from the rationality of the Enlightenment to the internationalist spirit of the League of Nations.[9]

Despite attacks by people like Nevins and the daily reports of the horrors of Nazi warfare, Anne, like her husband Charles, inspired the fervor and the admiration of American isolationists. The *Hartford Courant* rhapsodized over "the breadth, the scope of her intellectual powers," while the *Chicago Daily Tribune* hailed her "strong and courageous thinking and writing." But Anne changed her mind. After the death in 1944 of a man she loved, the French author and pilot Antoine de Saint-Exupéry, she felt great sadness that the "wrong of my book kept us from meeting again. I am sad that I never had the luxury of knowing whether or not he forgave us for our stand, forgave me for my book." Decades later, in 1973, she again expressed contrition, telling an interviewer that writing *The Wave of the Future* was "a mistake. . . . It didn't help anybody. . . . I didn't have the right to write it. I didn't know enough."[10]

"I think the re-election of President Roosevelt for a third term would be a *national evil* of the first magnitude!" John L. Lewis, the notoriously volatile president of the United Mine Workers and the Congress of Industrial Organizations (CIO), proclaimed to a nationwide radio audience. On October 25, 1940, ten days before the November election, Lewis, with his powerful miner's build, shaggy eyebrows, and permanent scowl, delivered what Robert Sherwood termed a "Hymn of Hate against Roosevelt."[11]

In his broadcast—supposedly sponsored by "Democrats for Willkie" but in reality paid for by James Rhodes Davis, an isolationist, arms trafficker, and oil speculator with deep ties to Nazi Germany who, on several occasions, had involved Lewis in shady missions and compromising deals—Lewis charged that the president "no longer hears the cries of the people!"[12] In a sulfurous barrage of personal insults and slurs, he portrayed FDR as "intellectually sterile," bent on war, and committed to the "deification of the state." The president, he railed, was determined to impose a dictatorship as well as his own "royal family" on the nation so that he could "continue to toy with the lives of men and the destiny of nations." The labor leader accused him of running for a third term because of his "personal craving for power, the overweening *abnormal and selfish craving for increased power. . . .* Are we to yield to the appetite for power and the vaunted ambitions of a man who plays with the lives of human beings for a pastime? I say 'no!'" Lewis's message to the "women of our race" was to oppose the candidate who would "make cannon fodder of your sons." And he had a pointed question for all the young men registering for the draft: "Have you cause to rejoice? You, who may be about to die in a foreign war, created at the whim of an international meddler, should you salute your Caesar?" Whim, meddler, Caesar: the subversive words and message were clear. The young men who were registering for the draft owed their future commander in chief neither confidence nor respect nor obedience.[13]

In 1936, Lewis had campaigned for FDR and even taken credit for bringing several million votes to the Democratic ticket. But in early 1937 he changed his tune when Roosevelt declined to intervene in support of a CIO-sponsored sit-down strike that closed many General Motors plants. No matter that the CIO, an umbrella organization of major industrial unions, owed its existence to New Deal bills like the Wagner Act. Although the breach between them widened, Lewis, with his usual extravagant sense of self-importance, told Roosevelt, probably in January 1940, that if the president chose him as his running-mate in 1940, he would support FDR for a third term. "Can you beat it?" FDR said in amazement, after recounting the conversation to Perkins. How did you answer him? Perkins asked. "Why, he didn't press me. He just asked me to think it over and give it consideration."[14]

In the fall of 1940, Lewis turned to Wendell Willkie, though virtually all he and the GOP candidate had in common was their mutual desire to defeat Franklin Roosevelt. In late September, the two men met and tentatively agreed on a quid pro quo: Lewis would endorse Willkie in exchange for Willkie's promise to make labor legislation a top priority. A few days later in Pittsburgh, Willkie memorably told a crowd that the position of secretary of labor was "a man's job."[15]

For his part, Lewis told his radio audience in October that Willkie was a "gallant American. . . . He is not an aristocrat. He has the common touch." As if he were trying to cast the Wall Street executive as an unemployed mechanic, Lewis portrayed the GOP candidate as a man who "has worked with his hands and has known the pangs of hunger." Of course, while he pounded the Democrats for their "unrestrained baiting and defaming of labor," Lewis had nothing to say about Willkie's relationship with labor when he was president of Commonwealth and Southern Corporation or about the GOP platform that threatened to undo the huge strides unions had made under the New Deal. Republicans in several states had already shown their party's true colors—in Minnesota recently passing a bill greatly weakening organized labor and in Wisconsin repealing the state's Labor Relations Act and passing an anti-labor "Employment Peace Act."[16]

When he reached the end of his speech, Lewis issued a stern ultimatum. He threatened that, if working men and women rejected his leadership, dismissed his advice, and elected Roosevelt, he would immediately resign his post in the CIO. "I will accept the result as being the equivalent of a vote of no-confidence and will retire," he declared, putting union members on interesting notice that the election of 1940 was a referendum not on Roosevelt but on himself.[17]

In Lewis's toxic anti-Roosevelt diatribe, Wendell Willkie was little more than a bit player. Even so, Willkie effusively expressed his gratitude for "the most eloquent address I ever heard." But in fact Lewis's caustic speech did nothing to bring labor to Willkie's side. Almost all of the labor movement's leaders and rank-and-file members dismissed the CIO president as a traitor and a turncoat. Lewis had gone over to the side "of the enemies of labor," declared Daniel Tobin, the president of the International Brotherhood of Teamsters.[18]

For almost a year, labor had been lining up to declare its support for Franklin Roosevelt. His New Deal had given to millions of working men and women jobs, social security, a minimum wage and maximum working hours, and, most important, the Wagner Act, guaranteeing the right of employees to join unions and bargain collectively through their own representatives. Labor was sticking with Roosevelt. In the months leading up to the election season, dozens of unions joined the third-term movement: the International Garment Workers Union, the Teamsters, the United Auto Workers, the Amalgamated Clothing Workers, the United Rubber Workers, the Textile Workers, the Steel Workers, and the Bakery Workers. Even the secretary-treasurer of the United Mine Workers, Lewis's own union, supported Roosevelt.[19]

Immediately after Lewis's October rant, more unions bucked his leadership and threw their strength to Roosevelt: dairy workers and glass and communications workers, boatmen, woodworkers and retail and wholesale employees, clothing cutters and electrical, radio, and machine workers, and the newspaper guild. Lewis, declared one union president, "stands exposed before the entire labor movement as a person who would cast labor's interests to the wind to satisfy his own swollen egotism."[20]

A week later, at a rally sponsored by the American Labor Party in Madison Square Garden, a crowd of eighteen thousand cheered as a dozen more labor leaders spewed out their contempt for Lewis and pledged their support for Roosevelt. "We will not follow John L. Lewis," shouted one union leader, "in his tantrum!"[21]

On the afternoon of Friday, November 1, tens of thousands of people began gathering in downtown Brooklyn, hoping to catch a glimpse of President Roosevelt later that day. It was already evening when the motorcade slowly made its way to the Brooklyn Academy of Music through the jammed streets, the smiling president waving from side to side at the cheering throngs. At 8:45 p.m., when the vanguard of motorcycle police signaled the approach of the president's car, the crowds at the Academy of Music yelled and whistled, waved flags and blew horns. The deafening clamor could be heard for blocks. Once inside the hall, FDR received a joyous ovation. Trying to quiet the audience, he held up his watch to indicate that radio time was slipping away, but the applause and cheers went on and on.[22]

He was in superb form. He opened his talk by gibing at the moving target proffered by the Republicans, wholly unable to decide where they stood on the critical issues of the day. "This is a funny campaign," Roosevelt began. "It is a strange campaign. Here it is almost the day of election and it is still impossible to determine what are the principles of the opposition party. What is it that the Republican leaders would do during the next four years if they were given a chance?" Without mentioning Willkie's name or the names of his supporters, he charged that they were all speaking on all sides of all questions. On Mondays they agreed with the administration's foreign policy, but on Tuesdays those same policies were condemned. And so it went. On Fridays they approved the gains that labor had made under the New Deal but on Saturdays, "we are told to weep because labor has been the principal sufferer under the New Deal." Bursting into laughter, the audience could hardly wait to hear the rest.

Those witty and telling observations were a prelude to a denunciation *not* of the well-meaning if perpetually shifting Willkie but rather of the "very strange assortment of political bedfellows" who sought shelter under the umbrella of the GOP. Willkie presented "so indistinct a target," Robert Sherwood remarked, that Roosevelt had not really been able to put his heart into the contest against him. But, Sherwood added, "a battle to discredit John L.

Lewis loomed as a real pleasure."[23] This "unholy alliance" of heterogeneous bedfellows, Roosevelt told the crowd in Brooklyn, was composed of extreme reactionaries and extreme radicals. The common ground on which radicals and reactionaries united was "their common will to power and their impatience with the normal democratic processes to produce overnight the inconsistent dictatorial ends that they, each of them, seek." While they accused the Roosevelt administration of stifling democracy and while they never tired of repeating that war would destroy American democracy, in truth it was they who wanted to kill democracy. Moderate Republicans, Roosevelt argued, did not realize the threat this "unholy alliance" posed.

"Something *evil* is happening in this country," Roosevelt gravely said, "when a full page advertisement against this Administration, paid for by Republican supporters, appears—where, of all places?—in the *Daily Worker,* the newspaper of the Communist Party." Repeating that sobering phrase, he went on: "Something *evil* is happening in this country when vast quantities of Republican campaign literature are distributed by organizations that make no secret of their admiration for the dictatorship form of government."

The spirit of democracy, Roosevelt emphasized, was one of tolerance and inclusivity. "We are a nation of many nationalities, many races, many religions—bound together by a single unity, the unity of freedom and equality," he said. As if responding to the anti-Semitism of some isolationists, he added that "whoever seeks to set one religion against another, seeks to destroy all religion." And as if throwing back at Lindbergh his demand that American leaders be wholly American and of pure, untainted American blood, the president declared that "the vote of Americans will be American—and only American."

A newspaper story published that morning supplied Roosevelt with a punch line, one that revealed how out of touch some GOP leaders were with American society. Columnist Arthur Krock reported that a prominent Republican member of the Philadelphia bar had commented that "the President's only supporters are paupers, those who earn less than $1,200 a year and aren't worth that, and the Roosevelt family."[24] Who were those "paupers"? FDR now demanded. "They are only millions and millions of American families . . . only the common men and women who have helped build this country, who have made it great, and who would defend it with their lives if the need arose." The Philadelphian's scorn for "paupers," the president said, expressed "the true sentiment of the Republican leadership in this year of grace."

Roosevelt ended his talk with more fighting words. In his famous campaign speech in October 1936 in Madison Square Garden, to the roaring approval of a tumultuous crowd, he had repeated the militant refrain: "For all these we have only just begun to fight!" Now in Brooklyn he reminded his listeners what he was fighting against and what, with his heart and soul, he was fighting for. "I am only *fighting* for a free America—for a country in which all men and women have equal rights to liberty and justice," he exclaimed. "I am *fighting* against the revival of Government by special privilege. . . . I am *fighting*, as I always have fought, for the rights of the little man as well as the big man. . . . I am *fighting* to keep this Nation prosperous and at peace. I am *fighting* to keep our people out of foreign wars, and to keep foreign conceptions of Government out of our own United States. I am *fighting* for these great and good causes. I am *fighting* to defend them against the power and might of those who now rise up to challenge them. And I will not stop *fighting*."[25]

But Wendell Willkie thought the president was fighting dirty. The next day he angrily charged that Roosevelt's remark about the "strange assortment of political bedfellows" in the GOP was aimed at stirring up hatred and division. As for FDR's mention of the Philadelphia Republican's derision of paupers, Willkie retorted that the remark, even if true, was made by someone with "no connection" to the Republican national ticket. Instead of discussing the "real issues" of the campaign, Roosevelt had invented "straw men," Willkie said, accusing the president of stooping to "the strategy of Hitler." But others, like *Time*, thought that in Brooklyn "the Roosevelt touch was sure."[26] And in Philadelphia, Democrats playfully adorned their lapels with buttons reading "Another Pauper for Roosevelt."

The climactic rally of Roosevelt's campaign swing took place in Cleveland the following day, Saturday, November 2. There had been little time to prepare his speech. On the train Friday night, after Hopkins went to bed, Rosenman and Sherwood huddled over their draft. All night long, munching on sandwiches and fortifying themselves with coffee, they worked on the speech. Finally, at six o'clock they had a draft and sent it to the president's car to be given to him with his breakfast. Then they caught a little sleep.[27]

Roosevelt joined them for lunch on the train Saturday. He looked gray and worn, Sherwood later recalled. "This is too much punishment to expect any man to take," he thought. "I almost hoped he would lose the election for it seemed that flesh and blood could not survive another six months—let alone four years—in this terrible job." But as Roosevelt reminisced about his old sailing days along the New Brunswick and New England coasts, he began to relax, and, to Sherwood's surprise, his grayness gave way to healthy color. After lunch, the president said, "Now! what have you three cutthroats been doing to my speech?" Together they worked for another six hours on the talk.

At small railroad stops along the way, Roosevelt left his speechwriting team, put on his leg braces and walked out to the back platform on the arm of Pa Watson to greet the crowds, usually factory workers and their wives. As the train pulled out of the various stations, they ran after it, shouting, "God bless you!"[28]

In Cleveland, people lined the streets five deep to watch the president drive by. Almost forty thousand Ohioans jammed into the huge Convention Hall, cheering their hearts out as Roosevelt made his way to the podium, continuing to applaud even after he started to speak. With "fatigue written on his face," FDR pulled all of his weapons out of his cache, wrote *Time* magazine, and kept the audience "spellbound."[29]

This time, instead of pounding the opposition, Roosevelt welcomed it. His adversaries in Congress and in the press, he said, provided "positive proof that what we have built and strengthened in the past seven years is democracy!" But he did assail the poisonous, defeatist assertion that democracy was finished. "Is this the end of a story that has been told?" he asked. "Is the book of democracy now to be closed and placed away upon the dusty shelves of time?

"My answer is this: All we have known of the glories of democracy—its freedom, its efficiency as a mode of living, its ability to meet the aspirations of the common man—all these are merely an introduction to the greater story of a more glorious future. We Americans of today—all of us—we are characters in this *living book of democracy*."

But Americans, he went on, were also the authors of that book. The New Deal was *their* creation. *They* were the vital agents of change who worked alongside him. "*You* provided work for free men and women in America who could find no work. . . . *You* wrote into the law the right of working men and women to bargain collectively. . . . *You* turned to the problems of youth and age. . . . *You* made safe the banks which held your savings." The future, he said, belongs to all Americans. "It is for us to design it; for us to build it."

Roosevelt rejected the backward path offered by the "doubters of democracy." Instead he called on all Americans to cherish their form of self-government. "For you can build ships and tanks and planes and guns galore," he said, "but they will not be enough. You must place behind them an invincible faith in the institutions which they have been built to defend. . . . We intend to keep our freedom—to defend it . . . against the forces of dictatorship, whatever disguises and false faces they may wear. . . . We will not be scared into retreating by threats from the doubters of democracy." Then he offered his own inspiring vision of the future—"an America devoted to our freedom—unified by tolerance, unified by religious faith, a people consecrated to . . . peace." Repeating the phrase "I see an America" seven times, he described a dynamic, prosperous, growing democracy, with freedom, opportunity, tolerance, and security for all. It was a society built on justice, not, as in fascist dictatorships, on want and fear. In his inaugural address in 1937, he had repeated the refrain "I see" eight times, but then it was to underscore the nation's incomplete recovery from the Depression, the millions trying to live on meager incomes, millions still ill-housed, ill-clad, ill-nourished.

For the first time that fall, Roosevelt confronted the third-term issue. As if he suddenly realized that defeat at the polls was possible, he asked voters to give him the opportunity to serve for another four years. There was a "great storm raging now," he reminded his listeners in Cleveland and across the nation, and that storm was the "true reason that I would like to stick by these people of ours until we reach the clear, sure footing ahead. . . . When that term is over," he assured the crowd, "there will be another President, and many more Presidents in the years to come." "No! No!" people cried out, unwilling to contemplate letting him go.[30]

"We will make it," he said. "And the world, we hope, will make it, too." With those muted words, Roosevelt evoked the efforts, hardships, struggles, and sacrifices that lay ahead. No one yet knew how the story would end. Five years later, Robert Sherwood would strike a similarly uncertain note in his script for *The Best Years of Our Lives*, winner of the Oscar for best movie of 1946. The film tells the story of soldiers and sailors returning home from the war, struggling to restart their lives. In the last scene, actor Dana Andrews, playing a decorated air force captain, tells his wife-to-be, played by Teresa Wright, that, although they are in love, a hardscrabble life awaits them. "We'll have to work, get kicked around." Those final, inconclusive words of the script suggested, as Roosevelt did in Cleveland, not an end but a rough and hopeful beginning.[31]

In the back of the platform behind the president sat Rosenman and Sherwood. Enthralled, Sherwood mouthed the words in unison with the president. Why didn't he stand up, too, and take a bow? Rosenman whispered to him. For seventeen years, from 1928 to 1945, Sam Rosenman listened to Roosevelt deliver speeches—but the one in Cleveland, he later wrote, topped the list. It was pitched "above the political battle," Rosenman explained. He and Sherwood had described the president's hopes, philosophy, and aspirations. The speech "laid out a blueprint for the America of the future as he would wish it. . . . It was unequaled."[32]

On the same evening that Roosevelt was inspiring the crowd in Cleveland with his panorama of a flourishing, egalitarian society, Wendell Willkie spoke in Madison Square Garden. People had begun arriving at 4:30 that afternoon;

by 6:00 the arena was packed with twenty-three thousand fans waiting patiently until the candidate arrived in the hall at 10:15.

"Well, I'm going to take you in on a little secret," Willkie began as he looked over the sea of cheering supporters waving American flags. "I just listened over the radio from Cleveland, Ohio. And I tell you, I listened, you're all either Communists or Fascists! I have that on the highest authority."

In fact, in his speech earlier that evening in Cleveland, Roosevelt had not repeated the attack he had made in Brooklyn on the strange assortment of extremist bedfellows who had gathered together in support of the GOP candidate. No matter: Willkie wanted to rouse his audience in collective outrage against Roosevelt. But that strategy again put the president in the central, starring role of Willkie's speech. "Wendell Willkie, the man," insisted Wendell Willkie the candidate that night in Madison Square Garden, "has little meaning in this campaign."

It was all about Roosevelt. Willkie pleaded with voters to think hard before satisfying the third-term candidate's "lust for power" with four more years in the White House. He quoted the memorable words from FDR's 1936 campaign speech in Madison Square Garden as an example of his arrogance—"I should like to have it said of my first administration that in it the forces of selfishness and of lust for power met their match. I should like to have it said of my second administration that in it these forces met their master"—and told the crowd that he, Willkie, had a different plea, to be the people's servant, not master. Then, for the moderates in the audience, he enumerated the many New Deal achievements with which he agreed: from collective bargaining and the minimum wage to social security and aid for the unemployed. He voiced approval, too, of the president's policy of giving aid to the "heroic British people" and, echoing Roosevelt, repeated that "there is no place in this crusade for Communists, Fascists or Nazis" or any of their fellow travelers.

Where then did Willkie part company with FDR? Only on the tired issues of budget deficits, "unlimited spending," bloated bureaucracy, and court-packing. What about Willkie's own positive agenda? "I will pledge to you, all of you," he declared in his conclusion, "a unity that you have not had in the last eight years. . . . And out of unity will come a confidence of man in man, and in each other's motives and in each other's hopes. Out of that confidence will grow the new America." Reinserting words that his speechwriters had rejected, he pledged equality and liberty for all, without discrimination of race, creed, or color. Unity, confidence, hope, tolerance, a new America. The words were heartfelt and idealistic—less eloquent than Roosevelt's, but the message was the same. The joyous crowd in Madison Square Garden clapped and blew horns.[33]

That night, on the other side of the East River, Mayor Fiorello La Guardia was speaking at Erasmus Hall High School in Brooklyn at a rally sponsored by the American Labor Party. For months, the energetic mayor had been stumping for FDR. Now he explained to the crowd of fourteen hundred people that there was a clear-cut division of thought in this election. "The progressives, liberals, working men and women, organized labor and patriots are all on one side and on the other the materialistic, greedy, selfish groups that believe in special privilege." When a photographer attempted to snap his picture, the mayor interrupted his speech and said, "Go away, I did not come here to have my picture taken." Then, turning to the audience, he added with a conspiratorial smile, "He thinks I'm Wendell Willkie!" While the audience roared its approval, La Guardia, in an ebullient mood, put on his own burlesque show. Bending down and pulling a lock of hair over his forehead and mimicking Willkie's husky voice, the mayor shouted, "I came up the hard way!" Then, in another aside to the audience, he said, "Some men have their hair mussed because their brains are working, others because the photographers are working!"[34]

On Sunday, November 3, two days before Americans headed to the polls, Willkie, his wife, and their son attended church. The rest of the day, the candidate relaxed in his apartment on Fifth Avenue, chatting with friends and receiving last-minute reports about his prospects. "Joe, how are we coming out?" he asked his campaign manager, Joe Martin. "We've got a chance to win, Wendell," Martin replied, explaining that twelve or fourteen important states were still up for grabs—states like Wisconsin, Illinois, New York, Indiana, Ohio, and Iowa. "They are going to be decided by a small margin. If we get what they call that last week's pay-up, we can win. If we don't, we won't." Willkie said nothing. "The difficulty that we're really under," Martin added as gently as he could, "is that we've got to take all of them." Martin was less candid with reporters, making the standard prediction that Willkie would win on Election Day. On Sunday evening, Willkie issued a last-minute statement—an attack, once again, on FDR. If elected president, he promised, he would propose a constitutional amendment limiting the tenure of office of any president to "eight years or less."[35]

That same Sunday, Roosevelt returned to Washington at noon. He issued a brief statement requesting that private employers release their workers early on Tuesday, as the federal government did, to give them time to vote. And he met with Cordell Hull and his deputy Sumner Welles to discuss the foreign situation. While they spoke in the White House, German bombers descended from the clouds to systematically machine-gun Sunday strollers, cyclists, buses, and motorists in towns northeast of London; Italian troops continued their raids on Salonika and other cities in Greece while Greek troops, aided by a few British bombers, fought back; and the Axis and Russians worked to reach an agreement on the Balkans.[36]

"It has been grand fun, hasn't it!" FDR said to Robert Sherwood and Sam Rosenman late Sunday evening, before boarding the train for Hyde Park. FDR pronounced those words, Sherwood dryly noted, "with more warmth than accuracy." Then the president reminded them that they and their wives were expected for supper in Hyde Park two days later on election night.[37]

On Monday the president motored through the mid-Hudson countryside in New York, waving to people from his open car and speaking to cheering crowds in Poughkeepsie, Newburgh, Kingston, and Rhinebeck.[38] In the evening, sitting in the quiet study of his home in Hyde Park where he had done his homework as a little boy, he spoke briefly to the nation on the radio. With microphones from every national broadcasting system placed on the desk, he talked intimately to Americans across the continent, addressing them not as a partisan candidate or party head but as the leader of all.

In their public talks and addresses, presidents often remind their followers of their deeds and accomplishments while hoping to inspire them with their visions for the future. And yet, leaders do not always need to hit the highest, loftiest notes on the scale; sometimes—perhaps especially in a violent, anarchic world—the mundane may be lovelier, more reassuring, and more moving than the extraordinary. On the eve of the election, Roosevelt connected with his followers by locating beauty, security, and freedom in the ordinary daily routines of ordinary Americans.

"As I sit here tonight with my own family," he said, "I think of all the other American families . . . sitting in their own homes. They have eaten their supper in peace, they will be able to sleep in their homes tonight in peace. Tomorrow they will be free to go out to live their ordinary lives in peace—free to say and do what they wish, free to worship as they please. Tomorrow, of all days, they will be free to choose their own leaders who, when that choice has been made, become in turn only the instruments to carry out the will of all the people.

"And I cannot help but think of the families in other lands—millions of families—living in homes like ours. On some of these homes, bombs of destruction may be dropping even as I speak to you. . . . We vote as free men. . . . In our polling places are no storm troopers or secret police to look over our shoulders as we mark our ballots." He then pictured Americans at those polls, discussing with one another "the state of the nation, the weather and the prospect for their favorite football team." With a smile, he remarked that "there will be a few warm arguments."

Democracy was not just a word to be shouted at political rallies, he emphasized. "It is a living thing—a human thing—compounded of brains and muscles and heart and soul." It was the birthright of every citizen, white and colored, Protestant, Catholic, and Jew. "Democracy is every man and woman who loves freedom and serves the cause of freedom."

Making no strong pitch for himself, the president merely thanked his supporters for their trust in his administration and remarked that he awaited the verdict of the electorate "in full confidence of vindication of the principles and policies on which we have fought the campaign." Both sides, he added, had conducted honorable campaigns. And he urged all Americans to vote. "Tonight," he said, "I should like to add that a free election is of no use to the man who is too indifferent to vote." Roosevelt had intended also to say "too lazy to vote," but Harry Hopkins pressed him to delete those words. "I don't think you ought to insult the people," he said, the offending adjective having reminded him of the accusations that the unemployed were too lazy to work. Roosevelt agreed. Ending his radio chat with the prayer he had recited years ago as a student at Groton, he asked for divine guidance to save the nation and its people "from violence, discord and confusion: from pride and arrogance and from every evil way."[39]

His talk, once again, had been composed by the master playwright.

On that last day before Americans went to the polls, Willkie rushed around New York City, speaking with supporters and giving three final talks. When reporters pointedly asked him how he would deal with isolationists if he won the presidency, he impatiently replied that, if he occupied the White House, *they* would have to cooperate with *him*.[40] The first of his three speeches that day was addressed to American women. They "built this country alongside their men," he said. Praising the important roles women play in American society, he recalled his own mother's pioneering career as a lawyer. In the concluding words of a meandering speech, he returned to the subject of his mother: he had fought the fight that his mother would have wanted him to fight. "I have kept faith as she would have had me keep it. I finished the course as she would have me finish it. . . . My purpose is to keep America out of war and to preserve American values. . . . Women of America, I ask you to help me to save these values."

Later that evening, Willkie took to the radio again. Like Roosevelt, he thanked his supporters, and like Roosevelt, he praised democracy: "Democracy cannot be neglected," he said. "It doesn't just take care of itself. You, the citizens of it, must take care of it." And, like Roosevelt, he said that it was the "sacred duty" of all Americans to vote.

But, firing off one last round at the president, he also called on voters not to permit Roosevelt to "thrust aside" the precious two-term tradition. "Let us remember," he warned, "that dictatorships always begin by asking people to give up some law or tradition." The Democratic Party, he suggested to its members, was an example—it had been "kidnapped" by a few men who had accumulated too much personal power. Moreover, to those who touted Roosevelt as the more experienced candidate to deal with a world crisis, he replied that Neville Chamberlain had also had great experience and that, like FDR, the prime minister had not wanted to give up power. "Yet the people of England deliberately chose a new government," Willkie said, neglecting to explain that, in fact, the people of England had played no role in the change in leadership that took place behind closed doors in Westminster Hall. The discredited Chamberlain, unable to form a national government, resigned; Winston Churchill took his place, leading a coalition government of the Conservative and Labor parties.

At the end of his talk, after quoting at length from Abraham Lincoln and George Washington, Willkie exhorted all Americans of all religions and ethnicities to unite. "We are bound together by the living laws of man and the living word of God," he said. "These are the bonds of brotherhood. In brotherhood—in brotherhood alone—we shall become strong."

Late on Monday night, politicians along with stage and screen stars spoke on radio shows for both candidates. The Democrats had control of the airwaves from 10:00 until midnight; the GOP from midnight until 2. Broadcasting from Carnegie Hall, the Democratic cast included Alexander Woollcott, Melvyn Douglas, and Walter Huston as well as Benny Goodman, Irving Berlin, Marian Anderson, Carl Sandburg, and Dorothy Thompson, with Mayor La Guardia presiding as master of ceremonies. "This is not a political meeting," La Guardia announced to the crowd. "The campaign is over. This is a victory meeting for the reelection of President Roosevelt!" Dorothy Thompson charged that the Republicans had on their side "the Stalinists, the Nazi boys and the Fascist boys," but Roosevelt, she confidently declared, would "preserve democracy in the United States and restore it to the world." Leaving the hall at the end of the show, La Guardia said that he was "going downtown on the sidewalks of New York to pick up a few more votes!"[41]

Appearing in the Republicans' show at the Ritz Theatre in New York was a motley crew, including a pair of pugilists—Joe Louis and John L. Lewis—and a contingent of former friends of the president like Al Smith and Raymond Moley. Robert Taft phoned in his message from Ohio, and Bing Crosby called from Hollywood to say that he was "personally against the third term and plenty of other people out here in California are too." A news flash was read to the audience, predicting that Willkie would carry eight midwestern states as well as New York, Pennsylvania, and Massachusetts. During Moley's talk, the shriek of sirens outside heralded the arrival of the candidate himself. The audience cried "We want Willkie," and Moley quickly ended his talk.

Mounting the stage, Willkie went over to chat with Joe Louis. Then Joe Martin introduced the GOP candidate as the "new champ." As Willkie stepped up to the microphone, the crowd roared its approval for twelve deafening minutes, chanting, "We want Willkie!" One last time warning Americans that the reelection of the "third-term candidate" would destroy America's "democratic way of life," Willkie pleaded earnestly, "Help me, help me, help me save it!" He was, by then, mentally and physically drained; his vocabulary failed him, and his speech fell flat. He ended by telling his listeners that "no man in all the history of time has ever felt a deeper dedication or sense of obligation to the cause that he has led than I feel to this cause that I lead. And we must win, we must win this cause tomorrow."[42]

That evening, Robert Sherwood heard another Republican commercial on the radio, addressed to the mothers of America, that he described as "bloodcurdling." Speaking in "the ominous, insidious tones of a murder mystery program," the announcer said, "When your boy is dying on some battle field in Europe and he's crying out 'Mother! Mother!'—don't blame Franklin D. Roosevelt because he sent your boy to war—blame YOURSELF, because YOU sent Franklin D. Roosevelt back to the White House!"[43]

Earlier that evening, as theatergoers were making their way through Times Square to see their plays—Cole Porter's *Du Barry Was a Lady* with Bert Lahr and Gypsy Rose Lee, Kaufman and Hart's *The Man Who Came to Dinner* with Monty Woolley, and Robert Sherwood's *There Shall Be No Night* with Alfred Lunt, Lynn Fontanne, and Sidney Greenstreet—they encountered young supporters of Roosevelt and Willkie facing off, each group trying to drown out the other with patriotic songs, booing, and hoarse invective. "We want Roosevelt! We want Roosevelt!" and "Back to Wall Street!" cried the president's fans, while their counterparts shouted back, "We want Willkie!" Traffic was tied up, police reinforcements arrived, and the spontaneous outdoor Broadway show made the front page of the *New York Times* on Election Day.[44]

Who would win the election on that day? In either case, the world would not lose. A cartoon in the *London Evening Standard*, endorsing both candidates, said it all. The drawing showed two campaign posters side by side outside a polling station, one reading "ROOSEVELT FOR PRESIDENT—AND A BLACK EYE FOR HITLER" and the other, "WILLKIE FOR PRESIDENT—AND A KICK IN THE PANTS FOR HITLER." In front of the polling booth stands Herr Hitler in person, with a worried expression on his face, wondering which way to vote. Either way, he loses.[45]

Chapter 18

Safe at Third

O N THE AFTERNOON OF ELECTION DAY, November 5, the president longed for relief from the tension of the day. After making a half-hearted attempt to work on his stamp collection, he decided to play poker with Harry Hopkins, Pa Watson, and Marvin McIntyre. In the early evening, Eleanor served a buffet dinner for all the guests—family, friends, staff, neighbors—at her nearby cottage, Val-Kill, while Roosevelt dined alone with his mother in the "big house," Springwood.[1]

After dinner, everyone returned to Springwood. The forty or so guests congregated in the library, chatting quietly or listening to the election returns on the radio. In another room off the front hall sat the president's mother with several old friends, sewing or knitting with the radio on softly. Robert Sherwood observed Eleanor in a red chiffon dress wandering from room to room, not paying attention to the election news. If asked, she replied impersonally, "I heard someone say that Willkie was doing quite well in Michigan," in exactly the tone of someone saying, "The gardener tells me the marigolds are apt to be a little late this year." The mood was tense, though the guests affected a gay confidence.[2]

In the dining room, converted into a workroom with extra telephones and news printers, Roosevelt sat alone at the big table, his jacket off, his tie hung low under his collar. Spread out before him as he kept score were a radio, charts, tally sheets, pencils, and a telephone. Missy LeHand brought him the latest "takes" from the teletype machines as they chattered out the returns. Henry Morgenthau, Sam Rosenman, Harry Hopkins, and Eleanor occasionally came in for a few minutes.

The first count to reach the president came from Nutbush township in North Carolina: Roosevelt, 24; Willkie, nothing. Reports from Connecticut arrived. In 1932, Roosevelt had failed to carry that neighboring state, but he had won it in 1936 and once again seemed to have it in his corner by a safe margin.[3] The next returns, however, were mixed. The first numbers from New York City were disappointing. According to one report, only Jewish neighborhoods were falling into the Roosevelt column. And in urban areas around the country, Willkie was doing better than had been expected, and he was also showing strength in the farm and dust bowl areas of the Midwest and in the key states of Ohio, Illinois, and Pennsylvania.

After a brief visit from an agitated Morgenthau, the president's nerves got the better of him. "Mike, I don't want to see anybody in here," Roosevelt said to Mike Reilly, the Secret Service chief. "Including your family, Mr. President?" the surprised Reilly asked. "I said 'anybody,'" FDR snapped in a grim voice, his jaw set tight. Reilly noticed that the president had broken into a heavy sweat. Succumbing to the strain of the evening, Roosevelt temporarily shut down the usually inexhaustible faucet of his charm.

Within a few minutes Morgenthau appeared again. "Mr. Secretary, the president doesn't want to see anybody. Sorry," Reilly said as Morgenthau's face fell. For the next hour Reilly stood guard at the door.[4]

On Tuesday morning, Wendell Willkie and his wife, Edith, voted at a public school near their apartment. He smiled and waved to the news cameras and to the small crowd of people cheering, "We want Willkie!" He spent the next few hours taking a drive through Central Park and then resting at home before leaving in the late afternoon for his headquarters at the Commodore Hotel.

In his fourteenth-floor suite at the Commodore, Willkie, in his usual rumpled suit, chatted with friends and relatives and read newspapers. In nearby rooms, his staff of statisticians analyzed the early returns. Chain-smoking, the presidential hopeful listened silently to the election returns on the radio, announced by Elmer Davis, the popular commentator. When a small lead for Roosevelt in Indiana was announced, Willkie walked around the room and then remarked that the returns had probably come from Gary, in the industrial northwest of the state, a region that had gone solidly for FDR in 1936. After finishing dinner, Willkie, still optimistic, sent a message to reporters in the hotel's press room. "I think it is a horse race," he wrote. "I don't think the result will be finally determined before sometime tomorrow."

But the unfavorable trend continued during the evening, and Willkie's mood turned grim. Then came in news that FDR was going to carry Ohio by one hundred thousand votes. It would be virtually impossible for the Republican candidate to win without that state, but he was not ready to give up. "I can still win," he said.[5]

Around midnight, he spoke with Joe Martin on the telephone. "It doesn't look as though we're going to make it, Joe," Willkie admitted. Then came a report that vice presidential candidate Charles McNary, in Salem, Oregon, had already conceded the race and congratulated Roosevelt and Wallace. "We shall try to afford Mr. Roosevelt and his associates a worthy and vigilant opposition," McNary stated, adding that the "trend" indicated a Republican victory in 1944. Listening to the broadcast, Willkie was quiet.[6]

As Roosevelt sat in the dining room, tallying the votes coming in, he knew that, earlier that day, millions of Americans had pronounced their verdicts on his eight long, rough years in the White House. There had been successes and failures, fireside chats, economic emergencies, key programs from social security to rural electrification, the fierce backlash on court-packing, another tumble into recession, and a misguided venture to "purge" the Democratic Party of conservatives in 1938. But perhaps weighing even more heavily on voters' minds that day were their hopes for the future, their fear of imminent war, and their confidence in Franklin Roosevelt, in his ability to steer the nation through the turbulent waters ahead.

Results from Pennsylvania—a state with six hundred thousand more Republicans than Democrats and one of the six states that had voted for Hoover in 1932—trickled in. To win there, Roosevelt had to hold on to the twenty-three coal and industrial counties—and thanks to the coal miners and steel workers of the CIO, it looked like he was carrying nineteen of them.[7]

More numbers poured in—the tide was cresting for FDR. At 9:40 p.m., Ed Flynn, the national Democratic Party chairman, called to say that the *Cleveland Plain Dealer* in the key battleground state of Ohio was calling the election for Roosevelt. He had cruised to another victory. Easily.

An elated Roosevelt called out to Mike Reilly to open the door, and, as family and friends strolled in, the celebrations began.

Around midnight, the president and his guests heard a commotion outdoors. Franklin; his mother, Sara; Eleanor; sons Franklin, Jr., and John and their wives; Harry Hopkins; and a few others walked outside to the portico of the big house to greet a festive torchlight parade. Hundreds of neighbors and townspeople along with a few reporters and movie cameramen had followed a town band to the house. The president laughed happily when a little boy held up a sign on which the words SAFE ON THIRD were scrawled over the words OUT STEALING THIRD. "We are facing difficult days in this country," Roosevelt told the well-wishers, "but I think you will find me in the future just the same Franklin Roosevelt you have known a great many years. . . . My heart has always been here. It always will be."[8]

When the evening's events were all over, Sara took Grace Tully aside and said in a sad voice, "Little Tully, a lot of my friends and some of my relatives are not going to like this at all tomorrow." It was more important, Tully countered, that tens of millions of people throughout the country and around the world were rejoicing.[9]

Indeed, in Europe and Asia, South America and Africa, people looked to Roosevelt for help. His White House had become "a symbolic lighthouse in the worldwide blackout of democracy," commented *Time*. While Roosevelt was greeting his neighbors in Hyde Park, German planes were dropping fifteen hundred bombs on London, destroying factories and railroad tracks, reducing the docks to rubble and buildings to smoking skeletons. "I did not think it right for me as a Foreigner to express any opinion upon American policies while the Election was on," Churchill wrote to Roosevelt the day after the election, "but now I feel you will not mind my saying that I prayed for your success and that I am truly thankful for it." On that fiftieth consecutive night of Nazi bombing raids over Britain, Churchill added that "we are entering upon a somber phase of what must evidently be a protracted and broadening war. . . . Things are afoot which will be remembered as long as the English language is spoken in any quarter of the globe."[10]

On the night before the election, poet Carl Sandburg had spoken out on the radio for Roosevelt, calling him "a not perfect man and yet more precious than fine gold." Three weeks later, thanking him for his words, the president expressed his satisfaction that so many American voters, including many without much education, "do have that final ability to decide our fate and the country's fate 'in the deep silence of their own minds.' "[11] Indeed, in casting their ballots for FDR, average citizens in the United States showed that they had no fears of a third-term dictatorship. On the contrary, they knew Roosevelt and trusted him, and they were still willing to follow him. He had helped them emerge from the Great Depression, and they hoped that, as Nazi bombers pounded cities in England and Scotland, he would once again guide them through days or years of struggle and sacrifice. Officially the United

States was at peace; but in the minds of Americans, the nation could hardly have been closer to war. And that was the decisive issue of the election of 1940.

At 12:30 a.m., Willkie took the elevator down to the Commodore ballroom. The crowd of five thousand supporters had dwindled to fifteen hundred. As he marched into the room, people erupted in cheers, chanting, "We want Willkie!" "Fellow workers," he began. "I first want to say to you that I never felt better in my life!" "That's my man!" someone shouted. The candidate thanked the crowd for being "a part of the greatest crusade of this century," promising that "the principles for which we have fought will prevail." There was no concession speech, no congratulations to his opponent. As if the battle were not over, Willkie exhorted his followers not to be "afraid or disheartened because I am not in the slightest. . . . I hear some people shouting to me 'Don't give up.' I guess those people don't know me. I must be going back upstairs, but I did want to come by to thank you. . . . Don't be afraid and never quit. Good night." Returning to his suite, he told reporters that he would have no statement to make until the following morning.[12]

Early on Wednesday, Willkie dictated a curt telegram to the president in Hyde Park. "Congratulations on your re-election as president of the United States. I know that we are both gratified that so many American citizens participated in the election. I wish you all personal health and happiness. Cordially, Wendell L. Willkie." Defeat had come hard.[13]

At noon, he released a brief statement conceding the race. He accepted "with complete good-will" the results of the election and pledged himself to work for American unity, preparedness, and aid to Britain. The statement appeared in a short seventeen-line article tucked away on page 24 of the *New York Times*. Two days past the election and Willkie was already yesterday's news. It was Alf Landon who made the front page, as if he, not Willkie, were the leader of the GOP who had the task of acknowledging the election results and generously pledging cooperation with the reelected president. "There is in the world tonight the unity of the machine gun," Landon stated at an "America United Rally" in New York's Carnegie Hall. "And then, there is the inspiring unity of a free people, behind a leader who is honest, and truthful, and frank as to the toil and hardships ahead. . . . Republicans and Democrats stand shoulder to shoulder for national defense, as always."[14]

Roosevelt had won by a substantial margin, but 1940 was not the 1936 landslide when Landon had carried only two small states; nor was it as lopsided as

1932 when Hoover won 6 states with 59 electoral votes to FDR's 472. This time the electoral vote was 449 to 82, with 38 states in FDR's camp and 10 in Willkie's. In addition to the Republican pillars of Maine and Vermont, Willkie carried his "home" state of Indiana, Henry Wallace's home state of Iowa, and six others, all deep in the interior of the nation—Michigan, Kansas, Nebraska, North Dakota, South Dakota, and Colorado. Willkie fared particularly well among wealthier Americans, while FDR's popularity among the upper-income groups sank from 42 percent in 1936 to 28 percent in 1940. The turnout at the polls was unusually large. In New York City more than 95 percent of registered voters had cast their ballots. The popular vote—27,303,945 for FDR; 22,347,744 for Willkie—decisive though it was, could give Willkie some solace. He had attracted five million more voters than Landon—in fact, more than any GOP candidate in American history. After the GOP's crushing defeat in 1936, it was back in the game and, fortunately, so was the two-party system.[15]

FDR's broad and inclusive coalition—blacks, ethnic minorities, Jews, immigrants, urban workers, organized labor, farmers, intellectuals, southerners, including white supremacists, and some independents—had stayed on board. With the exception of Cincinnati, he carried every large city in the country. As usual, he received his most extravagant support in the Deep South, climaxing in South Carolina, where he received 98 percent of the vote, and Mississippi, where he won 96 percent. And despite the threats of John L. Lewis, members of labor unions remained loyal to their true protector. According to Gallup's Institute of Public Opinion, 79 percent of CIO members and 71 percent of AFL members voted for Roosevelt, proving, as Gallup said, "the Administration owes its reelection to labor."[16] Three weeks after the election, just as he had threatened, Lewis resigned as CIO president, though he remained head of the United Mine Workers. Speaking of himself oddly in the third person in his swan song at the CIO convention, he said, with tears in his eyes, that "whether he was right or wrong, at least his heart was in the right place."[17]

Roosevelt rejected the fancy three-syllable word "inclusive," Frances Perkins later remarked. He preferred to say simply that in his government no one would be left out.[18] But while the president could capitalize on his wide spectrum of support, his opponent had been forced to struggle with a severely fractured minority party. It proved a daunting if not impossible task for the moderate and internationalist Willkie to appeal simultaneously to Republican progressives, conservatives, and isolationists as well as to independent voters and anti-third-term Democrats.

Nor had he succeeded in winning over the GOP establishment itself. "What beat Wendell was the Republican party," maintained Edward Willkie, a member of his brother's campaign entourage. Other friends of Willkie agreed that many Republican "regulars" and members of the Old Guard had dragged their heels during the campaign and even felt relief when the maverick lost. For his part, Democratic national chairman Ed Flynn added that Willkie had made the situation worse by taking "every opportunity he could to insult directly or indirectly the politicians in the Republican Party."

Second-guessing the campaign and playing the blame game over the next weeks, months, and years became a sport for Republicans. Some felt that it had been a campaign run by amateurs; some pinned responsibility on Willkie's foreign policy advisor Raymond Buell for pushing the candidate too far toward interventionism; others blamed Russell Davenport for clumsily slighting Old Guard Republicans and for not delegating more responsibility. Some expressed disgust that the likes of Father Coughlin, the German–American Bund, and other pro-fascist organizations had gravitated toward Willkie, hurting the candidacy of a man who was deeply committed to democratic ideals and principles of tolerance and equality.[19]

It was the fall of France and the Nazi bombings of Great Britain that defeated Wendell Willkie, Joe Martin contended. "There are times, and 1940 was one," he wrote, "when the party that seems best able to prosecute a war is invincible. In the last analysis, the people trusted Roosevelt's experience in coping with the situation that confronted the country." Moreover, Martin was convinced that, given the deep divisions in the GOP, Willkie would not have been able to lead the wartime government as effectively and skillfully as FDR could with the Democratic Party united behind him.[20]

Willkie had poured his heart, mind, body, soul, and vocal cords into his "crusade" —and later would apologize for having resorted to reckless accusations and misguided rhetorical ventures into isolationist territory. He had always stood up for the core programs of the New Deal and always contemptuously repudiated the support of hate-mongers like Father Coughlin. And, no less passionately than Roosevelt, he believed that America had to utterly reject the poison of fascism as well as do everything in its power to aid Britain. And, as much as Roosevelt, Willkie mistrusted the powerful isolationist bloc in the GOP. Although the *New York Times* reporter in London, Raymond Daniell, commented that the fifty American destroyers and American planes sent across the ocean by Roosevelt had impressed Britons more than Wendell Willkie's campaign utterances, a few days after the election, Churchill nevertheless complimented Willkie, whose pledge of material aid to Britain, Churchill said, had "deeply touched the British government and people." Later that week, writing to Sam Rosenman, FDR expressed relief that he had won, not because he doubted Willkie's internationalism, but because "there were altogether too many people in high places in the Republican campaign who thought in terms of appeasement of Hitler."[21] Willkie voiced that same fear. If the Republican Party let itself be recaptured by the "old-guard reactionaries" with their isolationist notions, he told newspaper columnist Mark Sullivan in late November, the result would be "tragic."[22]

"There is no doubt in my mind," Robert Sherwood later wrote, "that Roosevelt had far more admiration for Willkie than for any opponent he ever faced." The president respected Willkie's enormous courage, if not his political acumen, Sherwood commented, and was "profoundly and eternally grateful" for Willkie's persistent battle against isolationism. "I'm glad I won," said Roosevelt, "but I'm sorry Wendell lost."[23]

When Franklin and Eleanor's train arrived in Washington two days after the election, on the morning of November 7, a tumultuous crowd of two hundred thousand people turned out to greet them at Union Station. Army, navy, and marine bands played festive music. Government employees and schoolchildren, all on a half-day holiday, lined the parade route from the station to the White House, waving and cheering as the president, vice president–elect, and their wives drove down Pennsylvania Avenue in an open car. That street "has seen Presidents come and go," wrote the *New York Times*, "but never before a third term President." Back in the White House, the president took time to receive the office staff. "Everybody went in all smiles," wrote one excited secretary, Leila Stiles, to her mother that day. "I don't think there is a person that works here that doesn't adore him. . . . When I shook hands with him I leaned over and said, 'I did it. I voted twice!' He threw back his head and laughed and said, 'Grand!'"[24]

The following day, close to two hundred reporters jammed into Roosevelt's office. He was calmly smoking a cigarette.

"Mr. President," one reporter asked, "toward the end of the campaign you made certain statements that were regarded by many people as indicating that you would not accept a fourth term. Did you definitely mean that?"

"Well," responded FDR, "the question is this: Oughtn't you go back to grade school and learn English? It was perfectly clear to me and to almost everybody else in this country."

"That was your meaning?"

"Well, read it. I am not teaching you English. Read it."

"I have read it, sir."

"Well, read it again," Roosevelt said, with growing annoyance. "It was a statement, and perfectly plain English. Read it again."

The statement they were referring to came from FDR's campaign speech in Cleveland when he vowed that the country would make it through the storm before his next term ended. "When that term is over there will be another President, and many more Presidents in the years to come," he had said, "and I think that, in the years to come, that word 'President' will be a word to cheer the hearts of common men and women everywhere. Our future belongs to us Americans."

For failing to understand Roosevelt's "perfectly clear" meaning, the reporter was commanded to brush up on his English. And a dunce cap, too, might have hammered home the lesson.[25]

"Is not the result in the USA magnificent?" wrote the British Labor Party leader Clement Attlee jubilantly to Harold Laski two days after Roosevelt's reelection. But at Nazi headquarters on Wilhelmstrasse there were "long faces" when news of Roosevelt's victory reached Berlin, reported William Shirer. For his part, Shirer could hardly wait to leave Germany. "Ed Murrow promises to meet me at Lisbon," he noted in his diary on the day of his departure in early December. "My last night in a black-out. After tonight the lights . . . and *civilization*!"[26] Shortly after the election, the state secretary in the Foreign Ministry Office in Berlin, Ernst von Weizsaecker, rushed a list of talking points to his staff in Washington. If Hans Thomsen was asked about Roosevelt's win, Weizsaecker advised, "please say with cool reserve that the outcome was expected by us and we have reckoned with it for a long time." He had added another sentence but, on second thought, crossed it out: "The victorious outcome of the war for the Axis Powers will not be changed through the election."[27]

German propagandists had failed in their short-term aim of defeating Roosevelt, but they did not abandon their longer-term goals. It was essential, wrote an official in the Information Department in Berlin, that the Washington embassy continue its efforts to "undermine, by indirect and camouflaged actions, the psychological bases of the Anglo-American efforts to form a union." And by continuously working beneath the surface to influence the American "mood," he wrote, German propaganda would strive to "hamper [America's] warlike tendencies."[28]

The entry of the United States into the war, Ambassador Dieckhoff wrote a few weeks later, would have a "very unfavorable effect on Germany materially and psychologically." And so he recommended that Germany ignore any insults or provocations from America and instead remain "ice-cold and calm." Because Americans were "the most unpredictable people in the world," as demonstrated, he noted, by their panicked reaction to Orson Welles's famous 1938 radio broadcast about a Martian invasion of New York, they had to be kept calm, at all costs unagitated and unperturbed. This was, he concluded, "not a weak policy but a clever one."[29]

In the days and months following the election, Roosevelt would reward his loyal friends and toss aside disloyal ones. After the election, a reporter asked Frances Perkins whether it would be inappropriate to ask if she would accept a third appointment as labor secretary. "Very inappropriate," she said with a smile. Perkins would remain in the cabinet throughout FDR's time in the White House. Harold Ickes offered to resign in case the president wished to do some reshuffling, but the president declined. "That is mighty sweet of you and if I were a Frenchman I would kiss you on both cheeks. As an American, all I can say is 'you are a very good boy. Keep up the good work.'" Jimmy Byrnes and Robert Jackson would soon receive seats on the Supreme Court.[30]

But not everyone got kissed by FDR.

Jim Farley's split with Roosevelt over the third-term issue had been a bitter one for the two old friends. In the late summer of 1940, Farley exited the administration, replaced by a new postmaster general, Frank Walker—and he also stepped down that summer from the chairmanship of the Democratic National Committee. Still, after sulking for weeks, he accompanied FDR to two campaign rallies, and, as New York's Democratic state chairman, he made a last-minute appeal on November 3 to New York party workers to get out the vote for Roosevelt. And then he took on a new job—chairman of the Coca-Cola Export Corporation and the soft-drink's supersalesman around the world.[31]

Also thrown overboard—but with far less regret and far fewer warm memories—was Joe Kennedy. A few days after the election, Kennedy spoke with *Boston Globe* reporter Louis Lyons, one of his oldest journalistic friends, and Lyons's colleague Ralph Coglan, editor of the *St. Louis Post-Dispatch*. For an hour and a half, sitting in his suite at the Ritz-Carlton Hotel in Boston, in shirtsleeves with his suspenders hung around his hips as he munched on apple pie and American cheese, Kennedy held forth. He "poured out to us his views about America and the war in a torrent that flowed with the free, full power and flood of the Mississippi River," Lyons reported in the *Globe*, quoting the ambassador's remarks in a long and damning article that appeared in the Sunday edition on November 10, 1940.

The United States would enter the war, Kennedy blustered, "over my dead body. What would we get out of it?" He was willing, he said, "to spend all I've got left to keep us out of war. There's no sense in our getting in. We'd just be holding the bag." Was the ambassador determined to revive the inept statesmanship of his friend Neville Chamberlain, who died that week? It was "bunk," Kennedy said, that Britain was fighting for democracy. "She's fighting for self-preservation, just as we will if it comes to us." And a little icing on the cake: Eleanor Roosevelt always pestering him "to take care of the poor little nobodies who hadn't any influence. She's always sending me a note to have some little Susie Glotz to tea at the embassy."

That was good for a flurry of titters, but it was the ambassador's stark, unalloyed defeatism that proved utterly devastating. "Democracy is finished in England," he told Lyons. "It may be here." Two short, indelible sentences; one prestigious career in ruins. The casually spoken words could not be erased. His fate was sealed.

"I know more about Europe than anybody else in this country," Kennedy asserted as the interview drew to a close. "I'm going to make it a point to educate America to the situation. Well, I'm afraid you didn't get much of a story."[32]

As soon as the Sunday paper hit the newsstands, Kennedy issued a statement—more defiant than exculpatory. He did not retreat from or deny the substance of the points attributed to him in the *Globe*, but insisted that his controversial remarks had been "off the record," a contention that Lyons and his newspaper firmly denied.[33]

As if the interview in the *Globe* weren't bad enough, two days later Kennedy left for California, where he spoke with his old friends in the movie industry. At a grand luncheon at the Warner Brothers studio, he urged his audience of two hundred Hollywood insiders to stop making anti-Nazi films that could only antagonize the inevitable victor; and he warned the many Jews in the audience to cease their "warmongering" and avoid "hurting themselves." He had the movie moguls "pop-eyed," Drew Pearson reported in his newspaper column.[34]

"We'd better have him down here and see what he has to say," an irate Roosevelt told his wife in Hyde Park before Thanksgiving. His staff had looked into the *Globe* interview and determined that it was authentic. Eleanor met Kennedy's train at Rhinecliff and escorted Kennedy straight to the president. The election had passed, noted historian Michael Beschloss, and now Roosevelt "was freer to indulge the frustrations he had pent up for months." The two men spoke in private. Ten minutes later, the conversation was over. Eleanor had rarely seen her husband so angry. "I never want to see that son of a bitch again as long as I live!" the president exploded. "Get him out of here!" But they had invited Kennedy for the weekend, she reminded Franklin. "Then you drive him around Hyde Park, give him a sandwich, and put him on that train!" The episode was "the most dreadful four hours of my life," Eleanor later confided to a friend.[35]

On December 1, the ambassador went to the White House and officially tendered his resignation. Accepting it, the president made the pro forma request that he remain at his post until his successor was chosen. Kennedy issued a statement saying that, after a short holiday, he would "devote my efforts to . . . the preservation of the American form of democracy: that cause is to help the President keep the United States out of the war." In other words, commented Washington columnists Alsop and Kintner, "he really meant he was going to peddle appeasement all across the United States."[36]

In England, many people celebrated the ambassador's departure. "While he was here," wrote the *London News Chronicle*, "his suave monotonous smile, his nine over-photographed children and his all-fellow-well-met manner concealed a hard-boiled business man's eagerness to do a profitable business deal with the dictators, and he deceived many decent English people." Returning the compliment, Kennedy was overheard muttering, "I hate all of those goddamned Englishmen from Churchill on down."[37] But the headline in the *Chicago Daily News*, owned by Secretary of the Navy Frank Knox, read "WELL RID OF HIM," while Knox himself told a crowd in Boston that it did not "fit the American spirit" to talk appeasement in a world where "force and force alone determines the fate of nations." A pleased Lord Lothian told the Foreign Office in London that he found Knox "refreshingly outspoken."[38]

For half a day in early December, 345 members of the House of Commons listened to talks from the pacifists among them who urged negotiations with Hitler. At the end of the debate, 340 MPs voted against peace talks and only four in favor. It was a striking demonstration of the "vitality" of British democracy, editorialized the *New York Times*, adding that Joseph Kennedy's aspersions on the precious heritage that the British were fighting to preserve had assumed "the dimensions of a colossal insult."[39]

On January 20, 1941, Roosevelt named as his new ambassador to the Court of St. James a New Hampshire Republican named John Winant. A former history teacher, pilot, governor of New Hampshire, and first head of the Social Security Board, Winant was, most crucially, deeply committed to helping Churchill and Britain. While Winant would soon gain the enormous affection of the British people, Kennedy would enjoy noble stature among isolationists who embraced him as one of their own. The America First Committee invited him to be its leader. On the Senate floor, Senator Vandenberg hailed Kennedy as "one of the fundamental sources of reliable information." Praising his "first-class mind" and his "quick, Celtic insight and perceptiveness of atmosphere," conservative columnist Mark Sullivan expressed the hope that Kennedy would continue to "provide America with sound judgment." The ambassador had "suddenly become the hero of all the isolationists in the country," remarked newspaperman Frank Kent, "and of the groups which think it makes no particular difference which side wins the war."[40]

As Roosevelt was sorting out his new administration, one man would be warmly welcomed on his team: his rival, Wendell Willkie. On November 11, a week after the election, Willkie gave an Armistice Day talk, carried on the radio. The light of constitutional government had disappeared entirely from the continent of Europe, Willkie eloquently said. While darkness descended upon Europe, millions upon millions of Americans had flocked to the polls, keeping democracy "triumphantly alive." That shining example of free government gave hope to the besieged people "on the heroic island of Britain—in the ruined cities of France and Belgium."

And then he gave his audience a valuable political science lesson on the role of the loyal opposition as well as a lesson on character, for he was not willing to waste any time nursing his election wounds. He taught that it was essential for Americans to have a sense of national unity and purpose. "We have elected Franklin Roosevelt president. He is your president. He is my president," Willkie said. "And we pray that God may guide his hand during the next four years." But he also stressed that in an open democratic system in which two parties competed for power and the majority party governed, the minority had the obligation to be constructive rather than merely factious: "A vital element in the balanced operation of democracy is a strong, alert and watchful opposition . . . vigorous, loyal and public-spirited." The opposition party, he emphasized, must aim at strengthening the nation and making it more productive. "Let us not, therefore, fall into the partisan error of opposing things just for the sake of opposition. Ours must not be an opposition *against*—it must be an opposition *for.*"[41] Willkie also contributed his own postmortem of the election season. Hoping to still the waters that he himself had done much to stir, he noted that, in the heat of the campaign, "people became bitter. Many things were said which, in calmer moments, might have been left unsaid or might have been worded more thoughtfully." Interestingly, although Willkie's talk focused on the role of the loyal opposition and the minority party, he had not pronounced the words "Republican" or "GOP" a single time, perhaps indicating his own uncertainty or ambivalence about the strength of his party affiliation.

After Willkie's refusal to concede defeat on election night and his cold telegram of congratulations to the president the following day, his unusual call for national unity and a constructive opposition party were warmly welcomed in the White House. The day before Willkie's Armistice Day talk, his fellow Republican, Secretary of War Stimson, had written to him, telling him how much he appreciated "the courage and vision which it took for you to come out as clearly as you did in favor of helping the British and adopting the Selective Service act." And for his part, too, Roosevelt knew that, however bitter and divisive Willkie's campaign had ultimately been, both he and Willkie had taken lessons from Machiavelli's playbook. Overheated rhetoric, unrealistic promises, expressions of fealty to the god of no foreign wars, and unfortunate concessions to the isolationists had poured out of both campaigns. And yet, as one reporter correctly observed, the two campaigns "left no scars past healing" and "no unsportsmanlike recriminations. A will to unity is evident on all sides. Americans know how to close ranks."[42]

On Sunday, December 29, 1940, in his flat in east London, foreign correspondent Ernie Pyle heard the wail of the sirens and then the "boom, crump, crump, crump, of heavy bombs at their work of tearing buildings apart." From a high, darkened balcony, he and a couple of his friends saw London "ringed and stabbed with fire." It was a "dreadful masterpiece," he wrote. "Whole batches of incendiary bombs fell. We saw two dozen go off in two seconds. They flashed terrifically, then quickly simmered down to pinpoints of dazzling white, burning ferociously." More than ten thousand incendiary bombs had been dropped in one of the heaviest attacks of the war. On the same Sunday in Coventry, a vital industrial city one hundred miles northwest of London, scarcely a street escaped the pounding of five hundred German bombers.[43]

That evening, Roosevelt was wheeled into a small room in the White House jammed with a motley group of onlookers: Cordell Hull and other cabinet members, the president's mother, and movie stars Clark Gable and Carole Lombard. Seated at a desk covered with the microphones of the major networks, FDR gave one of his most important fireside chats. It was, in part, a response to Adolf Hitler's speech three weeks earlier in a munitions plant in Berlin. Speaking to twelve thousand armament workers, the Führer had declared that there were "two worlds that stand opposed to each other" and that he and his fellow Germans "cannot ever reconcile ourselves" to the democratic, capitalist nations.[44]

The president's message came through loud and clear. "The Axis not only admits but *proclaims* that there can be no ultimate peace between their philosophy of government and our philosophy of government," Roosevelt told the millions of people in the United States and around the world who were listening attentively to his words. The "Nazi masters of Germany," he continued, had made it plain that they were determined to enslave the whole of Europe "and then use the resources of Europe to dominate the rest of the world."

Turning to the isolationists, appeasers, defeatists, and fifth columnists in America, he rejected their insistent message that "the Axis powers are going to win anyway" and that the United States might just as well try to get the best deal it could. A negotiated peace! he scoffed. "Is it a negotiated peace if a gang of outlaws surrounds your community and on threat of extermination makes you pay tribute to save your own skins?" A nation could have peace with the Nazis, he said, "only at the price of total surrender." Sternly he warned Americans not to blind themselves to the "evil forces" that were "already within our own gates." Those forces sought to "reawaken long slumbering racial and religious enmities which should have no place in this country" and were doing "exactly the kind of work that the dictators want done in the United States." The American government, he underscored, knew all about them and was working to ferret them out.

But the nation faced an even more serious and urgent task. The president summoned American citizens and American industry to make their mightiest efforts to increase the production of munitions and war supplies. It was Harry Hopkins who provided the speech's key phrase. "We must become the great arsenal of democracy," FDR proclaimed. There would be "no bottlenecks," he emphasized, in America's determination to aid Great Britain, for Britain was fighting the fight of all democracies, including that of the United States. "If Great Britain goes down," he warned, "the whole world, our hemisphere included, would be run by threats of brute force." Of course there were perils in his strategy to keep America out of the war. "If we are to be completely honest with ourselves," he told Americans, "we must admit that there is risk in any course we may take." Indeed, despite his statement that his "sole purpose" was to avoid war, his election victory and the implications of his militant "arsenal of democracy" speech signaled to some perceptive observers that the entrance of the United States into the death struggle of democracies was likely if not inevitable.[45]

Roosevelt had really enjoyed working on that speech, commented Robert Sherwood, for, with the election over, he could finally throw out "namby-pamby euphemisms." For the first time, Sherwood wrote, the president felt free to mention the Nazis by name and "lash out against the apostles of appeasement" and the "American citizens, many of them in high places" who were abetting the work of foreign agents. Roosevelt knew that he was still the respected and confident voice of America and that it had fallen to him to express and defend the hopes of civilized humanity.[46]

"No, Fala, you can't go with me today," FDR said to his black Scottie, who vainly tried to accompany his master to the oath-taking ceremony at the Capitol. Tommy Qualters, the president's bodyguard, escorted the disappointed Scottie back into the White House. In high spirits, the president drove down Pennsylvania Avenue to the Capitol in an open car, chatting animatedly with House Speaker Sam Rayburn and waving his tall silk hat to the crowds. Shortly after sunrise on January 20, hundreds of thousands of people had begun collecting at the Capitol and along the parade route, willing to wait for hours in the bright sunshine and bitter cold until noon for the dramatic, precedent-shattering spectacle to unfold. People filled the reviewing stands, jammed the sidewalks, and even perched in trees. Near the inaugural stand, soldiers guarded every doorway and window, while, around the Capitol, five hundred marines with fixed bayonets assisted Washington police and Secret Service men.[47]

His hand on an opened page of an old family Bible, the president took, for the third time, the oath of office, intoned by Chief Justice Hughes. That oath, commented *New York Times* columnist Arthur Krock, "was more than a pact with his 130 millions of countrymen and countrywomen; it was a pact with mankind's ancient dream of freedom for the human spirit; it was a pact with free men everywhere."[48]

After making that sacred pact, the president turned to the immense shivering crowd and addressed them and the millions listening on the radio. His speech, this time, struck unusual notes. On March 4, 1933, under gray, gloomy skies and occasional sleet and snow, he had lifted the spirits of Americans crushed by the Depression by confidently promising to solve the nation's economic problems. In his inaugural talk four years later, in January 1937, he conceded that recovery was far from complete and that there remained more work to be done. This time he addressed a nation not yet at war and yet not at peace. Archibald MacLeish had submitted a draft of the speech that was full of optimism about democracy's victory, but Roosevelt told Sam Rosenman that he wanted a different tone. Instead he gave a philosophical talk: the subject was not fiscal chaos or the completion of the New Deal but democracy—its soul as well as its physical being—under attack.[49]

The "coordinate branches of the Government continue freely to function"; the Bill of Rights remained "inviolate." The freedom of elections was wholly maintained. And yet, the nation still had internal enemies. This time, he did not excoriate the "unscrupulous money changers" as he had in 1933 or the "private autocratic powers" as he had in 1937. In 1941, the danger came from the radical isolationists, the "prophets of the downfall of American democracy."

Just as America's first president, George Washington, had vowed to preserve "the sacred fire of liberty," Roosevelt too committed himself to keeping that fire alive. He would not permit it to be "smothered with doubt and fear." Promising to "protect and perpetuate the integrity of democracy," he stressed that the conflicts around the world were not just about territory or military superiority, but rather about preserving fundamental human liberties. Seeking to inspire the courage of Americans, he declared, "We do not retreat. We are not content to stand still. As Americans, we go forward, in the service of our country, by the will of God." There was nothing in his solemn and unifying address to which Wendell Willkie would not have subscribed.

After the inauguration, unlike in 1933 and 1937, there were no wild cheers, no victory balls—just a luncheon, a tea-time reception, and a family dinner in the White House. That day, Hitler and Mussolini met in Germany, and American newspapers carried reports of massive Axis attacks on the British aircraft carrier *Illustrious* anchored in Malta as well as attacks on Greece and the Suez Canal. On this Inauguration Day, no one was singing "Happy Days Are Here Again."[50]

Chapter 19

Roosevelt and Willkie: Almost a Team

O
N SUNDAY, January 19, 1941, the *New York Times* reported good
news and bad. The good news was that output of military aircraft in
the United States had dramatically increased and that Greek forces
had sunk a large Italian transport ship in the Adriatic; the bad was that German bombers had subjected London and Britain's eastern coast to a fierce
pounding and that Hitler and Mussolini were meeting in Germany to discuss
ways to forestall full American assistance to Britain.

That day, while Roosevelt, Rosenman, and Sherwood were putting the
finishing touches on the president's third inaugural address, an aide announced
that Wendell Willkie had just arrived in the White House. Glancing at his desk,
the president realized that it was clean of papers. "Give me a handful to strew
around on my desk," he said to Sherwood and Rosenman, "so that I will look
very busy when Willkie comes in."[1]

A week earlier, on January 12, Willkie had given a remarkable demonstration of patriotism, character, and vision. Just two months after his defeat at the
polls, he took the unusual step of issuing a statement to the press supporting
President Roosevelt's proposal for a new policy of "Lend-Lease." "It is the history of democracy," he wrote in his press release, "that, under such dire circumstances, extraordinary powers must be granted to the elected executive.
Democracy cannot hope to defend itself from aggression in any other way."
Free from the constraints and compromises of the campaign, as was Roosevelt, the Republican now openly hammered the "appeasers, isolationists, and
lip-service friends of Britain" who, he said, "will seek to sabotage" aid to the

United Kingdom. And a final plea addressed to Republicans: support Lend-Lease and put patriotism above partisanship.[2]

Those Republicans, however, probably noticed that in his statement, Willkie had referred to "the Republicans" rather than to "we Republicans," and they swiftly paid him back. The GOP's dismissive reply came from Alf Landon. Rejecting Willkie's position as no different from Roosevelt's, Landon denounced Lend-Lease as a "slick scheme," like "lending a cake of ice in July in Kansas," and said that "if Mr. Willkie had revealed that to be his position before the Republican national convention he would not have been nominated." Other Republicans felt betrayed. Before Willkie issued his press release, publisher Roy Howard had urged him to "blast" Lend-Lease and expose Roosevelt "as a dictator," and now Howard was furious. At a dinner party after Willkie's announcement, Howard threatened to use his newspaper empire to "tear your reputation to threads." Bruce Barton joined them and took the same line. Willkie later remarked that he managed to keep his temper "though if Howard wasn't such a little pipsqueak I'd have felt like knocking him down."[3]

Lend-Lease was FDR's key bill of 1941, a vital response to the urgent pleas of British leaders for essential war matériel that they acknowledged they could not pay for. "1941 will be a hard and difficult year," the British ambassador Lord Lothian had gravely told reporters upon returning to America from London in late November 1940. Admitting that Britain was running out of funds to purchase war supplies, he said that England needed planes, munitions, ships, and, he added, "perhaps a little financial help."[4] Determined to help keep Britain in the fight, Roosevelt proposed that the United States "lend" or "lease" the armaments and munitions the British needed. "What I'm trying to do," he had explained at a press conference on December 17, "is to eliminate the dollar sign . . . the silly old foolish dollar sign."

As reporters scribbled his words in their notebooks, the president made the memorable analogy of a friendly man with a garden hose whose neighbor's house is on fire. He could let his neighbor take the hose, connect it to a hydrant, and put out the fire. "Now what do I do?" Roosevelt asked. "I don't say to him before that operation, 'Neighbor, my garden hose cost me $15; you have to pay me $15 for it.' . . . I don't want $15—I want my garden hose back after the fire is over." If the hose was damaged, FDR explained, the neighbor would replace it later. His homey analogy, suggesting that there was nothing especially dangerous or radical about lending a hose to a neighbor, may have helped in the fight for Lend-Lease, as Robert Sherwood later argued.[5] But in fact isolationists virulently opposed Roosevelt's idea, depicting it as a blatant act of war. It would "plow under every fourth American boy," railed the ferociously isolationist Burton Wheeler. Shooting back just as hyperbolically, the president told reporters that he regarded Wheeler's remark "as the most untruthful, as the most dastardly, unpatriotic thing that has ever been said."[6]

Indeed, the Lend-Lease bill bore the patriotic label of H.R. 1776—though now 1776 evoked not separation from Britain but rather a marriage. That revolutionary number had been the brainstorm of Massachusetts representative John McCormack, the Democratic majority leader who introduced the bill in the House. An imaginative politician, McCormack pitched the bill to his constituents in Boston as aiming to rescue not Britain but the Catholic Church. "Madam, do you realize that the Vatican is surrounded on all sides by totalitarianism?" the congressman wrote to one resident of South Boston. "This is not a bill to save the English, this is a bill to save Catholicism."[7]

On the day that Willkie came out in support of Lend-Lease, January 12, he also announced that he would soon be leaving for Britain to get a close-up view of the European situation and "obtain a broader perspective." He had met with Secretary of War Stimson the previous day and also communicated with Secretary of State Hull about the trip. Now Roosevelt had a perfect opening, not only for a bipartisan foreign policy but for a chance to work with his former opponent. "I pray that if Mr. Roosevelt is elected," wrote columnist Dorothy Thompson on the eve of the election, "he will invite the collaboration of Wendell Willkie." That was about to happen.[8]

He has "lots of talent," FDR had said to Frances Perkins after the election, adding that Willkie "would have made a good Democrat. Too bad we lost him." The president had mulled over a place for Willkie in his administration—an important post though not a political one. Shortly after the election, Perkins phoned Willkie with an offer of the chairmanship of a new commission, the Defense Labor Board, created to settle labor disputes before they harmed the defense effort. Willkie declined. But in January, Roosevelt learned of Willkie's upcoming trip to England, and he reached out again to his old adversary.[9]

At their White House meeting on January 19, it was agreed that Willkie would serve informally as the president's personal representative to England. Then Roosevelt took out a sheet of his personal stationery and penned a message to Churchill. "Dear Churchill," the letter read, "Wendell Willkie will give you this. He is truly helping to keep politics out over here." The letter concluded with several lines from a poem by Longfellow.

Sail on, Oh Ship of State!
Sail on, Oh Union strong and great.
Humanity with all its fears
With all the hope of future years
Is hanging breathless on thy fate.

The president's spontaneous quotation of Longfellow's words greatly impressed Sherwood, who was present at the meeting. "Roosevelt never made a more graceful or effective gesture than that," he wrote. And Roosevelt was convinced that, rather than sending one of his political friends, the leader of the opposition party could best reassure Churchill about America's determination to aid Britain.[10]

"Well, I wouldn't take it," Joe Martin grumbled as he tried to dissuade Willkie from serving as Roosevelt's agent. "What are you going to get out of it?" Willkie wanted to see for himself Britain's destroyed buildings and factories, London's streets full of debris and suffering. "Anyhow I'm going," he said to Martin. "Roosevelt is just trying to win you over," the House minority leader warned. "This won't be well received by the Republicans." Another Republican outraged by the plan was isolationist congressman George Tinkham of Massachusetts, who demanded that Willkie be subpoenaed to appear immediately before the House Foreign Affairs Committee. Willkie laughed at Tinkham's statement, telling reporters that he would be delighted to appear but was busy getting "shots in the arm" and preparing for his departure. For his part, Senator Wheeler suggested that Roosevelt appoint Willkie ambassador to Great Britain "so we will have a completely war-minded administration."[11]

On January 22, two days after the president's inauguration, Willkie's plane left for England. He was accompanied by his friends John Cowles, a newspaper publisher, and Landon Thorne, a banker whose wife's cousin was Henry Stimson. After stops in the Azores and Portugal, Willkie arrived in London on January 26, incarnating American solidarity and determination to save Great Britain from defeat. "I want to do all I can to get the United States to give England the utmost aid possible in her struggle," he told reporters at the airport.[12]

He toured bombed-out sites in London, Coventry, Birmingham, and Liverpool, inspected war-production factories, drank beer and played darts in pubs, chatted with dockworkers, and, amid exploding bombs, descended into underground shelters. In those shelters thousands of people huddled: "I haven't seen one who was afraid," he said. And when, during a visit to the House of Commons, sirens shrieked, anti-aircraft guns thundered, and bombs exploded outside, Willkie noted that the members of Parliament never batted an eye. The spectacle of open debate in the Commons while Nazi planes pounded London was, he commented, "the most dramatic example of democracy at work anyone could wish to see." And the besieged people of Britain welcomed him warmly wherever he went; Londoners nicknamed him the "Indiana Dynamo."[13]

Churchill entertained him at 10 Downing Street as well as at his poorly heated country residence, Chequers, and he was the guest of honor at a dinner hosted by Lord Beaverbrook, the minister of aircraft production, attended by the prime minister and virtually all the government ministers. When Willkie met King George VI and Queen Elizabeth, the King kept his distance, but the American had more success with the Queen. "You see," Willkie said to her, "you are doing better with me than you did with Joe Kennedy." "Yes," the Queen replied, "and it wasn't because I failed to try with Mr. Kennedy either."[14] Willkie also spoke with Foreign Secretary Anthony Eden; Labor Party leader and Lord Privy Seal Clement Attlee; and A. V. Alexander, the first lord of the admiralty. Too, he visited with FDR's friend, the political scientist Harold Laski. "I had a couple of hours with your late rival, at his request," Laski wrote to Roosevelt. "I thought him shrewd, very agreeable and warm-hearted; but incredibly inexperienced in political argument." Still, softening his appraisal and raising Willkie's grade, he added that his "gesture of sympathy did good here" and observed that Willkie's trip probably ruled him out for the Republican nomination in 1944.[15] Willkie also flew to Dublin, where he failed to persuade Irish prime minister Eamon De Valera to ease his intransigent policy of neutrality and permit Churchill to use badly needed Irish ports.[16]

While Willkie was en route to London, Joseph Kennedy and Charles Lindbergh were giving strong testimony in Congress against Lend-Lease. "I'm against the bill in its present form," Kennedy had declared flatly to the House Foreign Affairs Committee on January 21, warning that Lend-Lease "confers upon the President authority unheard-of in our history." It was indeed true that the bill gave sweeping powers to the president: he would be able to direct government agencies to produce or procure "any defense article for the government of any country whose defense the President deems vital to the defense of the United States." Too, the president could sell or transfer or exchange or lease or lend or repair defense matériel for such governments. Kennedy's hope was that "less drastic ways" could be found to handle the problem of aid to Britain. In fact, Kennedy had somewhat softened his harsh stand against Lend-Lease after having recently met with the president, who did his best to defuse the ambassador's rage.[17]

Kennedy's first task in his testimony was to dispel the idea that he was a defeatist or an appeaser. On the contrary, he said, the truth was simply that helping England was not worth "exhausting our own resources so as to threaten our whole civilization." Passionately, he delivered to the members of the House committee his defense of isolationism. "We want to preserve our democracy. And, ladies and gentlemen, we are not going to preserve anything by getting into this war. It is said that we cannot exist in a world where totalitarianism rules. I grant you it is a terrible future to contemplate. But why should any one think that our getting into a war would preserve our ideals?" Even if America entered the war and triumphed, what would be the fruits of that costly victory? "Well, at the end of the war we win—so what?" Kennedy said. "Our taxes will be high; more people will be paying them; our national debt will be enormous. . . . This is not our war!"[18]

In answer to questions from committee members, the ambassador expressed concern that "we have done enough unneutral things to have war declared on us long ago." What exactly were those "unneutral" acts? asked one congressman. "I think turning over 50 destroyers to England was unneutral," Kennedy replied. "All of our efforts now are unneutral." His words prompted committee member Hamilton Fish to lavish praise upon him for being "the one man who, more than any other, is trying to keep the United States out of this war."[19] Roosevelt, who viewed Kennedy's testimony as a bizarre spectacle, was convinced, as he told his son-in-law afterward, that Kennedy thought that he and the other elite members of the "small capitalistic class" would be safer under Hitler than under Churchill.[20]

Soon it was Lindbergh's turn. It was a veritable media event. On January 23, several hundred people—including congressmen and Hollywood stars—jammed into the smoke-filled hearing room to listen to him state that Lend-Lease would force the United States to enter the European war. This time the once publicity-shy aviator didn't seem to mind the glare of klieg lights as he chatted amiably with reporters and cameramen before the hearings began.[21]

"Whom do you want to win the war?" Representative Wirt Courtney, Democrat from Tennessee, demanded point-blank to the boos and catcalls of isolationists in the visitors' galleries. "Neither side," Lindbergh calmly replied. "I think it would be a disaster to Europe if either side wins completely." The only resolution to the problem, he insisted, lay in a "negotiated" peace based on "realities." But would that be a "just peace?" another skeptical representative impatiently asked. Perhaps not a just peace "according to our standards," Lindbergh conceded. Had he ever expressed any opposition to Hitler? asked Representative Luther Johnson, a Democrat from Texas. "Yes, but not publicly,"

Lindbergh admitted. The aviator believed in complete neutrality. That meant apportioning blame equally between aggressors and their victims. "There is much I do not like that is happening in the world on both sides," he said. Moreover, between fascists and democrats, "there is not as much difference in philosophy as we have been led to believe."[22]

In private, Lindbergh told his friend Selden Rodman that he had an equally low opinion of Nazism and "democracy as practiced by the Roosevelt administration." "Who am I to tell the German people what kind of politics they should have?" he said to Rodman. "That is their business, and as far as I can understand it, they made the only choice possible for them to make in 1933." In an interview with historian Wayne Cole in June 1972, Lindbergh repeated that he had never wanted to denounce the Nazis. "He said it had become 'such a fetish to damn the enemy that I got disgusted with it,'" Cole noted. "He said he believes in being critical of your own people and asked how else could you improve."[23]

Hamilton Fish had invited Lindbergh to testify before the committee, but even the über-isolationist Fish, who always insisted that the United States was impregnable to attack, seemed skeptical of the aviator's extreme defeatism. "You do not want the impression to go out . . . that England couldn't win the war if it went on a long time and if we were willing to send 20 million men, we couldn't wear the Germans down?" Fish asked. "It's possible but not probable," Lindbergh replied, reminding him that Italy and Japan would team up with Germany against Britain. In fact, weeks earlier Fish had come out in favor of supplying Britain with airplanes and merchant vessels, and he would ultimately vote in favor of Lend-Lease. "The Congress will support President Roosevelt," Fish had stated in late December, "on all feasible measures short of war."[24] But another isolationist, Karl Mundt of South Dakota, elicited the aviator's high motives, his self-sacrificing patriotism. "Why," Mundt asked, "do you endanger your reputation by expressing these convictions? . . . You're willing to risk rebuke if you can help avoid war for us?" "I'm ready to risk anything!" Lindbergh exclaimed.

After four and a half hours, his testimony was over. The aviator was "visibly pleased," reporters noted, when members of the committee as well as several hundred spectators rose and applauded him as he left the witness stand.[25] In his testimony lay "the bankruptcy of American idealism," editorialized the *New York Times*. In London, the *Daily Herald* printed a photo of Lindbergh on the front page with the caption: "Lindbergh, Pro-Nazi." Official circles in Berlin, on the other hand, were predictably jubilant. "Hats off!"

said a spokesman for the Reich's Foreign Office, rhapsodizing about the aviator's courage and candor.[26]

While Willkie was in Dublin in late January, he received an urgent cable from Cordell Hull. Would he cut short his visit and hurry back to Washington "as soon as possible" to testify in favor of the Lend-Lease bill before the Senate Foreign Relations Committee? Hull needed Willkie to counter opposition from Kennedy and Lindbergh as well as from isolationist organizations like America First.[27] Willkie immediately agreed, and the State Department made arrangements for his return flight. While he was en route home, the House of Representatives approved the Lend-Lease bill on February 8 by a vote of 260 to 165. Now the bill's fate remained in the hands of the Senate.

"What the British desire from us is not men, but materials and equipment," Wendell Willkie told reporters after his plane touched down at La Guardia Airport on February 9. That day Churchill spoke on the radio, making public his response to the messages from Roosevelt conveyed by Willkie and by Harry Hopkins, who had also spent several weeks in England that winter. "Put your confidence in us," the prime minister memorably said. "We shall not fail or falter; we shall not weaken or tire. . . . Give us the tools and we will finish the job."[28]

"The people of Britain are united almost beyond belief," Willkie told the members of the Senate Foreign Relations Committee on February 11, two days after he returned from England. The huge, column-adorned Caucus Room was packed with more than a thousand people, including wives and friends of senators and interested citizens eager to witness the dramatic spectacle of a defeated presidential candidate coming to the assistance of his victorious opponent. The British "are a free people," Willkie said. "Millions of them will die before they give up that island. When the going gets tough they'll force that bunch of robbers to give up." The previous week, Lindbergh had dismissed the idea of American military aid for Britain when he testified before the Senate committee. "An English victory, if it were possible at all," Lindbergh had told the senators, "would necessitate years of war. . . . This is why I say that I prefer a negotiated peace."[29]

For thirty minutes Willkie read from his prepared text. A week before his forty-ninth birthday, he looked tired from his journey, but there was no fatigue in his voice. As photographers scrambled around looking for good shots and as camera lights flashed, the senators listened carefully. Willkie noted that the Lend-Lease bill gave the president new powers. "Now I'm as much opposed as any man in America to undue concentration of power in the chief executive. And may I say," he added with disarming charm, to the laughter of the spectators, "that I did my best to remove that power from the present executive." He would have preferred that the impetus for Lend-Lease had come from Congress rather than the White House, he said. But in any case, he now hoped that the bill would be adopted with a "non-partisan and almost a unanimous vote." Willkie's approach was nonconfrontational, informal, and impressionistic and seemed to correspond to some of the advice given to him by *New York Times* columnist Arthur Krock. "Avoid every aspect of cockiness on the stand," Krock wrote to Willkie on the day of his arrival back in the United States. "Disclaim any thought of posing as a military expert. Some very smart people will be laying for you. Take one or two fundamental tacks and decline to be diverted to others by questions that will be asked. Say you are simply giving your impressions . . . that you know nothing of military or aviation affairs from the expert viewpoint."[30]

The Senate committee's internationalists—chairman Walter George of Georgia, Pat Harrison of Mississippi, Tom Connally of Texas, all Democrats—were pleased and had no questions to ask. But Willkie was grilled by the committee's isolationists—conservative Republicans like Michigan's Vandenberg as well as progressive Republicans like North Dakota's Gerald Nye and California's Hiram Johnson and especially by Democrats like Iowa's Guy Gillette and Missouri's Bennett Champ Clark. Remaining collected throughout, lounging in his chair and smoking a cigarette, Willkie testified easily, fending off his foes with wit and candor.

"Is this all-out-aid-to-England policy," asked Senator Vandenberg as he leaned forward portentously, "a policy which, if necessary, . . . takes us into war in order to keep England afloat?" Only Congress can declare war, Willkie countered, adding that such a declaration needed overwhelming public sentiment behind it. "If Britain were to collapse," Willkie said, "we would be in war a month afterward. That's my guess." "One month?" exclaimed Senator Robert Reynolds, Democrat of North Carolina. "Well, a month or sixty days," he answered. Reminded by Senator Gillette that the 1940 Republican platform had stated that the party was "firmly opposed" to America's involvement in foreign wars, Willkie responded, "So am I," and explained that the best way to stay out of the war was to give all effective military aid to Britain.

"Mr. Willkie, you had already taken your position on this bill before you went abroad, had you not?" demanded Senator Clark, beginning his hostile cross-examination. "The point I am getting at is that you did not need to go on a tour of England and Ireland to make up your mind." Then, after dredging up criticism of Roosevelt from Willkie's campaign speeches, Clark accused Willkie of having become "the champion" of Roosevelt's foreign policy. For over an hour, Clark peppered him with argumentative questions. "Suppose the Germans got our bombers and used them against us?" Clark asked. "If all the hazards of war go against us, we will get whipped," Willkie responded. "You have flown halfway around the world to advise this committee," Clark finally said, returning to his theme of Willkie's trip. "I did not fly halfway around the world to advise this committee or anybody else. Let us be fair in this," Willkie said. When Clark slipped and addressed Willkie as "Mr. President," the crowd in the galleries burst into applause. "You merely speak of what should have been," Willkie said with an impish smile. Washington insiders had been licking their lips for weeks over what brazen-voiced Clark, known for public rudeness, would do with Willkie, columnists Joseph Alsop and Robert Kintner reported. But the senator was defeated by Willkie's reasonable, good-humored answers.[31]

Finally Gerald Nye pointedly remarked that during the campaign Willkie had asserted that if Roosevelt was reelected, America would be at war by April 1941.

"You ask me whether or not I said that?"

"Do you still agree that that might be the case?"

"It might be. It was a bit of campaign oratory," he responded dismissively, angering the isolationists in the GOP who felt that Willkie had tricked them. Then, with his usual quick wit, Willkie added, to laughter in the visitors' galleries, that he was glad that Nye had read his speeches because "Mr. Roosevelt said he didn't." Willkie's testimony left Nye fuming that the two presidential candidates had engaged in a "phony campaign" and a "circus for suckers." Their claim to oppose American participation in the war was a charade. "They were supposed to be wrestling to a finish to determine the 'Keep Out of War' championship," Nye later wrote. "When the whole thing was over, both men went out of the ring laughing."[32]

At ten o'clock that evening, after Willkie's long day of testimony, Willkie and Roosevelt met in the White House and dined in the president's study—Roosevelt had even asked for an outside chef to prepare a special meal. "Above all," FDR's secretary Grace Tully later wrote, "the Boss said he did not want to be disturbed by anyone." The two men were to have an "old cronies dinner" alone. "Willkie came and remained well on toward midnight and from the sounds of laughter in the Study where dinner was served," Tully remarked, "it was clear to me that the two men enjoyed being together." Afterward,

Willkie told reporters that he and the president had had "a very lively discussion," while denying rumors that he was about to accept a post in the Roosevelt administration.[33]

The next day the stock market suffered a "severe jolt," some analysts attributing the sell-off to Willkie's Senate testimony and his description of the gravity of the situation in Europe. That evening, the former GOP candidate spoke at a Lincoln Day dinner in New York, a black-tie Republican affair at the Waldorf-Astoria Hotel. He used the occasion to urge the GOP to lead the fight for aid to Britain. As the party's titular head, he feared that it was committing political suicide by refusing to recognize the totalitarian threats—especially when Gallup polls showed that 79 percent of Americans wanted Britain to fight until the Nazis were defeated. "Have you got it in you? Have you got it in you?" he cried to the crowd in the Waldorf's grand ballroom, quoting his drill sergeant in World War I. The Republican Party had come into existence as the champion of freedom and emancipation; it would not survive, he cautioned, if it became the party of "negation and failure and death." Still, while he called for cooperation with FDR on aid to Britain, he also sought to play the part of opposition leader by criticizing the White House's failure to "understand the basic functioning of the free enterprise system" and outlining his own agenda. The combination of an internationalist foreign policy and the revival of a free enterprise philosophy presented a "golden opportunity," he explained. "Have we the vision?" he asked, challenging Republicans to embrace the future. "Have we the ability? Have we the leadership to take America down this glorious path that is offered us?"[34]

GOP leaders quickly responded to Willkie's challenge. Robert Taft was still convinced that "Hitler's defeat is not vital to us" and denounced Lend-Lease as a "fraud." After all, he reckoned, if you lend chewing gum to someone, you "certainly do not want the same gum back." The fact that Willkie supported this Rooseveltian concoction, Taft held, proved that he had no right to speak for the party on foreign policy. Senator Nye, too, branded Willkie's backing of Lend-Lease a "betrayal" and then spoke for twelve hours on the Senate floor in an effort to stall the bill. In the House, Hamilton Fish charged that Willkie was "beating the war drums more furiously than the interventionists and war makers of the Democratic party." Willkie would be more helpful to the GOP, Fish added, "if he would refrain from public comment on such a vital foreign and constitutional issue." Pitching in for his friends in the GOP, Democrat Burton Wheeler, the Senate floor leader for the opposition to Lend-Lease, referred to Willkie as "the intrepid Trojan Horse of the Republican Party."[35] And for his part, Herbert Hoover told Joe Kennedy that Willkie's support of Lend-Lease "made practically no difference to the Republicans."[36] Among those who had aspired to the 1940 GOP nomination, Thomas Dewey alone joined Willkie in backing Lend-Lease. After denouncing the bill in January, he changed his mind in February, announcing that he was "satisfied" with the House version of Lend-Lease.[37]

Across the country, GOP bigwigs as well as members of grassroots organizations expressed annoyance with their standard-bearer. The isolationist *Chicago Daily Tribune* could not contain its fury, denouncing the "Barefoot Boy as a Barefaced Fraud." In burning editorials, it thundered that Willkie was a "Republican Quisling" who now carried "the Roosevelt banner" for the "Dictator Bill."[38] In Washington, spurred on by the German chargé d'affaires in Washington, Hans Thomsen, dozens of flag-waving women representing the "Women's Neutrality League" and "Paul Revere's Sentinels" hung a two-faced effigy—one side showing FDR, the other Wendell Willkie—in front of the British Embassy. Meeting in Omaha, GOP leaders from fourteen states issued a statement expressing confidence in House minority leader Joseph Martin, Senate minority leader Charles McNary, and the GOP congressional delegation—but not in Wendell Willkie.[39] Why was the Republican Party so determined "to plow under a fellow like this Willkie?" wondered journalist Raymond Clapper, adding that one should probably not expect better of "the kind of leaders who have run the Republican Party in recent years." The simple truth of the matter, wrote *New York Times* reporter Turner Catledge, was that the GOP was "floundering, confused and befuddled, divided by jealousies and suspicions."[40]

While many intransigent Republicans in Congress refused to stray from steadfast opposition to the Roosevelt administration, their 1940 candidate recognized that the United States faced one of the gravest crises in its history and urged action to provide Britain with aid; and he had won over a majority of Americans. A Gallup poll released in early March showed his stock still rising, prompting the British ambassador, Lord Halifax, to note that "he may well be the biggest dynamic force in our favour outside the White House." Many newspaper columnists and editorial boards also embraced Willkie wholeheartedly. "Willkie's Increasing Stature" and "Wendell Willkie—A Man!" read editorial headlines in the *Washington Post* and the *Atlanta Constitution*, newspapers that praised Willkie effusively for winning "the admiration of the entire nation" and for being "beyond question the greatest figure that has graced the Republican party in a decade."[41] Walter Lippmann lavished praise upon Willkie. "Surely Wendell Willkie was right," Lippmann wrote, "when he says that we have come to the end of isolationist thinking. . . .

We are compelled to deal today with the consequences of the isolationist policy that we adopted and followed for 20 years." Columnist Ralph McGill noted that when Republicans used to sneer about "That Man," they were referring to Roosevelt; now "to the Republicans Mr. Willkie is 'That Man.'" But, he added in a tribute to Willkie, "the new 'That Man' is a greater figure today than when, hoarse and weary, he went up and down the land campaigning for votes."[42]

After modifying the bill to give Congress final authority over appropriations for Lend-Lease supplies, the Senate passed Lend-Lease on March 10 by a vote of 60 to 31. Seventeen Republicans voted against it and only ten in favor. Senator Vandenberg, however, denied that the division in the Senate indicated any division "on the question of aid to Britain." In the House, the picture was not as bleak for GOP moderates. The following day, it approved the new version of Lend-Lease by a vote of 317 to 71, with 94 Republicans in favor and 54 against. At least some Republicans—including both the Senate and House minority leaders, McNary and Martin, who voted for Lend-Lease—were following Willkie's lead, and they, not the isolationists, were in tune with public opinion. Gallup polls in March showed that 56 percent of Americans backed the Lend-Lease bill—with support surging to 78 percent in the South and dropping to 46 percent in Ohio, Illinois, Indiana, and Michigan.[43]

But at the same time, isolationist Republicans, according to columnists Alsop and Kintner, were "already openly working to destroy Willkie's power in the party." The day after Willkie's testimony, Arthur Sulzberger, the publisher of the *New York Times*, which had endorsed Willkie in 1940, remarked to Harold Ickes that had Willkie been elected, he would not have been able to control his party in Congress. John Hamilton, the former GOP national chairman, also expressed his belief that the break between Willkie and the rest of the Republican Party was "irreparable."[44]

And Willkie did little to repair that breach. When a friend advised him to seek counsel on foreign policy issues from GOP congressional leaders before speaking out, he exploded. "Should I submit my ideas to others before enunciating?" Willkie tartly replied in mid-March. "I have not as yet found Bob Taft, Arthur Vandenberg or any of the rest submitting their ideas to me. . . . I doubt whether the country accepts those gentlemen as leaders as readily as they think they are."[45]

Two weeks after the Lend-Lease vote, Wendell Willkie traveled to Toronto, where hundreds of thousands of people filled the streets to cheer him. After a band played "God Save the King" and "The Star-Spangled Banner," Prime Minister William Lyon Mackenzie King expressed the gratitude of

Canadians for Willkie's support of Lend-Lease. Thanking the prime minister and the crowd, Willkie vowed that "Nazism and all it means as a menace to liberty must and shall be eradicated utterly and its leaders driven from power."[46]

Four days later, Roosevelt also paid a stunning tribute to the man he had run against. On March 29, speaking on the radio from his cabin on the *Potomac*, anchored in the harbor of Fort Lauderdale, he addressed Democrats across the nation attending their party's traditional and partisan Jackson Day dinners. But this year Roosevelt's message was strictly and idealistically non-partisan. Andrew Jackson, he told his audience, was a great American because he "placed his devotion to country *above* adherence to party." At this critical moment, with the world threatened by fascist domination, Americans' unity and determination were essential to block the totalitarian threat. And no one demonstrated that spirit better than his former opponent. "The leader of the Republican party himself—Mr. Wendell Willkie—in word and in action," FDR said, "is showing what patriotic Americans mean by rising above partisanship and rallying to the common cause." One pundit later commented that Willkie had the distinction of "being patted enthusiastically on the back by his erstwhile opponents and kicked in the rear with equal enthusiasm by his erstwhile friends."[47]

The unique post-election partnership between the two former adversaries provided some comic moments in March 1941 at the White House Correspondents Association's annual dinner, attended by both FDR and Willkie. One skit in a movie shown at the dinner had two mask-wearing newsmen playing the president and Willkie. Under the title "Bundling for Britain," the two men lay together in a double bed. When "Mr. Willkie" recognized his bedfellow, he sat up in fright. "Help me! Help me!" he cried, while a comfortable "Mr. Roosevelt" serenely puffed away on his cigarette. At that dinner, the real Willkie rose to his feet and applauded FDR's remarks on foreign policy, while House minority leader Joe Martin and other Republicans, according to columnists Alsop and Kintner, "sat on their hands and looked glum." But the quasi-partnership that bound the two former rivals seemed to bestow rewards on them both. According to a March 1941 Gallup poll, 60 percent of Americans now believed that Willkie "would have made a good president." And that month, Roosevelt's popularity also hit a record high: 72 percent of Americans approved of him as president.[48]

Still, between the real Roosevelt and Willkie it was apparently not all milk and honey. Years later family members, friends, and colleagues would comment on their relationship, some negatively, others positively. While Willkie's son, Philip, said that his father thought that FDR was "intellectually shallow,"[49] Irita Van Doren, who may have had the closest relationship to Wendell, affirmed that he always enjoyed talking with Roosevelt.[50]

As for FDR, in May 1941 he privately expressed annoyance that Willkie had gone over his head and communicated directly with Churchill about supplying Britain with ships, and in 1944 he remarked to a friend that Willkie's election in 1940 would have been "a rather dangerous experiment."[51] But Frances Perkins noted that FDR enjoyed Willkie's company and had "genuine regard" for him. "Whether it was Willkie's charm, sincerity or vigor, I cannot say," she wrote.[52] And once Robert Sherwood overheard Harry Hopkins make critical remarks about Willkie to the president. "Roosevelt slapped him with as sharp a reproof as I ever heard him utter," Sherwood wrote. "Don't ever say anything like that around here again. Don't even *think* it. You of all people ought to know that we might not have had Lend Lease or Selective Service or a lot of other things if it hadn't been for Wendell Willkie. He was a godsend to this country when we needed him most."[53]

If FDR and Willkie were more wary than fond of each other, such feelings would have been natural; if the opportunistic Roosevelt used Willkie to demonstrate bipartisan cooperation and political unity in a time of crisis, that would have been understandable; and if Willkie needed to attack some of FDR's policies in order to retain his Republican credentials and claim the title of GOP leader or simply to voice forthrightly his own objections, that too would have been pragmatic and politic. And if the defeated candidate felt any envy of the victor, that would have only been human. But for the good of the country and the survival of democracy around the world, the former rivals sought to work together and probably came to respect each other.

Just as the president had welcomed the skills of internationalist Republicans like Stimson and Knox, he also welcomed the talent of his 1940 opponent. In the end, Roosevelt and Willkie, the two former antagonists, were almost a team.

Chapter 20

Roosevelt and Willkie vs. Lindbergh

ENDELL WILLKIE WAS WINNING FRANKLIN ROOSEVELT'S gratitude and admiration, but between Roosevelt and Lindbergh there was nothing but hatred and bile. That vituperative clash did not end on November 5. In his Inaugural Address on January 20, 1941, the president unmistakably condemned the isolationist line of Lindbergh and his wife. The previous day, FDR, Sam Rosenman, Archibald MacLeish, and Robert Sherwood had been going over a draft of the speech. "I certainly wish we could use that terrible phrase, 'the wave of the future,'" said Sherwood, referring to Anne Lindbergh's bestselling book. "Why not?" FDR said calmly, and proceeded to dictate the words he would pronounce in his Inaugural Address. "There are men who believe that democracy, as a form of government and a frame of life, is limited or measured by a kind of mystical and artificial fate—that, for some unexplained reason, tyranny and slavery have become the surging wave of the future—and that freedom is an ebbing tide. But we Americans know that this is not true."[1]

That spring, Lindbergh and Roosevelt would trade more blows. Speaking at an America First rally in New York on April 23, the day that the Greek government fled Athens for Crete ahead of the unstoppable German invasion, the aviator denounced once again America's aid for Great Britain. The "United States cannot win this war for England," Lindbergh judged, "regardless of how much assistance we extend." He assured his audience that Germany was virtually certain to win, and the Reich's victory, he said, should be greeted with America's cooperation, friendship, and trade.[2]

Two days later, at a White House press conference on April 25, it was the president's turn to blast Lindbergh. It was just "dumb," he replied dismissively to a reporter's question, to think that a Nazi victory was inevitable. Lindbergh, he said, spoke just like the appeasers at Valley Forge, the men who had tried to persuade George Washington to quit. Why hadn't Lindbergh been called into service? another reporter inquired, pointing out that the flier held a commission in the Army Air Corps Reserve.

It was a question that Roosevelt had wanted to be asked and for which he had carefully prepared an answer. A few days earlier he had requested that John Franklin Carter, the author of several books on the New Deal as well as detective novels, do a little research for him. Carter also wrote a syndicated column, "We the People," under the pen name of Jay Franklin and would conduct secret investigations—especially on subversive fifth-column activities in the United States—for the president during the war.[3] This time, FDR asked him for information about the Civil War "copperheads"—the northerners who had sympathized with the South and believed that the North could not win the war. Thanks to the diligent Carter's fifty-page report, Roosevelt could now give reporters history lessons about Alexander the Great, Cromwell, and Clement Vallandigham of Ohio, the leader of the Civil War copperheads. Answering the reporter's question, Roosevelt emphasized that during the Civil War the Union declined to call the copperheads into service. "Are you still talking about Colonel Lindbergh?" a reporter asked. "Yes," the president replied coldly. His meaning was clear. Lindbergh was a Nazi-sympathizer for whom the American army air corps had no use.[4]

"My Dear Mr. President," a defiant Lindbergh wrote on April 28 in a letter he released to news agencies, "Since you, in your capacity as president of the United States and Commander in Chief of the Army, have clearly implied that I am no longer of use to this country as a reserve officer . . . I can see no honorable alternative to tendering my resignation as colonel in the United States Army Air Corps Reserve." Secretary of War Stimson promptly snapped up the offer.

But Lindbergh was not done. "Have we been given the opportunity to vote on the policy our government has followed? NO!" Lindbergh shouted at an America First rally on May 23 in Madison Square Garden, where the crowd of twenty-two thousand booed and hissed the names of Roosevelt and Willkie in equal measure. "We had no more chance to vote on the issue of peace and war last November than if we had been in a *totalitarian* state ourselves. We in America were given just about as much chance to express our beliefs at the election last Fall as the Germans would have been given if Hitler had run against Goering!" There was "an awakened spirit in our nation," he warned, putting Republicans as well as Democrats on stark notice that a popular uprising against both parties might erupt.[5]

Wide-open party conventions, energetic campaigns, a democratic election conducted by the book, and the clear verdict of American voters: none of that was enough to satisfy Lindbergh. "Is it not time for us to turn to new policies and to a *new leadership?*" he demanded seven months after the election. The aviator was questioning the legitimacy of that democratic election, hoping to undermine the president's authority; and he was also casting Wendell Willkie as Roosevelt's co-conspirator in a fraudulent contest. Apparently neither candidate sufficiently represented the "wave of the future."[6]

"There was once a time in America," he told the crowd at another America First rally in Minneapolis, "when we could impose our will by vote. Candidates . . . clearly stated their stand. . . . But it now seems doubtful that we even had two parties last November, at least as far as the Presidential candidates were concerned." Americans were denied "the freedom to vote on vital issues," he charged. So impressed were the Japanese by Lindbergh's attack on American democracy that a few weeks later they dropped leaflets containing excerpts from Lindbergh's talk along with bombs over Chungking, the seat of the Chinese Nationalist wartime government in the southwestern province of Szechuan.[7]

Of course, Lindbergh's views came as no surprise to the White House. Several months earlier, Robert Sherwood had reminded Americans that Lindbergh had "a Nazi's Olympian contempt for all democratic processes." Roosevelt, too, had lashed out at the isolationists like Lindbergh, who scorned the deliberative, orderly processes of a constitutional democracy. "Yes, the decisions of our democracy may be slowly arrived at," he said at a White House correspondents dinner on March 15. "But when that decision is made, it is proclaimed not with the voice of any one man but with the voice of one hundred and thirty millions. It is binding on us all. And the world is no longer left in doubt."[8]

Around the country, newspapers slammed the "perversity" of Lindbergh's assault on democracy. "In the interval between elections," editorialized the *Washington Post*, "all good citizens accept with at least some grace our existing leadership. Otherwise there would be chaos. . . . Mr. Lindbergh is evidently as lacking in decorum toward our institutions as he is lacking in any feeling of repugnance for Nazi institutions." The *New York Telegram* wondered if Lindbergh wanted to impeach Roosevelt "to get as a new president Henry Wallace" or if he simply had in mind imposing a Nazi dictatorship on the country. *Life* featured a photo of Lindbergh saluting the flag at the

Madison Square Garden rally, pointing out that his pose resembled the fascist salute. "Over 20,000 people in the audience booed Roosevelt, Willkie," *Life* wrote. "No one booed Adolf Hitler."[9]

Even General Robert Wood, the head of America First, was surprised by Lindbergh's criticism of the election. Warning the aviator that his call for new leadership "might be misconstrued by some extremists as advocating a revolution," Wood urged him to state that he stood by the American Constitution. Though Lindbergh would have preferred to stick to his own convictions—"I do not like to be held back by the question of influencing the mass of people," he had noted in his diary in February 1941—he complied with Wood's request, issuing a public statement that "neither I nor any one else on the America First Committee advocates anything but constitutional methods."[10]

A few days after Lindbergh's Madison Square Garden speech on May 23, he met with Herbert Hoover in New York, in the former president's apartment at the Waldorf Towers. "We discussed the possibility of Roosevelt being impeached before his term expires," Lindbergh wrote in his diary. But Hoover's tepid reaction disappointed him. "I do not believe he recognized the decadence in England," the aviator wrote, "or the *virility* in Germany."[11] As for the president's high crimes and misdemeanors, Lindbergh was convinced that Roosevelt's aims mirrored those of Hitler. It was clear to him, he told his friend Selden Rodman in July 1941, that Roosevelt, "with less *frankness*" than Hitler, "is attempting to impose *his* world order, in the guise of defending other peoples' freedom, and . . . he does not stop at any means—including . . . the starvation and ultimate destruction of millions of human beings to do it."[12]

On May 27, President Roosevelt issued a historic proclamation informing Americans that an "unlimited national emergency" existed and that, "unless the advance of Hitlerism is forcibly checked now, the Western Hemisphere will be within range of the Nazi weapons of destruction." Thus it was necessary to strengthen American defenses "to the extreme limit of our national power and authority." So dramatic was his nationwide radio address that it virtually shut down the country: baseball games and boxing matches came to a halt as spectators listened to the president over loudspeakers; audiences in movie theaters moved to the lobbies to hear his words; in towns and cities, small crowds gathered on the streets, listening to the speech through the open windows and doorways of shops and homes. Somberly Roosevelt declared that the United States "will expect all individuals and all groups to play their full parts, without stint, and without selfishness, and without doubt that our democracy will triumphantly survive."[13]

"Your voice filled me with happiness tonight," wrote the young congressman from Texas, Lyndon Johnson, to the president that night. "I hope to be battling for your friends and against your enemies on the Senate floor."[14] And also ready to answer the president's call and play his part was Wendell Willkie. On June 6, at a Unity Day rally in the Chicago Stadium, he told a crowd of twenty-two thousand people that in America's hour of national peril "it would be downright folly, *if not worse*, for any man to spend his time in criticizing and obstructing the efforts of the Administration. I shall continue with all my power to do what I can to *support the President* in his foreign policy." He urged all Americans, Republicans and Democrats, labor and management, to put an end to "petty politics" and join him on the Roosevelt defense team. The national emergency called for the organization of the whole American economy "into one vast, closely cooperating machine, . . . the whole thing ticking like a first-class watch. It can be done and it must be done."

Then, without mentioning Lindbergh's name, Willkie took sharp aim at the aviator's recent pronouncements. "We seem to have a few who are trying to run a kind of out-of-season political campaign of their own," Willkie declared. "We have been lately informed that this country needs a new leader. That is reckless and misguided talk. We in America do not choose new leaders between elections." Of course there was room in a democracy for dissent and "for honest differences of opinion," he added, noting that he himself had criticized Roosevelt "very severely" during the fall campaign. But it was another thing to challenge the results of a democratic election. "The American people expressed their views in a free election. They chose Franklin D. Roosevelt."[15]

"Reckless and misguided" isolationists, Willkie said, encouraged Americans to believe in the "myth of the invincibility of dictatorships" and in the delusion that Americans could find safety from the Nazi plague "by locking ourselves within our own walls." But in the real world, he explained, Americans faced a twofold task: a complete dedication to national defense and the prevention of a British defeat. Vividly, he painted a British victory as the "greatest affirmation" of democracy that history would ever know. "In all those silent places of the earth where men are enslaved and dictators now seem permanently in power there will be lifting of heads as there was more than a century ago when men first heard of the Declaration of Independence." In a magazine article Willkie had written a few weeks earlier, he underscored that the United

States bore a crucial responsibility for the fate of Britain as well as for many other nations. "The world cannot get along without the United States of America," he wrote. "Americans, stop being afraid!"[16]

In 1941, a ticket for the movies cost a quarter. On movie screens across the country, Charlie Chan, Dr. Kildare, Andy Hardy, W. C. Fields, Fred Astaire, Ginger Rogers, Bing Crosby, and Bob Hope investigated crimes, joked, romanced, danced, and sang. But there were darker films, too, in which fifth columnists and saboteurs filled the screen, movies like *Confessions of a Nazi Spy* with Edward G. Robinson, Hitchcock's *Foreign Correspondent*, and director Frank Borzage's *The Mortal Storm*. That film, starring Jimmy Stewart, Robert Young, and Margaret Sullavan, contained harrowing scenes of life in hate-filled Nazi Germany and a young couple's doomed effort to flee across the border. In *Escape*, which had opened in New York's Radio City a week before Election Day 1940, American Robert Taylor tries to smuggle his German-born mother out of a Nazi concentration camp with the help of a local countess played by Norma Shearer.[17]

In *Murder in the Air*, Ronald Reagan played an FBI agent tracking down foreign spies. Charlie Chaplin's audacious *The Great Dictator* showcased his devastating portrait of the fascist tyrant "Adenoid Hynkel" and Jack Oakie's sharp performance as "Benzino Napaloni." In *Sky Murder*, sleuth Nick Carter, played by Walter Pidgeon, smashes a Nazi spy ring. Gary Cooper won the Academy Award for his portrayal of Sergeant York, the pacifist Tennessee mountaineer who decided that sometimes violence is the only way to defend democracy and fought courageously in World War I.

Nazis, concentration camps, fifth columnists, heroic resistance, courageous soldiers and pilots: Hollywood's films clearly conveyed an antifascist message. Was there a Hollywood conspiracy to whip up war hysteria and propel the nation into war against Germany?

Isolationists thought so. A "little clique of Wall Street bankers, together with the motion picture industry, are trying to stir up sentiment to take us into war," charged Senator Burton Wheeler in late July 1941, a few weeks after *Sergeant York* opened in movie theaters around the country. Appeasers like Wheeler should be ousted from their Senate seats, proclaimed the real-life Sergeant Alvin York in Knoxville, who referred to Wheeler as "Neville."[18] For months, Wheeler had been threatening to muzzle Hollywood, unless, as he said, "the industry itself displays a more impartial attitude" and presents "both sides of each question." Now, in the summer of 1941, he believed that the time was ripe for federal regulation of the content of films. As a writer in the ultra-isolationist magazine *Scribner's Commentator* complained, "If you seek escape in a movie theatre there is a good chance that an added attraction will present a spy with a thick German accent stealing our latest bombing sights or planting TNT along the locks of the Panama Canal."[19]

Senator Nye went further, blaming not just Hollywood but the Jewish heads of the major studios. Speaking at an America First rally in St. Louis, Nye charged that Hollywood's films were "designed to drug the reason of the American people." He proceeded to read aloud the names of the studio heads as he pretended to stumble over the foreign-sounding syllables: Louis B. Mayer, George Schaefer, Adolph Zukor, Joseph Schenck, Darryl Zanuck, Murray Silverstone, Sam Goldwyn, Jack Warner, Sam Katz, and David Bernstein. "Are you ready to send your boys to bleed and die in Europe to make the world safe for this industry?" he asked. And in his next breath, he demanded a congressional investigation.[20]

As the chairman of the Senate Interstate Commerce Committee, Wheeler appointed a subcommittee, headed by Democrat Worth Clark of Idaho, to investigate the charge that Hollywood studios were producing propaganda movies.[21] The Motion Picture Producers and Distributors of America retained as their counsel—perhaps at the suggestion of the White House—one of the senior partners in the firm of Willkie, Owen, Otis and Bailly. His name was Wendell Willkie.[22]

The subcommittee proceedings were a silly, nasty sideshow during the explosive year of 1941, but fortunately Willkie provided a much-needed dose of realism and rationality. If the question under investigation was whether the movie industry was opposed to the Nazi dictatorship, Willkie stated in a public letter released to the committee, "there need be no investigation." In an unequivocal statement, he preemptively outlined the position of the studio heads. "They have watched with horror the destruction of a free life within Germany and the ruthless invasions of other countries by Nazis. On behalf of the motion-picture industry and its personnel, I wish to put on the record this simple truth: We make no pretense of friendliness to Nazi Germany nor to the objectives and goals of this ruthless dictatorship. We abhor everything which Hitler represents. . . . In simple terms, the United States stands for the right of an individual to lead a decent life. Hitler and his Nazis stand for the opposite. The motion-picture industry wants no compromise between these two concepts. . . . The industry desires to *plead guilty* to sharing, with their fellow citizens, a horror of Hitler's Nazis; and to plead guilty to doing everything within its power to help the national-defense program."

As for Nye's Jew-baiting and the anti-Semitism that lay at the core of the subcommittee's proceedings, Willkie noted that if the committee felt that the racial and geographical backgrounds of American citizens were a fit subject for investigation, then he would "frankly state" that, working in prominent as well as inconspicuous positions in the film industry, there were Nordics and non-Nordics, Jews and gentiles, Protestants and Catholics, native and foreign-born. And if the committee wanted film industry witnesses to testify to the accuracy of Hollywood's portrayal of the horrors of life under the Nazi dicta-torship or to document the "magnificent courage" of the English people un-der Nazi assault, Willkie offered to produce them. It was ironic, he added, that although isolationists were perpetually warning that America's entry into war would transform the nation into a totalitarian state, their attempt to abridge freedom of speech with censorship of the movies would indeed help install precisely such a dictatorial regime. "From the motion picture and radio industries it is just a small step to the newspapers, magazines and other peri-odicals. And from the freedom of the press it is just a small step to the free-dom of the individual to say what he believes. The United States, with England and its allies, remains the bulwark of the rights of the individual in the world today. The rights of the individual mean nothing if freedom of the press and freedom of speech are destroyed."[23]

As if underscoring Willkie's message about the importance of tolerance and the evil of dictatorships, that same day American newspapers reported on the persecution of Jews in Germany and in Nazi-occupied countries: Jews in the territory of the Reich were not allowed to appear in public without affixing to the left side of their chests a yellow, hexagonal "star of Judah"; in the north-ern German city of Hanover, Jews were evicted from their homes and herded into the local Jewish cemetery; in Amsterdam, Jews were arrested and re-moved to forced labor camps in France and in Germany; and in France, a few weeks after six thousand Jews in Paris and five thousand in Orléans were rounded up and sent to concentration camps, a hundred prominent Jews—former government officials, bankers, art collectors—were also summarily arrested.[24] Ironically, the anti-Nazi studio heads were cautious about drama-tizing the German persecution of Jews in their movies; in fact, *The Mortal Storm* was one of the few movies to include scenes of anti-Jewish violence.

Hearings on the movie industry began in Washington on September 9. Packed with isolationists, Clark's subcommittee had only one supporter of the administration, Ernest McFarland of Arizona, who repeatedly told his fellow committee members that he could "not see that we are accomplishing any-thing" and warned against censorship.[25] After Senator Clark announced that the sole purpose of the inquiry was to "ascertain the facts," Nye took over and read aloud a forty-one-page denunciation of Hollywood movies.

A quasi-pacifist, agrarian, and anticorporatist, Nye had conducted a Senate investigation in 1934 of what he considered a conspiracy of profit-seeking American arms manufacturers to push the nation into war in 1917.[26] But in 1941, he decided to focus on a different target. Instead of blaming war-profiteering industrialists for leading the country into war, this time he held responsible the four heads of the major Hollywood studios—all Jewish and three of them "foreign-born." While assuring his listeners that anti-Semitism was "foreign to my thinking," Nye charged that it was for "non-American" reasons that these nefarious Hollywood producers were injecting their antifascist bias into American films.[27]

When the senator finally reached the end of his statement, Willkie dryly remarked that Nye had ably demonstrated "without a bit of doubt, why this foolish show should be ended once and for all." Since Nye had admitted that he hadn't even seen the movies he condemned, Willkie offered to screen them in the committee room. "That will make a real movie show out of this!" Willkie said.[28] After sitting through more accusations against the film industry and being denied the right to cross-examine witnesses, Willkie released a statement to the press. Zeroing in on "the real object of the investigation," he charged that the subcommittee's aim was simply "the sabotage of the country's foreign policy."[29]

On September 16, three days after the committee subpoenaed Charlie Chaplin to testify about *The Great Dictator*, Roosevelt weighed in. At his press conference, he read aloud from a telegram received by a senator whose identity, he confided to reporters with a smile, he was not at liberty to disclose: "HAVE JUST BEEN READING BOOK CALLED THE HOLY BIBLE. HAS LARGE CIRCULATION. WRITTEN ENTIRELY BY FOREIGN BORN, MOSTLY JEWS. FIRST PART FULL OF WARMONGERING PROPAGANDA. SECOND PART CONDEMNED ISOLATIONISM WITH STORY ABOUT A GOOD SAMARITAN. SHOULD BE ADDED TO YOUR LIST AND SUPPRESSED."[30]

On the evening of September 11, during the hearings, Willkie invited Bernard Baruch and James Byrnes, the New Deal loyalist FDR had recently appointed to the Supreme Court, to his Washington hotel suite to listen to President Roosevelt's important fireside chat. In a talk condemning the Nazis' determination to seize control of the world's waterways, Roosevelt brought Americans back to earth from the diversion of what the *New York Times* called the Senate's "kangaroo court."[31]

A week earlier, on September 4, the American destroyer *Greer* had been sailing through the North Atlantic carrying American mail to Iceland. A British patrol plane signaled the *Greer* that a German submarine lay ten miles ahead. Speeding up, the *Greer* made sound contact with the U-boat and reported its precise location to the plane. Then the British plane attempted to drop missiles on the sub but missed. Two hours later, the U-boat, equally unsuccessfully, launched torpedoes at the *Greer*. Although the *Greer* had in fact sought out the U-boat, for Roosevelt's purposes it was a perfect incident to dramatize the Nazi menace and announce a major change in military policy.[32] According to Harold Ickes as well as to T. North Whitehead in the British Foreign Ministry, since April the president had been hoping that Germany would make just such a blunder that would justify a bolder American strategy.[33] Following Roosevelt's other policy initiatives—the destroyers-for-bases deal, Lend-Lease, and Roosevelt and Churchill's recent agreement on an Atlantic Charter, binding their nations together—he was now taking the country another step closer to war. And yet this new move was understandable and warranted, given the urgency of the world situation and the mortal threat that fascist aggression posed to American democracy.

In his fireside chat, the president reminded Americans that the *Greer* incident was only the latest of German submarine attacks on American ships and merchant vessels. He assured his listeners that "we are not becoming hysterical or losing our sense of proportion," but it was too late for the "tender whisperings of appeasers" and their "soporific lullabies" designed to convince the citizens of the United States that wide oceans could protect them from Hitler. It was time for realism. "It is now clear," Roosevelt said, "that Hitler has begun his campaign to control the seas by ruthless force and by wiping out every vestige of international law, every vestige of humanity." The Nazis wanted nothing more than America's passivity and silence to "give them the green light to go ahead on this path of destruction." It was time for "active defense."

"It is no act of war on our part when we decide to protect the seas that are vital to American defense. The aggression is not ours. Ours is solely defense." The commander in chief decided that, if German or Italian vessels of war entered waters deemed necessary for American defense, they would do so at their own peril. The sole responsibility, he noted, rested with Germany. "There will be no shooting unless Germany continues to seek it. . . . I have no illusions about the gravity of this step. I have not taken it hurriedly or lightly. It is the result of months and months of constant thought and anxiety and prayer."

The bottom line: shoot on sight. Fairly certain that Hitler would restrain his U-boats and not respond with full-scale war so long as his Russian campaign remained unsettled, Roosevelt had in effect declared naval war on Germany. And if anyone was uncertain about the president's intent, Secretary Knox eliminated that doubt four days later. "Beginning tomorrow," he said in a speech in Milwaukee, "the Navy is ordered to capture or destroy by every means at its disposal Axis-controlled submarines or surface raiders in these waters. That is our answer to Mr. Hitler."[34]

That same evening, September 11, America's most zealous isolationist, Charles Lindbergh, spoke at an America First rally in Des Moines. Earlier that evening, the crowd in the Municipal Coliseum had heard Roosevelt's talk by radio. When Lindbergh appeared, he was greeted by frenzied applause mixed with equally deafening boos and catcalls. In his speech, he first took a swipe at the president, charging that Roosevelt had manufactured "incidents" to propel the country into war. And reminding the crowd how consistent his own message had been, he took a swipe at Willkie, too: "We will not tell you tomorrow that it was 'just campaign oratory,'" he said. But his real target was neither Roosevelt nor Willkie. Quickly getting to the meat of his remarks, he told the crowd of eight thousand that it was time for the "naked facts." Certain groups of agitators, he charged, had planned a step-by-step campaign to involve the nation in war. "I must speak with utmost frankness," he stated, "for in order to counteract their efforts, we must know *exactly* who they are." And then he blurted out his true thoughts.[35]

"The British and the Jewish races," Lindbergh declared, "for reasons which are *not American*, wish to involve us in the war." The nation's enemy was an internal one, a Jewish one. "Their greatest danger to this country," he contended, "lies in their large ownership and influence in *our* motion pictures, *our* press, *our* radio, and *our* government." Now the booing drowned out the cheers, forcing him again and again to stop, wait out the catcalls, and start his sentences over again. Unlike Senator Nye, who had repeatedly denied the charge that he was anti-Semitic, Lindbergh's unambiguous message was that Jews living in the United States constituted a wealthy, influential, conspiratorial foreign "race" that had seized "our" media and infiltrated "our" political institutions. They were the alien out-group, hostile to "us." Lindbergh seemed to strike a note of compassion when he stated that "no person with a sense of the dignity of mankind can condone the persecution the Jewish race suffered in Germany," except that he predictably began his very next sentence with the word "but," the short yet portentous conjunction that signals an imminent reversal of direction. "*But* no person of honesty," he told his audience, "can look on *their* pro-war policy here today without seeing the dangers involved in such a policy both for *us* and for *them*."[36]

In 1790, George Washington had assured the Hebrew Congregation of Newport, Rhode Island, that all citizens "possess alike liberty of conscience and immunities of citizenship." The nation's first president audaciously rejected the notion of "toleration" because it implied, as he wrote, the "indulgence" of one class of people for another.[37] But a century and a half later, Lindbergh was immune to Washington's wisdom. "Instead of agitating for war," the aviator declared, "Jewish groups in this country should be opposing it in every possible way, for they will be among the first to feel its consequences. Tolerance is a virtue that depends upon peace and strength. History shows that it cannot survive war and devastation." Thus Lindbergh put American Jews on stark, intimidating notice that America's "tolerance" for them rested upon a fragile foundation. His accusations against the English—"we know that England is spending great sums of money for propaganda in America"—and against the Roosevelt administration—its power "depends upon the maintenance of a wartime emergency"—paled in comparison to his menacing condemnation of American Jews. A few weeks before his Des Moines speech, Lindbergh had confided to his friend Selden Rodman that Jews had only "themselves to blame. As in Germany, they control the press, the radio, and the movies—at least out of proportion to their numbers. . . . Instead of acting in the interests of their country . . . they are acting in the interest—or the presumed interest—of their race."[38]

"Lindbergh ought to be shipped back to Germany to live with his own people!" shouted a Texas state representative before the House of Representatives in Austin proceeded to pass a resolution informing the aviator that he was not welcome in the Lone Star State. In Washington, waving a copy of Adolf Hitler's *Mein Kampf* on the floor of the House of Representatives, Luther Patrick of Alabama exclaimed that "it sounds just like Charles A. Lindbergh!"[39] Across the country newspapers, columnists, politicians, and religious leaders lashed out at Lindbergh for sinning "against the American spirit," as the *New York Herald Tribune* put it. "The voice is the voice of Lindbergh, but the words are the words of Hitler," wrote the *San Francisco Chronicle* in an editorial that echoed dozens of others. "I am absolutely certain that Lindbergh hates the present democratic system," wrote columnist Dorothy Thompson. "I am absolutely certain that Lindbergh is pro-Nazi," she judged. "I am absolutely certain that Lindbergh foresees a new party along Nazi lines."[40] Thomas E. Dewey branded the aviator's talk "an inexcusable abuse of the right of freedom of speech," and Robert Taft called Lindbergh's reference to Jews as a foreign race "a grossly unjust attitude." Theologian Reinhold Niebuhr urged members of America First to dissociate themselves from Lindbergh and his utterances designed to incite racial and religious strife.[41]

Even Lindbergh's wife, Anne, admitted to a "profound feeling of grief." "It is very terrible for me to have him made the symbol of anti-Semitism in this country," she wrote in her diary. "Isn't it strange, there is no hate in him, and yet he rouses it and spreads it." Years later, the Lindberghs' daughter Reeve discovered her father's Des Moines speech and remarked on the "chilling distinction in his mind between Jews and other Americans."[42]

Lindbergh's defenders were few: Mussolini expressed solidarity with him, *Scribner's Commentator* praised him for identifying "the trinity of ugly forces," and the America First Committee dismissed the "false charges," insisting that the only real issue was that of war. But in fact America First never recovered from the calamity of Lindbergh's stop in Des Moines. Some of the members of the executive and national committees resigned, major contributors bailed out, and the head of the New York chapter, John T. Flynn, branded the speech "stupid." In Washington, Roosevelt asked his attorney general about the possibility of a grand jury investigation of the money sources behind America First.[43]

"Almost any problem can be discussed today in America except the *Jewish problem*," a perplexed Lindbergh bitterly wrote in his diary a few days after his sulfurous speech.[44]

With Lindbergh firmly anchored in the toxic universe of pro-Nazi appeasers, Willkie released his own statement just minutes after the aviator's speech, calling it "the most un-American talk made in my time by any person of national reputation." Referring to Roosevelt's fireside chat that same September evening, Willkie called on all Americans to rally behind their president and support his orders to the navy to "shoot on sight." "No man can say whether this will involve the United States in war," Willkie explained, "but any thoughtful person knows that if the president were less firm, disastrous war would be inevitable."[45]

On October 6, 1941, Willkie spoke at a National Republican Club dinner in the Grand Ballroom of the Waldorf-Astoria in New York. Still valiantly trying to wear the mantle of party leader and hoping to cleanse the GOP of what he called the "ugly smudge of isolationism," he implored his fellow Republicans to abandon that unilateralist outlook. The Republican Party had "the duty and opportunity," he told the crowd at the Waldorf, "to make America strong, preserve liberty at home, and help preserve liberty in the world." And he recommended a specific first step—the complete repeal of the Neutrality Act. That long-standing bill, he maintained, was the product of "hypocrisy and deliberate self-deception." It still hampered the delivery of goods to Britain, freedom on the seas, and America's ability to protect its own sailors. Roosevelt, too, wanted to eliminate restrictions on the ability of American ships to deliver war materials to countries fighting against Axis aggression, but he had asked for repeal only of certain key sections of the act, such as those banning the arming of American merchant vessels and preventing them from entering combat zones and docking in belligerent ports. But for his part, Willkie scoffed at such a "piecemeal" approach. Noting that the Democrats were thwarted by their own isolationists, "led by the Wheelers and the Clarks," he envisioned the GOP once again as a party of "world outlook."[46]

On October 17, a German submarine near Iceland torpedoed the American destroyer U.S.S. *Kearney*, killing eleven of her crew. Though news of the attack had not yet reached Washington, that same day members of the House of Representatives voted in favor of repeal of sections of the Neutrality Act by a healthy margin of 259 to 138. But the repeal legislation still had to come before the Senate.

On October 18, on nationwide radio, Willkie again implored Americans to stop "deluding" themselves and repeal completely the hypocritical neutrality laws. There remained no doubt, he said, that the governments in Berlin, Tokyo, and Rome were "irrevocably linked by the dangerous dream of world conquest." A year earlier, he had told a crowd in Cleveland that he was "for keeping out of war. I am for peace for America." But now he forthrightly declared that the moment had come to "abandon the hope of peace." Two days later, three Republican senators—Styles Bridges of New Hampshire, Warren Austin of Vermont, and Chan Gurney of South Dakota—took up Willkie's cause and introduced an amendment to the House bill calling for outright repeal of the entire Neutrality Act of 1939. The headline on the front page of the *New York Times* read, "A COUP FOR WILLKIE." On November 5—exactly one year after the presidential election—the former candidate toured a Pratt and Whitney airplane plant in Hartford and told reporters that it "would be a fine thing" if all the defeatists in the United States could also visit the plant.[47]

But despite Willkie's efforts and the internationalist stands taken by Bridges, Austin, and Gurney as well as by Republican governors Leverett Saltonstall of Massachusetts, Harold Stassen of Minnesota, and Henry Blood of Utah, the GOP remained largely a party of isolationists, in open rebellion against Willkie's claim to party leadership.

First of all, Alf Landon, who had recently accused Roosevelt and Willkie of collaborating to smother political debate, declared in a speech in Kansas City in mid-October that the one thing the GOP did not need was minority leaders who "break ice" for the president and "run interference for the party in power." Moreover, the Neutrality Act was not a "mausoleum of dead words," he insisted. On the contrary, he blamed the president for cutting "our ship of state from its moorings of early neutrality, and now we find ourselves in the middle of a Niagara."[48] In early November, Indiana representative Charles Halleck, Willkie's old fraternity brother who had placed his name in nomination at the GOP Convention, broke with his friend and called for the GOP to be the standard-bearer of peace. It was "a tragic thing," lamented Halleck, that there was so little understanding and common ground between Willkie and Republicans in Congress. "He doesn't see us, and we don't see him."[49]

Making a noisier splash, Representative Dewey Short of Missouri, an isolationist who had campaigned for Willkie in 1940, rose on the House floor on November 6, the day after Willkie's visit to the Pratt and Whitney plant, to read him out of the GOP. "May God forgive me for ever having supported such an impostor, this fifth columnist, this preposterous man, this Trojan horse who is seeking to split the Republican party wide open!" exclaimed Short, a former preacher, adding that Willkie couldn't even be elected dog-catcher. "Why then did you nominate him for the Presidency?" demanded John McCormack. "Because you Democrats palmed him off on us in the hopes of ruining us!" Short shouted back. When informed about the attack on him, Willkie calmly said that Short talked like "many men when they represent a dying cause."[50] Never to be left out of the isolationist clique, Hamilton Fish, the recipient of Nazi-tainted money, challenged Willkie to oppose President Roosevelt's unconstitutional "undeclared war." As if it wasn't bad enough that Fish had been photographed standing next to German-American Bund leader Fritz Kuhn or that he rented a house he owned in New York to the German consul general there, two weeks later, Fish's aide George Hill was indicted by a federal grand jury in Washington for lying about his associations with Nazi agents. The prosecutor labeled Hill a key figure in the distribution, under government frank, of propaganda "master-minded by foreign agents."[51]

On November 7, three weeks after the House voted to repeal sections of the Neutrality Act, the Senate also approved repeal, but only by a vote of 50 to 37 after acrimonious debate. A month before Pearl Harbor, few members of the GOP were willing to follow Willkie's lead: just 6 Senate Republicans voted for repeal and 21 voted against, including the usual cast of Nye, Vandenberg, McNary, Lodge, and Taft. And this time, the House passed the Senate bill by a narrow margin of 212 to 194, with only 22 Republicans favoring repeal and a vast majority of them—137—opposed.[52]

In December 1941, in an article for the *Nation*, Willkie noted that, by calling for repeal of the entire Neutrality Act, he and a handful of Republicans had actually taken "the ball away from the Administration leaders" and set the White House scrambling to catch up. But unless the GOP became aware of the totalitarian threat and recognized that America had to assume world leadership, Willkie warned, it would fade from the scene. That same issue of the *Nation* included an article by Robert Taft, who was not ready to embrace a bipartisan, internationalist foreign policy. "It is obvious," Taft crisply wrote, "that a party kills itself and removes any excuse for its existence when it adopts the principles of its opponents."[53]

An opinion poll showed that Willkie was still the favorite among Republican voters, and yet he was becoming more and more estranged from Republican leaders as he found greater common ground with Roosevelt than with them. "As soon as the election was over, the party leaders tossed him out," wrote journalist Raymond Clapper, scornful that the GOP did not recognize "a real leader when it had the luck to find one on its doorstep." Joe Martin, too, believed that Willkie's support for FDR's foreign policy destroyed his influence in the Republican Party, but, Martin judged years later, Willkie had acted for the good of the country. "This is Wendell Willkie's monument."[54]

A year after the election, as Willkie steadfastly pursued his internationalist course, it became clear that he had ventured too far ahead of most of the members of his party to lead it. And yet without the responsibilities and obligations of political office, he possessed the invaluable freedom to take courageous, principled, moral stands. "If I could choose between 'Here lies an unimportant president,' and 'Here lies one who contributed to saving freedom at a moment of great peril,'" he once wrote to a friend, "I would prefer the latter."[55]

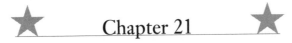

Chapter 21

Epilogue: One Nation Indivisible

I N THE EARLY AFTERNOON OF SUNDAY, December 7, 1941, as Roosevelt and Hopkins were finishing lunch, the phone rang. It was Frank Knox.

"Hello, Frank."

"Mr. President, it looks like the Japanese have attacked Pearl Harbor."

"No!"

There must be some mistake, thought Hopkins. Surely Japan would not attack Honolulu. Just six months earlier, General George Marshall had assured the president that Oahu, a mountainous island with fortifications and garrisons surrounded on all sides by a vast belt of water, was "the strongest fortress in the world."[1]

For weeks in the fall of 1941, Secretary Hull had been negotiating with the Japanese on the question of their merciless invasion of China and seizure of French Indochina. "I am not very hopeful," Roosevelt wired Churchill in late November, as the talks stalled, "and we must all be prepared for real trouble, possibly soon." The White House thought that Japan would probably strike the Philippines, Thailand, or British and Dutch possessions in the Pacific; and to the extent that they gave any thought at all to Hawaii, they considered Oahu the least probable target.[2] But now, on December 7, Roosevelt thought the report was probably true, and an hour later Admiral Harold Stark, the chief of naval operations, phoned to confirm the attack on Pearl Harbor.

At 3:00 p.m., the president met with Secretary Stimson, Secretary Hull, Secretary Knox, Admiral Stark, and General Marshall. Hopkins felt that the atmosphere in the meeting was "not too tense" because they all realized that the nation's most dangerous enemy was Hitler and, as he wrote, "that sooner or later we were bound to be in the war and that Japan had given us an opportunity."[3] Indeed, the relentlessly accurate Japanese torpedo and dive-bombers that mauled and sank battleships in Pearl Harbor, killed thousands of sailors, and ravaged barracks, aircraft, and airfields had ferociously propelled the United States into war. "We are in it," the president said repeatedly to his advisors. Conspiracy theories would later emerge, suggesting that the president had wanted and planned the attack, but, as historian James MacGregor Burns wrote, a better explanation is a "complacency theory" that takes into account the lazy security in Pearl Harbor and the poor communications arrangements of the American command.[4]

That evening, the radio correspondent Edward R. Murrow, on leave from London, and his wife, Janet, assumed that their dinner engagement at the White House was canceled. "We still have to eat," said Eleanor. While the president pored over the reports from Hawaii in his office and met with cabinet members and congressional leaders, Eleanor and the Murrows shared the Roosevelt family's traditional Sunday supper of scrambled eggs. Murrow and his wife were about to leave when FDR sent word that he wished to see him. As Murrow waited for the president, Hull, Stimson, Knox, and Hopkins grimly paraded past him into the Oval Office.

Finally, at one in the morning, Murrow and Roosevelt met. The president's face was ashen and drained, Murrow observed, but his demeanor was "calm and so steady." At first FDR said nothing about the attack, asking the reporter instead about London and how the British were bearing up. Then, in cold, controlled anger, the president reeled off the losses at Pearl Harbor, the ships lost, the planes destroyed, the dead and wounded. As he was leaving the White House, Murrow bumped into his CBS colleague Eric Severeid. "It's pretty bad," Murrow said.[5]

That afternoon in Pittsburgh, the America First Committee had held another rally, this one starring Senator Gerald Nye. Before the meeting began, a reporter for the *Pittsburgh Post-Gazette*, Robert Hagy, passed along to the senator the first bulletins to come over the AP wire. "It sounds terribly fishy to me," Nye told Hagy. Indeed, it was "as if nothing had happened," the reporter wrote, as speaker after speaker went ahead and denounced Roosevelt as a warmonger. While a Pennsylvania state senator was addressing the crowd, a reserve officer in the audience stood up and shouted, "Do you know that Japan has attacked Manila, that Japan has attacked Hawaii?" "Throw him out!" people yelled. When it was Nye's turn to speak, he asked the crowd, "Whose war is this?" In unison, they shouted, "Roosevelt's!" In the middle of Nye's speech, Hagy was called to the telephone and heard the news that the Japanese Imperial Government in Tokyo announced a state of war with the United States and Great Britain. When the rally was finally over, Hagy informed Nye that Roosevelt had convened a meeting of the cabinet and congressional leaders for 9:00 that evening. Nye appeared flustered. By then the fight had gone out of him, the reporter observed. But the senator still had the energy to take one more swipe at Roosevelt. "We have been maneuvered into this by the President," he said, "but the only thing now is to declare war and to jump into it with everything we have and bring it to a victorious conclusion."[6]

JAPAN WARS ON U.S. AND BRITAIN;
MAKES SUDDEN ATTACK ON HAWAII;
HEAVY FIGHTING AT SEA REPORTED

On December 8, 1941, the shocking eight-column three-row headline in the *New York Times* foretold an unprecedented global conflict and signaled to tens of millions of startled Americans that their lives had been irrevocably changed.

That day the president resolutely addressed Congress, asking for a declaration of war. "Yesterday, December 7, 1941—a date which will live in infamy," he stated, "the United States of America was suddenly and deliberately attacked by naval and air forces of the Empire of Japan." Secretary Hull had wanted him to summarize in his speech the whole history of American relations with Japan, but Roosevelt insisted on keeping the speech short—just five hundred words—and keeping the focus on the attack on Hawaii.

On the evening of December 9, Roosevelt addressed the nation in a fireside chat. "We may acknowledge that our enemies have performed a brilliant feat of deception, perfectly timed and executed with great skill," he said. "It was a thoroughly dishonorable deed, but we must face the fact that modern warfare as conducted in the Nazi manner is a dirty business. We don't like it—we didn't want to get in it—but we are in it and we're going to fight it with everything we've got." The message was simple, colloquial, realistic—and Americans accepted its accuracy and determination.[7]

"If we are to go forward, we must move as a trained and loyal army." Those words, spoken by Franklin Roosevelt in his first inaugural address in the bleak winter of 1933, had suddenly become relevant again. Now the trained and loyal army would face a military crisis, not an economic one.

"There is no politics now," declared Joe Martin, House minority leader. Senator McNary agreed; Republicans will "go along with whatever is done," he said. Even isolationists swiftly closed ranks with the Roosevelt administration—though most of them would never confess to error; indeed, they continued to believe that they had been right all along. "Nothing matters except VICTORY," wrote Senator Vandenberg, adding that "the 'arguments' must be postponed." In his diary, however, he penned, "We asked for it and we got it." Burton Wheeler, too, expressed the hope that all Americans would come together to win the war. "The only thing now is to do our best to lick hell out of them," he said, remarking that the Japanese military leaders "must have gone crazy." Arch-isolationist Hamilton Fish agreed that the time for debate and controversy had passed. How could he "best help promote unity, uphold your war program, serve my country?" he asked the president.[8] Also urging Americans to come together was Herbert Hoover. "We must have and will have unity in America," the former president declared. "We must have and will have support for the President of the United States in this war to defend America. We will have victory!" In private, however, Hoover blamed western democracies in general for objecting to Hitler's invasion of Poland and blamed Roosevelt in particular for deliberately taking a "series of provocative actions" that drove Japan to Pearl Harbor, like "a rat driven into a corner." The vote in the Senate to declare war on Japan was unanimous; in the House there was one dissenting voice.[9] The special subcommittee investigating anti-Nazi Hollywood films ended its hearings. Charlie Chaplin's testimony was canceled.

On December 11, Germany and Italy declared war against the United States. Unleashing a torrent of words that lasted for ninety minutes, Hitler railed that Roosevelt was a warmonger and a gangster who sought to create conflicts everywhere and who was, in his opinion, "insane." Furthermore, the Führer charged that the American president, in his pursuit of "world dictatorship," collaborated with Jews—and "we all know the intention of the Jews to rule all civilized states in Europe and America." Striking a spiritual note, Hitler expressed his gratitude to "God Almighty for having given me the strength and the knowledge to do what had to be done."[10]

This time Roosevelt did not go before Congress, but instead sent a brief message asking for a declaration of war. "The long known and long expected has thus taken place," his statement read. "The forces endeavoring to enslave the entire world now are moving toward this hemisphere. Never has there been a greater challenge to life, liberty, and civilization."[11]

That day, the American government shut down the German embassy and its seditious activities. The State Department would not have to apologize again to Germany for wayward American sailors who tore down swastika flags from German consulates.[12] The Keep America Out of the War Congress was quickly dissolved, and the America First Committee disbanded, permanently closing its offices and canceling Lindbergh's talk at a rally scheduled for the following day in Boston. "Our principles were right," read the committee's unyielding final public statement on December 11. "Had they been followed war could have been avoided." Taking a spiteful parting shot at President Roosevelt, General Wood, the organization's head, sniped, "Well, he got us in through the back door."[13]

And Charles Lindbergh? "How did the Japs get close enough to attack us?" he wrote in his diary on December 7, staggered by the news. Six months earlier, in a speech in the Hollywood Bowl—published under the rash title "Time Lies with Us" in the November issue of *Scribner's Commentator*—he had set out "to show you *conclusively* tonight" that the country was invulnerable to a foreign invasion and that "we would have plenty of warning of the approach of a hostile fleet." Though events had proved him utterly wrong, he nevertheless carped that "we have brought it on our own shoulders" and blamed the Roosevelt administration for dragging the country into war.[14] In late December, having already resigned his commission, he volunteered his services to the army air corps. No thanks, answered the War Department. "You can't have an officer leading men who thinks we're licked before we start," explained a White House intimate. "And that's that." A few weeks after Pearl Harbor, Mayor La Guardia called on veterans to melt down their service medals and return them to Italy and Germany in the form of bullets. He invited Lindbergh to throw his German medal into the pot, too, but the aviator defiantly declined—although, as Harold Ickes had noted in July 1941, Lindbergh had "no hesitation about sending back to the president his commission in the United States Army Air Corps Reserve. . . . But he still hangs on to the Nazi medal."[15]

Turned down by the heads of Pan American as well as by several other aircraft companies, Lindbergh would eventually work as a consultant at Henry Ford's Willow Run plant near Detroit, where B-24 bombers were built; and though he had no military rank, he would fly combat missions in the Pacific as a test pilot for United Aircraft Corporation. In 1954, after Lindbergh was awarded the Pulitzer Prize for his book, *The Spirit of St. Louis*, President Eisenhower restored his commission in the Air Force Reserve and promoted him to brigadier general. Three years later, *The Spirit of St. Louis* came out as a Hollywood film, directed by a German-Jewish refugee, Billy Wilder, and starring James Stewart. In 1962, the former America First spokesman and old friend of Ambassador Joseph Kennedy was a guest at a star-studded gala dinner at the White House, seated at President John F. Kennedy's head table.[16]

Until his death in 1974, Charles Lindbergh never wavered from his belief that the United States should never have entered World War II and was convinced, as his biographer A. Scott Berg wrote, that Roosevelt's policies "led to a series of failures and disasters almost unparalleled in history." Nor did he ever give up his theories of Anglo-Saxon racial superiority and his sour disgust with what he diagnosed as western bourgeois decadence. Ten days after Pearl Harbor, the *New York Post* reported that, in a brief talk at a New York dinner party, the aviator had deplored that the white race was "divided in this war" and contended that Britain and Germany should have combined forces to conquer Russia and Poland and use them as buffers against "the yellow race." And in late 1942, still unmoved by all the atrocities and suffering caused by fascist aggression, he told his wife that "war, dreadful as it is, is better than decay."[17]

After the war, he saw for himself the unspeakable horrors of the gas chambers and ovens of Nazi concentration camps. Though he knew that millions of human beings had been exterminated and tens of millions slaughtered on battlefields and ships and in shattered, smoldering cities, he remained skeptical that "German atrocities averaged worse than ours." Unlike his wife, who admitted that "we were both very blind . . . to the worst evils of the Nazi system," Lindbergh himself, as Berg underscored, never expressed remorse. On the contrary, decades later, in 1970, he told an interviewer that World War II "marks the beginning of our Western civilization's breakdown. Much of our Western culture was destroyed. We lost the genetic heredity formed through eons of many million lives." Lindbergh, the admirer of Nazi Germany and of the racial theories of Alexis Carrel, apparently tried to make up for that genetic loss when he fathered three children in the 1950s and '60s with his young German mistress in Munich.[18]

The services of Joseph P. Kennedy were equally unwelcome. "In this great crisis all Americans are with you. Name the Battle Post," the former ambassador hopefully wrote to Roosevelt after Pearl Harbor. "I'm yours to command." Roosevelt eventually responded cordially but made no job offer. When a reporter asked the president if he was thinking of bringing Kennedy back into his administration, he crisply replied, "No, no."[19] Roosevelt and Kennedy never reconciled, and Kennedy's bitterness toward the man he came to call "that crippled son of a bitch" never abated.[20] During the fall of 1944, he believed that it would be an "unpardonable crime" for Americans to continue Roosevelt in office. In 1945, as Kennedy sifted through his diplomatic files, he contemplated writing about his London years; it would be a book, he told Herbert Hoover, that would "put an entirely different color on the process of how America got into the war and would prove the betrayal of the American people by Franklin D. Roosevelt."[21] Until FDR's death he would rant about the "Jew-controlled" president, sneer at "Jew-ideas," and gripe that the Hopkins, Rosenman, and Frankfurter clique had surrounded the president with "Jews and Communists."[22]

Nor did the White House seek any contribution from Herbert Hoover, the man who had told a crowd in Salt Lake City in 1940 that the Roosevelt administration had "a pronounced odor of totalitarian government." After Pearl Harbor, as Hoover later wrote, "I at once supported the President and offered to serve in any useful capacity. . . . I thought my services might again be useful, however there was no response."[23] Indeed. "Well, I'm not Jesus Christ," FDR said caustically to Bernard Baruch. "I'm not going to raise Herbie from the dead."[24]

"If at any time I can be of service, I know you will feel free to command me," Jim Farley wrote to the president on December 9. "I knew I could count on you," the president replied, but no request to serve ever came from the White House. It was a bleak parting for the two old friends. Columnist Arthur Krock commented that Farley's bitter opposition to Roosevelt's run for a third term had placed him, like Joe Kennedy, on the White House blacklist of men who had incurred "high displeasure."[25]

Pearl Harbor galvanized the patriotism of Americans of all stripes and persuasions, eager to serve their country. On December 8, men from their teens to their sixties overwhelmed the recruiting stations of the U.S. Army, Marine Corps, Navy, and Coast Guard. Waiting to sign up to go to war, many stood in line the whole night while others dozed or spent the hours until morning laughing and joking in nearby restaurants, lobbies, and halls. "There is a war going on and I want to do my part," 24-year-old Edward Tung told a reporter in New York. A lieutenant in the Fire Department added that the country had been good to him and nothing he could sacrifice would be enough in return.[26]

Wendell Willkie also volunteered to do his part. On Friday, December 5, Roosevelt had penned a note to him, asking if he was interested in making a short exploratory trip to Australia and New Zealand. "There might be an armed clash at any moment if the Japanese continued their forward progress against the Philippines, Dutch Indies, or Malaya or Burma," FDR observed. "Perhaps the next four or five days will decide the matter." On December 15, Roosevelt and Willkie met for lunch in the White House and agreed that it was not an opportune moment for a trip to Australia and New Zealand. But as

Willkie left the White House, he told reporters, "In times like these, there is not any American who would not be willing to give everything he had in the service of his country."[27]

The next proposal for a foreign voyage came from Willkie. In the summer of 1942, he asked the president's permission to visit the Middle East, Russia, and China. FDR wholeheartedly agreed: Willkie would once again serve as his personal representative, demonstrating American unity, gathering information, and discussing with key heads of state plans for the postwar future. In his letter to the Chinese leader Chiang Kai-shek, FDR wrote, "As you know, Mr. Willkie was the candidate against me in the 1940 election and as such is the titular leader of the opposition. He has given unstinted support to the government in its foreign policy and the conduct of the war, and has helped to create the excellent state of unity that exists today."[28]

Willkie's book *One World*, based on his round-the-world journey and written with his companion Irita Van Doren, immediately jumped to the top of the best-seller list in the spring of 1943, selling a million copies in two months. In it, Willkie described his meetings with political and military leaders, recounted his conversations with average people, and gave his political opinions. The message of *One World*—the title itself was a rebuke to the very notion of isolationism—was that "this is one world; that all parts of it for their own well-being are interdependent on the other parts." He called for a new "declaration of interdependence among the nations of this one world" and for a "council today of the United Nations—a common council in which all plan together." Envisioning a future of racial justice in the United States as well as the reconstruction of Europe as an economically united region, Willkie wrote that in the postwar world the task of the United States would be to "unify the peoples of the earth in the human quest for freedom and justice." While Charles Lindbergh clung to his divisive theories of white racial purity, Willkie embraced the simpler purity of Jefferson's self-evident truth that all men were created equal. "The day is gone when men and women of whatever color or creed can consider themselves the superiors of other creeds or colors," Willkie wrote. "The day of equal peoples is at hand." *One World* was a "bull's eye title," poet Carl Sandburg enthused in a book review. Willkie had proven himself a "momentous figure," he wrote, "no matter how many nominations he loses, no matter what pails of vituperation are poured on his head."[29]

But a month after Willkie gave a ferociously liberal speech in Indianapolis, defending the right of workers to bargain collectively, the right of all citizens to be free of racial discrimination, and the government's "duty" to protect every citizen against economic calamity, the Republican crew distanced itself from his progressive vision and claim to party leadership. Reviewing *One World* on the first page of the *New York Times Book Review*, Minnesota's Harold Stassen, who had backed Willkie at the Philadelphia Convention, now withheld his seal of approval. While he allowed that the book was "picturesque" and that it gave a "good birdseye view," he criticized Willkie's "tendency to be dogmatic and belligerent" as well as his "understatement of the evils of communism." Stassen concluded his review by slamming the paucity of "concrete suggestions" in *One World*.[30]

Was Willkie interested in a return to politics? Perhaps he would run in 1944 for the Democratic nomination, Harold Ickes had mused in 1941. He would have a better chance as a Democrat than as a Republican, Ickes felt. For his part, Robert Sherwood hypothesized that if Willkie were to win the Republican nomination in '44, the president might not seek a fourth term. "I had no tangible basis for this belief," Sherwood later admitted, conceding that it was a highly unlikely scenario. "Greatly as the Old Guard lords of the Republican machine hated Roosevelt," Sherwood wrote, "they had come to hate Willkie even more."[31] Willkie did enter some of the GOP primaries in 1944. He won in New Hampshire but, after coming in last in the isolationist state of Wisconsin, pulled out of the race. The *Chicago Daily Tribune* applauded his decision, dismissed him as a "minor nuisance," and recommended that he "take a walk."[32] At the party convention, Willkie would be neither seated nor permitted to address the delegates.

In the spring of 1944, rumors circulated in Washington that FDR might dump Wallace and choose Willkie as his running-mate. Indeed, on many key issues Willkie was overtaking the White House, leading the demand for a second front in Europe, for the military to act more aggressively, and for the State Department to cease appeasing the Vichy government in France; he even wanted the president to ask Congress for large increases in taxes and revenues for war-related expenses, prompting Roosevelt to observe that he and the Republican leader thought alike.[33] Too, Willkie consistently attacked isolationism and colonialism, spoke out for labor rights, civil rights, and the government's obligation to provide citizens with economic security, and stood in the vanguard of the call for an international organization of nations. And so, that spring, before the Democratic Convention, the White House put out vague feelers to him about the vice presidency. The idea, however, went nowhere, as did New York senator Robert Wagner's plan to draft Willkie at the Democratic Convention. (In addition to Willkie's ambivalence and FDR's leaning toward Truman, both FDR and Willkie were legal residents of New York State, a pairing prohibited by the Twelfth Amendment to the Constitution.)

But Willkie did express interest in Roosevelt's suggestion that they join forces to realign the nation's two political parties. He agreed to meet with FDR's emissary Sam Rosenman and discuss the idea of bringing Democratic and Republican liberals and moderates together in a new progressive party.[34]

The plan greatly appealed to Willkie. In the late spring of 1942, bitterly frustrated by GOP conservatives, he had audaciously waged war against them. In a move that mirrored FDR's failed attempt in 1938 to purge reactionaries from the Democratic Party by intervening in party primaries, Willkie similarly tried and failed to liberalize the GOP by opposing congressmen like Hamilton Fish and Stephen Day. "I'll go into the elections or into the primaries in the states as I see fit," Willkie declared. "I can say now that if I was a citizen of Illinois I wouldn't vote for the reelection of Congressman Day. . . . I don't want to see the party today fall into the hands of the wrong leadership!" Unsurprisingly, FDR had lent his support to Willkie's purge, inviting him to lunch in February 1942 to discuss "the problem of Fish" and meeting with him again in April to discuss the congressman. "No greater disaster can happen to the Republican party than the election of men like . . . Fish," Willkie agreed.[35]

Roosevelt "wants to team up with you," Rosenman told Willkie in early July 1944 in a secret meeting in New York, "and he thinks the right time to start is immediately after this election . . . whether he wins or loses in November." Willkie agreed, lamenting that "both parties are hybrids." He was enthusiastic about forming a new progressive party and fighting with, rather than against, Roosevelt. "You tell the president that I'm ready to devote almost full time to this," Willkie said. "A sound, liberal government in the United States is absolutely essential to continued cooperation with the other nations of the world." In a letter he drafted to FDR, Willkie noted that he was "intensely interested" in the project and agreed that they should postpone talks until after the November election.[36]

In September and early October 1944, after having been prevented from speaking at the GOP Convention and furious that the party platform had refused to endorse a United Nations organization, Willkie remained noticeably neutral in the contest between Roosevelt and Dewey. Instead of campaigning for either candidate, he published two nonpartisan articles in *Collier's* magazine, the first one advocating greater international collaboration and an end to colonial empires, and the second, entitled "Citizens of Negro Blood," calling for a ban on poll taxes, an anti-lynching law, and an end to racial discrimination in the armed forces. He and his friend Walter White, the secretary of the NAACP, made plans to write a book together on the struggle for racial equality.

Unlike Roosevelt, who was forced to pirouette painfully around the issue of race in order to keep the solidly Democratic white South on board, Willkie was free from the constraints of electoral politics, free to speak out as a moral leader. Ahead of the White House, ahead of the Republican Party, and ahead of the times, he forcefully called for transformational civil rights legislation.[37]

On October 8, 1944, a day after his article on civil rights appeared in *Collier's*, the 52-year-old Willkie suffered a heart attack in a New York hospital where he was already being treated for a heart ailment. He died as he had lived, an idealist, a humanitarian—and a lone wolf. His "tremendous courage," the president wrote in a statement after his death, "prompted him more than once to stand alone. . . . In this hour of grave crisis the country loses a great citizen." Secretary of War Henry Stimson proposed that Willkie be given a hero's grave in Arlington National Cemetery, but Edith Willkie decided on a burial in Rushville.[38]

On March 1, 1945, in an address to Congress that echoed the message of *One World*, President Roosevelt proposed an "organization under which the peace of the world will be preserved and the forces of aggression permanently outlawed," an organization that, in October 1945, would come into existence as the United Nations.[39]

Almost a team in 1941, Roosevelt and Willkie were, posthumously, too, almost a team.

Five months after his November reelection to a fourth term, on April 12, 1945, the 63-year-old Roosevelt, too, would be dead—worn out, like George Washington, by the burdens of his high office.

In April 1948, London's Grosvenor Square was a display of colorful pageantry. It was on that leafy square that John Adams, the first United States minister to Great Britain, had lived. Now British and American flags hung from the Georgian houses, an American marine band played, and thousands of spectators lined the sidewalks, leaned out of windows, and sat on rooftops. Present, along with Eleanor Roosevelt, were the prime minister, Clement Attlee; Winston Churchill, now the leader of the opposition party; King George VI and Queen Elizabeth and their daughters, as well as dukes and duchesses, ambassadors, mayors, a former secretary of state, and Robert Sherwood. As silence fell over the crowd, Eleanor Roosevelt pulled a cord and unveiled a statue of Franklin D. Roosevelt. This monument, declared the King, would stand as a "permanent reminder of our comradeship with the American people in the dark days of the war." After the unveiling, Churchill, in formal dress and top hat, walked slowly around the base of the statue, his head thrown characteristically forward. He paused for a long moment. Then quietly he brushed at his eyes with his hands.

Later that evening, Churchill paid tribute to his American colleagues, to Wendell Willkie as well as to FDR. "Delighted to read your stirring speech," Churchill had wired Willkie in January 1941, after his courageous endorsement of Lend-Lease.[40] Now the former prime minister told the guests at a formal dinner that Franklin Roosevelt "changed decisively and permanently the moral axis of mankind by involving the New World inexorably and irrevocably in the fortunes of the Old. His life must therefore be regarded as one of the commanding events in human destiny. As a result of his personal influence and exertions, the principle of 'one world'—as his opponent Mr. Wendell Willkie called it—in which all the men in all the lands must play their part and do their duty, has been finally proclaimed and comprehended."

Grosvenor Square became a pilgrimage site for tens of thousands of people. Many left bouquets of flowers and note cards around the base of the statue.

"Lifelike, isn't it?" said one of them.

"Lovely," murmured a young schoolgirl.

"A grand man," said one man, looking up at the statue and shading his eyes against the midday sun. "There's no doubt about it. The world would be better off for a few more like him."[41]

Notes

Chapter 1: Mystery in the White House

1. See Grace Tully, *F.D.R., My Boss* (New York: C. Scribner's Sons, 1949), 240.

2. *Atlanta Constitution*, November 9, 1938, "President Sits Up for Vote Returns."

3. *New York Times*, November 6, 1940, "Roosevelt Looks to 'Difficult Days.'"

4. James MacGregor Burns, *Roosevelt: The Lion and the Fox* (New York: Harcourt, Brace, 1956), 451; *Time*, November 11, 1940, "The Presidency: Victory"; *New York Times*, November 6, 1940, "Roosevelt Looks to 'Difficult Days.'"

5. *New York Times*, August 18, 1940, "Willkie Accepts"; *Los Angeles Times*, October 9, 1940, "Willkie Asks Truth about War Moves"; *New York Times*, November 6, 1940, "Willkie Retires Refusing to Give Up." Philip graduated from Princeton in June 1941.

6. Charles A. Lindbergh, *The Wartime Journals of Charles A. Lindbergh* (New York: Harcourt Brace Jovanovich, 1970), November 5, 1940, 413–414.

7. *New York Times*, October 15, 1940, "Lindbergh Assails 'Present' Leaders."

8. Robert H. Jackson, *That Man: An Insider's Portrait of Franklin D. Roosevelt*, ed. John Q. Barrett (New York: Oxford University Press, 2003), 41.

9. Samuel Rosenman, *Working with Roosevelt* (New York: Harper and Brothers, 1952), 137.

10. *Los Angeles Times*, November 4, 1936, "Roosevelt Elected by Landslide"; *Chicago Daily Tribune*, November 4, 1936, "Roosevelt Wins: Landslide"; *Hartford Courant*, November 4, 1940, "Roosevelt Is Reelected by Landslide."

11. *Washington Post*, November 4, 1936, "Democrats Win 7 House Seats Now Held by Republicans."

12. *New York Times*, November 4, 1936, "Election Crowd in a Merry Mood."

13. In 1938, Republicans increased the number of their seats in the House from 88 to 169.

14. *Hartford Courant*, November 10, 1938, "Today and Tomorrow."

15. Robert Sherwood, *Roosevelt and Hopkins: An Intimate History*, rev. ed. (New York: Harper and Brothers, 1950), 179.

16. *New York Times*, November 4, 1940, "Result in Balance in Gallup Survey." See also *New York Times*, November 7, 1940, "Dr. Gallup Cites Survey's Success"; Steven Casey, *Cautious Crusade: Franklin D. Roosevelt, American Public Opinion, and the War against Nazi Germany* (New York: Oxford University Press, 2001), 18. For his part, FDR deeply distrusted Gallup, who had underestimated the number of votes FDR received in 1936.

17. *Chicago Daily Tribune*, October 8, 1940, "Dunn Poll Gives Willkie Victory"; *New York Times*, November 4, 1940, "Surveys of the Election"; *New York Times*, November 7, 1940, "Dr. Gallup Cites Survey's Success."

18. Joseph P. Lash, *Roosevelt and Churchill, 1939–1941: The Partnership That Saved the West* (New York: Norton, 1976), 235.

19. *Chicago Defender*, November 2, 1940, "President Roosevelt and Mr. Willkie."

20. *New York Times*, November 3, 1940, "President and Congress."

21. *Los Angeles Times*, November 3, 1940, "What We Do Not Know."

22. *Washington Post*, November 3, 1940, "Wendell Willkie's Great Campaign"; *Washington Post*, November 2, 1940, "On the Defensive"; *Hartford Courant*, November 2, 1940, "Indispensable to Foreign Affairs?"

23. *Los Angeles Times*, October 10, 1940, "Current Comment."

24. William L. Shirer, *Berlin Diary* (New York: Knopf, 1941), November 6, 1940, 560–561.

25. William Shirer, *20th Century Journey: A Memoir of a Life and the Times*, 3 vols. (Boston: Little, Brown, 1984), *The Nightmare Years, 1930–1940*, 2:523.

26. *New York Times*, October 22, 1940, "Britain, De Gaulle Hope of Frenchmen," by P. J. Philip.

27. *New York Times*, November 1, 1940—delayed account from October 24, 1940, "Democracy Dead, Laval Declares."

28. Sherwood, *Roosevelt and Hopkins*, 213; *Hartford Courant*, June 19, 1938, " 'President' Geo. M. Cohan Makes Theatrical History"; *New York Times*, October 12, 1937, "Cohan as 'Tap-Dancing Roosevelt.' " When FDR met Cohan in 1940 to present him with an award for composing patriotic songs, he said, "Well, how's my double?" *Washington Post*, May 2, 1940, "President Greets Cohan."

29. *Washington Post*, January 28, 1940, "President Roosevelt: A Birthday Portrait"; President Roosevelt's Press Conference, August 20, 1940, in Samuel I. Rosenman, ed., *Public Papers and Addresses of Franklin D. Roosevelt [PPA]*, 13 vols. (New York: Macmillan, 1941), 9:333.

30. *Los Angeles Times*, June 24, 1937, "Early Boom for Roosevelt"; *Time*, July 12, 1937, "The Presidency: Plague, Dunces, Du Ponts"; *New York Times*, June 30, 1937, "President Tells Third Term Questioner."

31. *Atlanta Constitution*, June 21, 1939, "President Evades Blunt Question"; see also *Chicago Daily Tribune*, June 21, 1939, "President Shies When Quizzed."

32. *New York Times*, November 26, 1939, "Roosevelt Jests."

33. *New York Times*, June 18, 1939, "All-Absorbing Political Riddle"; *Washington Post*, July 3, 1940, "Over the Coffee," by Harlan Miller.

34. *Washington Post*, November 18, 1939, "Today and Tomorrow."

35. *Los Angeles Times*, December 10, 1939, "Gridiron Club Kids 'Roosevelt the Sphinx.' "

36. *Christian Science Monitor*, December 12, 1939, "Intimate Message from Washington."

37. *Atlanta Constitution*, December 10, 1939, "Mrs. F.D.R. Shown as First Lady Hopeful."

38. *New York Times*, March 10, 1940, "News Women Solve Third Term Riddle"; William Carroll, *Gracie Allen for President* (San Marcos, Calif.: Coda Publications 1999), 14. Gracie Allen's book, *How to Become President*, replete with useful tips for American mothers, would be published in July 1940 by Duell, Sloan and Pearce.

39. Address at Jackson Day Dinner, January 8, 1940, in *PPA*, 9:25.

40. *Chicago Daily Tribune*, January 9, 1940, "3D Term Drums Beaten"; *Washington Post*, January 9, 1940, " '3 Empty Places' Steal the Show"; *Los Angeles Times*, January 22, 1940, "President May Run."

41. *Wall Street Journal*, January 10, 1940, "The Jackson Day Speech," italics added. See also *Christian Science Monitor*, January 9, 1940, "President Gay but Like Clam on Third Term"; *Hartford Courant*, January 29, 1940, "The Great Game of Politics"; *Hartford Courant*, April 7, 1940, "Sullivan Convinced Roosevelt Won't Run."

42. Harold L. Ickes, *The Secret Diary of Harold L. Ickes*, 3 vols. (New York: Simon and Schuster, 1953–1954), June 25, 1939, 2:659.

43. James MacGregor Burns, *Roosevelt: The Soldier of Freedom* (New York: Harcourt Brace Jovanovich, 1970), 9.

44. *New York Times*, February 2, 1936, "The President's Mystery Story"; Franklin D. Roosevelt, Fulton Oursler, and Rupert Hughes, *The President's Mystery Story: Propounded by Franklin D. Roosevelt, solved by Rupert Hughes, Samuel Hopkins Adams, Anthony Abbott, Rita Weiman, S. S. Van Dine, John Erskine* (New York: Farrar and Rinehart, 1936).

45. Morgenthau presidential diaries, January 1940, in Wayne Cole, *Roosevelt and the Isolationists, 1932–45* (Lincoln: University of Nebraska Press, 1983), 385.

46. FDR to John Boettiger, March 7, 1940, in Elliott Roosevelt, ed., *F.D.R.: His Personal Letters*, 4 vols. (New York: Duell, Sloan and Pearce, 1947–1950), 2:1006.

47. *New York Times*, February 4, 1940, "Roosevelt Enigma Overshadows All Else."

48. *New York Times*, July 11, 1937, "The Third Term Issue."

49. Sherwood, *Roosevelt and Hopkins*, 3.

50. Frances Perkins, *The Roosevelt I Knew* (New York: Viking, 1946), 126.

51. Reminiscences of Frances Perkins, 1955, pp. 379, 385, Columbia Center for Oral History Collection.

52. Paul Appleby, "Roosevelt's Third Term," *American Political Science Review*, 46, 3 (September 1952), 754–765.

53. Oral History Interview with Sam Rosenman, conducted by Jerry Hess, 1968 and 1969, Truman Library, p. 17. http://www.trumanlibrary.org/oralhist/rosenmn.htm.

54. Burton K. Wheeler with Paul F. Healy, *Yankee from the West* (Garden City, NY: Doubleday, 1962), 354.

55. December 10, 1939, in Amanda Smith, ed., *Hostage to Fortune: The Letters of Joseph P. Kennedy* (New York: Viking, 2001), 404.

56. Richard Lowitt, *George W. Norris: The Triumph of a Progressive* (Urbana: University of Illinois Press, 1978), 318. See also Doris Kearns Goodwin, *No Ordinary Time: Franklin and Eleanor Roosevelt: The Home Front in World War II* (New York: Simon and Schuster, 1994), 107.

57. Roy Jenkins, *Franklin Delano Roosevelt* (New York: Henry Holt, 2003), 109–110.

58. Sherwood, *Roosevelt and Hopkins*, 170. This scenario is similar to the one in Philip Roth's novel *The Plot against America*, in which he imagines Lindbergh winning the 1940 election and Roosevelt coming back to power afterward. Interestingly, Huey Long in 1935 flirted with the idea of denying Roosevelt a second term and pushing a Republican into the White House. Long's idea was that the Republican would make such a mess of things that the country would turn to the populist left and elect him, Long, in 1940. See James MacGregor Burns, *The Crosswinds of Freedom* (New York: Knopf, 1989), 80. In 1935, before his assassination, Huey Long published a book, *My First Days in the White House* (Harrisburg, Pa.: The Telegraph Press).

59. Kenneth S. Davis, *FDR: Into the Storm, 1937–1940* (New York: Random House, 1993), 584.

60. *New York Times*, April 5, 1940, "Roosevelt's Mother Uncertain on 3d Term." "My son is particularly well fitted in knowledge of his own country and other countries," she said, "but I cannot say whether I would want him to run again, unless he would do good by being President."

61. *New York Times*, March 23, 1940, "Kin Opposes Third Term." See also *New York Times*, July 3, 1938, "Doubts Roosevelt Race."

62. Eleanor Roosevelt, *This I Remember* (New York: Harper and Brothers, 1949), 212–214.

63. Harold Ickes to William Bullitt, November 17, 1939, in William Bullitt Papers, Manuscripts and Archives, Yale University, Box 41. Courtesy of J. Garry Clifford.

64. Jackson, *That Man*, 32–33.

65. James Farley Papers, July 6, 1939, Box 44, Manuscript Division, Library of Congress. Frances Perkins, who initially opposed FDR's quest for a third term because she didn't want to close the future to young Democratic activists, similarly found no other viable candidates. "Surveying the country, however, Frances saw no one with the stature to replace Roosevelt and continue the New Deal's momentum. She liked Jim Farley but didn't believe he had 'presidential timbre.' Her experience with Al Smith's 1928 candidacy had also convinced her that the public would not endorse Farley's Roman Catholicism. She did not trust James Byrnes, a former congressman who had become a senator. In her opinion, Byrnes, a southern conservative who had opposed the Fair Labor Standards Act, was a political manipulator. She thought he was so cynical that he could never

appreciate that some people actually worked for higher causes. She considered Paul McNutt, a former Indiana governor with presidential aspirations, a vain stuffed shirt. She thought Roosevelt bought his support by naming him to head the Social Security Board, telling Frances he gave Mc-Nutt 'something' to keep him in the president's corner." See Kristin Downey, *The Woman behind the New Deal: The Life of Frances Perkins* (New York: Nan A. Talese/Doubleday, 2009), 304–305.

66. James Farley Papers, July 6, 1939, Box 44, and Memorandum, October 20, 1939, Box 44, Farley Papers, Manuscript Division, Library of Congress. Courtesy of J. Garry Clifford.

67. In November 1939, Harold Ickes wrote: "The President neither likes nor trusts Garner. I can not believe that he will support him in any situation. . . . He is not for McNutt either." Ickes to William Bullitt, November 17, 1939, in William Bullitt Papers, Manuscripts and Archives, Box 41, Yale University. Courtesy of J. Garry Clifford.

68. According to Robert Jackson, FDR didn't believe that Farley should think about the presidency in 1940. FDR said to Jackson in the late fall of 1937, "He doesn't seem to see that if he would run for Governor of New York and serve a term, he would establish an independent record as an administrator. He could then go before the people as an administrator, a governor, but now he's a national political party chairman and a Postmaster General. I don't think the people would elect a national chairman president. He ought to establish an independent record. But Jim isn't in a position to do it. He's not going to do it and I wouldn't go to him about it at this time." Jackson, *That Man*, 32–33. See also James MacGregor Burns, *Roosevelt: The Lion and the Fox* (New York: Harcourt, Brace, 1956), 412.

69. James A. Farley, *Jim Farley's Story: The Roosevelt Years* (New York: Whittlesey House/McGraw-Hill, 1948), 184–186.

70. *Hartford Courant*, July 25, 1939, "Farley Says Goodbye."

71. *Christian Science Monitor*, July 25, 1939 "Intimate Message from Washington." See also *New York Times*, July 25, 1939, "Roosevelts Deed Library Site." Many people thought it unlikely that the president would run for a third term. He seemed to be spending more time in Hyde Park recently, busying himself with plans for his library, and he appeared—at least to some reporters—more cheerful and less harassed. See *Hartford Courant*, November 16, 1939, "Retirement of Roosevelt Seen Likely."

72. Burns, *Roosevelt: The Lion and the Fox*, 414–415.

73. Burns, *Roosevelt: The Lion and the Fox*, 409.

74. Roosevelt quoted in John Morton Blum, *Roosevelt and Morgenthau: From the Morgenthau Diaries* (Boston: Houghton Mifflin, 1972), 261–262.

75. *Hartford Courant*, February 15, 1940, "Today and Tomorrow," by Walter Lippmann.

Chapter 2: George Washington and Franklin Roosevelt: Duty or Ambition?

1. George Washington quoted in Joseph J. Ellis, *Founding Brothers: The Revolutionary Generation* (New York: Vintage, 2002), 123.

2. Washington to Madison, May 20, 1792, in Susan Dunn, ed., *Something That Will Surprise the World: The Essential Writings of the Founding Fathers* (New York: Basic Books, 2006), 66. Madison pleaded with Washington not to deprive the country of "the inestimable advantage of having you at the head of its councils." An alarmed Hamilton warned that Washington's retirement would be "the greatest evil, that could befall the country at the present juncture." If the president left office after just one term, Hamilton wrote, "much is to be dreaded." And while Hamilton and Jefferson agreed on almost nothing, Jefferson, too, exhorted Washington to remain "at the watch." "North and South will hang together," he wrote, "if they have you to hang on." Washington reluctantly agreed with his friends.

3. Washington to Lafayette, April 28, 1788, in Dunn, *Something That Will Surprise the World*, 51, italics added.

4. Mr. Randolph, June 1, 1787, Article 2, Section 1, Clause 1, in Founders Constitution, http://press-ubs.uchicago.edu/founders/documents/a2_1_1s4.html; Notes for June 1, 1787, in Wilbourn Benton, ed., *1787: Drafting the U.S. Constitution*, 2 vols. (College Station: Texas A & M University Press, 1986), 2:1108.

5. Benton, *1787: Drafting the U.S. Constitution*, 2:1122, 1175–1176. See also Founders Constitution, June 1, 1787, Article 2, Section 1, Clauses 2 and 3, http://press-pubs.uchicago.edu/founders/documents/a2_1_2-3s2.html; June 18, 1787, Chapter 8, Document 10, http://press-pubs.uchicago.edu/founders/documents/v1ch8s10.html.

6. July 19, 1787, in Benton, *1787: Drafting the U.S. Constitution*, 2:1133.

7. Niccolò Machiavelli, *The Discourses*, Book 3, Chapter 28.

8. Benton, *1787: Drafting the U.S. Constitution*, 2:1133–1135.

9. Benton, *1787: Drafting the U.S. Constitution*, 2:1136. The following summer, at the New York Ratifying Convention, Mr. R. R. Livingston similarly argued that the people were the best judges of who should be their leaders and that "to dictate and control them, to tell them whom they shall not elect, is to abridge their natural rights." See *Debate in New York Ratifying Convention*, June 2, 1788, in Jonathan Elliot, ed., *The Debates in the Several State Conventions*, 5 vols. (Philadelphia: Lippincott, 1937), 2:286–297, 301–309, 316–322.

10. See Hamilton, *Federalist* No. 65. See also Sara Forsdyke, "Exile, Ostracism, and the Athenian Democracy," *Classical Antiquity*, 10, 1 (October 2000), 232–263.

11. Jefferson to Alexander Donald, February 7, 1788, in Philip Kurland and Ralph Lerner, eds., *The Founders Constitution*, 3 vols. (Chicago: University of Chicago Press, 1987), 3:505.

12. Jefferson to John Taylor, January 6, 1805, in Jefferson, *Writings*, ed. Merrill Peterson (New York: Library of America, 1984), 1153; Jefferson to Lafayette, May 1805, in Paul Leicester Ford, ed., *The Writings of Thomas Jefferson*, 10 vols. (New York: G. P. Putnam's Sons, 1892–1899), 9:67.

13. *New York Times*, September 21, 1940, "Text of the President's Address at the University of Pennsylvania."

14. *Chicago Daily Tribune*, March 5, 1937, "Victory Dinner Speech by Roosevelt."

15. Elliott Roosevelt, ed., *F.D.R.: His Personal Letters*, 4 vols. (New York: Duell, Sloan and Pearce, 1947–1950), 2:966. See also *New York Times*, May 16, 1939, "Quezon Will Agree to a Second Term"; *Chicago Daily Tribune*, May 16, 1939, "Asks Philippines to Allow Second Term as Chief."

16. *Atlanta Constitution*, May 30, 1939, "Capital Parade," by Joseph Alsop and Robert Kintner.

17. James MacGregor Burns, *Roosevelt: The Lion and the Fox* (New York: Harcourt, Brace, 1956), 271, italics added.

18. Roosevelt, Fireside Chat, June 24, 1938, in Samuel I. Rosenman, ed., *Public Papers and Addresses of Franklin D. Roosevelt [PPA]*, 13 vols. (New York: Macmillan, 1941), 7:399, italics added.

19. *New York Times*, November 9, 1904, "Roosevelt."

20. TR to George Otto Trevelyan, June 19, 1908, in Hermann Hagedorn, ed., *The Roosevelt Treasury: A Self-Portrait from His Writings* (New York: G. P. Putnam's Sons), 193, italics added. He also wrote that he was causing deep chagrin to the many good men who believed that "they were losing quite needlessly the leader in whom they trusted."

21. James MacGregor Burns and Susan Dunn, *The Three Roosevelts: Patrician Leaders Who Transformed America* (New York: Atlantic Monthly Press, 2001), 122–123, 126.

22. Rexford Tugwell quoted in *New York Times*, September 22 1957, "The President He Knew."

23. See James MacGregor Burns, *The Deadlock of Democracy* (Englewood Cliffs, N.J.: Prentice-Hall, 1963), 175.

24. Alexander Hamilton, *Federalist* No. 72, in Dunn, *Something That Will Surprise the World*, 138–139, italics added.

25. Charles Lindbergh quoted in *New York Times*, August 5, 1940, "Text of Col. Lindbergh's Speech."

26. See Ellis, *Founding Brothers*, 135; Joseph J. Ellis, *His Excellency: George Washington* (New York: Knopf, 2004), 235ff. Washington's draft of his Farewell Address in George Washington, *Writings*, ed. John Rhodehamel (New York: Library of America, 1997), 945, italics added. See also Washington to Charles Carroll, May 1, 1796, in John C. Fitzpatrick, ed., *Writings of George Washington*, 39 vols. (Washington, D.C.: 1931–1939), 37:29–31.

27. Memorandum by George Beckwith on a Conversation with Alexander Hamilton, October 1789, in Dunn, *Something That Will Surprise the World*, 149. David Reynolds mentions that, in creating a close Anglo-American bond in 1940 and 1941, "the shared language, stripped of all extravagant

myths, proved particularly potent. It facilitated more extensive and more intensive personal relationships than would otherwise have been possible." David Reynolds, *The Creation of the Anglo-American Alliance 1937–1941* (Chapel Hill: University of North Carolina Press, 1982), 267.

28. Laski to Frankfurter, quoted in Isaac Kramnick and Barry Sheerman, *Harold Laski: A Life on the Left* (New York: Allen Lane, Penguin Press, 1993), 428.

29. Harold J. Laski, "The Democratic Convention," *The Nation*, 20, 492 (July 27, 1940), 81; Harold J. Laski, *The American Presidency* (New York: Harper and Brothers, 1940), 180, 275–276, respectively.

30. Alsop and Kintner comment on the dedication in *Atlanta Constitution*, May 1, 1940, "Capital Parade."

Chapter 3: Walking on Eggs

1. *New York Times*, August 12, 1936, "U.S. Will Keep Hands Off in Spain."

2. *New York Times*, August 15, 1936, "President Roosevelt's Chautauqua Address." He also said that in any new war, Americans would "face the choice of profits or peace" and hoped that they would choose peace.

3. FDR to Hull, 1935, quoted in James MacGregor Burns, *Roosevelt: The Lion and the Fox* (New York: Harcourt, Brace, 1956), 251–252.

4. *New York Times*, September 14, 1935, "Roosevelt Asserts Neutrality Resolution."

5. See Burns, *Roosevelt: The Lion and the Fox*, 250–255; David L. Porter, *The Seventy-Sixth Congress and World War II* (Columbia: University of Missouri Press, 1979), 20.

6. *New York Times*, March 1, 1936, "Roosevelt Renews Plea against Profits in War." See also Robert A. Divine, *The Illusion of Neutrality* (Chicago: University of Chicago Press, 1962). Divine argues in that book as well as in his *Roosevelt and World War II* (Baltimore, Md.: Johns Hopkins University Press, 1969) that FDR was an isolationist at least until the Munich conference because his priority was the New Deal and not stopping aggression in Asia or Europe prior to 1939.

7. Burns, *Roosevelt: The Lion and the Fox*, 61.

8. A week after his inauguration, however, his secretary of the navy undertook—quietly and slowly—a naval buildup.

9. *New York Times*, October 6, 1937, "President Hits Out." See also Robert Dallek, *Franklin D. Roosevelt and American Foreign Policy* (New York: Oxford University Press, 1979), 148. See also *New York Times*, October 8, 1937, "Two Foreign Policies."

10. Dorothy Borg, "Notes on Roosevelt's 'Quarantine' Speech," *Political Science Quarterly*, 72, 3 (September 1957), 423.

11. Frank Freidel, "FDR vs. Hitler: American Foreign Policy, 1933–1941," *Proceedings of the Massachusetts Historical Society*, 3rd Series, 99 (1987), 30.

12. *Washington Post*, October 6, 1937, "League's Bid for Positive Action"; *Atlanta Constitution*, October 6, 1937, "The President and Peace," italics added; *Saint Louis Globe Democrat* and *Cincinnati Inquirer* quoted in *New York Times*, October 6, 1937, "Nation-wide Press Comment on President Roosevelt's Address"; *New York Times*, October 10, 1937, "Policy in the Making." See also Borg, "Notes on Roosevelt's 'Quarantine' Speech," 405.

13. Samuel I. Rosenman, *Working with Roosevelt* (New York: Harper and Brothers, 1952), 166.

14. *Los Angeles Times*, October 10, 1937, "Neutrality Favored as Best Hope of Peace."

15. Harvey Cantril and Mildred Strunk, eds., *Public Opinion 1935–1946* (Princeton, N.J.: Princeton University Press, 1951), 966–967. See also James MacGregor Burns, *The Crosswinds of Freedom* (New York: Knopf, 1989), 153.

16. *Atlanta Constitution*, October 14, 1937, "Tinkham Talks Removal of F.D.R."; *Atlanta Constitution*, October 17, 1937, "Fish Asserts F.D.R. Should Be Ousted"; *Hartford Courant*, October 6, 1937, editorial; *New York Times*, October 6, 1937, "Nation-wide Press Comment on President Roosevelt's Address." The *New York Herald Tribune* also warned that the speech "was an appeal for a popular emotional mandate to the president to take whatever course in our international relations

that seemed to him best," in *Los Angeles Times*, October 6, 1937, "Editorial Comment Varies on President's Address."

17. Burns, *Roosevelt: The Lion and the Fox*, 318–319.

18. FDR to Endicott Peabody, October 16, 1937, and FDR to Edward House, October 19, 1937, in Elliott Roosevelt, ed., *F.D.R.: His Personal Letters*, 4 vols. (New York: Duell, Sloan and Pearce, 1947–1950), 1:716–719.

19. *New York Times*, October 12, 1937, "President Greets Mussolini's Son." FDR's mother also wrote to her son in 1937 from Italy, "The Duce sent me a grand bunch of flowers," quoted in James Roosevelt, *My Parents: A Differing View* (Chicago: Playboy Press, 1976), 240. It was also true that Roosevelt hoped to use Mussolini as a lever with which to restrain Germany. Lowenthal, "The Coming of the War: The Search for United States Policy 1937–1942," *Journal of Contemporary History*, 16, 3 (July 1981), 419.

20. *New York Times*, October 11, 1937, "Urge White House to Bar Duce's Son."

21. See Lowenthal, "The Coming of the War: The Search for United States Policy 1937–1942," 414–415. See also Borg, "Notes on Roosevelt's 'Quarantine' Speech," 405; John McV. Haight, Jr., "Roosevelt and the Aftermath of the Quarantine Speech," *Review of Politics*, 24, 2 (April 1962), 255.

22. Chamberlain quoted in Antony Best, *International History of the 20th Century* (New York: Routledge, 2003), 173.

23. John C. Donovan, "Congressional Isolationists and the Roosevelt Foreign Policy," *World Politics*, 3, 3 (April 1951), 304.

24. Burns, *Roosevelt: The Lion and the Fox*, 262.

25. *Los Angeles Times*, January 11, 1938, "War Vote Amendment Rejected in Congress"; *New York Times*, January 11, 1938, "Ludlow War Referendum Is Defeated."

26. FDR to Arthur Murray, February 10, 1938, in Roosevelt, *F.D.R.: His Personal Letters*, 2:757.

27. Although the stock market was down 11.2 percent during FDR's second term, the change in gross domestic product was a positive 3.1 percent, lower than the 6 percent growth during his first term and lower than the 17.3 percent growth during the third term. *New York Times*, March 23, 2012, "What Stocks and G.D.P. Say about Obama's Chances."

28. *New York Times*, September 4, 1938, "Bullitt Promises Unity with France"; *New York Times*, September 10, 1938, "Roosevelt Denies U.S. Is Allied with Europeans against Hitler."

29. *New York Times*, September 13, 1938, "'Oppression' Cited."

30. William L. Shirer, *Berlin Diary* (1941, repr. Baltimore, Md.: Johns Hopkins University Press, 2002), 126.

31. Robert Sherwood, *Roosevelt and Hopkins: An Intimate History*, rev. ed. (New York: Harper and Brothers, 1950), 100.

32. Burns, *Roosevelt: The Lion and the Fox*, 389.

33. Message to Czechoslovakia, Germany, Great Britain and France, September 27, 1938, in Samuel I. Rosenman, ed., *The Public Papers and Addresses of Franklin D. Roosevelt [PPA]*, 13 vols. (New York: Macmillan, 1941), 7:531–537.

34. See FDR, Address at Queen's University, Kingston, Ontario, Canada, August 18, 1938, in *PPA*, 7:491–494.

35. *Washington Post*, October 1, 1938, "London Gives Prime Minister Great Ovation." See Barbara Farnham, *Roosevelt and the Munich Crisis* (Princeton, N.J.: Princeton University Press, 1997).

36. Winston Churchill, "The Choice for Europe," May 9, 1938, in Winston Churchill, *Blood, Sweat and Tears* (New York: G. P. Putnam's Sons, 1941), 25–26.

37. Burns, *Roosevelt: The Lion and the Fox*, 385–387; see also J. P. Taylor, *Origins of the Second World War* (New York: Atheneum, 1962), 191. See also Lowenthal, "The Coming of the War," 418.

38. Press Conference, October 13, 1938, in Kenneth S. Davis, *FDR: Into the Storm, 1937–1940* (New York: Random House, 1993), 353; see also *New York Times*, October 14, 1938, "Roosevelt Moves to Rush Expansion of Army and Navy."

39. The chairman of FDR's Advisory Committee on Political Refugees in 1938, James McDonald, had better judgment than most.

40. *Chicago Daily Tribune*, October 29, 1936, "Text of President's Speech at Statue of Liberty."

41. The "Emergency Quota Act" of 1921 limited the number of immigrants admitted from any country annually to 3 percent of the number of residents from that same country already living in the United States; the act of 1924 reduced the quota even more, to 2 percent. The acts were especially punitive for Asians, southern and eastern Europeans, and Jews. See *Annual Report of the Commissioner General of Immigration to the Secretary of Labor, 1922*, 8–9. In his annual message of December 1931, President Hoover boasted that "immigration has been curtailed by administrative action. Upon the basis of normal immigration the decrease amounts to about 300,000 individuals who otherwise would have been added to our unemployment." On the immigration situation in the late 1930s, see *New York Times*, September 13, 1938, "German Refugees Fill Entry Quota"; *New York Times*, June 26, 1938, "German Immigration Far under the Quota"; *New York Times*, March 26, 1938, "Refugee Plan Is Extended by Roosevelt"; *Washington Post*, November 18, 1938, "Raised Quota Studied."

42. Gunnar Myrdal, *An American Dilemma: The Negro Problem and American Democracy*, 2 vols. (New York: Harper and Brothers, 1944), 1:1186, note 4.

43. Adolf Hitler, Speech at Nuremberg Party Conference, September 12, 1938, quoted in N. H. Baynes, ed., *The Speeches of Adolf Hitler*, 2 vols. (Oxford: Oxford University Press, 1942), 1:735. Dr. Robert Ley, the head of the German Labor Front, announced in June 1940 that, with France having just capitulated, the "Aryan" peoples of Europe now recognized that they had only one enemy, the Jew. "Europe must free itself of Jews and their minions. That is freedom." *New York Times*, June 26, 1940, "Nazis View France as Key to New Era."

44. *Wall Street Journal*, November 14, 1938, "What's News"; *New York Times*, November 14, 1938, "Extremists Sway Nazis."

45. *Washington Post*, November 16, 1938, "President Says U.S. Is 'Shocked' by War on Jews"; *New York Times*, April 29, 1938, "Immigration Quota for Austria Unchanged." British Colonial and Dominions Secretary Malcolm MacDonald also rejected appeals to relax the immigration quota in Palestine. See *Los Angeles Times*, November 25, 1938, "Britain Rejects Zionist Appeals." Historian and Roosevelt biographer Kenneth S. Davis wrote that FDR could suspend at will his "remarkable sensitivity. . . . He seems to have been able to turn empathy on or off at will, as if it were water in a faucet." Kenneth S. Davis, *FDR: The War President* (New York: Random House, 2000), 746–747.

46. *New York Times*, February 26, 1939, "100 Jews Each Day Must Leave Reich." The Committee for Assistance of Jews in Italy also called upon the United States to permit immediate entry of Italy's unwanted Jews.

47. *New York Times*, June 5, 1939, "Refugee Ship Idles off Florida Coast."

48. *Washington Post*, June 3, 1939, "Sub-committee Would Bar Aliens to 1944"; *Chicago Daily Tribune*, May 12, 1939, "Lash Roosevelt War Talk." See also *New York Times*, January 9, 1940, "Senate Votes Bill Sharpening Laws to Deport Aliens."

49. Sheldon Neuringer, "Franklin D. Roosevelt and Refuge for Victims of Nazism," in *Franklin D. Roosevelt: The Man, the Myth, the Era*, ed. Herbert Rosenbaum and Elizabeth Bartelme (New York: Greenwood Press, 1987), 87. The quote is from Neuringer's interview with Ernest Lindley in June 1976.

50. Richard Breitman, "FDR's 1938 Refugee Policy," unpublished article, May 2009; memorandum of Sumner Welles to Moffat, December 22, 1938, Welles Papers, Box 48, Folder 9, State Department European Affairs, 1938, Franklin D. Roosevelt Library (FDRL), Hyde Park, N.Y.; *New York Times*, January 6, 1939, "Mussolini Rebuffs Roosevelt on Jews."

51. Undersecretary of State Sumner Welles confirmed that the president himself was the author of the Evian conference. Welles to Alling, June 6, 1938, Welles Papers, Box 46, Folder 2 (IJ 1938), FDRL, Hyde Park, N.Y. Quoted in Richard Breitman, "FDR's 1938 Refugee Policy," unpublished article, 2009.

52. French delegate quoted in David S. Wyman, *Paper Walls: America and the Refugee Crisis, 1938–1941* (New York: Pantheon, 1985), 49.

53. Address at Meeting of Officers of the Intergovernmental Committee on Political Refugees, October 17, 1939, in *PPA*, 8:546–550; *New York Times*, October 22, 1939, "Refugee Proposal Irritates Allies."

54. The United States, in January 1941, rejected a plea from the Vichy government in France to permit hundreds of thousands of persons of many origins living in France, particularly Jews forced out of Luxembourg, Belgium, and Germany, to emigrate to the United States. *New York Times*, January 9, 1941, "U.S. Refuses French Plea to Take Refugees." It can also be argued that FDR chose relatively poor ambassadors to European nations, ambassadors who veered toward appeasement like his ambassador to Great Britain, Joseph Kennedy; his ambassador to Poland, Ireland, and Belgium, John Cudahy; and his ambassador to France, William Bullitt. Interestingly, FDR did take a keen interest in the fates of convicts who escaped from the French penal colony Devil's Island in South America. When the escaped convicts were imprisoned in Puerto Rico, the president tried unsuccessfully to find ways to circumvent immigration rules so that they could be allowed to enter the United States and then sent to west Africa to fight with General de Gaulle's "Free French" Army. On the island of Trinidad, however, British officials who caught escaped convicts harbored them for two weeks and then outfitted them with boats and sent them to sea to find some refuge as best they could. See Harold L. Ickes, *The Secret Diary of Harold L. Ickes*, 3 vols. (New York: Simon and Schuster, 1953–1954), January 19, 1941, 3:411; *Miami News*, June 15, 1941, "Roosevelt Unable to Save 38 Devil's Island Fugitives." The dramatic story of escaped convicts from Devil's Island was the plot of the 1944 movie *Passage to Marseille* directed by Michael Curtiz and starring Humphrey Bogart and Peter Lorre.

55. Burns, *Roosevelt: The Lion and the Fox*, 388.

56. *New York Times*, December 6, 1938, "Roosevelt's Address at Chapel Hill."

57. J. Garry Clifford, "A Note on the Break between Senator Nye and President Roosevelt in 1939," *North Dakota History*, 49 (Summer 1982), 14–17; *New York Times*, February 2, 1939, "Berlin Is Amazed." See also Davis, *FDR: Into the Storm*, 407–408; *Los Angeles Times*, January 31, 1939, "Hitler Gives Warning." A week before that White House meeting, a Douglas bomber crashed near Los Angeles, and it was discovered that a representative of the French Air Ministry had been a passenger on the plane. Senators wanted to know why the French mission was secret and if the War Department had approved the sale of planes to France. FDR called the meeting to appease the isolationists and stated publicly that he had given permission for the sale of planes to France. See Clifford, "Note on the Break between Senator Nye and President Roosevelt," 14. See also Warren Kimball, *The Most Unsordid Act: Lend-Lease 1939–1941* (Baltimore, Md.: Johns Hopkins University Press, 1969), 4–7. As for the frontier on the Rhine, in March 1945, American soldiers seized the bridge at Remagen and crossed the Rhine into Germany. Also, in December 1938, FDR asked Treasury Secretary Henry Morgenthau to supervise foreign arms purchases.

58. Press Conference, February 3, 1939, in *PPA*, 8:111–114. See also *Los Angeles Times*, February 4, 1939, "Roosevelt Hurls Lie." Isolationist senator Nye thought that FDR was referring to him as the "boob." See Wayne S. Cole, *Senator Gerald P. Nye and American Foreign Relations* (Minneapolis: University of Minnesota Press, 1962), 156; Nye, Memorandum, January 31, 1939, Gerald P. Nye Mss., Herbert Hoover Presidential Library, West Branch, Iowa, quoted in Clifford, "Note on the Break between Senator Nye and President Roosevelt," 16.

59. David Scott, March 22, 1939, quoted in David Reynolds, *The Creation of the Anglo-American Alliance 1937–1941* (Chapel Hill: University of North Carolina Press, 1982), 286.

60. William L. Shirer, *20th Century Journey: A Memoir of a Life and the Times*, 3 vols. (Boston: Little, Brown, 1984), *The Nightmare Years, 1930–1940*, 2:398.

61. *Atlanta Constitution*, April 16, 1939, "Hitler Decides to Reject."

62. Shirer, *20th Century Journey*, 2:397. That summer Shirer returned to Washington for a few weeks, only to hear Borah issue a public statement categorically affirming that there would be no war. Almost everyone in the capital seemed to agree with him, Shirer observed. Shirer, *20th Century Journey*, 2:410.

63. *Los Angeles Times*, April 29, 1939, "Text of Hitler's Answers." See also Shirer, *20th Century Journey*, 2:402.

64. *Washington Post*, April 29, 1939, "The Answer"; *Hartford Courant*, April 29, 1939, "Gloomy View Is Taken by Most Legislators"; *Atlanta Constitution*, April 29, 1939, "Fuehrer Lightens Tension of France"; *Los Angeles Times*, April 29, 1939, "Speech Regarded at Capital with Hope and Disappointment"; *New York Times*, April 29, 1939, "Congress Reaction to Hitler Varies."

65. Burns, *Roosevelt: The Lion and the Fox*, 394.

66. Marshall to Craig, September 19, 1939, in Mark A. Stoler, *George C. Marshall: Soldier-Statesman of the American Century* (New York: Twayne, 1989), 68–74; *New York Times*, September 9, 1939, "100,000 More Men"; John Morton Blum, *From the Morgenthau Diaries*, 3 vols. (Boston: Houghton Mifflin, 1959–1967), 2:140. See also Forrest C. Pogue, *George C. Marshall*, 4 vols. (New York: Viking, 1963–1987), 2:6, 10–11, 16–17.

67. James MacGregor Burns and Susan Dunn, *The Three Roosevelts: Patrician Leaders Who Transformed America* (New York: Atlantic Monthly Press, 2001), 420. In August 1914, at the dawn of the First World War, President Woodrow Wilson had communicated the opposite message when he asked Americans to be neutral in thought and in action. He said, "We must be impartial in thought as well as in action, must put a curb upon our sentiments as well as upon every transaction that might be construed as a preference of one party to the struggle before another." *Christian Science Monitor*, August 18, 1914, "President Wilson Bids All His Countrymen Be Neutral Both in Speech and Action."

68. *Washington Post*, September 4, 1938, "Roosevelt Told of Sinking." See also *Washington Post*, September 4, 1939, "Reich Signed 1936 Pledge."

69. *Hartford Courant*, September 9, 1939, "Emergency Proclaimed by Roosevelt"; *Christian Science Monitor*, September 15, 1939, "Roosevelt Pushes Sphere at Sea"; Richard W. Steele, "Franklin D. Roosevelt and His Foreign Policy Critics," *Political Science Quarterly*, 94, 1 (Spring 1979), 19–20.

70. *Hartford Courant*, September 9, 1939, "Emergency Proclaimed." See also Sherwood, *Roosevelt and Hopkins*, 134.

71. Message to Congress, September 21, 1939, in *PPA*, 8:521.

72. FDR to Frank Knox, October 4, 1939, and FDR to Lord Tweedsmuir, October 5, 1939, in Roosevelt, *FDR: His Personal Letters*, 2:933 and 934, italics added.

73. Porter, *The Seventy-Sixth Congress and World War II*, 23–85. Porter provides a detailed account of all the congressional negotiations on the neutrality legislation in 1939.

74. Steven Casey, *Cautious Crusade: Franklin D. Roosevelt, American Public Opinion, and the War against Nazi Germany* (New York: Oxford University Press, 2001), 23. See also Divine, *Illusion of Neutrality*, 297, 317–318.

75. Kimball, *Most Unsordid Act*, 17–19. Kimball points out that the Roosevelt administration—as well as the British and French themselves—had mistaken views about the finances of the Allies and that FDR might have uttered Borah's very words when he proposed Lend-Lease in 1941. Henry Morgenthau quoted Ambassador Joseph Kennedy as writing in the autumn of 1939, "England is busted now." Blum, *From the Morgenthau Diaries*, 2:104.

76. *Time*, March 18, 1948, "Books: The Sage of Kansas."

77. FDR to White, December 14, 1939, in Roosevelt, *F.D.R.: His Personal Letters*, 2:967–968.

78. *New York Times*, December 10, 1939, "'Is He or Ain't He?'"

79. Rexford Tugwell, Diary, February 6, 1940, in Rexford Tugwell Papers, FDRL, quoted in Wayne Cole, *Roosevelt and the Isolationists* (Lincoln: University of Nebraska Press, 1983), 367.

80. Burns, *Roosevelt: The Lion and the Fox*, 262, italics added.

81. Sherwood, *Roosevelt and Hopkins*, 126–127. In his book *My Parents: A Differing View*, the president's son James Roosevelt recounts a conversation in which his father said, "I had to educate the people to the inevitable, gradually, step by step, laying the groundwork for programs which would allow us to prepare for the war that was drawing us into it. . . . Jimmy, I would have loved to have said that as president I was in a position to know what was happening in the world much more than was the public or even the members of Congress. . . . But I couldn't say that because the public and congressmen didn't want to hear it and so wouldn't have believed it and would have turned on me." James Roosevelt, *My Parents: A Differing View*, 160–161.

82. FDR to John Cudahy, April 17, 1940, in Roosevelt, *F.D.R.: His Personal Letters*, 2:1017. For his part, Lord Lothian, the British ambassador to the United States, felt that the "intrinsic ugliness" of the Nazi aggression along with the risks taken by the British naval forces would cement American loyalty to the Allies. Lord Lothian, April 23, 1940, Reel 6, British Foreign Office Records, FO 371 series, Public Record Office. Courtesy of J. Garry Clifford. Ambassador Cudahy

would leave the State Department in 1940, become a "roving reporter" in Europe, and then join the America First isolationist movement in the United States. In June 1941, Harold Ickes would call him "a megaphone through which Hitler is graciously permitted to shout his obscenities into the ears of Americans." *New York Times*, June 11, 1941, "Ickes Says Cudahy Is Nazi 'Megaphone.'" Cudahy was the uncle of Harold Ickes's young wife, Jane, and did not approve of that marriage; that disapproval probably added to Ickes's dislike of Cudahy.

83. FDR to Cudahy, May 8, 1940, in Roosevelt, *F.D.R.: His Personal Letters*, 2:1024. John Cudahy was in Brussels and seemed pro-German. See his book, *The Armies March: A Personal Report* (New York: Scribner's, 1941). He died soon thereafter.

84. Burns, *Roosevelt: The Lion and the Fox*, 419.

85. Radio Address to Eighth Pan American Scientific Congress, Washington, May 19, 1940, in *PPA*, 9:187, italics added. See also *New York Times*, May 11, 1940, "America Angered."

86. Burns, *Roosevelt: The Lion and the Fox*, 419. See also FDR to Sumner Welles, June 1, 1940, in Roosevelt, *F.D.R.: His Personal Letters*, 2:1036.

87. Harold Ickes, unpublished diary, May 19, 1940, Manuscript Division, Library of Congress. Courtesy of J. Garry Clifford.

88. FDR to Anna, June 1, 1940, in Roosevelt, *F.D.R.: His Personal Letters*, 2:1034.

89. *New York Times*, July 21, 1940, "Job of President Grows Steadily Bigger"; *Time*, June 10, 1940, "The Presidency: Prelude to History."

90. Pogue, *George C. Marshall*, 2:30–31. James Farley wrote in 1939 that Morgenthau "has been a good soldier, loyal; and whatever views he has had, he expressed privately to the President and argued with him privately. But in his public attitude he has always given the impression of being thoroughly sympathetic with the President's viewpoints at all times." James Farley Papers, January 10, 1939, Box 43, p. 10, Manuscript Division, Library of Congress.

91. Pogue, *George C. Marshall*, 2:23–24, 31–32.

92. George C. Marshall, interviewed by Forrest C. Pogue, November 15, 1956, in Larry I. Bland, ed., *Papers of George Catlett Marshall*, 5 vols. (Baltimore, Md.: Johns Hopkins University Press, 1981–), 2:210–211. See also Ed Cray, *General of the Army George C. Marshall* (New York: W. W. Norton, 1990), 155. See also Harold Gullan, "Expectations of Infamy: Roosevelt and Marshall Prepare for War," *Presidential Studies Quarterly*, 28, 3 (Summer 1998), 518.

93. Bland, *Papers of George Catlett Marshall*, editorial notes, 2:210–211. Henry Morgenthau, FDR's acting director of procurement, wrote in May 1940: "We haven't got one airplane today that has got the things we need if they went up against a German plane." See Blum, *From the Morgenthau Diaries*, 2:138–143.

94. Another strategically situated island that worried him went unmentioned—the island of Fernando Noronha, a few hundred miles east of Brazil, in the South Atlantic, where less than two thousand miles separated Africa and South America.

95. FDR, Message to Congress, May 16, 1940, in *PPA*, 9:198–205, italics added.

96. FDR to Helen Rogers Reid, June 6, 1940, Reid Family Mss., Manuscript Division, Library of Congress, quoted in Clifford, "Note on the Break between Senator Nye and President Roosevelt in 1939," 15. See also Michael Leigh, *Mobilizing Consent: Public Opinion and American Foreign Policy, 1937–1947* (Westport, Conn.: Greenwood Press, 1976), Chapter 2.

97. *New York Times*, June 2, 1940, "Impact of the War on the Nation's Viewpoint"; *Atlanta Constitution*, June 23, 1940, "Republican, Democratic Views Almost Same"; Marquess of Lothian, June 1, 1940, No. 891, Telegram 811, A3223 B, Reel 6, British Foreign Office Records, FO 371 series, Public Record Office. Courtesy of J. Garry Clifford. A 1937 Gallup poll found that 55 percent of Americans chose England as their favorite European country; 11 percent chose France, 8 percent chose Germany, and 4 percent chose Ireland.

98. *New York Times*, June 2, 1940, "Impact of the War on the Nation's Viewpoint."

99. This point was made in a memo from Nelson Poynter, National Committee of Independent Voters, to Harry Hopkins, October 22, 1940, in George McJimsey, ed., *Documentary History of the Franklin D. Roosevelt Presidency*, 43 vols. (Bethesda, Md.: University Publications of America, 2001–2008), Document 122, 13:654.

100. Ickes, *Secret Diary*, August 4, 1940, 3:289, italics added.

101. Stoler, *George C. Marshall*, 75.

102. Mark S. Watson, *Chief of Staff: Prewar Plans and Preparations*, a volume in the multivolume and official *United States Army in World War II* (Washington, D.C.: Government Printing Office, 1950), 312. The planner quoted is then-Major (but later Lieutenant General and General Eisenhower's chief of staff) Walter Bedell Smith.

103. Sherwood, *Roosevelt and Hopkins*, 173; *Washington Post*, May 12, 1940.

104. Sam Rosenman Oral History, Harry S. Truman Library, p. 18; Reminiscences of Frances Perkins, Pt. 7, Session 1, p. 379, Columbia Center for Oral History Collection.

105. Robert Jackson Oral History, Columbia University, p. 42; *New York Times*, November 3, "Roosevelt Needed, Jackson Declares." The New York politico and soon-to-be chair of the National Democratic Party, Ed Flynn, agreed. "I myself had come to feel that it was the only possible decision to make," he later wrote. Edward J. Flynn, *You're the Boss* (New York: Viking, 1947), 155.

106. *New York Times*, July 6, 1940, "Roosevelt Names Five Basic Freedoms"; *Los Angeles Times*, October 24, 1940, "President Raps Liberty League." The reporter was Richard Harkness. See Sherwood, *Roosevelt and Hopkins*, 231; Roosevelt, Fireside Chat, "Arsenal of Democracy," December 29, 1940, in *PPA*, 9:639.

107. *New York Times*, December 6, 1940, "Nazis Envisage Chattel Slavery for People of Conquered Nations." The speech, given in May 1940, was leaked to *Life* magazine and printed seven months later in the *New York Times*. The *Times* noted that "there are satisfactory reasons for believing that the address is authentic as condensed here."

108. *New York Times*, September 11, 1932, "Roosevelt's View of the Big Job," by Anne O'Hare McCormick.

109. *New York Times*, December 6, 1940, "Nazis Envisage Chattel Slavery."

Chapter 4: Lindbergh and the Shrimps

1. FDR to Roger Merriman, professor of history and headmaster of Eliot House at Harvard, May 21, 1940, in Elliott Roosevelt, ed., *F.D.R.: His Personal Letters*, 4 vols. (New York: Duell, Sloane and Pearce, 1947–1950), 2:1028.

2. James MacGregor Burns, *Roosevelt: The Lion and the Fox* (New York: Harcourt, Brace, 1956), 419.

3. Burns, *Roosevelt: The Lion and the Fox*, 419.

4. Newspaper editor William Evjue, the editor of the *Madison Capital Times*, agreed. "There are always a number of dupes who lend their names to such committees but really running the show will be found the chronic Roosevelt haters who organize outfits like the 'America First Committee' in order to spread their anti-Roosevelt venom." John E. Miller, *Governor Philip F. La Follette, the Wisconsin Progressives, and the New Deal* (Columbia: University of Missouri Press, 1982), 169.

5. FDR's Christmas message, *New York Times*, December 25, 1943, "Text of Roosevelt Yule Message."

6. Address at the University of Virginia, June 10, 1940, in Samuel I. Rosenman, ed., *Public Papers and Addresses of Franklin D. Roosevelt [PPA]*, 13 vols. (New York: Macmillan, 1941), 9:261.

7. FDR later told Secretary of War Henry Stimson that Secretary of State Hull had strongly objected to the line about the dagger and FDR had taken it out of the speech. But on the train to Charlottesville, FDR was still fuming about Italy's attack, and Eleanor advised him to satisfy his conscience and put the line back in, which he did. Henry Stimson Diaries, December 29, 1940, vol. 32, Yale University Library, Manuscripts and Archives.

8. Roosevelt, Address at the University of Virginia, June 10, 1940, in *PPA*, 9:260. See also Eleanor Roosevelt, *This I Remember* (New York: Harper, 1949), 211–212.

9. *Time*, June 17, 1940, "The Presidency: Tenth of June."

10. Kenneth S. Davis, *FDR: Into the Storm, 1937–1940* (New York: Random House, 1993), 556–557.

11. Davis, *FDR: Into the Storm*, 556–557; *New York Times*, August 21, 1940, "Walsh Opposes Ship Sale"; *Chicago Daily Tribune*, June 20, 1940, "Walsh Assails Secret Sale"; Burns, *Roosevelt: The Lion and the Fox*, 421–422, 439; *Los Angeles Times*, June 25, 1940, "Text of Roosevelt Statement Halting Torpedo Boats Sale." Torpedo boats would be sent as part of the destroyers-for-bases deal in August 1940.

12. A Gallup poll taken in late June 1940, after the fall of France, showed that 57 percent of Americans approved of FDR's foreign policy; and on the question of a third term for Roosevelt, 46 percent of all Americans favored keeping him in office and a whopping 91 percent of Democrats said they would support a third term.

13. *New York Times*, May 22, 1927, "Crowd Roars Thunderous Welcome"; *Atlanta Constitution*, June 14, 1927, "Manhattan Pays Greatest of All Tributes to Lindbergh."

14. *New York Times*, May 20, 1940, "Text of the Speech"; *Los Angeles Times*, May 20, 1940, "Lindbergh Pleads."

15. *Washington Post*, May 19, 1940, "Nazis Smash through Belgium, into France"; *New York Times*, May 18, 1940, "Belgian Refugees Swarm into Paris"; *New York Times*, May 20, 1940, "Col. Lindbergh's Broadcast"; *New York Times*, May 20, 1940, "Text of the Speech," italics added. See also A. Scott Berg, *Lindbergh* (New York: G. P. Putnam's Sons, 1998).

16. FDR to Henry Stimson, May 21, 1940, in Robert Dallek, *Franklin D. Roosevelt and American Foreign Policy* (Oxford: Oxford University Press, 1979), 225.

17. *New York Times*, May 18, 1940, "British Face Crisis with Grim Resolve"; *New York Times*, May 20, 1940, "Text of the Speech," italics added. The Jewish people, Lindbergh would rail in an infamous speech in Des Moines in September 1941, posed a great "danger to this country . . . in their large ownership and influence in our motion pictures, our press, our radio, and our government." See *New York Times*, September 12, 1941, "Lindbergh Sees a 'Plot' for War."

18. See Susan Dunn, "French Anti-Semitism and the Cult of the Soil," *Partisan Review*, 61, 4 (Fall 1994), 592–599.

19. William L. Shirer, *Berlin Diary* (New York: Knopf, 1941), 593.

20. Dispatch of July 1940, in William Shirer, *The Rise and Fall of the Third Reich* (New York: Simon and Schuster, 1960), 749. Von Boetticher added, "I have repeatedly reported on the mean and vicious campaign against Lindbergh, whom the Jews fear as their most potent adversary." Walter Ross, *The Last Hero: Charles A. Lindbergh* (New York: Manor Books, 1974), 305.

21. H. and J. Warner to Roosevelt, May 20, 1940, Roosevelt Papers, OF 73, 1940 file, Box 4, Franklin D. Roosevelt Library, Hyde Park, N.Y. See also Todd Bennett, "The Celluloid War: State and Studio in Anglo-American Propaganda Film-Making, 1939–1941," in *International History Review*, 24, 1 (March 2002), 76. See also Richard W. Steele, "The Great Debate: Roosevelt, the Media and the Coming of the War, 1940–41," *Journal of American History*, 71, 1 (June 1984), 74.

22. *New York Times*, March 2, 1932, "Child Stolen in Evening"; *New York Times*, March 3, 1932, "Roosevelt Orders State Police Hunt"; *New York Times*, May 13, 1932, "Body Mile from Hopewell"; *New York Times*, October 9, 1934, "Col. Lindbergh Identifies Hauptmann by His Voice."

23. *New York Times*, January 3, 1935, "10 Hauptmann Case Jurors"; *New York Times*, February 24, 1935, "Aid to Hauptmann Seen in Interview"; *New York Times*, September 21, 1934, "Held as Extortionist."

24. *New York Times*, December 24, 1935, "Exiling Our Own Sons" (editorial); *New York Times*, December 24, 1935, "America Shocked by Exile Forced on the Lindberghs."

25. *New York Times*, December 29, 1935, "Voluntary Exile"; *New York Times*, December 24, 1935, "Comment in the German Press."

26. Anne Morrow Lindbergh, *The Flower and the Nettle: Diaries and Letters of Anne Morrow Lindbergh, 1936–1939* (New York: Harcourt Brace, 1976), 97.

27. *New York Times*, July 24, 1936, "Lindbergh in Reich Warns on Air War." On the opening day of the Berlin Olympics, Lindbergh sat near—but did not meet—the Führer. *New York Times*, August 3, 1936, "Lindbergh Ends Stay in Germany." See also Wayne Cole, *Roosevelt and the Isolationists* (Lincoln: University of Nebraska Press, 1983), 280–290; Cole, *Charles Lindbergh and the Battle against American Intervention in World War II* (New York: Harcourt Brace Jovanovich, 1974).

28. Kenneth S. Davis, *The Hero: Charles A. Lindbergh and the American Dream* (Garden City, N.Y.: Doubleday, 1959), 373.

29. Truman Smith, *Berlin Alert: The Memoirs and Reports of Truman Smith*, ed. Robert Hessen (Stanford, Calif.: Hoover Institution Press, 1984), 114–115.

30. Shirer, *Berlin Diary*, July 23, 1936, 64.

31. Lindbergh, *The Flower and the Nettle*, 100–102. See also David Gordon, "America First: The Anti-War Movement, Charles Lindbergh, and the Second World War, 1940–1941," originally presented at a joint meeting of the Historical Society and the New York Military Affairs Symposium, September 26, 2003, available at: http://libraryautomation.com/nymas/americafirst.html.

32. *New York Times*, August 3, 1940, "Lindy in Berlin 12 Days." See also Lindbergh, *The Flower and the Nettle*, 99; *New York Times*, August 2, 1936, "100,000 Hail Hitler"; *New York Times*, August 3, 1936, "Lindbergh Ends Stay in Germany."

33. William Shirer, *20th Century Journey: A Memoir of a Life and the Times*, 3 vols. (Boston: Little, Brown, 1976–1990), 2:236–237.

34. Lindbergh to Harry Davison, January 23, 1937, quoted in Cole, *Charles A. Lindbergh and the Battle against American Intervention*, 34–35.

35. Lindbergh to Breckinridge, September 23, 1936, and Lindbergh to Davison, October 28, 1937, in Cole, *Charles A. Lindbergh and the Battle against American Intervention*, 35, 38, italics added.

36. Alexis Carrel, *Man, the Unknown* (New York: Harper and Brothers, 1935), 177, 211, 251; David M. Friedman, *The Immortalists: Charles Lindbergh, Dr. Alexis Carrel, and Their Daring Quest to Live Forever* (New York: Ecco/HarperCollins, 2007), 45, 86–91. See also Andres Horacio Reggiani, "Alexis Carrel, the Unknown: Eugenics and Population Research under Vichy," *French Historical Studies*, 25, 2 (Spring 2002), 331–356. In the early 1930s, Carrel and Lindbergh had on occasion worked together at the Rockefeller Institute in New York. Only Carrel's death in 1944 prevented him from being tried for collaboration with the Nazis. In 1945, Lindbergh mourned his friend. Criticizing the "unfairness" of those who had attacked the eugenicist's racial theories, Lindbergh asked "what possible advantage" it would have been to France if Carrel "had refused to co-operate with the Germans." Charles A. Lindbergh, *The Wartime Journals of Charles A. Lindbergh* (New York: Harcourt Brace Jovanovich, 1970), May 16, 1945, 1941. See also *Time*, November 13, 1944, "Milestones."

37. *New York Times*, October 20, 1938, "Hitler Grants Lindbergh High Decoration"; *New York Times*, February 8, 2001, "Anne Morrow Lindbergh, 94, Dies."

38. Lindbergh, *Wartime Journals*, November 13, 1938, 115; Berg, *Lindbergh*, 379–380.

39. Lindbergh, *Wartime Journals*, December 16, 1938, 126.

40. Davis, *Hero*, 378–379.

41. Charles Lindbergh, "Aviation, Geography and Race," *Reader's Digest*, 35 (November 1939).

42. *Washington Post*, September 20, 1939, "On the Record," by Dorothy Thompson.

43. Lindbergh, *Wartime Journals*, March 20, 1939, 166; April 1, 1939, 173.

44. Ross, *Last Hero*, 276–277. Lindbergh met with Stanley Baldwin in 1937 and with Harold Nicholson in 1938 as well as with other foreign statesmen and prime ministers.

45. Lindbergh, *Wartime Journals*, July 10, 1939, 229. He wrote to General Arnold, chief of the Air Corps of the U.S. Army, and urged him to visit Germany. See Ross, *Last Hero*, 287.

46. Lindbergh, *Wartime Journals*, April 20, 1939, 187.

47. Lindbergh, *Wartime Journals*, April 20, 1939, 186; *Chicago Daily Tribune*, April 21, 1939, "Col. Lindbergh in Conference with President"; Max Wallace, *The American Axis: Henry Ford, Charles Lindbergh, and the Rise of the Third Reich* (New York: St. Martin's Press, 2003), 204–205. The implication was that FDR wanted to co-opt his isolationist adversary. But since such an offer was purported to have been extended to Lindbergh before his first nationwide radio address in September 1939, the rumors of a cabinet position were highly implausible. In his memoir, an isolationist who was a friend to Lindbergh, George Eggleston, insisted that Secretary of War Woodring offered a cabinet post as secretary of air to Lindbergh, if Lindbergh canceled his speaking plans. George T. Eggleston, *Roosevelt, Churchill, and the World War II Opposition* (Old Greenwich, Conn.: Devin-Adair, 1979), 77.

48. Lindbergh, *Wartime Journals*, April 20, 1939, 188.

49. Two Royal Air Force pilots visited Germany, were greatly impressed by German air-power, and reported on their findings in 1936. Their report was not used until Winston Churchill wanted to alert the British government to the danger of aerial attack. Vincent Orange, "The German Air Force Is Already 'The Most Powerful in Europe': Two Royal Air Force Officers Report on a Visit to Germany, 6–15 October 1936," in *Journal of Military History*, 70, 4 (October 2006), 1011–1028.

50. *New York Herald Tribune*, headline: "Lindbergh Reported Providing U.S. with Data on Reich Air Force." See also *Atlanta Constitution*, April 21, 1939, "Lindy Urges U.S. to Lead Aviation"; G. Pascal Zachary, *Endless Frontier: Vannevar Bush, Engineer of the American Century* (New York: Free Press, 1997), 100; "Engine Research Laboratory Urged by N.A.C.A.," *Science News-Letter*, 37, 3 (January 20, 1940), 44. See also James Phinney Baxter, *Scientists against Time* (Boston: Little, Brown and Company, 1946). Bush had also been the dean of engineering at MIT.

51. Vannevar Bush, Foreword, in Baxter, *Scientists against Time*, vii; *New York Times*, June 30, 1974, "Vannevar Bush Is Dead." On FDR's meeting with Bush, June 12, 1940, see Davis, *FDR: Into the Storm*, 562. Army Chief of Staff General George C. Marshall knew that in making proposals to the president "you have to intrigue his interest, and then it knows no limit." Two weeks later, Marshall wrote approvingly that "the Research Committee recently appointed by the President is going to be an important receptacle for several of our problems, especially inventions." George Marshall to Bernard Baruch, June 29, 1940, in Larry Bland, ed., *Papers of George C. Marshall*, 5 vols. (Baltimore, Md.: Johns Hopkins University Press, 1981–), 2:253.

52. Elliott Roosevelt, FDR's son, wrote that the appointment of Bush was "directly traceable" to Charles Lindbergh's "parlor preachments of German invincibility." Elliott wrote that when Bush heard Lindbergh speak at a private meeting, he felt impelled to approach Harry Hopkins and unveil plans for a National Defense Research Council. Hopkins introduced Bush to FDR. Elliott Roosevelt, *A Rendezvous with Destiny: The Roosevelts of the White House* (New York: Putnam, 1975), 270. See also Baxter, *Scientists against Time*; Zachary, *Endless Frontier*, 100.

53. Lindbergh, *Wartime Journals*, June 21, 1940, 360.

54. *Atlanta Constitution*, August 4, 1940, "Lindbergh Is Just Like His Father"; *New York Times*, April 5, 1913, "Progressives Meet as Fighting Force." See the review of Bruce L. Larson's "Lindbergh of Minnesota," a biography of Lindbergh, Sr., by Leroy Ashby, *Wisconsin Magazine of History*, 58, 2 (Winter, 1974–1975), 151–152. Anne Morrow Lindbergh wrote in her diary, "Charles tells me that his father was opposed to war with Germany . . . and that he was greatly criticized for it and called a traitor. Now the same thing is happening again, by an odd flick of chance." Lindbergh, *The Flower and the Nettle*, 496.

55. Charles A. Lindbergh, *Why Is Your Country at War?* (Washington, D.C.: National Capital Press, 1917), 15–31, 140–148. He attacked those who "value the perpetuation of property accumulation, more than the preservation of human integrity." Lindbergh, *Why Is Your Country at War?*, 31. And Lindbergh Sr. wanted government ownership of public utilities, especially ones that like the telephone and telegraph convey information, 140. See also Paul Seabury, "Charles A. Lindbergh: The Politics of Nostalgia," *History*, 2 (1960), 123–144; Wayne Cole interview with Charles Lindbergh, June 7, 1972, Army and Navy Club, Washington, D.C., Cole Papers, Hoover Presidential Library, West Branch, Iowa. Courtesy of J. Garry Clifford.

56. Anne Morrow Lindbergh, *War Within and Without: Diaries and Letters of Anne Morrow Lindbergh, 1939–1944* (New York: Harcourt Brace Jovanovich, 1980), xxiii.

57. Lindbergh, *Why Is Your Country at War?*, 8.

58. Charles Lindbergh told Wayne Cole in 1972 that "there was no relation between his father's anti-involvement efforts and his own" and he believed that his father envisaged "simple solutions for complex problems." Cole, interview with Lindbergh, June 7, 1972.

59. *New York Times*, August 5, 1940, "Text of Col. Lindbergh's Speech."

60. Lindbergh, *Wartime Journals*, March 31, 1939, and February 28, 1939, 161, 172. Lindbergh wrote that only if the "white race" was seriously threatened should Americans "fight side by side with the English, French and Germans but not with one against the other for our mutual destruction."

Hartford Courant, October 14, 1939, "Lindbergh Asks Embargo." See also Lindbergh, "Aviation, Geography, and Race," 64–66.

61. Lindbergh, *The Flower and the Nettle*, February 25, 1939, 534; Lindbergh, *Wartime Journals*, August 17, 1940, 79; Lindbergh, quoted in Berg, *Lindbergh*, 386. Also in 1939, Lindbergh wrote that "we must . . . limit to a reasonable amount the Jewish influence in the Educational agencies in this country—i.e. press, radio, and pictures." Berg, *Lindbergh*, 393.

62. Sir John Slessor, *The Central Blue: The Autobiography of Sir John Slessor, Marshal of the RAF* (New York: Frederick Praeger, 1957), 218–222. William Shirer agreed that Lindbergh was "gullible." For Shirer, he was "a civilian pilot of genius but with no real military training or knowledge." Shirer, *20th Century Journey*, 2:367. Rodman also wrote: "One can not help but admire his great courage and rocklike integrity. But the fact remains that we don't speak the same language politically; and though he has none of the brass jingoism or sadistic power-worship that make the Nazis so unspeakable, he seems bound to end up in their camp. Perhaps it is because he has been cut off for so long from the common man, that he is incapable of being stirred by the degradation of the masses under fascism. Perhaps it is simply because his initial isolationism and the memory of his father's martyrdom drive him logically as well as emotionally into the 'enemy' camp. . . . Probably it is something of each of the causes, but whatever it is, it is a national as well as a personal tragedy. Lawrence of Arabia had less courage but more wisdom to keep out of politics. He pretended, hypocritically, that he was a failure and could do nothing supremely well; deep down he must have understood that his kind of fame and genius were a peril to society." Selden Rodman Diary, July 22, 1941, Sterling Library, Yale University. Courtesy of J. Garry Clifford.

63. *New York Times*, August 5, 1940, "Text of Col. Lindbergh's Speech."

64. Lindbergh to Joseph Kennedy, November 9, 1938, in Truman Smith, *Berlin Alert: The Memoirs and Reports of Truman Smith*, ed. Robert Hessen (Stanford, Calif.: Hoover Institution Press, 1984), 158. In May 1940, Hitler's man in Danzig, Arthur Greiser, delivered a similar message about the natural dominance of "master states": "Only great nations with a high Kultur," declared the future organizer of the Holocaust in Poland, "are called to leadership; small nations are useful only under the protection and leadership of great nations." *New York Times*, May 12, 1940, "Nazi World Revolution Is Hitler's Objective." In 1938 Kennedy called for the European democracies and fascist dictatorships to cease "emphasizing their differences" and reestablish good relations. See Cole, *Roosevelt and the Isolationists*, 289–290.

65. Lindbergh, *War Within and Without*, June 24, 1940, 117.

66. Robert Sherwood, *Roosevelt and Hopkins: An Intimate History*, rev. ed. (New York: Harper and Brothers, 1950), 153. Sherwood declared that Lindbergh was "simply a Nazi with a Nazi's Olympian contempt for all democratic processes." *New York Times*, December 12, 1940, "Calls Lindbergh 'a Nazi.'" See also Burns, *Roosevelt: The Lion and the Fox*, 436.

67. *New York Times*, August 26, 1940, "Sherwood Assails Ford, Lindbergh." Janet Murrow, the wife of the CBS foreign correspondent in London Edward R. Murrow wrote home, "Beware Mr. C. A. Lindbergh. He's a good disciple of National Socialism." Joseph Persico, *Edward R. Murrow: An American Original* (New York: McGraw-Hill, 1988), 151.

68. Historian Wayne S. Cole, who wrote important studies of Lindbergh, isolationism, and the America First Committee and interviewed the aviator at length in the early 1970s, found him "frank, honest, candid, proud, thoughtful, reflective, intelligent, balanced, tolerant." Cole was undoubtedly influenced by his personal contact with Lindbergh and may also have sympathized with his outsider status. Cole, interview with Lindbergh, June 7, 1972. See also Cole, *Charles A. Lindbergh and the Battle against American Intervention*, 143–153.

69. Morgenthau Diary, May 20, 1940, quoted in Davis, *FDR: Into the Storm*, 504.

70. *New York Times*, July 15, 1941, "Lindbergh Called Nazi Tool by Ickes"; *Chicago Daily Tribune*, April 14, 1941, "Ickes Lambastes America First." Jim Farley once said that Ickes sent up "trial balloons" for Roosevelt. James Farley Papers, January 10, 1939, Box 43, p. 13, Manuscript Division, Library of Congress. Courtesy of J. Garry Clifford.

71. Cole, *Charles A. Lindbergh and the Battle against American Intervention*, 144.

Chapter 5: Isolationists: The War Within

1. Hitler quoted in William L. Shirer, *20th Century Journey: A Memoir of a Life and the Times*, 3 vols. (Boston: Little, Brown, 1984), 2:427.

2. Arthur Schlesinger, Jr., "Back to the Womb? Isolationism's Renewed Threat," *Foreign Affairs*, 74, 4 (July–August 1995), 2–8.

3. *New York Times*, December 22, 1940, "Production Speed Vital, Hoover Says." See also George Nash, ed., *Freedom Betrayed: Herbert Hoover's Secret History of the Second World War* (Stanford, Calif.: Hoover Institution Press, 2011).

4. Ralph Smuckler, "The Region of Isolationism," *American Political Science Review*, 47, 2 (June 1953), 386–401. There would be hardly any America First chapters in the South; and the few southerners who were isolationists, Wayne Cole writes, "were driven to silence." Wayne S. Cole, *America First: The Battle against American Intervention, 1940–1941* (Madison: University of Wisconsin Press, 1953), 31; Alexander DeConde, "The South and Isolationism," *Journal of Southern History*, 24, 3 (August 1958), 343; *New York Times*, September 22, 1940, "Sentiment to Aid Britain Is Growing."

5. Charles A. Lindbergh, *The Wartime Journals of Charles A. Lindbergh* (New York: Harcourt Brace Jovanovich, 1970), October 3, 1940, 396.

6. *Washington Post*, February 9 1939, "Sen. Walsh Addresses Navy Sponsors Here"; *New York Times*, June 13, 1940, "Wheeler Makes a Threat to Bolt." Holt demanded an investigation of the financial investments of newspapers that supported military aid for the Allies.

7. See Frank Freidel, *Franklin D. Roosevelt: The Triumph* (Boston: Little, Brown, 1956), 136–137. See also John Thomas Anderson, "Senator Burton K. Wheeler and United States Foreign Relations," Ph.D. thesis, 1982, University of Virginia, 100–101, 104; Robert Bendiner, "Men Who Would Be President: Burton K. Wheeler," *The Nation*, 150, April 27, 1940, 534.

8. Robert Sherwood, *Roosevelt and Hopkins: An Intimate History*, rev. ed. (New York: Harper and Brothers, 1950), 173. See Leroy Rieselbach, "The Basis of Isolationist Behavior," *Public Opinion Quarterly*, 24, 4 (Winter 1960), 645–657.

9. *New York Times*, February 13, 1940, "Republicans Call for 'Lincoln's Way.'"

10. Justus Doenecke, *Storm on the Horizon: The Challenge to American Intervention, 1939–1941* (Lanham, Md.: Rowman and Littlefield, 2000), 2; James T. Patterson, *Congressional Conservatism and the New Deal* (Lexington: University of Kentucky Press, 1967), 101. Borah echoed Lindbergh in denouncing the "powerful interests" [read Jews] who were trying to draw America into the European conflict. *Chicago Daily Tribune*, September 11, 1939, "Borah Reviews Huge Losses." See also *Los Angeles Times*, August 5, 1940, "Lindbergh Proposes Accord for America and Germany." In September 1939, Harold Ickes wrote to William Bullitt, the ambassador to France: "Our old friend, Hiram [Johnson], whom you and I have seen swing from the liberal position to that of extreme conservatism, will be sounding the old alarums and Borah will be shaking his shaggy mane while fighting the battle of twenty years ago. . . . Little Gerald Nye, with simulated pomposity, will go about delivering the speeches that have been so popular and so profitable before the women's clubs of the country." Ickes to Bullitt, September 18, 1939, in William Bullitt Papers, Manuscripts and Archives, Yale University, Box 41. Courtesy of J. Garry Clifford.

11. *New York Times*, April 29, 1939, "Congress Reaction to Hitler Varies," italics added.

12. Wayne S. Cole, *Senator Gerald P. Nye and American Foreign Relations* (Minneapolis: University of Minnesota Press, 1962), 169–170.

13. *Los Angeles Times*, October 21, 1939, "American Fear of Hitler Scored."

14. Richard Norton Smith, *Thomas E. Dewey and His Times* (New York: Simon and Schuster, 1982), 302. See also *New York Times*, June 23, 1939, "Air Expansion Bill Approved by House."

15. In 1939, FDR asked Hutchins to head the SEC. *Chicago Daily Tribune*, March 24, 1939, "Hutchins Asked by Roosevelt." In October 1940, FDR also asked Hutchins to head Selective Service. Charles Beard, "The Myth of Rugged American Individualism," *Harper's Magazine*, December 1931, 13.

16. *New York Times*, February 10, 1938, "Need for Big Navy Derided by Beard." See also *Life*, February 21, 1938, "Life on the American Newsfront: Historian and Admiral Join the War Debate."

17. Charles A. and Mary Beard, *America in Midpassage* (New York: Macmillan, 1939), 452–453. Other historians hammered Beard for burying his head in the sand. Harold Laski slammed his "noble escapism" in the *New Statesman*, 18, 452 (October 21, 1939), 562. See Manfred Jonas, *Isolationism in America, 1925–1941* (Ithaca, N.Y.: Cornell University Press, 1966), 153. Columbia University historian Allen Nevins reviled Beard's "frigid indifference" to the people who were dying under bombs and machine guns, people who "speak the language we speak" (*New York Times*, May 26, 1940, "Two Views of America's Part"). Max Lerner also ridiculed his "candid policy of tending to our own garden" (*New Republic*, June 3, 1940, "In the Hour of Decision").

18. J. Garry Clifford and Samuel R. Spencer, Jr., *The First Peacetime Draft* (Lawrence: University Press of Kansas, 1986), 143. In 1939, Beard also published *Giddy Minds and Foreign Quarrels: An Estimate of American Foreign Policy* (New York: Macmillan, 1939).

19. *New York Times*, November 21, 1940, "Ickes Warns U.S. of Propagandists."

20. Justus D. Doenecke, "The Isolationist as Collectivist: Lawrence Dennis and the Coming of World War II," *Journal of Libertarian Studies*, 3, 2 (Summer 1979), 195; *New York Times*, June 18, 1940, "Roosevelt Called 'No. 1 Isolationist'"; Lawrence Dennis, *The Dynamics of War and Revolution* (New York: Weekly Foreign Letter, 1940), xxiv.

21. Raymond Buell, Memorandum on Foreign Affairs for Henry Luce, January 8, 1941, p. 33, Raymond Leslie Buell Papers, Manuscript Division, Library of Congress. Courtesy of J. Garry Clifford.

22. TR to Henry Ford, February 9, 1916, in Theodore Roosevelt, *Letters and Speeches* (New York: Library of America, 2004), 700.

23. Sherwood, *Roosevelt and Hopkins*, 281. See also *Washington Post*, November 30, 1998, "Ford and GM Scrutinized for Alleged Nazi Collaboration." See also Ken Silverstein, "Ford and the Führer," *The Nation*, January 24, 2000. In June 1940, Ford's son Edsel agreed that Ford would build nine thousand Rolls-Royce engines for British planes, but Henry Ford forced cancellation of the deal. *New York Times*, July 4, 1940, "Packard Assumes Rolls-Royce Job."

24. *Washington Post*, November 30, 1998, "Ford and GM Scrutinized for Alleged Nazi Collaboration."

25. *New York Times*, May 26, 1939, "Auto Leader Urges World Trade Accord"; *New York Times*, December 15, 1939, "France to Give US Order for Tools"; *Washington Post*, November 30, 1998, "Ford and GM Scrutinized for Alleged Nazi Collaboration"; Reinhold Billstein, Karola Fings, Anita Kugler, and Nicholas Levis, *Working for the Enemy: Ford, General Motors and Forced Labor during the Second World War* (New York: Berghahn, 2000), 37–44.

26. *Los Angeles Times*, November 9, 1940, "Design for New World." See also Graeme Howard, *America and a New World Order* (New York: Scribner's, 1940).

27. *Washington Post*, August 13, 1940, "Linked to Westrick, Head of Texas Oil Company Quits"; Jacques R. Pauwels, "Torkild Rieber, 'Profits Uber Alles!' American Corporations and Hitler," *Labour/Le Travail*, 51 (Spring 2003), 232.

28. Justus Doenecke, "Non-Interventionism of the Left: The Keep America Out of the War Congress," *Journal of Contemporary History*, 12, 2 (April 1977), 222–223, 230–231.

29. See John Milton Cooper, *The Vanity of Power: American Isolationism and the First World War, 1914–1917* (Westport, Conn.: Greenwood, 1969). Cooper points out that most of the arguments made by isolationists in the 1930s had already been made during World War I.

30. Bernard Bellush and Jewel Bellush, "A Radical Response to the Roosevelt Presidency: The Communist Party (1933–1945)," *Presidential Studies Quarterly*, 10, 4 (Fall 1980), 649–655; Irving Howe and Lewis Coser, *The American Communist Party: A Critical History* (Boston: Beacon Press, 1957), 384–411; *Hartford Courant*, March 9, 1940, "Views Are Presented on Election"; *Washington Post*, June 30, 1941, "U.S. Communist Party Appeals for Aid to Reds"; *Washington Post*, June 22, 1941, "White House Pickets Stop." See also Manfred Jonas, *Isolationism in America* (Ithaca, N.Y.: Cornell University Press, 1966); Harvey Klehr, John Earl Haynes, and Fridrikh Igorevich Firsov, *The Secret World of American Communism* (New Haven, Conn.: Yale University Press, 1995).

31. America First statement, June 23, 1941, in Cole, *America First*, 85–86.

32. *Atlanta Constitution*, July 2, 1941, "Hitler Better Ally than Reds, Lindbergh Says."

33. *Hartford Courant*, September 16, 1939, "Lindbergh for Neutrality"; *Washington Post*, October 14, 1939, "Text of Col. Lindbergh's Radio Address"; Charles Lindbergh, "What Substitute for War?" in *Atlantic Monthly*, March 1940. See also Paul Seabury, "Charles A. Lindbergh: The Politics of Nostalgia," *History*, 2 (1960), 132; Charles Lindbergh, "Aviation, Geography and Race," *Reader's Digest*, 35 (November 1939); Lindbergh, *Wartime Journals*, January 7, 1939, 136; A. Scott Berg, *Lindbergh* (New York: G. P. Putnam's Sons, 1998), 394, italics added; Kenneth S. Davis, *The Hero: Charles A. Lindbergh and the American Dream* (Garden City, N.Y.: Doubleday, 1959), 401. In 1972, Charles Lindbergh told historian Wayne Cole that he "believes very much in race. He says 'it enriches life' and he likes the diversity of different races. He does not favor artificial barriers between races. He believes it would be unfortunate to mix races thus doing away with that racial diversity; and it would be unfortunate to build fences around the different races. . . . So far as inferiority or superiority of any particular race or races, Lindbergh believes that depends on the frame of judgment one uses to view the races." Wayne Cole interview with Charles Lindbergh, June 7, 1972, Army and Navy Club, Washington, D.C., Cole Papers, Hoover Presidential Library, West Branch, Iowa. Courtesy of J. Garry Clifford. One isolationist author who seemed to agree with Lindbergh's racialism was the occultist writer Alice A. Bailey.

34. David Gordon, "America First, the Anti-War Movement, Charles Lindbergh and the Second World War": http://libraryautomation.com/nymas/americafirst.html.

35. Cole, *America First*, 10. Pelley contended that Washington should support Hitler to prevent "Jewish Bolshevism" from taking over. Pelley would be tried for high treason and sedition in 1942. Those charges were dropped, and he was convicted of other charges and sentenced to fifteen years in prison. See Geoffrey S. Smith, "Isolationism the Devil, and the Advent of the Second World War," *International History Review*, 4, 2 (February 1982), 75; Donnell Portzline, "William Dudley Pelley and the Silver Shirt Legion of America," unpublished doctoral dissertation, Ball State University, Muncie, Indiana, 1965.

36. Doenecke, *Storm on the Horizon*, 7.

37. David Gordon, "America First, the Anti-War Movement, Charles Lindbergh and the Second World War": http://libraryautomation.com/nymas/americafirst.html.

38. *Wall Street Journal*, June 12, 1940, "A Plea for Realism," italics added. The *Journal* editorialized that "Stop Hitler Now" ads were unrealistic. "All the armed democracies of Europe combined have not been able to stop Hitler's mechanized military might. 'Stop Hitler now!' What with? Our bare hands and the bared breasts of our youth?" Doenecke, *Storm on the Horizon*, 139–149. See also John T. Flynn, "Can Hitler Beat American Business?" *Harper's*, February 1940, 321–328; *New York Times*, September 12, 1941, "Lindbergh Sees a 'Plot' for War"; *Los Angeles Times*, June 21, 1941, "Text of Lindbergh Plea for Isolation."

39. *Chicago Daily Tribune*, June 28, 1936, "Text of President Roosevelt's Speech."

40. Gary Dean Best, *Herbert Hoover, the Postpresidential Years, 1933–1964*, 2 vols. (Stanford, Calif.: Hoover Institution Press, 1983), 1:119.

41. *New York Times*, March 3, 1940, "Roosevelt Leaning to War"; *New York Times*, May 21, 1940, "Strict Neutrality Demanded by Taft." See also Taft to A. Kirk, April 10, 1940, and Taft to Mary Truesdale, April 30, 1940 in James T. Patterson, *Mr. Republican: A Biography of Robert A. Taft* (Boston: Houghton Mifflin, 1972), 200, 216.

42. General Robert Wood and Douglas Stuart, founders of America First. See Cole, *America First*, 82–84.

43. *New York Times*, June 16, 1940, "Text of Colonel Lindbergh's Address."

44. *New York Times*, August 26, 1940, "Sherwood Assails Ford, Lindbergh"; Roosevelt, Radio Address Announcing Unlimited National Emergency, May 27, 1941, in Samuel I. Rosenman, ed., *Public Papers and Addresses of Franklin D. Roosevelt [PPA]*, 13 vols. (New York: Harper and Brothers, 1941), 10:190–191.

45. Michael R. Beschloss, *Kennedy and Roosevelt: The Uneasy Alliance* (New York: Norton, 1980), 193. See also Doenecke, *Storm on the Horizon*, 31.

46. Wheeler, June 26, 1941, quoted in Doenecke, *Storm on the Horizon*, 203.

47. Doenecke, *Storm on the Horizon*, 31.

48. *Washington Post*, March 26, 1939, "Borah Calls Britain Best Ally of Hitler."

49. *Christian Science Monitor*, March 13, 1940. See also Thomsen to Foreign Ministry, June 15, 1940, in *Documents on German Foreign Policy, 1918–1945*, Series D (1937–1945), 13 vols. (Washington, D.C.: United States Government Printing Office, 1947–), Document 441, 9:576. The committee helped pay for the costs of Charles Lindbergh's radio broadcast on June 15, 1940.

50. Thomsen to Foreign Ministry, June 15, 1940, in *Documents on German Foreign Policy*, Series D, Document 441, 9:576. See also Thomsen to Foreign Ministry, June 19, 1940, in *Documents on German Foreign Policy*, Series D, Document 492, 9:624–625.

51. Arthur M. Schlesinger, Jr., ed., *History of American Presidential Elections, 1789–1968*, 2 vols. (New York: Chelsea House Publishers, 1971), "1940 Election" by Robert E. Burke, 2:2922.

52. Justus D. Doenecke, ed., *In Danger Undaunted: The Anti-Interventionist Movement of 1940–1941 as Revealed in the Papers of the America First Committee* (Stanford, Calif.: Hoover Institution Press, 1990), 7, 9, 19, 89. Ford soon resigned from the AFC, unwilling to risk his job as an assistant football coach at Yale. See Kingman Brewster to R. Douglas Stuart, Jr., July 1940, Document 2, 89. In an interview with J. Garry Clifford, May 29, 1983, New Haven, Brewster said that in retrospect he was glad that the isolationists lost. Brewster acknowledged that the Yale elite in 1940 was consciously or unconsciously anti-Semitic. He also mentioned Sargent Shriver in that interview. Courtesy of J. Garry Clifford. See also Cole, *America First*, 1off. Ronald Reagan would appoint Douglas Stuart ambassador to Norway.

53. Cole, *America First*, 12–15. Wood would insist that American intervention in the war would result in "the end of capitalism all over the world." Cole, *America First*, 83.

54. Doenecke, *In Danger Undaunted*, 8, 10, 11, 16, 37, 41, 409. On La Follette, see John E. Miller, *Governor Philip F. La Follette, the Wisconsin Progressives, and the New Deal* (Columbia: University of Missouri Press, 1982), 168.

55. Cole, *America First*, 30, 95, 99, 167–169.

56. Doenecke, *In Danger Undaunted*, 10, 28. See also Seabury, "Charles A. Lindbergh: The Politics of Nostalgia," 138.

57. Cole, *America First*, 132; Doenecke, *In Danger Undaunted*, 14–15. See also David Gordon, "America First, the Anti-War Movement, Charles Lindbergh and the Second World War": http://libraryautomation.com/nymas/americafirst.html.

58. Doenecke, *In Danger Undaunted*, 26, 36–37. See also Cole, *America First*, 131–139. Even Arthur Schlesinger, Jr. confessed that in 1940 he "sympathized with part of the isolationist case: that the United States was not commissioned a world savior and should not intervene militarily where vital interests were not at stake." Arthur M. Schlesinger, Jr., *A Life in the Twentieth Century: Innocent Beginnings, 1917–1950* (Boston: Houghton Mifflin, 2000), 243.

59. Doenecke, "Non-Interventionism of the Left," 230.

60. *New York Times*, April 20, 1940, "10,000 Here Join in Peace Rallies."

61. Harold L. Ickes, *The Secret Diary of Harold L. Ickes*, 3 vols. (New York: Simon and Schuster, 1953–1954), June 12, 1940, 3:205.

62. FDR, Address to American Youth Congress, February 10, 1940, *PPA*, 9:92–93.

63. *New York Times*, February 10, 1940, "Anti-Reds Balked in Floor Scuffles."

64. Hugh Ross, "John L. Lewis and the Election of 1940," *Labor History*, 17, 2 (1976), 177.

65. *New York Times*, September 22, 1940, "Sentiment to Aid Britain Is Growing."

66. *Williams Record*, April 20, 1938. See also *New York Times*, April 25, 1938, "Will Buy Vienna Books." See also Stephen Norwood, *The Third Reich in the Ivory Tower* (New York: Cambridge University Press, 2009), 227. "Where books are burned, people eventually will be burned as well," predicted the German poet Heinrich Heine in 1821 in his poem "Almansor." "*Dort wo man Bücher verbrennt, verbrennt man auch am Ende Menschen.*"

67. *New York Times*, June 21, 1940, "Hull, at Harvard"; *New York Times*, June 21, 1940, "The Text of Secretary Hull's Address at Harvard"; *Hartford Courant*, June 21, 1940, "'Menacing

Shadow Falls Blacker' Says Hull." Dr. A. Lawrence Lowell said that the war is "a struggle over conflicting ideas of civilization, to which we cannot be indifferent." He asked if America could gaze on the struggle "with a cold, impartial eye, as if we lived on another planet" and added that Americans should not assume that the totalitarian states would have no designs on us. "Nations are sometimes asked questions which they must, at their peril, answer at once and answer right. What shall we answer now?" Not all schools were as enlightened. In October 1940, Columbia's president Nicholas Murray Butler declared that his university had taken a firm stand in the "war between beasts and human beings" and thrown all its resources into the national defense effort. Therefore he invited members of the faculty who were defeatists, isolationists, and pro-fascists to resign. The purpose of the university, Butler said, was to follow "the paths of reason," and above and beyond academic freedom came the university's commitment to "pursue its high ideals." *New York Times*, October 4, 1940, "Dr. Butler's Address"; *New York Times*, October 4, 1940, "Dr. Butler Warns His Faculty." The British ambassador Lord Lothian, in his weekly political summary to the Foreign Office, noted that "Butler has started something resembling an anti-totalitarian heresy hunt . . . and has been taken to task by H. G. Wells." Lothian to Foreign Office, October 8, 1940, Telegram 2138, Reel 6, Records of British Foreign Office. Courtesy of J. Garry Clifford. William Castle, Jr., also complained about Harvard University. On February 28, 1941, he wrote, "It seems quite obvious that free speech in the University is a good bit restricted because [President] Conant is so violent in his beliefs." William R. Castle, Jr., Diary, Houghton Library, Harvard University. Courtesy of J. Garry Clifford.

68. *Hartford Courant*, June 21, 1940, "'Menacing Shadow Falls Blacker' Says Hull." On Elliott's denunciation of Hitler, see W. Y. Elliott, "The Pragmatic Revolt in Politics: Twenty Years in Retrospect," *Review of Politics*, 2, 1 (January 1940), 9. The Williams, Yale, and Harvard rallies were all sponsored by the Military Training Camps Association. See *New York Times*, June 7, 1940, "College Drive Due for Preparedness." Meetings were also held at Brown, Amherst, and Princeton. See also *New York Times*, June 13, 1940, "Conscription Aid Seen at 4 Colleges"; *New York Times*, June 18, 1940, "Yale, Brown Urge Military Training"; and *Christian Science Monitor*, June 20, 1940, "Solemnities at Harvard."

69. *Christian Science Monitor*, June 17, 1940, "Yale Seniors Heed Baccalaureate Call"; *Christian Science Monitor*, June 17, 1940, "Problems Exceed World War, Stimson Tells United States"; *New York Times*, June 20, 1940, "Text of Lothian's Address to Yale Alumni."

70. *New York Times*, June 17, 1940, "20,000 at Boston Ask Aid to Allies."

71. *New York Times*, January 6, 1940, "200 Organize to Aid White Committee."

72. Marcia Davenport, *Too Strong for Fantasy* (New York: Scribner, 1967), 289.

73. *New York Times*, June 12, 1940, "Roosevelt Praises 'Stop Hitler' Ad"; *New York Times*, June 16, 1940, "Appeasement Here Assailed by White." Another group of interventionists advocated sending the Allies not just material assistance but American troops as well. This was the Century Club Group, whose members included Joseph Alsop, Henry Luce, Dean Acheson, Allen Dulles, James Conant, Walter Wanger, and Robert Sherwood. See William Tuttle, "Aid-to-the Allies Short-of-War versus American Intervention, 1940: A Reappraisal of William Allen White's Leadership," *Journal of American History*, 56, 4 (March 1970), 840–858.

74. *New York Times*, June 27, 1940, "Historians Urge Help for Allies." The historians included Henry Steele Commager of Columbia University; Bernadotte Schmitt of the University of Chicago; Edward Mead Earle of Princeton; Carl Becker of Cornell; Allan Nevins of Columbia; and Dumas Malone, the editor-in-chief of Harvard University Press. Reinhold Niebuhr, "Pacifism and 'America First,'" in *Love and Justice: Selections from the Shorter Writings of Reinhold Niebuhr*, ed. D. B. Robertson (Philadelphia: Westminster Press, 1957), 285–286.

75. *New York Times*, June 1, 1940, "Plan to Help Allies Is Widely Supported." The words appeared in a telegram that was placed in the *Congressional Record*. A few weeks later, she presided over the graduation ceremonies at Smith College, at which the poet W. H. Auden addressed the graduates. Ridiculing the isolationists' argument that America could remain remote from the havoc in Europe and rejecting the fascist credo that the collective will of the people trumped the precious right of the individual to "realize his potential nature to the full," Auden told the graduates

that "whatever political label we may choose to wear, we have either to adapt to an open society or perish." *New York Times*, June 18, 1940, "Bids Smith Class Seek 'Open Society.'"

76. Anne Morrow Lindbergh, *War Within and Without: Diaries and Letters of Anne Morrow Lindbergh, 1939–1944* (New York: Harcourt Brace Jovanovich, 1980), October 27, 1940 and June 2, 1940, 148, 97, respectively. On June 19, 1940, Charles and Anne had lunch with Alexander Kirk, who had been counselor of the American Embassy in Berlin in 1939–1940 and who had just returned to the United States. Anne wrote that she did not agree with Kirk's point of view, but added, "I might have if I had not married Charles." Lindbergh, *War Within and Without*, 113; *New York Times*, November 28, 1940, "White Gives Story on Warships' Sale."

Chapter 6: Dark Horse

1. *Atlanta Constitution*, April 5, 1939, "Washington Correspondents See G.O.P. as 2–1 Choice."

2. Kuhn was jailed not for treason but rather for embezzlement. Dewey was famous for winning all but one of his seventy-three cases.

3. *New York Times*, April 16, 1939, "'Garner' Made Hero by Gridiron Club."

4. *New York Times*, February 23, 1939, "In the Nation," by Arthur Krock.

5. Memo on Cohen's conversation with Willkie, December 11, 1939, included in Cohen, Memo to Missy LeHand, June 29, 1940, PSF, Cohen, Roosevelt Mss., Franklin D. Roosevelt Library (FDRL), Hyde Park, N.Y. Courtesy of J. Garry Clifford.

6. *New York Times*, June 19, 1940, "Willkie Was Democrat Until '39." See also Steve Neal, *Dark Horse: A Biography of Wendell Willkie* (Garden City, N.Y.: Doubleday, 1984). Willkie did not publicly reveal his new party affiliation until January 1940, when he began his run for the GOP nomination.

7. *Chicago Daily Tribune*, December 6, 1935, "Roosevelt Vote Donor Accepts Refund."

8. Willkie to Bob (no last name), August 17, 1936, Barnard Mss., Manuscripts Department, Lilly Library, Indiana University, Bloomington. Courtesy of J. Garry Clifford.

9. Willkie, June 12, 1940, National Press Club in Washington, in Ellsworth Barnard, *Wendell Willkie: Fighter for Freedom* (Marquette: Northern Michigan University, 1966), 166.

10. *New York Times*, September 18, 1938, "Republicans Set for Dewey Draft"; *New York Times*, October 21, 1938, "Dewey Fighting Talk Cheers Republicans"; *New York Times*, October 30, 1938, "Dewey Acclaims His Party Ticket." See also Gary Dean Best, *Herbert Hoover: The Post-presidential Years, 1933–1964*, 2 vols. (Stanford, Calif.: Hoover Institution Press, 1983), 1:118.

11. Richard Norton Smith, *Thomas E. Dewey and His Times* (New York: Simon and Schuster, 1982), 273. See also *New York Times*, September 30, 1938, "Dewey Put in Line for 1940 Presidency."

12. *Atlanta Constitution*, January 7, 1940, "Dewey Lead Grows." See also *New York Times*, May 8, 1940, "Popularity Gain Shown by Willkie."

13. *New York Times*, April 14, 1940, "Roosevelt and Dewey Take 1940 Front Rank."

14. Neal, *Dark Horse*, 60. See also Smith, *Thomas E. Dewey*, 285–301.

15. *Washington Post*, April 15, 1940, "The Once Over."

16. Neal, *Dark Horse*, 70.

17. *Life*, April 22, 1940, "Wendell Willkie Exhibits Versatility."

18. *Los Angeles Times*, May 31, 1940, "Poll Charts Willkie Gain."

19. *Los Angeles Times*, June 12, 1940, "Willkie Gains Second Place."

20. *New York Times*, June 18, 1940, "Dewey Demands Strong War Steps."

21. Smith, *Thomas E. Dewey*, 304.

22. *New York Times*, March 31, "Shun Peace Talks."

23. Charles Peters, *Five Days in Philadelphia: The Amazing "We Want Willkie!" Convention of 1940* (New York: PublicAffairs, 2005), 19. See also Smith, *Thomas E. Dewey*, 303.

24. *Chicago Daily Tribune*, May 28, 1940, "Dewey Warns America: Shun Foreign Wars."

25. *New York Times*, June 22, 1940, "Dewey Denounces Roosevelt on War." See also *New York Times*, March 27, 1940, "Split in Wisconsin." Colonel Theodore Roosevelt was a manager of the Dewey campaign.

26. Smith, *Thomas E. Dewey*, 297; *Chicago Daily Tribune*, May 12, 1940, "America Wants to Stay Out of It, Says Dewey"; *New York Times*, December 2, 1939, "Dewey Opens Drive"; *New York Times*, June 22, 1940, "Dewey Denounces Roosevelt on War."

27. Rexford G. Tugwell, *The Democratic Roosevelt: A Biography of Franklin D. Roosevelt* (Garden City, N.Y.: Doubleday, 1957), 538.

28. James T. Patterson, *Mr. Republican: A Biography of Robert A. Taft* (Boston: Houghton Mifflin, 1972), 190; Taft, Speech to the Lions Club, March 1, 1940, in Clarence E. Wunderlin, Jr., ed., *Papers of Robert A. Taft*, 4 vols. (Kent, Ohio: Kent State University Press, 1997–2006), 2:120–121.

29. *New York Times*, May 21, 1940, "Strict Neutrality Demanded by Taft." See also *Wall Street Journal*, May 24, 1940, "Speaking of Infiltration." See also Patterson, *Mr. Republican*, 217.

30. Herman Klurfeld, *Winchell: His Life and Times* (New York: Praeger, 1976), 75.

31. *Christian Science Monitor*, October 28, 1939, "Neutrality Vote in Senate"; Patterson, *Mr. Republican*, 202; *New York Times*, May 21, 1940, "Strict Neutrality Demanded by Taft." See also *Christian Science Monitor*, May 21, 1940, "Taft Insists on Caution"; *New York Times*, June 20, 1940, "Excess Gains Levy Voted by Senate"; *New York Times*, June 23, 1940, "Tax Bill Is Passed to Pay for Arming."

32. Taft to Paul Walter, December 20, 1940, in Wunderlin, *Papers of Robert A. Taft*, 2:211.

33. *New York Times*, April 21, 1939, "Roosevelt Seizes War Crisis"; *Los Angeles Times*, May 21, 1940, "Taft Criticizes Roosevelt Talk"; *New York Times*, May 19, 1940, "Taft Asks Nation to Turn from War."

34. Patterson, *Mr. Republican*, 200.

35. *New York Times*, May 21, 1940, "Strict Neutrality Demanded by Taft"; *Chicago Daily Tribune*, May 21, 1940, "Taft Wants U.S. to Stop Playing." See also Patterson, *Mr. Republican*, 199, 219.

36. Vandenberg Diary, November 27, 1938, in Neal, *Dark Horse*, 57.

37. *New York Times*, April 9, 1940, "2 Primaries Today"; Neal, *Dark Horse*, 59.

38. *American Mercury*, January 1940, "The New Deal Must Be Salvaged." See also Neal, *Dark Horse*, 58.

39. *New York Times*, June 6, 1939, "Vandenberg Cites Way to Recovery"; *New York Times*, May 17, 1940, "Vandenberg Urges 'Insulated' America"; *Washington Post*, June 10, 1940, "President's Talk to Be Broadcast"; *New York Times*, May 26, 1940, "War's Turn Upsets Republicans' Race." See also C. David Tompkins, *Senator Arthur H. Vandenberg: The Evolution of a Modern Republican* (Lansing: Michigan State University Press, 1970), 174.

40. *New York Times*, June 27, 1936, "Text of Roosevelt Address"; William Leuchtenburg, *Herbert Hoover* (New York: Times Books/Henry Holt, 2009), 109, 113, 132–134.

41. Arthur Schlesinger, Jr., *The Age of Roosevelt: The Crisis of the Old Order, 1919–1933* (Boston: Houghton Mifflin, 1957), 241. See also Herbert Hoover, *Memoirs*, vol. 3, *The Great Depression: 1929–1941* (New York: Macmillan, 1952), 195.

42. *New York Times*, December 6, 1939, "Hoover Will Organize Relief for Finland"; *New York Times*, May 16, 1940, "Hoover Again Head of Belgium Relief"; *Hartford Courant*, October 1, 1939, "Hoover Urges Nation Shun Moves to Put America into War."

43. *Hartford Courant*, October 1, 1939, "Hoover Urges Nation Shun Moves to Put America into War"; *Los Angeles Times*, October 21, 1939, "Hoover Demands Armament Policy Protect Civilians." See also *Saturday Evening Post*, October 28, 1939, "We Must Keep Out"; Best, *Herbert Hoover*, 1:125, 134–135.

44. George H. Nash, ed., *Freedom Betrayed: Herbert Hoover's Secret History of the Second World War and Its Aftermath* (Stanford, Calif.: Hoover Institution Press, 2011), 830; *New York Times*, May 18, 1940, "Hoover and Dewey Back Defense Plan." See also Best, *Herbert Hoover*, 1:145–148. See also *Washington Post*, May 18, 1940, "White House Gratified by Cooperation"; *Washington Post*, May 26, 1940, "Voters Like Way F.D.R. Handles Foreign Affairs." Hoover, Landon, Dewey, and Taft supported FDR on war preparedness. Landon said, "I pledge to support our President in his announced efforts to strengthen the Nation against attack and to continue to cooperate with him in all efforts for complete unity on foreign policy." Hoover agreed, declaring

that "there can be no partisanship upon the principle of national defense." Dewey recommended a national defense board "completely removed from politics." Taft also gave support: "We must have completely adequate preparedness for defense at once to cope with any eventuality." Willkie agreed with FDR but said that the New Deal's "continuous attacks on the American industrial system the last seven years will hamper the drive to expand armament production."

45. *Washington Post*, May 26, 1940, "Voters Like Way F.D.R. Handles Foreign Affairs."

46. Best, *Herbert Hoover*, 1:121–130.

47. *Hartford Courant*, July 20, 1940, "Today and Tomorrow."

48. *Christian Science Monitor*, June 10, 1940, "Willkie Backs Drive to Ban Isolationist Plank." See also *New York Times*, May 5, 1940, "Willkie No 100% Foe of New Deal Policy"; Willkie to Gardner Cowles, April 3, 1940, in Neal, *Dark Horse*, 55. Taft in particular was "blind, foolish and silly," Willkie said. Neal, *Dark Horse*, 75.

49. *New York Times*, February 7, 1937, "Republican Leaders Chided by Hoffman."

50. *Hartford Courant*, October 28, 1939, "How Senate Voted"; *New York Times*, December 7, 1937, "Gov. Aiken Urges Republican Purge"; *Christian Science Monitor*, October 4, 1938, "GOP Unity in Massachusetts"; Milton Plesur, "The Republican Congressional Comeback of 1938," *Review of Politics*, 24, 4 (October 1962), 556.

51. Neal, *Dark Horse*, 2; Herbert Parmet, *Never Again: A President Runs for a Third Term* (New York: Macmillan, 1968), 56.

52. Neal, *Dark Horse*, 9; Peters, *Five Days in Philadelphia*, 27.

53. Lois E. Fenn to Willkie, January 27, 1930, "Correspondence—45," from Special File, Barnard Mss.

54. Donald Johnson, *The Republican Party and Wendell Willkie* (Urbana: University of Illinois Press, 1960), 50.

55. Neal, *Dark Horse*, 11. Willkie gave a graduation talk about the failure of Indiana's state government to regulate banks and businesses.

56. Peters, *Five Days in Philadelphia*, 29.

57. Parmet, *Never Again*, 56.

58. *Hartford Courant*, February 6, 1939, "Utilities Feud with TVA Ended." See also *Time*, February 13, 1939, "Public Utilities: TVA Deal"; *New York Times*, August 16, 1939, "TVA Takes Title to Power for State of Tennessee; $78,000,000 Paid Willkie."

59. *Washington Post*, January 7, 1938, "Low Prices, High Wages Sought by New Deal Spokesman." Willkie expressed "the viewpoint of the small businessman who has earned every dollar he has," enthused the Laramie [Wyoming] *Republican and Boomerang*. "We need a president with that viewpoint!" Parmet, *Never Again*, 97. On the other end of the spectrum, the *New York Daily News* commented that a man residing at 1010 Fifth Avenue didn't have a chance. "All we can say is they don't know the Mississippi Valley." Parmet, *Never Again*, 118.

60. *Hartford Courant*, July 1, 1940, "Willkie Has Appearance of Scholar," by Joseph Alsop and Robert Kintner. Frances Perkins was also pleased that the GOP in 1940, at least on much domestic policy, had almost become the "me, too" party, willing to go along with Democratic programs— but promising to administer them better. "Well, now I think we can sleep quietly and peacefully," she said. "The Republicans have adopted our platform and that means that our program is permanent." Frances Perkins Oral History, Part 7, Session 1, p. 698 of Columbia University Libraries Oral History Research Office.

61. Neal, *Dark Horse*, 47; Barnard, *Wendell Willkie: Fighter for Freedom*, 149; *New York Times*, May 19, 1939, "Need for Free Enterprise"; *Time*, July 31, 1939, "Utilities: Indiana Advocate." Willkie was highly unusual in not having previously run for or held public office. William Howard Taft had served as Theodore Roosevelt's secretary of war but had never run for public office before being elected president. Similarly Herbert Hoover had been secretary of commerce in the Harding and Coolidge administrations but had never run for office before the election of 1928.

62. Neal, *Dark Horse*, 48. See also Smith, *Thomas E. Dewey*, 293; Marcia Davenport, *Too Strong for Fantasy* (New York: Scribner, 1967), 259.

63. Davenport, *Too Strong for Fantasy*, 262ff; Neal, *Dark Horse*, 49; Alan Brinkley, *The Publisher: Henry Luce and His American Century* (New York: Knopf, 2010), 253. See also Davenport, *Too Strong for Fantasy*, 259.

64. *New York Times*, June 19, 1940, "Willkie Warns U.S. to Keep Out of War."

65. Willkie to David Lawrence, June 12 and May 22, 1939, respectively, in Neal, *Dark Horse*, 47.

66. Wendell L. Willkie, "Idle Money, Idle Men," *Saturday Evening Post*, June 17, 1939. See also Willkie, "Brace Up, America!," *Atlantic Monthly*, June 1939; Willkie, "The Faith That Is America," *Reader's Digest*, December 1939.

67. *Christian Science Monitor*, January 30, 1940, "Willkie Says He Could Not Refuse to Run."

68. Harold L. Ickes, *The Secret Diary of Harold L. Ickes*, 3 vols. (New York: Simon and Schuster, 1953–1954), February 17, 1940, 3:137.

69. Davenport to Willkie, February 18, 1940, in Neal, *Dark Horse*, 66; Davenport, *Too Strong for Fantasy*, 268.

70. Hugh Ross, "Was the Nomination of Wendell Willkie a Political Miracle?," *Indiana Magazine of History*, 58, 2 (June 1962), 83.

71. *New York Times*, April 9, 1940, "2 Primaries Today"; *New York Times*, April 11, 1940, "Gains in Primaries Elate Republicans"; Warren Moscow, *Roosevelt and Willkie* (Englewood Cliffs, N.J.: Prentice-Hall, 1968), 33; James Ceaser, *Presidential Selection: Theory and Development* (Princeton, N.J.: Princeton University Press, 1979), 229; James Beniger, "Winning the Presidential Nomination: National Polls and State Primary Elections, 1936–1972," *Public Opinion Quarterly*, 41, 1 (Spring 1976), 24, 36. Primaries became binding only after the contentious 1968 Democratic National Convention. Robert E. Burke, "Election of 1940," in *History of American Presidential Elections, 1789–1968*, 4 vols., ed. Arthur M. Schlesinger, Jr. (New York: Chelsea House, 1971), 4:2930; Peters, *Five Days in Philadelphia*, 45–46. See also Neal, *Dark Horse*, 51.

72. Brinkley, *The Publisher*, 249, 252–253; Clare Boothe, *Margin for Error* (New York: Random House, 1940).

73. Wendell Willkie, "We, the People," *Fortune*, April 1940; Guy Lemmon, Interview, Barnard Mss.; Burke, "Election of 1940," 4:2927.

74. Neal, *Dark Horse*, 68.

75. Oren Root, *Persons and Persuasions* (New York: Norton, 1974), 35. See also Peters, *Five Days in Philadelphia*, 39–40; *Time*, June 10, 1940, "Cockiest Fellow."

76. Parmet, *Never Again*, 121; Neal, *Dark Horse*, 71. Raymond Clapper wrote a series of columns about Willkie for the Scripps-Howard newspaper chain. Another of the many Republicans whom Willkie impressed was William Castle, Herbert Hoover's undersecretary of state and a member of the GOP national committee. "What a candidate he would make!" Castle said after meeting him for the first time in April. "He is the most typically American looking of men. He speaks well and with entire belief in what he is saying." William R. Castle, Jr., Diaries, Houghton Library, Harvard University, April 16, 1940, p. 18. Courtesy of J. Garry Clifford.

77. Root worked for a Wall Street firm headed by John W. Davis, who ran for president in 1924. Raymond Buell mentioned that Root was present when Willkie spoke on March 24, 1940, at the Lawyers Club in New York, and expressed his admiration for Willkie and said that Willkie should be president. Raymond Buell, unpublished memoir, p. 8, Box 13, Raymond Leslie Buell Papers, Manuscript Division, Library of Congress. Courtesy of J. Garry Clifford.

78. Beniger, "Winning the Presidential Nomination," 36; Root, *Persons and Persuasions*, 20.

79. Neal, *Dark Horse*, 69; Root, *Persons and Persuasions*, 24.

80. Peters, *Five Days in Philadelphia*, 48; Root, *Persons and Persuasions*, 31ff.

81. Root, *Persons and Persuasions*, 31; *New York Times*, April 15, 1940, "Boom for Willkie Reported Gaining"; Parmet, *Never Again*, 89, 90, 94.

82. Johnson, *Republican Party and Wendell Willkie*, 68; *Washington Post*, June 19, 1940, "'We Must Stay Out,' Willkie Says."

83. *Hartford Courant*, May 12, 1940, "Democracies Aid Favored by Willkie"; *New York Times*, May 12, 1940, "Willkie Condemns 'Commission' Rule"; Janet Flanner, "Rushville's Renowned

Son-in-Law," *New Yorker*, October 12, 1940, 39. Willkie told Flanner that the enthusiastic reaction made him run.

84. *Wall Street Journal*, May 13, 1940, "Mid-Western Politics"; *New York Times*, May 19, 1940, "Willkie Shedding 'Dark Horse' Role"; *Time*, June 10, 1940, "Cockiest Fellow."

85. *Hartford Courant*, July 1, 1940, "Willkie Has Appearance of Scholar," by Joseph Alsop and Robert Kintner; Flanner, "Rushville's Renowned Son-in-Law."

86. Wendell Willkie, "Fair Trial," *New Republic*, 102, 12 (March 18, 1940), 370–372.

87. *New York Times*, March 12, 1941, "U.S. Reading Habits Praised by Willkie." Willkie also lamented the "one-year-in-four" attitude toward politics held by Americans in general, who only got interested during an election year and the rest of the time left politics in the hands of party "professionals." Edward Weeks Interview, December 9, 1957, "Campaign—103," Barnard Mss. See also *New York Times*, May 9, 1940, "Students Form Willkie League." Willkie's invitation to review a book by Justice Frankfurter for the *Harvard Law Review* is mentioned in Ben Cohen memorandum, December 11, 1939, PSF, filed under Willkie, FDRL.

88. *Washington Post*, April 21, 1940, "Wendell Willkie: From Main Street to Wall Street"; *Time*, July 8, 1940, "Gentleman from Indiana"; *New York Times*, October 27, 1940, "The Next First Lady?"; *Christian Science Monitor*, June 12, 1940, "Edith Willkie—Wife of Leading Republican 'Dark Horse.'"

89. *New York Times*, August 20, 1940, "Ickes Belittles Willkie"; Tugwell, *Democratic Roosevelt*, 538.

90. Neal, *Dark Horse*, 38–39, 43–44. Neal quotes Shirer. Janet Flanner reported that Willkie frequented the literary salons of Dorothy Thompson and Irita Van Doren. Flanner, "Rushville's Renowned Son-in-Law."

91. John Culver and John Hyde, *American Dreamer: A Life of Henry A. Wallace* (New York: Norton, 2000), 234.

92. Peters, *Five Days in Philadelphia*, 35. In the 1948 movie *State of the Union*, Katharine Hepburn played the role of Mrs. Willkie, Spencer Tracy played that of Willkie, and Angela Lansbury played Irita Van Doren.

93. *New York Times*, May 29, 1940, "Ask Allies' Needs, Willkie Suggests."

94. Parmet, *Never Again*, 82; Wendell Willkie, "Five Minutes to Midnight," *Saturday Evening Post*, June 22, 1940.

95. *New York Times*, April 26, 1940, "Willkie Cautions on New Deal Aims"; *New York Times*, March 4, 1940, "Willkie Asks Fight."

96. Willkie, May 4, 1938, in James H. Madison, ed., *Wendell Willkie* (Bloomington: Indiana University Press, 1992), viii, 157–167; Willkie, "Five Minutes to Midnight."

97. *New York Times*, May 16, 1940, "Willkie Asks Rise in National Spirit"; *New York Times*, May 29, 1940, "Ask Allies' Needs, Willkie Suggests."

98. *Time*, June 29, 1942, "The People's Choice"; *New York Times*, December 4, 1938, "Republicans Restore Old Guard in Command"; Neal, *Dark Horse*, 89.

99. *Hartford Courant*, June 16, 1940, "W. A. White Says Willkie Has Appeal." On Liberty League, see Frederick Rudolph, "The American Liberty League, 1934–1940," *American Historical Review*, 56, 1 (October 1950), 19–33.

100. *Christian Science Monitor*, June 7, 1940, "Mirror of World Opinion: An Estimate of Wendell Willkie."

101. *New York Times*, June 19, 1940, "Willkie Warns U.S. to Keep Out of War."

102. *New York Times*, May 17, 1940, "Willkie Is Called 'Dark Horse.'"

103. Davenport, *Too Strong for Fantasy*, 227.

104. *Atlanta Constitution*, May 16, 1940, "Dorothy Thompson Asks G.O.P. to Let F.D.R. Run Unopposed"; *Washington Post*, April 5, 1940, "The Candidates on Parade" by Dorothy Thompson. For her opinions in the *Herald Tribune*, Thompson was fired, and she moved to the *New York Post*. See Lynn D. Gordon, "Why Dorothy Thompson Lost Her Job," *History of Education Quarterly*, 34, 3 (Fall 1994), 281–303.

105. FDR to Morris Ernst, May 18, 1940, in Elliott Roosevelt, ed., *F.D.R.: His Personal Letters*, 4 vols. (New York: Duell, Sloane and Pearce, 1947–1950), 2:1026.

106. *Atlanta Constitution*, May 16, 1940, "Dorothy Thompson Asks G.O.P. to Let F.D.R. Run Unopposed."

107. Raymond Buell, Foreign Affairs Memorandum to Henry Luce, December 11, 1940, Raymond Leslie Buell Papers, Manuscript Division, Library of Congress. Courtesy of J. G. Clifford.

108. *New York Times*, May 26, 1940, "Two Views of America's Part."

109. J. Garry Clifford and Samuel Spencer, *The First Peacetime Draft* (Lawrence: University Press of Kansas, 1986), 99–100. See also Raymond Buell, unpublished memoir, p. 11, Box 13, Raymond Leslie Buell Papers, Manuscript Division, Library of Congress. Courtesy of J. Garry Clifford.

110. Peters, *Five Days in Philadelphia*, 21; Johnson, *Republican Party and Wendell Willkie*, 106, note. See Patterson, *Mr. Republican*, 220.

111. *New York Times*, May 26, 1940, "War's Turn Upsets Republicans' Race." A month later, another *Times* reporter judged that a conservative isolationist stood a better chance to win the nomination than Willkie. *New York Times*, June 21, 1940, "Stimson and Knox Disowned by Party."

112. *New York Times*, April 14, 1940, "1940 Baffles Owls of Gridiron Club."

Chapter 7: Home Run for the White House

1. *New York Times*, May 25, 1940, "President Derides Talk of Coalition"; *Washington Post*, May 25, 1940, "Coalition Cabinet"; *Hartford Courant*, May 25, 1940, "FDR Spikes Coalition."

2. Fireside Chat on National Defense, May 26, 1940, in Samuel I. Rosenman, ed., *Public Papers and Addresses of Franklin D. Roosevelt [PPA]*, 13 vols. (New York: Macmillan, 1941), 9:239.

3. *New York Times*, October 3, 1936, "Denies Roosevelt Averted a Revolt"; *New York Times*, September 3, 1936, "Knox Sees 'Aliens' Ruling Democrats"; *New York Times*, October 8, 1936, "Knox Warns Labor against New Deal." On the campaign trail, Knox oscillated between charging that the president's "squandering" of public money was the "recourse of a dictator" (*New York Times*, October 8, 1936, "Knox Warns Labor against New Deal") and allowing that the New Deal "is not planning a dictatorship; it just has delusions of grandeur" (*New York Times*, September 8, 1936, "Knox Warns Labor to Shun 'Iron Hand'").

4. Reminiscences of Frances Perkins, p. 315, Columbia Center for Oral History Collection (CCOHC); Frances Perkins, *The Roosevelt I Knew* (New York: Viking, 1946), 5–6.

5. *Chicago Daily News*, October 6, 1937, quoted in Steven M. Mark, *An American Interventionist: Frank Knox and United States Foreign Relations*, unpublished Ph.D. dissertation, University of Maryland, 1977, 192.

6. *Chicago Daily News*, September 2 and 7, 1939, in Mark, *American Interventionist*, 211.

7. Knox to White, May 28, 1940, quoted in Mark, *American Interventionist*, 230.

8. *New York Times*, May 12, 1940, "Knox Demands Defense Arming"; *New York Times*, May 18, 1940, "Col. Knox to Form Air 'Plattsburgs'"; *New York Times*, February 1, 1941, "Secretary Knox's Statement to Senate Group."

9. *New York Times*, July 3, 1940, "Knox Urges Every Possible Aid to Great Britain"; *Los Angeles Times*, January 2, 1940, "Knox Offered Navy Post"; Knox, Memorandum of Conversation with President Roosevelt on December 10, 1939, at White House, in Wayne Cole, *Roosevelt and the Isolationists* (Lincoln: University of Nebraska Press, 1983), 369.

10. See FDR to Edison, October 9, 1939, and FDR to Henry Knox, December 29, 1939, in Elliott Roosevelt, ed., *F.D.R.: His Personal Letters*, 3 vols. (New York: Duell, Sloan and Pearce, 1947–1950), 2:936–937, 975–976.

11. Knox, memorandum of his conversation with FDR, December 10, 1939, quoted in Mark, *American Interventionist*, 233–234. Historian John Morton Blum wrote that Edison was not only a tepid New Dealer but "worse than tepid as an administrator." John Morton Blum, ed., *From the Morgenthau Diaries*, 3 vols. (Boston: Houghton Mifflin, 1959–1967), 2:165. Harold Ickes wrote in his diary that at a White House meeting, "I remarked in an undertone to Harry [Hopkins] that

Edison seemed to me to be a very stupid person and unfitted for the job that he held. Harry cheerfully acquiesced." Harold Ickes, unpublished diary, June 15, 1940, Manuscript Division, Library of Congress. Courtesy of J. Garry Clifford.

12. Robert Sherwood, *Roosevelt and Hopkins: An Intimate History*, rev. ed. (New York: Harper and Brothers, 1950), 136. See also *New York Times*, December 31, 1939, "Edison Appointed Naval Secretary."

13. *New York Times*, July 3, 1940, "Knox Urges Every Possible Aid to Great Britain"; *New York Times*, June 21, 1940, "Knox Once Severe as New Deal Critic."

14. James MacGregor Burns, *Roosevelt: The Lion and the Fox* (New York: Harcourt, Brace, 1956), 424; Ed Cray, *General of the Army: George C. Marshall* (New York: Norton, 1990), 161. See also Blum, *From the Morgenthau Diaries*, 2:166.

15. Kenneth S. Davis, *FDR: Into the Storm, 1937–1940* (New York: Random House), 572. On Patterson, see J. Garry Clifford, ed., *The World War I Memoirs of Robert P. Patterson* (Knoxville: University of Tennessee Press, 2012).

16. Burns, *Roosevelt: The Lion and the Fox*, 121–122.

17. Reminiscences of Henry L. Stimson, 1949, p. 21, CCOHC.

18. Burns, *Roosevelt: The Lion and the Fox*, 251–252, 424; Sherwood, *Roosevelt and Hopkins*, 163; Davis, *FDR: Into the Storm*, 500; *New York Times*, March 7, 1939, "Ex-Secretary Stimson's Letter on Foreign Relations." See also Blum, *From the Morgenthau Diaries*, 2:166.

19. Davis, *FDR: Into the Storm*, 572.

20. Harold L. Ickes, *The Secret Diary of Harold L. Ickes*, 3 vols. (New York: Simon and Schuster, 1953–1954), February 7, 1940, 3:133 and 136; Harold Ickes, unpublished diary, June 12, 1940, Library of Congress. Courtesy of J. Garry Clifford. In his unpublished diary, Ickes wrote in early June 1940: "Pa [Watson] admitted to me at luncheon yesterday that, from the beginning, he did not believe that the President would force Woodring out and that is just about my own state of mind. On the other hand, Ross McIntire thinks that he will and that the chances of his offering the place to me are good. . . . I heard the other day that Woodring was telling people that the President would not dare to fire him because he and Morgenthau and Bill Bullitt knew too much about the extent to which the president had broken the law in shipping supplies to the Allies." Harold Ickes, unpublished diary, June 12, 1940.

21. Mark A. Stoler, *George C. Marshall: Soldier-Statesman of the American Century* (New York: Twayne, 1989), 63, 72.

22. James Farley Papers, January 10, 1939, Box 43, p. 10, Manuscript Division, Library of Congress. Courtesy of J. Garry Clifford.

23. William R. Castle, Jr., Diaries, Houghton Library, Harvard University, February 3, 1940, p. 13. Though Castle would become a national committee member of America First, he believed in loyalty and felt that neither Woodring nor Joseph Kennedy showed the proper loyalty to the commander in chief. Castle Diary, October 30, 1940, p. 383. See also Wayne S. Cole, *America First: The Battle against American Intervention, 1940–1941* (Madison: University of Wisconsin Press, 1953), 22. Ickes wrote: "I have always regarded Woodring as poor stuff and if he could strike back at the president without hurting himself, in my opinion, he would do it without hesitation." Harold Ickes, unpublished diary, June 23, 1940, Library of Congress. Courtesy of J. Garry Clifford.

24. Sherwood, *Roosevelt and Hopkins*, 135, 137; Burns, *Roosevelt: The Lion and the Fox*, 416.

25. FDR to Woodring, March 11, 1940, in Roosevelt, *F.D.R.: His Personal Letters*, 2:1007; Ickes, *Secret Diary*, May 19, 1940, 3:180.

26. Robert Dallek, *Franklin D. Roosevelt and American Foreign Policy, 1932–1945* (New York: Oxford University Press, 1979), 228; Davis, *FDR: Into the Storm*, 554; Burns, *Roosevelt: The Lion and the Fox*, 420.

27. Davis, *FDR: Into the Storm*, 573; FDR to Woodring, in Roosevelt, *F.D.R.: His Personal Letters*, 2:1044; J. Garry Clifford and Samuel Spencer, *The First Peacetime Draft* (Lawrence: University Press of Kansas, 1986), 92; Morgenthau Interview, April 25, 1946, Box 391, Morgenthau Papers, quoted in Thomas G. Paterson, J. Garry Clifford, and Deborah Kisatsky, *American Foreign Relations: A History*, 2 vols. (Lexington: Heath, 1995), 2:113.

28. Harold Ickes, unpublished diary, June 29, 1940, Library of Congress. Courtesy of J. Garry Clifford. *New York Times*, March 21, 1940, "Edison to Be Jersey Candidate."

29. Mark, *American Interventionist*, 243–244; Burns, *Roosevelt: The Lion and the Fox*, 424; Henry Stimson Diaries, June 25, 1940, Reel 6, vol. 29, p. 56, Yale University Library, Manuscripts and Archives; Henry L. Stimson and McGeorge Bundy, *On Active Service in Peace and War* (New York: Harper and Brothers, 1948), 323. After hearing FDR's speech in Charlottesville on June 10, 1940, Knox wrote to his wife, "From now on we are in the war until Germany and her jackal partner Italy are well licked." A few days later he wrote, "The sooner we declare war the sooner we will get ready." Knox to Mrs. Knox, June 11 and June 15, 1940, quoted in Warren Kimball, *The Most Unsordid Act: Lend-Lease 1939–1941* (Baltimore, Md.: Johns Hopkins University Press, 1969), 59.

30. Clifford and Spencer, *First Peacetime Draft*, 89; Stimson and Bundy, *On Active Service*, 324. Stimson also mentioned that he wanted Robert Patterson as his assistant secretary, an appointment that got delayed later on. See Henry Stimson Diaries, June 25, 1940, vol. 29, Reel 6, p. 56, Yale University Library, Manuscripts and Archives. See also Larry Bland, ed., *The Papers of George Catlett Marshall*, 5 vols. (Baltimore, Md.: Johns Hopkins University Press, 1981–), 2:251, editorial note; Godfrey Hodgson, *The Colonel: The Life and Wars of Henry Stimson* (New York: Knopf, 1990), 214.

31. *New York Times*, June 21, 1940, "Capital Surprised," italics added.

32. George C. Marshall, letter to his wife, June 28, 1940, in Bland, *Papers of George Catlett Marshall*, 2:252; Stoler, *George C. Marshall*, 73.

33. David Reynolds, "Lord Lothian and Anglo-American Relations, 1939–1940," *Transactions of the American Philosophical Society*, New Series, 73, 2 (1983), 4; Clifford and Spencer, *First Peacetime Draft*, 93.

34. *New York Times*, June 21, 1940, "Capital Surprised"; *Atlanta Constitution*, June 23, 1940, "Master Stroke by Roosevelt Stuns G.O.P."; *Chicago Daily Tribune*, June 21, 1940, "Changes in the Cabinet."

35. *New York Times*, June 22, 1940, "Senate Hearings Ordered on Stimson's Nomination"; *Chicago Daily Tribune*, June 22, 1940, "Roosevelt War Policy Arouses Growing Storm"; *Los Angeles Times*, June 22, 1940, "Woodring Blast Starts Battle"; Wayne S. Cole, *Senator Gerald P. Nye and American Foreign Relations* (Minneapolis: University of Minnesota Press, 1962), 173.

36. Joe Martin, *My First Fifty Years* (New York: McGraw-Hill, 1960), 153.

37. Clifford and Spencer, *First Peacetime Draft*, 91.

38. *New York Times*, June 22, 1940, "Senate Hearings Ordered."

39. *Hartford Courant*, June 23, 1940, "White Sees Naming of Knox, Stimson as 'Time Bomb.'" The Senate went on to confirm Knox by a vote of 66 to 16, with 17 Republicans voting for him, and only 5 against. Stimson did not fare as well. He was confirmed in the Senate by a vote of 56 to 28, with 10 Republicans voting for him and 12 against.

40. *New York Times*, May 22, 1940, "Hoover on Record against Coalition"; *New York Times*, June 21, 1940, "Action on Cabinet Attacked by Dewey."

41. Ickes, *Secret Diary*, June 23, 1940, 3:215.

Chapter 8: The Republicans in Philadelphia

1. *New York Times*, June 23, 1940, "Candidates Stage Battle of Stunts."

2. *New York Times*, June 25, 1940, "Heat, Noise, Music"; *Time*, July 8, 1940, "The Sun Also Rises."

3. *New York Times*, June 25, 1940, "Heat, Noise, Music."

4. Charles Peters, *Five Days in Philadelphia: The Amazing "We Want Willkie!" Convention of 1940* (New York: PublicAffairs, 2005), 59.

5. *Washington Post*, May 21, 1940, "Willkie Bids for 'Write-In'"; *Chicago Daily Tribune*, June 24, 1940, "Willkie Claims Vote Promises from 45 States." See also Peters, *Five Days in Philadelphia*, 69.

6. Cowles Interview, p. 27, Barnard Mss., Manuscripts Department, Lilly Library, Indiana University, Bloomington. Courtesy of J. Garry Clifford.

7. "Someday they will write about how naive I was," Willkie said, "but I didn't want to spoil their illusions." Donald Johnson, *The Republican Party and Wendell Willkie* (Urbana: University of Illinois Press, 1960), 79, note.

8. *Atlanta Constitution*, June 25, 1940, "The Capital Parade," by Joseph Alsop, Robert Kintner; *New York Times*, June 24, 1940, "New Gains for Willkie."

9. *Christian Science Monitor*, June 25, 1940, "'Advance with Determination'"; *Chicago Daily Tribune*, June 25, 1940, "Build Defense, Walk in Peace, Stassen Tells Convention." See also Peters, *Five Days in Philadelphia*, 75.

10. Charles de Gaulle, *War Memoirs*, 3 vols. (New York: Viking Press, 1955–1960), 1:73. See also Robert Paxton, *Vichy France: Old Guard and New Order* (New York: Knopf, 1972), 9; William Shirer, *20th Century Journey: A Memoir of a Life and the Times*, 3 vols. (Boston: Little, Brown, 1976–1990), 2:544.

11. *New York Times*, June 25, 1940, "Nazi Bugle Blares Tidings to the World."

12. Shirer, *20th Century Journey*, 2:524.

13. Albert Speer, *Inside the Third Reich* (New York: Macmillan, 1970), 172.

14. *New York Times*, August 13, 1941, "Text of Pétain's Broadcast." See also Kenneth S. Davis, *FDR: Into the Storm, 1937–1940* (New York: Random House, 1993), 561. A French aircraft carrier loaded with forty-four American dive-bombers and sixty-two other planes never made its way to France and docked instead in Martinique, where its cargo would spend the rest of the war, but hundreds of thousands of rifles, artillery guns, and machine guns got through to England. Willkie's foreign policy advisor Raymond Buell later thought that FDR might pull an "October Surprise" and seize Martinique in the final days of the campaign.

15. Virginia Cowles, "Flight from Paris, June 1940," in *Reporting World War II*, 2 vols. (New York: Library of America, 1995), 1:53–54.

16. William L. Shirer, *Berlin Diary* (New York: Knopf, 1941), June 17, 1940, 410.

17. *New York Times*, June 24, 1940, "Churchill Warned against Terms"; *New York Times*, June 26, 1940, "Churchill Bitter"; *New York Times*, June 26, 1940, "Nazis View France as Key to New Era."

18. *New York Times*, June 28, 1940, "Convention Called Marvel in This Age," by Anne O'Hare McCormick; *Los Angeles Times*, June 25, 1940, "Control Lost by Party Leaders."

19. *New York Times*, June 28, 1940, "Convention Called Marvel in This Age."

20. Steve Neal, *Dark Horse: A Biography of Wendell Willkie* (Garden City, N.Y.: Doubleday, 1984), 108.

21. *New York Times*, June 19, 1940, "Lewis Defends the Hoover Regime." See also Hugh Ross, "John L. Lewis and the Election of 1940," *Labor History*, 17, 2 (1976), 177; *New York Times*, June 20, 1940, "Effort Is Started to Block Willkie"; *New York Times*, June 22, 1940, "Quits Lewis Group in Third Term Row." See also Neal, *Dark Horse*, 101; *New York Times*, July 12, 1940, "Roosevelt Willing." Hans Thomsen, the German chargé d'affaires in Washington, informed his Foreign Ministry of Lewis's helpful activities, reporting that he was "determined to make ruthless use of his influence . . . not indeed because of any pro-German sentiments, but because he fears that America's involvement in a war would mean . . . the placing of his organization under emergency laws." Thomsen to Foreign Ministry, July 4, 1940, *Documents on German Foreign Policy, 1918–1945*, Series D (1937–1945), 13 vols. (Washington, D.C.: United States Government Printing Office, 1947–), Document 108, 10:120–121.

22. Peters, *Five Days in Philadelphia*, 58; *New York Times*, June 26, 1940, "Convention Uses Lungs"; *Time*, July 8, 1940, "The Sun Also Rises."

23. *New York Times*, June 26, 1940, "Text of Former President's Address"; *Chicago Daily Tribune*, June 27, 1940, "Furious Battle Rages"; *Time*, July 8, 1940, "The Sun Also Rises." See also Gary Dean Best, *Herbert Hoover: The Postpresidential Years, 1933–1964*, 2 vols. (Stanford, Calif.: Hoover Institution Press, 1983), 1:159–161.

24. *Hartford Courant*, June 26, 1940, "Mr. Hoover's Stirring Address." Hoover and the *Courant*'s editor, Maurice Sherman, were friends. *Washington Post*, June 2, 1940, "Mr. Hoover's Message."

25. *New York Times*, June 25, 1940; *Los Angeles Times*, June 26, 1940, "Page Advertisements Summon Nation." Years later, documents came to light indicating that the German embassy had

helped pay for the ads. See Thomsen to Foreign Ministry, June 12, 1940, in *Documents on German Foreign Policy*, Series D, Document 417, 9:550–551. For his part, Fish later said he regretted that the Nazis had not spent more to ensure American nonparticipation in the war. He also provided use of his office for the mailing activities of a Nazi agent, George Sylvester Viereck (Herbert Parmet, *Never Again: A President Runs for a Third Term* [New York: Macmillan, 1968], 139).

26. Thomsen to Foreign Ministry, June 12, 1940, in *Documents on German Foreign Policy*, Series D, Document 417, 9:551. See also Alton Frye, *Nazi Germany and the American Hemisphere* (New Haven, Conn.: Yale University Press, 1967), 136–137. The expenses were authorized by Berlin. See Thomsen to Foreign Ministry, July 3, 1940, in *Documents on German Foreign Policy*, Series D, Document 91, 10:101–102. See also Ross, "John L. Lewis and the Election of 1940," 175–177.

27. Thomsen to Foreign Ministry, June 12, 1940, in *Documents on German Foreign Policy*, Series D, Document 417, 9: 551. See also Thomsen to Foreign Ministry, June 19, 1940, in *Documents on German Foreign Policy*, Series D, Document 493, 9:625–626. See also Frye, *Nazi Germany and the American Hemisphere*, 136; Ross, "John L. Lewis and the Election of 1940," 174.

28. Ross, "John L. Lewis and the Election of 1940," 175.

29. *New York Times*, June 27, 1940, "Peace Made Issue"; *New York Times*, June 26, 1940, "Ban Intervention." Any other slant would have ratified Roosevelt's policies and his appointment of Stimson and Knox, so the GOP predictably adhered to its isolationist stance. *New York Times*, June 23, 1940, "Republicans Confused on Eve of Convention."

30. *Time*, July 8, 1940, "The Sun Also Rises."

31. *New York Times*, June 27, 1940, "Peace Made Issue."

32. *Time*, July 1, 1940, "The Trumpets Blow."

33. Raymond Clapper, column, June 27, 1940, in Raymond Clapper, *Watching the World*, ed. Mrs. Raymond Clapper (New York: Whittlesey House/McGraw Hill, 1944), 156.

34. *New York Times*, June 22, 1940, "White Hails Choice of Knox, Stimson."

35. *New York Times*, July 17, 1940, "Platform Is Ready"; *New York Times*, July 6, 1940, "Democrats Seek Platform for All"; Alfred Landon to Roy Howard, July 20, 1940, in Alfred M. Landon Papers, Kansas Historical Society, Topeka. Courtesy of J. Garry Clifford.

36. Robert A. Divine, *Foreign Policy and U.S. Presidential Elections, 1940–1948* (New York: New Viewpoints, 1974), 28. *New York Times*, June 27, 1940, "War Plank Called Shaky Compromise"; *New York Times*, June 26, 1940, "Ban Intervention."

37. *New York Times*, June 25, 1940, "Willkie Is Opposed." See also Neal, *Dark Horse*, 97–98. See also *Atlanta Constitution*, June 25, 1940, "Willkie Halted."

38. Peters, *Five Days in Philadelphia*, 69; *Time*, June 3, 1940, "Candidates and the War."

39. Harold Ickes, unpublished diary, June 5, 1940, Manuscript Division, Library of Congress. Courtesy of J. Garry Clifford.

40. *Hartford Courant*, June 22, 1940, and June 25, 1940, "Today and Tomorrow," by Walter Lippmann. See also Robert Sherwood, *Roosevelt and Hopkins: An Intimate History*, rev. ed. (New York: Harper and Brothers, 1950), 174.

41. Joe Martin, *My First Fifty Years in Politics* (New York: McGraw-Hill, 1960), 159.

42. Peters, *Five Days in Philadelphia*, 69. See also *Chicago Daily Tribune*, June 24, 1940, "Willkie Claims Vote Promises from 45 States"; *Time*, July 8, 1940, "The Sun Also Rises." See Neal, *Dark Horse*, 83, 87. To another group Willkie said, "I haven't any trades to make. Take me or leave me." Neal, *Dark Horse*, 96.

43. Hugh Ross, "Was the Nomination of Wendell Willkie a Political Miracle?," *Indiana Magazine of History*, 58, 2 (June 1962), 83. Iowa's first ballot votes, for instance, would go to Hanford MacNider, a diplomat who had served in the Coolidge and Hoover administrations—even though Dewey won seventy-four of the seventy-six straw polls held in Iowa cities; Pennsylvania's votes would go to Governor Arthur James on the first ballot; Massachusetts's unpledged delegates would back House minority leader Joe Martin on the first two ballots, though a group of delegates, led by Henry Cabot Lodge and Governor Saltonstall, let it be known that they would switch to Willkie on the third ballot; New Hampshire's delegates would go for Senator Styles Bridges on the

first ballot; Kansas's to 75-year-old senator Arthur Capper on the first ballot, after which delegates were expected to follow the lead of Alf Landon; and, in Connecticut, Governor Raymond Baldwin, his state's favorite son, agreed to lead his delegation to Willkie on the second ballot.

44. *Los Angeles Times*, June 15, 1940, "Illinois G.O.P. Convention Sidetracks Pledge for Dewey"; *Los Angeles Times*, June 16, 1940, "Willkie Gains as Dark Horse"; *Wall Street Journal*, June 7, 1940, "Presidential Politics: Taft, Dewey First Ballot Strength about Even"; *Chicago Daily Tribune*, June 15, 1940, "76 Iowa Towns Pick Dewey"; Ross, "Was the Nomination of Wendell Willkie a Political Miracle?," 85–88.

45. *Washington Post*, June 9, 1940, "Outcome of G.O.P. Convention Uncertain," by Mark Sullivan.

46. *New York Times*, June 23, 1940, "Crowds Welcome 'Big Three' of Race." "Doesn't that mean war?" an onlooker asked Willkie. "That's a matter of opinion," Willkie said, skirting a direct answer. *Chicago Daily Tribune*, June 24, 1940, "Willkie Claims Vote Promises from 45 States." Without that isolationist edge in Willkie's Brooklyn speech, however staged and calculated it was, Raymond Buell later commented, "Willkie could not have been nominated." Raymond Buell, unpublished memoir, p. 11, Box 13, Raymond Leslie Buell Papers, Manuscript Division, Library of Congress. Courtesy of J. Garry Clifford.

47. Knox to Willkie, March 23, 1940, in Neal, *Dark Horse*, 69.

48. James H. Madison, *Wendell Willkie, Hoosier Internationalist* (Bloomington: Indiana University Press, 1992), 24; *Chicago Daily Tribune*, June 25, 1940, "G.O.P. Convention Cheers 'American Way.'"

49. Harold Stassen interview, Washington, D.C., December 28, 1956, in Barnard Mss.; *New York Times*, June 24, 1940, "Gains for Willkie"; Ross, "Was the Nomination of Wendell Willkie a Political Miracle?," 91.

50. Arthur Vandenberg, "Inside Stuff—Real History," Vandenberg scrapbooks and diaries, vol. 12, Bentley Historical Library, University of Michigan, Ann Arbor. Vandenberg wrote that he said, "Tell Dewey that I think the Vice Presidency is very important and that if I were not a Senator I would take it, but I think—as I did in 1936—that my place on the Senate floor is more important than on the Senate rostrum." See also Arthur Vandenberg, *The Private Papers of Senator Vandenberg*, ed. Arthur Vandenberg, Jr. (Boston: Houghton Mifflin, 1952). See also *Washington Post*, June 25, 1940, "Lots of Spinach." In response to "stop Willkie" moves, Vandenberg declared that the only "stop" movement he knew of was one to "stop Roosevelt." *Hartford Courant*, June 24 1940, "Baldwin Will Back Willkie."

51. Best, *Herbert Hoover*, 1:152; *Chicago Daily Tribune*, June 27, 1940, "Furious Battle." When Willkie heard that Hoover might oppose him, he jumped into a taxi, went to Hoover's hotel, and talked with Hoover face to face, later commenting only that their conversation had been "pleasant and highly satisfactory." *New York Times*, June 30, 1940, "Willkie's 'Miracle' Rise."

52. *New York Times*, June 27, 1940, "4 Are Nominated."

53. *New York Times*, May 17, 1940, "Gannett Says Speech Indicates a Failure."

54. Charles Halleck Oral History, conducted by James T. Patterson, December 1969, p. 75, Oral History Project, Indiana University. See also Ross, "Was the Nomination of Wendell Willkie a Political Miracle?," 70–100.

55. Martin, *My First Fifty Years in Politics*, 151.

56. Halleck Oral History, pp. 82, 101, 80, respectively.

57. *Chicago Daily Tribune*, June 17, 1940, "Nominating Speeches." See also *New York Times*, June 27, 1940, "4 Are Nominated." Sam Pryor, a wealthy Connecticut politico who was in charge of the convention's important arrangements committee, later admitted that he had given most of the spectator tickets to Willkie activists. Johnson, *Republican Party and Wendell Willkie*, 92. See also Neal, *Dark Horse*, 105; *Hartford Courant*, June 2, 1940, "'See Sam Pryor' Becomes Philadelphia Watchword."

58. Marquis Childs, in Neal, *Dark Horse*, 44.

59. *New York Times*, June 28, 1940, "New Gallup Survey Is Not Yet Ready"; James Beniger, "Winning the Presidential Nomination: National Polls and State Primary Elections, 1936–1972,"

Public Opinion Quarterly, 41, 1 (Spring 1976), 29. Willkie topped Dewey only in the last of sixteen polls taken before the nomination.

60. Parmet, *Never Again*, 145; Peters, *Five Days in Philadelphia*, 98.

61. *New York Times*, June 27, 1940, "In the Nation"; *Hartford Courant*, June 26, 1940, "Today and Tomorrow," by Walter Lippmann.

62. *Christian Science Monitor*, June 29, 1940, "Intimate Message from Philadelphia."

63. *New York Times*, June 28, 1940, "Fighting Pledge Made by Willkie."

64. Peters, *Five Days in Philadelphia*, 101; Richard Norton Smith, *Thomas E. Dewey and His Times* (New York: Simon and Schuster, 1982), 308–309; *New York Times*, June 24, 1940, "New Gains for Willkie"; Neal, *Dark Horse*, 109.

65. *New York Times*, June 28, 1940, "Rivals Worn Down."

66. *Washington Post*, June 28, 1940, "Willkie Rises after Parley in Elevator"; Neal, *Dark Horse*, 97.

67. Peters, *Five Days in Philadelphia*, 102; *New York Times*, June 28, 1940, "Rivals Worn Down."

68. Diary of Courtney Letts de Espil, insert to p. 1191 (June 28, 1940), Courtney Letts de Espil Mss., Manuscript Division, Library of Congress. Courtesy of J. Garry Clifford.

69. *New York Times*, June 28, 1940, "Rivals Worn Down."

70. Interview with Harold J. Gallaher, September 18, 1953, in Barnard Mss., "Nomination."

71. Martin, *My First Fifty Years*, 155.

72. Neal, *Dark Horse*, 112.

73. Peters, *Five Days in Philadelphia*, 102–103; Neal, *Dark Horse*, 112.

74. Martin, *My First Fifty Years*, 156; Neal, *Dark Horse*, 113. Johnson, in *Republican Party and Wendell Willkie*, 99, writes that Willkie was a little dejected after the fifth ballot, saying, "Well, he [Taft] might get it. At least I scared them."

75. Martin, *My First Fifty Years*, 156.

76. Parmet, *Never Again*, 155.

77. *Time*, July 8 1940, "The Sun Also Rises"; Neal, *Dark Horse*, 114.

78. Martin, *My First Fifty Years*, 157; Oren Root, *Persons and Persuasions* (New York: Norton, 1974), 41.

79. Peters, *Five Days in Philadelphia*, 106–109; Neal, *Dark Horse*, 115–116; Halleck Oral History, p. 80. On the sixth ballot, Hoover had nine votes and Dewey eight.

80. Marcia Davenport, *Too Strong for Fantasy* (New York: Scribner, 1967), 273; Peters, *Five Days in Philadelphia*, 108.

81. *New York Times*, June 28, 1940, "Rivals Worn Down."

82. *New York Times*, June 29, 1940, "Opinion of Newspapers on the Nomination of Willkie."

83. Clapper, *Watching the World*, June 28, 1940, 158–159.

84. *New York Times*, June 29, 1940, "Opinion of Newspapers on the Nomination of Willkie"; *Time*, July 8, 1940, "The Sun Also Rises." Only the contrarian Harold Ickes had a different take on Willkie's nomination. In his mind, it was a "masterful piece of work" engineered by the big financial interests and stage-managed by able advertising executives, to "make the people believe that it was an uprising on their part." Harold L. Ickes, *The Secret Diary of Harold L. Ickes*, 3 vols. (New York: Simon and Schuster, 1953–1954), July 18, 1940, 3:268.

85. *New York Times*, June 28, 1940, "Convention Called Marvel in This Age." Sherwood, *Roosevelt and Hopkins*, 173.

86. Gardner Cowles, Willkie's supporter, said this years later. Cowles, interview conducted by Neal, in Neal, *Dark Horse*, 120.

87. "I would not accept a nomination on a platform in which I did not believe," Willkie wrote to Arthur Krock in December 1939. But in his April 1940 *Fortune* article, "We, the People," he wrote that Americans were rightly suspicious of political platforms, even those of the winning party, because they were often forgotten after the election.

88. Neal, *Dark Horse*, 119–120; *New York Times*, June 30, 1940, "Our Isolation Over." The *Yorkshire Post* described Willkie's nomination as "one of those minor miracles of which the Allied

cause stands in need. . . . The isolationists are defeated. Both Republicans and Democrats as a whole are in favor of swift and extensive aid to the Allies."

89. Thomsen to the Foreign Ministry, June 28, 1940, in *Documents on German Foreign Policy*, Series D, Document 47, 10:48–49; Thomsen to the Foreign Ministry, July 3, 1940, in *Documents on German Foreign Policy*, Series D, Document 91, 10:101–102. See also Ross, "John L. Lewis and the Election of 1940," 175; Saul Friedländer, *Prelude to Downfall: Hitler and the United States, 1939–1941* (New York: Knopf, 1967), 101.

90. *New York Times*, July 28, 1940, "British and Nazis View Our Election"; *New York Times*, October 26, 1940, "Wallace Charges Nazis Are Ordered to Assist Willkie."

91. *Hartford Courant*, June 24, 1940, "Baldwin Will Back Willkie."

92. Ickes, *Secret Diary*, June 29, 1940, 3:222; *New York Times*, June 29, 1940, "GOP Closes Convention"; Martin, *My First Fifty Years in Politics*, 160.

93. *New York Times*, June 25, 1940, "Willkie Is Opposed by Congress Group"; Neal, *Dark Horse*, 93.

94. Ickes, *Secret Diary*, June 29, 1940, 3:222. See also Neal, *Dark Horse*, 118; Martin, *My First Fifty Years*, 160; *New York Times*, June 29, 1940, "Senator Drafted." See also Peters, *Five Days in Philadelphia*, 110.

95. Martin, *My First Fifty Years*, 160; Neal, *Dark Horse*, 118; Halleck Oral History, p. 91.

96. *New York Times*, June 29, 1940, "Delegates at Final Session."

97. *Atlanta Constitution*, June 29, 1940, "Willkie Sounds Call."

98. *New York Times*, June 29, 1940, "Willkie Breaks Party Tradition."

99. *New York Times*, June 29, 1940, "Text of Willkie's Address"; *Hartford Courant*, June 29, 1940, "Willkie Says Campaign to Be Crusade."

100. Philip Willkie Interview, August 6, 1953, "Loyal Opposition—8," Barnard Mss.

101. *New York Times*, June, 29, 1940, "Senator Drafted." See also Neal, *Dark Horse*, 121.

102. Neal, *Dark Horse*, 119. Taft to Richard Scandrett, November 15, 1940, in Clarence Wunderlin, Jr., ed., *Papers of Robert A. Taft*, 4 vols. (Kent, Ohio: Kent State University Press, 1997–2006), 2:202; Charles A. Lindbergh, *The Wartime Journals of Charles A. Lindbergh* (New York: Harcourt Brace Jovanovich, 1970), September 17, 1940, 390.

103. *Atlanta Constitution*, July 12, 1940, "Capital Parade."

104. Frances Perkins, quoted in Kristin Downey, *The Woman behind the New Deal: The Life of Frances Perkins* (New York: Nan A. Talese/Doubleday, 2009), 309.

105. Sherwood, *Roosevelt and Hopkins*, 174.

106. *Washington Post*, October 2, 1940, "Willkie's Text, Pledging Jobs."

107. *New York Times*, July 9, 1940, "The Third Term"; *Washington Post*, October 10, 1940, and July 2, 1940, "Today and Tomorrow," by Walter Lippmann; *Washington Post*, July 7, 1940, "Roosevelt Ponders Third Term Course," by Ernest Lindley.

108. Ross Gregory, "Politics in an Age of Crisis: America, and Indiana, in the Election of 1940," *Indiana Magazine of History*, 86, 3 (September 1990), 262.

109. Sherwood, *Roosevelt and Hopkins*, 176. See also *New York Times*, July 2, 1940, "Willkie Is Hopeful of Roosevelt Race." *Washington Post*, July 15, 1940, "Democrats against Third Term." Willkie expressed hope that President Roosevelt would run for a third term. "Why?" he was asked. "Because I want to beat him," he replied.

110. *New York Times*, June 29, 1940, "GOP Closes Convention."

Chapter 9: Roosevelt's Game

1. John Adams to Abigail, May 29, 1775, in James MacGregor Burns and Susan Dunn, *George Washington* (New York: Times Books/Henry Holt, 2004), 23, italics added.

2. George Washington, Address to the Continental Congress, June 16, 1775, in Susan Dunn, ed., *Something That Will Surprise the World: The Essential Writings of the Founding Fathers* (New York: Basic Books, 2006), 36.

3. Washington to Martha Washington, June 18, 1775, in Dunn, *Something That Will Surprise the World*, 36–38.

4. Acceptance of Nomination, July 19, 1940, in Samuel I. Rosenman, ed., *The Public Papers and Addresses of Franklin D. Roosevelt [PPA]*, 13 vols. (New York: Macmillan, 1941), 9:296–297.

5. James MacGregor Burns, *Roosevelt: The Lion and the Fox* (New York: Harcourt, Brace, 1956), 161, italics added

6. Burns, *Roosevelt: The Lion and the Fox*, 101.

7. *New York Times*, March 31, 1940, "Holds Roosevelt Risks Party Ruin." See also *Washington Post*, March 1, 1940, "Roosevelt's Silence Scored by Johnson."

8. Robert Sherwood, *Roosevelt and Hopkins: An Intimate History*, rev. ed. (New York: Harper and Brothers, 1950), 99; Harry Hopkins Papers, Georgetown University, Box 46, Folder 2, June 1939. See also Herbert Parmet, *Never Again: A President Runs for a Third Term* (New York, Macmillan, 1968), 19. FDR always had Hopkins at his elbow in 1938, wanting him to be included in photographs at baseball parks and fishing cruises. Even Eleanor Roosevelt wrote in her "My Day" column: "He is one of the few people in the world who gives me the feeling of being entirely absorbed in doing his job well."

9. Robert H. Jackson, *That Man: An Insider's Portrait of Franklin D. Roosevelt*, ed. John Q. Barrett (New York: Oxford University Press, 2003), 31–32. See also FDR's speech at the Democratic Victory dinner, March 4, 1937: "My great ambition on January 20, 1941, is to turn over this desk and chair in the White House to my successor, whoever he may be, with the assurance that I am at the same time turning over to him as President, a nation intact, a nation at peace, a nation prosperous." *PPA*, 6:114.

10. Cordell Hull, *Memoirs of Cordell Hull*, 2 vols. (New York: Macmillan, 1948), 1:859. Frances Perkins considered Paul McNutt, a former Indiana governor with presidential aspirations, a vain stuffed shirt. She thought Roosevelt bought his support by naming him to head the Social Security Board. FDR told Perkins that he gave McNutt "something" to keep him in the president's corner. See Kristin Downey, *The Woman behind the New Deal: The Life of Frances Perkins* (New York: Nan A. Talese/Doubleday, 2009), 304–305; Ross Gregory, "Politics in an Age of Crisis: America, and Indiana, in the Election of 1940," *Indiana Magazine of History*, 86, 3 (September 1990), 256ff; Burton K. Wheeler and Paul Healy, *Yankee from the West* (Garden City, N.Y.: Doubleday, 1962), 353ff.

11. Burns, *Roosevelt: The Lion and the Fox*, 412. See also FDR to Herbert Lehman, March 26, 1940, in Elliott Roosevelt, ed., *F.D.R.: His Personal Letters*, 3 vols. (New York: Duell, Sloan and Pearce, 1947–1950), 2:1009.

12. James MacGregor Burns, *Leadership* (New York: Harper and Row, 1978), 39–40. See also Michael Beschloss, *Kennedy and Roosevelt: The Uneasy Alliance* (New York: Norton, 1980), 201.

13. Burns, *Roosevelt: The Lion and the Fox*, 411–413. See also *New York Times*, April 21, 1940, "Many Signs Now Point to a Roosevelt 'Draft.'" Paul McNutt dropped out of contention in late May, saying that the country needed FDR to run again.

14. Burns, *Leadership*, 39. See also *Hartford Courant*, February 15, 1940, "Today and Tomorrow," by Walter Lippmann; *New York Times*, May 12, 1940, "Men and Issues in Doubt."

15. Reminiscences of Frances Perkins, Pt. 7, Columbia Center for Oral History Collection.

16. *Washington Post*, August 11, 1939, "Roosevelt Will Bolt."

17. FDR to Henry Horner, March 27, 1940, in Roosevelt, *F.D.R.: His Personal Letters*, 2:1011. Historian Bernard F. Donahoe argues that the New Deal had been weakened in the late 1930s, by FDR's court-packing scheme, the recession of 1937, and his 1938 attempted purge of southern conservatives from the Democratic Party. Because of the weakened liberal position, Donahoe believes that FDR's principal motivation in running for the third term was indeed to preserve the New Deal. See Bernard F. Donahoe, *Private Plans and Public Dangers: The Story of FDR's Third Nomination* (Notre Dame, Ind.: University of Notre Dame Press, 1965). But I maintain that FDR probably knew that because of the international crisis, the New Deal would be more or less shelved anyway. As it turned out, the huge increase in defense production and employment solved many of the nation's wrenching domestic problems.

18. Harold L. Ickes, *The Secret Diary of Harold L. Ickes*, 3 vols. (New York: Simon and Schuster, 1953–1954), 3:235. See also Parmet, *Never Again*, 34; Eleanor Roosevelt, *This I Remember* (New York: Harper and Brothers, 1949), 212–213.

19. Ickes, *Secret Diary*, 3:201.

20. Press Conference, March 19, 1940, in *PPA*, 9:109. FDR told reporters that the story "was made completely out of whole cloth—obviously. But that is not the point. Of course I never said such a thing about Jim Farley." His press secretary Steve Early repeated that the president "has no time right now to give to the preparation of political statements." *Washington Post*, May 25, 1940, "Coalition Cabinet."

21. *New York Times*, April 21, 1940, "Many Signs Now Point to a Roosevelt 'Draft'"; *New York Times*, March 12, 1940, "Roosevelt Is Reported Seeking Delegates So As to Hold Control"; *New York Times*, July 5, 1940, "Say Hull Will Run with Roosevelt"; *Wall Street Journal*, March 13, 1940, "Roosevelt Held to Have No Intention of Running."

22. Roosevelt, *This I Remember*, 226; *New York Times*, April 29, 1940, "First Lady 'in Vacuum' Concerning Third Term." "I believe he did not honestly want the nomination," she later wrote.

23. Perkins Oral History, Part 7, Session 1, p. 378.

24. James A. Farley, *Jim Farley's Story: The Roosevelt Years* (New York: Whittlesey House/McGraw-Hill, 1948), 246–251. See also Burns, *Roosevelt: The Lion and the Fox*, 424ff; Kenneth S. Davis, *FDR: Into the Storm, 1937–1940* (New York: Random House, 1993), 591ff.

25. *New York Times*, July 8, 1940, "Roosevelt Tells Farley His Stand on Third Term." See also Parmet, *Never Again*, 174; Charles Peters, *Five Days in Philadelphia: The Amazing "We Want Willkie!" Convention* (New York: PublicAffairs, 2005), 128ff.

26. James Farley, Memoranda, October 20, 1939, and June 17, 1940, Farley Papers, Box 44 and Box 45, Manuscript Division, Library of Congress. Courtesy of J. Garry Clifford. See also *New York Times*, April 24, 1940, "Farley Bars War as Campaign Issue."

27. *New York Times*, May 12, 1940, "Men and Issues in Doubt"; *New York Times*, July 12, 1940, "77 House Members Urge 3d Term." Out of the 269 Democratic members of the House, 77 had gone on record urging FDR to run for a third term. In 1939, Jim Farley explained that Democrats were playing up the prospect of a third term out of self-interest. "After Roosevelt leaves Washington," he wrote, "they will be out of the picture and they know it." James Farley, Memorandum, July 5, 1939, Farley Papers, Box 44.

28. Edward J. Flynn, *You're the Boss* (New York: Viking Press, 1947), 154. See also Donahoe, *Private Plans and Public Dangers*.

29. James Farley, Memorandum, July 5, 1939, Farley Papers, Box 44.

30. Harold Ickes, "I Want Roosevelt," in *Look*, June 20, 1939.

31. Sherwood, *Roosevelt and Hopkins*, 117; *New York Times*, June 17, 1939, "Hopkins Declares for 3d Term."

32. *New York Times*, January 9, 1940, "R. H. Jackson Urges President to Wait"; *Hartford Courant*, June 24, 1939, "The Great Game of Politics"; *Hartford Courant*, January 9, 1940, "Jackson Day Sets Drums to Beating."

33. *New York Times*, June 22, 1939, "Third Term Backed by Three Senators." See also Max Lerner, "Franklin D. Roosevelt," *The Nation*, 150, 25 (June 22, 1940), 752–755; *Hartford Courant*, August 12, 1939, "Loud Shouts Raised for Third Term."

34. *U.S. News*, July 12, 1940, 24; *New York Times*, March 12, 1940, "Roosevelt Is Reported Seeking Delegates"; *New York Times*, March 15, 1940, "Anti-3D Term Plea Works in Reverse."

35. *New York Times*, January 6, 1940, "Books of the Times"; R. G. Tugwell, "Must We Draft Roosevelt?," *New Republic*, 102, 20 (May 13, 1940), 630. Tugwell is summarizing remarks he made at a *Herald Tribune* Forum debate in October 1938.

36. Davis, *FDR: Into the Storm*, 595; Sherwood, *Roosevelt and Hopkins*, 171; *New York Times*, July 19, 1940, "Burke Bolts Party over Third Term"; *Washington Post*, June 4, 1940, "3d-Term Foes in Senate Quit."

37. *Hartford Courant*, November 18, 1939, "Great Game of Politics"; *Hartford Courant*, July 26, 1940, "The Great Game of Politics."

38. See Bruce G. Peabody and Scott E. Gant, "The Twice and Future President: Constitutional Interstices and the Twenty-Second Amendment," *Minnesota Law Review*, 83 (February 1999), 565–635.

39. *Los Angeles Times*, August 7, 1938, "Landon Sees Roosevelt Defeat If He Runs Again."

40. *New York Times*, August 22, 1940, "Willkie Flies Here"; *New York Times*, July 25, 1940, "Roosevelt Ends Hyde Park Holiday."

41. *Washington Post*, July 6, 1940, "Pointing His Own Moral."

42. Eugene Lyons, "Beware the Third Termites!," *American Mercury*, 47, 188 (August 1939), 385–391. The Republican-controlled state legislature of Rhode Island—with the support of the state's Democratic senator Peter Gerry—called for federal legislation banning a third term. *Chicago Daily Tribune*, March 15, 1940, "Storm Gathers in Senate Over 3D Term Issue." In a pamphlet published for the "No Third Term Association," one person insisted that the two-term custom was "the moral bar to indefinite self perpetuation of presidents in office." Thomas H. Reed, "The Fundamental Issue: A Brief against the Third Term," Prepared for the No Third Term Association, Arthur T. Vanderbilt, Chairman, October 1940, 2. Senator "Cotton Ed" Smith of South Carolina said he would "walk out and stay out" of the Democratic Party if FDR was renominated. *Chicago Daily Tribune*, March 15, 1940, "Storm Gathers in Senate over 3D Term Issue."

43. *Atlanta Constitution*, September 26, 1895, "Cleveland and the Third Term." http://www .presidency.ucsb.edu/ws/index.php?pid=29586#axzz1SUEgkpjA.

44. William Allen White, *A Puritan in Babylon: The Story of Calvin Coolidge* (New York: Macmillan, 1938), 361. See also David Greenberg, *Calvin Coolidge* (Times Books/Henry Holt, 2006), 138.

45. *Wall Street Journal*, February 11, 1928, "Senate Adopts La Follette Resolution"; *New York Times*, February 8, 1928, "Senate in Spirited Four-Hour Debate"; *New York Times*, December 12, 1907, "No Third Term for Roosevelt." See also *New York Times*, December 10, 1907, "Third Term Resolution." The resolution concerning Grant passed by a vote of 234 to 18.

46. *New York Times*, February 8, 1928, "Senate in Spirited Four-Hour Debate on Third Term Ban."

47. *Washington Post*, February 11, 1928, "Ban on Third Term Adopted in Senate by Vote of 56–26"; *Los Angeles Times*, October 19, 1940, "McNary Charges New Dealers."

48. *New York Times*, July 24, 1940, "Ban on Third Term Opposed in Survey."

49. "Senses of Cinema," by Brian Darr: http://archive.sensesofcinema.com/contents/cteq/05/35/great_mcginty.html.

50. *Hartford Courant*, August 18, 1940, "Gag Writers Bearing Down"; *New York Times*, August 31, 1940, "Melvyn Douglas and Loretta Young." Melvyn Douglas and his wife, the future congresswoman Helen Gahagan Douglas, were fervent New Dealers.

Chapter 10: The Democrats in Chicago

1. Harold L. Ickes, *The Secret Diary of Harold L. Ickes*, 3 vols. (New York: Simon and Schuster, 1953–1954), July 5, 1940, 235. Two weeks before the Democratic National Convention was scheduled to begin in Chicago, the president continued to maintain his sphinx-like silence about a possible third term. *Chicago Daily Tribune*, July 3, 1940, "Roosevelt Goes on Dodging." "Are the Sphinx's lips moving?" read the caption on a cartoon in the "Over the Coffee" column in the *Washington Post* on July 3, 1940.

2. *Christian Science Monitor*, July 10, 1940, "Third Term Still Secret; 'Sphinx' to Be in Bed"; *New York Times*, July 10, 1940, "President Parries 3D Term Inquiries." At another press conference three days later, FDR said he would not attend the convention and refused to state whether he would accept the party's nomination. *New York Times*, July 13, 1940, "President Refuses to Tell Press."

3. James MacGregor Burns, *Roosevelt: The Lion and the Fox* (New York: Harcourt, Brace, 1956), 426.

4. *New York Times*, July 9, 1940, "Garner's 'Cowboys' Whoop into Chicago"; *New York Times*, May 1, 1940, "Wheeler Will Run If Roosevelt Quits"; *New York Times*, July 9, 1940, "Farley Off to Chicago."

5. *Christian Science Monitor*, July 17, 1940, "Intimate Message from Chicago"; *New York Times*, July 16, 1940, "Hits Back at G.O.P."

6. *New York Times*, July 16, 1940, "Delegates Cheer Leaders' Speeches."

7. *New York Times*, July 12, 1940, "Roosevelt Willing"; *New York Times*, July 16, 1940, "Delegates' Spirits Subdued."

8. James A. Farley, *Jim Farley's Story: The Roosevelt Years* (New York: Whittlesey House/McGraw-Hill, 1948), 271–272; Homer Cummings Diary, July 13, 1940, Homer Cummings Papers, University of Virginia, Charlottesville. Courtesy of J. Garry Clifford. *Atlanta Constitution*, June 30, 1940, "Nine out of Every 10 Democrats for F.D.R."; Harold Ickes, unpublished diary, June 30, 1940, Manuscript Division, Library of Congress. Courtesy of J. Garry Clifford.

9. *New York Times*, July 16, 1940, "Chairman Farley's Address to the Democratic Convention"; Jonathan Mitchell, "Chicago: Family Stuff," *New Republic*, 103, 5 (July 29, 1940), 137–138; *New York Times*, February 15, 2010, "Tallulah's Back in Town."

10. *New York Times*, July 16, 1940, "Text of Speaker Bankhead's Keynote Address." Bankhead pronounced the names of Washington, Jefferson, Madison, and Hamilton along with Secretary of State Cordell Hull. Bankhead's speech was a "most miserable flop," Raymond Clapper wrote. "Roosevelt's handling of this thing would make me weep, if I didn't feel that he had been so smart alecky about it." Raymond Clapper to his wife, Monday, 12:30 a.m., in Clapper Collection, Box 49, Manuscript Division, Library of Congress. Courtesy of J. Garry Clifford.

11. *New York Times*, July 15, 1940, "Chicago Strains for Some Verve"; *Time*, July 22, 1940, "Mystery Story"; Ickes, *Secret Diary*, 3:243.

12. *New York Times*, June 28, 1940, "Convention Called Marvel in This Age"; *New York Times*, July 15, 1940, "Chicago Strains for Some Verve."

13. *New York Times*, July 14, 1940, "At the Convention"; *New York Times*, July 15, 1940, "Chicago Strains for Some Verve"; Mitchell, "Chicago: Family Stuff." See also Edward J. Flynn, *You're the Boss* (New York: Viking, 1947), 156: "The 1940 Democratic Convention in Chicago was not a very cheerful gathering." There were few FDR posters or banners.

14. *Los Angeles Times*, July 18, 1940, "Writer Fears Disastrous Class Struggle at Polls"; *New York Times*, July 14, 1940, "Delegates Circle in Wide Doldrums"; *New York Times*, July 7, 1940, "New Dealers Speed Up Drive for Roosevelt."

15. *New York Times*, July 14, 1940, "Delegates Circle in Wide Doldrums"; *Los Angeles Times*, July 14, 1940, "Roosevelt Dominated Convention at Chicago"; *New York Times*, July 14, 1940, "At the Convention."

16. *Los Angeles Times*, July 17, 1940, "Chicago Stadium Is Crowded for Fateful Announcement."

17. Ickes, *Secret Diary*, 3:246–249.

18. James Farley, January 10, 1939, Box 44, Farley Papers, p. 15, Manuscript Division, Library of Congress.

19. FDR to Wendell Willkie, in Robert Sherwood, *Roosevelt and Hopkins: An Intimate History*, rev. ed. (New York: Harper and Brothers, 1950), 3.

20. Sherwood, *Roosevelt and Hopkins*, 176–179; Reminiscences of Samuel I. Rosenman, Columbia Center for Oral History Collection (CCOHC); Herbert Parmet, *Never Again: A President Runs for a Third Term* (New York: Macmillan, 1968), 182; Eleanor Roosevelt, *This I Remember* (New York: Harper and Brothers, 1949), 218; Samuel Rosenman, *Working with Roosevelt* (New York: Harper, 1952), 206; Paul Appleby, "Roosevelt's Third Term," *American Political Science Review*, 46, 3 (September 1952), 755.

21. *New York Times*, July 17, 1940, "President Explains Why He Has Kept Silence on Third Term Till Now."

22. *Christian Science Monitor*, July 17, 1940, "Intimate Message"; *New York Times*, July 17, 1940, "Chicago Stadium Is Crowded for Fateful Announcement"; *New York Times*, July 17, 1940, "Choice Left Open."

23. *Washington Post*, July 17, 1940, "Delegates Go Wild at Name of Roosevelt"; *New York Times*, July 17, 1940, "Chicago Stadium Is Crowded"; *Chicago Daily Tribune*, July 17, 1940, "Move to Pick F.D.R. Tonight"; *Christian Science Monitor*, July 17, 1940, "Intimate Message from Chicago."

24. *New York Times*, July 17, 1940, "Choice Left Open"; *Hartford Courant*, July 17, 1940, "Declaration Follows Wild Demonstration."

25. *Chicago Daily Tribune*, July 17, 1940, "Move to Pick F.D.R. Tonight"; *New York Times*, July 17, 1940, "President Explains Why He Has Kept Silence"; *New York Times*, July 21, 1940, "Third Term?"

26. *Los Angeles Times*, July 17, 1940, "Third-Term Drive Pushed"; *New York Times*, July 17, 1940, "Clamor for Draft Sweeps the Floor"; *Washington Post*, July 18, 1940, "Convention as Exciting as Africa."

27. *New York Times*, July 17, 1940, "Clamor for Draft Sweeps the Floor."

28. *Hartford Courant*, July 7, 1940, "Declaration Follows Wild Demonstration."

29. *Chicago Daily Tribune*, July 18, 1940, "Protests Gag of Efforts to Hit 3d Term."

30. *New York Times*, July 17, 1940, "Platform Is Ready"; *New York Times*, July 6, 1940, "Democrats Seek Platform for All"; Alfred Landon to Roy Howard, July 20, 1940, in Alfred M. Landon Papers, Kansas Historical Society, Topeka. Courtesy of J. Garry Clifford.

31. *Washington Post*, July 16, 1940, "17 Men Working on Foreign Plank."

32. Thomsen to the Foreign Ministry, July 19, 1940, in *Documents on German Foreign Policy, 1918–1945*, Series D (1937–1945), 13 vols. (Washington, D.C.: United States Government Printing Office, 1947–), Document 190, 10: 250–251. See also Hugh Ross, "John L. Lewis and the Election of 1940," *Labor History*, 17, 2 (1976), 176.

33. *New York Times*, July 15, 1940, "Chicago Strains for Some Verve"; *New York Times*, July 1, 1940, "Wheeler Warns His Party on War"; *New York Times*, July 13, 1940, "Two Direct 'Draft.'" See also John Thomas Anderson, "Senator Burton K. Wheeler and United States Foreign Relations," Ph.D. thesis, University of Virginia, 1982, 105ff.

34. *Chicago Daily Tribune*, July 18, 1940, "Jam Galleries to Overflowing."

35. *New York Times*, July 17, 1940, "Third-Term Foes Gain in Solidarity"; *New York Times*, July 18, 1940, "By Acclamation." On July 12, 1940, FDR met with his former attorney general Homer Cummings in the White House, who wrote later that day that the president "spoke about the report that Senator Glass was going to Chicago to nominate Farley. He expressed his distaste for this idea. He did not say whether he was going to accept the nomination or not and I did not ask him. I think I know, and I think he knows I know." Homer Cummings Diary, Cummings Papers, University of Virginia, Charlottesville. Courtesy of J. Garry Clifford.

36. John B. Connally, *In History's Shadow: An American Odyssey* (New York: Hyperion, 1993), 76–77.

37. Kenneth S. Davis, *FDR: Into the Storm, 1937–1940* (New York: Random House, 1993), 598.

38. *New York Times*, July 13, 1940, "Two Direct 'Draft.'"

39. *Washington Post*, July 19, 1940, "'We Are Not Afraid': Democrats Convince Themselves."

40. *New York Times*, August 11, 1940, "Hopkins: Right-Hand Man"; *Washington Post*, July 18, 1940, "Over the Coffee."

41. Burton K. Wheeler with Paul F. Healy, *Yankee from the West* (Garden City, N.Y.: Doubleday, 1962), 365; Davis, *FDR: Into the Storm*, 598.

42. Wheeler, *Yankee from the West*, 366–367; Ickes, *Secret Diary*, 3:258, 262.

43. Rosenman, *Working with Roosevelt*, 205; John C. Culver and John Hyde, *American Dreamer: The Life and Times of Henry A. Wallace* (New York: Norton, 2000), 217; *New York Times*, July 14, 1940, "Second Place Talk Buzzes in Chicago"; *New York Times*, July 15, 1940, "Many Are Hopeful of Vice Presidency"; *Atlanta Constitution*, July 16, 1940, "F.D.R. Phones Byrnes."

44. Frances Perkins, *The Roosevelt I Knew* (New York: Viking, 1946), 130–133; Appleby, "Roosevelt's Third Term," 759; Kristin Downey, *The Woman behind the New Deal: The Life of Frances Perkins* (New York: Nan A. Talese/Doubleday, 2009), 304–305.

45. Culver and Hyde, *American Dreamer*, 228.

46. Rosenman, *Working with Roosevelt*, 212–213; Grace Tully, *F.D.R., My Boss* (New York: C. Scribner's Sons, 1949), 239; *New York Times*, July 19, 1940, "Sharp Floor Fight." See also Appleby, "Roosevelt's Third Term," 759.

47. Rosenman, *Working with Roosevelt*, 215; Davis, *FDR: Into the Storm*, 599.

48. Rosenman, *Working with Roosevelt*, 214; Ickes, *Secret Diary*, July 18, 1940, 3:258, 262, 268; Sherwood, *Roosevelt and Hopkins*, 178. According to one insider, Ickes even threatened to bolt the party.

49. *New York Times*, July 19, 1940, "But Silence Came as Leader Spoke"; Farley, *Jim Farley's Story*, 302. A few days before the convention had begun, Homer Cummings had warned the president that even if he was able to put over an unpopular choice, it would be met with "sullen acquiescence." Homer Cummings Diary, July 12, 1940, in Cummings Papers; Burns, *Roosevelt: The Lion and the Fox*, 429.

50. Roosevelt, *This I Remember*, 214.

51. *New York Times*, July 19, 1940, "Delegates Were Impatient."

52. *Hartford Courant*, July 19, 1940, "First Lady Goes before Convention"; Reminscences of Frances Perkins, 1955, Pt. 7, Session 1, pp. 469, 471, CCOHC; Downey, *Woman behind the New Deal*, 307–308; Rosenman, *Working with Roosevelt*, 214; Farley, *Jim Farley's Story*, 302; Davis, *FDR: Into the Storm*, 601.

53. *New York Times*, July 19, 1940, "Delegates Were Impatient"; James Roosevelt, *My Parents: A Different View* (Chicago: Playboy Press, 1976), 162.

54. Sherwood, *Roosevelt and Hopkins*, 179; *New York Times*, July 19, 1940, "But Silence Came as Leader Spoke"; *Chicago Daily Tribune*, July 19, 1940, "Wild Disorder Marks Democrat Revolt."

55. *New York Times*, July 19, 1940, "Delegates Were Impatient."

56. Booth Mooney, *Roosevelt and Rayburn: A Political Partnership* (Philadelphia: J. B. Lippincott, 1971), 136; *New York Times*, July 19, 1940, "Delegates Were Impatient."

57. Reminscences of Frances Perkins, Pt. 7, Session 1, pp. 467–477, CCOHC; Burns, *Roosevelt: The Lion and the Fox*, 429; *Chicago Tribune*, July 19, 1940, "Wild Disorder Marks Democrat Revolt"; Mitchell, "Chicago: Family Stuff."

58. Rosenman, *Working with Roosevelt*, 215.

59. Burns, *Roosevelt: The Lion and the Fox*, 429; Rosenman, *Working with Roosevelt*, 215–217.

60. Rosenman, *Working with Roosevelt*, 215–217.

61. Papers of Claude Wickard, Document 28, "The 1940 Convention," p. 15, Franklin D. Roosevelt Library (FDRL), Hyde Park, N.Y.; Davis, *FDR: Into the Storm*, 601; David Robertson, *Sly and Able: A Political Biography of James F. Byrnes* (New York: Norton, 1994), 294; *New York Times*, July 19, 1940, "Sharp Floor Fight." See also Wickard Diary, p. 15, Box 14, FDRL.

62. Rosenman, *Working with Roosevelt*, 218.

63. *New York Times*, July 19, 1940, "Delegates Were Impatient"; *New York Times*, July 19, 1940, "Sharp Floor Fight"; *Time*, July 29, 1940, "A Tradition Ends." Davis, *FDR: Into the Storm*, 601, incorrectly states that no one moved that the nomination be made unanimous.

64. *New York Times*, July 19, 1940, "Sharp Floor Fight"; *Chicago Daily Tribune*, July 19, 1940, "Wild Disorder Marks Democrat Revolt"; Mooney, *Roosevelt and Rayburn*, 138. See also Wickard Diary, p. 17, FDRL.

65. *Time*, July 29, 1940, "Campaign" and "A Tradition Ends."

66. Rosenman, *Working with Roosevelt*, 219.

67. *Time*, July 29, 1940, "A Tradition Ends."

68. Memorandum by Ambassador Dieckhoff, July 21, 1940, *Documents on German Foreign Policy*, Series D, Document 199, 10:259–260.

69. *New York Times*, August 18, 1940, "'No Real Choice' Left, Says Norman Thomas"; Wheeler, *Yankee from the West*, 354. Wheeler wrote to Saul Haas in 1939, "I expect to support [FDR] wholeheartedly." Quoted in Robert E. Burke, "A Friendship in Adversity: Burton K. Wheeler and Hiram W. Johnson," *Magazine of Western History*, 36, 1 (Winter 1986), 20–22; Wheeler would also cast his vote against Lend-Lease in 1941. *Atlanta Constitution*, March 4, 1941,

"Capital Parade." See also Anderson, "Senator Burton K. Wheeler and United States Foreign Relations," 105ff.

70. J. Garry Clifford and Samuel R. Spencer, Jr., *The First Peacetime Draft* (Lawrence: University Press of Kansas, 1986), 151; *Christian Science Monitor*, August 14, 1940, "Knox Declares Draft Vital."

71. Wayne Cole interview with Charles Lindbergh, June 7, 1972, Army and Navy Club, Washington, D.C., Cole Papers, Hoover Presidential Library, West Branch, Iowa. Courtesy of J. Garry Clifford. Lindbergh to Truman Smith, August 1, 1941, in Lindbergh Papers, Box 249, Smith 1941, Sterling Library, Yale University. Courtesy of J. Garry Clifford.

72. *New York Times*, August 26, 1940, "Sherwood Assails Ford, Lindbergh."

73. Walter Winchell, *Winchell Exclusive* (Englewood Cliffs, N.J.: Prentice-Hall, 1975), 126; Steve Neal, *Dark Horse: A Biography of Wendell Willkie* (Garden City, N.Y.: Doubleday, 1984), 122.

Chapter 11: Willkie Runs Alone

1. Steve Neal, *Dark Horse: A Biography of Wendell Willkie* (Garden City, N.Y.: Doubleday, 1984), 128; *Chicago Daily Tribune*, July 18, 1940, "Willkies Attend Festival"; *Christian Science Monitor*, July 18, 1940, "Choice of Roosevelt Pleases Willkie"; *Hartford Courant*, July 20, 1940, "Convention Is Stamped Ditto Mark."

2. *New York Times*, June 30, 1940, "Willkie on Cruise"; Raymond Buell, unpublished memoir, p. 12, Box 13, Raymond Leslie Buell Papers, Manuscript Division, Library of Congress. See also Lord Lothian, Survey of American Press, December 6, 1940, BPS No. 86, Reel 13. Courtesy of J. Garry Clifford. See also Justus Doenecke, *Storm on the Horizon: The Challenge to American Intervention, 1939–1941* (Lanham, Md.: Rowman and Littlefield, 2000), 3. Roosevelt seemed to agree with Buell about Roy Howard. In June 1940, FDR invited Howard to lunch at the White House and asked him to go to South America and see what could be done about combating the fifth-column activities of the Germans. Howard declined. Ickes wrote that "in his heart" FDR "despises" Howard. Harold Ickes, unpublished diary, June 9, 1940, Manuscript Division, Library of Congress. Courtesy of J. Garry Clifford.

3. Press Conference, August 20, 1940, in Samuel I. Rosenman, ed., *Public Papers and Addresses of Franklin D. Roosevelt [PPA]*, 13 vols. (New York: Macmillan, 1941), 9:332–333.

4. *Washington Post*, August 9, 1940, "Willkie Lashes at Machine Rule"; *Los Angeles Times*, July 25, 1940, "Willkie Lauds West's Spirit"; *New York Times*, July 26, 1940, "West for Willkie"; *New York Times*, July 11, 1940, "Willkie Busy Man in Day of Loafing"; *New York Times*, July 28, 1940, "Nominees Busy 'on Vacation'"; Herbert Parmet, *Never Again: A President Runs for a Third Term* (New York: Macmillan, 1968), 211.

5. *New York Times*, August 2, 1940, "Drift to Willkie Seen by W. A. White."

6. *New York Times*, July 27, 1940, "Willkie Will Drive for Votes in South"; *Time*, August 5, 1940, "Republicans"; see also Frederick Bradlee, "Thomas Jefferson Coolidge," *Proceedings of the Massachusetts Historical Society*, 3rd series, 72 (October 1957–December 1960), 373–378; *Time*, January 26, 1936, "The Cabinet: Exeunt."

7. *New York Times*, July 28, 1940, "Nominees Busy 'On Vacation,'" italics added; Charles Halleck Oral History, p. 92, conducted by James T. Patterson, December 1969, Oral History Project, p. 75, Indiana University. Courtesy of J. Garry Clifford.

8. *New York Times*, August 3, 1940, "Willkie Is Willing to Give President Position on Draft"; Neal, *Dark Horse*, 127. In his diary entry of August 12, 1940, Charles Lindbergh wrote that he phoned Willkie's headquarters in order to speak with Hoover (not Willkie) and was "cut off several times before I could get through. The place sounded like a madhouse, and the voices answering the phone, as my call was switched first to one place and then to another, seemed out of patience and exhausted." Charles A. Lindbergh, *The Wartime Journals of Charles A. Lindbergh* (New York: Harcourt Brace Jovanovich, 1970), 377–378.

9. Neal, *Dark Horse*, 131; Halleck Oral History.

10. Gary Dean Best, *Herbert Hoover: The Postpresidential Years, 1933–1964*, 2 vols. (Stanford, Calif.: Hoover Institution Press, 1983), 1:172; *New York Times*, November 17, 1940, "Hits Hoover's Plan."

11. *New York Times*, August 12, 1940, "Willkie Invites Elliott Roosevelt to Pay Him a Call in His Hotel"; *Los Angeles Times*, August 12, 1940, "Willkie Sees Hoover and Elliott Roosevelt"; *Time*, August 19, 1940, "Fellow Amateurs"; *New York Times*, July 25, 1940, "Calls Vote Issue Clear"; *Atlanta Constitution*, August 13, 1940, "Willkie Bids Goodbye to F.D.R.'s Son"; *New York Times*, August 13, 1940, "Hoover Will Make Willkie Speech"; Neal, *Dark Horse*, 130.

12. *Los Angeles Times*, August 12, 1940, "Willkie Sees Hoover and Elliott Roosevelt"; *New York Times*, November 1, 1940, "Hoover Declares Roosevelt Unsafe"; Best, *Herbert Hoover*, 1:167, 170–172.

13. Joseph Persico, *The Imperial Rockefeller: A Biography of Nelson A. Rockefeller* (New York: Simon and Schuster, 1982), 32; *Hartford Courant*, June 29, 1940, "Convention Pestered by Rumors."

14. Karl A. Lamb, "John Hamilton and the Revitalization of the Republican Party, 1936–1940," *Papers of the Michigan Academy of Science, Arts, and Letters*, 45 (1960), 236; Milton Plesur, "The Republican Congressional Comeback of 1938," *Review of Politics*, 24, 4 (October 1962), 532; Neal, *Dark Horse*, 123.

15. Henry Evjen, "The Willkie Campaign: An Unfortunate Chapter in Republican Leadership," *Journal of Politics*, 14, 2 (May 1952), 246.

16. Joe Martin, *My First Fifty Years in Politics* (New York: McGraw-Hill, 1960), 103, 106, 120; Charles Peters, *Five Days in Philadelphia: The Amazing "We Want Willkie!" Convention of 1940* (New York: PublicAffairs, 2005), 120.

17. *Time*, September 9, 1940, "Mr. Willkie's Man Farley."

18. Martin, *My First Fifty Years*, 105–109.

19. Alfred Landon to Harold B. Johnson, October 17, 1940, in Papers of Alfred M. Landon, Kansas Historical Society, Topeka. Courtesy of J. Garry Clifford. See also *New York Times*, October 2, 1940, "Landon Distrusts President on Peace."

20. Martin, *My First Fifty Years*, 110.

21. Neal, *Dark Horse*, 126.

22. *Hartford Courant*, July 20, 1940, "Isolationism Is Not Issue." Several years later, Willkie would still be wrestling with the same problem. "I agree with you," he wrote to William Allen White in 1943, "that I should be very careful in extemporaneous speech." Willkie to White, July 6, 1943, "Correspondence—43," Barnard Mss., Manuscripts Department, Lilly Library, Indiana University, Bloomington. Courtesy of J. Garry Clifford.

23. *New York Times*, September 8, 1940, "Willkie Pledges a 'No-War' Policy"; *New York Times*, August 18, 1940, "Man of the Middle West"; *New York Times*, August 4, 1940, "Unorthodox Campaign Is Mapped by Willkie.'"

24. *New York Times*, August 18, 1940, "Man of the Middle West."

25. *New York Times*, July 28, 1940, "Elwood Prepares for a Big Day."

26. *New York Times*, August 18, 1940, "Elwood Visitors Nearly Swamp It." See also Neal, *Dark Horse*, 133; Marcia Davenport, *Too Strong for Fantasy* (New York: Scribner, 1967), 275. "The whole thing was hell," wrote Davenport. See also Neal, *Dark Horse*, 136.

27. Martin, *My First Fifty Years*, 113. See also Robert A. Divine, *Foreign Policy and U.S. Presidential Elections, 1940–1948* (New York: New Viewpoints, 1974), 46ff.

28. *New York Times*, August 18, 1940, "Offer to Meet Rival."

29. In his memoir, Raymond Buell notes that when he first read Willkie's original draft of his speech, the candidate had come out for conscription but criticized aspects of the selective service bill that had been introduced in the Senate and House by Burke and Wadsworth. Buell convinced him to change his mind on this. Raymond Buell, unpublished memoir, p. 25, Box 13, Raymond Leslie Buell Papers, Manuscript Division, Library of Congress. Courtesy of J. Garry Clifford.

30. *New York Times*, August 18, 1940, "Willkie Accepts," italics added; *Chicago Daily Tribune*, June 29, 1940, "Fight for National Unity!" *New York Times*, August 18, 1940, "Text of the Address of Wendell Willkie."

31. *New York Times*, August 1, 1940, "Elwood Visitors Nearly Swamp It."

32. *Hartford Courant*, August 18, 1940, "GOP Lauds"; *Atlanta Constitution*, August 21, 1940, "Ohio Leaning toward Willkie"; *New York Times*, August 2, 1940, "Drift to Willkie Seen by W. A. White."

33. *New York Times*, August 19, 1940, "Reaction to Speech Pleases Willkie."

34. Martin, *My First Fifty Years*, 113; Halleck Oral History, p. 90; *Time*, August 26, 1940, "The Crowd at Elwood"; *New York Times*, August 20, 1940, "Difference between Speech-Writing and Speech-Making."

35. *Hartford Courant*, August 20, 1940, "None Helped with Speech at Elwood"; *Hartford Courant*, August 18, 1940, "GOP Lauds, Foes Scoff."

36. *New York Times*, August 20, 1940, "Text of Secretary Ickes's Address." Ickes's belief that criticism of FDR was abusive and a help to Hitler was echoed by U.S. Representative Francis Myers of Philadelphia. *New York Times*, August 24, 1940, "Says Willkie Aids Hitler."

37. *New York Times*, July 1, 1940, "Willkie Returning Today to Quit Post as Utilities Head"; *Chicago Daily Tribune*, August 20, 1940, "Willkie Slams Back at Ickes." In fact, Willkie asked New Hampshire senator Styles Bridges to issue a reply and "polish off Ickes." Answering that call, Bridges dismissed Ickes as a "Hitler in short pants" and a "political hatchet man" and reminded his listeners that while Hitler rearmed, Roosevelt and Chamberlain slept. *New York Times*, August 19, 1940, "Reaction to Speech Pleases Willkie"; *New York Times*, August 21, 1940, "Ickes Is Assailed."

38. Wayne Cole, *Roosevelt and the Isolationists* (Lincoln: University of Nebraska Press, 1983), 395; Robert Jackson, *That Man: An Insider's Portrait of Franklin D. Roosevelt*, ed. John Q. Barrett (New York: Oxford University Press, 2003), 31. See also Stimson Diary, August 20, 1940, Stimson Papers, Yale University. Courtesy of J. Garry Clifford.

39. *New York Times*, August 28, 1940, "M'Nary Promises in His Acceptance End to 'Disunity'"; *New York Times*, August 25, 1940, "M'Nary Will Speak Only 4 or 5 Times."

40. *Chicago Daily Tribune*, August 30, 1940, "Who's He Running against, Hitler?"; *Atlanta Constitution*, August 30, 1940, "Text of Wallace's Speech." Governor Lehman of New York, addressing the New York State Democratic Convention on September 30, 1940, said that "nothing that could happen in the United States could give Hitler, Mussolini, Stalin or the Government of Japan more satisfaction than the defeat of . . . Franklin D. Roosevelt." *New York Times*, October 1, 1940, "Text of Gov. Lehman's Address." FDR virtually contradicted Wallace's point when he said in a speech in Philadelphia that Germany had "suddenly wiped out" the right of free elections and free choice of heads of government, and that the cornerstone of American democracy was "periodic free elections." In them rested "the complete and the enduring safety of our form of government." *New York Times*, September 21, 1940, "Text of President's Address at University of Pennsylvania." For his part, Willkie responded on October 12, 1940, in a speech in Boston: "Do any of you care what foreign rulers think about American government? Are you going to take a dictator in to the voting booth with you next November?" *New York Times*, October 12, 1940, "Willkie's Boston Speech."

41. *Chicago Daily Tribune*, August 30, 1940, "Wallace Talk Cuts Off Game."

42. *New York Times*, August 23, 1940, "Willkie to Visit 18 States."

43. *New York Times*, August 20, 1940, "Willkie Pledges Indiana Loyalty"; *New York Times*, August 22, 1940, "Willkie Flies Here to Work Out Plans." See also Neal, *Dark Horse*, 135ff.

44. *New York Times*, August 19, 1940, "Reaction to Speech Pleases Willkie."

45. *Time*, September 9, 1940, "Mr. Willkie's Man Farley."

46. *New York Times*, August 19, 1940, "Reaction to Speech Pleases Willkie"; *New York Times*, August 20, 1940, "Willkie Prefers Land to Securities"; Neal, *Dark Horse*, 137.

47. Halleck Oral History, p. 92.

48. Robert Sherwood, *Roosevelt and Hopkins: An Intimate History*, rev. ed. (New York: Harper and Brothers, 1950), 184–185.

49. *New York Times*, July 3, 1940, "Gifts or Willkie to Buy No Favors."

50. *Hartford Courant*, August 27, 1940, "Today and Tomorrow" by Walter Lippmann; *Chicago Daily Tribune*, September 3, 1940, "Democratic: Willkie Ignores Party Pledges."

51. James MacGregor Burns, *Roosevelt: The Lion and the Fox* (New York: Harcourt, Brace, 1956), 443.

52. Martin, *My First Fifty Years in Politics*, 103–107. When newspaper columnist George Sokolsky met briefly with Willkie in New York in August and suggested that the candidate confer with McNary, Vandenberg, and Taft to coordinate positions with them on foreign and domestic policy, Sokolsky wrote, "he listened to my suggestion but did not respond." Willkie was doing nothing, Sokolsky lamented, to assert party leadership and rally Republican leaders behind him. George Sokolsky to Herbert Hoover, August 24, 1940, in Post-Presidential Subject-Campaign 1940-Candidates, Willkie, Herbert Hoover Presidential Library, West Branch, Iowa.

53. *New York Times*, July 3, 1940, "Gifts for Willkie to Buy No Favors"; Evjen, "Willkie Campaign," 249. See also Donald Johnson, *The Republican Party and Wendell Willkie* (Urbana: University of Illinois Press, 1960), 132.

54. Alan Brinkley, *The Publisher: Henry Luce and His American Century* (New York: Knopf, 2010), 258–259. See also Neal, *Dark Horse*, 138; Luce, Foreword, in John F. Kennedy, *Why England Slept* (New York: W. Funk, Inc., 1940), xv, italics added.

55. *Foreign Correspondent* opened in New York on August 16, 1940.

56. Patrick McGilligan, *Alfred Hitchcock: A Life in Darkness and Light* (New York: Harper, 2003), 270–272.

57. *Hartford Courant*, June 10, 1940, "Britons Told to Guard Bikes from Parachutists."

Chapter 12: An Army of Citizen Soldiers

1. J. Garry Clifford and Samuel R. Spencer, Jr., *The First Peacetime Draft* (Lawrence: University Press of Kansas, 1986), 43.

2. FDR to Grenville Clark, May 18, 1940, in Elliott Roosevelt, ed., *F.D.R.: His Personal Letters*, 4 vols. (New York: Duell, Sloan and Pearce, 1947–1950), 2:1026; FDR memo to Watson, June 14, 1940, OF 4065, Franklin D. Roosevelt Library (FDRL), Hyde Park, N.Y. See also Clifford and Spencer, *First Peacetime Draft*, 98.

3. Message to Congress Asking Additional Appropriations for National Defense, May 16, 1940, in Samuel I. Rosenman, ed., *Public Papers and Addresses of Franklin D. Roosevelt* [*PPA*], 13 vols. (New York: Macmillan, 1941), 9:198–204.

4. Press Conference, May 28, 1940, in *PPA*, 9:242–243, italics added.

5. Message to Congress, May 31, 1940, in *PPA*, 9:251.

6. Eleanor Roosevelt, "My Day," July 11, 1940. Comprehensive electronic edition of her "My Day" columns: http://www.gwu.edu/~erpapers/myday/.

7. *New York Times*, June 5, 1940, "Capital Is Uneasy on Latin America"; *New York Times*, June 5, 1940, "In the Nation," by Arthur Krock; *New York Times*, June 8, 1940, "Conscription Idea Wins Wide Backing." On June 7, 1940, FDR wrote to Lewis Douglas, "So you see, I am doing everything possible—though I am not talking very much about it because a certain element of the Press, like the Scripps-Howard papers, would undoubtedly pervert it." FDR to Douglas, June 7, 1940, in Roosevelt, *F.D.R.: His Personal Letters*, 2:1038.

8. Clifford and Spencer, *First Peacetime Draft*, 98.

9. Clifford and Spencer, *First Peacetime Draft*, 99. See also *Chicago Daily Tribune*, June 19, 1940, "U.S. Training for All Youths"; *New York Times*, June 19, 1940, "Roosevelt Proposes Training for Youths." See also Kenneth S. Davis, *FDR: Into the Storm* (New York: Random House, 1993), 605.

10. *New York Times*, June 20, 1940, "Hillman Will Map Training of Youth," italics added. The program mentioned by Early would *not* be run by the military but rather by the civilian agencies like the Civilian Conservation Corps and the National Youth Administration. Steve Early Press Conference, June 19, 1940, Box 40, Early Mss., FDRL. See also Clifford and Spencer, *First Peacetime Draft*, 98.

11. Clifford and Spencer, *First Peacetime Draft*, 52, 28, 13, 5, respectively; *Los Angeles Times*, June 23, 1940, "Sentiment for Compulsory Training Shows Sharp Rise."

12. Clifford and Spencer, *First Peacetime Draft*, 59; *New York Times*, September 19, 1936, "Pledge to Fight for Truth."

13. Clifford and Spencer, *First Peacetime Draft*, 14–15; *New York Times*, May 23, 1940. See also John G. Clifford, "Grenville Clark and the Origins of Selective Service," *Review of Politics*, 35, 1 (January 1973), 17–40.

14. George Marshall Interview, January 22, 1957, in Larry Bland, ed., *The Papers of George Catlett Marshall*, 5 vols. (Baltimore, Md.: Johns Hopkins University Press, 1981–), 2:263. See also Mark Stoler, *George C. Marshall: Soldier-Statesman of the American Century* (Boston: Twayne, 1989), 75–76. "I very pointedly did not take the lead," Marshall remarked some years afterward. "I wanted it to come from others. . . . Then I could take the floor and do all the urging that was required. But if I had led off with this urging, I would have defeated myself before I started." As a military leader, Marshall realized that he should not give the impression of "trying to force the country into a lot of actions which it opposed."

15. Marshall, Speech to Veterans of Foreign Wars, June 19, 1940, in Bland, *Papers of George Catlett Marshall*, 2:247–249.

16. Clifford and Spencer, *First Peacetime Draft*, 231.

17. *New York Times*, July 30, 1940, "Roosevelt Asks a Year's Training of National Guard."

18. Clifford and Spencer, *First Peacetime Draft*, 85, 262, note.

19. Clifford and Spencer, *First Peacetime Draft*, 84.

20. Clifford and Spencer, *First Peacetime Draft*, 103–104, italics added; *New York Times*, July 4, 1940, "Pershing, Conant Back Training Bill."

21. Henry Morgenthau to FDR, May 15, 1940, and Marshall to Charles Graham, September 23, 1941, in Bland, *Papers of George Catlett Marshall*, 2:214 and 2:616. See also Stoler, *George C. Marshall*, 76; *New York Times*, July 13, 1940, "Training Planned." See also Clifford, "Grenville Clark and the Origins of Selective Service," 30–31; Bland, *Papers of George Catlett Marshall*, 2:263–264; *New York Times*, August 17, 1940, "Marshall Warns of Big Army Need."

22. *Atlanta Constitution*, July 13, 1940, photo display, "They Have Eyes"; *New York Times*, July 13, 1940, "Training Planned"; Stoler, *George C. Marshall*, 76–78.

23. *New York Times*, August 1, 1940, "Great Peril Seen."

24. Robert Dallek, *Franklin D. Roosevelt and American Foreign Policy, 1932–1945* (New York: Oxford University Press, 1979), 248; *New York Times*, July 19, 1940, "Text of President's Speech Accepting 3d Nomination."

25. *Christian Science Monitor*, August 2, 1940, "Draft Backed by Roosevelt"; *Washington Post*, August 2, 1940, "Charges Platform to Tussle with Holt"; *Washington Post*, August 5, 1940, "Just Poppycock?" by Ernest Lindley.

26. *Los Angeles Times*, July 31, 1940, "Plea against Draft Fails"; Clifford and Spencer, *First Peacetime Draft*, 148–149. Polluting the coverage of the debate on selective service were phony news stories concocted by Joseph Goebbels's Nazi propaganda machine, like the report that "Selective Service is designed to make American cannon fodder on the Continent for the sake of Jewry." Sidney A. Freifeld, "Nazi Press Agentry and the American Press," *Public Opinion Quarterly*, 6, 2 (Summer 1942), 222.

27. *New York Times*, June 16, 1940, "Lindbergh Charges War Designs"; Charles A. Lindbergh, *The Wartime Journals of Charles A. Lindbergh* (New York: Harcourt Brace Jovanovich, 1970), 375; *New York Times*, August 5, 1940, "Lindbergh Urges We 'Cooperate' with Germany"; *Atlanta Constitution*, August 5, 1940, "Cooperate with Nazis"; *Life*, August 19, 1940, "Appeasers and Anti-Conscriptionists." In 1941, Lindbergh proposed a laissez-faire approach to military service, writing that "we should not be conscripting our youth for a foreign war they do not wish to fight." Charles Lindbergh, "Letter to Americans," *Collier's*, March 29, 1941.

28. Clifford and Spencer, *First Peacetime Draft*, 172.

29. *New York Times*, July 28, 1940, "Compulsory Drill Seen Gaining Favor"; *Washington Post*, August 11, 1940, "Voters in All States Favor Conscription by 2 to 1."

30. Press Conference, August 2, 1940, in *PPA*, 9:317–321; FDR to Eleanor Roosevelt, August 5, 1940, quoted in Dallek, *Franklin D. Roosevelt and American Foreign Policy*, 248.

31. Clifford and Spencer, *First Peacetime Draft*, 172–173, 279, note 98; Barkley to FDR, August 8, 1940, Box 8, OF, 1413, FDRL.

32. Clifford, "Grenville Clark and the Origins of Selective Service," 33; *Atlanta Constitution*, September 3, 1940, "The Capital Parade," by Joseph Alsop and Robert Kintner.

33. *New York Times*, August 7, 1940, "Clash on Draft"; *Hartford Courant*, August 7, 1940, "Bitter Senate Debate Delays Final Vote"; *Chicago Daily Tribune*, August 7, 1940, "Charges Slush Fund."

34. *New York Times*, August 14, 1940, "Army Plans Upset by Delay"; *New York Times*, September 15, 1940, "Draft Fund Asked"; *New York Times*, August 28, 1940, "Draft Bill Upheld in First Test Vote"; *New York Times*, August 15, 1940, "Senate Lifts Pay in Army"; *New York Times*, August 13, 1940, "Norris Says Draft Would Lead Nation into Dictatorship." *Congressional Record*, August 21, 1940, 10663–10665, and August 27, 1940, 11014–11015. See Clifford and Spencer, *First Peacetime Draft*, 289, note 35.

35. Thomas T. Connally, *My Name Is Tom Connally* (New York: Crowell, 1954), 238ff.

36. *New York Times*, August 20, 1940, "Tydings Speaks Up for Conscription."

37. Clifford and Spencer, *First Peacetime Draft*, 182–183, 189. In the Senate Military Affairs Committee, members quickly voted against an amendment designed to weaken the bill by limiting the number of draftees to one million. *Christian Science Monitor*, August 2, 1940, "Draft Backed by Roosevelt."

38. *Time*, August 12, 1940, 13; Clifford, "Grenville Clark and the Origins of Selective Service." On August 23, 1940, in a formal ceremony, King George VI of England stripped both Mussolini and King Victor Emmanuel of Italy of British honorary knighthoods. *Chicago Daily Tribune*, August 24, 1940, "British Honors Stripped from Duce and King."

39. Dallek, *Franklin D. Roosevelt and American Foreign Policy*, 243–244; James MacGregor Burns, *Roosevelt: The Lion and the Fox* (New York: Harcourt Brace, 1956), 438; FDR to Knox, July 22, 1940, in Roosevelt, *F.D.R.: His Personal Letters*, 2:1049.

40. Bland, *Papers of George Catlett Marshall*, 2:295, note 2; *Time*, July 29, 1940, "The Strategic Geography of the Caribbean Sea." See also Alan Brinkley, *The Publisher: Henry Luce and His American Century* (New York: Knopf, 2010), 262–263; Warren Kimball, "Franklin D. Roosevelt and World War II," *Presidential Studies Quarterly*, 34, 1 (March 2004), 87.

41. Harold L. Ickes, *The Secret Diary of Harold L. Ickes*, 3 vols. (New York: Simon and Schuster, 1953–1954), 3:283.

42. FDR to David Walsh, August 22, 1940, in Roosevelt, *F.D.R.: His Personal Letters*, 2:1057; *Washington Post*, September 7, 1940, "Isolationist Bloc Continues Silence on Destroyer Deal."

43. Clifford and Spencer, *First Peacetime Draft*, 190; Dallek, *Franklin D. Roosevelt and American Foreign Policy*, 245.

44. Richard Norton Smith, *Thomas E. Dewey and His Times* (New York: Simon and Schuster, 1982), 329. See also John Callan O'Laughlin, Memorandum, August 15, 1940, in collection of the Manuscript Division, Library of Congress, O'Laughlin Box 45. O'Laughlin wrote: "Mr. Hoover told me he had in the meantime telephoned to Willkie and had induced him to withhold any reference to the Destroyers in his speech."

45. Dallek, *Franklin D. Roosevelt and American Foreign Policy*, 246–247; Bland, *Papers of George Catlett Marshall*, 2:295, note 2.

46. *New York Times*, August 10, 1940, "Willkie Bars Link to Foreign Policies"; *New York Times*, August 18, 1941, "Text of the Address of Wendell Willkie"; Joe Martin, *My First Fifty Years in Politics* (New York: McGraw-Hill, 1960), 110; Clifford and Spencer, *First Peacetime Draft*, 193. See also Steve Neal, *Dark Horse: A Biography of Wendell Willkie* (Garden City, N.Y.: Doubleday, 1984), 139.

47. *Chicago Daily Tribune*, August 30, 1940, "Don't Sovietize U.S"; Clifford and Spencer, *First Peacetime Draft*, 201.

48. *New York Times*, August 18, 1940, "Speech 'Satisfies' Taft"; *Atlanta Constitution*, August 12, 1940, "Draft Measure Backers See Willkie Boost"; Clifford and Spencer, *First Peacetime Draft*, 192, 196; Johnson to his son, Hiram Johnson, Jr., August 30, 1940, in Neal, *Dark Horse*, 139.

49. *New York Times*, August 18, 1940, "U.S.-Canada Ties Welded by President and Premier"; Henry Stimson Diaries, August 17, 1940, Reel 6, vol. 30, p. 98, Yale University Library, Manuscripts and Archives.

50. Mackenzie King Diaries, August 17, 1940, p. 866, Libraries and Archives of Canada, www .collectionscanada.gc.ca; Clifford and Spencer, *First Peacetime Draft*, 200.

51. Clifford and Spencer, *First Peacetime Draft*, 202.

52. Press Conference, August 23, 1940, in *PPA*, 9:337–340; *New York Times*, August 25, 1940, "Senate Dallying on Draft Continues."

53. FDR to L. B. Sheley, August 26, 1940, in Roosevelt, *F.D.R. His Personal Letters*, 2:1058; *New York Times*, August 27, 1940, "Willkie Demands Chief for Defense Board."

54. *Washington Post*, August 29, 1940, "How Senate Voted on Conscription"; *Hartford Courant*, August 27, 1940, "Today and Tomorrow," by Walter Lippmann.

55. Clifford and Spencer, *First Peacetime Draft*, 289, note 41; FDR, Speech to Teamsters Union Convention, Washington D.C., September 11, 1940, in *PPA*, 9:414–415; *New York Times*, September 12, 1940, "Roosevelt Backs Draft of Industry."

56. *New York Times*, August 30, 1940, "Willkie Assails Plant-Seizure Plan"; *Time*, September 9, 1940, "Mr. Willkie's Man Farley"; *Chicago Daily Tribune*, September 3, 1940, "Willkie Ignores Party Pledges."

57. *Washington Post*, September 7, 1940, "Willkie Calls Destroyer Deal 'Dictatorial'"; *Chicago Daily Tribune*, September 3, 1940, "Willkie Ignores Party Pledges"; Arthur M. Schlesinger, Jr., ed., *History of American Presidential Elections*, 4 vols. (New York: Chelsea House, 1971), 3:2743; *Washington Post*, September 6, 1940, "Willkie Favors Limited Draft of Industry."

58. *Hartford Courant*, August 29, 1940, "Senate Roll Call on Conscription." McNary did not actually cast a vote but was recorded as in favor of the draft and "paired" with Democrat Guy Gillette, who was against the bill. George Marshall had believed that McNary's vote was "in the bag." Marshall to Mrs. Butler Ames, August 16, 1940, in Bland, *Papers of George Catlett Marshall*, 2:290, note 2.

59. Hershey Interview, December 15, 1967, in Clifford, "Grenville Clark and the Origins of Selective Service," 31–32.

60. *New York Times*, September 4, 1940, "Roosevelt Hails Gain of New Bases."

61. Burns, *Roosevelt: The Lion and the Fox*, 440; Kimball, "Franklin D. Roosevelt and World War II," 87, 97; Dallek, *Franklin D. Roosevelt and American Foreign Policy*, 244–245.

62. *New York Times*, September 4, 1940, "Roosevelt Hails Gain of New Bases"; Robert H. Jackson, *That Man: An Insider's Portrait of Franklin D. Roosevelt*, ed. John Q. Barrett (New York: Oxford University Press, 2003), 93–103. Jackson wrote that FDR "had shown uncanny foresight in expecting my legal opinion to draw the heat away from his deal. The opinion became the focus of much of the public controversy that ensued, and opposing quarters with equal extravagance threatened the Attorney General with everything from immortality to impeachment." Jackson, *That Man*, 102. See also William Casto, "Attorney Robert Jackson's Brief Encounter with the Notion of Preclusive Presidential Power," *Pace Law Review*, 30, 2 (Winter 2010), 373; Charles A. Lofgren, "*United States v. Curtiss-Wright Export Corporation*: An Historical Reassessment," *Yale Law Journal*, 83, 1 (November 1971), 1–32.

63. *New York Times*, September 4, 1940, "Ruling by Jackson"; Jefferson to John C. Breckinridge, August 12, 1803, in Susan Dunn, ed., *Something That Will Surprise the World: The Essential Writings of the Founding Fathers* (New York: Basic Books, 2006), 313.

64. Press Conference, September 3, 1940, in *PPA*, 9:379, 381.

65. *Washington Post*, September 7, 1940, "Today and Tomorrow" by Walter Lippmann; FDR to King George VI, November 22, 1940, in Roosevelt, *F.D.R.: His Personal Letters*, 2:1084. Some interventionist Democrats had urged the president to bypass Congress, warning him that some senators, including McNary, would stall the bill by insisting on "a few months debate on it." Robert Shogan, *Hard Bargain: How FDR Twisted Churchill's Arm* (New York: Scribner, 1995), 210.

66. *Time*, September 16, 1940, "What the Bases Mean." See also William Langer and S. Everett Gleason, *The Challenge to Isolation*, 2 vols. (New York: Harper Torchbooks, 1952), 2:770–776;

David Reynolds, *The Creation of the Anglo-American Alliance 1937–1941* (Chapel Hill: University of North Carolina Press, 1982), 121–131.

67. *Atlanta Constitution*, September 4, 1940, "Destroyers-Bases"; *Christian Science Monitor*, September 4, 1940, "A Stroke for Defense"; *Chicago Daily Tribune*, September 9, 1940, "Col. M'Cormick Hails Isle Bases as Defense Aid." The *St. Louis Post-Dispatch* was virtually alone in denouncing the deal, editorializing that FDR "committed an act of war." *New York Times*, September 4, 1940, "Comment by Press on British Accord," 13.

68. David Lilienthal, *The Journals of David Lilienthal*, 7 vols. (New York: Harper and Row, 1964), 1:209; Grace Tully, *F.D.R., My Boss* (New York: C. Scribner's Sons, 1949), 244.

69. *New York Times*, August 21, 1940, "Isle Leases Urged." See also Langer and Gleason, *Challenge to Isolation*, 2:775.

70. *Los Angeles Times*, September 6, 1940, "Voters Back Warship Deal."

71. *Hartford Courant*, September 4, 1940, "Naval Deal Is Assailed by Danaher." Congress had been "interpreted out" of the proceedings," objected the *Wall Street Journal*, darkly warning that "by this road government in America approaches the political outskirts of Berlin." *Wall Street Journal*, September 5, 1940, "In Strictest Confidence"; Frank Knox to Alf Landon, November 4, 1939, in Alfred M. Landon Papers, Kansas Historical Society, Topeka. Courtesy of J. Garry Clifford.

72. *New York Times*, September 7, 1940, "Willkie Condemns Destroyers Trade." "We don't know what the President may trade away next," Willkie said. "He may trade away the Philippines." While Willkie recognized that the country approved of the deal, he warned that, in a time of struggle in the world between democracy and totalitarianism, it was crucial to follow democratic processes to the letter.

73. Arthur M. Schlesinger, Jr., *The Imperial Presidency* (Boston: Houghton Mifflin, 1973), 107; Neal, *Dark Horse*, 140.

74. *Chicago Daily Tribune*, September 10, 1940, "First American Destroyers Join England's Navy."

75. Clifford and Spencer, *First Peacetime Draft*, 211; *New York Times*, September 4, 1940, "Industrial Draft Chief House Issue."

76. *Atlanta Constitution*, September 5, 1940, "Fist Fight Flares"; *New York Times*, September 5, 1940, "Draft Call Nov. 7, Wadsworth Says"; *Los Angeles Times*, September 5, 1940, "Fist Battle Stirs House in Draft Row"; Clifford and Spencer, *First Peacetime Draft*, 213.

77. *New York Times*, September 4, 1940, "Industrial Draft Chief House Issue"; *New York Times*, September 7, 1940, "Roosevelt Prods Congress"; *New York Times*, September 11, 1940, "Willkie Opposes Delaying of Draft"; Clifford and Spencer, *First Peacetime Draft*, 219.

78. Clifford and Spencer, *First Peacetime Draft*, 219–220; *New York Times*, September 8, 1940, "Capital Is Shaken."

79. *New York Times*, September 15, 1940, "Final Roll Calls on Draft Bill"; *New York Times*, September 15, 1940, "Draft Fund Asked." In the Senate, seven Republicans voted for the bill and ten against. *New York Times*, August 13, 1941, "Vote Is 203–202."

80. *Los Angeles Times*, September 18, 1940, "War Boosts Roosevelt"; *New York Times*, September 17, 1940, "Proclamation Calling for Draft"; Clifford and Spencer, *First Peacetime Draft*, 223; Bland, *Papers of George Catlett Marshall*, illustration 32, opposite 2:261.

81. Clifford and Spencer, *First Peacetime Draft*, 224–225; *Fortune*, 30 (March 1946), "Grenville Clark: Statesman Incognito."

82. Samuel Rosenman, *Working with Roosevelt* (New York: Harper, 1952), 225.

83. Bland, *Papers of George Catlett Marshall*, 2:308–312. Speech delivered on CBS radio at 10:15 p.m. on September 16, 1940.

84. Campaign button in "Freedom from Fear: F.D.R., Commander in Chief" exhibit in 2006 at FDRL. See *New York Times*, February 3, 2006, "F.D.R. and the Stuff of His War."

85. *New York Times*, August 12, 1940, "Sergeant York for Draft"; *Atlanta Constitution*, November 26, 1940, "Hero York in Dilemma as Draft Board Leader." But on November 15, 1940, the *New York Times* reported that eight young divinity students who refused to register for the draft, even though they would have been granted conscientious objector status or been exempt from ser-

vice, were found guilty under the Selective Service Training Act and sentenced to one year and one day in jail. *New York Times*, November 15, 1940, "8 Draft Objectors Get Prison Terms."

Chapter 13: Campaigning 101

1. *New York Times*, July 19, 1940, "Text of President's Speech"; FDR to Edward J. Kelly, August 28, 1940, in Elliott Roosevelt, ed., *F.D.R.: His Personal Letters*, 4 vols. (New York: Duell, Sloan and Pearce, 1947–1950), 2:1060; Press Conference, August 27, 1940, in Samuel I. Rosenman, ed., *Public Papers and Addresses of Franklin D. Roosevelt [PPA]*, 13 vols. (New York: Macmillan, 1941), 9:353.

2. *New York Times*, September 12, 1940, "Text of President Roosevelt's Address on Labor"; *New York Times*, September 12, 1940, "Roosevelt Backs Draft of Industry." The Democratic National Committee was obliged to pay for the airtime for a political speech by FDR but not for a policy speech.

3. *New York Times*, September 3, 1940, "Text of Roosevelt's Speech at the Chickamauga Dam Dedication"; *New York Times*, September 3, 1940, "New Day, New Arms."

4. FDR to John Boettiger, October 1, 1940, in Roosevelt, *F.D.R.: His Personal Letters*, 2:1069; *Time*, October 14, 1940, "Getting Restless."

5. FDR to Francis Maloney, August 3, 1940, in Roosevelt, *F.D.R.: His Personal Letters*, 2:1053.

6. *Washington Post*, September 23, 1940, "Mrs. Roosevelt to Broadcast New Deal Show"; *Los Angeles Times*, September 23, 1940, "Authors Back Third Term"; *New York Times*, September 14, 1940, "Actors to Aid President"; *Washington Post*, October 31, 1940, "Campaign Broadcasts"; *New York Times*, October 11, 1940, "Roosevelt, Jr. Praises Ability of 'My Old Man'"; FDR to Franklin Roosevelt, Jr., October 4, 1940, in Roosevelt, *F.D.R.: His Personal Letters*, 2:1070.

7. John C. Culver and John Hyde, *American Dreamer: The Life and Times of Henry A. Wallace* (New York: Norton, 2000), 235–240; FDR to Henry Wallace, August 29, 1940, in Roosevelt, *F.D.R.: His Personal Letters*, 2:1062; Harold L. Ickes, *The Secret Diary of Harold L. Ickes*, 3 vols. (New York: Simon and Schuster, 1953–1954), 3:324.

8. Charles Peters, *Five Days in Philadelphia: The Amazing "We Want Willkie!" Convention of 1940* (New York: PublicAffairs, 2005), 130; Culver and Hyde, *American Dreamer*, 83; Robert Jackson, *That Man: An Insider's Portrait of Franklin D. Roosevelt*, ed. John Q. Barrett (New York: Oxford University Press, 2003), 43.

9. Culver and Hyde, *American Dreamer*, 232.

10. Jackson, *That Man*, 42–44; Reminiscences of Frances Perkins, Pt. 7, Session 1, p. 709, Columbia Center for Oral History Collection (CCOHC).

11. Steve Neal, *Dark Horse: A Biography of Wendell Willkie* (Garden City, N.Y.: Doubleday, 1984), 44; *American Heritage*, "The FDR Tapes," 33, 2 (February/March 1982), 2, 12, 33. Perkins Reminiscences, Pt. 7, Session 1, p. 708. William O. Douglas wrote in his memoirs that the Democrats were willing to use letters they had between Willkie and Van Doren if the Willkie team made public the letters they had in their possession written by Henry Wallace to a religious mystic, the letters written to "Dear Guru." See Neal, *Dark Horse*, 144.

12. Paul Block of the *Pittsburgh Post Gazette* had the guru letters and had already commissioned an article about them. See Jackson, *That Man*, 45; Joe Martin, *My First Fifty Years in Politics* (New York: McGraw-Hill, 1960), 117. Sam Rosenman maintained that it was Willkie's decision. See Reminiscences of Samuel I. Rosenman, 1957–1960, p. 231, CCOHC; *Time*, September 23, 1940, "Wallace on the Way"; Culver and Hyde, *American Dreamer*, 239, note.

13. Robert Sherwood, *Roosevelt and Hopkins: An Intimate History*, rev. ed. (New York: Harper and Brothers, 1950), 174, and note on 945.

14. Sherwood, *Roosevelt and Hopkins*, 99; Frances Perkins, *The Roosevelt I Knew* (New York: Viking, 1946), 115–116.

15. *New York Times*, October 9, 1940, "Willkie Demands Roosevelt Tell If He Plans War"; *New York Times*, October 20, 1940, "F.D.R. vs. W.L.W."; *Washington Post*, September 17, 1940,

"Complete Text of Wendell Willkie's Address Given at Coffeyville, Kansas"; *New York Times*, September 17, 1940, "Willkie Predicts Dictatorship Here"; *New York Times*, September 22, 1940, "Campaign Puzzles Remain."

16. *Chicago Daily Tribune*, September 9, 1940, "Willkie's Party Will Travel on Train of 12 Cars"; Neal, *Dark Horse*, 143; *New York Times*, September 1, 1940, "Pattern of the Campaign Now Set."

17. *New York Times*, October 28, 1940, "Willkie Chance Seen in *Fortune*'s Survey"; *Christian Science Monitor*, October 30, 1940, "Willkie, Roosevelt Seen Neck and Neck"; *Los Angeles Times*, November 4, 1940, "State by State Standing in Final Gallup Poll."

18. Neal, *Dark Horse*, 147; *Time*, September 23, 1940, "While London Burned"; *Time*, October 7, 1940, "The Road Back." Dr. Harold Barnard was Willkie's throat specialist.

19. Grace Tully, *F.D.R., My Boss* (New York: C. Scribner's Sons, 1949), 239–240; *New York Times*, November 2, 1940, "Willkie Hopes Are Up."

20. *New York Times*, September 3, 1940, "Flynn Challenges Willkie on Labor"; *New York Times*, September 5, 1940, "Retorts to Willkie." Flynn also charged that the National Labor Relations Board had found two of the companies guilty of interfering with the rights of their employees. *New York Times*, September 4, 1940, "Willkie Denounces Labor Spies Story"; *New York Times*, September 7, 1940, "Willkie Shift Seen."

21. Raymond Buell, unpublished memoir, p. 40, Box 13, Raymond Leslie Buell Papers, Manuscript Division, Library of Congress. Courtesy of J. Garry Clifford. *Time*, September 23, 1940, "While London Burned"; *Washington Post*, September 14, 1940, "Willkie Hits Tax Evasion Deals." See also Buell, unpublished memoir, p. 36.

22. Buell, unpublished memoir, p. 33; *New York Times*, September 17, 1940, "Willkie Predicts Dictatorship Here If Roosevelt Wins."

23. *New York Times*, September 17, 1940, "Willkie Predicts Dictatorship If Roosevelt Wins"; *Washington Post*, September 17, 1940, "Willkie Sees Dictatorship Peril in U.S."; *Hartford Courant*, September 17, "Totalitarian Ends Seen to Third Term"; *Time*, September 23, 1940, "While London Burned."

24. *New York Times*, September 18, 1940, "Willkie Asks Vote of South."

25. *Los Angeles Times*, September 20, 1940, "Wendell Willkie Given Wild Ovation"; Marquis Childs, "The Education of Wendell Willkie," in Milton Crane, ed., *The Roosevelt Era* (New York: Boni and Gaer, 1947), 475.

26. *Washington Post*, September 23, 1940, "Willkie Shies from Hoover"; *Hartford Courant*, September 22, 1940, "Willkie Urges U.S. Aid"; *New York Times*, September 22, 1940, "Varied Receptions Given to Willkie"; *Hartford Courant*, September 22, 1940, "Willkie Urges U.S. Aid to Britain"; *New York Times*, September 27, 1940, "Text of Wendell Willkie's Address at Omaha on the Farmer's Problem."

27. Edward Levinson to Jerome Frank, chair of the SEC, October 3, 1940, Jerome Frank Manuscripts, Yale University; *Chicago Daily Tribune*, October 3, 1940, "Willkie Invades 'Tough Spots' in Industrial Cities"; *Los Angeles Times*, October 3, 1940, "Crowds Clog Willkie's Way in Cleveland"; *New York Times*, October 3, 1940, "Pontiac's Apology Is Sent to Willkie; *New York Times*, October 4, 1940, "Held in Basket Throwing"; *Chicago Daily Tribune*, October 3, 1940, "Michigan's Rotten Eggs"; *New York Times*, October 3, 1940, "Willkie Charges Defense 'Politics.'"

28. Neal, *Dark Horse*, 165; *New York Times*, October 12, 1940, "Willkie Hit by Potato When He Enters Boston." In the Dorchester section of Boston, Willkie was booed and pelted with more soft fruit. *Washington Post*, October 12, 1940, "War Dragged into Campaign, Willkie Says."

29. *New York Times*, October 4, 1940, "Text of Willkie's Address in Pittsburgh"; Perkins, *The Roosevelt I Knew*, 116–117; Perkins Oral History, Part 7, Session 1, p. 699. Jim Farley agreed with Willkie. Farley wrote that Perkins "has just never been able to catch on with the public. . . . I think if we had had a good strong man in the Labor position, such as Ed McGrady, there never would have been a break in labor." Memorandum of January 10, 1939, Farley Papers, Box 44, p. 16, Manuscript Division, Library of Congress. Courtesy of J. Garry Clifford.

30. *New York Times*, October 31, 1940, "Text of Willkie's Baltimore Address"; *Los Angeles Times*, October 1, 1940, "Text of Willkie's Address to G.O.P. Women at Detroit"; *New York Times*, October 26, 1940, "Willkie Inquires about '4th Term.'"

31. Memorandum of Eliot Janeway, n.d., in George McJimsey, ed., *Documentary History of the Franklin D. Roosevelt Presidency*, 40 vols. (Bethesda, Md.: University Publications of America, 2001–2008), Document 71, 13:404; Democratic National Committee, "Third Term Catechism," in McJimsey, *Documentary History of the Franklin D. Roosevelt Presidency*, Document 49, 13:282–289.

32. *New York Times*, October 12, 1940, "Willkie's Boston Speech"; *Hartford Courant*, October 9, 1940, "Willkie Hits at Flynn in Bronx"; *Los Angeles Times*, October 9, 1940, "Willkie Asks Truth about War Moves."

33. *Washington Post*, October 26, 1940, "Text of Willkie's Speech"; *New York Times*, September 18, 1940, "Willkie Asks Vote of South"; *New York Times*, October 5, 1940, "Text of Willkie Speech on Defense"; *Washington Post*, September 17, 1940, "Complete Text of Wendell Willkie's Address Given at Coffeyville, Kansas"; *New York Times*, October 13, 1940, "The Text of Willkie Speech at Albany."

34. *New York Times*, October 4, 1940, "Willkie Presents 7-Point Labor Plan"; *New York Times*, October 4, 1940, "Text of Willkie's Address in Pittsburgh"; *Washington Post*, September 24, 1940, "Text of Willkie's Seattle Speech"; *New York Times*, September 27, 1940, "Willkie Promises Help to Farmers by Pushing Trade"; *New York Times*, October 20, 1940, "Willkie Indicates He Would Abandon AAA's Crop Curbs"; *New York Times*, September 27, 1940, "Text of Wendell Willkie's Address at Omaha on the Farmer's Problem."

35. *New York Times*, October 23, 1940, "Willkie Questions Roosevelt Pledge to Avoid War Entry"; *New York Times*, October 22, 1940, "Text of Willkie's Address in Milwaukee."

36. *New York Times*, August 18, 1940, "Willkie Accepts," italics added; *New York Times*, October 1, 1940, "Willkie Puts Ban on Brain Truster"; Neal, *Dark Horse*, 153.

37. Walter Lippmann to Gould, November 20, 1940, Lippmann Manuscripts, Yale University. Courtesy of J. Garry Clifford; *New York Times*, September 17, 1940, "Mr. Willkie at Coffeyville."

38. *Washington Post*, September 17, 1940, "Willkie Taken to Task"; *New York Times*, September 17, 1940, "The Text of Willkie's First Major Speech"; *New York Times*, September 15, 1940, "Willkie Says That Roosevelt 'Promoted' the Munich Pact." Raymond Buell guiltily commented that a memo he had written for Willkie's speech had mistakenly contained the word "telephone." Buell, unpublished memoir, pp. 40–41. Courtesy of J. Garry Clifford.

39. *New York Times*, September 15, 1940, "Willkie Says That Roosevelt 'Promoted' the Munich Pact."

40. Address of Robert H. Jackson on CBS, October 9, 1940, in McJimsey, *Documentary History of the Franklin D. Roosevelt Presidency*, Document 94, 13:555; *Christian Science Monitor*, October 10, 1940, "G.O.P. Has Nothing to Give America, Jackson Declares."

41. *New York Times*, November 1, 1940, "Willkie Warns U.S. of One-Man Rule."

42. *Atlanta Constitution*, September 25, 1940, "Willkie's Most Striking Gains with Independents"; *New York Times*, September 20, 1940, "Roosevelt Passes Willkie in Survey"; *Washington Post*, September 20, 1940, "The Pendulum Swings," by Ernest Lindley. Two months after the election, the *New York Times* reported that major Republican donors—the Du Pont, Rockefeller, and Pew families—had contributed to Willkie's campaign only 25 percent of what they had bestowed on the GOP in 1936. See *New York Times*, January 18, 1941, "Republican Gifts by Three Families Reached $276,725."

43. Buell, unpublished memoir, pp. 26, 18, 19, respectively.

44. *Atlanta Constitution*, September 21, 1940, "Roosevelt Leads in 38 States"; *New York Times*, September 15, 1940, "Election Prospects"; *Atlanta Constitution*, September 21, 1940, "Wilting Willkie"; *Washington Post*, September 20, 1940, "The Pendulum Swings," by Ernest Lindley.

45. *New York Times*, August 31, 1940, "Willkie Backing by Dailies Heavy"; Roy Howard to Joseph Pulitzer, September 27, 1940, and Roy Howard to Alf Landon, September 27, 1940, in Alfred M. Landon Papers, Kansas Historical Society, Topeka. Courtesy of J. Garry Clifford.

46. *Atlanta Constitution*, September 28, 1940, "Growing Sentiment"; *Hartford Courant*, September 30, 1940, "Supporting Willkie in Tennessee"; *Washington Post*, September 29, 1940, "The Real Issue"; *Christian Science Monitor*, October 3, 1940, "More than One Emergency."

47. *Time*, October 7, 1940, "The Road Back."

48. Neal, *Dark Horse*, 152; Raymond Clapper, *Watching the World*, ed. Mrs. Raymond Clapper (New York: Whittlesey House/McGraw-Hill, 1944), September 20, 1940, 160. The whole campaign could be titled "Organized Chaos," agreed Russell Davenport's wife, Marcia, who accompanied her husband on the campaign trail. Marcia Davenport, *Too Strong for Fantasy* (New York: Scribner, 1967), 274–275; *Hartford Courant*, October 18, 1940, "President's Supporters Are Uneasy," by Joseph Alsop and Robert Kintner.

49. Edward J. Flynn, *You're the Boss* (New York: Viking, 1947), 169; *Chicago Daily Tribune*, September 23, 1940, "Willkie Enters Home State of Running Mate"; Neal, *Dark Horse*, 166. McNary and FDR had also forged a cordial working relationship.

50. Buell, unpublished memoir, pp. 10, 19. From what Buell could tell, Willkie had "only contempt" for Martin—as well as for other Republicans like Hoover and Landon.

51. *New York Times*, August 25, 1940, "Willkie Holds Lead in Gallup Test"; *New York Times*, October 6, 1940, "Roosevelt's Lead Mounts"; *Time*, October 7, 1940, "The Road Back." So dramatic were those numbers that some Republicans, like Michigan's Senator Vandenberg, were tempted to jump ship. "We ought to do everything possible to save Michigan's Republican representation anyway," Vandenberg wrote to his son, quoted in Robert A. Divine, *Foreign Policy and U.S. Presidential Elections, 1940–1948* (New York: New Viewpoints, 1974), 58.

52. Ben Cohen, memorandum, "Conversation at Luncheon with Mr. Wendell Willkie," December 11, 1939, PSF, filed under Willkie, Franklin D. Roosevelt Library, Hyde Park, N.Y.; *New York Times*, September 8, 1940, "Willkie Pledges a 'No-War' Policy"; Rexford G. Tugwell, *The Democratic Roosevelt: A Biography of Franklin D. Roosevelt* (Garden City, N.Y.: Doubleday, 1957), 539; Sam Pryor interview, August 9, 1955, "Campaign—100," Barnard Mss., Manuscripts Department, Lilly Library, Indiana University, Bloomington. Courtesy of J. Garry Clifford. Neal, *Dark Horse*, 159.

53. *Chicago Daily Tribune*, October 9, 1940, "Explain Stand on War! Willkie Challenges FDR"; *Los Angeles Times*, October 9, 1940, "Willkie Asks Truth about War Moves." In his address at the *Herald Tribune* Forum in late October, Willkie said, "In Nazi Germany the ownership of most business is left in private hands, but management is rigidly controlled. Here in America we have a rapidly growing parallel. . . . Four years from now America may have gone so far along the road toward State domination that it will be too late to turn back." *New York Times*, October 24, 1940, "Text of Wendell L. Willkie's Address."

54. *Los Angeles Times*, October 9, 1940, "Willkie Asks Truth about War Moves"; Kenneth S. Davis, *FDR: Into the Storm* (New York: Random House, 1993), 189; *Christian Science Monitor*, January 10, 1938, "House Blocks Vote of People."

55. *New York Times*, October 19, 1940, "Mr. Willkie on the Upswing"; *New York Times*, September 17, 1940, "Willkie at Coffeyville"; Weekly Political Summary, Telegram No. 95, October 14, 1940, Records of British Foreign Office, Reel 6. Courtesy of J. Garry Clifford. *Christian Science Monitor*, October 12, 1940, "Responsibility-Unity-Work"; *New York Times*, October 15, 1940, "Illinois, Indiana, Michigan Shift to Willkie."

56. *New York Times*, October 15, 1940, "Text of Willkie's Address at Rally in Syracuse"; *Wall Street Journal*, October 15, 1940, "Presidential Politics"; *Chicago Daily News*, October 18, 1940, "New Deal Stirs War"; *Chicago Daily News*, October 18, 1940, "Willkie's Address on America's 'World Role,'" italics added. Willkie made a similar argument in Yonkers on September 28. *New York Times*, September 29, 1940, "Text of Willkie's Address at Yonkers Rally"; *Los Angeles Times*, October 18, 1940, "Willkie Tells Road to Peace."

57. *Washington Post*, September 22, 1940, "Text of Willkie Speech"; *Washington Post*, October 3, 1940, "Willkie Urges Aid to Britain"; *New York Times*, October 12, 1940, "Willkie Declares New Deal Regime Is 'Irresponsible'"; *New York Times*, October 18, 1940, "Willkie Declares We Can Aid British Only by Producing"; *New York Times*, October 18, 1940, "Shift to Willkie."

58. *New York Times*, October 23, 1940, "Willkie Questions Roosevelt Pledge to Avoid War Entry"; *New York Times*, October 22, 1940, "Text of Willkie's Address in Milwaukee."

59. Willkie to Vandenberg, October 22, 1940, in Divine, *Foreign Policy and U.S. Presidential Elections*, 67.

60. *New York Times*, October 23, 1940, "Nazi Fliers Foiled."

61. *New York Times*, October 19, 1940, "Text of the Willkie Speech Warning of State Socialism."

62. *Time*, October 14, 1940, "Willkie's Case"; Neal, *Dark Horse*, 149–152.

63. Buell, unpublished memoir, pp. 47–49.

64. Sherwood, *Roosevelt and Hopkins*, 184.

Chapter 14: Enter Robert Sherwood

1. The first meeting of Sherwood and Hopkins was in September 1938, also during a Long Island weekend; they met again in early 1940. Robert Sherwood, *Roosevelt and Hopkins: An Intimate History*, rev. ed. (New York: Harper and Brothers, 1950), 3, 172; *New York Times*, April 30, 1940, "The Play in Review."

2. Sherwood, *Roosevelt and Hopkins*, 49–50.

3. Sherwood, *Roosevelt and Hopkins*, 122. See also the Reminiscences of Samuel I. Rosenman, 1957–1960, p. 180, Columbia Center for Oral History Collection (CCOHC). Rosenman recalled that in October 1940, "We had to have somebody who could write effectively, and someone who agreed with Roosevelt's foreign policy at that time. Remember October, 1940, was the time when Lindbergh and the America First group were quite influential with the people of the United States. Not everyone agreed with Roosevelt's foreign policy, even some good old New Dealers didn't agree. So we had to find somebody who combined all of these characteristics: was a New Dealer, could write, and agreed wholly with his foreign policy." Reminiscences of Rosenman, p. 180, CCOHC.

4. *New York Times*, November 15, 1955, "Robert E. Sherwood Dead"; *New York Times*, October 13, 1940, "Up to 'There Shall Be No Night.'"

5. Sherwood, *Roosevelt and Hopkins*, 194; Reminiscences of Rosenman, p. 51, CCOHC.

6. *New York Times*, October 12, 1940, "We Can Avoid War."

7. Address on Hemisphere Defense, October 12, 1940, in Samuel I. Rosenman, ed., *Public Papers and Addresses of Franklin D. Roosevelt [PPA]*, 13 vols. (New York: Macmillan, 1941), 9:460–467.

8. Sherwood, *Roosevelt and Hopkins*, 213–217.

9. Samuel I. Rosenman, *Working with Roosevelt* (New York: Harper and Brothers, 1952), 234.

10. Rosenman, *Working with Roosevelt*, 234, 238; Sherwood, *Roosevelt and Hopkins*, 217–218, 197, respectively. Sherwood wrote, "As one who has had considerable experience in the theater, I marveled at the unfailing precision with which [FDR] made his points, his grace in reconciling the sublime with the ridiculous, as though he had been rehearsing these lines for weeks and delivering them before audiences for months. . . . Referring again to my experience in the theater, I can testify that he was normally the most untemperamental genius I have ever encountered. That is one of the reasons why he was able to sleep so well at night." Sherwood, *Roosevelt and Hopkins*, 218. When FDR met Orson Welles in 1944, he told Welles that they were the "two best actors in the world." David Gergen, *Eyewitness to Power: The Essence of Leadership, Nixon to Clinton* (New York: Simon and Schuster, 2000), 244.

11. Sherwood, *Roosevelt and Hopkins*, 217.

12. *Chicago Daily Tribune*, October 10, 1940, "Dunn Poll Picks Willkie"; *New York Times*, October 18, 1940, "Shift to Willkie"; *New York Times*, October 23, 1940, "Survey Finds Roosevelt's Lead Is Result Solely of War."

13. Telegram, October 24, 1940, from Alice Clements to Stephen Early, and Telegram, October 25, 1940, from the Iowa Committee for Agriculture to Stephen Early, in George McJimsey, ed., *Documentary History of the Franklin D. Roosevelt Presidency*, 43 vols. (Bethesda, Md.: University

Publications of America, 2001–2008), Documents 133 and 137, 13:716, 722; Sherwood, *Roosevelt and Hopkins*, 187–188.

14. *Hartford Courant*, October 18, 1940, "President's Supporters Are Uneasy." Judge M. A. Musmanno sent a telegram: "I cannot emphasize too strongly for the President in his next speech to smash and smash hard Willkie." Congressmen Lyndon Johnson of Texas and Adolph Sabath of Illinois also urged FDR to give some tough fighting speeches. McJimsey, *Documentary History of the Franklin D. Roosevelt Presidency*, Documents 177, 160, and 176, 13:869, 809, 868, respectively. See also Clyde Eastus, U.S. Attorney in Fort Worth, to Steve Early, October 16, 1940, in McJimsey, *Documentary History of the Franklin D. Roosevelt Presidency*, Document 107, 13:600–601. Herbert Brunner of Jackson Heights, N.Y., urged the White House to come up with a slogan to counter the "No Third Term" slogan. He recommended "Willkie promises like a Huey Long." McJimsey, *Documentary History of the Franklin D. Roosevelt Presidency*, Document 150, 13:775. The National Committee of Independent Voters for Roosevelt and Wallace gave advice on recovering the German-American vote. McJimsey, *Documentary History of the Franklin D. Roosevelt Presidency*, Document 168, 13:836–837.

15. Herbert Parmet, *Never Again: A President Runs for a Third Term* (New York: Macmillan, 1968), 247, and see McJimsey, *Documentary History of the Franklin D. Roosevelt Presidency*, Document 85, 13:528–531.

16. James MacGregor Burns, *Roosevelt: The Lion and the Fox* (New York: Harcourt, Brace, 1956), 445ff; Harold L. Ickes, *The Secret Diary of Harold L. Ickes*, 3 vols. (New York: Simon and Schuster, 1953–1954), 3:351–352.

17. FDR to Robert S. Allen, October 22, 1940 in Elliott Roosevelt, ed., *F.D.R.: His Personal Letters*, 4 vols. (New York: Duell, Sloan and Pearce, 1847–1950), 2:1073. Allen wrote with Drew Pearson the syndicated column "Washington Merry-Go-Round."

18. *New York Times*, October 24, 1940, "Peace Set as Goal"; *PPA*, 9:487; *New York Times*, October 27, 1940, "President Back in Role of Joyful Campaigner"; Sherwood, *Roosevelt and Hopkins*, 186.

19. *New York Times*, October 24, 1940, "Peace Set as Goal."

20. *New York Times*, January 11, 1935, "Peace an Illusion, Writes Mussolini"; *Washington Post*, October 31, 1940, "Nazis Back Italians."

21. *Hartford Courant*, October 29, 1940, "Roosevelt Assails GOP"; *Washington Post*, October 29, 1940, "As 25,000 Cheer."

22. The Greeks would soon counterattack successfully, driving the Italian troops back into Albania. But Nazi Germany would invade and conquer Greece in April 1941.

23. Sherwood, *Roosevelt and Hopkins*, 189.

24. Rosenman, *Working with Roosevelt*, 242; Sherwood, *Roosevelt and Hopkins*, 189–190.

25. Campaign Address at Madison Square Garden, October 28, 1940, *PPA*, 9:508, italics added.

26. Burns, *Roosevelt: The Lion and the Fox*, 255; *New York Times*, September 1, 1935, "Neutrality Law Is Signed."

27. Sherwood, *Roosevelt and Hopkins*, 189, 201.

28. *Chicago Daily Tribune*, October 22, 1940, "Democratic: Stimson Exposes Willkie Smear"; Sherwood, *Roosevelt and Hopkins*, 201.

29. Radio Address on the Occasion of the Drawing of Numbers, October 29, 1940, in *PPA*, 9:510–514.

30. *Hartford Courant*, October 30, 1940, "Draft Numbers Drawn in Dramatic Ceremony"; *Time*, November 11, 1940, "The Draft: Only the Strong"; J. Garry Clifford and Samuel R. Spencer, Jr., *The First Peacetime Draft* (Lawrence: University Press of Kansas, 1986), 1.

31. Henry Stimson Diaries, October 29, 1940, Reel 6, vol. 31, p. 89, Manuscripts and Archives, Yale University Library. The British ambassador, Lord Lothian, feared that the timing of the lottery was a mistake, but "if so," he added, "it was a bold and honourable one." Lord Lothian, November 3, 1940, Weekly Political Summary, No. 2557, Telegram No. 2441, Reel 6, Records of British Foreign Office. Courtesy of J. Garry Clifford. Robert A. Divine, *Foreign Policy and U.S.*

Presidential Elections, 1940–1948 (New York: New Viewpoints, 1974), 69; Sherwood, *Roosevelt and Hopkins*, 188; *Los Angeles Times*, October 30, 1940, "Added Willkie Gains Shown"; *Atlanta Constitution*, August 4, 1940, "Willkie Leading Roosevelt."

Chapter 15: Franklin and Joe

1. Michael R. Beschloss, *Kennedy and Roosevelt: The Uneasy Alliance* (New York: Norton, 1980), 215. James Farley wrote in 1939, "I never trusted [Kennedy]. I always thought and felt he was a lone-wolf who could be loyal only to Kennedy; that he would stay on only as long as the Administration could be helpful to Kennedy, and no longer." James Farley Papers, Box 44, Memorandum of January 10, 1939, p. 21, Manuscript Division, Library of Congress. Courtesy of J. Garry Clifford.

2. Beschloss, *Kennedy and Roosevelt*, 213, 216; Robert A. Divine, *Foreign Policy and U.S. Presidential Elections, 1940–1948* (New York: New Viewpoints, 1974), 77. In August 1940, Wood had been reluctant to assume the role of AFC chair, fearing that his association with the committee would handicap Willkie. See Wayne Cole, *America First* (Madison: University of Wisconsin Press, 1953), 168; Steve Neal, *Dark Horse: A Biography of Wendell Willkie* (Garden City, N.Y.: Doubleday, 1984), 168.

3. John H. Davis, *The Kennedys: Dynasty and Disaster* (New York: McGraw-Hill, 1984), 99–100; *Atlanta Constitution*, October 8, 1940, "Capital Parade."

4. Breckinridge Long Diary, October 11, 1940, in Beschloss, *Kennedy and Roosevelt*, 214. See also Wayne Cole, *Roosevelt and the Isolationists* (Lincoln: University of Nebraska Press, 1983), 290; Joseph P. Kennedy, *I'm for Roosevelt* (New York: Reynal and Hitchcock, 1936).

5. Will Swift, *The Kennedy Family amidst the Gathering Storm* (Washington, D.C.: Smithsonian Books, 2008), 220. When Harry Hopkins was in England in January 1941 as FDR's representative and meeting with Churchill, Anthony Eden, and other cabinet ministers and military leaders, he received a message from Lady Astor, inviting him for a weekend at Cliveden and informing him that he had been making great mistakes in meeting with the wrong people. Robert Sherwood, *Roosevelt and Hopkins: An Intimate History*, rev. ed. (New York: Harper and Brothers, 1950), 260.

6. Dirksen's memo quoted in Max Wallace, *The American Axis: Henry Ford, Charles Lindbergh, and the Rise of the Third Reich* (New York: St. Martin's Press, 2003), 167–168. Kennedy was not the only ambassador with tendencies toward appeasement of Hitler. It can be argued that FDR chose other poor ambassadors to European nations, like John Cudahy, his ambassador to Poland, Ireland, and Belgium, and William Bullitt, his ambassador to the Soviet Union and France. In 1935, at a meeting in Moscow with James G. McDonald, the League of Nations high commissioner for refugees, Bullitt "insisted on a long discussion of the reasons [i.e., justifications] for anti-Semitism." James G. McDonald, *Refugees and Rescue: The Diaries and Papers of James G. McDonald, 1935–1945*, ed. Richard Breitman, Barbara McDonald Stewart, and Severin Hochberg (Bloomington: Indiana University Press, 2009), 18–19. Upset about the lack of support that he was receiving about the refugee problem, McDonald resigned in protest. Ambassador to Germany Hugh Wilson wrote in 1938 that certain people in the United States wanted to involve the nation in war for reasons "which do not appeal to the vast majority of the American people as real cause for war." As Richard Breitman explains, Wilson's suggestion was that there was a Jewish conspiracy determined to provoke war with Germany. Richard Breitman, "FDR's Refugee Policy, 1938," unpublished essay.

7. Truman Smith, *Berlin Alert: The Memoirs and Reports of Truman Smith* (Stanford, Calif.: Hoover Institution Press, 1984), 154–155. The letter of September 22, 1938, was especially important. See also Swift, *Kennedy Family amidst the Gathering Storm*, 92, 123; Beschloss, *Kennedy and Roosevelt*, 163, 175; *Hartford Courant*, September 15, 1938, "American Ambassador Calls on Chamberlain."

8. Herman Klurfeld, *Winchell: His Life and Times* (New York: Praeger, 1976), 80–81.

9. Charles A. Lindbergh, *The Wartime Journals of Charles A. Lindbergh* (New York: Harcourt Brace Jovanovich, 1970), 72–79; Cole, *Roosevelt and the Isolationists*, 283.

10. Cole, *Roosevelt and the Isolationists*, 283–284. See also David Nasaw, *The Patriarch: The Remarkable Life and Turbulent Times of Joseph P. Kennedy* (New York: Penguin, 2012), 331; *New York Times*, September 3, 1938, "Religious Freedom Urged by Kennedy."

11. James MacGregor Burns, *Leadership* (New York: Harper and Row, 1978), 34; *New York Times*, October 20, 1938, "Kennedy for Amity with Fascist Bloc." See also Amanda Smith, ed., *Hostage to Fortune: The Letters of Joseph P. Kennedy* (New York: Viking, 2001), editor's note, 228; Knox to Hull, October 25, 1938, in Cole, *Roosevelt and the Isolationists*, 290.

12. Kenneth S. Davis, *FDR: Into the Storm* (New York: Random House, 1993), 487; Harold L. Ickes, *The Secret Diary of Harold L. Ickes*, 3 vols. (New York: Simon and Schuster, 1953–1954), September 9, 1939, 2:712.

13. Kennedy to FDR, September 3, 1939, in Smith, *Hostage to Fortune*, 385–386; Kennedy to Missy LeHand, October 3, 1939, in *New York Times*, July 29, 2010, "In Roosevelt Archive, History as He Made It."

14. John Morton Blum, ed., *From the Morgenthau Diaries*, 3 vols. (Boston: Houghton Mifflin, 1959–1967), 2:102; Cole, *Roosevelt and the Isolationists*, 290. In February 1939, Father Charles Coughlin named Joseph Kennedy "The Man of the Week" in his ferociously anti-Semitic weekly, *Social Justice*.

15. Beschloss, *Kennedy and Roosevelt*, 212; Sherwood, *Roosevelt and Hopkins*, 150; Diaries of William R. Castle, Jr. Houghton Library, Harvard University, February 21, 1940, p. 14. Courtesy of J. Garry Clifford. Kennedy confided to Joseph Patterson that there was no one in the world who wanted more to see Germany beaten than he, but he believed that the United States needed to adopt a realistic policy. Kennedy to Joseph Medill Patterson, August 22, 1940, in Smith, *Hostage to Fortune*, 462.

16. John F. Kennedy, *Why England Slept* (New York: Wilfred Funk, 1940), 230, 224. See also Michael Meagher, "'In an Atmosphere of National Peril: The Development of John F. Kennedy's World View,'" *Presidential Studies Quarterly*, 27, 3 (Summer 1997), 467–479.

17. *New York Times*, September 2, 1940, "Best Sellers of the Week"; *New York Times*, November 19, 1969, "Kennedy, Financier and Diplomat"; Kennedy, *Why England Slept*, 229–231; italics are in Kennedy's text.

18. *Wall Street Journal*, August 1, 1940, "Executives' Bookshelf"; *New York Times*, August 11, 1940, "Why Britain Slept"; Smith, *Hostage to Fortune*, 233; Kennedy to Rose Kennedy, September 10, 1940, 467; Kennedy to Hull, August 7, 1940, in Smith, *Hostage to Fortune*, 459; Kennedy to FDR, August 27, 1940, in Smith, *Hostage to Fortune*, 463.

19. Beschloss, *Kennedy and Roosevelt*, 213. Joe Jr. wrote that his father was tired of "letting the Jewish columnists in America kick his head off." Swift, *Kennedy Family amidst the Gathering Storm*, 121. Swift records Joe Sr.'s anti-Semitic outbursts after he left the ambassadorship. Swift, *Kennedy Family amidst the Gathering Storm*, 165.

20. FDR to Kennedy, October 17, 1940, in Smith, *Hostage to Fortune*, 475; Beschloss, *Kennedy and Roosevelt*, 214; Divine, *Foreign Policy and U.S. Presidential Elections, 1940–1948*, 77.

21. *Hartford Courant*, October 28, 1940, "Kennedy Talks with FDR"; FDR to Kennedy, October 26, 1940, in Smith, *Hostage to Fortune*, 480.

22. *New York Times*, October 28, 1940, "Kennedy Sees Roosevelt at White House"; Beschloss, *Kennedy and Roosevelt*, 215ff.

23. Beschloss, *Kennedy and Roosevelt*, 216–217; Kennedy diary entry, October 27, 1940, in Smith, *Hostage to Fortune*, 481.

24. Kennedy diary entry, October 27, 1940, in Smith, *Hostage to Fortune*, 481; Beschloss, *Kennedy and Roosevelt*, 217; Arthur M. Schlesinger, Jr., *Robert Kennedy and His Times* (New York: Ballantine Books, 1979), 35–36.

25. Kennedy diary entry, October 27, 1940, in Smith, *Hostage to Fortune*, 483. Beschloss, *Kennedy and Roosevelt*, 218, 221, 218, respectively.

26. Beschloss, *Kennedy and Roosevelt*, 219.

27. Kennedy's position that Chamberlain was correct in agreeing to the Munich Pact foreshadowed revisionist histories such as A. J. P. Taylor's 1961 book, *The Origins of the Second World*

War. Taylor praised Chamberlain's policy of appeasement, ignoring the fact that Chamberlain abandoned appeasement in the spring of 1939 after Hitler took over the rest of Czechoslovakia.

28. *Washington Post,* October 30, 1940, "Text of Talk for Roosevelt by Kennedy." In July 1940, Chamberlain wrote in his diary, "Saw Joe Kennedy, who says everyone in the U.S.A. thinks we shall be beaten before the end of the month." Beschloss, *Kennedy and Roosevelt,* 208.

29. October 29, 1940, in Smith, *Hostage to Fortune,* 489.

30. *Time,* November 11, 1940, "The Last Seven Days"; *Los Angeles Times,* October 31, 1940, "Roosevelt's Boston Address."

31. *New York Times,* November 3, 1940, "Embattled Candidates in a Mood of Victory"; Sherwood, *Roosevelt and Hopkins,* 191. See also Blum, *From the Morgenthau Diaries,* 2:196.

32. *Christian Science Monitor,* October 31, 1940, "Roosevelt Favors 12,000 More Planes."

33. *Los Angeles Times,* October 31, 1940, "Order Pushed by President"; Sherwood, *Roosevelt and Hopkins,* 191; Blum, *From the Morgenthau Diaries,* 2:196.

34. *New York Times,* October 13, 1940, "17% of U.S. Voters Seen Favoring War"; Gallup, "Influencing and Evaluating Public Opinion," lecture on November 7, 1940, Army War College Records, quoted in J. Garry Clifford, review essay, "Both Ends of the Telescope: New Perspectives on FDR and American Entry into World War II," *Diplomatic History,* 13, 2 (April 1989), 229; Sherwood, *Roosevelt and Hopkins,* 299.

35. *New York Times,* October 31, 1940, "Willkie Cites Past." Robert Sherwood wrote that when Harry Hopkins was in England in early 1941, the English couldn't grasp that only Congress in the United States could declare war. Sherwood wrote that "there persisted the belief in London that Roosevelt would have the United States in the war by May 1, 1941. This strange misapprehension may have been due in part to the prediction made by Willkie . . . that if Roosevelt were re-elected we would be at war in April." Sherwood, *Roosevelt and Hopkins,* 263; *Christian Science Monitor,* October 31, 1940, "Roosevelt Favors 12,000 More Planes."

36. "When the Red Red Robin" was written by Harry Woods in 1926. Jolson placed a $20,000 bet that Roosevelt would be reelected. *Washington Post,* November 4, 1940, "The New Yorker," by Leonard Lyons.

Chapter 16: The Fifth Column

1. *New York Times,* October 1, 1940, "Gov. Lehman Asks 3D Term"; *New York Times,* October 1, 1940, "Hitler Is the Issue"; *New York Times,* October 4, 1940, "Dictators on Way"; *New York Times,* October 8, 1940, "Mr. Mathews Expelled." By November 24, 1940, Matthews was back in Rome, reporting for the *New York Times.*

2. Thomsen to Foreign Ministry, February 7, 1940, in *Documents on German Foreign Policy, 1918–1945,* Series D (1937–1945), 13 vols. (Washington, D.C.: United States Government Printing Office, 1947–), Document 597, 8:748.

3. *Documents on German Foreign Policy,* Series D, Document 597, 8:749. See also Francis MacDonnell, *Insidious Foes: The Axis Fifth Column and the American Home Front* (New York: Oxford University Press, 2005), 27.

4. Thomas H. Etzold, "The (F)utility Factor: German Information Gathering in the U.S. 1933–1941," *Military Affairs,* 39, 2 (April 1975), 77–78; *New York Times,* September 1, 1940, "Fifth Columnists Active in America."

5. Thomsen to Foreign Ministry, April 19, 1940, in *Documents on German Foreign Policy,* Series D, Document 139, 9:206; Thomsen to Foreign Ministry, May 14, 1940, in *Documents on German Foreign Policy,* Series D, Document 243, 11:339; see also Thomsen to Foreign Ministry, March 27, 1940, in *Documents on German Foreign Policy,* Series D, Document 13, 9:30.

6. Thomsen to Foreign Ministry, October 4, 1940, in *Documents on German Foreign Policy,* Series D, Document 147, 11:243–244; see also Thomsen to Foreign Ministry, July 5, 1940, in *Documents on German Foreign Policy,* Series D, Document 112, 10:125–126.

7. Wayne Cole, *Roosevelt and the Isolationists* (Lincoln: University of Nebraska Press, 1983), 144. See also Thomsen to Foreign Ministry, September 24, 1939, in *Documents on German Foreign*

Policy, Series D, Document 129, 8:127. Any contact between Thomsen and Father Coughlin, a German propagandist later said, would have smeared Coughlin and destroyed "his integrity." Wayne Cole, *America First* (Madison: University of Wisconsin Press, 1953), 118. See also Heribert Von Strempel, "Confessions of a German Propagandist," *Public Opinion Quarterly,* 10, 2 (Summer 1946), 221, 225. See also Alfred M. Beck, *Hitler's Ambivalent Attaché: Lt. Gen. Friedrich von Boetticher* (Washington, D.C.: Potomac Books, 2005), 162.

8. Memorandum by Ambassador Dieckhoff, July 21, 1940, in *Documents on German Foreign Policy,* Series D, Document 199, 10:259–260. See also Warren Kimball, "Dieckhoff and America," *Historian,* 27, 2 (February 1965), 220.

9. *New York Times,* October 16, 1940, "Roosevelt Leads to War, Nazi Says."

10. *New York Times,* October 12, 1940, "Willkie's Boston Speech." Sidney A. Freifeld, "Nazi Press Agentry and the American Press," *Public Opinion Quarterly,* 6, 2 (Summer 1942), 234–235, 222, 226, 230, respectively. Freifeld was the Rome correspondent for the *New York Herald Tribune* and the *London Times and News Chronicle.* In 1941, former ambassador John Cudahy, representing the North American Newspaper Alliance, and Karl van Wiegand, chief correspondent of the Hearst Sunday newspapers, were "awarded" interviews with Hitler and Goering.

11. Von Strempel, "Confessions of a German Propagandist," 233. Strempel, however, told the War Crimes Commission that the New York consulate did continue to maintain relations with the German-American Bund.

12. Ambassador Dieckhoff to Foreign Ministry, June 2, 1938, in *Documents on German Foreign Policy,* Series D, Document 454, 1:708; *New York Times,* November 15, 1940, advertisement for Quincy Howe, *The News and How to Understand It* (Display Ad 66), 18.

13. *New York Times,* January 3, 1941, "Five-Cent Hitlers"; *New York Times,* January 2, 1941, "Bares Bund Creed."

14. *New York Times,* February 21, 1939, "22,000 Nazis Hold Rally in Garden"; *New York Times,* September 4, 1939, "Kuhn Says Hitler 'Can Lick World'"; *Atlanta Constitution,* February 26, 1939, "On the Record" by Dorothy Thompson; *Chicago Daily Tribune,* February 21, 1939, "Fight Nazis in Big N.Y. Rally."

15. *New York Times,* February 23, 1949, "Kuhn Is Freed by German Court." After the war, Kuhn was convicted under German law as a "major Nazi." He served two years in prison before his sentence was commuted. See also Richard W. Steele, "Franklin D. Roosevelt and His Foreign Policy Critics," *Political Science Quarterly,* 94, 1 (Spring 1979), 17; Robert Dallek, *Franklin D. Roosevelt and American Foreign Policy* (New York: Oxford University Press, 1979), 225. See also Arthur M. Schlesinger, Jr., "A Comment on 'Roosevelt and His Foreign Policy Critics,'" *Political Science Quarterly,* 94, 1 (Spring 1979), 33–35.

16. Thomsen to Foreign Ministry, September 18, 1939, in *Documents on German Foreign Policy,* Series D, Document 88, 8: 89–91.

17. Thomsen to Foreign Ministry, June 19, 1940, in *Documents on German Foreign Policy,* Series D, Document 493, 9:626.

18. Fish in fact complained that the Nazis were too tightfisted with their funds. Herbert Parmet, *Never Again: A President Runs for a Third Term* (New York: Macmillan, 1968), 139; Thomsen to Foreign Ministry, June 12, 1940, in *Documents on German Foreign Policy,* Series D, 9:551. See also Alton Frye, *Nazi Germany and the American Hemisphere, 1933–1941* (New Haven, Conn.: Yale University Press, 1967), 136–137. The expenses were authorized by Berlin. See Thomsen to Foreign Ministry, July 3, 1940, in *Documents on German Foreign Policy,* Series D, Document 91, 10:101–102. See also Hugh Ross, "John L. Lewis and the Election of 1940," *Labor History,* 17, 2 (1976), 175–177.

19. Ross, "John L. Lewis and the Election of 1940," 174; Thomsen to Foreign Ministry, June 15, 1940, in *Documents on German Foreign Policy,* Series D, Document 441, 9:576; Thomsen to Foreign Ministry, June 19, 1940, in *Documents on German Foreign Policy,* Series D, Document 492, 9:624–625; Justus D. Doenecke, ed., *In Danger Undaunted: The Anti-Interventionist Movement of 1940–1941 as Revealed in the Papers of the America First Committee* (Stanford, Calif.: Hoover Institution Press, 1990), 36.

20. Cole, *America First*, 118–130.

21. Thomsen to Foreign Ministry, June 19, 1940, in *Documents on German Foreign Policy*, Series D, Document 493, 9:626; Frye, *Nazi Germany and the American Hemisphere*, 140–141; John Roy Carlson, *Under Cover: My Four Years in the Nazi Underworld of America* (New York: E. P. Dutton, 1943), 121; Thomsen to Foreign Ministry, July 18, 1940, in *Documents on German Foreign Policy*, Series D, Document 186, 10:243; *Washington Post*, April 27, 1939, "Forego Any Neutrality Laws"; Frye, *Nazi Germany and the American Hemisphere*, 161; Niel M. Johnson, *George Sylvester Viereck: German-American Propagandist* (Urbana: University of Illinois Press, 1972), 219–220, 227.

22. Johnson, *George Sylvester Viereck*, 221, 204, respectively; Phyllis Keller, "George Sylvester Viereck: The Psychology of a German-American Militant," *Journal of Interdisciplinary History*, 2, 1 (Summer 1971), 92–93, 97. See also Geoffrey S. Smith, *To Save a Nation: American Countersubversives, the New Deal, and the Coming of World War II* (New York: Basic Books, 1973), 166–168. Another book by Viereck, published in 1930, *Salome, the Wandering Jewess*, deals with a modern woman's revolt against her bondage to the male principle. That book along with *The Invincible Adam* (1932) constituted Viereck's "trilogy of love." Keller, "George Sylvester Viereck," 93.

23. Johnson, *George Sylvester Viereck*, 218, 198, 200, 216, respectively; Smith, *To Save a Nation*, 167. Republican congressman Stephen Day of Illinois also helped Viereck.

24. *Congressional Record* of June 22, 1940, in Robert Shogan, *Hard Bargain: How FDR Twisted Churchill's Arm* (Boulder, Colo.: Westview Press, 1999), 141. See also William Shirer, *The Rise and Fall of the Third Reich* (Greenwich, Conn.: Fawcett, 1960), 748; *Atlanta Constitution*, June 15, 1940, "F.D.R. Scoffs At Nazi Pledge"; Thomsen to Foreign Ministry, June 27, 1940, in *Documents on German Foreign Policy*, Series D, Document 39, 10:40. See also Carlson, *Under Cover*, 87. A new book was published in the fall of 1940, *Fifth Columnists Active in America* by George Birtt, an editorial writer for the *New York World Telegram*.

25. *Congressional Record*, August 20, 1940, and September 3, 1940, pp. 11378ff.

26. Thomsen to Foreign Ministry, September 1, 1940, in *Documents on German Foreign Policy*, Document 2, 11:1–2.

27. Saul Friedlander, *Prelude to Downfall: Hitler and the United States, 1939–1941*, trans. Aline B. Werth (New York: Knopf, 1967), 76; *New York Times*, March 30, 1940, "Berlin Accuses U.S."; Thomsen to Foreign Ministry, June 19, 1940, *Documents on German Foreign Policy*, Series D, Document 492, 9:624–625; *New York Times*, April 2, 1940, "Fish Asks Inquiry of Nazi White Book"; *Christian Science Monitor*, April 2, 1940, "Congress Cool"; *Chicago Daily Tribune*, April 4, 1940, "Our Hot Ambassadors"; Frye, *Nazi Germany and the American Hemisphere*, 134.

28. Thomsen to Foreign Ministry, August 7, 1940, *Documents on German Foreign Policy*, Series D, Document 300, 10:427–428; *New York Times*, October 28, 1940, "Best Sellers of the Week"; Justus D. Doenecke, *Storm on the Horizon: The Challenge to American Intervention, 1939–1941* (Lanham, Md.: Rowman and Littlefield, 2000), 163; Justus D. Doenecke, "The Isolationist as Collectivist: Lawrence Dennis and the Coming of World War II," *Journal of Libertarian Studies*, 3, 2 (Summer 1979), 200; Von Strempel, "Confessions of a German Propagandist," 222.

29. Thomsen to Foreign Ministry, June 13,1940, in *Documents on German Foreign Policy*, Series D, Document 422, 9:559; and June 16, 1940, in *Documents on German Foreign Policy*, Series D, Document 455, 9:585; *Atlanta Constitution*, April 27, 1941, "Stay Out of War"; *Hartford Courant*, August 28, 1940, "A Timely Warning"; *Washington Post*, March 16, 1940, "Arms and the Man"; *New York Times*, August 20, 1940, "'Peace Bloc' Assails Conscription"; *Hartford Courant*, June 2, 1940, "Kathleen Norris Regrets Suggestion"; *New York Times*, April 23, 1941, "Lindbergh to Lead Anti-Convoy Rally"; *Chicago Daily Tribune*, April 23, 1941, "Fears of Few Peril Millions, Kathleen Norris Warns"; Frye, *Nazi Germany and the American Hemisphere*, 137.

30. Von Strempel, "Confessions of a German Propagandist," 218–219, 228–230; William Shirer, "Berlin: September 1940," in *Reporting World War II*, 2 vols. (New York: Library of America, 1995), 1:129; Frye, *Nazi Germany and the American Hemisphere*, 145, 97, 163, respectively; *New York Times*, March 31, 1940, "Allies Come to Grips with Reich Propaganda"; *Atlanta Constitution*, April 11, 1940, "White Discovers Some British Converts of Nazi Propaganda." In March 1941, the head of the German News Agency, Manfred Zapp, was indicted for failing to register as a foreign agent.

31. *New York Times*, June 29, 1949, "William Griffin, Publisher, Was 51"; Thomsen to Foreign Ministry, November 4, 1940, in *Documents on German Foreign Policy*, Series D, Document 284, 11:463–464.

Chapter 17: Final Days, Final Words

1. *New York Times*, October 15, 1940, "Lindbergh Assails 'Present' Leaders," italics added. In "Backwash from the Wave of the Future," published in the ultraconservative, isolationist periodical *Scribner's Commentator*, 10 (June 1941), Jane Ellsworth warned that America, under the Roosevelt administration, was allowing the "blood of an entirely different culture to be injected into her veins." The result of pollution via Jewish blood, she wrote, is "a weakening, stunting, confused reaction."

2. Charles A. Lindbergh, *The Wartime Journals of Charles A. Lindbergh* (New York: Harcourt Brace Jovanovich, 1970), August 24, 1940, 381; Lindbergh, *Wartime Journals*, November 5, 1940, 414.

3. Anne Morrow Lindbergh, *War Within and Without: Diaries and Letters of Anne Morrow Lindbergh, 1939–1944* (New York: Harcourt Brace Jovanovich, 1980), 119–120, italics added.

4. *New York Times*, June 18, 1940, "Roosevelt Called 'No. 1 Isolationist'"; Lawrence Dennis, *The Dynamics of War and Revolution* (New York: Weekly Foreign Letter, 1940), xxiv. Willkie's foreign policy advisor, Raymond Buell, who was also an editor at *Fortune*, met with Dennis and afterward wrote that Dennis and Lindbergh were close friends who both believed that "the war is a product of the Wall Street plutocracy, Jews, etc. and Dennis figures that if a small number of intellectuals have been 'right' on this war issue and have a clear-cut fascist alternative, they will be able to seize power." Raymond Buell, Memorandum on Foreign Affairs for Henry Luce, January 8, 1941, p. 34, Raymond Leslie Buell Papers, Manuscript Division, Library of Congress. Courtesy of J. Garry Clifford.

5. Anne Morrow Lindbergh, *The Wave of the Future: A Confession of Faith* (New York: Harcourt, Brace, 1940), 11–12, 18–21, 24, 34, italics added. "Are we afraid," she wrote, "not only of German bombers but also of change, of responsibility, of growing up?" In the text of his August 4, 1940, speech, Charles Lindbergh also referred to "democracy" and the "so-called democratic nations." *New York Times*, August 5, 1940, "Text of Col. Lindbergh Speech." See also *New York Times*, January 6, 1941, "Hits Fear in Book by Mrs. Lindbergh."

6. Anne Morrow Lindbergh to Elizabeth Morrow, September 4, 1940, in Lindbergh, *War Within and Without*, 143.

7. *Los Angeles Times*, November 1, 1940, "Text of Willkie's Address," italics added.

8. *Hartford Courant*, October 6, 1940, "Anne Lindbergh Writes Her 'Confession of Faith'"; *Chicago Daily Tribune*, October 2, 1940, "A Modern Philosophy"; Wayne Cole, *Roosevelt and the Isolationists* (Lincoln: University of Nebraska Press, 1983), 461. See also *Chicago Daily Tribune*, April 14, 1941, "Ickes Lambastes America First."

9. Allan Nevins, "Or Is It 'The Wave of the Past'?," *New York Times Sunday Magazine*, December 29, 1940, 12. Thomas W. Lamont, a partner of J. P. Morgan and Co., gave a speech on November 15, 1939, in which he said: "What we have been witnessing in Germany since 1933 . . . has been a violent social revolution. A German friend described it to me in terms of a great tidal wave. It came rolling in . . . overwhelming the country, bore out to sea and oblivion the stable elements of the community, leaving cast upon the shore all the strange creatures of the undersea world of society." Lamont, "Economic Peace Essential to Political Peace," in *Vital Speeches of the Day*, 6, 108–110.

In her "My Day" newspaper column of April 18, 1949, Eleanor Roosevelt mentioned a book by Reuben Markham entitled *The Wave of the Past*, published in 1941 by the University of North Carolina Press. Markham's book, ER wrote, "is apparently inspired by Anne Lindbergh's book, *The Wave of the Future*. Mr. R. H. Markham writes that 'the past has its mark and the future has its mark. The one is slavery and the other is freedom.' I think you will find both of these books of interest." "My Day," April 18, 1941.

10. *New York Times*, October 3, 2004, "Inside the List"; Lindbergh, *War Within and Without*, October 8, 1944, 450. But for his part, Charles Lindbergh insisted in 1972 that his wife's book was correct. He told Wayne Cole that "reviewers and critics left out the 'scum' part—giving a totally false impression of what she wrote." Wayne Cole interview with Charles Lindbergh, June 7, 1972, Army and Navy Club, Washington, D.C., Cole Papers, Hoover Presidential Library, West Branch, Iowa. Courtesy of J. Garry Clifford.

11. *New York Times*, October 26, 1940, "Text of John L. Lewis's Appeal for the Support of Wendell Willkie." Robert Sherwood, *Roosevelt and Hopkins: An Intimate History*, rev. ed. (New York: Harper and Brothers, 1950), 193.

12. *New York Times*, November 1, 1940, "Willkie Warns U.S. of One-Man Rule"; Melvyn Dubofsky and Warren Van Tine, *John L. Lewis* (Urbana: University of Illinois Press, 1986), 331–332, 345–346, 446. In 1933, with Hitler's approval, James Rhodes Davis had built an oil refinery in Hamburg to which he shipped oil from Mexico. But in 1938, Davis's business suffered a reverse. Mexico nationalized foreign oil leases, expropriating Davis's holdings. Under mysterious circumstances, Davis convinced John L. Lewis to intervene on his behalf with the Mexican government. Lewis traveled to Mexico and successfully persuaded the government to grant Davis exclusive commercial rights to the nationalized oil of Mexico, which Davis's tankers shipped to Germany and Italy. *New York Times*, December 31, 1940, "Davis Arranged in 1938." See also Hugh Ross, "John L. Lewis and the Election of 1940," *Labor History*, 17, 2 (1976).

In 1939, when the British blockade shut off German oil imports from Mexico, Davis concocted another bizarre plan: he would convince Roosevelt to negotiate a peace settlement in Europe and thus end the blockade, a scheme that had the approval of Hermann Goering. Once again Davis called on Lewis for help, and in September 1939, the labor boss managed to set up an appointment for Davis with President Roosevelt. When the two met on September 15, Davis presented himself as Goering's personal representative and peace emissary, and, according to a memo written by Roosevelt's aide and assistant secretary of state Adolf Berle, assured the president that Goering would soon be in control of Germany and was bent on peace. FDR immediately directed the FBI to monitor Davis—as well as all his contacts with Lewis. Ross, "John L. Lewis and the Election of 1940," 165; James V. Compton, *The Swastika and the Eagle: Hitler, the United States, and the Origins of World War II* (Boston: Houghton Mifflin, 1967), 165. See also Saul Friedlander, *Prelude to Downfall: Hitler and the United States, 1939–1941*, trans. Aline B. Werth (New York: Knopf, 1967).

Then Davis left for Berlin. Meeting with Goering and other high German officials, Davis convinced them that Lewis wielded tremendous political influence in the United States. Davis claimed not only that Lewis had great sway over Roosevelt but that no Democratic presidential candidate could win without the labor boss's financial backing, and that Lewis therefore could guide the outcome of the 1940 election. *New York Times*, October 23, 1946, "Rogge Ties Lewis to Nazis in Politics."

Apparently taken in by Davis's outlandish claims, Goering encouraged the oilman to persuade Lewis to turn the election against Roosevelt if the president refused to negotiate a peace deal acceptable to Germany. Goering would even assign a young Nazi "supervisor" named Joachim Hertslett to accompany Davis back to the United States. Goering promised Hertslett a post in Germany's Washington embassy and instructed him to raise with Lewis the possibility of organizing a general strike in the United States in the event that war appeared likely. Hertslett, however, was stopped in Bermuda, his forged Swedish passport confiscated; barred from entering the United States, he made his way to Mexico. In March 1940, shadowed by FBI agents, Hertslett gained entrance to the United States and took up residence at the German embassy in Washington. He met several times with Lewis at the United Mine Workers headquarters in Washington and spent a weekend with Davis and Lewis at Davis's home in Scarsdale, N.Y. Hertslett informed Lewis of Goering's hope to defeat FDR in the election. According to what Hertslett told interviewers after the war, Lewis promised to throw his full weight against Roosevelt if he ran for a third term. *New York Times*, January 1, 1941, "Marshall Defies U.S."; Ross, "John L. Lewis and the Election of 1940," 165–166, 172, note; *New York Times*, December 31, 1940, "Verne Marshall Tells of an Offer of Peace"; Alton Frye, *Nazi Germany and the American Hemisphere, 1933–1941* (New Haven,

Conn.: Yale University Press, 1967), 144; Ladislas Farago, *The Game of the Foxes: The Untold Story of German Espionage in the United States and Great Britain During World War II* (New York: D. McKay, 1971), 373.

In the fall of 1940, through the intermediacy of Sam Pryor, Willkie met with Davis in Indiana. Davis informed Willkie that he was willing to pay for Lewis to make a nationwide radio speech endorsing Willkie. Herbert Parmet, *Never Again: A President Runs for a Third Term* (New York: Macmillan, 1968), 233–234.

In late October, Lewis gave his speech for Willkie on the radio with Davis paying $55,000 for the broadcast time. Frye, *Nazi Germany and the American Hemisphere*, 144, note 21. When Lewis was informed much later of Davis's connections to the Nazis, he reacted defensively, pointing out that many respectable American businessmen had ties to Germany in the 1930s. Ross, "John L. Lewis and the Election of 1940," 187.

13. *New York Times*, October 26, 1940, "Text of John L. Lewis's Appeal for the Support of Wendell Willkie," italics added.

14. Frances Perkins, *The Roosevelt I Knew* (New York: Viking, 1946), 127.

15. Parmet, *Never Again*, 233–234; Ross, "John L. Lewis and the Election of 1940," 184.

16. Arthur M. Schlesinger, Jr., ed., *History of American Presidential Elections*, 4 vols. (New York: Chelsea House, 1971), 4:2961; William Millikan, *A Union against Unions: The Minneapolis Citizens Alliance and Its Fight against Organized Labor, 1903–1947* (St. Paul: Minnesota Historical Society Press, 2001), 349. The bill was signed on April 22, 1939. See also *New York Times*, March 19, 1939, "Minnesota Swings Far to the Right"; *Christian Science Monitor*, October 20, 1939, "Labor Finds Little Grist from Legislative Mills."

17. *New York Times*, October 26, 1940, "Text of John L. Lewis's Appeal for the Support of Wendell Willkie"; *Washington Post*, October 28, 1940, "Lewis Sits Down" by Ernest Lindley. At a White House meeting on October 26, Assistant Secretary of State Adolf Berle heard FDR say that "until John Lewis had made his speech, he had had less than no enthusiasm for this campaign at all, and did not greatly care how it came out; but after Lewis had uncorked this singularly dirty line of demagogy he wanted to be re-elected if only to put Lewis out of public life." *Navigating the Rapids, 1918–1971: From the Papers of Adolf A. Berle*, ed. Beatrice Bishop Berle (New York: Harcourt Brace Jovanovich, 1973), 346.

18. Kenneth S. Davis, *FDR: Into the Storm* (New York: Random House, 1993), 618; Dubofsky and Van Tine, *John L. Lewis*, 358–359; Donald Bruce Johnson, *The Republican Party and Wendell Willkie* (Urbana: University of Illinois Press, 1960), 155; *New York Times*, October 26, 1940, "Tobin Puts Lewis on Side of 'Enemy.'"

19. *New York Times*, November 3, 1940, "Experts Ponder Labor Vote"; *New York Times*, March 29, 1940, "Tobin Urges Third Term"; *New York Times*, July 11, 1940, "Auto Union Urges Roosevelt to Run"; *New York Times*, May 21, 1940, "Clothing Workers Demand 3D Term"; *New York Times*, July 14, 1940, "Three Stand Firm"; *New York Times*, May 4, 1940, "Pennsylvania Labor Urges Third Term."

20. *New York Times*, October 27, 1940, "Lewis Repudiated, Backed by Labor"; *New York Times*, October 27, 1940, "Labor's Response to Lewis Diverse"; *New York Times*, October 27, 1940, "C.I.O Denunciation Pours on J. L. Lewis"; *Christian Science Monitor*, October 28, 1940, "Wide Split Seen in C.I.O"; *New York Times*, November 1, 1940, "Secretary of C.I.O. Supports Roosevelt"; *New York Times*, October 27, 1940, "C.I.O Denunciation"; *New York Times*, November 2, 1940, "Lewis Is Repudiated by 24 of News Guild."

21. *New York Times*, November 1, 1940, "Willkie Warns U.S. of One-Man Rule"; *Atlanta Constitution*, November 1, 1940, "Capital Parade"; *New York Times*, November 3, 1940, "Experts Ponder Labor Vote." Also at that rally were Henry Wallace, Mayor La Guardia, New York's governor Herbert Lehman, and Senator James Mead. Mead reminded the audience of Willkie's labor record when he was president of Commonwealth and Southern Corporation. Mead said it was a "grim story of hired labor spies, tear gas, company unions, as well as coercion and intimidation of union workers." *New York Times*, November 1, 1940, "Willkie Warns U.S. of One-Man Rule."

22. *New York Times*, November 2, 1940, "Ovation in Kings."

23. Sherwood, *Roosevelt and Hopkins*, 192.

24. *New York Times*, November 1, 1940, "In the Nation," by Arthur Krock.

25. Campaign Address at Brooklyn, November 1, 1940, in Samuel I. Rosenman, ed., *Public Papers and Addresses of Franklin D. Roosevelt [PPA]*, 13 vols. (New York: Macmillan, 1941), 9:530–539. See also *New York Times*, November 1, 1940, "In the Nation," by Arthur Krock.

26. *New York Times*, November 3, 1940, "President's Talk Scored by Willkie"; *Time*, November 11, 1940, "The Last Seven Days." Chester Bowles, a member of America First and future ambassador to India and governor of Connecticut, wrote to Douglas Stuart, Jr., on October 22, 1940, "If I thought that Willkie would keep us out of war and that Roosevelt would put us into war, I would, of course, vote for Willkie. At the same time, if we were actually at war, I believe I would rather have Roosevelt as President than Willkie. All of which is very confusing to me personally!" America First Collection, Box 285, Hoover Institution Archives, Stanford, Calif. Courtesy of J. Garry Clifford.

27. Samuel I. Rosenman, *Working with Roosevelt* (New York: Harper and Brothers, 1952), 248–250; Sherwood, *Roosevelt and Hopkins*, 195ff. Sherwood later wrote that the work that was put into writing FDR's speeches was "prodigious"; his most important speeches sometimes required a week or more of hard labor, with every word judged by its effectiveness over the radio. FDR understood that his words would constitute a major part of his legacy. Sherwood, *Roosevelt and Hopkins*, 212, 215.

28. Sherwood, *Roosevelt and Hopkins*, 195–196.

29. *Time*, November 11, 1940, "The Last Seven Days."

30. Campaign Address in Cleveland, November 2, 1940, in *PPA*, 9:544–553, italics added; Sherwood, *Roosevelt and Hopkins*, 196.

31. Campaign Address in Cleveland, November 2, 1940, in *PPA*, 9:552.

32. Rosenman, *Working with Roosevelt*, 248.

33. *New York Times*, November 3, 1940, "Text of Willkie's Address and the Final Rally"; *New York Times*, November 3, 1940, "Ovation to Willkie"; Marcia Davenport, *Too Strong for Fantasy* (New York: Scribner, 1967), 282. An armed man who approached to within feet of the platform where Willkie had just finished speaking at Madison Square Garden was arrested after a woman told police that he had a loaded revolver. He was a 78-year-old doctor who said he just wanted to get a better look at Willkie. *New York Times*, November 3, 1940, "Armed Man Seized Near Willkie."

34. *New York Times*, November 3, 1940, "Mayor Ridicules Willkie's Record"; *New York Times*, September 13, 1940, "Mayor La Guardia Backs Roosevelt."

35. Joe Martin, *My First Fifty Years in Politics* (New York: McGraw-Hill, 1960), 119; *New York Times*, November 4, 1940, "Pledge by Willkie"; *Chicago Daily Tribune*, November 4, 1940, "Willkie Plea: Bar 3D Terms."

36. *New York Times*, November 4, 1940, "Nazis Machine Gun Streets of London"; *New York Times*, November 4, 1940, "Drive on Koritza"; *New York Times*, November 4, 1940, "The International Situation."

37. Robert Sherwood, *Roosevelt and Hopkins*, 198.

38. *Los Angeles Times*, November 5, 1940, "President Confident of Third Term."

39. *New York Times*, November 5, 1940, "Hyde Park Appeal"; Rosenman, *Working with Roosevelt*, 254; Sherwood, *Roosevelt and Hopkins*, 198.

40. Steve Neal, *Dark Horse: A Biography of Wendell Willkie* (Garden City, N.Y.: Doubleday, 1984), 172.

41. Sherwood, *Roosevelt and Hopkins*, 199; *Washington Post*, November 5, 1940, "Dorothy Thompson, Stage, Screen Stars Go on Air."

42. *New York Times*, November 5, 1940, "Flood of Oratory Ends Willkie Drive"; *New York Times*, November 5, 1940, "Texts of Willkie Radio Addresses on Eve of the Election"; *Washington Post*, November 5, 1940, "Dewey, Lewis and Louis"; Neal, *Dark Horse*, 173.

43. Sherwood, *Roosevelt and Hopkins*, 198.

44. Theater advertisements, *New Yorker*, October 12, 1940, 34; *New York Times*, November 5, 1940, "Times Sq. Bedlam of Boos and Cheers."

45. David Low, *Years of Wrath: A Cartoon History: 1931–1945*, ed. Quincy Howe (New York: Simon and Schuster, 1946), pages unnumbered but in chronological order. See also *New York Times*, November 5, 1940, "Cartoon Depicts Hitler as a Puzzled Voter Here."

Chapter 18: Safe at Third

1. *Washington Post*, November 6, 1940, "President, Neighbors Hail Victory."

2. Robert Sherwood, *Roosevelt and Hopkins: An Intimate History*, rev. ed. (New York: Harper and Brothers, 1950), 199; James MacGregor Burns, *Roosevelt: The Lion and the Fox* (New York: Harcourt, Brace, 1956), 451.

3. *Hartford Courant*, November 6, 1940, "Roosevelt Ballots at Hyde Park"; Grace Tully, *F.D.R., My Boss* (New York: C. Scribner's Sons, 1949), 240.

4. Michael Francis Reilly, *Reilly of the White House* (New York: Simon and Schuster, 1947), 66. According to Reilly, Morgenthau was "slightly hysterical" on election night.

5. *New York Times*, November 6, 1940, "Willkie Retires Refusing to Give Up"; Steve Neal, *Dark Horse: A Biography of Wendell Willkie* (Garden City, N.Y.: Doubleday, 1984), 174.

6. Joe Martin, *My First Fifty Years in Politics* (New York: McGraw-Hill, 1960), 120; *Washington Post*, November 10, 1940, "Nation Heals Battle Scars." Willkie's wife had given up hope. "I wish Wendell would get ready to go home," she said. *New York Times*, November 6, 1940, "Willkie Retires Refusing to Give Up."

7. Hugh Ross, "John L. Lewis and the Election of 1940," *Labor History*, 17, 2 (1976), 188.

8. *New York Times*, November 6, 1940, "Roosevelt Looks to 'Difficult Days'"; James MacGregor Burns, *Roosevelt: The Soldier of Freedom* (New York: Harcourt Brace Jovanovich, 1970), 3; Kenneth S. Davis, *FDR: Into the Storm* (New York: Random House, 1993), 625.

9. Tully, *F.D.R., My Boss*, 241.

10. *Time*, November 11, 1940, "To the Lighthouse"; *New York Times*, November 6, 1940, "Heavy Raiding Reported"; Burns, *Roosevelt: The Soldier of Freedom*, 9–10; Churchill to Roosevelt, November 6, 1940, in Warren F. Kimball, ed., *Churchill and Roosevelt: The Complete Correspondence*, 3 vols. (Princeton, N.J.: Princeton University Press, 1984), 1:81.

11. FDR to Carl Sandburg, December 3, 1940, in Elliott Roosevelt, ed., *F.D.R.: His Personal Letters*, 4 vols. (New York: Duell, Sloan and Pearce, 1947–1950), 2:1086.

12. *New York Times*, November 6, 1940, "Willkie Retires Refusing to Give Up."

13. *Time*, November 11, 1940, "The Losers."

14. *New York Times*, November 7, 1940, "From Mr. Willkie"; *New York Times*, November 7, 1940, "Mrs. Willkie Takes Loss Cheerfully"; *New York Times*, November 7, 1940, "Lincoln-Like Plea of Benet."

15. *Los Angeles Times*, December 8, 1940, "Significant Trends Shown." *Time*, November 11, 1940, "The Presidency: Victory."

16. In South Carolina, FDR won 95,470 votes compared to just 1,727 for Willkie; in Mississippi, FDR won 168,267 votes to 7,364 for Willkie. *New York Times*, November 6, 1940, "Maine and Vermont Stay in Republican Fold but Their Pluralities Are Reduced Heavily"; *Washington Post*, December 6, 1941, "The Gallup Poll: Labor Defection from Roosevelt"; Robert A. Divine, *Foreign Policy and U.S. Presidential Elections, 1940–1948* (New York: New Viewpoints, 1974), 85. See also Irving Bernstein, "John L. Lewis and the Voting Behavior of the C.I.O.," *Public Opinion Quarterly*, 5 (June 1941), 233–249.

17. *New York Times*, November 23, 1940, "Philip Murray Replaces Lewis."

18. Frances Perkins, *The Roosevelt I Knew* (New York: Viking, 1946), 113.

19. Raymond Buell, unpublished memoir, p. 26, Box 13, Raymond Leslie Buell Papers, Manuscript Division, Library of Congress; Ben Allen to Herbert Hoover, November 19, 1940, Post-Presidential Subject-Campaign 1940-Candidate, Willkie, Herbert Hoover Presidential Library, West Branch, Iowa. In the Barnard Mss., Manuscripts Department, Lilly Library at Indiana University, Bloomington, see the following: George Roberts Interview, August 10, 1955, "Campaign—100";

Bartley Crum Interview, August 15, 1955, "Campaign—101"; Donald Thornburgh Interview, "Campaign—103"; Edward Willkie Interview, "Campaign—95"; Pierce Butler Interview, "Campaign—103." Butler, the son of Pierce Butler, Jr., who was with Willkie on the campaign train, said that his father was with Dewey on election night and recalled that Dewey was drunk and definitely not depressed by Willkie's defeat. Barnard Mss., Manuscripts Department, Lilly Library, Indiana University, Bloomington. Courtesy of J. Garry Clifford. See also Ellsworth Barnard, *Wendell Willkie: Fighter for Freedom* (Marquette: Northern Michigan University Press, 1966), 365; Edward J. Flynn, *You're the Boss* (New York: Viking, 1947), 148, 168; Heribert Von Strempel, "Confessions of a German Propagandist," *Public Opinion Quarterly*, 10, 2 (Summer 1946), 224; Neal, *Dark Horse*, 151–152; William R. Castle, Jr., Diary, Houghton Library, Harvard University, November 6, 1940, p. 383. Courtesy of J. Garry Clifford. *New York Times*, August 29, 1940, "Bund Backs Willkie"; *New York Times*, September 8, 1940, "Says Bigot Groups Support Willkie." Willkie's advisor Raymond Buell later wrote that he "heaved a genuine sigh of relief that Willkie had been defeated, although of course I kept this feeling dark." Buell, unpublished memoir, p. 64. For his part, Harold Ickes indulged in second-guessing of the Democratic side. On Election Day, a nervous Ickes complained to his diary, "We haven't deserved to win. It actually seemed at times to me that important people in our ranks were trying to throw victory away while the president seemed to be utterly indifferent. I have never seen such incompetent and inept management." Four days later, he admitted that he had been "very anxious. . . . There were too many elements of doubt and uncertainty in it to suit me." Harold L. Ickes, *The Secret Diary of Harold L. Ickes*, 3 vols. (New York: Simon and Schuster, 1954), November 5, 1940, and November 9, 1940, 3:361–362.

20. Martin, *My First Fifty Years in Politics*, 120, 101, respectively. Bernard F. Donahoe concluded his book *Private Plans and Public Dangers: The Story of FDR's Third Nomination* (Notre Dame, Ind.: University of Notre Dame Press, 1965) with the remark that "the voting in the 1940 election seems to indicate that no Democrat except Roosevelt could have defeated Willkie," 195.

21. *New York Times*, November 7, 1940, "Joy Voiced Abroad"; *New York Times*, November 10, 1940, "Hard Road Ahead, Churchill Warns"; FDR to Rosenman, November 13, 1940, in Roosevelt, *F.D.R.: His Personal Letters*, 2:1078.

22. Willkie to Mark Sullivan, November 24 and 25, 1940, quoted in Neal, *Dark Horse*, 179; Herbert Parmet, *Never Again: A President Runs for a Third Term* (New York: Macmillan, 1968), 278.

23. Sherwood, *Roosevelt and Hopkins*, 635; *Washington Post*, October 2, 1940, "On the Record"; James Roosevelt, *My Parents: A Differing View* (Playboy Press, 1976), 164. Henry Luce wrote that Willkie was "as unprecedented as the Third Term." Alan Brinkley, *The Publisher: Henry Luce and His American Century* (New York: Knopf, 2010), 260. FDR did not have such fond feelings for his adversary in the 1944 presidential election, New York governor Thomas Dewey. "I still think he is a son of a bitch," FDR said to his aide William Hassett after Dewey conceded the election. Burns, *Roosevelt: The Soldier of Freedom*, 530. Robert Sherwood also wrote that the election of 1940 was the political battle the president liked least to remember. It had the atmosphere of a "dreadful masquerade" in which the two candidates disguised the fact that they agreed with each other on the basic issues. Sherwood, *Roosevelt and Hopkins*, 200.

24. *New York Times*, November 8, 1940, "Washington Hails Roosevelt Return"; Leila Stiles, November 7, 1940, Leila Stiles file, Franklin D. Roosevelt Library (FDRL), Hyde Park, N.Y. Courtesy of J. Garry Clifford.

25. Press Conference, November 8, 1940, in Samuel I. Rosenman, ed., *Public Papers and Addresses of Franklin D. Roosevelt [PPA]*, 13 vols. (New York: Macmillan, 1941), 9:560. See also *Wall Street Journal*, November 9, 1940, "First Press Conference of a Third Term."

26. Attlee to Laski, November 7, 1940, quoted in David Reynolds, "Roosevelt, the British Left and the Appointment of John G. Winant as United States Ambassador to Britain in 1941," *International History Review*, 4, 3 (August 1982), 398; William L. Shirer, *Berlin Diary* (New York: Knopf, 1941), November 6, 1940, and December 5, 1940, 561, 596, italics added.

27. Circular of the State Secretary, November 8, 1940, in *Documents on German Foreign Policy, 1918–1945*, Series D (1937–1945), 13 vols. (Washington, D.C.: United States Government Printing Office, 1947–), Document 305, 11:499.

28. Memorandum by an Official of the Information Department, November 19, 1940, in *Documents on German Foreign Policy*, Series D, Document 359, 11:624–625. This memorandum was unsigned but showed the name of Dr. von Trott zu Solz of the Information Department at the top.

29. Memorandum by Ambassador Dieckhoff, January 9, 1941, in *Documents on German Foreign Policy*, Series D, Document 633, 11:1061–1063.

30. On November 25, 1940, an erroneous article appeared on the front page of the *New York Times*, headlined "Miss Perkins Quits Cabinet; Views Her Job as Finished"; *New York Times*, November 6, 1940, "Common Sense; Praised"; FDR to Ickes, November 8, 1940, in Roosevelt, *F.D.R.: His Personal Letters*, 2:1077. The *New York Times* erroneously reported that the president intended to accept the resignation of Colonel Stimson. *New York Times*, November 8, 1940, "Ickes Offer to Quit Hint to the Others."

31. *Los Angeles Times*, December 9, 1941, "Unions Vow Loyal Work"; *New York Times*, November 23, 1940, "Philip Murray Replaces Lewis"; *New York Times*, November 4, 1940, "Farley Asks Aides to Get Out Vote"; *New York Times*, June 10, 1976, "James A. Farley, 88, Dies."

32. *Boston Globe*, November 10, 1940, "Kennedy Says Democracy"; *New York Times*, August 9, 1940, "Farley Withdraws from the Cabinet"; *Atlanta Constitution*, December 6, 1940, "The Capital Parade," by Joseph Alsop and Robert Kintner; Will Swift, *The Kennedy Family amidst the Gathering Storm* (Washington: Smithsonian Books, 2008), 293; *New York Times*, November 12, 1940, "Kennedy Disavows Interview on War"; *Atlanta Constitution*, November 14, 1940, "Capital Parade," by Joseph Alsop and Robert Kintner; Isaac Kramnick and Barry Sheerman, *Harold Laski: A Life on the Left* (New York: Allen Lane/Penguin, 1993), 430. "I think he must be planning on resigning his post," commented Charles Lindbergh after reading the Kennedy interview. Charles A. Lindbergh, *The Wartime Journals of Charles A. Lindbergh* (New York: Harcourt Brace Jovanovich, 1970), November 11, 1940, 415. Anne Morrow Lindbergh wrote in her diary that Kennedy was "evidently very irritated at the president. . . . It almost gave you confidence to be with a man with so much sheer sense of power even though you know some of it—maybe most of it?—was self-inflated. I felt he was the most powerful person in the United States at this moment." Anne Morrow Lindbergh, *War Within and Without: Diaries and Letters of Anne Morrow Lindbergh, 1939–1944* (New York: Harcourt Brace Jovanovich, 1980), November 12, 1940, 152–153. A few weeks after Kennedy's interview, three pacifist members of the British House of Commons introduced a motion calling for immediate peace and compromise with Germany. Their motion was voted down, 342 to 4. Because these appeasers were permitted to speak in Parliament, the *New York Times* editorialized, "What now becomes of the fatuous idea that British democracy is dead or dying? Can any free country do better than this to prove that its freedom still lives?" *New York Times*, December 6, 1940, "Democracy at Its Best."

33. *New York Times*, November 12, 1940, "Kennedy Disavows Interview on War." Other newspapers jumped to the *Globe*'s defense, mocking the cry of "I was misquoted!" Columnists Joseph Alsop and Robert Kintner reported that *Globe* editors had twice phoned Kennedy, read him the article before it went to press, and asked him to approve the quotations, which he did. *Washington Post*, December 5, 1940, "Capital Parade."

34. David Koskoff, *Joseph P. Kennedy: A Life and Times* (Englewood Cliffs, N.J.: Prentice-Hall, 1974), 303–304; Michael R. Beschloss, *Kennedy and Roosevelt: The Uneasy Alliance* (New York: Norton, 1980), 226. In 1945, Herbert Hoover had a private conversation with Kennedy and reported that "Kennedy told me that in the campaign Roosevelt had sent for him to come back, told him that he did not propose to get the country into the war at all. Kennedy said that he believed Roosevelt and went out and made a speech in Roosevelt's support. When Kennedy realized that these promises had no meaning, he went out and made two speeches denouncing Roosevelt and his proposals to get into the war." George H. Nash, ed., *Freedom Betrayed: Herbert Hoover's Secret History of the Second World War and Its Aftermath* (Stanford, Calif.: Hoover Institution Press, 2011), 829.

35. Beschloss, *Kennedy and Roosevelt*, 228–230; Gore Vidal, "Eleanor," *New York Review of Books*, 17, 8 (November 18, 1971).

36. *New York Times*, December 2, 1940, "Kennedy Resigns as London Envoy to Combat War"; *Atlanta Constitution*, December 6, 1940, "The Capital Parade" by Joseph Alsop and Robert Kintner.

37. Kennedy was overheard saying this in early January 1941 to Franklin Roosevelt, Jr., in a plane from Palm Beach to Washington. Beschloss, *Kennedy and Roosevelt*, 234–235.

38. *New York Times*, December 7, 1940, "Kennedy Is Attacked by British Writer." *Time*, however, insisted that "Britons saw him off with sincere regret." *Time*, November 4, 1940, "Foreign Relations: Good-by Joe"; Koskoff, *Joseph P. Kennedy*, 303–305; *New York Times*, November 15, 1940, "Knox in Warning of Perilous Times Denounces Hitler"; Lord Lothian, Weekly Political Summary, November 19, 1940, Telegram 2632, Reel 6, Records of British Foreign Office. Courtesy of J. Garry Clifford.

39. *New York Times*, December 8, 1940, "Suing for Peace."

40. Burns, *Roosevelt: The Soldier of Freedom*, 73. See also Reynolds, "Roosevelt, the British Left and the Appointment of John G. Winant," 393–413; Sherwood, *Roosevelt and Hopkins*, 269; Koskoff, *Joseph P. Kennedy*, 305–306; *New York Times*, December 2, 1940, "Kennedy Resigns as London Envoy to Combat War"; Wayne Cole, *America First: The Battle against Intervention, 1940–1941* (Madison: University of Wisconsin Press, 1953) 17; *Hartford Courant*, December 9, 1940, "The Great Game of Politics"; *Washington Post*, December 3, 1940, "Continue, Mr. Kennedy."

41. *New York Times*, November 12, 1940, "Text of the Willkie Address Urging 'Loyal Opposition,'" italics added. Willkie echoed the words of the Massachusetts Federalist politician Fisher Ames, who, after the Federalists' loss of the White House in the election of 1800, wrote that the opposition should be "a champion who never flinches, a watchman who never sleeps." Ames to Theodore Dwight, March 19, 1801, in Seth Ames, ed., *Works of Fisher Ames*, 2 vols. (Boston: Little, Brown, 1854), 1:293–294. See also Richard Hofstadter, *The Idea of a Party System* (Berkeley: University of California Press, 1969), 145.

42. Stimson to Willkie, November 10, 1940, Willkie Manuscripts, Manuscripts Department, Lilly Library, Indiana University, Bloomington. Courtesy of J. Garry Clifford. James MacGregor Burns, *The Deadlock of Democracy: Four-Party Politics in America* (Englewood Cliffs, N.J.: Prentice-Hall, 1963), 173; *Washington Post*, November 10, 1940, "Nation Heals Battle Scars."

43. Ernie Pyle, "London on Fire," December 29, 1940, in *Reporting World War II*, 2 vols. (New York: Library of America, 1995), 1:147–148; *Christian Science Monitor*, December 30, 1940, "Buildings Smashed." See also Sherwood, *Roosevelt and Hopkins*, 228.

44. *New York Times*, December 11, 1940, "Hitler Challenges World Democracy." See also Burns, *Roosevelt: The Soldier of Freedom*, 27.

45. December 29, 1940, in *PPA*, 9:633–644; Sherwood, *Roosevelt and Hopkins*, 226.

46. Sherwood, *Roosevelt and Hopkins*, 219.

47. *Los Angeles Times*, January 21, 1941, "President's Scottie Wanted to Go, Too"; *New York Times*, January 21, 1941, "Up and Down Pennsylvania Avenue"; *New York Times*, January 21, 1941, "President Finds It Exhilarating Day"; *Los Angeles Times*, January 21, 1941, "Half Million Visit Capital"; *Chicago Daily Tribune*, January 21, 1941, "Roosevelt Calm and Assured as He Repeats Oath."

48. *New York Times*, January 21, 1941, "In the Nation," by Arthur Krock.

49. *New York Times*, January 21, 1941, "Third-Term Induction Presents Sharp Contrasts"; Samuel Rosenman, Diary, January 17, 1941, Rosenman Papers, FDRL. Courtesy of J. Garry Clifford.

50. *Chicago Daily Tribune*, November 8, 1940, "Roosevelt Rides thru Capital as Conquering Hero"; *New York Times*, January 21, 1941, "Wider Nazi Help Expected in Rome"; *New York Times*, January 20, 1941, "15 Planes Downed by Malta Defense"; *New York Times*, January 20, 1941, "The International Situation."

Chapter 19: Roosevelt and Willkie: Almost a Team

1. Robert Sherwood, *Roosevelt and Hopkins: An Intimate History*, rev. ed. (New York: Harper and Brothers, 1950), 234; *New York Times*, January 20, 1941, "President Cordial"; *Time*, January 27, 1941, "Critical Collaboration."

2. *New York Times*, January 13, 1941, "Willkie Statement on the War Aid Bill"; *Christian Science Monitor*, January 13, 1941, "Willkie's Statement Supporting President." The isolationist *Chicago Daily Tribune* took a different stand. Roosevelt's proposal, the *Tribune* editorialized, "is a

bill for the destruction of the American Republic" and for "unlimited dictatorship." *Chicago Daily Tribune*, January 12, 1941, "A Bill to Destroy the Republic."

3. *New York Times*, January 12, 1941, "Landon Denounces 'Slick' Lease Plan"; *Chicago Daily Tribune*, January 13, 1941, "Willkie's View—and Landon's"; Steve Neal, *Dark Horse: A Biography of Wendell Willkie* (Garden City, N.Y.: Doubleday, 1984), 187, 189–190. Also memorandum dated January 16, 1941, by a guest at a dinner party at Irita Van Doren's apartment attended by Willkie, Robert Kintner, Harold Guinzburg, and Dorothy Thompson. PSF: Willkie, Franklin D. Roosevelt Library (FDRL), Hyde Park, N.Y. On February 21, 1941, former GOP congressman and Willkie supporter Bruce Barton wrote to Russell Davenport, expressing his opposition to aid for Britain and his hope that "Wendell might make a clear cut distinction between himself and Roosevelt." Willkie Mss., Manuscripts Department, Lilly Library, Indiana University, Bloomington. Courtesy of J. Garry Clifford.

4. Churchill to FDR, December 2, 1940, quoted in Robert Dallek, *Franklin D. Roosevelt and American Foreign Policy, 1932–1945* (New York: Oxford University Press, 1979), 254; *New York Times*, November 24, 1940, "Envoy Flies Here." Often-repeated stories that Lothian remarked, "Well, boys, Britain's broke. It's your money we want," seem to be fictional. David Reynolds finds no evidence that Lothian said this nor do I. See Reynolds, "Lord Lothian and Anglo-American Relations, 1939–1940," *Transactions of the American Philosophical Society*, New Series, 73, 2 (1983), 48. The headline in the *Chicago Daily Tribune*, however, was "Envoy Lothian Claims Britain Going Broke," November 24, 1940.

5. Sherwood, *Roosevelt and Hopkins*, 3, 172. Sherwood also noted that Roosevelt's speeches and talks were "subjected to the process of simplification or even oversimplification that he demanded. He was happiest when he could express himself in the homeliest, even tritest phrases, such as 'common or garden,' 'clear as crystal,' 'rule of thumb,' 'neither here nor here,' 'armchair strategists,' or 'simple as ABC.' " Sherwood, *Roosevelt and Hopkins*, 213. Historian Warren Kimball points out that Ickes first used the fire-next-door analogy in August 1940 in a personal letter to Roosevelt in which he wrote, "It seems to me that we Americans are like the householder who refuses to lend or sell his fire extinguishers to help put out the fire in the house that is right next door although that house is all ablaze and the wind is blowing from that direction." Ickes to Roosevelt, August 2, 1940, FDRL. A few days later, FDR spoke with Ambassador William Bullitt and asked, "How do you think the country and the Congress would react if I should put aid to the British in the form of lending them my garden hose?" Warren Kimball, *The Most Unsordid Act: Lend-Lease 1939–1941* (Baltimore, Md.: Johns Hopkins University Press, 1969), 77. In his November 22, 1940, syndicated column, Frank R. Kent also stated, "With her cash exhausted, we could begin to give, and not sell, England the materials which she needs to save herself and, incidentally, protect us." *Los Angeles Times*, November 22, 1940, "The Great Game of Politics."

6. Press Conference, January 14, 1941, in Samuel I. Rosenman, ed., *Public Papers and Addresses of Franklin D. Roosevelt* [*PPA*], 13 vols. (New York: Macmillan, 1941), 9:711–712. Wheeler also released to the press some statistics about American air strength that, as Warren Kimball notes, had probably been presented in closed executive session with General Marshall. His violation of executive testimony led FDR to comment that the disclosures were surely interesting to Hitler. Kimball, *The Most Unsordid Act*, 188.

7. Thomas G. Paterson, J. Garry Clifford, and Kenneth J. Hagan, *American Foreign Relations: A History*, 2 vols. (Lexington, Mass.: Heath, 1995), 2:184. See also Kimball, *Most Unsordid Act*, 153, note 5.

8. *Christian Science Monitor*, January 13, 1941, "Willkie Going to England"; Henry Stimson Diaries, January 11, 1941, Reel 6, vol. 32, p. 98, Manuscripts and Archives, Yale University Library; Hull to Willkie, January 10, 1941, Willkie Mss., Manuscripts Department, Lilly Library, Indiana University, Bloomington, Courtesy of J. Garry Clifford. Hull's letter concerns passports and visas for Willkie, Thorne, Cowles, and Davenport. *Washington Post*, November 6, 1940, "The Winner's Task."

9. Frances Perkins, *The Roosevelt I Knew* (New York: Viking, 1946), 117–119. The British ambassador, Lord Lothian, told Walter Lippmann after the election that it was "most desirable that Willkie should realize how urgently his full assistance is needed." Lippmann to Lewis Doug-

las, November 28, 1940, in Lippmann Manuscripts, Box 67, Yale University. Courtesy of J. Garry Clifford.

10. Perkins, *The Roosevelt I Knew*, 118; Sherwood, *Roosevelt and Hopkins*, 234.

11. Joe Martin, *My First Fifty Years in Politics* (New York: McGraw-Hill, 1960), 129; *New York Times*, January 19, 1941, "OPM Head for Bill"; *Chicago Daily Tribune*, January 14, 1941, "Wheeler Calls Willkie as War Minded as F.D.R."

12. *New York Times*, January 27, 1941, "Willkie Arrives in London." Henry Stimson wrote to the British minister of shipping, Sir Arthur Salter, on January 14, 1941, paving the way for Willkie as well as for Landon Thorne, "who is not only a close friend of Mr. Willkie's but of mine." Willkie Mss., Manuscripts Department, Lilly Library, Indiana University, Bloomington. Courtesy of J. Garry Clifford. After meeting with Willkie on January 11, 1941, Stimson wrote, "Willkie is all right but he is rather a prima donna and not a student; and with a careful, thorough man like Thorne along . . . there is a great chance to steady Willkie. . . . So I talked it over with Thorne after Willkie had gone." Henry Stimson Diaries, January 11, 1941, Reel 6, vol. 32, p. 99, Yale University Library, Manuscripts and Archives.

13. Neal, *Dark Horse*, 194, 201; *New York Times*, January 29, 1941, "Willkie Unshaken."

14. Sherwood, *Roosevelt and Hopkins*, 255; Guest list, Lord Beaverbrook's Dinner, January 28, 1941, Willkie Mss., Manuscripts Department, Lilly Library, Indiana University, Bloomington; Marquis Childs to Joseph Pulitzer, February 12, 1941, Joseph Pulitzer Papers, Reel 102, Library of Congress. Courtesy of J. Garry Clifford. When Harry Hopkins was in London in early January and met with Churchill, the prime minister also criticized Kennedy. Sherwood, *Roosevelt and Hopkins*, 238.

15. Laski to FDR, February 18, 1941, OF, 4040, FDRL, quoted in Gary Dean Best, *Harold Laski and American Liberalism* (New Brunswick, N.J.: Transaction, 2005), 111.

16. Neal, *Dark Horse*, 199. According to Harold Ickes, columnist Robert Kintner had dinner with Willkie upon his return from Europe and Willkie said that he had been "brutally frank with De Valera. . . . De Valera complained that arms and munitions that Ireland had desired of England had not been forthcoming and Willkie told him 'of course not,' that Ireland could not expect help when it refused to give help. . . . He told De Valera flatly that it was foolish to think that Ireland could escape involvement in this conflict simply by remaining neutral and that Hitler would strike Ireland just whenever he got ready." Harold L. Ickes, *The Secret Diary of Harold L. Ickes*, 3 vols. (New York: Simon and Schuster, 1954), February 22, 1941, 439–440.

17. Michael R. Beschloss, *Kennedy and Roosevelt: The Uneasy Alliance* (New York: Norton, 1980), 235–238. This time Kennedy's rage was directed at those he branded the White House's "hatchetmen." As Warren Kimball noted, Kennedy's testimony was confused and contradictory. He "refused either to condemn or support the Lend-Lease Bill but instead repeatedly stated that Britain had to be aided as quickly and efficiently as possible. Yet during the same testimony he expressed the fear that America might be drawn into a war for which she was not prepared." Kimball, *Most Unsordid Act*, 191.

18. *New York Times*, January 19, 1941, "Text of Kennedy's Address"; *Chicago Daily Tribune*, January 22, 1941, "Kennedy Warns"; *New York Times*, January 22, 1941, "Kennedy Opposes Full Power Given in Lease-Lend Bill"; *Washington Post*, January 22, 1941, "Retiring Envoy Opposes Grant of New Powers to Chief Executive."

19. *Chicago Daily Tribune*, January 22, 1941, "Kennedy Warns"; *New York Times*, January 22, 1941, "Kennedy Opposes Full Power Given in Lease-Lend Bill"; *Washington Post*, January 22, 1941, "Retiring Envoy Opposes Grant of New Powers to Chief Executive."

20. FDR to John Boettiger, February 1941, quoted in Doris Kearns Goodwin, *No Ordinary Time: Franklin and Eleanor Roosevelt: The Home Front in World War II* (New York: Simon and Schuster, 1994), 211. The *New York Times*'s London correspondent, Raymond Daniell, wrote in 1941 that if England fell, thereby discrediting FDR's interventionist policy, "wouldn't the way be open for some demagogue, some American Quisling, to campaign and win on a platform of collaboration with Hitler's new order for the sake of trade, prosperity, and lower taxes?" Raymond Daniell, *Civilians Must Fight* (Garden City, N.Y.: Doubleday, Doran and Company, 1941), 320.

21. *Washington Post*, January 24, 1941, "Lone Eagle Grows Gregarious."
22. *Chicago Daily Tribune*, January 24, 1941, "Lindbergh Hits Hysteria."
23. Selden Rodman Diary, July 22, 1941, Sterling Library, Yale University. Courtesy of J. Garry Clifford. Wayne Cole interview with Charles Lindbergh, June 7, 1973, Army and Navy Club, Washington, D.C., Cole Papers, Hoover Presidential Library, West Branch, Iowa. Courtesy of J. Garry Clifford.
24. *New York Times*, December 28, 1940, "Wheeler Defines His 'Just' Peace."
25. Wayne Cole, *Charles Lindbergh and the Battle against American Intervention in World War II* (New York: Harcourt Brace Jovanovich, 1974), 130; *Chicago Daily Tribune*, January 24, 1941, "Lindbergh Hits Hysteria"; *New York Times*, January 24, 1941, "Urges Neutrality"; *Atlanta Constitution*, January 24, 1941, "U.S. Could Not Hope to Win"; *Washington Post*, January 24, 1941, "Collapse of Reich Only Chance"; *Washington Post*, January 24, 1941, "Applause Pleases Lindbergh." Lindbergh also stated that he saw "the fault of the war about evenly divided in Europe." See also Kenneth S. Davis, *The Hero: Charles A. Lindbergh and the American Dream* (Garden City, N.Y.: Doubleday, 1959), 398. Two weeks later, on February 6, Lindbergh testified again before the Senate Foreign Relations Committee, repeating the same arguments, urging defeat of the Lend-Lease bill because Britain was fighting "a war which I do not feel she possibly can win" regardless of how much help Britain received from the United States. See *Los Angeles Times*, February 7, 1941, "Lindbergh Talks Again." Herbert Hoover also opposed Lend-Lease. In March 1941, he wrote to William Castle it was "a war bill, yet 95 percent of the people think it is only aid to Britain. . . . [It] empowers the President to become a real dictator." George H. Nash, ed., *Freedom Betrayed: Herbert Hoover's Secret History of the Second World War and Its Aftermath* (Stanford, Calif.: Hoover Institution Press, 2011), 215.
26. *New York Times*, January 24, 1941, "Peace When There Is No Peace"; *New York Times*, January 24, 1941, "Lindbergh Called Pro-Nazi in Britain"; *New York Times*, January 25, 1941, "Lindbergh Praised by Reich Official."
27. *Atlanta Constitution*, February 1, 1941, "Plea to Return"; Wayne S. Cole, *America First: The Battle against American Intervention, 1940–1941* (Madison: University of Wisconsin Press, 1953), 47–49.
28. *Chicago Daily Tribune*, February 10, 1941, "Tells of F.D.R.'s Letter." Willkie's traveling companion, Landon Thorne, Stimson's wife's cousin, met with Stimson and General Marshall on the evening of February 9. "Thorne told us all that he could . . . of what had happened and it made a very thrilling experience," Stimson wrote. Stimson Diaries, February 9, 1940, Reel 6, vol. 33, p. 18, Manuscripts and Archives, Yale University Library.
29. James MacGregor Burns, *Roosevelt: The Soldier of Freedom* (New York: Harcourt Brace Jovanovich, 1970), 48; *New York Times*, February 7, 1941, "Lindbergh's Statement before the Foreign Relations Committee."
30. *Time*, February 24, 1941, "The Undefeated"; Krock to Willkie, February 9, 1941, Willkie Mss., Manuscripts Department, Lilly Library, Indiana University, Bloomington. Courtesy of J. Garry Clifford. For his part, Raymond Buell complained that Willkie "swallows the bill whole with one or two unimportant suggestions. . . . Mr. Willkie has not discharged the intellectual responsibility which falls on the Opposition leader at the present time." Buell to Henry Luce, January 15, 1941, Foreign Affairs Memorandum, Raymond Leslie Buell Papers, Manuscript Division, Library of Congress. Courtesy of J. Garry Clifford.
31. *New York Times*, February 12, 1941, "Verbatim Testimony of Wendell Willkie"; *New York Times*, February 12, 1941, "Warns U.S. of Axis"; *Time*, February 24, 1941, "The Undefeated"; *Atlanta Constitution*, February 14, 1941, "The Capital Parade." Vandenberg had written to Willkie on November 25, 1940, "You and I will not always agree on everything—but I seriously doubt whether we ever seriously disagree on fundamentals. . . . I think, however, we should 'talk things over.'" Willkie Mss., Manuscripts Department, Lilly Library, Indiana University, Bloomington. Courtesy of J. Garry Clifford.
32. Cole, *America First*, 178; *Los Angeles Times*, February 12, 1941, "Senators Ask; He Answers." See also Sherwood, *Roosevelt and Hopkins*, 187; Martin, *My First Fifty Years*, 128. See

also Gerald P. Nye Papers, Box 50, "Willkie," no date, Herbert Hoover Presidential Library, West Branch, Iowa. Nye kept detailed records of every antiwar statement that Willkie made during the presidential campaign and during his trip to Britain and Ireland. See "Willkie in London" and "1940 Campaign Speeches by Wendell Willkie on Keeping Out of War," Box 50, Willkie, Wendell, in Gerald P. Nye Papers, Herbert Hoover Presidential Library, West Branch, Iowa.

33. Grace Tully, *F.D.R., My Boss* (New York: C. Scribner's Sons, 1949), 58. Tully erroneously placed the dinner in January, before Willkie's trip to England. According to *Time*, Willkie stayed at the White House for two hours. See *Time*, February 24, 1941, "The Undefeated"; *New York Times*, February 12, 1941, "Reports on Talks."

34. *New York Times*, February 12, 1941, "Financial Markets"; *New York Times*, January 31, 1941, "Few Voters Back Lindbergh Views"; Wendell Willkie, "The Future of the Republican Party," *Nation*, 153, 24 (December 13, 1941), 609–612; *New York Times*, February 13, 1941, "Asks Positive Plan"; *Los Angeles Times*, February 13, 1941, "Willkie Challenges Republicans"; *Christian Science Monitor*, February 13, 1941, "Text of Willkie Talk to Republicans"; *New York Times*, January 31, 1941, "Few Voters Back Lindbergh Views."

35. James T. Patterson, *Mr. Republican: A Biography of Robert A. Taft* (Boston: Houghton Mifflin, 1972), 247, 244, 243, respectively. See also *New York Times*, February 13, 1941, "Asks Positive Plan"; *Chicago Daily Tribune*, January 22, 1941, "Acts to Block Dictator Bill"; *New York Times*, March 1, 1941, "Wheeler Asserts Aid Bill Seeks War."

36. Joseph P. Kennedy, Diary Notes, January 21, 1941, in Amanda Smith, ed., *Hostage to Fortune: The Letters of Joseph P. Kennedy* (New York: Viking, 2001), 524.

37. *Washington Post*, February 13, 1941, "Dewey Backs Lend-Lease." See also *New York Times*, January 11, 1941, "Hoover and Dewey Criticize Aid Bill"; *New York Times*, February 19, 1941, "War Is Pictured."

38. *Chicago Daily Tribune*, January 15, 1941, "G.O.P. Disturbed"; *Chicago Daily Tribune*, February 13, 1941, "Nye Calls Willkie's Support of Dictator Bill a Betrayal"; *Chicago Daily Tribune*, February 13, 1941, "The Barefoot Boy as a Barefaced Fraud"; *Christian Science Monitor*, February 13, 1941, "G.O.P. Leaders Differ on Willkie"; *Chicago Daily Tribune*, March 3, 1941, "Report War Aim of President Is World New Deal."

39. *New York Times*, February 14, 1941, "Women Hang Effigy"; *New York Times*, January 31, 1941, "Party 'Anger' Reported"; *New York Times*, February 3, 1941, "Midwest Leaders to 'Watch' Willkie"; Saul Friedländer, *Prelude to Downfall: Hitler and the United States, 1939–1941* (New York: Knopf, 1967), 173.

40. Raymond Clapper, *Watching the World*, ed. Mrs. Raymond Clapper (New York: Whittlesey House/McGraw-Hill, 1944), February 12, 1941, 166–167; *New York Times*, February 16, 1941, "Republicans Confused."

41. *Washington Post*, March 2, 1941, "Popularity of Willkie Has Risen, Poll Shows"; *Washington Post*, February 23, 1941, "Willkie's Increasing Stature" by Ernest Lindley; *Atlanta Constitution*, February 13, 1941, "Wendell Willkie—A Man!"; Lord Halifax, Weekly Political Summary for British Foreign Office, No. 991, Telegram No. 8870, Reel 1. Courtesy of J. Garry Clifford.

42. *Washington Post*, February 27, 1941, "Today and Tomorrow"; *Atlanta Constitution*, February 7, 1941, "One Word More." Willkie's internationalist worldview was the "historical and traditional position of the Republican Party," wrote Gardner Cowles, Jr., to Willkie. "It is only comparatively recently that a few leaders within the party have turned it down the path of narrow isolationism," he remarked, encouraging Willkie to emphasize even more that "the true and historic Republican program" is internationalism. "Doesn't this make sense?" Gardner Mike Cowles, Jr., to Willkie, September 22, 1941, Willkie Mss., Manuscripts Department, Lilly Library, Indiana University, Bloomington. Courtesy of J. Garry Clifford.

43. *New York Times*, March 11, 1941, "President and Congress Clear Way for British Aid"; *Christian Science Monitor*, March 10, 1941, "Senate Lend-Lease Vote"; *Washington Post*, March 12, 1941, "House Concurs in Lease-Lend." Nye spoke for twelve hours, trying to stall the bill in the Senate. *Washington Post*, March 12, 1941, "The Gallup Poll." See also *Washington Post*, February 14, 1941, "The Gallup Poll." As Kimball noted, between January 22 and March 7, 1941,

eighteen polls were taken on Lend-Lease and each one had at least 50 percent of those polled in favor of the bill's passage. The last poll, on March 7, had 61 percent in favor. Even in the isolationist Midwest, support for Lend-Lease was 50 percent in March. Kimball, *Most Unsordid Act*, 191–192.

44. *Washington Post*, December 19, 1940, "Capital Parade"; Ickes, *Secret Diary*, February 16, 1941, 3:432; Hamilton Interview, "Lend-Lease," 17, Barnard Mss., Lilly Library, Indiana University; Neal, *Dark Horse*, 187.

45. Willkie to John Hollister, March 7, 1941, "Correspondence—20," Barnard Mss.

46. *New York Times*, March 25, 1941, "Canadians Cheer Plea by Willkie." "To preside at a meeting of Willkie's in Toronto," the prime minister wrote in his diary, "would be very helpful in every way—in Britain, in the States, and elsewhere." Diaries of Mackenzie King, March 20, 1941, Library and Archives Canada, online, p. 3, http://www.collectionscanada.gc.ca/databases/king/index-e.html.

47. Neal, *Dark Horse*, 214; Irving Stone, *They Also Ran* (New York: Doubleday, Doran, 1943), 342. When Willkie and Frank Knox were both awarded honorary degrees by Dartmouth College in June 1941, the president of Dartmouth said to Willkie: "In political defeat you have become a greater force for unity than would have been possible for you in victory." *New York Times*, June 16, 1941, "Dartmouth Head Extols Willkie."

48. *New York Times*, March 16, 1941, "Movie Pokes Fun at the President"; *Atlanta Constitution*, March 22, 1941, "The Capital Parade"; *New York Times*, March 2, 1941, "Popular Esteem for Willkie Rising"; *New York Times*, March 15, 1941, "Roosevelt Trend at Record High."

49. Philip Willkie Interview, August 1952 and August 1953, "Relations with Roosevelt," 2–3, Barnard Mss. Willkie's wife, Edith, later claimed that her husband felt that Roosevelt "doesn't have any moral sense." Edith Willkie Interview, November 1, 1960, "Relations with Roosevelt, 14," in Barnard Mss., and interview, August 2, 1955, Barnard Mss. Willkie's college classmate George Henley would claim that Willkie hated Roosevelt "like the Devil hates holy water." George Henley Interview, June 18, 1959, in Barnard Mss. Journalist Roscoe Drummond, who had become close to Willkie, would tell an interviewer that Willkie had neither an "understanding or alliance or allegiance with Roosevelt." Roscoe Drummond Interview, "Relations with Roosevelt," 10, in Barnard Mss.

50. Irita Van Doren Interview, December 30, 1954, New York City, "Relations with Roosevelt," Barnard Mss. Jim Farley remembered that, in a meeting in late 1938, "Willkie professed great admiration for the President and his program." James Farley, *Jim Farley's Story: The Roosevelt Years* (New York: Whittlesey House/McGraw-Hill, 1948), 157. In the fall of 1941, a thoughtful Willkie took the trouble to pen a note of sympathy to the president, whose mother had recently died. "My heart goes out to you," he wrote. "Messages like yours are a real comfort at such a time," FDR responded. "Relations with Roosevelt," 12, Barnard Mss.

51. Neal, *Dark Horse*, 207–208; Roosevelt to Hamilton Holt, November 20, 1944, OF 4040, FDRL. Robert Jackson interestingly made a similar comment about Willkie, writing that "although I liked him personally, I did not feel that he had much knowledge of the world. . . . This would have been a rather dangerous experiment in 1940." Robert Jackson, *That Man: An Insider's Portrait of Franklin D. Roosevelt*, ed. John Q. Barrett (New York: Oxford University Press, 2004), 45.

52. Perkins, *The Roosevelt I Knew*, 117, 119. According to Eleanor Roosevelt, her husband "liked Wendell Willkie very much. He never felt the bitterness toward him that he felt toward some of his other opponents." Eleanor Roosevelt, *This I Remember* (New York: Harper, 1949), 220–221. Willkie also defended Eleanor Roosevelt against criticism, and in 1943 said that she was "one of the most intelligent women in America." Ellsworth Barnard, *Wendell Willkie: Fighter for Freedom* (Marquette: Northern Michigan University Press, 1966), 434.

53. Sherwood, *Roosevelt and Hopkins*, 635. On November 5, 1940, Election Day, Harold Ickes was home in Washington. FDR's attack dog wrote in his diary during the day, "I desperately want the President to win. I am horribly afraid of Willkie. I believe him to be unscrupulous, unfair, reckless to the point of daring, and greedy for power. If he should be elected, I would honestly fear for the future of my country." Ickes, *Secret Diary*, November 5, 1940, 3:361.

Chapter 20: Roosevelt and Willkie vs. Lindbergh

1. Samuel I. Rosenman, *Working with Roosevelt* (New York: Harper and Brothers, 1952), 270; Inaugural Address, January 20, 1941, in Samuel I. Rosenman, ed., *Public Papers and Addresses of Franklin D. Roosevelt* [*PPA*], 13 vols. (New York: Harper and Brothers, 1950), 10:3–6.

2. *New York Times*, April 24, 1941, "The International Situation"; *New York Times*, April 26, 1941, "President Defines Lindbergh's Niche." In July in San Francisco, Lindbergh said, "I would a hundred times rather see my country ally herself with England, or even with Germany, with all her faults, than the cruelty, the godlessness and the barbarism that exists in soviet Russia." *Christian Science Monitor*, July 2, 1941, "Lindbergh Prefers Nazis to Reds." Even Lindbergh's former attorney Henry Breckenridge denounced his ex-client. "He who spreads the gospel of defeatism is an ally to Hitler," Breckenridge said. Lindbergh, he added, was like Norway's Quisling. *New York Times*, April 27, 1941, "Strikes at Lindbergh."

3. See Francis McDonnell, *Insidious Foes: The Axis Fifth Column and the American Home Front* (New York: Oxford University Press, 1995), 141–142.

4. *New York Times*, April 26, 1941, "President Defines Lindbergh's Niche." See also Press Conference, April 25, 1941, in *PPA*, 10:136–138; Wayne Cole, *Charles A. Lindbergh and the Battle against American Intervention in World War II* (New York: Harcourt Brace Jovanovich, 1974), 130–131; *New York Times*, April 27, 1941, "Strikes at Lindbergh." On Carter, see Steven Casey, "Franklin D. Roosevelt, Ernst 'Putzi' Hanfstaengel and the 'S-Project,' June 1942–June 1944," *Journal of Contemporary History*, 35, 3 (July 2000), 339–359.

5. *New York Times*, April 29, 1941, "Lindbergh Quits Air Corps"; *New York Times*, May 24, 1941, "Lindbergh Joins in Wheeler Plea to U.S. to Shun War"; *New York Times*, May 24, 1941, "Texts of the Addresses by Lindbergh and Wheeler." Attending the rally in Madison Square Garden was Joseph McWilliams, the leader of the pro-fascist American Destiny Party, and his followers.

6. *New York Times*, May 30, 1941, "Lindbergh Assails Roosevelt Speech," italics added; *Christian Science Monitor*, May 31, 1941, "Lindbergh Says Roosevelt Seeks Domination." On May 10, speaking in Minneapolis, Lindbergh said, "There was once a time in America when we could impose our will by vote. . . . The people of this nation were not given the chance to vote on the greatest issue of our generation—the issue of a foreign war. . . . We have been asked to fight abroad for the 'Four Freedoms.' But there are other freedoms that our President did not mention. One is the freedom to vote on vital issues." *Chicago Daily Tribune*, May 11, 1941, "U.S. Democracy Totters, Warns Col. Lindbergh."

7. *New York Times*, May 11, 1941, "War Choice Denied"; *Chicago Daily Tribune*, May 11, 1941, "U.S. Democracy Totters, Warns Col. Lindbergh"; *New York Times*, June 6, 1941, "Japanese Drop Lindbergh Leaflets." Wisconsin's former governor Phil La Follette, a progressive in the 1930s, agreed with Lindbergh and declined to vote for either presidential candidate in 1940, arguing that it was a fixed fight between two liberal internationalists. John Miller, *Governor Philip F. La Follette* (Columbia: University of Missouri Press, 1982), 166–167.

8. *New York Times*, December 12, 1940, "Calls Lindbergh 'A Nazi.'" Address at Annual Dinner of White House Correspondents' Association, March 15, 1941, in *PPA*, 10:63.

9. *Washington Post*, June 1, 1941, "Mr. Lindbergh's Reply"; Max Wallace, *The American Axis: Henry Ford, Charles Lindbergh, and the Rise of the Third Reich* (New York: St. Martin's Press, 2003), 284. See also *New York Times*, June 3, 1941, "What 'New Leadership'?"; *Time*, June 2, 1941, "Freedom of the Seas"; *Life*, June 9, 1941, "People," 56.

10. Wood to Lindbergh, June 2, 1941, and Wood to Lindbergh, August 12, 1941, in Cole, *Charles A. Lindbergh and the Battle against American Intervention*, 146; Charles A. Lindbergh, *The Wartime Journals of Charles A. Lindbergh* (New York: Harcourt Brace Jovanovich, 1970), February 27, 1941, 452; *New York Times*, June 10, 1941, "Speech Distorted, Lindbergh Holds."

11. Lindbergh, *Wartime Journals*, May 31, 1941, 498, italics added. For its part, even America First discouraged talk of impeachment, although Douglas Stuart was interested in its possibility and some chapter heads called for the impeachment of Frank Knox. Wayne Cole, *America First*

(Madison: University of Wisconsin Press, 1953), 176–177. On the Lindbergh-Hoover meeting, see J. Garry Clifford, "A Connecticut Colonel's Candid Conversation with the Wrong Commander-in-Chief," *Connecticut History*, 28 (November 1987), 24–38. For his part, Hoover sympathized with Lindbergh and wrote that he was the object of the interventionists' "almost unbelievable smear and vilification." George H. Nash, ed., *Freedom Betrayed: Herbert Hoover's Secret History of the Second World War and Its Aftermath* (Stanford, Calif.: Hoover Institution Press, 2011), 199.

    12. Selden Rodman Diary, July 22, 1941, Sterling Library, Yale University. Courtesy of J. Garry Clifford.

    13. Roosevelt, Radio Address Announcing Unlimited National Emergency, May 27, 1941, in *PPA*, 10:193–194; *New York Times*, May 28, 1941, "Speech Echoes in a Hushed City."

    14. LBJ to FDR, May 27, 1941, PPF 6149, Franklin D. Roosevelt Library (FDRL), Hyde Park, N.Y.

    15. *New York Times*, June 7, 1941, "Text of Willkie Attack"; *New York Times*, June 7, 1941, "Willkie Berates Roosevelt Critics." A month earlier, Willkie had criticized the president for making a personal attack on Lindbergh by calling him a copperhead. *New York Times*, May 4, 1941, "Willkie Declares Patrol Inadequate."

    16. Wendell Willkie, "Americans, Stop Being Afraid!," *Collier's*, May 10, 1941, 65–66. Also in that article, Willkie wrote, "The democratic process spoke. I believe in the democratic process. I accept its verdicts."

    17. The director of *Confessions of a Nazi Spy*, Anatole Litvak, and the star Edward G. Robinson were members of Hollywood's Anti-Nazi League. The film was the first anti-Hitler film and fifth-column exposé produced in Hollywood and was banned in much of Europe. McDonnell, *Insidious Foes*, 64–71; *New York Times*, November 3, 1940, "Problem in Defense." William R. Castle, Jr., a member of the America First Committee, the GOP national committee, and Hoover's undersecretary of state, saw *The Mortal Storm* in July 1940 and wrote: "It is a most deadly indictment of Nazi philosophy and acts arising therefrom. It is terribly sad, and terribly real. It is admirably acted and has none of the usual Hollywood exaggeration. But it does make one loathe the Nazis and all they stand for with a very personal and energetic loathing." William R. Castle, Jr., Diary, July 21, 1940, Houghton Library, Harvard University.

    18. *New York Times*, August 1, 1941, "Wheeler Charges Movies Want War"; *Atlanta Constitution*, July 12, 1941, "Oust Wheeler from Senate, York Urges"; *New York Times*, May 31, 1941, "Must Fight to Keep Liberty, Says York."

    19. *Chicago Daily Tribune*, January 14, 1941, "Wheeler Warns Film Makers"; *New York Times*, January 19, 1941, "Shall the Screen Remain Free?"; Wheeler to Hays, January 13, 1941, in Todd Bennett, "The Celluloid War: State and Studio in Anglo-American Propaganda Film-Making, 1939–1941," *International History Review*, 24, 1 (March 2002), 95. Already in 1940 the motion picture industry had volunteered, on a free or cost basis, to make recruiting shorts, morale-boosting movies, and training movies for the government. Darryl Zanuck, a lieutenant-colonel in the Reserve Corps and vice president of Twentieth Century-Fox, helped organize cooperation between the movie industry and the government. See George Marshall, Memorandum for General Sheed, January 31, 1941, and see editor's notes, in Larry Bland, ed., *Papers of George Catlett Marshall*, 5 vols. (Baltimore, Md.: Johns Hopkins University Press, 1981–), 2:402–403. See also Ronald Lora and William Henry Longton, eds., *The Conservative Press in Twentieth-Century America* (Westport, Conn.: Greenwood Press, 1999), 276; *New York Times*, January 19, 1941, "Shall the Screen Remain Free?"

    20. Bennett, "Celluloid War," 97.

    21. The previous week, on July 25, 1941, the *New York Times* had reported that, using his congressional franking privilege, Wheeler had mailed out a million postcards, many addressed to American soldiers, containing excerpts from speeches by Hoover, Joseph Kennedy, Senator Nye, and Charles Lindbergh and asking soldiers to "write today to President Roosevelt . . . that you are against our entry into the European war." It was an act that came close to subversion, if not treason, remarked Secretary of War Stimson, while General Marshall pointed out that army regulations forbade soldiers from engaging in activities intended to influence legislation. *New York Times*, July

25, 1941, "Wheeler Franked Anti-War Speeches"; *Los Angeles Times*, July 26, 1941, "Wheeler Post-cards Assailed by President."

22. Zanuck to Steve Early, November 28, 1941, quoted in Bennett, "Celluloid War," 99.

23. *New York Times*, September 9, 1941, "Willkie Attacks Inquiry on Films." See also *Propaganda in Motion Pictures*, Hearings before a Subcommittee of the Committee on Interstate Commerce, U.S. Senate, 77th Congress, Sessions on S. Res. 152, September 1941 (Washington, D.C.: United States Government Printing Office, 1942), 18–19. In August 1940, Jack Warner of Warner Brothers as well as Joseph and Nicholas Schenck, the heads of Loew's Incorporated, Metro-Goldwyn-Mayer's parent company, had offered to produce any film projects related to defense that the administration wanted, regardless of the cost. One film, released in October 1940, was called *Eyes of the Navy*, a patriotic portrait of the activities on naval air bases, from basic training and courses in aviation to recreational sailing and fishing. "Patient instructors, eager cadets, flying high wide and handsome," says the narrator. "Those who qualify become wings of the Navy. We don't rush them through, they have got to be good. Thumbs up! Young America is going places!" *Los Angeles Times*, November 1, 1940, "Power Film to Be Shown."

24. *New York Times*, September 9, 1941, "100 Leading Jews Seized in Paris"; *Washington Post*, September 9, 1941, "Nazis Round Up Hannover Jews for Eviction"; *Atlanta Constitution*, September 10, 1941, "Riots Reported in Berlin."

25. *Time*, September 22, 1941, "Hollywood in Washington." For McFarland's remarks, see *Propaganda in Motion Pictures*, 203, 205, 409.

26. *New York Times*, January 18, 1936, "Glass Assails Nye on Wilson Charge"; Wayne S. Cole, *Senator Gerald P. Nye and American Foreign Relations* (Minneapolis: University of Minnesota Press, 1962). At one point in those hearings, Virginia's senator Carter Glass, responding furiously to Nye's charge that Woodrow Wilson had led the quest for war profits and spoils, beat his desk with his knuckles until they bled. Economic historian Roland Stromberg analyzed the different attitudes of the American business community toward war and isolationism in the late 1930s. Roland Stromberg, "American Business and the Approach of War, 1935–1941," *Journal of Economic History*, 13, 1 (Winter 1953), 63, 71.

27. *Propaganda in Motion Pictures*, 6, 11. Nye then singled out for reprobation the most egregious pro-war movies—films like *The Great Dictator*, *Escape*, and the recently released *Sergeant York*. *New York Times*, September 10, 1941, "Movies Feed Propaganda." As for the *March of Time* documentary newsreels produced by Henry Luce's Time, Inc., Nye labeled them the "purest form of manufactured propaganda." As for his own blatant anti-Semitism, Nye predictably announced that he had "splendid Jewish friends, in and out of the moving picture business." *Propaganda in Motion Pictures*, 17, 37. See also *Christian Science Monitor*, September 10, 1941, "Eight Films Listed by Nye." In fact, in 1936, MGM had purchased the screen rights to film Sinclair Lewis's 1935 antifascist novel *It Can't Happen Here*, but ultimately the studio declined to make the movie, causing Lewis to denounce MGM's decision as "a fantastic exhibition of folly and cowardice." See McDonnell, *Insidious Foes*, 30–31.

28. *New York Times*, September 10, 1941, "Movies Feed Propaganda"; *Propaganda in Motion Pictures*, Senate Hearings, 54.

29. *New York Times*, September 10, 1941, "Movies Feed Propaganda"; *Time*, September 22, 1941, "Hollywood in Washington." The committee also heard from John T. Flynn, chairman of the New York chapter of America First, indignant that "not a single foot of film" presented the "anti-war side." *New York Times*, September 12, 1941, "Flynn Says Films Bar Peace Side." See also *Propaganda in Motion Pictures*, Senate Hearings, 54.

30. *Hartford Courant*, September 14, 1941, "Chaplin Is Summoned"; *New York Times*, September 17, 1941, "President Denies Movies Pressure."

31. *New York Times*, September 10, 1941, "The Movies Go before a Kangaroo Court," by Arthur Krock.

32. James MacGregor Burns, *Roosevelt: The Soldier of Freedom* (New York: Harcourt Brace Jovanovich, 1970), 139.

33. Harold L. Ickes, *The Secret Diary of Harold L. Ickes*, 3 vols. (New York: Simon and Schuster, 1953–1954), April 12, 1941, 3:466; T. North Whitehead, ca. April 30, 1941, memo attached to Lord Halifax, Memorandum, Reel 16, A3153/384/45, Records of British Foreign Office. Courtesy of J. Garry Clifford.

34. Burns, *Roosevelt: The Soldier of Freedom*, 141. Even before Roosevelt had selected him to be the new secretary of the navy, Knox had proposed, in a letter to Henry Stimson, that the United States take control of the Atlantic "by the use of our fleet combined with the remnants of the British and French navies." Knox to Stimson, May 22, 1940, Henry L. Stimson Papers, Sterling Library, Yale University, as quoted in Steven M. Mark, *An American Interventionist: Frank Knox and United States Foreign Relations*, unpublished Ph.D. dissertation, University of Maryland, 1977, 229–230. When it came out some years later, after the war, that FDR had withheld vital details on the *Greer* incident—namely, that the *Greer* had signaled to the British the U-boat location—there was a backlash and FDR was accurately portrayed in the press as devious.

35. *Chicago Daily Tribune*, September 12, 1941, "F.D.R. Creating War Incidents"; *New York Times*, September 12, 1941, "Lindbergh Sees a 'Plot' for War"; *Washington Post*, May 20, 1940, "Lindbergh Calls Fears 'Hysterical,'" italics added.

36. *Chicago Daily Tribune*, September 12, 1941, "F.D.R. Creating War Incidents," italics added. Lindbergh said that he had worded his Des Moines speech "carefully and moderately." Geoffrey S. Smith, *To Save a Nation: American Countersubversives, the New Deal, and the Coming of World War II* (New York: Basic Books, 1973), 179.

37. George Washington, "To the Hebrew Congregation in Newport, Rhode Island," August 18, 1790, in Susan Dunn, ed., *Something That Will Surprise the World: The Essential Writings of the Founding Fathers* (New York: Basic Books, 2006), 62.

38. *New York Times*, September 12, 1941, "Lindbergh Sees a 'Plot' for War"; *Chicago Daily Tribune*, September 12, 1941, "F.D.R. Creating War Incidents"; *Washington Post*, May 20, 1940, "Lindbergh Calls Fears 'Hysterical.'" On May 1, 1941, Lindbergh wrote in his diary: "Most of the Jewish interests in the country are behind war, and they control a huge part of our press and radio and most of our motion pictures." Lindbergh, *Wartime Journals*, 481. A defense of Lindbergh's speech is made by James P. Duffy, *Lindbergh vs. Roosevelt: The Rivalry That Divided America* (Washington, D.C.: Regnery, 2010), 196ff. See also Anne Morrow Lindbergh, *War Within and Without: Diaries and Letters of Anne Morrow Lindbergh, 1939–1944* (New York: Harcourt Brace Jovanovich, 1980), 221. Lindbergh's Des Moines speech echoed his speech on May 19, 1940, when he warned against a "small minority" that controlled "much of the machinery of influence and propaganda" and was determined to propel the nation into war. Selden Rodman Diary, July 22, 1941, Sterling Library, Yale University. Courtesy of J. Garry Clifford.

39. *Atlanta Constitution*, September 19, 1940, "Texas Solons Flay Lindbergh in Resolution"; *Washington Post*, September 19, 1941, "Texas House Asks Lindbergh to Stay Away"; *New York Times*, September 20, 1941, "Hitler and Lindbergh Linked in House Talk."

40. *New York Herald Tribune*, September 22, 1941, "Jew Baiting"; *Des Moines Register and Tribune*, quoted in Kenneth S. Davis, *The Hero: Charles A. Lindbergh and the American Dream* (Garden City, N.Y.: Doubleday, 1959), 414–415; *Chicago Defender*, October 4, 1941, "The Spirit of K.K.K. and Col. Lindbergh"; *San Francisco Chronicle* in Cole, *Charles A. Lindbergh and the Battle against American Intervention*, 174; "Lindbergh's Nazi Pattern," *New Republic*, 105, 12 (September 22, 1941), 360–361; Dorothy Thompson, *Look*, November 18, 1941.

41. Cole, *Charles Lindbergh and the Battle against American Intervention*, 180; *New York Times*, September 15, 1941, "Dewey Denounces Lindbergh's Talk"; *New York Times*, September 14, 1941, "Lindbergh Is Accused." Herbert Hoover also told Lindbergh that he felt the speech was a mistake. Lindbergh, *Wartime Journals*, October 6, 1941, 546.

42. Lindbergh, *War Within and Without*, September 14, 1941, September 15, 1941, September 17, 1941, 223–229. Two days after Lindbergh's Des Moines speech and before he had returned home to the north shore of Long Island, Selden Rodman and several friends had dinner with Anne in her secluded house. Afterward, they commented on "the extraordinary charm and dignity of our

fragile hostess, but especially the sadness in her eyes, her tragic isolation." Selden Rodman Diary, September 13, 1941, Sterling Library, Yale University. Courtesy of J. Garry Clifford. *Time*, June 14, 1999, "The Flyer, Charles Lindbergh," by Reeve Lindbergh.

43. Cole, *America First*, 148, 151–154, 162; Cole, *Charles Lindbergh and the Battle against American Intervention*, 129, 177; Lora and Longton, *Conservative Press*, 277. See also *New York Times*, September 26, 1941, "The Un-American Way"; *New York Times*, October 11, 1941, "Rome Defends Lindbergh."

44. Lindbergh, *Wartime Journals*, September 15, 1941, 539–541. In 1972, historian Wayne S. Cole interviewed Lindbergh. They spoke about anti-Semitism, and Cole came away from the interview "convinced that Lindbergh is NOT anti-Semitic and that he is impressively balanced and mature on the subject. In this conversation I found less evidence of anti-Semitic views than I found in interviews with Nye, Wheeler, Wood, [R. Douglas] Stuart, [arch-isolationist Verne] Marshall, or really any of the others I have interviewed." Wayne Cole interview with Charles Lindbergh, June 7, 1972, Army and Navy Club, Washington, D.C., Cole Papers, Hoover Presidential Library, West Branch, Iowa. Courtesy of J. Garry Clifford.

45. Cole, *Charles A. Lindbergh and the Battle against American Intervention*, 175; *New York Times*, September 12, 1941, "Willkie Applauds."

46. *New York Times*, October 22, 1941, "Willkie Rallies His Party on War, Appeal Signed"; *New York Times*, October 7, 1941, "Willkie Rallies His Party on War, Urges Republicans Take Lead." See also Wendell Willkie, Arthur H. Vandenberg, Harold E. Stassen, and Robert A. Taft, "The Future of the Republican Party," *Nation*, 153, 24 (December 13, 1941), 609–612.

47. *New York Times*, October 3, 1940, "Text of Willkie's Address at Cleveland"; *New York Times*, October 19, 1941, "Willkie Calls Idea of Peace 'Delusion'"; *New York Times*, October 21, 1941, "A Coup for Willkie"; *New York Times*, November 6, 1941, "Willkie Hails Work at United Aircraft."

48. *New York Times*, August 31, 1941, "Landon Hits Attempt 'to Smother Debate'"; *New York Times*, October 18, 1941, "Text of Landon's Speech."

49. *Washington Post*, November 3, 1941, "Willkie Leadership Is Challenged in Home State"; *Hartford Courant*, November 5, 1941, "GOP Is Seen Unwilling to Oust Willkie"; Charles Halleck, Memorandum including Frank McNaughton to David Hulburg, "Isolationists' Effort to Read Willkie Out of the Party," November 6, 1941, Raymond Leslie Buell Papers, Box 14, Manuscript Division, Library of Congress. Courtesy of J. Garry Clifford.

50. *New York Times*, November 7, 1941, "Short Denounces Willkie in House." See also Donald Bruce Johnson, *The Republican Party and Wendell Willkie* (Urbana: University of Illinois Press, 1960), 196ff.

51. *New York Times*, November 20, 1940, "Nazi Bribe Article Denounced by Fish"; *New York Times*, October 6, 1941, "Newman Clubs Cheer Fish's Talk on War"; *New York Times*, October 25, 1941, "Fish's Aide Indicted as Perjurer." The aide would be convicted in 1942. *Atlanta Constitution*, October 25, 1941, "Perjury Laid to Secretary of Hamilton Fish."

52. *Hartford Courant*, November 8, 1941, "Neutrality Bill Vote in Senate"; *Atlanta Constitution*, November 14, 1941, "House Sends Neutrality Revisions to Roosevelt."

53. Willkie, "Future of the Republican Party," 609; Taft, "Future of the Republican Party," 612.

54. Johnson, *Republican Party and Wendell Willkie*, 201; Raymond Clapper, *Watching the World*, ed. Mrs. Raymond Clapper (New York: Whittlesey House/McGraw-Hill, 1944), January 30, 1942, 97; Joe Martin, *My First Fifty Years* (New York: McGraw-Hill, 1960), 129.

55. In 1942, Willkie wanted the United States to act more aggressively militarily. In late 1943, Willkie was about to publicly criticize the State Department for what he considered its appeasement of Vichy, but Stimson implored him to desist and Willkie ultimately refrained from making his harsh criticism known. In 1944, he complained that the nation wasn't raising enough revenue. Burns, *Roosevelt: The Soldier of Freedom*, 222, 297, 434; Steve Neal, *Dark Horse: A Biography of Wendell Willkie* (Garden City, N.Y.: Doubleday, 1984), 324.

1. James MacGregor Burns, *Roosevelt: The Lion and the Fox* (New York: Harcourt Brace, 1956), 461; Robert Sherwood, *Roosevelt and Hopkins: An Intimate History*, rev. ed. (New York: Harper and Brothers, 1950), 430–431; Jean Edward Smith, *FDR* (New York: Random House, 2007), 506. See also Gordon W. Prange, *At Dawn We Slept: The Untold Story of Pearl Harbor* (New York: McGraw-Hill, 1981), 122.

2. James MacGregor Burns, *Roosevelt: The Soldier of Freedom* (New York: Harcourt, 1970), 156, 160. Henry Stimson wrote on February 7, 1941, that Hawaii was a high priority and the "best equipped of all our overseas departments." On April 24, 1941, he wrote that "Marshall felt that Hawaii was impregnable whether there were any ships left there or not. . . . He was strongly of the opinion that the psychological benefit of moving the Fleet to the Atlantic would far outweigh any encouragement that it would give to Japan." Henry Stimson Diaries, Reel 6, vol. 33, pp. 183–185, Manuscripts and Archives, Yale University Library. Marshall wrote that "dispersions" of the fleet "might lessen our power to operate effectively . . . in the principal theatre—the Atlantic." George Marshall, Memorandum for Admiral Stark, November 29, 1940, in Larry I. Bland, ed., *Papers of George Catlett Marshall*, 5 vols. (Baltimore, Md.: Johns Hopkins University Press, 1981–), 2:361. However, on February 6, 1941, Marshall asserted that American defenses in Hawaii were insufficient and ordered improvements. On February 7, in a letter to General Short, he added that the navy's demands for additional strategic positions in the Pacific were making it difficult to meet the requirements of Hawaii. "The risk of sabotage and the risk involved in a surprise raid by Air and by submarine, constitute the real perils of the situation." Bland, *Papers of George Catlett Marshall*, 2:410–413.

3. Prange, *At Dawn We Slept*, 122; Sherwood, *Roosevelt and Hopkins*, 430–431; Jean Edward Smith, *FDR* (New York: Random House, 2007), 506.

4. Sherwood, *Roosevelt and Hopkins*, 431; Burns, *Roosevelt: The Lion and the Fox*, 461. See also James MacGregor Burns, *The Crosswinds of Freedom* (New York: Knopf, 1989), 174–175.

5. Joseph Persico, *Edward R. Murrow: An American Original* (New York: McGraw-Hill, 1988), 194.

6. Robert Hagy, "The Worst News That I Have Encountered," in *Reporting World War II*, 2 vols. (New York: Library of America, 1995), 1:236–240.

7. Sherwood, *Roosevelt and Hopkins*, 432, 437.

8. *New York Times*, December 8, 1941, "Capital Dissensions Fade Out"; *Chicago Daily Tribune*, December 8, 1941, "Wheeler Urges Declaration of War on Japan"; *Christian Science Monitor*, December 8, 1941, "Nation Unites as One Man to Repel Attack"; Wayne Cole, *Roosevelt and the Isolationists, 1932–45* (Lincoln: University of Nebraska Press, 1983), 504, 507; *New York Times*, December 8, 1941, "Wheeler Backs a War on Japan"; *Los Angeles Times*, January 16, 1942, "Jury Convicts Fish Secretary."

9. *Chicago Daily Tribune*, December 9, 1941, "U.S. Must Fight with All It Has, Hoover Asserts"; Hoover, "My Attitude toward Japan," November 26, 1944, in George H. Nash, ed., *Freedom Betrayed: Herbert Hoover's Secret History of the Second World War and Its Aftermath* (Stanford, Calif.: Hoover Institution Press, 2011), 824, 830–831. Representative Jeanette Rankin of Montana dissented. She had also voted against the First World War.

10. *New York Times*, December 12, 1941, "Textual Excerpts from the War Speech of Reichsfuehrer in the Reichstag."

11. Message to Congress, December 11, 1941, in Samuel I. Rosenman, ed., *Public Papers and Addresses of Franklin D. Roosevelt [PPA]*, 13 vols. (New York: Harper and Brothers, 1950), 10:532.

12. Alton Frye, *Nazi Germany and the American Hemisphere, 1933–1941* (New Haven, Conn.: Yale University Press, 1967), 158. Already in June 1941, German assets in the United States were frozen and the German Library of Information and German consulates closed. Though the embassy remained open, Thomsen and his staff came under close scrutiny. *New York Times*, January 20, 1941, "U.S. Regret Voiced in Nazi Flag Case."

13. Justus D. Doenecke, "Non-Interventionism of the Left: The Keep America Out of the War Congress, 1938–41," *Journal of Contemporary History*, 12, 2 (April 1977), 233; Wayne Cole, *America First: The Battle against Intervention, 1940–1941* (Madison: University of Wisconsin Press, 1953), vii, 195; *New York Times*, December 12, 1941, "America First Acts to End Organization"; *New York Times*, January 9, 1942, "Wood Ordnance Adviser"; A. Scott Berg, *Lindbergh* (New York: G. P. Putnam's, 1998), 431. The House Un-American Activities Committee, led by Texas congressman Martin Dies, had begun investigating America First in mid-November 1941. After Pearl Harbor, Wood would go on to join the staff of the army's Chicago Ordnance District as a full-time advisor; Douglas Stuart would serve with distinction overseas in the army; Kingman Brewster, who had resigned from America First in early 1941, would serve as a navy pilot during the war before becoming president of Yale and ambassador to Great Britain. The rabidly isolationist magazine *Scribner's Commentator* also immediately ceased publication.

14. Charles Lindbergh, *The Wartime Journals of Charles A. Lindbergh* (New York: Harcourt Brace Jovanovich, 1970), December 7 and 8, 1941, 560–561; Paul Seabury, "Charles A. Lindbergh and the Politics of Nostalgia," *History*, 2 (1960), 143; *Los Angeles Times*, June 21, 1941, "Text of Lindbergh Plea for Isolation." As late as November 1941, Lindbergh published an article in the isolationist magazine *Scribner's Commentator*, 88–93, making the argument that "England and France were never in a position to win this war" and that "the only way our American life and ideals can be preserved is by staying out of this war."

14. *New York Times*, December 31, 1941, "Mr. Lindbergh Volunteers"; Kenneth S. Davis, *The Hero: Charles A. Lindbergh and the American Dream* (Garden City, N.Y.: Doubleday, 1959), 416; Walter Ross, *The Last Hero: Charles A. Lindbergh* (New York: Harper Collins, 1976), 281; *Hartford Courant*, July 25, 1941, "Ickes Reply to Lindbergh Letter." See also *New York Times*, April 20, 1941, "Stimson Permits Lindbergh to Quit."

16. Berg, *Lindbergh*, 437–439; Davis, *The Hero*, 420; *Hartford Courant*, February 18, 1954, "Ike Restores Commission"; *Los Angeles Times*, May 12, 1962, "Lindberghs Attend Gala Dinner at White House"; *Vanity Fair*, June 2010, 167. See also Berg, *Lindbergh*, 516.

17. Berg, *Lindbergh*, 441; *New York Post*, January 9, 1942, "Lindbergh Regrets White Race Is 'Divided in This War' "; Anne Morrow Lindbergh, *War Within and Without: Diaries and Letters of Anne Morrow Lindbergh, 1939–1944* (New York: Harcourt Brace Jovanovich, 1980), December 12, 1942, 310.

18. Berg, *Lindbergh*, 469–470, 502–517; *New York Times*, August 30, 1970, "Lindbergh Says U.S. 'Lost' World War II"; *New York Times*, November 29, 2003, "DNA Proves Lindbergh Led a Double Life"; *New York Times*, August 2, 2003, "A Newspaper Reports Lindbergh Fathered 3 Children in Germany." Some newspapers reported that Lindbergh had fathered other children with his mistress's sister. *The Telegraph* (London), May 29, 2005, "Aviator Lindbergh 'Fathered Children by Three Mistresses.' "

19. *Atlanta Constitution*, May 25, 1941, "War Argument False, Kennedy Says Here"; Cole, *Roosevelt and the Isolationists*, 503; Michael R. Beschloss, *Kennedy and Roosevelt: The Uneasy Alliance* (New York: Norton, 1980), 244ff. Some discussions between the White House and Kennedy continued to take place; Kennedy was offered possible positions that he deemed unworthy of his talents. See Beschloss, *Kennedy and Roosevelt*, 249ff. During the war, Kennedy griped about "the appointment of so many Jews in high places in Washington." David Koskoff, *Joseph P. Kennedy: A Life and Times* (Englewood Cliffs, N.J.: Prentice-Hall, 1974), 319.

20. Michael Beschloss, *The Conquerors: Roosevelt, Truman and the Destruction of Hitler's Germany* (New York: Simon and Schuster, 2002), 162. See also Joseph P. Kennedy to Kathleen Kennedy Hartington, May 1, 1945, in Amanda Smith, ed., *Hostage to Fortune: The Letters of Joseph P. Kennedy* (New York: Viking, 2001), 616.

21. Hoover and Kennedy conversation, May 15, 1945 in Nash, *Freedom Betrayed*, 828–830; Beschloss, *Kennedy and Roosevelt*, 252–253.

22. Joseph P. Kennedy, Diary Notes on the 1944 Political Campaign, in Smith, *Hostage to Fortune*, 608–609. See also Beschloss, *Kennedy and Roosevelt*, 257–259.

23. Hoover, Salt Lake City, November 1, 1940, in Gary Dean Best, *Herbert Hoover: The Post-presidential Years, 1933–1964,* 2 vols. (Stanford, Calif.: Hoover Institution Press, 1983), 1:172; Hoover to Harry Truman, quoted in Richard Norton Smith, "Hoover and Truman, a Presidential Friendship," http://www.trumanlibrary.org/hoover/intro.htm. See also Leonard Benardo and Jennifer Weiss, *Citizen-in-Chief: The Second Lives of American Presidents* (New York: William Morrow, 2009), 268.

24. Thomas Fleming, *The New Dealers' War: FDR and the War within World War II* (New York: Basic Books, 2001), 103. In March 1941, however, Hoover pointed out to the War Department that the turnaround for British ships in American ports was three weeks, and if that delay were shortened, it would amount to the addition of two million tons of shipping for Britain. Roosevelt thought it a fine, constructive idea and asked Stimson to compliment Hoover on his proposal. See Henry Stimson Diaries, March 4, 1941, Reel 6, vol. 33, Manuscripts and Archives, Yale University Library. Courtesy of J. Garry Clifford.

25. *New York Times,* February 24, 1942, "Farley Proposed for High War Job"; *New York Times,* February 20, 1942, "In the Nation," by Arthur Krock. "I think that Jim Farley ought to be down in Washington helping in this war effort," Senator Connally declared three months after Pearl Harbor at a Democratic Party dinner.

26. *New York Times,* December 9, 1941, "Rush of Recruits Crowds Stations."

27. FDR to Willkie, December 5, 1941, in Elliott Roosevelt, ed., *F.D.R.: His Personal Letters,* 4 vols. (New York: Duell, Sloan and Pearce, 1947–1950), 2:1249–1250; *New York Times,* December 16, 1941, "Roosevelt Talk Heartens Willkie." See also Steve Neal, *Dark Horse: A Biography of Wendell Willkie* (Garden City, N.Y.: Doubleday, 1984), 216–220. Willkie sought to preserve his political independence by declining several invitations to serve in the Roosevelt administration in a variety of positions, but he was not offered the one position he did covet, chairman of the War Production Board. Sherwood, *Roosevelt and Hopkins,* 475; *New York Times,* January 18, 1942, "Naming of Nelson Hailed by Willkie." Also Rolland Marvin Interview, August 29, 1953, "Loyal Opposition—8," Barnard Mss., Manuscripts Department, Lilly Library, Indiana University, Bloomington. Courtesy of J. Garry Clifford. In early 1942, Willkie approached Jim Farley with a proposal for a "unity" government and bipartisan agreement on the renomination and reelection of senators and congressmen who supported the president's foreign policy. Farley thought it a doomed plan and persuaded him that it could not be successfully carried out. Jim Farley, *Jim Farley's Story: The Roosevelt Years* (New York: Whittlesey House/McGraw-Hill, 1948), 346. In December 1941, before Pearl Harbor, America First was interested in electing isolationist congressmen in 1942 regardless of political affiliation. See Cole, *America First,* 179.

28. FDR to Marshall, July 31, 1942, in Roosevelt, *F.D.R.: His Personal Letters,* 2:1336; *New York Times,* October 18, 1942, "Willkie Spoke for Self"; FDR to Chiang, August 21, 1942, in Barnard Mss. In late 1942, Roosevelt proposed that Willkie be honored with an award presented by a Jewish organization. "I cast my vote for Hon. Wendell E. Willkie," wrote Roosevelt, "because he is working so consistently throughout this war and in other nations for tolerance and better understanding." Accepting the award in December for "promotion of better understanding between Christians and Jews in America," Willkie went a step further than the president and rejected the word "tolerance." "It is not tolerance that one is entitled to in America; it is the right of every citizen in America to be treated by other citizens as an equal." The concept of tolerance, he explained, assumed the superiority of one group over others. "Our liberties," he said, "are the equal rights of every citizen." Did he know that he was echoing the very words that George Washington penned in 1790 to the Hebrew Congregation in Newport, Rhode Island? "All possess alike liberty of conscience and immunities of citizenship," wrote Washington. "It is now no more that toleration is spoken of, as if it was by the indulgence of one class of people, that another enjoyed the exercise of their inherent natural rights."

29. Wendell L. Willkie, *One World* (New York: Simon and Schuster, 1943), 161, 171–172, 191, 198; *Time,* May 4, 1942, "A Light for the People"; *Washington Post,* August 1, 1943, "Willkie, Book and Man." See also James H. Madison, *Wendell Willkie, Hoosier Internationalist* (Bloomington: Indiana University Press, 1992), 134.

30. *New York Times*, February 12, 1943, "Willkie Demands Lend-Lease Be Kept"; *New York Times*, April 11, 1943, "Report on a Wakening World."

31. Harold L. Ickes, *The Secret Diary of Harold L. Ickes*, 3 vols. (New York: Simon and Schuster, 1953–1954), February 8, 1941, 3:427; Sherwood, *Roosevelt and Hopkins*, 830–831. William Allen White wrote to Willkie on January 11, 1941: "The [Republican] National Committee, which always stinks and I have known it for more than forty years, will try to gang up on you and our Congressional organization will not be for you. Nevertheless, you can lick them in the convention when the time comes, if you want to, either for yourself or for anyone else." Willkie Mss., Manuscripts Department, Lilly Library, Indiana University, Bloomington. Courtesy of J. Garry Clifford.

32. *Chicago Daily Tribune*, April 6, 1944, "The End of Mr. Willkie"; *New York Times*, April 9, 1944, "Willkie Withdraws." Willkie came in behind three other candidates, Dewey, Harold Stassen, and General Douglas MacArthur. *New York Times*, June 17, 1944, "Spengler Invites Willkie, But as a Spectator Only"; *New York Times*, June 16, 1944, "Republicans Ask Willkie to Chicago"; Neal, *Dark Horse*, 311.

33. Burns, *Roosevelt: The Soldier of Freedom*, 297, 222, 434, respectively; *Washington Post*, February 5, 1944, "Roosevelt, Willkie Think Alike."

34. Ellsworth Barnard, *Wendell Willkie: Fighter for Freedom* (Marquette: Northern Michigan University Press, 1966), 478–479; Neal, *Dark Horse*, 309, 313–318. George Norris expressed fierce opposition to an FDR-Willkie ticket, and on July 17, 1944, FDR wrote to him: "I don't think there is any possible danger of Willkie, though feelers were put out about a week ago." FDR to Norris, July 17, 1944, in Roosevelt, *F.D.R.: His Personal Letters*, 2:1522–1523. After the death of Frank Knox in April 1944, the White House had also put out feelers to Willkie about possibly becoming secretary of the navy. Barnard, *Wendell Willkie*, 487.

35. *New York Times*, August 10, 1942, "Willkie Sees Fish as Party Menace"; *New York Times*, July 13, 1942, "Willkie Will Fight Party's Isolationists"; FDR to Willkie, February 21, 1942, in Roosevelt, *F.D.R.: His Personal Letters*, 2:1287. Both Fish and Day were reelected in 1942 but lost in 1944. Still, in 1942 Willkie succeeded in getting the Republican National Committee to adopt a moderately internationalist stand. Neal, *Dark Horse*, 229; Burns, *Roosevelt: The Soldier of Freedom*, 275.

36. Rosenman, *Working with Roosevelt*, 465–466; Draft of a letter from Willkie to FDR, July 20, 1944, Willkie Mss., Manuscripts Department, Lilly Library, Indiana University, Bloomington. Courtesy of J. Garry Clifford. The letter was drafted but was never mailed.

37. Wendell L. Willkie, "Citizens of Negro Blood," *Collier's*, 114 (October 7, 1944), 11, 47, 49; Neal, *Dark Horse*, 322; Susan Dunn, *Roosevelt's Purge: How FDR Fought to Change the Democratic Party* (Cambridge, Mass.: Harvard University Press, 2010), 236–239; Willkie to Krock, August 28, 1944, quoted in Neal, *Dark Horse*, 320.

38. *New York Times*, October 8, 1944, "His Illness Brief"; *Atlanta Constitution*, October 9, 1944, "Roosevelt, Dewey Join in Tribute"; Neal, *Dark Horse*, 323.

39. *Christian Science Monitor*, March 1, 1945, "Roosevelt Reports to Congress on Yalta."

40. Telegram from Churchill to Willkie, January 13, 1941, Willkie Mss., Box 15, Lilly Library, Manuscripts Department, Indiana University, Bloomington. Courtesy of J. Garry Clifford.

41. *Chicago Daily Tribune*, April 13, 1948, "Unveil London F.D.R. Statue"; *Washington Post*, April 13, 1948, "Roosevelt Altered Moral Axis of Mankind, Says Churchill"; *New York Times*, April 13 1948, "The Text of Roosevelt Tributes by Churchill and King"; *New York Times*, April 17, 1948, "Britons Make Shrine of Roosevelt Statue," by Clifton Daniel.

Acknowledgments

I AM VERY GRATEFUL FOR THE SUPERB ASSISTANCE AND WISE COUNSEL I received on this project from many friends and colleagues. With astounding generosity, J. Garry Clifford at the University of Connecticut, the co-author of *The First Peacetime Draft* and *American Foreign Relations: A History*, shared his monumental archive of historical documents with me and advised me on numerous key questions relating to military and diplomatic history. Mark Stoler, George Marshall scholar and editor of *The Papers of George Catlett Marshall*, offered expert advice on questions of military and foreign policy. Milton Djuric once again contributed his vast knowledge of the period and gave me indispensable help and encouragement at every stage of this project. Michael Beschloss, author of *Kennedy and Roosevelt*, contributed key insights about Joseph Kennedy and his relations with isolationists as well as with FDR. James T. Patterson at Brown University, author of *Congressional Conservatism and the New Deal* and *Mr. Republican: A Biography of Robert Taft*, carefully read my manuscript and gave me many astute and invaluable suggestions. Bruce Miroff, author of *Icons of Democracy*, also skillfully guided me in work relating to presidential elections and leadership. And colleagues in the Mathematics Department at Williams College—Edward Burger and Cesar Silva—cordially interpreted statistical and polling data for me. Robert Clark, the supervisory archivist at the Franklin D. Roosevelt Library in Hyde Park, once again steered me through miles of documents at the library.

I'm also indebted to Robin Keller in the Faculty Secretarial Office for aiding me countless times and to Alison O'Grady, Jo-Ann Irace, Susan Lefaver, Wendy Sherman, Linda McGraw, Rebecca Ohm, Walter Komorowski, and

Sylvia Brown at the Williams College Library. My students Grace Rehnquist, Ryan Ford, and Tyler Hull did excellent research for me in Williamstown and in Hyde Park; Martin Hochdorf helped me translate German documents; and Terri-Lynn Hurley, Lynn Melchiori, and Bruce Wheat at the Williams Office of Information Technology rescued me and my Mac during fraught moments of electronic crisis. And my warmest appreciation goes to three Deans of Faculty at Williams College—Peter Murphy, William Wagner, and Thomas Kohut—for their collegial support of my research and my teaching.

I am also indebted to my outstanding editor at Yale University Press, William Frucht, and to my wonderful, enthusiastic agents, Ike Williams and Katherine Flynn.

And my deepest gratitude and love go to James MacGregor Burns. His brilliant and pioneering work on Franklin D. Roosevelt—*Roosevelt: The Lion and the Fox* and *Roosevelt: The Soldier of Freedom*—and his Rooseveltian generosity of spirit inspired this book.

Index

Blood, Henry, 304
Bloom, Sol, 160
Boetticher, Friedrich von, 48
Bogart, Humphrey, 71, 191
Borah, William, 33, 35, 58, 64, 130
Borzage, Frank, 296
Bowles, Chester, 58, 381n26
Breckinridge, Henry, 68–69
Brewster, Kingman, 65, 338n52, 397n13
Bricker, John, 114, 115
Bridges, Styles, 79, 111, 304, 361n37
Britain. See Great Britain
Brundage, Avery, 66
Buell, Raymond, 90, 151, 152, 200, 202, 205, 265, 360n29
Bullitt, William, 26, 28, 33, 238
Burke, Edward, 98, 128, 152, 170
Burke-Wadsworth bill. See Compulsory military service; Selective Training and Service Act
Burns, James MacGregor, 12–13, 25, 68, 164, 308
Burton, Harold, 174–175
Bush, Vannevar, 53, 333n52
Butler, Nicholas Murray, 339n67
Byrd, Harry, 128, 135
Byrnes, James: on Burke-Wadsworth bill, 171, 174; as FDR's manager at Democratic convention, 136, 139, 144, 147–148; as possible presidential candidate, 321n65; as possible vice-presidential candidate, 142, 143; Supreme Court appointment of, 268, 299

Carrel, Alexis, 50–51, 55, 56, 242, 312, 332n36
Carter, John Franklin, 292
Castle, Jr., William, 65, 96, 343n76, 346n23, 392n17
Catledge, Turner, 91, 287
Chamberlain, Neville: and appeasement, 27–28; as byword in U.S. for appeasement, 108, 176, 199, 296; and German invasion of Norway, 36; Kennedy and, 222–223, 227, 269, 375n28; resignation of, 37, 256; on U.S. assistance, 25; Willkie on, 256
Chaplin, Charlie, 296, 299, 310

Chiang Kai-shek, 314
Churchill, Winston: as advocate of aid to Britain, 37, 45–46, 176–177, 283; on appeasement, 27; appointment as prime minister, 37, 158–159, 256; and Atlantic Charter, 300; and destroyers-for-bases deal, 176–178, 182, 184; and fall of France, 45, 37, 104; on FDR's election victory, 262; on FDR statue, 317–318; and Kennedy, 223, 226, 270; on U.S. economy and world peace, 203; on Willkie, 265, 318; Willkie on, 199, 203, 256; and Willkie's visit to Britain, 278–280
Cincinnatus, 122, 233
Clapper, Raymond: on FDR, 356n10; on GOP estrangement from Willkie, 287, 306; on GOP platform, 107; on isolationism, 35; on Republicans' predicted victory, 71; on Willkie's campaign, 201; on Willkie's nomination, 115, 119–120; on Willkie's popularity, 73
Clark, Bennett Champ, 61, 99, 176, 181, 284–285, 304
Clark, Grenville, 94, 167, 169–171, 175, 178, 185, 186–187
Clark, Worth, 139, 297, 298
Cleveland, Grover, 128, 129
Clifford, J. Garry, 169, 170, 185
Cliveden Set, 98, 221, 373n5
Coglan, Ralph, 268
Cohan, George M., 5, 320n28
Cohen, Benjamin, 72, 202
Cole, Wayne, 237, 282, 334n68, 337n33, 395n44
Committee to Defend America by Aiding the Allies, 68–69
Committee to Keep America Out of Foreign Wars, 106, 236
Commonwealth and Southern Corp., 72, 194, 246
Compulsory military service: FDR and, 167–169, 172, 174, 180; first lottery for, 218–219; Grenville Clark's leadership for, 169–170, 175, 186–187; isolationist opposition to, 103, 108, 172–173; public opinion on, 169, 173–174; Stimson and, 98, 169, 171, 186–187; Willkie and, 158, 178–179, 185. See also Preparedness; Selective Training and Service Act

Hopkins, Harry: and Democratic convention, 136, 138, 141–142; and election night, 259, 261; as envoy to Churchill, 283, 373n5; as FDR speechwriter, 207–215, 228, 255, 273; on military preparedness, 27; and Pearl Harbor attacks, 307–308; as possible presidential candidate, 123; and Sherwood, 207, 208; and third term for FDR, 127, 136; on Wallace as vice-presidential candidate, 143–144; and Wallace's "guru" letters, 191; on Willkie, 3, 290

Horner, Henry, 124–125

Howard, Graeme, 60

Howard, Roy: as isolationist, 151–152, 359n2; on Lend-Lease, 277; and Willkie, 84, 110, 197, 200, 205, 277

Hughes, Charles Evans, 274

Hull, Cordell: on isolationism, 68; and Kennedy's request for home leave, 224; and Pearl Harbor, 307–309; as possible presidential candidate, 12, 123, 127, 135, 141; in vice-presidential candidate pool, 125, 142, 143; and Willkie's support of Lend-Lease, 283; and Willkie's visit to Britain, 278

Hurd, Charles, 180

Hutchins, Robert Maynard, 59, 61, 64, 142–143

Ickes, Harold: on Anne Lindbergh, 244; on Charles Lindbergh, 56, 311; on Cudahy, 328–329n82; and Democratic convention, 131, 134, 135–136, 140; on Dennis, 59; on Farley's presidential aspirations, 11; on FDR's campaign, 382n19; on German attacks on U.S. ships, 300; as interventionist, 31, 37, 40, 98–99; on isolationists, 335n10; on Kennedy, 223; and Lend-Lease, 386n5; as possible FDR running mate, 143, 144; post-election role of, 268; on Stimson and Knox appointments, 100; and third term for FDR, 8, 125, 127; on Wallace, 144, 191; on Willkie, 82, 160, 315, 351n84; 361n37; 390n53; on Woodring, 96, 97, 346n20, 346n23

Immigration to U.S., 28–31, 326n41

Ingalls, Laura, 237

Internationalists: and Committee to Defend America by Aiding the Allies, 68–69; in Congress, 79, 175–176, 284; and conscription, 169–170, 176; demographics of, 69; and FDR, 20, 25, 42, 59, 163, 183, 217; in FDR's administration, 92–99, 100, 102–103, 290; Knox as, 93, 99, 102, 347n29, 394n34; and preparedness, 172; Republicans as, 75, 79, 93, 98, 99, 100, 102, 304, 389n42; Stimson as, 95, 98–99; students as, 67–68; at Williams College, 67–68; Willkie as, 1, 80, 83–84, 89, 110, 163, 192, 217, 264, 265–266, 286, 306. *See also* White, William Allen

Isolationism: and anti-Semitism, 47–48, 62, 66, 238, 241–242, 248, 297–298, 301–303; defeatism and, 4, 63, 149, 203, 210, 223, 227, 242–243, 248, 269, 270, 275, 281, 291; democracy and, 47, 52, 59–60, 61, 63, 67, 74–75, 175–176, 203, 212–213, 227, 242–243, 269, 270, 275; in Democratic Party, 57, 58, 139–140, 303; eugenics in, 50–51, 241–242; FDR's, in 1940 campaign, 192, 216–218, 229–230, 272; of Lindbergh, 46–47, 57, 61–63, 70, 169, 208, 334n62; and preparedness, 44, 52, 65–66, 106, 172–173, 341–342n44; in Republican Party, 24, 57, 58–59, 65–66, 78–79, 106–107, 115–116, 163–164, 265–266, 303–304, 309–310; Willkie and, in presidential campaign, 158, 192, 199–200, 202–205, 217–218, 265, 272, 285. *See also* America First Committee; Isolationists; Lindbergh, Anne; Lindbergh, Charles

Isolationists: after Pearl Harbor, 309–311; and aid to Britain, 64–65, 74, 75, 177, 184, 223, 280; America First Committee and, 65–66, 75, 220, 237, 270–271, 291, 292, 293, 294, 297, 301, 311; and American Youth Congress, 67; and British appeasers, 27, 28, 33, 75, 173, 222, 266, 270; and Committee to Keep America Out of Foreign Wars, 106, 236; communists as, 57, 61; in Congress, 33, 58–59, 175–176, 284, 305; conscription opposed by, 103, 108, 172–173, 184;

Remarque, Erich Maria, 61

Republican National Convention (1940), 101–120; isolationist platform at, 106–107, 112, 116; presidential nomination battle at, 107–116; role of German Embassy at, 106, 140; vice-presidential nomination at, 116–117, 349n43

Reynaud, Paul, 45

Reynolds, Robert, 30, 238, 284

Rieber, Torkild, 60–61

Rivers, Ed, 144–145

Robinson, Edward G., 296

Rochambeau, Jean-Baptiste, Count de (General), 242

Rockefeller, Nelson, 154

Rockwell, Norman, 243

Rodell, Fred, 128

Rodman, Selden, 55, 282, 294, 302, 334n62

Roerich, Nicholas, 191

Rogers, Edith, 30

Roosevelt, Anna, 10, 37

Roosevelt, Archibald, 67

Roosevelt, Eleanor: on conscription, 168, 174; at Democratic convention, 145, 146; and election day, 1, 259, 261; and fall campaign, 190; as first lady, 7, 10, 30, 87; and FDR tribute in London, 317; and Hauptmann trial, 48; and Kennedy, 269–270; and Pearl Harbor attack, 308; and third term for FDR, 7, 10, 125

Roosevelt, Elliott, 142, 145, 147, 153–154, 333n52

Roosevelt, Franklin D.: acceptance speech to Democratic convention by, 148–149; and aid to Britain, 31, 32, 40, 116, 178, 229, 230, 273, 276–277, 280; American Youth Congress, 67; and compulsory military service, 167–169, 172, 174, 180; death of, 317; on democracy, 63, 149, 183, 210, 212, 230–231, 248, 250–251, 255, 273, 274–275, 291, 293; and destroyers-for-bases deal, 176–178, 182–184, 226, 265; on election day, 1–2, 259–262; and fourth term, 317; Hollywood's support for, 48, 190–191; isolationist positions of, in campaign, 192, 216–218, 229–230, 272; on isolationists, 25, 42, 44, 59, 183; and Kennedy, 123–124, 221, 225–227,

269–270, 312–313, 397n19; labor union support for, 246–247, 264; Lend-Lease proposal by, 276–277, 386n5; Lindbergh on, 2, 47, 52, 241–242, 294, 312; and Lindbergh, 291–295, 332n47; on Lindbergh, 47, 56, 230, 248, 292, 293; London monument to, 317–318; meetings with Willkie of, 276, 278, 285–286, 316; and Mussolini, 25, 44, 330n7; and Neutrality Acts, 22, 23–24, 25, 31–32, 216–217; 1940 inauguration of, 274–275, 279; nomination of, 140–142; and Pearl Harbor attack, 307–309; and plans for new progressive party, 316; political coalition of, 264; polls in campaign on, 3, 159, 193–194, 200, 202, 203, 211, 212, 219; and post-election relations with Willkie, 276–290; and preparedness, 38, 167–169, 172, 174, 180, 189, 190; on presidential tenure, 17–19; and retirement, 8–10, 12, 122, 126, 233; speechwriters for, 207–219; and strategy for fall campaign, 189–190, 192–193, 211–212; and Wallace vice-presidential nomination, 143–149; wartime treatment of isolationists by, 310–313; on Willkie, 90, 266, 278, 290, 315, 317. *See also* Speeches of FDR; Third term for FDR

Roosevelt, Franklin D., Jr., 44, 191, 212, 261

Roosevelt, James, 226

Roosevelt, John, 261

Roosevelt, Sara, 1, 10, 261–262

Roosevelt, Theodore: decision to retire in 1908, 18–19, 124, 130; as interventionist, 22, 53, 60; and Knox, 92–93; presidential tenure of, 18, 128, 129; and progressivism, 155, 157; and Taft succession, 18, 124; Willkie on, 86, 88, 157

Root, Oren, Jr., 84–85

Rosenman, Samuel I.: on compulsory military service, 187; and Democratic convention, 139, 143–144, 147–148; and election night, 259; as FDR speechwriter, 208–210, 213, 216, 228, 229, 249, 251, 274, 276, 291; on FDR's vice-